EUROPE IN THE
TWENTIETH CENTURY

Robert O. Paxton

Columbia University

EUROPE IN THE TWENTIETH CENTURY

 Harcourt Brace Jovanovich, Inc.
New York   Chicago   San Francisco   Atlanta

ISBN: 0-15-524718-2

Library of Congress Catalog Card Number: 74-25090

Printed in the United States of America

The author wishes to thank the following for permission to reprint copyrighted material:

CHATTO & WINDUS LTD for a selection from "Dulce et Decorum Est" from *The Collected Works of Wilfred Owen,* edited by C. Day Lewis, 1963. Reprinted by permission of Chatto & Windus Ltd and the Executors of the Estate of Harold Owen.

COLLINS-WORLD PUBLISHERS, INC. for a selection from "Left March" from Vladimir Mayakovsky, *The Bedbug and Selected Poetry.*

FABER AND FABER LTD for selections from "The Waste Land" and "The Hollow Men" from T. S. Eliot, *Collected Poems, 1909–1962,* and "1914. Peace" from Rupert Brooke, *The Poetical Works of Rupert Brooke.* Reprinted by permission.

HARCOURT BRACE JOVANOVICH, INC. for selections from "The Waste Land" and "The Hollow Men" from T. S. Eliot, *Collected Poems, 1909–1962.* Reprinted by permission.

MACMILLAN PUBLISHING COMPANY, INC. for a selection from "Red Front" by Louis Aragon from Maurice Nadeau, *The History of Surrealism.* Translated by Richard Howard. Translation copyright © Macmillan Publishing Co., Inc., 1965. Reprinted by permission.

NEW DIRECTIONS PUBLISHING CORPORATION for a selection from "Dulce et Decorum Est" from Wilfred Owen, *Collected Poems.* Copyright Chatto & Windus, Ltd. 1946, © 1963. Reprinted by permission of New Directions Publishing Corporation.

PANTHEON BOOKS for a selection from "Blessed are . . ." from Charles Péguy, *Basic Verities: Prose and Poetry,* translated by Ann and Julien Green. Copyright 1943 by Pantheon Books, Inc. Reprinted by permission of Pantheon Books, a Division of Random House, Inc.

LAURENCE POLLINGER LIMITED for a selection from "Left March" from Vladimir Mayakovsky, *The Bedbug and Selected Poetry.* Reprinted by permission of Laurence Pollinger Limited and Collins-World Publishers, Inc.

Maps drawn by Rino Dussi

PREFACE

Europe is the foreign region Americans are likely to think they know best. It is the origin of more than 80 percent of our citizens. It is the overseas area most often visited by American tourists. American society, economy, and culture began as offshoots of Europe, so that an American dealing with a European businessman, playwright, or philosopher is likely to take common presumptions for granted.

Yet, while recognizably kin, Europeans live in a profoundly different world. They are conscious of a far longer history than Americans, a past marked by more ups and downs. Europeans are likely to be aware of the transience of empire and the ambiguity of humanity's efforts to improve itself and the world. They have inherited a more complicated hierarchy of social ranks and classes, a more formal intellectual tradition, and more overtly ideological politics than Americans. Sooner or later one will encounter an educated European convinced that while he can easily understand rootless, straightforward, homogeneous America, Americans have too little historical sense or cultural sophistication to fathom complex Europe. Like most caricatures, that view contains a germ of truth.

It is my belief that Americans can best acquire a sensitive appreciation of Europe by giving some thought to the past experience of Europeans. This book provides an introduction to their experience since 1914. Those sixty years were clamorous with war, revolution, and economic crisis. During that time social ranking, the cultural climate, popular attitudes, and Europeans' consciousness of their place in the world all changed at a dizzying rate.

Historians nowadays pay more attention than before to matters outside the familiar realms of war, diplomacy, and politics. Social mobility, family relationships, deep-seated popular values, and the lives of common men and women are beginning to be more frequent subjects for serious historical enquiry than they were when most of us now teaching recent European history were trained. These new concerns are reflected on many pages of this book, although there is not yet a canon of standard works on which a textbook author can comfortably draw. At the same time, the traditional matters of war, revolution, economy, and struggles over liberty and authority still occupy a large place here. It could not be otherwise without distorting Europeans' experience in this violent and uncertain century.

I have tried to present the essential core of the subject, the major themes of public and private life in Europe since 1914, without overburdening detail. I hope that readers will be tempted to deepen their knowledge by exploring the riches of more specialized works of European literature and the arts. If this introduction makes these works more accessible and more fun, my efforts will have been worthwhile.

Many people helped me along the way. Among those deserving special thanks are Thomas A. Williamson, Editor in Chief of the College Department of Harcourt Brace Jovanovich, who launched this project and sustained it with his loyal support. He was ably seconded by William J. Wisneski, History Editor at Harcourt Brace Jovanovich. Virginia Joyner disentangled syntax and clarified meaning with the rigor, moderated by good humor, that makes her perhaps the champion manuscript editor in the business. Irene Pavitt, aided by Peter Kaldheim, copyedited and prepared the manuscript for the press with exemplary care. Carla Hirst Wiltenburg was tireless and resourceful in her search for unhackneyed illustrations. And Pat Smythe combined words and pictures into a pleasing design.

The following scholars read the manuscript in various stages and offered valuable suggestions: Gerald D. Feldman of the University of California at Berkeley; Vojtech Mastny of the University of Illinois; James J. Sheehan of Northwestern University; F. Roy Willis of the University of California at Davis; and Robert Wohl of the University of California at Los Angeles. Any errors and shortcomings of the final versions are, of course, my own.

Finally, I dedicate this book to the students of my first decade of teaching, the 1960s. They sharpened my perceptions by their questions, exposed my ignorance by their probing curiosity, and quickened my conscience by their concern for the world.

Robert O. Paxton

CONTENTS

Preface   *v*

1 Europe at Zenith, 1914   *3*

Europe and the World   4
European Landscapes: Urban and Rural   12
The Rich and the Poor   15
The Family   23
Political Systems and Mass Movements   27
Inherited Creeds   34
Toward a New Consciousness   39

2 The Coming of War   *49*

The July Crisis of 1914   51
Escalation: From Local War to Continental War   60
A Longer View of the Causes of War   67

3 The Marne and After, 1914–1917   *75*

War Fever   75
The First Battle of the Marne   79
The Eastern Front   82
The Search for a Breakthrough in the West   86

The Widening War   92
The War at Sea   94
The United States Enters the War   95

4 The Impact of Total War   97

Adjusting to a War of Attrition   98
War Governments: A Comparative Look   99
The Social Impact   110
The Economic Impact   114
The Impact on Internal Order   116
The Intellectual Impact   121

5 Revolution, 1917–1920   125

The Russian Revolutions, 1917   126
The Bolshevik Regime   133
Revolutionary Stirrings in
    Western Europe, 1917   142
The German Revolution, 1918–19   145
The Dissolution of Austria-Hungary, 1918–19   150
Britain, France, Italy: The Unrest of 1919–20   156
Aftermath and Results   159

6 The Versailles Peace Settlement   165

The Setting: Ideals, Interests, and Ideology   166
The Settlement   173
The League of Nations Covenant   175
The Western European Settlement   177
The Eastern European Settlement   180

7 Revolution Against Revolution: Fascism   190

Fascism in Italy   192
National Socialism in Germany   201

Counterrevolution in Hungary   *206*
A Closer Look at Fascism   *208*

8 The Versailles System in Practice, the 1920s   *217*

The Years of Coercion, 1919–24   *218*
The Years of Conciliation, 1924–29   *225*
A New Diplomacy?   *235*

9 "Normalcy": Europe in the 1920s   *240*

A Return to "Normalcy"   *241*
Britain   *244*
France   *250*
Weimar Germany   *253*
Eastern Europe   *260*
The Iberian Peninsula   *266*
Fascist Italy   *268*
Revolutionary Russia in a Stabilized World   *269*
A Fragile Stability: Neoliberalism Assessed   *275*

10 Mass Culture and High Culture Between the Wars   *279*

Mass Culture: The Age of Radio and Movies   *280*
The New Leisure   *285*
The Effects of Mass Culture and Leisure   *290*
High Culture Between the Wars   *293*
The Settings of Interwar Culture   *300*

11 Depression Politics, 1929–1936   *310*

The Origins and Course of the
   Great Depression   *313*
Depression Remedies   *316*
Depression Politics in the Liberal States   *319*

Depression Politics in the Authoritarian States   *330*

Conclusion   *339*

12 The Spread of Fascism: The Authoritarian 1930s   *342*

Germany: National Socialism in Power   *344*

Clerical Authoritarianism   *354*

Fascism in Eastern Europe   *360*

Fascist Minorities in Western Europe   *363*

The Appeal of Fascism   *370*

13 The European Left in the Popular Front Era, 1934–1939   *373*

From "Class Against Class" to Popular Front   *373*

The Popular Front in France   *381*

Spain: Republic, Revolution, and Civil War   *389*

European Intellectuals and the Popular Front   *397*

The European Left After the Popular Front   *398*

14 The Versailles System Dismantled: Expansion and Appeasement, 1933–1939   *402*

Hitler's First Moves   *403*

The Remilitarization of the Rhineland, March 1936   *405*

Italy Shifts Sides   *408*

Hitler's Designs in the East   *411*

Czechoslovakia and Appeasement, 1938   *415*

The Polish Crisis, 1939: Descent into War   *424*

The Origins of the Second World War   *428*

15 Hitler's Europe: Conquest, Collaboration, and Resistance, 1939–1942   *433*

The Nature of the Conflict in 1939   *434*

War in the East, 1939–40   *436*

War in the West, 1940   438
War in the East, 1941–42   445
Hitler's "New Order"   448
Collaboration   453
Resistance   457

16 From Hot War to Cold War, 1942–1949   *467*

American Hegemony in the West   468
Soviet Hegemony in the East   476
The Big Three and the Future of Europe   482
Origins of the Cold War   490
First Battlegrounds of the Cold War   495
A World in Two Blocs, 1947–49   502

17 Ruin and Reconstruction, 1945–1953   *506*

The Work of Reconstruction   509
The Labour Government in Britain,
    1945–51   514
The French Fourth Republic   518
Postwar Italy   521
The Two Germanies   524
Eastern Europe: Successor States
    as Russian Satellites   528
Reconstruction and Orthodoxy
    in the Soviet Union   535

18 Europe in the Cold War: Between the Superpowers, 1947–1962   *539*

Europe Under the Mushroom Cloud   540
Western Europe: Cold War Politics at Home
    and Abroad   543
Western Europe: The Movement for Union   549
The Soviet Union: From Stalin
    to Khrushchev   559

Eastern Europe: Consolidation and Rebellion,
1948–56   *563*

19 The "New Europe": Consumer Societies
and Mass Culture in the 1960s   *570*

Consumer Societies   *572*
Politics in Consumer Societies, 1953–68   *582*
Discontents in Consumer Societies Since 1968   *585*
Mass Culture and High Culture
in the "New Europe"   *596*

20 Europe in the World Today   *604*

The Cold War Thaw   *605*
Polycentrism in the Communist World   *606*
The Emerging Western "Third Force"   *609*
West Meets East: Willy Brandt and Ostpolitik   *619*
Decolonization and "Informal Empire"   *622*
Europe in the 1970s   *626*

Picture Credits   *631*
Index   *633*

EUROPE IN THE
TWENTIETH CENTURY

The upper class at leisure: the beach at Villerville, photographed in 1908 by the French photographer Jacques Henri Lartigue.

EUROPE AT ZENITH, 1914

1

Europeans who took stock of themselves as the twentieth century opened were aware that their continent played a very special role in the world, a role out of all proportion to its size. A dense, highly skilled population; massive industrial productivity; a culture that rewarded creative novelty; and a near monopoly of modern military force: these qualities gave Europeans a commanding position on the globe in 1914. Europeans thought of themselves as "the civilized world"; and insofar as other peoples were increasingly influenced by European ways of doing things, the future seemed to promise the eventual Europeanization of the world.

In 1914 there were proportionally more Europeans in the world than ever before, or since.[1] The population explosion that erupts in Asia, Africa, and Latin America today began in Europe around the year 1750.

---

[1]Europeans constituted 25 percent of the world's population in 1914. Thereafter, their share of the world's people began to drop. By 1970, only 19 percent of the world's people were Europeans. (W. S. Woytinsky and E. S. Woytinsky, *World Population and World Production* [New York, 1953], p. 36.)

After having grown a mere 3 percent from 1650 to 1750, the European population then leapt over 200 percent: from 188 million in 1800 to 401 million in 1900. It spilled over into the rest of the world, sending, by 1900, 1 million emigrants a year to new settlements, chiefly in the Americas and Asiatic Russia. Along with them went another mass of "temporary emigrants": the missionaries, soldiers, teachers, and entrepreneurs who were setting the stamp of Europe on the face of the rest of the world. By 1914 there were 100 million persons of European origin in North America and 40 million in Latin America, and there were smaller outpost populations in the European colonies of Africa, Asia, and the Pacific.

Europe and the World

It was not through their numbers, however, but through their dynamism that Europeans dominated the world in 1914. "While the major part of the globe remained fixed in its customs," wrote the French poet and essayist Paul Valéry, "this little cape on the Asiatic continent . . . set itself clearly apart from the rest."

> Wherever the European spirit prevails, one sees the maximum of needs, the maximum of work, the maximum of capital, the maximum of production, the maximum of ambition, the maximum of power, the maximum of modification of external nature, and the maximum of communications and exchanges.[2]

During the nineteenth century Europeans had become the first people on earth to alter their physical environment almost beyond recognition. They substituted the frenetic rhythms of steam-driven factories, huge cities, and rail travel for the slow seasons of agriculture, the routine of village life, and the pace of a man on foot. In 1914, despite the recent upsurge of Japan and the United States as industrial powers, Europe still retained a decisive economic lead. Europe produced 56 percent of the world's coal (although the United States alone produced another 38 percent of it), and 60 percent of the world's iron and steel (against a United States share of 32 percent). Europe accounted for 62 percent of the world's exports (while the United States accounted for 14 percent). To be a European meant to be living in the world's first industrial complex: the oldest in terms of time and still the first in rank.

European Traders, Travelers, and Investors

The rest of the world was being increasingly drawn into a single world economy with Europe at its hub. Wherever goods were traded by means other than simple barter, European mercantile practices came into play.

[2]Paul Valéry, "Caractères de l'esprit européenne," *La Revue universelle,* Vol. 18, No. 8 (July 1, 1924): 133, 142.

The international gold standard, according to which governments promised to exchange their currencies freely for gold at a fixed rate, made it easy to settle commercial accounts for goods sold in one currency but paid for in another. International accounts for companies all over the world were usually settled in London. Because the British pound had been freely convertible into gold since 1821 (most other advanced countries had followed Britain in adopting the gold standard by the 1870s) and because British clearing houses, insurance brokers, and shipping agents were the largest, cheapest, and most experienced in the world, London had evolved into the *de facto* capital of a stable, unified world-trading system. In 1914, London handled the clearing of 70 percent of American companies' foreign accounts. And British firms owned 70 percent of the world's shipping.

Freer international trade was the capstone of this "classical-liberal" system. For a brief period, from 1860 to 1879, the world's major trading nations imposed almost no tariffs on foreign goods, and other kinds of restrictions on trade virtually vanished. Never had the movement of people and goods from one country to another been subject to so little government regulation.

The British economist John Maynard Keynes looked back from the 1920s with nostalgia on this prewar London-centered world economy. He recalled that

the inhabitant of London could order by telephone, sipping his morning tea in bed, the various products of the whole earth, in such quantity as he might see fit, and reasonably expect their early delivery upon his doorstep; he could at the same moment and by the same means adventure his wealth in the natural resources and new enterprises of any quarter of the world, and share, without exertion or even trouble, in their prospective fruits and advantages; or he could decide to couple the security of his fortunes with the good faith of the townspeople of any substantial municipality in any continent that his fancy or information might recommend.

He could secure forthwith, if he wished it, cheap and comfortable means of transit to any country or climate without passport or other formality, could despatch his servant to the neighborhood office of a bank for such supply of the precious metals as might seem convenient, and could proceed abroad to foreign quarters, without knowledge of their religion, language, or customs, bearing coined wealth upon his person, and would consider himself greatly aggrieved and much surprised at the least interference. But, most important of all, he regarded this state of affairs as normal, certain, and permanent, and any deviation from it as aberrant, scandalous, and avoidable.[3]

Dynamic Europeans were not content merely to trade with and travel to the rest of the world. They also invested their money there. In 1914 Europe was the source of 83 percent of the world's foreign investments, in both developed and underdeveloped areas: Canadian mines, American railroads, South American electric companies, Senegalese ground-

[3]John Maynard Keynes, *The Economic Consequences of the Peace* (New York, 1920), p. 12. These varied opportunities were open, of course, only to the wealthy.

nut plantations, Egyptian cotton farms, South African gold mines, Shanghai trading companies, and the like. Of the Latin American countries, only Chile owned its railroads in 1914. Even the new American giant, the United States, was deeply in debt to European investors. On the eve of the First World War, European investments in the United States totaled nearly $7 billion, while United States investments in Europe totaled a mere tenth of that figure.[4]

Imperialism

Could Europeans trade, travel, or invest abroad in full confidence, however, unless they had some means of forcing local governments to protect them and their property? In the case of the modernized states, diplomatic pressure might have been enough to protect European business and travel. Many British traders and investors were content in the mid-nineteenth century with what has been called "informal empire," or "free-trade imperialism." The more the Europeans' energies overflowed into underdeveloped regions, however, the more risks they ran from bandits, hostile populations, and the whims of local rulers. In underdeveloped regions, Europeans chose increasingly in the late nineteenth century to safeguard their access to markets, raw materials, and returns on their investments by seizing outright political and military control.

European imperialism—the acquisition of empires—was not new to the late nineteenth century. Europeans had begun establishing outposts at the edges of the world's oceans as early as the fifteenth century.[5] They had set up lucrative mines and trading posts in Latin America and Asia in the sixteenth and seventeenth centuries. They had forced foreign rulers to grant "capitulations," the right of European citizens to be ruled by their own laws, in enclaves like Shanghai and in whole regions like the Ottoman Empire. But all these efforts seemed insignificant compared with the enterprise of the late nineteenth century: the direct seizure of immense tracts of land around the world. Between the 1850s and 1911 the Europeans carved up into colonies almost the entire underdeveloped world. They parceled out among themselves all of Africa except Liberia and Ethiopia. The French completed their conquest of Indochina in the 1880s. After 1897 Europeans began staking out spheres of influence in China. By 1914 Britain had an empire 140 times its own size; Belgium, an empire 80 times its size; Holland, 60 times; and France, 20 times. Russia established itself as a major Pacific Ocean power with the completion of the Trans-Siberian Railroad (1891–1903). Ger-

---

[4]Harold U. Faulkner, *The Decline of Laissez-Faire* (New York, 1951), p. 87.
[5]The first European colony of modern times was Ceuta, an outpost on the northern coast of present-day Morocco. It was founded in 1402, partly for booty and partly for the religious purpose of making contact with Prester John, the legendary Christian emperor and priest, whose kingdom was believed to be beyond the Moslem world—that is, in Ethiopia.

EUROPEAN IMPERIAL EXPANSION IN ASIA

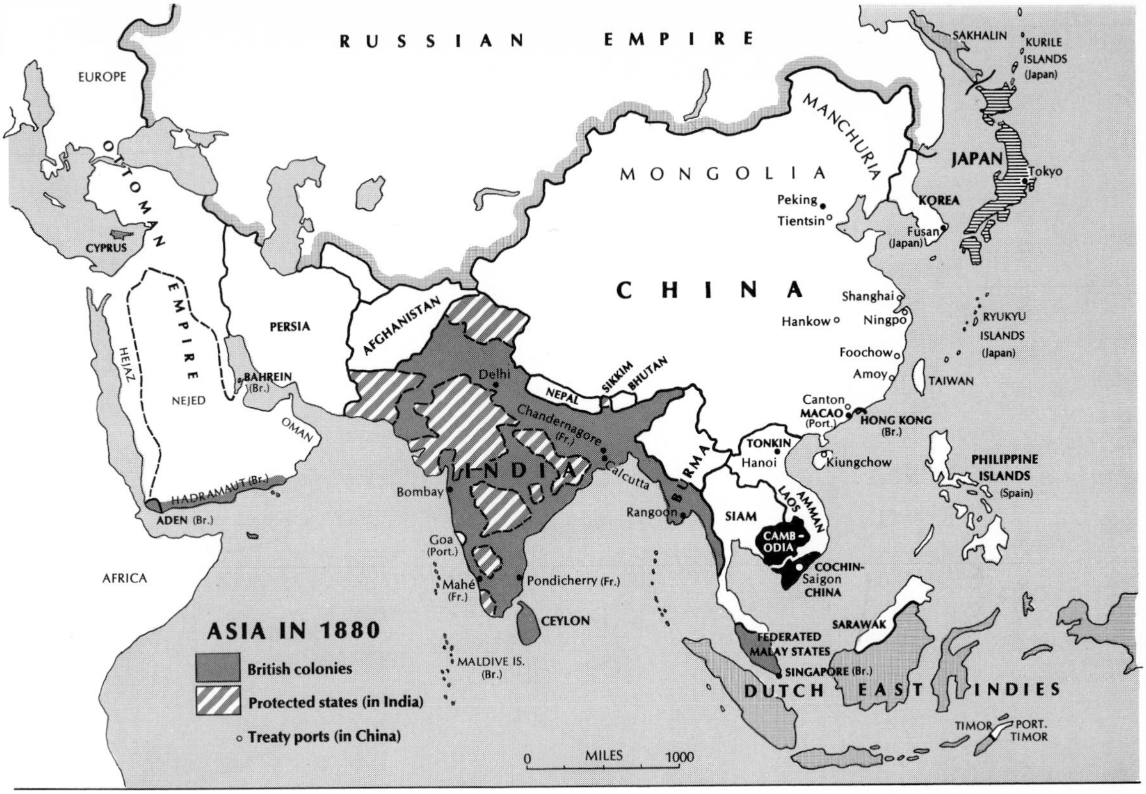
ASIA IN 1880
British colonies
Protected states (in India)
Treaty ports (in China)
RUSSIAN EMPIRE
EUROPE
OTTOMAN EMPIRE
CYPRUS
HEJAZ
NEJED
PERSIA
BAHREIN (Br.)
OMAN
HADRAMAUT (Br.)
ADEN (Br.)
AFRICA
AFGHANISTAN
Delhi
NEPAL
SIKKIM
BHUTAN
Chandernagore (Fr.)
INDIA
Calcutta
Bombay
Goa (Port.)
Mahé (Fr.)
Pondicherry (Fr.)
CEYLON
MALDIVE IS. (Br.)
BURMA
Rangoon
SIAM
TONKIN
Hanoi
LAOS
AMMAN
CAMBODIA
COCHIN-CHINA
Saigon
FEDERATED MALAY STATES
SINGAPORE (Br.)
SARAWAK
DUTCH EAST INDIES
TIMOR
PORT. TIMOR
PHILIPPINE ISLANDS (Spain)
MONGOLIA
MANCHURIA
CHINA
Peking
Tientsin
Shanghai
Hankow
Ningpo
Foochow
Amoy
Canton
MACAO (Port.)
HONG KONG (Br.)
Kiungchow
TAIWAN
RYUKYU ISLANDS (Japan)
KOREA
Fusan (Japan)
JAPAN
Tokyo
SAKHALIN
KURILE ISLANDS (Japan)
0 MILES 1000

ASIA IN 1914
British colonies
Protected states (in India)
Treaty ports (in China)
RUSSIAN EMPIRE
EUROPE
OTTOMAN EMPIRE
CYPRUS
HEJAZ
NEJED
RUSSIAN SPHERE OF INFLUENCE
PERSIA
BRITISH SPHERE OF INFLUENCE
KUWAIT (Br.)
BAHREIN (Br.)
OMAN
YEMEN
HADRAMAUT (Br.)
ADEN (Br.)
AFRICA
AFGHANISTAN
Delhi
NEPAL
SIKKIM
BHUTAN
Chandernagore (Fr.)
INDIA
Calcutta
Bombay
Goa (Port.)
Mahé (Fr.)
Pondicherry (Fr.)
CEYLON
MALDIVE IS. (Br.)
TIBET
BURMA
Rangoon
Bangkok
SIAM
TONKIN
Hanoi
LAOS
AMMAN
CAMBODIA
FRENCH INDO-CHINA
COCHIN-CHINA
Saigon
FEDERATED MALAY STATES
SINGAPORE (Br.)
BR. NORTH BORNEO
BRUNEI
SARAWAK
DUTCH EAST INDIES
TIMOR
PORT. TIMOR
PHILIPPINE ISLANDS (U.S.A.)
OUTER MONGOLIA
INNER MONGOLIA
MANCHURIA
Mukden
Peking
Tientsin
Weihaiwei
Port Arthur (Japan)
Kiaochow
REPUBLIC OF CHINA
Soochow
Shanghai
Ningpo
Hankow
Hangchow
Chungking
Foochow
Amoy
Canton
MACAO (Port.)
HONG KONG (Br.)
Kiungchow
TAIWAN
RYUKYU ISLANDS (Japan)
Vladivostok
KOREA
JAPAN
Tokyo
SAKHALIN
KURILE ISLANDS (Japan)
0 MILES 1000

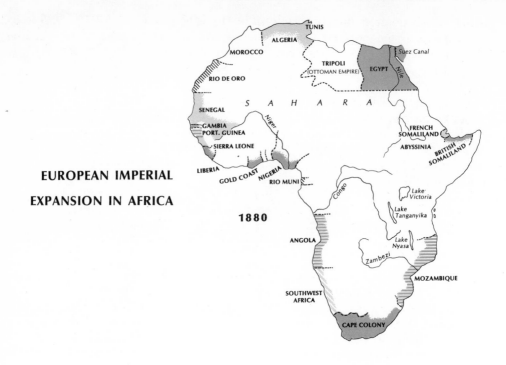

EUROPEAN IMPERIAL

EXPANSION IN AFRICA

1880

TUNIS
ALGERIA
MOROCCO
TRIPOLI
(OTTOMAN EMPIRE)
EGYPT
Suez Canal
RIO DE ORO
S A H A R A
Nile
SENEGAL
GAMBIA
PORT. GUINEA
FRENCH
SOMALILAND
SIERRA LEONE
ABYSSINIA
BRITISH
SOMALILAND
LIBERIA
GOLD COAST
NIGERIA
RIO MUNI
Congo
Lake
Victoria
Lake
Tanganyika
ANGOLA
Lake
Nyasa
Zambezi
MOZAMBIQUE
SOUTHWEST
AFRICA
CAPE COLONY

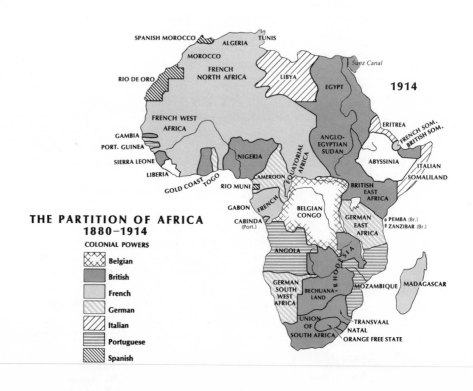

THE PARTITION OF AFRICA
1880–1914

COLONIAL POWERS

SPANISH MOROCCO
ALGERIA
TUNIS
MOROCCO
FRENCH
NORTH AFRICA
RIO DE ORO
LIBYA
EGYPT
Suez Canal
1914
FRENCH WEST
AFRICA
ERITREA
FRENCH SOM.
BRITISH SOM.
GAMBIA
PORT. GUINEA
ANGLO-
EGYPTIAN
SUDAN
ABYSSINIA
SIERRA LEONE
NIGERIA
ITALIAN
SOMALILAND
LIBERIA
GOLD COAST
TOGO
RIO MUNI
CAMEROON
EQUATORIAL AFRICA
BRITISH
EAST
AFRICA
GABON
FRENCH
BELGIAN
CONGO
GERMAN
EAST
AFRICA
PEMBA (Br.)
ZANZIBAR (Br.)
CABINDA
(Port.)
ANGOLA
RHODESIA
GERMAN
SOUTH
WEST
AFRICA
BECHUANA-
LAND
MOZAMBIQUE
MADAGASCAR
UNION
OF
SOUTH AFRICA
TRANSVAAL
NATAL
ORANGE FREE STATE

Belgian	
British	
French	
German	
Italian	
Portuguese	
Spanish	

many, which entered the competition late, in 1885, made up for the relatively restricted empire it had obtained in East and southwest Africa and on the China coast with gigantic investments in the less-developed parts of Europe and with the hasty construction of a powerful fleet after 1900. Only Japan managed to stem the European tide by adopting European industrial techniques with such success that the "capitulations" granted to foreign traders in 1858 could be revoked in 1894.

The explanation of the gigantic burst of energy that was late nine-teenth-century European imperialism is a central historical controversy. Some historians believe that imperialism was primarily a cultural phenomenon: the zeal of missionaries for converts, of engineers for new rivers to bridge, and of soldiers for glory. In Indochina, it was certainly Catholic missionaries who called for the help of the French Navy; and it was the naval officers who, in turn, exceeded their instructions and established French control in Indochina between the 1850s and the 1880s.

Other students of imperialism are convinced that economic drives were far more fundamental. They point to the French occupation of Tunisia in 1881, when French bondholders were faced with the loss of their assets, and to the British occupation of Egypt in 1882, when European investors could no longer collect interest on their loans to the spendthrift ruler of Egypt, Khedive Ismail. Some colonies were almost purely commercial propositions: Sir George Goldie's United African Company of 1879 spread the British presence into what is today Nigeria. The Italian conquest of Lybia from the Ottoman Empire in 1911 promised land as well as glory to the overpopulated south.

Explanations of imperialism based on simple trade or settlement are not fully satisfying. For one thing, the territories acquired in the 1885 to 1914 rush were rarely suitable for European settlement. Furthermore, the imperialist powers traded more with one another than with their colonies. The economic interpretation of imperialism rests on a far more basic judgment of capitalism's inherent faults. A British liberal economist, John A. Hobson,[6] angered by the British war in South Africa, the Boer War (1899–1902), first attributed imperialism in a systematic way to contradictions in capitalism. Hobson suggested that low wages and the maldistribution of wealth left European workers with such low purchasing power that capitalists could escape periodic depression only by a search for richer markets and higher investment returns overseas.

The Russian Marxist Nikolai Lenin pushed Hobson's arguments much further in *Imperialism: The Highest Stage of Capitalism* (1916). Lenin believed that capitalists must turn to monopoly when their rates of profit fall in the face of competition and ever more expensive technology. When the monopolies scramble for the last overseas opportunities, the capitalist states inevitably go to war, and sooner or later destroy one

[6]John A. Hobson, *Imperialism, A Study* (London, 1902).

another in a conflict like the one that raged while Lenin was writing. Lenin seriously underestimated the extent to which capital continued to be invested in the advanced countries, even during the imperialist rush of 1885 to 1914. Nevertheless, no interpretation of imperialism can fail to assign some role to economic aims.

Once begun, for whatever combination of motives, imperial expansion tended to take on a self-sustaining momentum as the last available territories were snapped up. Contemplating this escalation of imperialism in the 1880s and 1890s, Ronald Robinson and John Gallagher[7] have maintained that strategic considerations were uppermost in the British government's decisions to occupy Egypt. According to this account, the British took control of Egypt in 1882 in order to protect their stake in India. The very existence of a colony, in other words, creates the strategic necessity for controlling access to it. Critics of this theory have not failed to point out that the British were in India in the first place for reasons largely, if not wholly, economic. In any event, by 1914 the net result of imperialism was a world in which the Western powers had established themselves competitively on every continent. After the American Robert Peary had reached the North Pole in 1908, and after Roald Amundsen had raised the Norwegian flag at the South Pole in 1911, no corner of the earth had not felt the impress of imperialist energies in some form.

The Europeans were able to defend their world empires in 1914 because of their near monopoly of modern military force. Colonial armies, officered by Europeans and equipped by means of an ingenious technology, made short work of Oriental potentates, Muslim kingdoms, and African tribes. It was almost unheard of for native forces to gain more than a temporary advantage over the Europeans. The defeat of an Italian force by Ethiopians at Adowa in 1895 was the outstanding exception. The British imperial poet Rudyard Kipling could afford to be magnanimous to the hard-fighting Zulu warriors:

> An', 'ere's to you, Fuzzy-Wuzzy, . . .
> For you broke a British square.[8]

For, so far, the British had never failed to get what they wanted in the end.

The rising industrial powers outside Europe did not even attempt to build armed forces on a European scale. For example, the primary function of the United States' armed forces in the 1880s was simply to subdue the last of the Indian resisters. At that time, the great land armies of France, Germany, Austria-Hungary, and Russia had no equals on earth except one another. Thus, it was with a shock of premonition that many Europeans watched the United States wrest a colonial empire from Spain in 1898 and saw Japan defeat Russia in 1905.

[7]Ronald Robinson and John Gallagher, *Africa and the Victorians* (London, 1967).
[8]Rudyard Kipling, *Ballads and Barrack Room Ballads* (London, 1892), p. 150.

The glory of empire. Lord Curzon, viceroy of India, and Lady Curzon among Indian notables at the turn of the century.

European Artists and Scientists

European influence in the world was by no means entirely material. European arts and sciences were as much a lodestar to the rest of the world as European commerce and technical skill. The Americans who traveled abroad in Henry James' novels did so not to see quaint sights but to acquire European polish and learning. No American physicist or chemist expected to excel in his field without European study. Hundreds of Americans studied medicine each year in Germany, even after such American universities as Johns Hopkins introduced the Ph.D. degree and graduate seminars modeled on German university practice in the 1870s. So it was not mere ritual politeness that led the Harvard philosopher William James to open his lectures at Edinburgh in 1901 on "The Varieties of Religious Experience" by saying:

> To us Americans, the experience of receiving instruction from the living voice, as well as from the books, of European scholars is very familiar. . . . It seems the natural thing for us to listen while Europeans talk. The contrary habit, of talking while the Europeans listen, we have not yet acquired; and in him who first makes the adventure it begets a certain sense of apology being due for so presumptuous an act.[9]

[9]William James, *The Varieties of Religious Experience* (New York, 1958), p. 21.

European Landscapes: Urban and Rural

Europe was the most urban of the continents by 1914. Northern and Western Europe, the first region to shift a majority of its working population from agriculture to industry, was also the first region in which a majority of the population lived in towns and cities. While the total population soared, the rural portion of it remained stable or even declined; the excess poured into cities and towns.

Between 1800 and 1900, the number of European cities with populations of over 100,000 increased from 22 to 120. The fastest growing cities and towns were the newer, industrial ones (the population of Essen in Germany, for example, expanded by thirty times between 1800 and 1900). But, even the populations of the preindustrial capitals—Paris, London, Vienna—expanded by three or four times in the course of the nineteenth century. In 1848, only London and Paris contained more than 1 million inhabitants. In 1914, six European cities had more than 1 million inhabitants, compared with three in the United States, three in Asia, and two in Latin America. Even in the 1960s, Europe still had almost one-half of the world's cities of over 100,000: 300, compared with 215 in Asia and 155 in the Americas.[10] To be a European meant to live in or near great cities, particularly in the north and west of the Continent. In England, the most urban corner of Europe, four-fifths of the population lived in towns or cities. In Germany, the Low Countries, and parts of northern France and northern Italy, over one-half lived in urban areas. These cold facts, however, are less important than the social and intellectual impacts of urban living.

Life in the City

Cities were among the most glorious of European creations and, at the same time, among the most squalid. Since medieval times cities had attracted lavish concentrations of money, power, and artistic expression in Europe, as well as pestilential slums. The Industrial Revolution had poured more crowds into these slums, had added miles of hastily built tenements, and had overlaid it all with smoke and grime. In 1857 Charles Dickens described a "debilitated old house" in London that

> wrapped in its mantle of soot, and leaning heavily on the crutches that had partaken of its decay and worn out with it, never knew a healthy or cheerful interval. . . . You should alike find rain, hail, frost, and thaw lingering in that dismal enclosure, when they had vanished from other places; and as to snow, you should see it there for weeks, long after it had changed from yellow to black, slowly weeping away its grimy life.[11]

Nineteenth-century builders also contributed to those parts of European cities that were centers of elegance and spectacle. But unlike their predecessors, who had carefully laid out Napoleonic Paris, ecclesiastical Rome, and the great squares of Venice and Florence, the nineteenth-century city builders operated, in ways proper to the century of

[10] J. M. Houston, *Social Geography of Europe* (London, 1963), pp. 152, 155.
[11] Charles Dickens, *Little Dorritt* (1857).

middle-class prosperity, with a maximum of speculative real estate development and a minimum of planning, except to locate the new wealthy quarters west, or upwind, of the old city centers. Among the more carefully planned projects were the new *grands boulevards* of Paris, cut through the slums by Napoleon III in the 1850s and 1860s. Beginning in 1858, the old city walls of Vienna were torn down and replaced by the broad *Ringstrasse,* with its Opera and elegant cafés. Among the least planned were Berlin's great new commercial avenues like the *Kurfürstendamm* and its highly profitable villa developments in the former pine woods and potato fields west of the capital.

No wonder the Europeans' reaction to their cities at the opening of the twentieth century was ambivalent. On the one hand, critics of the cities pointed not only to the obvious squalor of urban slums but to the climate of human indifference and the loss of purpose and meaning that blighted so many urban lives. It is striking how frequently the theme of moving to the city occurs in nineteenth-century novels and how badly the fictitious urban immigrants fared. The prototype was perhaps Julien Sorel in Stendhal's *The Red and the Black* (1831). Increasingly calculated love affairs led him finally to Paris and to exection for having tried to kill his mistress. Many real Europeans among the millions who moved into towns and cities also found moral decadence and loneliness as well as physical misery. While social critics deplored urban poverty, conservatives attacked cities as warrens of uprooted cosmopolitan civilization. The heroes of Maurice Barrès' French novel *The Uprooted* (1897) lost their moral bearings in Paris and committed murder. Writing during the First World War, the German social commentator Oswald Spengler lamented that

> in place of a type-true people, born of and grown in the soil, there is a new sort of nomad, cohering unstably in fluid masses, the parasitical city-dweller, traditionless, utterly matter-of-fact, religionless, clever, unfruitful, deeply contemptuous of the countryman and especially that highest form of countryman, the country gentleman.[12]

In the midst of its magnificence the city seemed to many a human wasteland:

> Unreal City,
> Under the brown fog of a winter dawn,
> A crowd flowed over London Bridge, so many,
> I had not thought death had undone so many.
> Sighs, short and infrequent, were exhaled,
> And each man fixed his eyes before his feet.[13]

On the other hand, European cities were still irresistible magnets as the twentieth century opened. The largest crowd that had ever visited a single display, nearly 51 million persons—more than the total popula-

---

[12]Oswald Spengler, *The Decline of the West,* Vol. 1 (New York, 1926), p. 107.
[13]T. S. Eliot, "The Waste Land," in *The Complete Poems and Plays* (New York, 1952), p. 39.

tion of France—went to the Paris World's Fair during 1900. Millions were still moving into the cities. The ambitious moved because cities offered far wider opportunities for wealth and fame than the countryside. The rural poor moved because a bad job was better than none. Those in trouble moved for the city's anonymity. The artistically creative praised the variety and excitement of cities, as their predecessor Charles Baudelaire had done in the 1860s, as places of both "multitude and solitude," a "spree of vitality," an inebriating world of "feverish joys" where the soul could "give itself utterly, with all its poetry and charity, to the unexpectedly emergent, to the passing unknown."[14] Much of European creativity could not be imagined without the environment of towns and cities.

Life in Peasant Europe

A traveler crossing the Elbe River into Eastern Europe entered a world radically different from the efficient commercial farms and urbanized majorities of Western and northern Europe. Vast aristocratic estates inefficiently cultivated by a population of landless laborers stretched beyond the horizon. The Radziwills owned 500,000 acres in Poland; the Esterházys, 750,000 acres in Hungary. Four thousand great proprietors owned about a third of Hungary in 1895.[15] The Russian nobility and gentry, even after large losses of land to middle-class purchasers in the late nineteenth century, still owned about 14 percent of the land; the imperial family by itself owned another 1 percent of that vast country.[16] The same was true in southern Europe. Southern Italy and southern Spain were dominated by enormous estates, or latifundia. About 2 percent of the population owned 66.5 percent of the land in the southern Spanish province of Andalusia.[17] Small gentry and new middle-class rich imitated the life styles of the greatest landowners as well as they could. Landowners exercised social and economic sway in their regions far beyond the power that came from holding local political office.

Agriculture was grossly inefficient in Eastern and southern Europe in 1914. One-third of Russian peasant holdings still lacked steel ploughs. The ancient three-crop rotation system still kept large areas of land fallow. At the turn of the century, Russian peasants produced about 8.9 bushels of spring wheat per acre, while German peasants produced 27.5, and English farmers, 35.4.[18] Vast tracts of land in Andalusia were set aside as bullraising farms or hunting preserves. With many hands

---

[14]Charles Baudelaire, "Petits Poèmes en prose," in *Oeuvres completes*, Vol. 2, ed. Jacques Crépet (Paris, 1924), p. 163.
[15]C. A. Macartney, *The Hapsburg Empire, 1790–1918* (New York, 1969), p. 713.
[16]Geroid Tanquary Robinson, *Rural Russia Under the Old Regime* (New York, 1932), p. 268.
[17]Edward E. Malefakis, *Agrarian Reform and Peasant Revolution in Spain* (New Haven, Conn., 1970), p. 29.
[18]Robinson, p. 130.

devoted to seasonal tasks without the use of modern tools, the huge rural population in Eastern and southern Europe was underemployed. Peasants were desperate for some land of their own. In Western and northern Europe, where independent family farms were the rule, peasant proprietors were a conservative counterweight to urban and labor unrest in the late nineteenth century. In Eastern and southern Europe, however, a mass of land-hungry peasants formed a powder keg of unrest and anger on the eve of the First World War.

There remains one more European rural landscape—the remote hill villages of Mediterranean Europe and the Balkans, many of which practiced a primitive, subsistence agriculture almost beyond the reach of modern markets and the modern state. Here, peasants often owned some land, although their pockets of rocky, terraced hillside could not really sustain them. Others paid tribute to rapacious small landlords. The physician and painter Carlo Levi, an urban northern Italian exiled to a hill village in southern Italy by Mussolini's fascist regime, later wrote that Christian civilization itself, everything that had happened since Greek times, seemed to him to have never penetrated up beyond the last market town.[19] Other timelessly ancient hill villages survived in the Balkans, as described in the Yugoslav writer Milovan Djilas' recollections of his home town in Montenegro, *Land Without Justice* (1958). Only after 1945 were the last of these relics of subsistence economy drawn into the larger society.

Class and Social Rank

Society was highly stratified in Europe in 1914. Even after a century of middle-class expansion and hesitant steps toward political democracy, social distances remained very great. They were also quite visible. A European's social position was instantly evident in his clothes, size, complexion, and subtle traits of posture. Manual laborers on the Continent usually wore blue smocks over rough trousers and a cloth cap or beret; married lower-class women, especially those in the south and east, were usually dressed in rough black dresses and shawls. Wooden clogs were the common footwear of the rural poor. Although body size had begun to increase with better nutrition in the late nineteenth century, poor men, even in England, averaged three inches shorter than the wealthy.[20] Hard work and dangerous machinery left their marks on mutilated bodies. Sun-darkened faces and necks were still a caste mark of poverty, not a badge of leisure. A British officer, watching troops

**The Rich
and the Poor**

[19]Carlo Levi, *Christ Stopped at Eboli* (New York, 1947).
[20]Emanuel Le Roy Ladurie dates the "end of the anthropological 'Old Regime'" at around 1860, when the visible "proletariat" of diminutive Europeans began to disappear and average height began to rise from around five feet to the nearer six feet of today. (*Annales: économies, sociétés, civilisations* [July–October 1972]: 1234.)

bathing in a river during the First World War, is supposed to have turned in astonishment to a fellow officer with the remark, "I had no idea their bodies were so white."

Smell and voice completed the outward marks distinguishing the lower classes. George Bernard Shaw's comedy *Pygmalion* (1900) turns on the relation of accent and class. As Shaw remarked in the play's preface, "It is impossible for an Englishman to open his mouth without making some other Englishman despise him." The idly rich linguist Henry Higgins and his friend Colonel Pickering find Eliza Doolittle, a cockney flower girl, at the Covent Garden open market in London. "You see this creature with her kerbstone English," says Higgins, "the English that will keep her in the gutter to the end of her days. Well, sir, in three months I could pass that girl off as a duchess at an ambassador's garden party. I could even get her a place as a lady's maid or a shop assistant, which requires better English."

The social gradations in England so easily mocked by Shaw in 1900 were nevertheless quite real. Society was even more stratified in Eastern and southern Europe, where only a small middle class in the rare market towns stood between the landed aristocracy and the peasants.

The Poor

Most Europeans were poor in 1914. But the standard was at least higher than it had been in the past. Northern and Western Europe (along with its extension in North America) was the first region on earth where a

majority of the population could expect to be able to earn a bit more than what was needed for bare survival. Elsewhere in the world, unremitting labor for all one's days merely kept one alive, and not for long, or in good health.

Historians still argue about whether workers' living standards went up or down with the introduction of the first factories in the early nineteenth century, but real wages certainly rose substantially in the late nineteenth century. Purchasing power almost doubled in England, France, and Germany between 1880 and 1914. By that time, bread and potatoes were often supplemented by meat on working families' tables.[21] Many workers could afford simple factory-made clothes; and there was even a little left over in many a family's budget for beer, the café being the main recreation available after the normal fifty-to-sixty-hour work week.

The nineteenth century's massive increase in both agricultural and industrial productivity shifted the most urgent problem from quantity of production to distribution of the product. Since Europeans now produced some surplus, a new era was at hand, an era in which all citizens could demand a share in that surplus as rightfully theirs.

Despite the Europeans' very real material progress in the generations before 1914, dire poverty was still widespread in even the richest regions in 1914. The best information comes from the English provincial city of York, where Seebohm Rowntree devoted a lifetime to gathering precise data on the way his fellow citizens lived. The indefatigable Rowntree,

[21]John Burnett, *Plenty and Want: A Social History of Diet in England from 1815 to the Present* (London, 1966).

Watching a horse race at Ascot before the First World War. Hats and positions in the stands mark social classes very clearly. The upper class, in top hats, occupies the top rows; middle-class men appear in bowlers and straw hats. Working-class men, excluded from the stands, wear cloth caps.

conducting a house-to-house survey in 1899, found that nearly 28 percent of the inhabitants of York lived in such irreducible want that "total earnings were insufficient to obtain the minimum necessaries for the maintenance of merely physical efficiency."[22] A similar study of London at about the same time showed that 30.7 percent of its residents lived in poverty.

In plain words, in the richest city of the richest country in the world, in about 1900, nearly one-third of the people felt acute hunger, slept in their clothes for warmth, and looked forward only to death in a charity hospital or on the street and a pauper's burial in an unmarked grave. On the Continent, poverty was no less widespread in the most prosperous areas—northern France, the Low Countries, western Germany—than it was in England. In the more backward areas of Eastern and southern Europe, bare subsistence or less was still the lot of the majority. In 1900, for example, the average life expectancy was under thirty-five years in the Balkans and in Spain.[23]

Even those wage earners who lived above the bare subsistence level had to endure the most inescapable quality of working-class life: permanent insecurity. Social-welfare arrangements were only in their infancy. Germany led the way, after 1883, with compulsory state-run health- and retirement-insurance plans. France followed, far more tentatively, with voluntary social-insurance arrangements in the 1890s. In Britain, the Liberal party under the leadership of David Lloyd George replaced the trade unions' voluntary insurance schemes with a national, compulsory health- and unemployment-insurance system in 1911. Even so, many of the poor were not covered, notably the self-employed, agricultural workers, and domestics. Most working families had known poverty before and expected to know it again: illness, accidents, drunkenness, gambling, death of the principal wage earner, filled most ordinary working lives with uncertainty.

The Rich

The distance from poor to rich was planetary. In the same year that the fictitious Professor Higgins met Eliza Doolittle selling flowers at Covent Garden, the real landlord of the Covent Garden market, the Duke of Bedford, is supposed to have received £15,000 in rent for that property alone.[24] The guests who gathered every weekend in the great country houses or shooting lodges of England or Andalusia or Hungary took for granted the care given them by the hundreds of servants who unpacked

[22]Seebohm Rowntree, *Poverty* (London, 1901), pp. 86, 117. Rowntree also conducted a follow-up study in the depression year of 1936 and, in 1951, when he was eighty years old, a study of life under the welfare state. He found 31 percent living in poverty in York in 1936, although its cause had shifted from low wages to unemployment. The big breakthrough came after the Second World War. The 3 percent in poverty in York in 1951 were all aged. See Chapter 19, p. 576.

[23]P. Guillaume and J. P. Poussou, *Démographie Historique* (Paris, 1970), p. 341.

[24]About $75,000 at 1900 exchange rates. Of course, the Duke of Bedford also owned many other properties, including great expanses of farmland.

their bags and stood behind each of them at dinner. In that pre–income tax era, the most prodigal social display was possible. Count Robert de Montesquiou, the model for the Count de Charlus in Marcel Proust's *Remembrance of Things Past* (1913–27), held a musical gala in Paris in the early 1900s. He had rooms massed with roses and aigrettes, and placed a Wagnerian soprano "in a cloud of grey irises with a poinsettia here and there to remind us of the fire-theme." One of the guests, Countess Greffulhe, appeared "in a dress embroidered with golden lilies; a string of pearls, twisted in her hair, fell to her waist. She was going on to dine with the Queen of England."[25]

The very rich belonged, technically speaking, to one of two classes: the aristocracy or the wealthy middle class. Inherited noble title still mattered in the Europe of 1914. The great majority of those large landowners who monopolized social, economic, and political power in Eastern and southern Europe were titled aristocrats. On his Hungarian estate, a Prince Esterházy was virtually royal. The German aristocracy, concentrated on the great estates of Prussia, enjoyed almost total control of the German officer corps and of the top government positions. Even in urban-industrial England, every prime minister up to 1902 except Disraeli and Gladstone had been a peer.

Only in France and Italy was aristocratic title seriously diminished as a key to political power. The French revolutions of 1789, 1830, and 1848 had abolished the legal (although not the social) distinctions of birth, so that aristocrats were subject to the same laws and restricted to the same political rights as other citizens. The number of nobles in the two French houses of parliament declined from nearly a third of the total in 1871 to a mere handful in 1914.[26] The unification of Italy, from 1859 to 1871, had swept away the local kingdoms and the ruling houses to which the aristocrats had been attached, thereby diminishing their political roles. But even in France and Italy, aristocrats were still accorded enormous social deference; and although no longer powerful in electoral politics, they remained strong in the Army, the Church, and in diplomacy.

The wealthiest industrial and commercial tycoons were equal or superior to the aristocrats in everything except hereditary title. Traditionally, the possessors of great new fortunes did their best to acquire landed estates, aristocratic manners, and, eventually, a noble title itself for their children or grandchildren, if not for themselves. By 1900, however, many of the very wealthy had become less interested in buying their way into the aristocracy. As income from agriculture underwent a relative decline in the late nineteenth century, title more often needed wealth than wealth needed title. To recoup their fortunes, some aristocrats married American heiresses: Lord Randolph Churchill, Winston Churchill's father, married Jennie Jerome of New York; the French Count Boni de Castellane married the daughter of the American

[25]Philippe Jullian, *Prince of Aesthetes: Count Robert de Montesquiou* (New York, 1965), pp. 198–200.
[26]Mattei Dogan, "Political Ascent in a Class Society," in Dwaine Marvick, ed., *Political Decision Makers* (New York, 1961).

railroad entrepreneur Jay Gould. By 1900 the titled and untitled wealthy merged for every practical purpose, except, perhaps, that of inviting each other to dinner.

The Middle Class

Between the few very rich and the many poor lay the broad middle class. In its upper reaches, the European middle class was composed of comfortably established business and professional men, about whose smug self-confidence and intellectual narrowness the English novelist Arnold Bennett complained:

> Their assured, curt voices, their clothes, the similarity of manners, all show that they belong to a caste, and that the caste has been successful in the struggle for life.[27]

In early twentieth-century literature, the supreme example is the solid Hamburg merchant family whose rise and decline over several generations are described in Thomas Mann's novel *Buddenbrooks* (1902). The creators of the Buddenbrooks firm were sober, hard-working men, careful with their money, confident of its value, contemptuous of the frivolous, spendthrift ways of the aristocracy as much as of the coarse ways of the poor. Their highest aim was to instruct their sons in love of the family business. "I pray to God that I shall be able to turn over the business to you in its present state," old Johann Buddenbrooks wrote to his son. "Work, pray, and save."

Middle-class European life styles were intended to display respectability. Propriety was more highly valued than gaudy display, which was more characteristic of the *nouveau riche* or of the frivolous nobleman. The stiffness of clothing, the formality of meals, and the elaborate rituals of entertaining and leaving calling cards were expensive and painful ways of demonstrating to the outside world that one knew the proprieties and could afford to maintain them. Early twentieth-century novels of family life are filled with the "ceremonies of respectability," such as the savage description of Victorian child-rearing in Samuel Butler's *The Way of All Flesh* (1903), whose young hero was "taught to kneel . . . before he could well crawl."

Below the solid upper middle class ranged a large population that struggled, at the edge of insecurity, to keep up as many of the outward signs of respectability as it could. Shopkeepers, some rising skilled workers, and marginal professional men clung to middle-class values and signs, even though the gnawing knowledge that one bad break could send them into poverty dogged their lives, just as it did the lives of the wage earners.

The exact size of the European middle class in 1914 is impossible to measure because of that group's shadowy edges. At the top, the middle class merged into the aristocracy; at the bottom, it merged into the working class. By reputation, the nineteenth century had been the

[27]Quoted in Peter Laslett, *The World We Have Lost* (London, 1965), pp. 211–12.

century of middle-class triumph, and it would be easy to assume that by
1914 most residents of the more prosperous nations of Europe fell into
this category. But if we consider only those who were established in a
secure middle-class status and exclude those who merely aped its life
styles from below, the European middle class was still a minority in 1914.

The situation in England illustrates this point. One measure of the
solid middle class in England was the payment of income tax.[28] The rate
before 1914 was 5 percent on income over £150;[29] only about 300,000
persons (1 Englishman in 170) paid income tax, and they grumbled
about it. Not all these households could afford the outward signs of
middle-class life without struggling. From what we know of the distribution of wealth in England in 1914, some 120,000 households owned
about two-thirds of the capital wealth of the country: the real estate and
investments that made up the country's capital stock. Among them were
perhaps 40,000 landowners who owned 27 of the 34 million acres in the
country. At the other end of the scale, about two-thirds of the English
population disposed of only 5 percent of the national wealth.[30]

Another measure of the solid middle class was the employment of
servants. In 1901, those employed in domestic service formed the largest
occupational group in England, larger than mining, engineering, or
agriculture, if both men and women are counted. Among working
women, domestic service was by far the major occupation, employing
about 1.5 million of the 4 million English women who worked for
wages.[31] Harold Macmillan, Conservative prime minister of Britain in
the late 1950s, recalled his childhood home, the home of a prosperous
but austerely Methodist publisher, as one without frills; but there were
still seven servants.[32] Further down the scale, marginally middle-class
families struggled to keep one servant, for the woman who scrubbed and
cooked alone for her family, without the aid of gas or electric appliances,
inevitably looked and felt lower class. The Marx family, exiled in
London, barely scraped by in two rooms in Soho, with occasional income
from Karl Marx's articles for the New York *Tribune* and with help from
his friend Friedrich Engels. Even at the edge of poverty, however, the
Marxes still had their faithful servant, Frau Demuth.

The ultimate sign of the solid middle class was something less
measurable: the extent to which one could control one's life. Roger
Vailland's penetrating French novel *The Law* (1957), while actually set in
a primitive southern Italian village after the Second World War, is a

---

[28]First levied in England to pay for the Napoleonic Wars, the income tax was widely
adopted in Europe in the late 1880s and early 1890s. By 1910, only France, the United
States, Belgium, and Hungary had not yet levied taxes on income. The United States
adopted a national income tax in 1913. The First World War, or its immediate aftermath,
brought the income tax to all modern states.
[29]About $750 at 1914 exchange rates.
[30]Laslett, pp. 214–16.
[31]*Ibid.*, p. 226.
[32]Harold Macmillan, *The Winds of Change* (London, 1966), p. 39.

timeless essay on the meaning of class. Vailland's characters know that status is not simply a matter of wealth but of everyday human relations, of who "makes law" for others, who calls the tune. In Vailland's village no one "makes law" for the decayed nobleman Don Cesare. The aggressive entrepreneur Matteo Brigante subjects most of the villagers to his will, while he is humiliated by a few more independent than he. The rest of the villagers live, by and large, in a state of perpetual humiliation from which they do not have the money, nor the wit, nor the will to free themselves.

Most Europeans were too habituated to certain fundamental constraints—family obligations, sexual roles, and conformity to national styles and values—to notice how they controlled their lives. And an increasing proportion of Europeans were subjected to the results of many major decisions made by large companies or bureaucracies. The number of independent artisans had declined by 1900 to the irreducible 10 percent or so of carpenters, plumbers, and the like that has persisted through the twentieth century. Factory workers had become the most rapidly growing element of European populations in the late nineteenth century until their numbers leveled off around 1900 to the approximately one-third of the population that they still represent today. Their place as the fastest growing element at the turn of the century was taken by white-collar workers: clerical employees; workers in distribution, sales, and communications; and lower-level civil servants, such as teachers and postmen. Although many white-collar workers struggled to maintain a middle-class appearance, their lives were also subject to the decisions of others and to the dimly understood forces of the marketplace or of society.

It is an error, therefore, to believe that after a century of the "rise of the middle class" a majority of Europeans were established as independent middle-class men and women. Peter Laslett estimates that in England, the most highly developed urban and industrial region of Europe, only about 20 to 30 percent of the population could be called solidly middle class. An Englishman who was born within that charmed circle, or who reached it by his own efforts, could well reflect with Winston Churchill that "lapped in the accumulated treasure of the long past, the old world in its sunset was fair to see."[33] Outside that charmed circle lay a penumbra of those who struggled to imitate it. And then came the poor majority. If we extend the same analysis to the Continent, we would find rather similar social hierarchies in the most highly urbanized and industrialized regions: northern France, the Low Countries, western Germany, Sweden, and perhaps northern Italy. Further east and south, the middle class was restricted to a meager few merchants and moneylenders in the sparse market towns; here, the aristocrats and the peasant mass confronted each other across even sharper and steeper social gradations.

[33]Winston Churchill, *The World Crisis, 1911–1914* (London, 1923), p. 199.

How easily might a European move from one level to another in his lifetime? Clearly, European classes were not castes. One's lifelong social position was not immutably set by birth. Whereas inherited title and upper-class birth still lent enormous social prestige, wealth already counted for more, and that could be attained in a lifetime, given luck and will. However, the way up was narrowing. Studies of successful French businessmen show that more of them had risen out of the artisan ranks in the early stages of industrialization, before 1850, than was the case at the end of the nineteenth century, when it took more capital to launch a big enterprise. It was highly exceptional for a European to climb into a higher class in one generation: moves upward usually took several generations. Most Europeans in 1914 could expect to finish out their days in about the same social position as they had begun.

A move upward, moreover, could involve very painful personal experiences of isolation and rejection. In *Howard's End* (1910), E. M. Forster's novel about the workings of class distinctions in England, young Leonard Bast.

> stood at the extreme verge of gentility. He was not in the abyss, but he could see it, and at times people whom he knew had dropped into it. . . . Had he lived some centuries ago, in the brightly colored civilizations of the past, he would have had a definite status, his rank and income would have corresponded. But in his day the angel of Democracy had arisen, enshadowing the classes with leathern wings, and proclaiming: "All men are equal—all men, that is to say, who possess umbrellas." And so he was obliged to assert gentility.[34]

Bast's rather crude efforts to acquire "culture" and the misguided attempts of two wealthy young women to assist his social ascent destroyed him. The women suffered only slightly. The moral seemed to be, "There's never any great risk, as long as you have money."

Population Control   **The Family**

Europe at the turn of the twentieth century had passed one of the major turning points in social history: the "demographic transition," or the "fertility transition." In its simplest terms, this was the trend toward small families.

Traditional societies may pass through several demographic stages. In the first, population is kept approximately stable because very high birth rates are balanced by very high death rates. In the second stage, improved health conditions and better food supplies diminish the death rate, and population soars. Northern and Western Europe reached this

[34]E. M. Forster, *Howard's End* (New York, 1954), pp. 45–46, 60.

stage in the seventeenth, eighteenth, and early nineteenth centuries (and the Third World is reaching it today).

It was at this stage, in the nineteenth century, that Europeans began to see the advantages of having a small number of children.[35] In the first place, there was less reason to have many babies because improved living conditions meant that most of one's children could survive, an experience previously unknown. Second, children were expensive. Although more children may have meant more income on the farm, factory workers discovered, after limitations had been imposed on child labor, that more children only meant higher expenses for food and clothing. And as public education became widespread, the cost of education made children even more expensive. The lower middle class found that the "respectable" middle-class life style would be easier to reach with fewer children. Finally, the state's assumption of care of the aged dispelled the notion that one must have many children to support one's old age.

The move to have fewer children first became widespread soon after 1800 in the French middle and lower middle class: the first people in the world to practice birth control on a massive scale. Smaller families became more common in England, Germany, and Scandinavia in the 1870s and after. The trend toward smaller families did not correspond clearly to religious teaching, for it was nominally Catholic France that had led the way. Nor did it correspond to the availability of birth-control devices. Some means of preventing births had long been known, especially late marriage and *coitus interruptus*. To be sure, modern industry and medical knowledge made effective devices available: the diaphragm and rubber condoms were manufactured in the late nineteenth century. But, before cheap latex condoms were developed in the 1930s, such devices were too expensive for most people.[36] The important change, then, was not a technical one but a change in values. The possibility of attaining a middle-class existence now seemed within the grasp of many more families, provided they had fewer children.

As a result of this major shift in social attitudes, the birth rate in northern and Western Europe declined by half over the forty years after 1890. European populations as a whole leveled off. For example, Danish women born between 1840 and 1844 had an average of 4.4 children, with 60 percent of their fertility occurring after the age of thirty; Danish women born between 1905 and 1909 had an average of 2.25 children, with 60 percent of them being born before the women were thirty.[37]

[35]There is no guarantee that societies will enter this third stage. Where industrial development is weak, families may continue to be large, and, as in India and Egypt, population growth will far outstrip productivity. If there is high infant mortality, parents will continue to have many children, and there will be no hope of the population leveling off, except through catastrophe.

[36]The pill, which had important social effects both because it was inexpensive and because it was taken at the woman's initiative, was a development of the 1960s.

[37]I. C. Mattiessen, "Replacement for Generations of Danish Females, 1840/44–1920/24," in D. V. Glass and Roger Revelle, *Population and Social Change* (London, 1972).

Similar changes were taking place in all the modernized nations of Europe.

This shift in social attitudes has been called "one of the outstanding events of modern times,"[38] and it was working itself out through all the social institutions in Europe during the years covered by this book.

One traditional means of birth control in Europe had been late marriage. Many women in nineteenth-century Europe either married late or not at all; unmarried women were at their most numerous in nineteenth-century European societies, and not just in such novels as Jane Austen's *Pride and Prejudice* (1813). Married women, by contrast, continued to bear children late in life, as long as large families remained desirable. The changes at the turn of the century were manifold. People began to marry younger in Europe in the twentieth century, and women bore their children earlier in life; at the same time, their life expectancy was longer. The previously mentioned Danish women born between 1905 and 1909 could expect to live to the age of sixty-eight, while their predecessors born between 1840 and 1844 lived only an average of forty-seven years. Having finished childbearing at around the age of thirty, many of these modern women yearned to lead interesting and constructive lives in other ways.

The Woman's Place

Men were still absolute rulers of their households, however. The Napoleonic Code, which was the law not only in France but in many other European countries that had modernized their statute books in the nineteenth century, reinforced this traditional authority of the husband and father. Wives could not own property by themselves, make decisions concerning the domicile or the education of their children, or testify in court against their husbands. The father in the German upper–middle-class household in which the sociologist Max Weber grew up was probably no more authoritarian than most. Perhaps more than most, however, Weber's mother chafed against her husband's authority after her last child entered school in 1886, because much of the family's wealth came from her dowry, and yet she could not use it on the charities in which she wanted to express her Calvinist personality.

> Thus, in the fifth decade of her life, Helene [Weber], in accordance with the tradition of these circles, had at her disposal neither a fixed household allowance nor a special sum for her personal needs. Rather, with her expense books . . . she must request what she needs for the house and for herself from case to case. She is thus subject to continual control and—equally typically under this regimen—to the frequent criticism and amazement of her husband at the great expenditure, whose inevitability he cannot really judge. Since over half the family income flows from her own estate, she experiences this situation as increasingly contradictory and burdensome.[39]

[38] *Ibid.*
[39] Arthur Mitzman, *The Iron Cage* (New York, 1970), p. 45

By all that we can learn of working-class life in this period, the father's authority was, if anything, more absolute the further one descended in the social scale. A young Englishman recently recalled the life style of his grandparents at the end of the nineteenth century. The grandfather, a boot and shoe worker, seems to have been somewhat more harsh and less provident than many English working-class men, but the deference of his wife, who bore eleven children in fourteen years, was probably not exceptional.

> The womenfolk had always danced a most slavish attendance upon their men. In the house the men did nothing. They were not expected to carry the coal or to chop sticks or to carry the dustbin through the house to be placed on the pavement for collection. . . . When Edwin came home from work his chair had to be vacated immediately. He would throw down his kit-bag and coat on the floor for her to pick up and without a word he would sit down and lift each boot in turn for her to undo the laces and pull them off, resting his foot as he did so on the darned and faded pinafore that she always wore in the house. . . . When he died, the attention which he had received all his life devolved upon the only male then living at home.[40]

The woman's role began to change first in political terms in the years before 1914. Since women could already vote in Australia (1902),

[40]Jeremy Seabrook, *The Unprivileged* (London, 1967), pp. 17–18.

Suffragettes being arrested during a demonstration at Buckingham Palace, May 21, 1914.

Finland (1907), and Norway (1913), as well as in some states of the United States, such as Wyoming (1869), women's suffrage was already on the agenda. The issue was most energetically pressed in England, where between 1910 and 1914 the determined Mrs. Emmeline Pankhurst, her daughters, and her followers conducted demonstrations for the vote that led to hundreds of arrests and at least one death. The electoral barrier did not break down in England and Germany until after the First World War, however, and not in France and Italy until after the Second World War.

As for the question of women's rights in employment and within the family, the great increase in women's labor during the First World War was only the beginning of a long evolution in Europe toward the expectation that women might lead more independent lives. A much more profound shift of values had to take place before the French Napoleonic Code, for example, could be revised in the 1960s to give full juridicial equality to married women.

Political Systems and Mass Movements

The basic European political unit in 1914 was the sovereign nation-state. Sovereignty—a political concept developed in sixteenth-century Europe to justify absolute monarchy against the claims of feudal nobles and the Church—was that quality of a state that had a single source of power within and accepted no legal sanctions from without. Sovereignty stood in opposition to the medieval notion that all earthly authority is answerable to a universal divine, or natural, law. Even when the absolute authority of a prince had been replaced by popular sovereignty, it was axiomatic in 1914 that a state was the final judge of its own interests and that it dealt with other states in accordance with those interests. Even though states might accept some international agreements in pre-1914 Europe for their own convenience (for example, international postal conventions, the Red Cross, the rules of war, and the voluntary international arbitration machinery set up at the Hague Conference of 1899), they were still a law unto themselves in their dealings with one another. Those states that commanded sufficient power to prevent any outside intervention in their affairs, in fact as well as in theory, were considered Great Powers. In 1914, the Great Powers included Britain, France, Germany, Russia, Austria-Hungary, and perhaps Italy, but no longer Spain or the Ottoman Empire.

The Monarchy

Most European states were monarchies in 1914. Among the Great Powers, only France was a republic. Spain, which experimented briefly with a republic in 1873, reestablished the monarchy in 1875. Throughout the nineteenth century, newly independent states had tended to call in some unemployed German princeling to express national unity beyond the reach of any faction: Prince Leopold of Saxe-Coburg for Belgium in 1830, Otto of Bavaria for Greece in 1832 (and a Danish prince when Otto was deposed in 1862), Charles of Sigmaringen-Hohenzollern to become the Romanian King Carol in 1881, Alexander of Battenberg followed by Ferdinand of Saxe-Coburg for Bulgaria in 1879 and 1886, and so forth.

Outright republicanism was an exceptionally radical political position everywhere outside France and Switzerland up to 1914. In England, the royal house was more sincerely beloved under Victoria and Edward VII than it had been under George IV or William IV earlier in the nineteenth century. Most Italian liberals accepted the Piedmontese royal house that had unified Italy, and almost all German liberals accepted the Prussian Hohenzollerns as emperors of the proud new German Reich. To be republican in the empires of Austria-Hungary and Russia up to 1914 was to be revolutionary.

Although monarchy seemed an unquestioned fixture of most European states, great and small, it was equally accepted in 1914 that it should have constitutional limitations. Here too there was a gradation from west to east. In Britain, Scandinavia, and the Low Countries the king reigned but did not rule; in Italy, Germany, and Eastern Europe limitations on royal authority were both newer and narrower. In 1914, it was clear that Kaiser Wilhelm II of Germany, Emperor Franz Josef of Austria-Hungary, and Tsar Nicholas II of Russia still personally had the last word on national policy.

Even in these empires, however, there was a persistent trend toward some degree of constitutional limitation. The German Empire's *Reichstag* (parliament) had decisive budgetary power in many realms, although it had lost the all-important struggle to obtain control over the military budget in 1886 and 1887. Prime ministers of the Habsburg Empire, as in the German Empire, had to obtain the consent of parliaments in Austria and Hungary for their internal policies. Even the autocrat of all the Russias was obliged to establish a parliament (Duma) after the revolution of 1905. Limited though its authority was, the Duma did have legislative powers, and its consent was required to appropriate funds other than those for the military budget and the emperor's own purse. These developments encouraged Russian constitutional liberals like Paul Miliukov and reformist socialists like Aleksandr Kerensky to believe that their country would eventually be governed like the Western European constitutional monarchies.

For Miliukov and Kerensky, and for European constitutional liberals in general, the political issue in 1914 was still the issue first posed clearly by the French Revolution of 1789: how to replace hereditary authority with careers open to talent. Constitutional liberals in prewar Europe looked to a parliament on the British model as the best instrument to curb hereditary powers.

Prewar royalty. Kaiser Wilhelm II of Germany greets King Victor Emmanuel III of Italy aboard the yacht Hohenzollern *in the lagoon at Venice.*

The Role of Parliaments

Parliaments were being transformed by two parallel developments in the generation before the First World War. First, as states expanded their activities into new social and economic fields, parliaments simply had more to do. With an increase in the scope and complexity of legislation, members of parliaments became less dilettantish, and annual sessions took up a greater part of the year. The British House of Commons, for example, which sat an average 116 days a year in the mid-nineteenth century, was sitting an average 146 days a year on the eve of the First World War.

Second, more Europeans were receiving the right to vote for members of their parliaments. Britain had extended the vote to most adult males in 1884. Universal male suffrage had been established in France in 1848, and was effectively exercised after 1871. It was extended to Belgium in 1893, Spain in 1890, Norway in 1898, Sweden and Austria in 1907, and Italy in 1912.[41]

This development lagged in central and Eastern Europe. Although the German *Reichstag* was elected by all adult males from the time of the Reich's creation in 1871, the powerful upper house, the *Bundesrat,* was appointed. And Prussia, whose power far outweighed that of the other states in the German federal system, did not join the lesser German

[41]See page 27 for the right of women to vote.

states in granting universal manhood suffrage for state governments. Prussia maintained a three-class voting system that allowed the wealthiest handful of citizens, those who paid the top third of the taxes, to elect a third of the deputies. Hungary and most of the Balkan States had limited suffrage until the First World War. The Russian Empire seemed to be taking steps backward in the decade before 1914. The electoral law that permitted nearly all adult males to vote for the first and second Dumas in 1904 and 1906 was drastically curtailed for the elections of the third and fourth Dumas in 1907 and 1912. But liberal optimists could consider these temporary eddies in an inevitable tide of constitutional government.

In most of Europe directly elected lower houses gained ground against less democratically chosen upper houses. (There had been no upper house at all in France since 1871.) The most striking victory was that of the British House of Commons over the House of Lords. When the Lords opposed the welfare provisions in the Liberal leader Lloyd George's budget in 1909, they emerged from the conflict shorn of their absolute veto over bills passed by the Commons.

There were other subtler but no less important expansions of popular control over legislatures, such as the spread of the secret ballot and salaried parliament seats. The Australian, or secret, ballot provided envelopes and private voting booths for voters. Its introduction in France in 1913 reduced the pervasive influence of local "notables" over their lesser neighbors in political matters. The provision of a salary of £400 per year for all members of the British House of Commons in 1911 made it possible for men without private incomes to serve in that body, long one of the most gentry-dominated of European parliaments.

The progress of parliamentary institutions in European politics was still very uneven in 1914. The persistent growth of such institutions made it possible to assume that the trend of the future lay in the direction of broader electoral democracy. But vigorous counterattacks came from both old autocrats and new nationalists. Efforts to broaden the Prussian three-class voting system met with the most resolute opposition of the kaiser, as well as of many German liberals who had been converted by Bismarck's successes into believing that a strong state was more important than civil liberties. "What good would social reforms do us," said the German liberal Friedrich Naumann, "if the Cossacks come?"[42] The Austrian Parliament had been paralyzed off and on since 1899 by demonstrations begun by Czech and German deputies over the extension of minority language rights in the schools and courtrooms of the multinational empire. The Russian tsar was successfully rolling back the reforms he had been obliged to grant in 1905. In retrospect, it looks as if the decade before the First World War was not the dawn but the twilight of parliamentary regimes, the last moment before the economic complexities of the postwar years replaced parliaments with bureaucra-

---

[42]James J. Sheehan, *The Career of Lujo Brentano* (Chicago, 1968), p. 148.

tic planners and before nationalist passion for state "efficiency" replaced them with dictators.

The Socialist Movement

Social justice and economic rights emerged as new and pressing issues alongside the constitutional ones before the First World War. The horrors of the early factory system and the early industrial towns had helped provoke revolutionary outbursts in 1848 and in the Paris Commune of 1871. During the generation before the First World War, however, pressures for fundamental change in the capitalistic economic system were more sustained, for they came from new permanent institutions: labor unions and socialist parties.

Trade unions—fraternities of skilled workers banding together to protect their interests—had broadened into labor unions made up of whole industrial populations in the late nineteenth century. Although many governments had ceased to forbid the existence of labor unions (Britain in 1825; France in 1884), their rapid growth in both numbers and permanent cadres after the 1890s alarmed middle-class liberals as well as conservatives. British and German unions had over 2 million members, or about 30 percent of the male labor force, by 1914. German unions far exceeded those of other countries in the wealth and size of their permanent staffs, which grew ten times—from 290 to 2867—

A socialist rally in France, addressed in 1913 by the leading figure of the French socialist movement, Jean Jaurès.

between 1900 and 1914. French unions, which had organized less than 6 percent of the French work force and had far smaller strike funds, made up in militancy what they lacked in organization. The French government used the Army repeatedly to help control major strikes from 1906 to 1909.

New socialist parties made use of broadening voting rights to bring the mass of wage earners into politics independently, as a class. The influence of Karl Marx, who had died in 1883, became predominant among organized factory workers by the 1890s (except in Britain), displacing both the liberal reformers and the Catholic socialists who had attempted to lead earlier movements for economic justice. Marx's followers after the 1890s interpreted his strategy as the conquest of European democracies through the sheer numbers of the growing and voting proletariat. Their program did not seem futile in 1914. The German Social Democratic party with 110 seats and one-third of the votes cast in the elections of 1912, was the largest single party in the *Reichstag.* That was only the most conspicuous success of the socialist electoral strategy. The French Socialist party elected 103 of the 602 deputies in 1914, with about 1.5 million votes. The British Labour party won 29 seats out of 670 in the elections of 1906; the Austrian Social Democrats won 87 out of 516 in 1907; and at their high-water point in the second Duma of 1906, the Russian Social Revolutionaries (agrarian revolutionaries) and Social Democrats (Marxists) together held 103 out of 520 seats.

The impact of electoral socialism on European politics on the eve of war in 1914 was immense. In some cases, when socialists and liberal reformers joined forces, important social reforms were legislated. In England, Labour and Liberal votes combined in 1911 to enact a worker's insurance program. But, for many liberals as well as conservatives the rapid growth of Marxist parties lit up the political sky with the lightning flashes of a coming storm. In the German *Reichstag,* the huge Social Democratic delegation refused to stand for the traditional cheer of "Kaiser hoch!," and the kaiser spoke quite openly of their leaders as anti-German elements *(Deutschfeinde).* The outbreak of war in 1914 interrupted a gathering battle as to whether European liberals, who had traditionally put all their faith in the creation of parliamentary institutions, would let those institutions be captured by Marxists.

The Nationalist Movement

Nationalism stirred more hearts in Europe in 1914, including those of many workers, than did socialism. The idea of popular sovereignty led very easily to the notion that the people should be not only sovereign but enthusiastic citizens. In Western Europe after 1789, emotional loyalty to the nation supported the consolidation of large, homogeneous nation-states. The fervent citizen-armies of the French Revolution had been only the first spectacular example of nationalism ranged against the traditional internationalism of aristocrats and the clergy. Spreading outward from France, nationalism had aroused the dispersed German- and Italian-speaking peoples of Europe to create nation-states in the mid-nineteenth century where there had been only petty principalities before. The young Italian Fabrizzio in Stendhal's novel *The Charterhouse of Parma* (1839) wanted to join Napoleon on the battlefield because he thought the emperor represented the triumph of great national units over backward provinces like the Duchy of Parma. The revolutionaries in Germany in 1848 felt the same contempt for the hundreds of small German states that had survived Napoleon's campaigns.

After the unifications of Germany and Italy by 1871, universal education and mass communication gave both new and old states in Western Europe the means to make citizens more homogeneous and more loyal. Western European states typically used universal education to extirpate regional dialects as well as to teach patriotism. The Bretons, Basques, Welsh, and speakers of Provençal and of various German dialects were absorbed into larger communities; maps showing Europe divided into large areas of unshaded primary colors reflected, not inaccurately, this growing cultural homogeneity. Uprooted populations of the new cities, in need of some kind of emotional attachment, responded warmly to parades and patriotic speeches. Thus by 1914 nationalism tended to reinforce the homogeneity of the Great Powers in Western Europe.

In Eastern Europe, nationalism played an opposite role in the generation before 1914. As long-submerged peoples—like the Czechs, Poles, and Hungarians—as well as other ethnic groups that had never formed their own states—like the Slovaks, Slovenes, Albanians, and South Slavs—rediscovered the worth of their own languages and cultures, the trend toward a single state language was reversed. The Czech historian František Palacký, for example, had felt compelled to begin publishing his pioneering history of the Czech people—*History of Bohemia*—in 1836 in German, the language of learning throughout Eastern Europe. Only in 1848 was the publication of a Czech version begun. Such rediscovered national loyalties generated separatist movements. The Ottoman Empire, by 1913, had lost all but a few square miles of its European holdings to new nationalities: the Greeks, Albanians, Bulgarians, and Romanians. The multinational Habsburg Empire conceded special status to the Hungarians in 1867 by creating a "dual monarchy" in which Emperor Franz Josef governed simultaneously as emperor of Austria and king of Hungary, with the two states administering their own internal matters. After that one great national concession, however, Hungarian intransigence prevented similar concessions to the other major Habsburg subject nationalities: the Czechs, Poles, and South Slavs. This refusal only sharpened the thirst of these peoples for national autonomy, and eventually drove them beyond autonomy to demands for total independence during the First World War.

The dominant nationalities of the threatened empires responded with heightened ethnic feelings of their own. Pan-Germans dreamed of uniting all German-speaking peoples of Eastern Europe within the Reich. Pan-Slavs in Russia reasserted their ancient traditions against Western teaching and dreamed of uniting all Slavs under the tutelage of Holy Mother Russia; pan-Slavs in the Balkans wanted both unity and independence. Pan-Turanians, who tried to modernize the failing Ottoman Empire in 1908, wanted to recover all the original Turkish lands in central Asia and unite them under a revivified Ottoman rule.

Far from reinforcing existing states, therefore, Eastern European nationalism kept bursting the shell of the old dynastic empires of Turkey, Austria-Hungary, and Russia. Revolutions in Greece in the 1820s, in Poland in 1848 and 1863, in Bulgaria in 1875, and the Balkan Wars of 1912 to 1913 were only some of the more notable eruptions of ethnic nationalism and expansionism in nineteenth-century Eastern Europe. It seemed likely in 1914 that neither increased parliamentary democracy within the existing empires nor the traditional diplomacy of balancing the empires off against one another could be expected to contain these boiling ethnic pressures indefinitely.

Inherited Creeds   *Liberalism*

At the opening of the twentieth century, a great many Europeans—mostly members of the middle class or aspirants to it—took for granted the values of nineteenth-century liberalism.[43] Liberal thought was first formulated by the French *philosophes* of the late eighteenth century and the progressive rationalists of the early nineteenth century. But by 1900, their heroic battles had long been over, and all that remained was a pervasive set of easy assumptions that many middle-class Europeans felt were self-evident.

The first assumption was that the world was fully knowable. The universe was an orderly material system operating according to laws whose detailed workings were being uncovered bit by bit by scientists. This point of view had been dramatized by the discovery of Sir Isaac Newton (1642–1727) that the same gravitational laws accounted for both the fall of an apple and the orbits of the planets; it had been popularized in the eighteenth century by *philosophes* like Voltaire. The evident progress of science gave that point of view further currency in the nineteenth century.

A second assumption was that human beings were by nature capable of fully understanding this orderly universe. Human beings possessed a fixed, innate quality called "reason," which, when liberated by education from the dark bondage of superstition, could recognize an objective

---

[43]Current American usage of the word *liberal* to refer loosely to the far left may create confusion. The word *liberal* refers in this book to the faith in progress, individualism, and laissez-faire that permeated the European middle class when the twentieth century opened.

truth on which all men, if properly instructed, would agree. As the British liberal philosopher John Stuart Mill wrote in *On Liberty* (1859):

> There is, on the whole, a preponderance among mankind of rational opinions and rational conduct . . . owing to a quality of the human mind, . . . namely that his errors are corrigible. He is capable of rectifying his mistakes, by discussion and experience. . . . Wrong opinions and practices gradually yield to fact and argument. . . . If the lists are kept open, we may hope that if there be a better truth, it will be found when the human mind is capable of receiving it.[44]

Mill died in 1873, but his cautious hope that free discussion would lead to higher truth was widely taken for granted in 1900.

From these two axioms of liberal thought flowed the corollaries of liberal practice. The basic liberal weapon was schooling. Its fundamental duty was to free all persons from religious superstitions and inherited social distinctions that blocked the full development of reason's capacities—hence, the European middle class's drive for universal, secular, and free primary instruction in the late nineteenth century. Free and obligatory primary schooling had been achieved in Western Europe by the 1880s and was accepted as a goal even in Tsarist Russia by 1913, although large areas of illiteracy remained in Spain and Italy as well as in Russia.

Once an individual's reason had been set free by education, that person became a *citizen,* to use the term devised in the French Revolution to express the common membership of equally rational human beings in a free society. Citizens could be expected to share in political decisions without becoming playthings of demagoguery or prejudice—hence, the gradual conversion of European liberals to universal manhood suffrage during the nineteenth century, as literacy became more widespread. A citizen in an ideal liberal state also enjoyed equal status before the law and equal opportunity to enter the career best suited to his or her talents. It followed that a society of citizens would be naturally harmonious and that the state would need only a bare minimum of machinery to assure order.

In the economic realm, liberals assumed that reasonable persons would serve their own enlightened self-interest in a way so attuned to natural harmony that all of society would benefit. "Economic man," the business subspecies of rational man, if left free from clumsy state interference, would produce an ever-better product at an ever-lower price, thereby serving the community as well as himself. Temporary maladjustments in employment, wages, or prices would settle themselves, as if by an "invisible hand," to use the phrase dear to liberal economist Adam Smith (1723–90) and his nineteenth-century successors. This classical-liberal economy was, of course, nowhere in practice in 1914 Europe, not least because businessmen wanted state protection from foreign competition and from organized workers. But liberal economists still fought against tariffs and business cartels in 1914,

[44]John Stuart Mill, *On Liberty,* ed. R. B. McCallum (Oxford, 1948), pp. 17–18.

convinced that a self-adjusting world–free-trade system was the most efficient way to cheap abundance.

The conspicuous successes of science and technology in the nineteenth century, the rapid spread of literacy, the expansion of political liberties, and unprecedented economic growth encouraged hopes of indefinite progress toward human perfectibility. The French poet Victor Hugo wrote in 1859, after watching the ascent of a balloon, that it represented "the great *élan* of progress toward the heavens."

> Toward the divine, pure future, toward virtue,
> Toward beckoning science,
> Toward the end of evil, toward generous forgiveness,
> Toward abundance, peace and laughter, and a happy Mankind.[45]

Hugo's poem suggested that human mastery of the air would replace the old "diversity of languages, of reason, of laws, of customs," with a new, twentieth-century world of human harmony. The conquest of "so much sky would abolish the Nations." As late as 1895, the French scientist Marcellin Berthelot could still proclaim his faith in the nineteenth century's positivist dream that the certainties of science would be extended to every aspect of human knowledge, bringing with them not only material but ethical improvement. "The universal triumph of science will assure to mankind the most possible happiness and morality."[46]

But by the time that Europeans had actually begun to master the air (the Frenchman Louis Bleriot flew across the English Channel in 1909, only six years after the first brief airplane flight at Kitty Hawk), Victor Hugo's vision of human harmony through flight was already highly dubious. Science seemed as likely to favor the warmakers as the peacemakers, or as likely to permit human beings to become slack and decadent as "happy and moral": the two futures promised in H. G. Wells's most popular science fiction novels, *The War of the Worlds* (1898) and *The Time Machine* (1895). The American essayist Henry Adams, visiting the machinery exhibits at the Paris World's Fair of 1900, wrote that he

> would sit by the hour over the great dynamos watching them run noiselessly and smoothly as planets and asking them—with infinite courtesy—where the Hell they are going. They are marvelous. The Gods are not in it. Chiefly the Germans. . . . I can already see that the fellow who gets to 1930 will wish he hadn't.[47]

Such forebodings, however, were still the exception as the new century opened. The French philosopher Jean-Paul Sartre recalled in childlike terms (Sartre was nine years old in 1914) the hopeful view of human destiny that he had absorbed from his grandfather on the eve of the First World War.

[45]Victor Hugo, "Le Vingtième Siècle: Pleine mer; plein ciel," in *La Légende des Siècles* (1859).
[46]Marcellin Berthelot, "Science et Morale," *Revue de Paris* (February 1, 1895): 469.
[47]Henry Adams, *The Education of Henry Adams* (Boston, 1918), p. 379, and *Selected Letters,* ed. Newton Arvin (New York, 1951), p. 220.

There had been kings, emperors. They were very, very wicked. They had been driven out; everything was happening for the best.[48]

37

INHERITED
CREEDS

It was not only children who absorbed the liberal confidence in reason and progress in 1914. The Cambridge mathematician and philosopher Bertrand Russell, who was forty-two years old in 1914 and reputed to be the keenest skeptical mind in England, later recalled that "we all felt convinced that nineteenth-century progress would continue, and that we ourselves would be able to contribute something of value."[49] In the words of a more recent Cambridge graduate, Leonard Woolf:

> The main difference in the world before 1914 from the world after 1914 was in the sense of security and the growing belief that it was a supremely good thing for people to be communally and individually happy. . . . It seemed as though human beings might really be on the brink of becoming civilized.[50]

Conservatism

Conservatism was the accepted value system of kings, aristocrats, most priests, and many of their lesser supporters, especially in Eastern and southern Europe. European conservatives were pessimistic about human nature. They believed that "depraved" humanity was best guided by its natural leaders. Not all conservatives still believed that natural leaders were provided by God; a growing number of secular conservatives argued that natural leaders had been provided by history. Human society, in their view, was the product of a long, evolutionary process. Its parts fit together like a living biological organism, according to the favorite conservative analogy. To hack away at the limbs of that social organism in the name of some abstract principle was, according to conservatives, worse than a crime: it was pointless folly.

It should not be imagined that European conservatism at the beginning of the twentieth century was merely a pale nostalgia for things medieval. Modern conservatism began as a vigorous counterattack against the French Revolution of 1789. By 1914, the threat of socialism and of social revolution (as in France in 1871 and Russia in 1905) had been added to the older threat of democracy and of the abolition of all inherited status.

Modern conservatism underwent a vigorous rebirth shortly before 1914. A new generation of conservative propagandists and organizers moved conservatism out of the *châteaux* and pulpits and into the streets. They adapted it to the age of mass politics by adding a number of mass enthusiasms—nationalism, anticapitalism, and anti-Semitism—to the older values of social hierarchy, the organic interpretation of society, and the teachings of religion. While more traditional conservatism reigned in the villages and castles of peasant–aristocratic Eastern and

[48]Jean-Paul Sartre, *The Words* (New York, 1966), p. 15.
[49]Alan Wood, *Bertrand Russell, The Passionate Skeptic* (London, 1957), p. 31.
[50]Leonard Woolf, *Beginning Again* (London, 1964), pp. 36, 44.

southern Europe, new conservative leaders appeared in two capitals—
Paris and Vienna—where liberal values had been undermined by
national decline, fear of socialism, and concern about cultural decadence.

In Paris, Charles Maurras' *Action française* movement was traditionally
conservative in its call for a return to monarchy and the Church as the
only way to arrest France's slothful decline under the Third Republic.
But Maurras also struck a number of new notes. His was a call to action,
with high value placed on athletic vigor, and even violence, in life and in
politics. His strong-arm squad, the *Camelots du roi,* made up of university
students and disgruntled members of the lower middle class, beat up
liberal professors and broke up leftist meetings. Maurras appealed to
shopkeepers threatened by debt and modern competition with a blend
of anti-Semitism and a selective anticapitalism aimed at banks and
department stores. His militant nationalism was designed to paper over
class conflict with a single mass enthusiasm. The *Action française* was a
genuine innovation in the way in which it brought together traditional
conservatives and frightened ex-liberals in a movement that was most
conspicuous for what it was against: national disunity, social conflict, and
cultural decadence.

Georg von Schönerer's German-National movement in Vienna
came out of the animosities on the borderlands of Eastern Europe,
where German-speaking peoples found their old preeminence challenged by the rise of Slavic nationalism and socialist claims. Schönerer,
the son of a liberal aristocrat, scoffed at his father's formulas for
moderate constitutional monarchy. Unlike traditional conservatives,
however, he had little faith in the existing social hierarchies under which
the Habsburg Empire was slowly drifting into decay. With the sharp
aggressiveness characteristic of the new right, Schönerer mobilized
students, shopkeepers, and fervent nationalists around a new populist,
anti-Semitic demagoguery in the 1880s.[51] The influence of Schönerer
was still vivid in Vienna in the early 1900s, when a young art student
named Adolf Hitler was living a marginal existence there.

Organized Religion

Most Europeans still professed a religious creed in 1914. Organized
religion, however, was certainly weaker than it had been two generations
earlier. In the villages, credulity had diminished with the spread of
schooling and movement into cities. A widespread positivism, the belief
that science would continue to find material explanations for everything,
made the cultural climate inhospitable to the claims of religious faith.

No great religious thinkers were able to breast the tide of positivism in
the nineteenth century. Among the educated, organized religion had
not yet recovered from such humiliations as the public debate between

---

[51]This new right will be discussed more thoroughly when its fascist offspring is examined
in Chapter 7.

the brilliant Darwinian protagonist Thomas Henry Huxley and Bishop Samuel Wilberforce of Oxford in the 1860s. The Bishop of Oxford thought he had demolished Huxley by asking whether "it was through his grandfather or his grandmother that he claimed his descent from a monkey"; but it was clearly Huxley who won the day.

The main buttresses of organized religion at the opening of the twentieth century were reduced to social backwardness and social conformity. Religious practice remained fairly vigorous in those villages least penetrated by modernist ideas, and among the middle class that had renounced the scepticism of its fathers and flocked to church as a manifestation of respectability and support for the social order. The churches of Europe emerged as a mainstay of the social order, which did them little good among the resentful poor. The Orthodox Church of Russia was headed by the tsar's appointee, the Procurator of the Holy Synod, and received most of its funds from the state. The Catholic Church, strongest in southern Europe and the Rhineland, was international, but its social doctrines lent vigorous support to established authority. The Protestant state churches (such as the Church of England and the Lutheran churches in Germany and Scandinavia) functioned primarily as arenas for a weekly display of social correctness by the upper class.

Toward a New Consciousness

The inherited creeds discussed above were the commonplace assumptions of many ordinary, educated Europeans in 1914. Intellectuals, however, began to reject these commonplaces as early as the mid-nineteenth century. At that early stage, challenges came only from isolated individuals: the religious anguish of the Danish theologian Sören Kierkegaard, the self-scrutinizing sensitivity of the French poet Charles Baudelaire, and the scorn of the German philosopher Friedrich Nietzsche for the flabby mediocrity of contemporary liberal and Christian values. These lone seekers did not begin to be appreciated until the 1890s. After 1900, intellectual rejection of nineteenth-century ways of understanding human experience swelled into broad movements. By 1914, nothing less than revolutions were underway in science, aesthetic vision, and basic beliefs about the place of reason in human affairs.

The Revolution in Science

In contrast to the easily grasped technical triumphs of the nineteenth century, the most striking scientific achievements of the new century were both difficult to understand and disquieting.

Physicists' assumptions about the very nature of matter were challenged as the twentieth century opened. Like Democritus in 490 B.C., nineteenth-century physicists had supposed that matter was composed of irreducible material particles, or atoms. The accidental discovery of

X-rays by the German physicist Wilhelm Roentgen in 1895 set off a train of investigations of their properties; the results were difficult to reconcile with earlier assumptions. The British physicist J. J. Thompson discovered in 1897 that when X-rays were passed through a gas, they dislodged tiny electrically charged particles that left traces on a photographic plate. The uniformity of these particles under various strengths of radiation suggested to Thompson that they must be component parts of the atoms of gas. Subsequent researchers called these particles "electrons." It became clear that atoms were not irreducible, but were whole worlds in themselves. These discoveries opened the entirely new field of atomic physics.

At about the same time, the German physicist Max Planck, unable to account by conventional mechanical calculations for the way energy was distributed along the spectrum of radiant heat, proposed the hypothesis in 1900 that energy was not a continuous flow, but a periodic emission of packets of energy, or quanta. His quantum theory turned out to have far-wider applications than Planck had anticipated. Most importantly, it cleared away many difficulties in explaining the results of experiments in atomic physics. By applying quantum theory to the internal structure of the atom, J. J. Thompson's co-worker Ernest Rutherford (1911) and the Danish physicist Niels Bohr (1913) were able to work out a model of the way electrons whirled about the proton within an atom of matter like a miniature solar system.

For a time, the Newtonian solar system remained a persuasive analogy for describing the movement of subatomic particles. But Bohr continually found puzzling indications of randomness. In 1928, the German physicist Werner Heisenberg proposed the theory that atomic structures were "indeterminate." Since physicists had to work with instruments that were moving relatively to the subatomic movements being studied, Heisenberg reasoned, it was impossible for them to measure the position of electrons without distorting their speed, or to measure their speed without distorting their position.

Heisenberg's indeterminancy theory presented the world with a universe far different from the comfortable regularities of the Newtonian system. Physicists were now explaining the universe in terms of statistical probabilities rather than mechanical certainties. The physicist's intuition and something akin to an aesthetic flair became essential to the elegant mathematical language with which the universe was interpreted, a language incompatible with the kind of material certainty science had once seemed to embody.

The indeterminancy theory was deeply influenced by the work of Albert Einstein on relativity. Einstein was puzzled by late–nineteenth-century experiments that showed that the velocity of light was constant in whatever direction it was emitted. Either the earth was not moving, or the universe was not uniform. In his special theory of relativity (1905) and his general theory of relativity (1916), Einstein showed mathematically that absolute space and time could not exist in any straightforward mechanical sense. The observed behavior of light could be accounted for only on the hypothesis of curved space, and of space and time as relative to each other and forming a single continuum. Einstein received notoriety in 1919 when the Royal Astronomical Society proved during a solar eclipse that light rays were, indeed, curved when passing through the sun's magnetic field. This widely publicized experiment gave relativity theory much public attention that Einstein had not sought. Many people leaped to conclusions that the universe could be understood only in subjective terms and that there were no certainties in science.

The Revolution in Art and Thought

No less far reaching than the revolution in physics was the revolution in aesthetics taking place in the decade before 1914. The two revolutions were not entirely unrelated. Wassily Kandinsky, a Russian living in Munich, wrote that it was when he learned there were particles smaller than atoms that he began to rethink the whole nature of reality in the arts. He claimed to have made the first purely abstract painting in 1910: a watercolor composed of colored areas crisscrossed by lines. Although experimental artists had been arbitrarily distorting nature in order to heighten effects since the time of Vincent van Gogh (1853–90), Paul Gauguin (1848–1903), and Paul Cézanne (1839–1906), Kandinsky wanted to create an art of pure inwardness without reference to external nature. Kandinsky's book *Concerning the Spiritual in Art* (1912) was the first justification for pure abstraction: the abolition of any representational element at all.

Painting, for Kandinsky, is communication from the painter's soul through the feelings aroused by color and shape. The painter's emotions are transmitted by his feelings to the forms on the canvas, which "call forth a basically similar emotion in the soul of the spectator." Kandinsky thought that of all the arts painting should most resemble music, the art form that attempts least to represent anything else, and in which the composer is free to express himself directly in the language of rhythm and melody. For Kandinsky, colors, like sounds, had emotional values: yellow, for example, was a "strident trumpet blast." Painting was "color music."[52]

Kandinsky and his friends of the *Brücke* (bridge) and *Blaue Reiter* (blue rider) schools in Munich created one of the main prewar modern art movements in Europe—expressionism, the attempt to transmit strongly charged feelings by violent color and subject matter, arbitrary distortion, and abstract form.

Paris was the other center of aesthetic experiment before the First World War. A group of painters in Paris who called themselves the *Fauves* (wild beasts) set out in 1905 to smash the "slickness of over-refined art" through the violence of their color and distortion of forms.

[52]Wassily Kandinsky, *Concerning the Spiritual in Art,* trans. Michael Sadleir *et al.* (New York, 1947), pp. 23, 46.

A costume party in 1913 in the Paris studio of the painter Kees Van Dongen. Henri Matisse, the most celebrated of the Fauves, is the bearded man in front.

The best known of the *Fauves,* such as Henri Matisse (1869–1954), still retained some representational elements in their work, but their arbitrary use of flat, unmodeled areas of brilliant color carried them much farther from observed nature than their predecessors the impressionists, whose dappled canvases had been an attempt to present light scientifically.

Another major artistic innovation in pre-1914 Paris was cubism, practiced by, among others, the Frenchman Georges Braque (1882–1963) and the Spaniard Pablo Picasso (1881–1973). Cubism was still a way of representing nature, but it was nature utterly transformed by the painter's inner eye. All painting is a distortion by which depth is represented on a flat surface. The cubists chose to emphasize that distortion by presenting objects or human bodies seen simultaneously from many angles and arbitrarily rearranged by the artist.

The futurist movement, while it produced artistic work of less-enduring interest, also contributed to the climate of artistic ferment in prewar Paris. The Futurist Manifesto of 1911, the work of two Italians, Filippo Marinetti and Umberto Boccioni, called for a new aesthetic of violence and speed to replace stale, academic culture: "A speeding automobile is more beautiful than the Winged Victory of Samothrace." The futurists wanted to burn libraries and museums; they exalted war and the "subordination of women."

Despite their highly individual differences, the artistic rebels of the last decade before 1914 shared a number of common values. They broke completely with the artistic tradition begun in the Western world during the Renaissance, and maintained to some degree even by the impressionists of the late nineteenth century, that the business of art was to represent a universally understood external nature. In so doing, the dissident painters also broke with the very idea of learned technique, of artistic skills transmitted by teachers. Artistic expression became totally subjective; as such, it was without universally applicable standards.

Now that each artist's private creative drives took precedence over learned techniques, the sources of creativity became a matter of heightened interest. European artists were inclined to seek inspiration in childhood spontaneity or primitive feeling, outside the realms of reason and learning. Gauguin had urged painters to go beyond the horse in the Parthenon friezes to a child's rocking horse for inspiration. An exhibit of African masks in Paris in 1905 had a profound effect on the *Fauves* and the cubists, and the Munich expressionists studied primitive art in ethnographic museums. Since art was no longer a learned skill, it was now theoretically open to nonbourgeois Europeans for the first time. The customs collector Henri Rousseau was hardly proletarian, nor was he genuinely naive, but the childlike vision of his paintings delighted those who looked for new aesthetic inspiration.

It was not only European artists who were rediscovering subjective realities as the twentieth century opened. The French philosopher Henri Bergson (1859–1941), for example, had broken with the mathematical and mechanistic interests of his youth while puzzling about the nature of time. The irreconcilable difference between the physicist's *measured* time and each individual's subjective experience of the *duration* of time so struck the young Bergson that he spent the rest of his career as professor of philosophy working out the importance of intuition in human thought. Bergson argued that a whole realm of reality, of which the duration of time was merely one example, could only be known by direct, sympathetic comprehension or intuition. It could not be known directly by the symbolic language of mathematics or physics.

Bergson began lecturing in Paris in 1897 and won an enthusiastic following of students after the publication of *Creative Evolution* in 1907. His later lectures, exalting the human "vital impulses" (*élan vital*) that came "gushing out unceasingly . . . from an immense reservoir of life," and his mystical allusions to immortality won him a society audience. Ultimately, Bergson's influence was felt in the return of some French intellectuals to religion before 1914, and in the subtle probing of time and memory in Marcel Proust's *Remembrance of Things Past,* the first volume of which was published in 1913.

The most seminal thinker in the "recovery of the unconscious"[53] at the beginning of the twentieth century was unquestionably Sigmund Freud. Freud began practicing medicine in Vienna in the 1880s as a neurologist; his training had led him to treat the nervous system in physiological and even mechanistic terms. Cases of mental illness that seemed to have no physiological basis were then attracting the attention of some of Freud's colleagues, one of whom successfully treated several cases with hypnosis. In 1892 Freud worked on the case of Fraulein Elizabeth von R., who had shown no progress under hypnosis. In treating her, Freud experimented with the technique of getting the patient to recall the remote incidents behind her troubles by intense concentration and free association while lying on a couch with her eyes closed, a process Freud called "psychical analysis." During the 1890s, Freud became convinced from his clinical practice that much mental illness could be traced back to childhood sexual development. He believed that many of these illnesses could be treated by intense sessions of what he now called "psychoanalysis." In psychoanalysis, the patient recalled past experiences by free association, and the doctor took note of the ways in which the patient resisted revealing the most sensitive points and "transferred" his emotions to less-charged substitute issues.

Confident that a powerful unconscious mental life could be studied and treated scientifically, Freud subjected himself to psychoanalysis, through which he discovered his own inner resentments of his father. Freud also studied the importance of dreams and of what we now call "Freudian slips" in language, as clues to the mind's unconscious life. His book *The Interpretation of Dreams* (1899) used dramatic analogies like the Oedipus legend to illustrate the unconscious sexual jealousy and rivalry Freud perceived between sons and fathers, and to reveal how dependent conscious rational thought is on the unconscious mental life.

Freud's two central discoveries—the force of the unconscious mental life and the importance of childhood sexuality to personality development—arose simply from attempts to understand and treat mental illness. The fuller impact of his work had to await the passing of a generation and the revelations of human irrationality in the First World War. In time, it became clear that Freud had made obsolete the notions that reason controls the behavior of at least the educated portion of mankind, and that humans are fully aware of why they do what they do.

The Reaction to Cultural Revolution

The people and the movements singled out for discussion here were still only dissident minorities in 1914. They aroused violent animosity then, and established intellectual institutions had the power to shut them out.

[53]The phrase is from H. Stuart Hughes's basic work on European culture in this period, *Consciousness and Society* (New York, 1958).

Public opinion was much less tolerant of innovation in the arts and in thought in 1914 than it has been since the total victory of the modernists. Moreover, intellectual life was much more rigidly institutionalized in Europe before 1914 than it has been since.

In Paris, for example, the *Ecole des Beaux Arts* had a virtual monopoly of formal instruction in painting, sculpture, and architecture, and its instructors were appointed by the Ministry of Education. As late as 1881, the state exercised control over the Society of French Artists, which showed a selection of approved new paintings each year at its annual *Salon.* But even after the French state granted greater freedom of association, the official *Salon* rejected anything that did not conform to the derivative classicism still taught in the schools. Experimental artists had to show their works separately, at the *Salon des Indépendants* (after 1884) or the *Salon d'Automne* (after 1903), and they depended for support on friends and on a few adventurous purchasers.

The arts were even more tightly in the hands of conservatives in England. The classicist Lord Leighton, who insisted that art was the "representation of objects visible and tangible to the painter," ran the Royal Academy of Arts for nearly half a century, until 1893. The staff of the Royal Academy, consisting of forty "academicians" who chose their own successors, monopolized art instruction until the Slade School of Fine Arts was founded at the end of the century in the University of London. Experimental artists in Berlin and Vienna faced the same obstacles to being seen and appreciated; they formed "secession" showings when the established art shows were closed to them. No wonder modernism in the arts rejected the very idea of learned technique and perpetuation of historic styles.

Museums, whose very principle of creation in the nineteenth century was awe before the classics, were also closed to experimenters as a source of moral or material support. Many of those in power, both liberal and conservative, were shocked by a "cultural decadence" in modernism that seemed to threaten morals as well as good taste. The German Kaiser Wilhelm II dismissed the director of the Berlin Fine Arts Museum in 1908 for having dared to purchase some works of modern painting. The German empress blocked the production of Richard Strauss's naturalistic opera *Salome* (1905). She also prevented the opening of his *Der Rosenkavalier* (1911) in Berlin, although that opera's delicate treatment of the wistful feelings of approaching middle age was hardly daring, even at that time.

Scientists enjoyed more autonomy in their university laboratories, although Einstein had to do his early work outside the university establishment, while employed as an examiner of patent applications in Berne, Switzerland. Even after Einstein received the recognition of a university research appointment in Berlin, popularized notions of what he had done were attacked as Jewish cultural depravity in the 1920s. Freud was never accepted by his colleagues in Vienna.

The cultural revolutions of the generation before 1914 had succeeded, nevertheless, in putting in place the main elements of a new consciousness that was to become much more commonly accepted after the First World War. We are so close to their achievements today, and their experimentation was so individualistic and variegated, that it is easy to see cultural life on the eve of 1914 only as a kind of brilliant, intellectual pinwheel, without precise meaning. We can single out the main threads, however. A new aesthetic of personal sensibility had replaced the more objective aesthetic of representing external nature. Human consciousness was revealed as possessing unknown depths, and the place of reason in it had been called into question. Nature itself seemed susceptible to interpretation only by the most subjective hypotheses. It was what historian Carl Schorske had called a "great revaluation":

> The primacy of reason in man, the rational structure of nature, and the meaningfulness of history were all brought before the bar of personal psychological experience for judgment.[54]

This revaluation was not achieved without considerable cost. Those who shared in the new consciousness gave up the support of both tradition and any sense of integrated wholeness. They were subject to the loneliness and anxiety of being adrift in a meaningless universe. There remained only the heightened excitement of private artistic experience or piecemeal scientific discovery to cling to. As the French poet Charles Baudelaire had said earlier, "The intoxication of Art is the best thing of all for veiling the terrors of the Pit; . . . genius can play a part at the edge of the tomb with a joy that prevents it from seeing the tomb."[55]

The explorers of the new consciousness had no ready defenses against finding the same excitement in violence or cruelty that they found in artistic experience, as they were about to discover in the global war then brewing. Some people in the comfortable middle-class Europe of 1914 half hoped for some kind of apocalyptic wave of violence that would sweep away dull, bourgeois mediocrity. In the summer of 1913, the young English novelist D. H. Lawrence wrote to friends:

> My religion is a belief in the blood, the flesh, as being wiser than the intellect. We can go wrong in our minds. But what the blood feels and believes and says is always true.[56]

---

[54]Carl E. Schorske, "The Idea of the City in European Thought," in Oscar Handlin, ed., *The Historian and the City* (Cambridge, Mass., 1963), p. 109.
[55]Baudelaire, pp. 94–95.
[56]*The Portable D. H. Lawrence*, ed. Diana Trilling (New York, 1947), p. 563. It is only fair to add that Lawrence, married to a German woman, remained a pacifist during the war.

Suggestions for Further Reading*

The most useful introduction to all aspects of European life in the decade before 1914 is Oron J. Hale, *The Great Illusion, 1900–1914** (1971). Carleton J. H. Hayes, *A Generation of Materialism, 1871–1900** (1941) is still valuable. See also the illuminating essay by Geoffrey Barraclough, *An Introduction to Contemporary History** (1964), and J. Kim Munholland, *Origins of Contemporary Europe, 1890–1914** (1970).

Good recent general histories of the individual European states include: Robert K. Webb, *Modern England: From the Eighteenth Century to the Present** (1969); Pauline Gregg, *Modern Britain: A Social and Economic History Since 1760,** 5th ed. (1967); Trevor Lloyd, *Empire to Welfare State: English History, 1906–1967** (1970); and Eric Hobsbawm, *Industry and Empire** (1968), which concludes with suggestive graphs and charts.

Gordon Wright, *France in Modern Times: 1760 to the Present* (1960) is a model text with helpful bibliographical chapters on changing interpretations. Alfred Cobban, *A History of Modern France*, vol. 3: *1871–1962** (1965) is a sound short survey. Theodore Zeldin, *France 1848–1945*, vol. 1: *Ambition, Love, and Politics* (1973) contains brilliant essays on French social structure and public life.

For Germany see Hajo Holborn, *A History of Modern Germany*, vol. 3: *1840–1945* (1969), and Koppel S. Pinson, *Modern Germany*, 2nd ed. (1966). Arthur Rosenberg, *Imperial Germany: The Birth of the German Republic, 1871–1918** (1964) remains as indispensable as when first published in 1928.

Raymond Carr, *Spain 1808–1939* (1966) is the most detailed survey. Richard Herr, *Spain** (1971) is a suggestive discussion of the modern period. Gerald Brenan, *The Spanish Labyrinth,** 2nd ed. (1960) is a scintillating introduction to modern Spanish politics. See also Stanley G. Payne, *A History of Spain and Portugal*, 2 vols. (1973).

For Portugal see A. H. de Oliveira Marques, *History of Portugal*, vol. 2: *From Empire to Corporate State* (1972), and the same author's penetrating essay "Revolution and Counterrevolution in Portugal—Problems of Portuguese History, 1900–1930" (in English) in Manfred Kossok, ed., *Studien über die Revolution* (1969).

Christopher Seton-Watson, *Italy from Liberalism to Fascism, 1870–1925* (1967) is the most comprehensive narrative. The view of Denis Mack Smith, *Italy: A Modern History*, rev. ed. (1969) that liberalism had failed in Italy even before Mussolini may be compared with the more positive assessment of the parliamentary monarchy in A. William Salamone, *Italian Democracy in the Making: The Political Scene in the Giolittian Era* (1960).

T. K. Derry, *A History of Modern Norway, 1814–1972* (1973); Stewart Oakley, *A Short History of Sweden* (1966); Ingvar Andersson, *A History of Sweden*, 2nd ed. (1970); W. Glyn Jones, *Denmark* (1970); and John H. Wuorinen, *A History of Finland* (1965) are the best recent works on the Scandinavian countries.

For the Habsburg Empire see C. A. Macartney, *The Hapsburg Empire, 1790–1918* (1969). For the nationalities and attempts at

*Suggestions for Further Reading appear at the end of each chapter. The works cited are limited to some basic recent books and durable classics readily available in English. Many of them contain fuller, more specialized bibliographies. Books available in paperback form are marked with an asterisk.

federal reform, see Robert A. Kann, *The Multinational Empire: Nationalism and National Reform in the Habsburg Monarchy, 1848–1914*, 2 vols. (1950).

L. S. Stavrianos, *The Balkans Since 1453* (1958), and Robert L. Wolff, *The Balkans in Our Time** (1967) are the best treatment of this area.

For Russia see Hugh Seton-Watson, *The Russian Empire, 1801–1917* (1967); Donald W. Treadgold, *Twentieth Century Russia*, 2nd ed. (1964); and Nicholas V. Riasanovsky, *A History of Russia,* 2nd ed. (1969).

Guido de Ruggiero, *The History of European Liberalism** (1927) is still indispensable. See also J. S. Schapiro, *Liberalism: Its Meaning and History** (1958). David Sidorsky, ed., *The Liberal Tradition in European Thought** (1970), and Alan Bullock and Maurice Shock, eds., *The Liberal Tradition** (1956) are useful compilations, the latter drawn entirely from British examples.

David Caute, *The Left in Europe Since 1789** (1966) is a trenchant brief introduction, with unusual illustrations. G. D. H. Cole, *A History of Socialist Thought*, 5 vols. (1953–60) is the standard treatment. Julius Braunthal, *History of the International*, 2 vols. (1967) is sympathetic to the Second International, of which the author was an official. Outstanding works on the left in particular countries include Eric J. Hobsbawm, "Trends in the British Labour Movement since 1850," in Hobsbawm, ed., *Labouring Men** (1965); J. Peter Nettl, *Rosa Luxemburg,** abridged ed. (1969); Carl E. Schorske, *German Social Democracy, 1905–1917** (1955; reprint ed., 1970); and Harvey Goldberg, *The Life of Jean Jaurès* (1962).

Elie Kedourie, *Nationalism** (1966) is the best introduction. See also Boyd C. Shafer, *Faces of Nationalism: New Realities and Old Myths* (1972), the reworking of a standard book, and, for the nineteenth-century background, Hans Kohn, *The Idea of Nationalism,** rev. ed. (1961).

The starting point for modern European economic history is David S. Landes, *The Unbound Prometheus: Technological Change and Industrial Development in Western Europe from 1750 to the Present** (1969). Karl Polanyi, *The Great Transformation** (1944) is still suggestive.

D. K. Fieldhouse, *Colonial Empires** (1971) is the latest survey. In *Economics and Empire, 1830–1914* (1973) Fieldhouse minimizes economic motives. John A. Hobson, *Imperialism, A Study** (1902), and V. I. Lenin, *Imperialism: The Highest Stage of Capitalism** (1917) are the classic economic interpretations of empire. Hans-Ulrich Wehler, "Bismarck's Imperialism," *Past and Present*, No. 48 (August 1970) is the most sophisticated modern restatement of the socioeconomic interpretation. See also the superbly illustrated Heinz Gollwitzer, *Europe in the Age of Imperialism, 1880–1914** (1969).

T. B. Bottomore, *Classes in Modern Society** (1966) and *Elites and Society** (1964) are excellent introductions. See also the essay "Citizenship and Social Class," in *Class, Citizenship, and Social Development: Essays by T. H. Marshall* (1964).

T. H. Hollingsworth, *Historical Demography* (1969) is the most useful introduction to studies of population and family structure. See also Alfred Sauvy, *Fertility and Survival** (1963). D. V. Glass and Roger Revelle, eds., *Population and Social Change* (1972) contains a number of valuable articles on contemporary European demography.

Raymond Williams, *The Country and the City* (1973) explores literary and artistic reactions to urbanization. The *Journal of Contemporary History*, Vol. 4, No. 3 (July 1969) is devoted to contemporary European urban development.

The most comprehensive account of the Church is Kenneth Scott Latourette, *Christianity in a Revolutionary Age,** 5 vols. (1958–63; reprint ed., 1973).

A basic work on shifts in social thought at the beginning of the twentieth century is H. Stuart Hughes, *Consciousness and Society** (1958).

Among the flood of works on modern painting, Herbert Read, *A Concise History of Modern Painting** (1959), and the simple but effective *The Story of Art,** 12th ed. (1972) by E. H. Gombrich deserve to be singled out. Henry-Russell Hitchcock, *Architecture: Nineteenth and Twentieth Centuries,** 2nd ed. (1963) is a good starting point.

For science, see the outstanding bibliography in the work by Oron J. Hale cited at the beginning of this note.

THE COMING
OF WAR

2

"It seemed as though human beings might really be on the brink of becoming civilized," the British writer and social critic Leonard Woolf remembered having felt before the First World War.[1] The Great War—as many Europeans have continued to call it, even after the Second World War—put an end to such facile illusions. Europe, the most prosperous and most sophisticated civilization on earth, was unable to avoid a civil war among its Great Powers in 1914. The four-year struggle that followed was the bitterest, bloodiest, and costliest war in Europe since the Thirty Years' War of the seventeenth century. And since the same participants went to war again in 1939 after a shaky armed truce of twenty years, twentieth-century Europe could be said to have experienced its own thirty years' war.

[1]Leonard Woolf, *Beginning Again* (London, 1964), p. 44.

The First World War was not merely a barbaric bloodletting and a wanton destruction of what Winston Churchill called "the accumulated treasure of the long past."[2] It snuffed out the bravest and most promising part of a whole generation. It so distorted the world economy that Europeans could not be sure of earning the basic necessities until sustained prosperity returned in the 1960s. And it became a global war. Unable to dominate one another alone, the Great Powers involved the non-European United States and Japan and the semi-European Russia in an escalation that deprived the European states of sovereign control over their own destinies, perhaps forever.

No one in Europe had expected in 1914 that such a dark age was at hand. To be sure, many Europeans had feared war during periodic international crises that seemed to grow more ominous in the new century. The most frightening of these crises had been the confrontations between France and Germany over control of Morocco in 1905 and again in 1911. It was reassuring, however, that the Great Powers appeared determined to settle such confrontations by diplomatic negotiation after some ritual saber rattling. When lesser European states went to war among themselves, as in the two Balkan Wars of 1912 and 1913, the Great Powers showed their determination to work together to keep such wars localized, in the nineteenth-century diplomatic tradition of the Concert of Europe.

If war did come, Europeans, touched by liberal optimism, believed that modern weapons would make it quick and decisive. Long wars, like long sieges, were supposed to have disappeared along with medieval military technology. The Hundred Years' War of the fourteenth century had been followed by the Thirty Years' War of the seventeenth century. The twenty-three–year long Napoleonic Wars of 1792 to 1815 had been followed by short, decisive campaigns that made maximum use of rapid railway movement. The Prussian wars against Denmark (1864), Austria (1866), and France (1870–71) seemed to reinforce the positivist notion that science and complex technology made quick knock-out blows possible and long wars impossible to sustain. The kind of war that many Europeans feared in 1905 and in 1911 bore little resemblance to the horrors of the war they finally got from 1914 to 1918.

That catastrophe called into question the validity of what modern Europeans had accomplished. This accounts for the passion with which the search for the causes of the First World War has been pursued ever since. The emotions of war first produced highly personal explanations, like the "hang the kaiser" sentiment widespread in Britain in 1918. The publication of many volumes of diplomatic documents after the war led to a more sophisticated focus on the techniques of diplomacy under stress. It may be that fallible statesmen, bombarded with too many rapid communications and overwhelmed by tension and fatigue, simply lost control of the situation. In a still larger perspective, it may be that some

---

[2]Winston Churchill, *The World Crisis, 1911–1918* (London, 1923), p. 199.

fatal tragic flaw in the very dynamism of liberal, capitalist Europe was at work. It is the whole European achievement that is placed on trial when one considers the outbreak of the First World War.

The July Crisis of 1914

It is necessary first to distinguish between the Austro-Serbian war with which the confrontation began in July 1914, and the subsequent escalation that brought in all the Great Powers. For European statesmen had successfully contained local confrontations like this one a number of times in the recent past.

The crisis began with a political assassination, an act that has not usually led to war. A nineteen-year-old student, Gavrilo Princip, shot and killed the nephew of the Habsburg Emperor Franz Josef and heir to the throne, the Archduke Franz Ferdinand, and his wife, on June 28, 1914, in Sarajevo, where the archduke was on an inspection tour of the province of Bosnia. At first glance, it looked like a purely internal matter: an Austro-Hungarian subject had killed the Habsburg heir on Austro-Hungarian territory. Princip, however, was a Bosnian activist passionately committed to the ideal of uniting Bosnian and all other South Slavic peoples around the Kingdom of Serbia, the only independent South Slav state. From 1876 to 1878, the people of the provinces of Bosnia and Herzegovina had revolted against crumbling Turkish rule, but their aspirations for independence had been frustrated when the Great Powers put them under Austrian administration at the Congress of Berlin in 1878. That frustration was further embittered when Austria annexed Bosnia and Herzegovina outright in 1908. Princip had been armed and trained by the Black Hand, a terrorist group working underground from Serbian bases for South Slav independence and unity.

The heart of the matter, then, is the extent to which the Kingdom of Serbia was involved in Princip's act. For the first month, from the assassination on June 28 to the Russian mobilization on July 29, the crisis revolved around Serbian complicity and Austro-Hungarian efforts to punish the Serbians for it. But to understand the crisis it is necessary to take a brief look back at the origins of the conflict.

The Political Background

Complicated Balkan conflicts during the late nineteenth century lay behind the Austrian–Serbian confrontation. The Balkans were the one area of Europe whose state boundaries were radically redrawn in the late nineteenth century. The Ottoman Empire, which had stood at the very gates of Vienna in the 1680s, was slowly rotting from within. One Balkan province after another had asserted its national autonomy or independence from the Turks: local autonomy for Serbia in 1817, and for Wallachia and Moldavia in 1829; independence for Greece in 1832;

The Bosnian student Gavrilo Princip seized by police moments after he shot the heir to the Habsburg throne, the Archduke Franz Ferdinand, and his wife at Sarajevo, June 28, 1914.

independence for Serbia, and for Wallachia and Moldavia (united to form Romania), in 1878; local autonomy for Bulgaria in 1878 and independence in 1908.

National independence for the European provinces of the Ottoman Empire posed both advantages and dangers for the neighboring Great Powers, especially Austria-Hungary and Russia. Both could expect to acquire new political and cultural protégés and new trading partners in the area. However, neither Great Power could afford to see the other gain predominance on its doorstep. The emergence of one new weak but independent people after another in the Balkans brought the Austro-Hungarian and Russian empires into almost continuous conflict in the late nineteenth century.

Russian aid to the Bulgarian war for independence (1875–78) opened forty years of smoldering confrontation in the Balkans between Austria and Russia. The other Great Powers, led by Bismarck's Germany, worked to neutralize this conflict by balancing gains. At the Congress of Berlin in 1878, Russia's new client state in Bulgaria was sharply trimmed in size, and Austria found compensation in powerful indirect influence in the Kingdom of Serbia and the right to administer a semiautonomous Bosnia and Herzegovina. Imperial ambitions could be tempered, it seemed, by patient diplomacy and by the Great Powers' reluctance to permit any one of them to establish Balkan hegemony.

But imperial ambitions and fears were not the only destabilizing aspect of the Balkan transformations. Because no traditional or natural frontiers separated the new Balkan States, they bickered with one another over borders and over ethnic minorities in that polyglot region. Serbia, Greece, Bulgaria, and Montenegro, for example, all claimed parts of Macedonia and sent secret terrorist groups, *comitaji* societies, into that largest remnant of Turkish territory on the European Continent. There was always some risk that these squabbles could draw in one or another of the Great Powers and lead to a greater confrontation.

Another problem was that each newly independent or autonomous Balkan people was aglow with triumphant nationalism. Both Austria-Hungary and Russia had much to fear from ethnic revivals. Russia ruled over huge and restless Polish-speaking areas in the north, over large Ukrainian- and Turkish-speaking regions, and over Bessarabia, the region just east of the mouth of the Danube that Russia had seized from the Turks in 1812 and that the Romanians now claimed on grounds of national identity. The nationalist challenge to Russia was only a pinprick, however, compared with the nationalist threat to Austria-Hungary's

ETHNIC/LINGUISTIC COMPOSITION OF AUSTRIA-HUNGARY, 1914

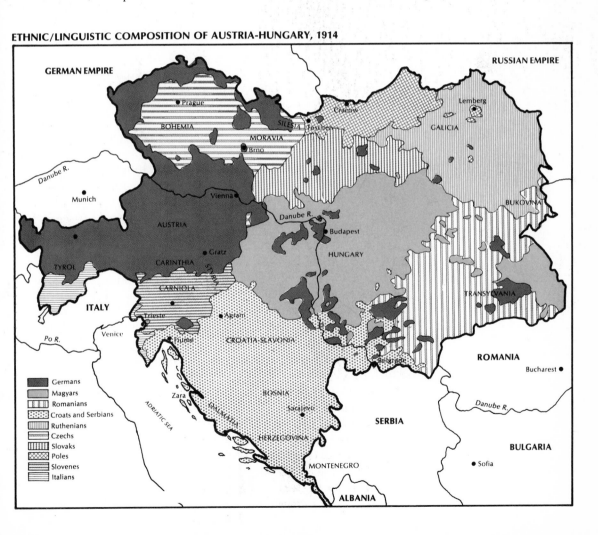

very existence. The southeastern half of Hungary, Transylvania, contained a large Romanian population; the southwestern tip of Hungary was inhabited by Croats, and the north by Slovaks. In Austria, an apprehensive German population maintained a precarious dominance over Czechs and Poles in the north, and over Slovenes, Bosnians, and other South Slavic people in the south. Austro-Hungarian internal politics in the late nineteenth century was a delicate balancing act in which the Hungarian Magyars ruthlessly controlled their minorities, and the Austrian Germans sought allies in one or another nationality against the rest. It was not enough for the Austro-Hungarians to keep the Russians out of their kindred Slavic areas in the Balkans. Austro-Hungarian security depended on blocking the creation of one large independent Slavic state on the southern border. That meant blocking the enlargement of Serbia.

Serbia was the only Balkan nation to threaten a Great Power directly. Following a change of dynasties in Serbia in 1903, the aggressive Serbian leader Nicholas Pashich adopted an openly anti-Austrian policy. The Austro-Hungarian government retaliated with tariff barriers against the main Serbian exports, pigs and plum brandy, in what has been called the "Pig War." More seriously, the Serbians could or would do little to stop the activities of the anti-Austrian secret society, the Black Hand. Serbia had become after 1903 "a jackal snapping at the Austro-Hungarian Achilles heel."

The Austrian foreign minister, Baron Alois von Aehrenthal, became convinced that unless Austria decided to "grasp the nettle and make a final end to the pan-Slav dream" the Austro-Hungarian Empire would continue to "sink miserably step by step."[3] Aehrenthal's first move to block future Serbian growth was to begin a railroad southward to the Aegean that would cut Serbia off from other Slavic areas and from the Adriatic Sea. When this kind of "informal empire" seemed insufficient, Aehrenthal decided in 1908 to annex Bosnia and Herzegovina outright so that they could never become part of a greater Slavic state on the Austrian southern border. The moment seemed propitious, for Russia had just been humiliated in the Russo-Japanese War of 1905, and Turkey was too preoccupied with domestic reform under the Young Turk movement even to protest Bulgarian accession to full independence in 1908.

Aehrenthal negotiated the annexation of Bosnia-Herzegovina with the Russian foreign minister, Alexander Izvolsky, in advance. In the most careful secrecy, the two foreign ministers agreed that in exchange for Russian acquiescence to the annexation the Austro-Hungarian Empire would support Russia's acquisition of the right to move warships through the Straits at Constantinople. Before Izvolsky had finished negotiating his new Straits rights with the other Great Powers, Aehrenthal announced the annexation of Bosnia-Herzegovina. Unable to

[3]Wayne S. Vucinich, *Serbia Between East and West* (Stanford, Calif., 1954), p. 229; Sidney B. Fay, *The Origins of the World War*, Vol. 1 (New York, 1929), p. 395.

Bulgarian artillery during the First Balkan War, 1912.

achieve his side of the bargain, Izvolsky felt betrayed. "The dirty Jew has deceived me," Izvolsky cried to the German chancellor, Prince Bernhard von Bülow, in Berlin where he heard the news. "He lied to me, he bamboozled me, that frightful Jew."[4] Izvolsky's desire to bring Russia to war with Austria over Bosnia-Herzegovina was blocked mainly by a private German threat to release the information that Izvolsky had agreed to the deal earlier in secret. After the Bosnian humiliation of 1908, no Russian statesman could afford to appear to yield an inch to Austria-Hungary.

But even Aehrenthal had not achieved his aim. The Kingdom of Serbia continued to expand. In 1912, Serbia joined the other Balkan States adjoining Turkish Macedonia—Greece, Montenegro, and Bulgaria—in a lightning war of aggression to take Macedonia from the Ottoman Empire. This First Balkan War profited the aggressors handsomely in the spoils of Macedonia, but Austria-Hungary's insistence that Albania be set up as an independent state under a German prince blocked Serbian access to the Adriatic Sea once again. Within a few months, the victors of the First Balkan War were quarreling over the spoils. Taking advantage of a Bulgarian general's unauthorized attack on Serbian and Greek positions, Serbia, Greece, and Montenegro, now joined by Romania and Turkey, forced Bulgaria to give up some territory in the Second Balkan War.

The unedifying Balkan Wars of 1912 and 1913 may have lulled Europeans into thinking that since the Great Powers had kept these two

[4]Bernhard von Bülow, *Memoirs,* Vol. 2 (Boston, 1931–32), p. 440.

conflicts localized by working together in the last exercise of the Concert of Europe, they could keep Balkan conflicts localized indefinitely. In Vienna, however, the Balkan Wars proved to a frightened Austro-Hungarian leadership that no further successes must be allowed Serbia, "that viper's nest."

It was against the background of narrowed tolerance between Austria-Hungary and Serbia, on the one hand, and between Russia and Austria-Hungary, on the other, that young Princip assassinated the Habsburg heir at Sarajevo in June 1914.

The Austro-Hungarian government had no conclusive proof that the Serbian government had any foreknowledge of the plans of Princip and his helpers. Even today, the most one can say is that some members of the Serbian cabinet and the military command were aware of a number of terrorist plots, and that the Serbian government had little zeal and even less power to put a stop to them. In any event, the government in Vienna seized on the assassination as "the moment . . . to render Serbia innocuous once and for all by a display of force."[5] For men like the Austro-Hungarian Army's chief of staff, General Conrad von Hötzendorf, who had been urging a preventive war against Serbia since 1908, it was time to put aside such half-way measures as the "Pig War," the Aegean railroad, and the creation of an independent Albania. The Habsburg government decided to wage a punitive war directly on Serbia. The Austro-Hungarian leaders bear the heavy responsibility of having made the first decision to go to war in July 1914.

Germany's "Blank Check"

It was important to the Austro-Hungarian plan that this war be limited. There was a serious danger of Russian intervention on Serbia's side. Only a German counterthreat could neutralize the Russians. On July 5, therefore, Aehrenthal's successor as Austro-Hungarian foreign minister, Count Leopold Berchtold, sent a top career diplomat to Berlin to give Kaiser Wilhelm II a personal letter from Emperor Franz Josef urging German support of Austrian intentions that Serbia "be destroyed as a power factor." The net of involvements had already begun to ensnare other Great Powers.

The German government had previously helped restrain the Austrians. This time, however, Kaiser Wilhelm extended to the Habsburg Empire what has been commonly called a "blank check." He assured Berchtold's envoy that Austria-Hungary could count on Germany's "full support . . . even if matters went to the length of a war between Austria-Hungary and Russia."[6] Furthermore, in the days that followed, the German Imperial chancellor, Theobald von Bethmann-Hollweg,

---

[5]Austrian foreign minister, Count Leopold Berchtold, quoted in Fay, Vol. 2, p. 228. Among Habsburg leaders, only the Hungarian prime minister, Count Tisza, made temporary objections to the idea of a war with Serbia on the ground that the Habsburg Empire contained too many Slavs already.

[6]Imanuel Geiss, *Julikrise und Kriegsausbruch*, Vol. 1 (Hannover, 1963–64), p. 84.

and other German officials actively goaded the Austrians to action with remarks about proving themselves a Great Power and remaining an ally worthy of Imperial Germany. The working papers of the German government captured after the Second World War show beyond doubt that the kaiser and his chancellor wanted a local Austro-Serbian war to reverse the decline of Germany's only ally. Did they see the broad implications of that position? Did they expect or want a wider war? These questions lie at the heart of the debate over the German "blank check" of July 5, 1914.

According to the German state papers of July 1914 that survive, the German leaders knew that Russia might intervene if Austria made war on Serbia. Evidently both civilian and military leaders regarded that as an acceptable risk for Germany. Russia might be only bluffing, and it could be counterbluffed. Impressed by signs of internal unrest in Russia following the Revolution of 1905, the kaiser thought that the Russian government would be unable to wage war. The German leaders also had to take into account the Franco-Russian Alliance, formed in 1892 and tightened since then. The Germans believed that French intervention was doubtful, since the French had not come automatically to the aid of the Russians either in the Russo-Japanese War of 1905 or in the Bosnian annexation crisis of 1908.

The German leaders seemed to have believed that whatever risks were involved were more than counterbalanced by possible strategic gains. The kaiser was obsessed with the belief that Germany had been "encircled," a word that recurs in his papers. The opportunity offered itself in July 1914 to prove that Germany and Austria could break out of the ring, and "to make Austria preponderant in the Balkans at the expense of Russia," as the kaiser wrote in the margin of one of his papers.[7] His Army chief of staff, General Helmut von Moltke, nephew of the general who had defeated the French in 1870, assured him that even if the worst happened Germany was in a better position to fight both Russia and France in 1914 than would be the case later. By 1917, the Russian rearmament program of 1908 would be completed and France would have adjusted to the new three-year military service law of 1913. Some of Moltke's statements lend themselves to the interpretation that he wanted a preventive war against Russia and France while there was still time. At the very least, his advice made the risks of war seem acceptable considering the possible gains. As German leaders saw their strategic position in July 1914, they must act vigorously to assert their growing world power or reconcile themselves to eventual decline.

Austria's Ultimatum to Serbia

Their backs stiffened by German prodding through the middle weeks of July, the Austro-Hungarian leaders set about making a public case for

---

[7]Fritz Fischer, *Germany's Aims in the First World War* (New York, 1967), p. 67.

Serbian guilt. They prepared an ultimatum, quite consciously designed to make demands that Serbia could not accept. Once Serbia rejected the ultimatum, Austria-Hungary would have justification for military action. While Europe returned to midsummer tranquility, and the kaiser departed on a yachting vacation off Norway, this time bomb was being slowly prepared in Vienna. There was no hurry, for the Austrians had decided not to present the ultimatum until July 23, to avoid coinciding with the state visit to St. Petersburg of French President Raymond Poincaré and Prime Minister René Viviani. The timing shows that the Austrians knew they were going to the brink.

The "timed note," as the ultimatum was prudently called, accused Serbia of "culpable tolerance" of terrorist and secessionist movements within the Habsburg lands, which obliged Austria to take on "the duty of putting an end to the intrigues which form a perpetual menace to the tranquility of the monarchy."[8] There followed ten demands, some of which merely required Serbia to suppress anti-Austrian movements and punish the guilty parties. Other demands were far less compatible with Serbian sovereignty. Austria insisted that Serbia dismiss officials and army officers whom the Austrians chose to designate, and that Austrian officials take part in the investigation of a conspiracy in Serbia leading up

[8]Geiss, Vol. 1, document N⁰. 155.

**BALKAN
CONFLICTS
1878–1914**

to the assassination. Unconditional acceptance of all demands was required within forty-eight hours. This ultimatum was delivered in Belgrade at 6:00 P.M. on July 23 by an Austrian ambassador who was already packing in anticipation of Serbian rejection.

The Serbian reply, delivered just before the deadline on July 25, was masterfully drafted to arouse sympathetic European opinion. The Serbians rejected out of hand only the demand for Austrian participation in the investigation within Serbia. They made conciliatory replies to the other demands. At the same time, however, the Serbian Army was mobilized.

Despite signs of a slackening will in Vienna at the end of July, the Austro-Hungarian ambassador kept to the plan and broke relations with Serbia on receiving its reply. The German chancellor and foreign minister did their best to keep alive the "spirit of Sarajevo," although they were eager to keep Austria's punitive action localized.

The last week of July was a testing time for traditional Great Power diplomacy. The Great Powers had managed to prevent war between Austria and Russia over Bosnia in 1908, and they had localized the Balkan Wars of 1912 and 1913. This crisis, however, was neither a Great Power confrontation, as in 1908, nor a war among lesser states, as in 1912 and 1913. This was an attempt by one Great Power, supported by

another, to change decisively its power position in the Balkans. That kind of conflict was much more difficult for the other Great Powers to stop.

The British government proposed a mediation that would forestall any military action between Austria and Serbia. But the Germans blocked all efforts at conciliation: they wanted a local war, not no war at all. This time, localization, as the British diplomat Arthur Nicolson pointed out, meant "holding the ring while Austria quietly strangles Serbia,"[9] without intervention by Russia on Serbia's behalf.

On July 28, the Austro-Hungarian Empire declared war on Serbia. The Austrian Army shelled Belgrade on July 29. For the first time since 1878, a Great Power was at war on the European Continent. Would the other Great Powers inexorably be drawn in?

Escalation: From Local War to Continental War

Austria and Germany had wanted the Austro-Serbian war to remain localized, another Balkan war. But military alliances and Great Power rivalries[10] threatened from the beginning to widen the conflict. The German government was prodding its ally Austria-Hungary to seize the opportunity for major gains in the Balkans. Russia, determined to prevent further Austrian aggrandizement, drew confidence from a mutual defense treaty with France. France, in turn, had informal defense agreements with Britain. But alliances are not always honored, and it was not yet clear whether other Great Powers would be drawn into actual fighting. The degree of escalation depended on the skill of statesmen who were working to prevent it, their control over information and over their own complex military machines, and their view of the unfolding choices between fighting and humiliation.

Russia's Mobilization

Russia was the Great Power most immediately affected by the news of the Austrian ultimatum to Serbia, for Russia could not permit a repeat of the Bosnian humiliation of 1908. After that crisis Russia had launched a massive rearmament program that was designed to bring its Army to 2.2 million men. Izvolsky, who had borne the brunt of the humiliation, had been removed as foreign minister and named ambassador to allied France. His successor, Sergei Sazanov, was particularly sensitive to charges by Russian pan-Slav patriots that he showed weakness in foreign disputes. In July 1914, exhilarated as well as exhausted by the toasts and speeches of the state visit by French President Poincaré, Sazanov was in

[9]Fay, Vol. 2, p. 355.
[10]European Great Power alliances in 1914:
The Central Powers: Germany and Austria-Hungary, allied since 1879, were more loosely tied to Italy since 1882 in the Triple Alliance.
The Allies, or the Entente Powers: France and Russia were allied since 1892; France was linked to Britain by the *Entente cordiale* of 1902.

no state to deal calmly with the Austro-Serbian situation. The Russian government could barely restrain itself from ordering partial mobilization against Austria on learning the terms of the ultimatum to Serbia on July 24. Russia rushed to arms when Austria declared war on Serbia on July 28. Austrian assurances to the Russians that they planned no permanent annexation of Serbian territory only showed how determined the Austrians were to complete their punitive expedition. At 11:00 A.M. on July 29, the four Russian military districts fronting Austria-Hungary were mobilized.

With this partial mobilization of the Russian Army military technology first took on a decisive role in the unfolding crisis. The preparation of a modern mass army for action had become a feat of prodigious complexity. It took minute planning to recall millions of reservists, to get them to the proper units along with supplies and equipment, and to move these massive assemblages of men and matériel by railroad to the front. Last minute changes in mobilization plans threatened to throw the whole procedure awry. Improvisation could be fatal. One had to follow the plan or become hopelessly snarled.

The Russian General Staff had worked out mobilization plans according to purely technical considerations, without taking into account the diplomatic implications of their elaborate timetables and emplacements. They had arranged for mobilization against Germany and Austria simultaneously. The generals assured Sazanov and the tsar that there was no way to carry out a partial mobilization against Austria alone without throwing the whole armed force into chaos. Furthermore, it was notorious that the creaking Russian bureaucracy needed a head start to match the military preparedness of Germany. If full mobilization were not ordered soon, Russia would never be ready to deal with a possible German attack.

Faced with these technical rigidities, the reluctant tsar ordered full mobilization later in the day of July 29. Just before midnight he revoked his order after receiving a warning telegram addressed to "Nicky" from his cousin "Willy" in Berlin.[11] After frantic appeals by the generals and Sazanov, he reinstated full mobilization on the morning of July 30, lest possible war with Germany be lost in advance. A second Great Power had committed itself irrevocably to a war stance.

France's Intentions

The French role in Russia's decision to mobilize is still highly controversial. The crucial point is whether the French, as Russia's only continental ally,[12] encouraged Russian belligerence in the hopes that a European war might permit them to recover the provinces of Alsace and

[11]Both Tsar Nicholas II of Russia and Kaiser Wilhelm II of Germany were grandsons of British Queen Victoria, through their mothers.
[12]Although Russia and Great Britain had resolved all existing differences in 1907, no formal alliance existed between them.

Lorraine, lost to Germany in 1871. As we have seen, French President Poincaré and Prime Minister Viviani had been in St. Petersburg on a state visit just before the Austrian demands on Serbia became known. The ritual toasts and parades of the visit no doubt stimulated Russian faith in the Franco-Russian Alliance at that crucial moment. Moreover, the two chief leaders of France were insulated from any direct role in events from July 23 until July 29, when the battleship *France* finally returned them home. In their absence, Justice Minister Jean-Baptiste Bienvenu-Martin was both inexperienced and uninfluential as acting head of government. These accidents left an unusually large amount of responsibility in the hands of the French ambassador to St. Petersburg, Maurice Paléologue. Apparently without precise instructions from home, Ambassador Paléologue allowed his enthusiasm for Russian court life and the excitement of the recent state visit to warp his judgment. He effusively promised Sazanov unconditional French support. At the same time, he failed to inform his own government of the ramifications of Russian mobilization on both the German and Austrian frontiers, a failure that prevented the French government from understanding the full implications of its support.

As an ardent patriot and a native of lost Lorraine, President Poincaré has been suspected of willingness to risk a war that promised to return his native province. There is only circumstantial evidence for such an allegation, however. After returning to Paris on July 29, Poincaré did continue to promise Russian Ambassador Izvolsky that "France was ready to fulfill all her treaty obligations" to aid Russia in case of a German attack.[13] The treaty obligations required only that France come to Russia's aid in case of German attack, or of Austrian attack supported by Germany. Heretofore, the French had carefully withheld support from Russia's Balkan adventures, as in the 1908 Bosnian crisis. To stand aside once more while Russia underwent another Balkan humiliation would probably have meant the end of the Franco-Russian Alliance. Because he did not want France to be left to face Germany alone, Poincaré did not prevent the Russians from taking military steps that put the Germans' backs to the wall.

The French government also was coming under pressure from the technical requirements of its own Army. General Joseph Joffre, commander in chief of the French armies, warned the government that unless French troops were put on a war footing with sufficient lead time, he would be unable to defend France against a sudden German attack westward. On July 30, therefore, the French "covering force"—the first-line frontier troops—were mobilized, although they were held six miles behind the frontier to avoid provocation. However little French leaders contemplated a preventive war, they were determined not to be caught again, as they had been caught in 1870, without allies and mobilized too late.

---

[13]Geiss, Vol. 2, p. 404.

Germany Declares War

63

ESCALATION:
FROM LOCAL
WAR TO
CONTINENTAL
WAR

The news of general Russian mobilization late on July 30 presented the German government with a military emergency and gave the generals a dominant voice in what followed. General Moltke was not placated by Russian Foreign Minister Sazanov's assurances that general Russian mobilization did not mean that any Russian troops would cross the frontier. Moltke was keenly aware of the lead time needed for German mobilization to catch up with that of the Russians. He told his government that noon on July 31 was the latest the Army could wait and still be assured of matching the Russian mobilization.

The military machines now began to set their own timing on decisions, and it was therefore of little importance that some German statesmen were beginning to recoil before the general war they had so cavalierly risked earlier. Returning from his Norwegian cruise on July 28, Kaiser Wilhelm had finally read the Serbian reply to Austria and had decided that "the grounds for war had now fallen away." At the last moment, Berlin proposed that the Austrian armies "halt in Belgrade" and merely hold Serbian territory as a bargaining counter. Sazanov held out the promise that the Russians would cancel mobilization in return for Austrian withdrawal from Serbia. Austria, for its part, was willing to accept mediation and to promise to annex no Serbian territory, but not to renounce its punitive operation altogether.

All these last-minute proposals, like the four-power mediation constantly urged by the British foreign secretary, had one flaw: they offered peace only at the cost of leaving the gradual Austrian decline in the Balkans unchecked by the kind of conspicuous success both Germans and Austrians had looked forward to after July 5. The decisive opinion offered in Berlin late on July 31 was General Moltke's, and it resulted in a German ultimatum to Russia. Germany gave the Russians twelve hours to renounce all military preparations against Austria and Germany. When the ultimatum expired the next day, Germany declared war on Russia at 5:00 P.M. on August 1.

The major question now was whether the French could stand aside while Germany and Russia fought in the east. There is every reason to think that Poincaré and Viviani were supported by public opinion in their determination to accept war rather than isolation from Russia or further German success. France did not feel responsible for war, wrote the centrist mass-circulation daily *Le Matin* on the morning of August 1, but "if it comes, we shall meet it with high hopes. We are convinced that it will bring us the restitutions which are our right."

The Schlieffen Plan

The question of whether France would stand aside was an academic one on August 1. For German military planners had decided long ago that the road to St. Petersburg ran through Paris. Assuming that the

Franco-Russian Alliance was rigid, the German military planners helped to make it more so by arranging to attack the French first. General Alfred von Schlieffen, German chief of staff from 1891 to 1907, had responded to the Franco-Russian Alliance by shaping all his plans to fit a two-front war. Schlieffen reasoned that France, which could mobilize more quickly than Russia, could be defeated in six weeks by throwing almost the entire German Army westward in a rapid scythelike swing through Holland and Belgium into western France, while only a few covering units held the eastern front. Then the more numerous but slower Russians could be dealt with at leisure by the whole German Army.

Although Schlieffen's successor, General Moltke, reduced the scope of the wheeling maneuver in order to leave Holland neutral, he did not abandon the essential pattern of the Schlieffen Plan. When the German twelve-hour ultimatum was dispatched to Russia late on July 31, the German generals had to assume that Paris would be their first target. Moltke could not wait to learn about French intentions before deciding which way to move his forces, for improvising on the Schlieffen Plan risked throwing the whole German war machine into confusion. So a simultaneous ultimatum went out to Paris on July 31: France must declare its neutrality within eighteen hours.

THE UNEXECUTED SCHLIEFFEN PLAN

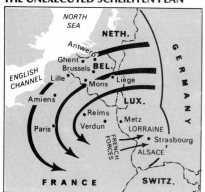

French code-breakers learned that the Germans intended to demand the frontier fortresses of Toul and Verdun as surety for France's neutrality. Whatever doubts might have been felt in Paris about Russian general mobilization now disappeared. The French government declared general mobilization on the afternoon of August 1, without awaiting news of German general mobilization, which was announced at about the same time. Although France first declared war on Germany on August 3, the Germans, by assuming that war with France was inevitable, had helped bring it about.

Britain's Role

There were several reasons why Britain might have considered Germany an enemy in 1914. Germany's enormous warship construction program since 1898 had required Britain to construct a powerful new class of battleships, Dreadnoughts, in order to keep control of the seas. The kaiser's support of the Boers in their war against the British in South Africa from 1899 to 1901 and commercial rivalry in the Near East, China, and Latin America had greatly sharpened the British public's awareness of Germany as an enemy. Finally, Britain had been engaged in joint military planning with France since 1902, and had settled all differences with France's ally Russia in 1907.

But no hard and fast agreements obliged the British to aid either France or Russia in case of a war with Germany. And, in fact, in 1914 British–German relations were more cordial than they had been at any time in the recent past. In that very July, Britain and Germany had agreed to share responsibility for building the Berlin-to-Baghdad Railway, heretofore a major focus of imperial and commercial rivalry. A British naval unit was visiting the German base at Kiel when the news broke of the Austrian ultimatum to Serbia. Wilhelm II's brother was assured by his cousin and fellow yachtsman, King George V, that England wished to remain neutral. It is characteristic of Wilhelm's view of the world that he based his tough policy on those royal words long after they had been contradicted by such underlings as foreign ministers and ambassadors.

The British foreign secretary, Sir Edward Grey, has been blamed for not using British power more decisively to stave off conflict. It has been suggested that if he had warned Germany sooner that Britain could not stand aside if France were attacked, the kaiser would have assessed the risks far more soberly in mid-July. To Grey's credit, he high-mindedly thought that any threat to make war only made war that much more likely. But having failed to give Germany a clear warning until July 29 that Britain would not remain neutral if France were drawn in, as the French urged, Grey also refused to bring pressure on Russia to demobilize, as the Germans urged. Instead, Grey devoted all his energies to a futile effort to arrange Great Power mediation of the Austro-Serbian dispute. During July he made four mediation proposals, all of which were doomed by German insistence that the conflict be "localized," that is, allowed to take place without Russian intervention. The French could not lend warm support to Grey's attempts at conciliation for fear of casting doubt in St. Petersburg on the reliability of their support as allies.

When events began to move rapidly in late July, the British government found itself thrust into the very position that it had hoped to avoid through its mediation efforts. It had to decide how to respond if the French were drawn into the war. British independence from continental allies had greatly diminished in the decade before 1914. The German naval challenge had led to a fateful British decision in 1912 to concentrate British naval forces in the English Channel, leaving the Mediterranean to control by the French Navy. Henceforth, British mastery of the seas depended on a friendly France to assure access to India and to the Middle East oil on which the British Navy was now dependent, having begun to convert from coal to oil in 1911. Even Britain had been forced by the cost of the early–twentieth-century armaments race to count on allies.

Sir Eyre Crowe, the senior career diplomat in the British Foreign Office, drew up a memorandum on July 25 outlining very clearly the alternatives for British world power. If Russia and France were determined to take up the gauntlet, Crowe argued, it would be fatal for Britain to stand aside. If Germany and Austria won, there would be no

French fleet; Germany would occupy the channel coast; and "what would be the position of a friendless England?" If France and Russia won without British support, "what would then be their attitude toward England? What about India and the Mediterranean?"[14] There had never been any real possibility of British neutrality if Germany went to war with France, and the stubborn belief of the kaiser and of Chancellor Bethmann-Hollweg in British neutrality was one of the most fatal blunders of the July crisis.

Crowe's reasoning shows why the last-minute German offer not to use naval units against the French channel coast failed to work its expected relief in London. It also shows that the British did not really go to war

[14]*British Documents on the Origins of the World War*, Vol. 11, p. 101.

The last meeting of Kaiser Wilhelm II of Germany (left) and King George V of Britain, before the First World War. The two monarchs, both grandsons of Britain's Queen Victoria, are seen here on a family occasion, preparing to review the garrison at the royal palace at Potsdam before the marriage of Kaiser Wilhelm's daughter in 1913. As usual, the Kaiser has taken pains to hide his withered left arm.

over a mere "scrap of paper," the Belgian Neutrality Treaty of 1839, as Bethmann-Hollweg furiously charged on learning that his plan for a localized war was exploding into a Continental war. It is true that a German ultimatum to Belgium on August 2 united British public opinion behind a dreaded war more effectively than Crowe's brand of geopolitical reasoning could have done. But British statesmen clearly understood well before August 2 that the real issue was not Belgian neutrality and the sanctity of treaties but the place of the British Empire in the world.

Britain declared war on an amazed Germany at 11:00 A.M. on August 4, after the expiration of an ultimatum demanding German withdrawal from Belgium.

Of the major European powers, only Italy stood aside from the conflict. Although formally linked to Germany by treaty since 1882, and informally linked by major economic investments, Italy had drawn more closely into the French economic sphere in the early twentieth century. More importantly, Italian national ambitions centered on the upper Adriatic Sea and its Balkan shores, areas once ruled by the independent Republic of Venice. These ambitions naturally threw Italy increasingly into conflict with Austrian interests in the years before 1914. In July and August 1914, therefore, Italian treaty links to Germany counted for less than potential gains from an Austrian defeat. For the moment, Italy remained neutral.

With that exception, all the European Great Powers were at war on August 4, 1914, for the first time since 1815, in a way no one would have believed possible only a month before.

A Longer View of the Causes of War

We have looked at close range at that hectic week of accelerating crisis that led from the announcement of Austria's demands on Serbia on July 24 to the declarations of war from August 1 to 4. From that perspective, one sees flawed and fallible men struggling to understand the rush of events and to take the right steps on short notice. From that perspective, it is tempting to place responsibility on individual personalities or on individual failures to make diplomacy work. For none of the Great Powers got what their leaders wanted in July and August 1914. Germany and Austria did not get their therapeutic little local war for Balkan advantage; the Russians did not get their limited war against Austria; the Germans did not get British neutrality in their war with France and Russia; the French and the British could not maintain the *status quo* that was probably the preference of a majority of their people. The diplomacy of July and August 1914 makes a tale of almost unmitigated failure. Was the First World War, then, a tragic accident, the result of human error that interrupted the course of an otherwise promising civilization?

From a longer point of view, it seems unlikely that so massive a calamity could flow from so ephemeral a cause. It is often argued that inherent flaws in liberal, capitalist society made a general European war unavoidable, sooner or later. The system of sovereign states provided no outside tribunal to settle differences, and rising ethnic nationalism made those differences more frequent. Moreover, imperialist rivalry among capitalist powers and increasing class conflict within capitalist societies made war an attractive choice for European leaders. According to these determinist positions, even if the Great Powers had scraped through the Austro-Serbian crisis as they had earlier crises, a major war was unavoidable in the long run within the existing system.

Sovereignty and a Nation's Honor

The system of sovereign states in Europe and the world allowed for no recourse to a higher tribunal for arbitration or mediation when any two states were on a collision course. Since the sovereign nation-state was accepted as the ultimate human authority, its welfare became a supreme value. "In questions of honor and vital interests," wrote the kaiser in the margin of a memorandum submitted to him, "you don't consult others."[15] European statesmen considered the state morally as well as legally sovereign; war was an acceptable course of action to save a state from decline, in the view of all but a tiny minority of pacifists in Europe in 1914.

All the European leaders knew recent examples in which restraint had produced national humiliation: Russia in the Bosnian crisis of 1908, Germany in the second Moroccan crisis in 1911, and Austria in the Balkan Wars. All of them knew other recent cases in which going to the brink had saved national honor, as in the case of France in the second Moroccan crisis of 1911. A continent crowded with sovereign nations that recognized no higher interest than the state's success seemed bound to be jostled into a major war sooner or later.

Imperialist Considerations

The sharpened commerical and colonial rivalries of the generation before 1914 would necessitate war eventually, in the opinion of some. Lenin's *Imperialism: The Highest Stage of Capitalism,* for example, argued that as capitalism ripened into monopoly, capitalism's profits would decline. Therefore, European monopolies would seek higher rates of yield outside their own countries in a world-wide race for profits that was bound to lead to war.

No one can deny the importance of colonial and commercial rivalries in statesmen's calculations of July and August 1914. The German historian Fritz Fischer has shown how frustrations in German commercial expansion eastward and southward in Europe contributed to the German leaders' sense of encirclement in 1914. If they did not build the Berlin-to-Baghdad Railway, someone else would. General Friedrich von

---

[15]Geiss, Vol. 1, p. 349.

Bernhardi's 1912 essay on Germany's choice—"World Power or Decline"—measured "world power" in cultural and commercial terms as well as in military terms.[16]

The two clearest instances in which colonial–commercial rivalry sharpened conflict between eventual belligerents of 1914 were the Moroccan crises of 1905 and 1911, and the German–British naval race. Both France and Germany had substantial investments in Morocco in the early twentieth century. Germany's deliberate challenge in 1905 to growing French political and military power there clearly heightened French nationalism and military expenditure in the following years. The second clash over Morocco in 1911, in which combined British and French pressure forced the Germans to back down, led General Moltke to write in his memoirs that another such display of weakness would make him despair of the future of the German Reich. The German–British naval race forced the British to admit that even their new fleet of Dreadnoughts could not guarantee access to the British Empire without French help. The web of economic interest and military calculation was tightening in the years before 1914.

It would be a mistake, however, to regard commercial and colonial rivalries as solely determining an inevitable war in 1914. German and British commercial interests recognized that they were each other's best trading partners and that trade prospers best in peace, as they proved by agreeing to the joint construction of the Berlin-to-Baghdad Railway in July 1914. London merchants and bankers were opposed to war during the July crisis. Colonial rivalries did not necessarily determine the alignments of 1914. After all, bitter colonial rivalries had pitted Britain against France in Africa and the Near East, and Britain against Russia in Iran and Afghanistan. Britain and Germany had cooperated in colonial settlements in central and North Africa and in the Far East, while even France and Germany had avoided colonial rivalry between 1871 and 1905. Indeed, it was the Russian turn away from colonial interests in the Far East after losing a war to Japan in 1905 that dangerously heightened rivalries in the Balkans, within Europe itself.

Internal Dissent

Did the breath of revolution at home stir some European statesmen to a more bellicose posture abroad? Internal strife certainly rose sharply in a number of European states on the eve of 1914. In France, strikes had reached unprecedented proportions from 1906 to 1909, and after conservatives had succeeded in 1913 in increasing military service to three years, the elections of 1914 threw the whole issue open again by returning a left majority. The German Social Democrats had become the largest party in the *Reichstag* in 1912, and the Prussian three-class voting system was under bitter attack. The Italian "Red Week" of June 1914

---

[16]Friedrich von Bernhardi, *Deutschland und der nächste Krieg* (1912), summarized in Fischer, pp. 34–35.

was the bloodiest strike wave in that country's history. As for Austria-Hungary, where the insoluble problem of dissident ethnic minorities festered beneath the brilliant surface of Viennese culture, wits said that its situation was desperate but not serious. The Russian tsar, aristocrats, and conservatives watched in constant dread for a new revolution following the unsuccessful uprising of 1905. Even that citadel of calm gradualism, Great Britain, was shaken in 1913 and 1914 by three different movements that took their anger into the streets: the mass protests for women's suffrage; the strike wave that was about to culminate in a general strike in August 1914; and, on the right, the army officers and English landowners in Ulster (Northern Ireland) who threatened civil war rather than accept the new laws providing for Irish Home Rule.

The important point is not whether these states were actually nearing a revolutionary situation in 1914, but whether national leaders thought so and what they proposed to do about it. Some statesmen, both liberal and conservative, feared that the dislocations of a war would "mean a state of things worse than that of 1848."[17] But even the conviction that war would heighten the revolutionary danger may have encouraged the kaiser to believe that the Russians would not dare fight Austria. Other statesmen, mostly conservative, believed that the jingoistic nationalism stimulated by a successful foreign war or warlike bluff was the most effective remedy for internal dissent. Some Austrian leaders believed in "mastering internal troubles by prosecuting an active foreign policy."[18] Russian Foreign Minister Sazanov told the tsar that "unless he yielded to the popular demand and unsheathed the sword on Serbia's behalf, he would run the risk of revolution and perhaps the loss of his throne."[19]

Only the most determinist of historians would suggest that capitalism's late stages must inevitably produce conservative efforts to distract class conflict by external war. Nor is there a clear case of any European statesman manufacturing a national emergency for purely internal purposes. What can be said, however, is that when an international emergency was thrust on them, some European statesmen took risks more willingly, in the belief that foreign success could only strengthen the ruling circle at home. At the very least, they knew that international humiliation produced revolution, as in Russia when revolution followed defeat at the hands of the Japanese in 1905. Even the British Liberal Prime Minister Herbert Asquith found some consolation as he contemplated "the most dangerous situation of the last forty years" in the Balkans on July 26: "It may incidentally have the effect of throwing into the background the lurid picture of civil war in Ulster."[20]

[17]Sir Edward Grey, quoted in Arno J. Mayer, "Domestic Causes of the First World War," in Leonard Krieger and Fritz Stern, eds., *The Responsibility of Power* (New York, 1967), p. 321.
[18]German Ambassador to London Prince Karl von Lichnowsky, opposing that remedy, quoted in *Ibid.,* p. 320.
[19]Quoted in Hans Rogger, "Russia in 1914," *Journal of Contemporary History,* Vol. 3 (1966): 243.
[20]Quoted in Cameron Hazlehurst, *Politicians at War* (New York, 1971), p. 32.

Other serious defects in the European system had devloped in the past generation to narrow the choices open to leaders in 1914. Both the Franco-Russian and the Austro-German alliances had been made more binding in the years before the war. It was not the firmer language of the alliance treaties that was dangerous, however, for the Great Powers had not felt obliged in practice to support their allies under any condition contrary to their own interests. France had not given the Russians assurances of help during the Bosnian crisis of 1908, for example. What was dangerous was the growing sense among the Great Powers that their security depended on the continued power of an ally. Unlike Bismarck before 1890, who had brought both Russia and Austria into a loose mutual cooperation, the German rulers after 1890 committed themselves to Austria and Italy in the Triple Alliance. As ties with Italy grew slack, the German leaders felt quite alone with Austria-Hungary by 1914, and bound to that empire's uncertain fate. France had no possibility of holding its own against the more numerous Germans without Russian support; if the Russians went to the brink against Germany, the French could not risk future isolation by giving an impression of doubtful support. Even Britain, unfettered by any explicit military obligations, could not imagine a secure future without a strong and friendly France. Increasingly powerful weapons having made them all more vulnerable, the Great Powers had to support their allies even when those allies took risks.

The War Machines

The industrialization of war also narrowed the statesmen's choices in 1914. European war machines had not only doubled in size between 1890 and 1914, raising military expenditures to the unprecedented level of nearly 5 percent of national income,[21] but they had also become enormously complex. The use of railroads in war in the 1860s put a new premium on speed, without reducing the older emphasis on numbers. Millions of reservists and vast quantities of artillery, ammunition, and supplies had to be moved in a few hours by a rail network that first had to be shifted from its normal commercial routes. Mobilization had to be begun early enough to meet dangers that were still only potential, although the very act of mobilization made those dangers more acute. Moreover, existing plans had to be followed whether or not they fit the current crisis, since improvisation was likely to produce chaos.

It has been noted how these technical requirements forced diplomacy

[21]Military expenditures during the pre-1914 arms race, while greater than they had ever been before, were still comparatively modest by current standards. The Great Powers spent nearly 10 percent of national income on arms in 1937. The Super Powers' armaments expenditure reached 13 to 15 percent of gross national product in the Cold War 1950s. (Quincy Wright, *A Study of War,* 2nd ed. [Chicago, 1964], pp. 667–72; Charles J. Hitch and Roland N. McKean, *The Economics of Defense in the Nuclear Age* [Cambridge, Mass., 1965], pp. 37, 98.)

out of control in the cases of general Russian mobilization on July 30, of the German commitment to the Schlieffen Plan, and of the early mobilization of the French "covering force" on July 30. Even in Britain, First Lord of the Admiralty Winston Churchill took the exceptional step of not dispersing the fleet from its usual summer maneuvers in July. The fear of being caught unprepared in the railroad age was sharper than the fear of slipping uncontrollably into overreaction.

The Exercise of Choice

We have seen how many features of the European state, economic, and military systems and the perfervid nationalisms of 1914 narrowed statesmen's choices. So more was involved in the failures of July and August 1914 than mere miscalculation, fatigue, or haste. However, most historians would feel uncomfortable if such emphasis were placed on predetermining conditions for war in 1914 that the free choices of European leaders were ignored. Historians should be as interested in the exercise of choice as in the conditions that limit choice. In July and August 1914, the Austrian leaders chose to punish Serbia for matters going far beyond the assassination of a royal heir. The German kaiser and chancellor supported Austria in a local war in order to reassert German vitality. The Russians had resolved as long ago as 1908 to forbid any further successes to Austria. French and British leaders decided, as the British foreign minister told the House of Commons on August 3, that "if we are engaged in war, we shall suffer, but little more than we shall suffer if we stand aside."[22]

These choices, it must be realized, were not simple selections between pure states of "peace" and "war." Decisions were made, step by step, between acceptable increments of war risk and unacceptable increments of risk of national humiliation, isolation, or decline. At each stage, the war risk seemed all the more acceptable because no European in 1914 had the faintest idea what sort of war the Great Powers could wage in the twentieth century. The length, fanaticism, and violence of what was to come was beyond human imagining as the first eager troops rushed to the front.

---

[22]Quoted in A. J. P. Taylor, *English History, 1914–45* (Oxford, 1965), p. 4.

Suggestions for Further Reading

L. C. F. Turner, *Origins of the First World War** (1970) is the best short introduction to debate and to bibliography. Laurence Lafore, *The Long Fuse** (1965) is a lucid brief discussion of the background to the First World War. Among more comprehensive treatments, the Italian newspaper editor Luigi Albertini's *Origins of the War of 1914,* 3 vols. (1952–57) provides an incomparable sweep of narrative detail, thorough on Balkan conditions and favorable to Italian intervention. Despite the uncovering of new information since the Second World War, the principal works of interwar American scholarship are still impressive. Sidney B. Fay, *The Origins of the World War,* 2 vols. (1929) shifts much of the blame from Germany to Serbia and Russia. Bernadotte E. Schmitt, *The Coming of the War* (1930) is more critical of the Central Powers.

Day-to-day developments during the final crisis can be followed in Imanuel Geiss, *July 1914* (1969), a selection of documents with commentary. The British decision to go to war has been reexamined most recently by Cameron Hazlehurst, *Politicians at War* (1971). A major new biography of a leading participant is Konrad Jarausch's study of Bethmann Hollweg, *The Enigmatic Chancellor* (1973).

Vladimir Dedijer, *The Road to Sarajevo* (1966) defends the idealism of Princip and his comrades and comes as close as may be possible to determining the degree of complicity of Serbian officers and ministers in the assassination of the Archduke Franz Ferdinand.

Arno J. Mayer, "Domestic Causes of the First World War," in Leonard Krieger and Fritz Stern, eds., *The Responsibility of Power** (1967) adds an important dimension.

The most interesting development since the Second World War has been Fritz Fischer's revival of the thesis of major German responsibility, in *Germany's Aims in the First World War** (1967). Fischer argued that most German political and military leaders were convinced in 1914 that they had to grasp for world power or decline. The passionate debate provoked by Fischer can be sampled in H. W. Koch, ed., *The Origins of the First World War** (1972), and in Gerald D. Feldman, *German Imperialism 1914–1918** (1972). Although there is no comparable new work on French war aims, see V. H. Rothwell, *British War Aims and Peace Diplomacy 1914–1918* (1971).

A. J. P. Taylor, *The Struggle for Mastery in Europe** (1954) contains the most authoritative bibliography of late–nineteenth-century diplomacy. As the last restrictions are lifted from European archives, research continues on prewar diplomacy and military preparation. Among important newer works are George Monger, *The End of Isolation, 1900–1907* (1963), an account of British policy, and Christopher Andrew, *Théophile Delcassé and the Making of the Entente Cordiale* (1968).

The German military are the subject of several master works: Gerhard Ritter, *The Sword and the Scepter,* vol. 2: *1890–1914* (1970); the same author's *Schlieffen Plan* (1958); and Gordon A. Craig, *The Politics of the Prussian Army, 1640–1945** (1955). Samuel R. Williamson, Jr., examines the Entente's military preparations in *The Politics of Grand Strategy: Britain and France Prepare for War, 1900–1914* (1969).

Arthur J. Marder, *The Anatomy of British Sea Power* (1940) may be supplemented with his comprehensive *From the Dreadnought to Scapa Flow: The Royal Navy in the Fisher Era, 1904–1919,* 5 vols. (1961–70). Eckhart Kehr's 1930 classic, *Battleship Building and Party Politics in Germany, 1894–1901,* is now available in English on microfilm (1973). More accessible is Jonathan Steinberg, *Tirpitz and the Birth of the German Battle Fleet* (1968).

Jubilant Berlin civilians escort their soldiers to the train, August 1914. Note the civilian at the far right who has traded his straw hat for a soldier's rifle and helmet.

THE MARNE
AND AFTER
1914–1917

3

During the first days of August 1914, more than 5 million young European men responded almost without opposition to military call-up. Many of them boarded the troop trains with genuine enthusiasm. The bands, banners, and young women with flowers were not mere window dressing. Popular animosities were already enflamed enough, and they were soon fanned by government propaganda and by nationalist intellectuals.

Each government had been remarkably successful in portraying the other side as the aggressor. The English poet Robert Graves, who had German uncles and a German middle name, recalled being persecuted in high school around 1910 because "German" meant "dirty German." "It meant 'cheap, shoddy goods competing with our sterling industries.'"

War Fever

It also meant military menace, Prussianism, useless philosophy, tedious scholarship, loving music, and sabre-rattling."[1] When the war broke out, German shops were damaged in London, German music was dropped from orchestra programs, and German sauerkraut was renamed "liberty cabbage." Stories of atrocities in Belgium, culminating in the German execution of the English nurse Edith Cavell in October 1915, fed those hatreds.

On the German side, many people felt they were defending virile German *Kultur* against the sly, mercantile English and the decadent Slavs and French. The German economist Werner Sombart, who had called himself socialist not long before, explained the war to his fellow citizens in 1915 as a contest between materialism and idealism, between British "Merchants" and German "Heroes."

> That is why, for us, who are imbued with militarism, the war is holy, the most sacred thing on earth.[2]

Most Frenchmen went to war convinced that they were defending humanitarian liberty against the booted Prussians. Only one major French public figure, novelist Romain Rolland, tried to keep his pacifist, internationalist values intact—"above the melee." He felt he could do so only by moving to Switzerland. All the ethnic groups of the troubled Austro-Hungarian Empire except some South Slavs and Czechs rallied with enthusiasm to the war against Tsarist Russia. Even Russians, deep in the throes of near-revolution in the summer of 1914, turned away from strikes and domestic opposition in August to face a common enemy. For every Russian who took part in the enthusiastic parades before the tsar's palace as the war began, there were probably many who merely accepted war sullenly. But the degree of popular enthusiasm surprised even the Russian rulers.

Beyond the national enmities and the arguments of national defense against aggressors, feeling of release from cramping bourgeois restraints gave war a positive allure for some soldiers. The draftees in Jules Romains' novel *Verdun* (1940) felt that "they were setting off for a noisy, bustling, rough sort of holiday, a real schoolboy expedition." The mediocre old world had been too full of "brittle things" that had to be tended politely.

> Here was a chance to live care-free for a while and irresponsibly to stretch the limbs in an orgy of crude action with never a thought for the brittle things that might be broken. Life would be better for some such "primitive" cure, for relapsing into simpler ways, for losing touch with the manners of refinement.[3]

Romain Rolland had been troubled as early as 1912 that "the children of the nation who had never seen war except in books had no difficulty in

[1] Robert Graves, *Goodbye to All That* (London, 1960), p. 38.
[2] Werner Sombart, *Händler und Helden* (Munich, 1915), p. 88.
[3] Jules Romains, *Verdun* (New York, 1940), pp. 4–5.

endowing it with beauty. Weary of peace and ideas, they hymned the anvil of battle on which, with bloody fists, action would one day new-forge the power of France."[4]

Exultation was all the easier in August 1914 because everyone believed that the war would be short. Every European conflict since 1815 had been decided in a few weeks. The growing complexity of military machines and of civilian economies suggested that a modern society could not support the cost of large-scale destruction for very long. The German chief of staff, General Alfred von Schlieffen, wrote in 1909 that a long war had become "impossible in an age when the existence of the nation is founded upon the uninterrupted continuation of trade and industry."[5] The French economist Paul Leroy-Beaulieu proved mathematically that a war in Europe could not last more than six months. The British Admiralty had stocked a six-months' supply of naval fuel oil, believing that no war could continue beyond that time. Most of the soldiers who boarded troop trains in August 1914 were certain that they would be home by Christmas.

A Dilemma for the Socialists

The patriotic surge of August 1914 confronted the European left with decisions of excruciating difficulty. The socialist parties of Europe had been planning during the decade before 1914 to call a general work stoppage in the event of an outbreak of the imperialist war that Marxist analysis had taught them to expect. The Workers' International,[6] the worldwide association of socialist parties in which the European socialists were dominant, had placed war prevention high on its agenda since 1904. The Moroccan crises of 1905 and 1911, the Bosnian crisis of 1908, and the Balkan Wars of 1912 and 1913 lent an urgent note to their plans. When the European governments began to rush to the brink of war in 1914, the permanent bureau of the International held a special meeting in Brussels on July 29, and the German Social Democratic leader Hermann Müller came to Paris on July 30 to confer with his fellow socialists in France. The European armies and police forces prepared to arrest socialist leaders in case mobilization was opposed by a general strike.

The war at hand in August 1914, however, resembled none of the hypothetical wars of overt aggression against which the International had plotted. Each European socialist party became convinced that its country was the victim of aggression and that its enemy's victory would set socialism back. The German Social Democratic party, the largest party in Germany and the most elaborately organized socialist party in

---

[4]Romain Rolland, *Jean Christophe*, Book 3, trans. Gilbert Cannan (New York, 1913), p. 458.
[5]Gerhard A. Ritter, *The Schlieffen Plan* (New York, 1958), p. 47.
[6]Technically, the Second International, founded in 1889, since the First International had broken down in 1874 in a dispute between followers of Marx and Bakunin.

the world, decided that German socialism was threatened by the danger of

> the victory of Russian despotism, which has stained itself with the blood of the best of its own people. Our task is to ward off this danger, to safeguard the culture and independence of our own country.[7]

The German trade unions decided on August 2 to call off their anticipated strike, and the Social Democratic party leaders voted 78 to 14 to support the German government. In the *Reichstag*, the deputies voted unanimously for special war appropriations on August 4. In France, the trade unions had decided against a strike as early as July 31. From Paris, the victory of autocratic Germany seemed a greater threat to French socialists than anything their government was likely to do to them. The only socialist parliamentary votes against war appropriations in Europe were two Social Democratic nays in Serbia and the walkout of fourteen Russian Social Democrats, both reformists and revolutionaries (Bolsheviks), and of eleven members of Aleksandr Kerensky's reformist Labor party. The Italian socialists largely approved their government's decision to stay out of the war, a course that spared them the difficult choices their European colleagues had been forced to make. No general strikes materialized in any belligerent country.

War and Social Peace

With hindsight, some critics have accused the European socialist leaders of betraying their followers at the crucial moment in August 1914. In fact, the mass of European workers were no less convinced of the duty to fight reactionary aggressors than were the socialist leaders. In France, where the General Staff had predicted that 10 percent of draftees would refuse the call, there was a refusal rate of only 1.5 percent, and the government decided not to arrest the socialist leaders whose names appeared on its secret list, "Carnet B." The British case was even more striking. Labour party leaders Ramsay MacDonald and Philip Snowden, who opposed British entry into the war, were disavowed by the rank and file on August 5 and forced to resign.

Nor was there any relation between revolutionary fervor and pacifism in 1914 among socialist leaders. British pacifism was as strong a minority current in the Liberal party as in the Labour party. On the Continent, reformists like the German Edouard Bernstein were pacifist in 1914, while the most militant prowar faction came from the ranks of revolutionary syndicalists like the French journalist Gustave Hervé and the Italian Benito Mussolini, men who by temperament welcomed violent solutions.

Assured of the support of most of its working class, every European belligerent entered the war in a mood of enthusiastic national unity.

---

[7]Speech of German Social Democratic leader Hugo Haase, August 4, 1914, before the *Reichstag*.

Volunteers flock to a British recruiting office in 1915, before the introduction of the draft.

French politicians proclaimed a *union sacrée,* a sacred union of Frenchmen around the flag. Kaiser Wilhelm II announced that he perceived no more enemies within the state; foreign war had created domestic peace (*Burgfrieden,* the internal truce of a besieged fortress). The embittered Russian factory workers and peasantry were the acid test of patriotic union. They ended strikes at the beginning of August, obeyed the draft call more or less without incident, and expressed little discernible opposition through the first months of the war. Internal harmony would never again be as complete as it was in August 1914.

On August 4, eager German armies crossed the Belgian frontier, and Moltke's slightly modified version of the Schlieffen Plan began to be executed. Five hundred trains a day ran up to the Belgian border. The Germans threw seven of their eight armies into a vast encircling movement designed to knock France out of the war in one blow. Despite the Belgians' heroic defense of their fortresses, by August 14 the Germans were sweeping in a great arc toward Paris.

As the German planners had hoped, the French Army launched the

The First Battle of the Marne

A color guard of cadets at the French military academy at Saint-Cyr in the white gloves and plumed shakos in which they fought in 1914.

bulk of its forces eastward in an effort to recapture Alsace-Lorraine. This opening campaign of the First World War was, in a sense, the last gesture of chivalric soldiery against the impersonal efficiency of mechanized warfare. The French troops, brightly clad in red trousers and blue tunics and led by young Saint-Cyr military school graduates who had taken an oath to wear their parade-ground headgear and white gloves in the first charge, were decimated by artillery and machine-gun fire. The French offensive gained no permanent ground, leaving the lost provinces to be recaptured only in the last days of the war. More importantly, the French headlong rush toward the Rhine played into the hands of Schlieffen's successors, who hoped to enfold as many French troops as possible into the pocket of their wheeling forces as far to the east of Paris as possible.

By the first week of September the Germans had reached the River Marne and the French government had fled Paris for Bordeaux. Schlieffen's dream of a lightning decision in the west appeared close to realization. Then came the French–British counterattack from September 6 to 10, which has become known as the First Battle of the Marne. It was one of the great deliverances of history.

General Joseph Joffre, a phlegmatic French commander whose legendary appetite and sound sleep during the German advance helped steady French nerves, coolly waited for the moment to strike back. The German advance created its own problems. Some units covered twenty to thirty miles a day on foot and outstripped their artillery and supplies in the effort to draw the immense trap shut. Moltke, ill and indecisive, could keep only distant contact with his army commanders; communications were made even more difficult by the distances that the mounted couriers of the day had to cover. Finally, General Alexander von Kluck, commander of the outermost wing, the German First Army, exposed two vulnerable spots to the watchful Joffre. In accordance with Moltke's retrenched version of the Schlieffen Plan, Kluck wheeled east of Paris, exposing his flank to the French forces in Paris that were now left outside the trap. Next, when he turned part of his army to face the danger from Paris, he opened a gap between his own force and the next German army to the east. On September 6, the French reserves in Paris were rushed out in the city's entire taxi fleet to attack Kluck's exposed flank; meanwhile, the first units of the British Expeditionary Force pushed cautiously into the gap between Kluck and the German Second Army. By September 10, the Germans had fallen back to the Marne, and Paris was saved.

It is true that Joffre was unable to turn this pause into a full German retreat. Indeed, neither army was able to dislodge the other from the trenches that both now began to dig for shelter. Instead, each tried to outflank the other in a series of "end runs" that moved ever more westward and northward until they reached the coast, a movement that is usually misnamed "the race to the sea." By mid-October, the line of combat stretched from the Belgian North Sea coast to the borders of Switzerland along three hundred miles of trenches defended by fast-firing weapons and earthworks. They were locked in that tactical immobility where they would remain for the next four years. As historian A. J. P. Taylor notes, "The machine gun and the spade had changed the course of European history."[8]

The First Battle of the Marne set the conditions that prevailed on the major front for the rest of the war. First of all, it ended the expectation that the troops would be home by Christmas. Not only would the war be a long one, but the home fronts would be gradually drawn into the business of making war. Furthermore, it meant that the rest of the war in the west would be dominated by

The French commander in chief, General Joseph Joffre (left), converses with the commander of the British forces in France, Sir John French, and Sir Douglas Haig (right).

[8]A. J. P. Taylor, *The Struggle for Mastery in Europe, 1848–1914* (Oxford, 1954), p. 531.

the search for a way to break through the crust of trenches and restore the decisive war of movement. That search was eventually to bring the whole world into the war. And it was to produce the brutalizing horrors of trench warfare in which boredom alternated with carnage.

At the Marne, it was neither France nor Germany that had been defeated but prewar European society, which now had to be transformed into one vast warmaking machine.

General Paul von Hindenburg watches the battle of Tannenberg through a field periscope, 1914. General Erich Ludendorff (second from right) stands by.

The Eastern Front

The long eastern front never bogged down in trench warfare. But the resulting war of movement was no more decisive and no less costly in life than in the west. The Germans had expected to contain the slowly mobilizing Russians with one-eighth of their armed forces while knocking France out of the war; the Austrians, similarly, had hoped to annihilate the Serbs before any serious threat arose on the Russian front. Neither expectation was realized, and the Russians were able to advance into East Prussia and Austrian Poland (the province of Galicia) in the opening weeks of the war. These successes were only temporary, however.

Tannenberg and the Masurian Lakes, 1914

The victory denied the Germans on the Marne was won in East Prussia. There, during the same weeks, the outnumbered Germans brought off a daring maneuver by separating two Russian armies and defeating them one at a time, one at Tannenberg on August 30, and the other at the Masurian Lakes on September 15. General Paul von Hindenburg and his chief of staff, General Erich Ludendorff, made themselves formidable reputations. Germany was heartened to fight on harder than ever, and the Russians never again seriously menaced German territory in the north.

One Russian soldier attempts to stop two deserters during the Russian retreat from Galicia, 1915.

The Austrian Fronts, 1914–15

The Austrians, meanwhile, were dealing less successfully with a two-front war. General Conrad von Hötzendorf was obliged to draw off his best troops from the Serbian front to meet an unexpectedly strong Russian showing in Galicia. The result was losses on both fronts. The Russians took all of Galicia in 1914 and threatened the Hungarian Plain across the Carpathian Mountains. By December 1914, on the southern front, the Serbians had thrown Austrian troops off Serbian soil twice, after very hard fighting. In May 1915, Italy joined the war on the Entente side[9] and opened an additional southern front against Austria-Hungary. The punitive expedition against Serbia with which Austria had begun the war was now swallowed up in a far graver struggle for Austro-Hungarian survival.

[9]See below, p. 93.

Russian soldiers fleeing before a German cavalry advance.

In 1915 the Germans came to the aid of their allies in the east. Since the stalemate on the western front seemed to offer no opportunity for a decisive thrust, Hindenburg and Ludendorff used their new prestige to extract reinforcements from the High Command. A fresh German–Austrian force battered an opening in the Russian line in Galicia on May 2, 1915, initiating one of the great retreats of Russian history. Demoralized and short of ammunition, the tsar's armies reeled back out of Galicia 300 miles into Russian territory, until winter finally terminated operations. Less spectacular than the losses of 1812 and 1941, the great Russian retreat of 1915 nevertheless cost European Russia 15 percent of its territory, 10 percent of its railroads, 30 percent of its industries, and nearly 20 percent of its population. The Russian Army's casualties are said to have amounted to 2.5 million killed, wounded, or captured.

Austria's threat from the south, meanwhile, became more urgent with the landing in April 1915 of a British–French expeditionary force at Gallipoli, at the tip of the peninsula south of Constantinople, in an effort to force the Straits. That landing was one of the most controversial operations of the war. In the opinion of its supporters, such as First Lord of the Admiralty Winston Churchill, putting a force ashore at the southern entrance to the Straits had the combined advantages of answering the Russian appeal for relief from attack by Turkey (newly allied with Germany) and bypassing the stalemated western front with a daring naval maneuver. It replaced brute force with mobility. In the opinion of its opponents, such as French General Joffre, it drained precious forces from the major front where decision would eventually be reached by piling mass on mass. In the end, the combined British and French force failed to fight its way out of the rocky peninsula of Gallipoli, not to speak of forcing the Straits and putting Turkey out of the war.

The Central Powers acquired a decisive advantage when Bulgaria, impressed by German successes in Russia, and no less thirsty for territorial gain at Serbian expense than in 1875 or 1912, agreed in September 1915 to join Germany and Austria-Hungary in a final attack on Serbia. The Allied response of transferring most of the Gallipoli contingent to the Greek port of Salonika did not redress the balance, and in fact led to the entrapment of a considerable Allied force there for most of the rest of the war.

Taken from both front and flank, the Serbian Army was forced into an agonizing retreat through the defiles of the Albanian mountains to the Adriatic Sea, where some 100,000 survivors were picked up by Allied ships. It has been estimated that Serbia lost one-sixth of its population to battle, epidemic, and famine in the course of this campaign. Serbia had been amply punished for the murder of the Archduke Franz Ferdinand, but the South Slav idea was no less militant for all that.

Early in 1916, the new German chief of staff, Erich von Falkenhayn, turned his main attention back to the western front. Hötzendorf was now left to follow his own plan of a major offensive against Italy. The most important result of his campaign in the Trentino in June 1916 was to leave the Russian front covered so thinly that Alexei Brusilov, the

After the defeat of his country's armies by the Austrians, King Peter of Serbia, seventy- one years old and nearly blind, retreats into exile.

most capable Russian general in that war, was able to rout the Austrians and recover much of the Galician ground lost in 1915. Brusilov received no help from other Russian armies to the north, however, and shortages of ammunition kept him from exploiting his skillful breach into Hungary. It was the final spurt of energy from the Russian war machine and the last great campaign of the war on the eastern front.

The Search for a Breakthrough in the West

The post-Marne stalemate in the west was a tactical novelty to which political and military leaders adapted only slowly. Moltke and Falkenhayn, no less than the French commanders Joffre and Ferdinand Foch, had been schooled in the war of movement and maneuver. British commanders, like John French and Douglas Haig, had been cavalry generals in the Boer War. After the Marne, the war in the west was an attempt to get back to the familiar tactic of movement. All the military staffs, prodded by an impatient and uncomprehending public opinion, tried for the next three years to "break the crust."

Assaults "Over the Top"

The basic problem in making an assault was how to open a gap in the opposing armies in the face of machine-gun fire, and then pour enough men and equipment through the gap to turn the exposed flanks. It was tempting to try to solve the problem with sheer mass: with numbers of men and quantities of artillery shells.

At first, the belligerents sent every available man to the front. The French even stripped essential armaments plants of their manpower for the anticipated decisive blow. The numbers of men in battle had been enormously increased by European population growth, the principle of universal military service, and the tactics of trying to strike a decisive first blow. Waterloo (1815) had been fought by 170,000 men; Sedan (1870) by 300,000. The First Battle of the Marne involved over 1 million men. But the firepower of artillery, modern rifles, and particularly the machine gun reduced these masses of men to crouching behind earthworks.

The trenches that had been hastily dug in 1914 developed into elaborate systems of defense, doubled or tripled in depth, and reinforced by concrete machine-gun emplacements. Command posts were housed in dugouts, which might be more or less dry as well as secure from all but direct hits. The connecting trenches, however, were too rat infested and muddy for the rough wood flooring to give much comfort. Above all, there was always a risk of being picked off by a sniper or a random mortar shot, even between offensives. "The front is a cage in which we must await fearfully whatever may happen," wrote the German war veteran Erich Maria Remarque in his novel *All Quiet on the Western Front* (1929). "We lie under the network of arching shells and

A German photograph illustrates three reasons why battle casualties ran far higher in the First World War than in earlier wars: artillery-scarred trenches, poison gas, and the machine gun.

live in a suspense of uncertainty. Over us Chance hovers."[10] In front of the trenches were systems of barbed wire, often thirty yards wide and three to five feet high, laced to iron stakes and trestles. And in front of that, "no man's land," the space between enemy lines, where patrols operated silently at night and where each side waited to see the enemy surge forward.

The assault "over the top" under these conditions required a massive preliminary softening up by artillery. Consumption of shell ran beyond any prewar staff officer's wildest imagining. The French General Staff had expected to expend about 13,000 shells a day. In the first days of the war, they actually used 120,000 shells a day. In 1916, the British used one gun for every twenty yards on a fourteen-mile front and 1.5 million shells to prepare for the Somme campaign. In April 1917, the French offensive in the Champagne was prepared by firing 6 million shells on a twenty-mile front. The problem with this method of "softening up" was that each artillery barrage warned the enemy of the location of the next offensive in time to reinforce the stunned and battered defenders. The result was generally an expensive but sterile engagement with only a few square yards of advance to show for high casualties. "Still the little piece of convulsed earth on which we lie is held. We have yielded no more than a few hundred yards of it as a prize to the enemy. But on every yard there lies a dead man."[11]

The assaults of 1915 on the western front were inconclusive. Even at Ypres, in Belgian Flanders, where the Germans first introduced mustard gas on April 22, they were prevented from following up their success because their reserves had been moved to the major eastern offensive.

[10]Erich Maria Remarque, *All Quiet on the Western Front* (New York, 1966), p. 63.
[11]*Ibid.*, p. 84.

French soldiers crouching in a trench during shelling at Verdun, 1916. The stiff body at the right may date from earlier fighting, for the dead often went unburied.

On neither side had impatient politicians or generals learned to solve the problem of stalemate other than by ever increasing masses of shells and men. Even greater trench battles were mounted in 1916 and early 1917. The most significant of these, which forever marked the First World War as the utter limit of human endurance, were the German offensive at Verdun in 1916, the British campaign on the Somme in 1916, and the quixotic offensive of the French General Robert Nivelle in the Champagne in April 1917. Here the tragic futility of trench warfare reached its climax.

Major Offensives: Verdun, the Somme, the Champagne

At the end of 1915, after brilliant gains on the eastern front, Moltke's successor, Falkenhayn, proposed to reopen the campaign in the west with a plan calculated to increase the French casualty rate. If the Germans singled out for attack a French position that "touched national honor and pride," he wrote in a December 1915 memorandum to the kaiser, the French would defend it at all cost. "If they do so, they will bleed to death." The target chosen was the fortress city of Verdun: strategically, the vital hinge where the front turned southward along the Meuse River; morally, a historic strongpoint whose loss would cripple French spirit.

On February 21, 1916, the Germans began a massive artillery barrage designed to obliterate the French trenches before Verdun. Joffre took the challenge, and for the next ten months the two sides shelled, took, lost, and retook a few square miles of heavily fortified terrain. General Phillippe Pétain, the elderly local commander who had been slated for an early retirement until he showed his methodical coolness in the first battles, held on with a grim determination that was the climax of French military effort in this century. "Ils ne passeront pas" (They shall not pass) was his laconic instruction to his troops. For ten months, the bottle-shaped salient of Verdun was supplied under shellfire along a single narrow road by a continuous truck convoy, bringing shells in and wounded out. Week after week the ground was dug and redug by millions of shells. Jules Romains' novel *Verdun* describes an officer stumbling across a corpse on leaving his dugout and then noticing that it was wearing a different uniform than the one he had stumbled across a few hours earlier.

In the end, the Germans did not pass, but the cost was staggering. Those who escaped with their lives were often maimed physically and mentally with what the French sardonically called "Poincaré tattoos." Nearly 700,000 on both sides did not escape with their lives. Falkenhayn had had his way, with one major amendment: the German Army had been bled white as well as the French. This greatest of all First World War battles had consumed the young men of a medium-sized town each morning and afternoon for ten months.

Aftermath of the Somme offensive, 1916.

The British turn came in July 1916 with the Somme campaign. It was designed to relieve the pressure on the French at Verdun and to achieve the elusive breakthrough by sheer mass. Poet Robert Graves was told by his colonel to forget the trenches and prepare for the war of movement that would follow when the British cavalry got behind the German trenches.[12] Sir Douglas Haig prepared the classic piercing operation. A ferocious artillery barrage of eight days' duration was supposed to open the way for three cavalry divisions to pass through. When the charge came, one-half of the men and three-quarters of the officers were either killed or wounded. The British gained a mere 120 square miles for 400,000 casualties, and the cavalry could never go into action. "For every yard of the 16-mile front from Gommecourt to Montauban there were two British casualties."[13]

As 1917 began, the quest for a decisive battle led the French cabinet to replace Joffre as commander in chief with the more flamboyant Robert Nivelle, a glib cavalry general who had been successful in some local advances at Verdun. Nivelle promised to "break the crust" once and for all with a grand offensive in the Champagne. The Nivelle offensive, which aroused the highest hopes beforehand in Paris and the deepest despondency afterward, was tactically no different from Haig's Somme offensive of the previous summer. The results were even poorer, for Hindenburg and Ludendorff, who had replaced the now discredited Falkenhayn, quietly withdrew the German line a few miles before Nivelle began his artillery preparation in April 1917. Punching at empty space, Nivelle was caught off balance and nearly routed in a campaign that left the French Army at the brink of insurrection.

As in the preceding year, British forces tried to divert the Germans in this emergency by attacking northward along the North Sea coast in Flanders. The usual week of artillery preparation opened the dikes, so that men and machines floundered for three indecisive months in the mud around Passchendaele and Ypres. The British strategist Basil H. Liddell-Hart tells of a staff officer who burst into tears upon seeing the area later, exclaiming, "My God, did we send men to fight in that?"[14] At the price of 240,000 men, Haig gained fifty square miles and the reputation of a callous squanderer of human life.

New Weapons

Inevitably, the search for a breakthrough led to ideas other than ever more violent assaults "over the top." Modern technology was applied to the problem of restoring offense to an equal footing with defense. The British introduced the first tank on September 15, 1916, near the end of the Somme campaign, in an attempt to give mobility and protection to the attacker of a fortified trench position. After a dubious beginning,

[12]Graves, p. 146.
[13]Martin Middlebrook, *The First Day on the Somme: 1 July 1916* (New York, 1972), p. 245.
[14]Basil H. Liddell-Hart, *The Real War, 1914–18* (Boston, 1930), p. 337.

British soldiers blinded by gas near Béthune, in northern France, during the final German offensive of April 1918, lead each other toward an advanced dressing station.

tanks finally became effective in the campaigns of 1918. The Germans first used poison gas at Ypres in April 1915, and the flame thrower at Verdun in February 1916.

The most dramatic new weapon was the airplane. Initially aircraft were used for observation and artillery ranging. When it became necessary to protect spotter planes from enemy aircraft, air combat took on a life of its own. In October 1915 the Dutch designer A. H. G. Fokker developed machine guns that were synchronized to fire between the propeller blades. With that invention began a brilliant period of individual air duels. Aces like the German "Red Baron," Manfred von Richthoven, the Frenchman Georges Guynemer, and the Englishman Albert Ball were revered by their publics for daring feats with Immelmann turns and other desperate aerial acrobatics.

Improved aircraft also increased each side's capacity to bomb the enemy's cities. The lighter-than-air German dirigibles that threw panic into British cities in 1916 had actually been quite vulnerable because they were so easy to shoot down. By 1918, more effective bombing planes were in use against London (1414 persons were killed by bombs in England during the war) and to a lesser extent in France and Germany (746 Germans were killed by bombs). In this way the widening net of the war began to ensnare civilians far behind the lines in the sufferings of combat.

The Widening War Both sides tried to break the stalemate by drawing new allies into the war. Turkey had come under German military and commercial influence before the war. It became for all practical purposes a belligerent on August 10, 1914, when the German cruisers *Goeben* and *Breslau,* fleeing from British warships in the Mediterranean, received refuge in the supposedly neutral Dardanelles. On October 29, these ships, formally purchased by Turkey but under the command of German officers, shelled the Russian Black Sea ports of Odessa and Sevastopol. When Russia declared war on Turkey on November 2, Britain and France soon followed suit.

THE FIRST WORLD WAR: THE FRONTS

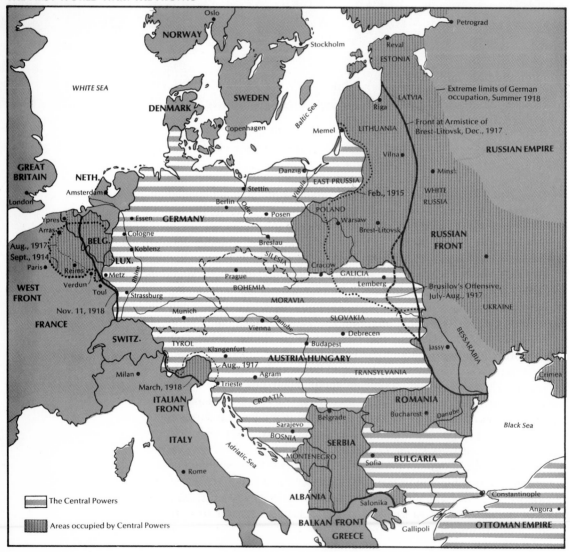

The Turkish sultan declared a holy war against the infidel and launched a double offensive: one army attacked through the Caucasus toward the oil fields of Baku and, at least in the proclamations of its general, toward India; the other moved on the Suez Canal. The Entente not only found itself blocked from sea contact with Russia but saw its colonial holdings threatened. It was at this point that the British and French reacted with the landing at Gallipoli in April 1915. After Bulgaria's entry into the war and Serbia's defeat in October 1915, the peninsula was considered untenable, and the Allied forces were withdrawn from Gallipoli in January 1916. The only remnant of the abandoned Balkan front was the Entente force that was more or less bottled up at the Greek port of Salonika.

Farther south, Britain moved energetically to stave off the threat to its Middle Eastern position. The tough "Anzacs"—the Australia-New Zealand Army Corps—sufficiently reinforced British units in Egypt to hold off a German–Turkish assault on the Suez Canal in February 1915. The kaiser's dreams of Egyptian and Indian revolts against the British were disappointed, for Britain maintained control over its colonial subjects. The British were able to mobilize Arab nationalism against the Ottoman Empire by extending vague promises of independence to the sherif of Mecca. And a British–Indian force was brought to the head of the Persian Gulf to block any enemy advance through Mesopotamia toward the oil installations at Abadan. The war was taking the whole world for its theater.

The Allies also successfully outbid the Central Powers in the effort to bring Italy into the war. Italy had renewed its adherence to the Triple Alliance with German and Austria-Hungary in 1902. But the original reasons for Italy's joining that alliance—support against France and for imperial expansion, and the possibility of neutralizing Austrian influence in the Balkans and at the Vatican—had become less compelling than the Italian–Austrian rivalry in the Alps and around the Adriatic. The alliance bound Italy to aid its allies only if they were attacked by other powers, and it was clearly Austria-Hungary that had taken the initiative in 1914. Italy declared its neutrality on August 3, 1914, thereby greatly easing the Allied naval position in the Mediterranean.

As the stalemate developed in the west, however, Italian participation in the war became more desirable to both the Allies and the Central Powers. Since the Entente could accede to Italian ambitions in the Austrian alpine and Adriatic regions, Italian Foreign Minister Sidney Sonnino signed the secret Treaty of London with Britain and France on April 26, 1915. In exchange for declaring war on the Central Powers, Italy was to receive important gains in the Alps (the Italian-speaking Trentino and part of the German-speaking Tirol up to the Brenner Pass), the head of the Adriatic Sea, the Dodecanese Islands, and the south coast of Turkey, as well as compensation in Africa if Britain and France made gains there. The Holy See was to be excluded from eventual peace negotiations. In the short run, the opening of an additional front against Austria was immensely important to the eastern front, where, as we have seen, it helped the Brusilov offensive of 1916. By 1917, however, Allied reinforcements had to be sent to Italy, and the balance on the western front had not swung to the Allies.

The War at Sea

The combatants sought at sea the decision denied them on land. From the first hours of war, Britain and France used their naval superiority to destroy German warships. The heavy German cruisers *Scharnhorst* and *Gneisenau,* which had caused concern in Britain by sinking a British naval force off Chile, were finally run down and sunk by a superior British force off the Falklands in December 1914, and the *Dresden* was sunk off Chile in March 1915. There remained no effective obstacles to an Allied blockade of Germany and Austria-Hungary. It was expected that the Central Powers would be unable to sustain a long modern war without imports from overseas.

In retaliation, Germany used its submarine fleet to impose a counter-blockade. On February 4, 1915, the German government declared the area around Britain, Ireland, and northern France a war zone within which any ship, even neutral, would be torpedoed without warning. Although there were too few U-boats to interfere seriously with shipping to the British Isles, the sinking of some passenger ships had the effect of creating a strong current of prowar opinion in the United States. This was especially true after the Cunard liner *Lusitania* was sunk off the southern coast of Ireland on May 7, 1915, with a loss of nearly 2000 lives, many of them American. The following September, German submarine action in the Atlantic was restricted in order to avoid further complications with Washington.

Throughout the first two years of the war, the British and German battle fleets had avoided contact. The British maintained their blockade from afar, while the Germans were reluctant to engage their smaller force. Early in 1916 Admiral Reinhard Scheer, commander of the German High Seas Fleet, proposed to bait the British Grand Fleet into an all-out battle that might change the whole balance of sea power and, with it, the outcome of the war. The result was the Battle of Jutland, the one major naval battle of the war and the last involving the maneuvering of battleships to fire their fifteen-inch guns without the intervention of aircraft or submarines. Churchill nostalgically called it "the culminating manifestation of naval force in the history of the world."

The battle actually worked no strategic change in the war. Scheer sent Admiral Franz von Hipper with five cruisers off the Norwegian coast in order to draw Admiral John Jellicoe and the British Dreadnoughts out of the naval base of Scapa Flow in Scotland. Scheer then poised his main fleet to intercept them. Throughout two days of maneuvering west of Denmark, May 30 to June 2, the opposing fleets damaged each other without ever decisively bringing the other into position to be demolished. Scheer, conscious of his inferiority, kept drawing away, and Jellicoe, nervous about torpedo attacks, failed to seize the opportunity to cut Scheer off from his home port. In the end, the British suffered somewhat heavier losses, but the relative strengths of the two navies remained the same. Neither side tried to engage the other directly again until 1918, and the Dreadnoughts remained a deterrent rather than an offensive weapon for the rest of the war.

For Germany, it was tempting to resort once again to submarine warfare to evade British control of the sea's surface. By the end of 1916, the kaiser had been convinced by Hindenburg and Ludendorff, now in supreme command of the German military forces, that the advantages of unrestricted submarine warfare outweighed the disadvantages. Germany needed relief from growing internal strain, the aid from the United States to Britain had to be diminished, and the possibility of the United States intervening effectively in the European combat was only slight. On February 1, 1917, German submarines were ordered to sink all merchantmen on sight. Losses to British shipping, which had mounted from a monthly average of 51,000 tons in 1914 to 103,000 tons in 1916, now climbed to over 300,000 tons in February 1917 and more than 400,000 tons in June 1917. Only the adoption of the convoy system kept the British Atlantic life line functioning.

The United States Enters the War

The announcement of unrestricted submarine warfare led the United States to break off diplomatic relations with Germany on February 3, 1917. The forces that had tended to keep the United States neutral were gradually falling away: the antagonism of Washington to British blockade measures was now totally overshadowed by the German sinking of Allied and neutral ships; American doubts about the Entente's war aims were diminished by the replacement of the tsar's autocracy with a democratic regime in Russia in February 1917, which the United States recognized on March 20; the financial and industrial stake of the United States in the war effort of Britain and France had grown to enormous proportions, while Germany, the first to borrow from the United States in 1914, was prevented by the blockade from calling on American economic power.

Finally, what remained of isolationist sentiment was dispelled by the British Admiralty's decipherment of the so-called Zimmermann Note, instructions from the German Secretary of State for Foreign Affairs Arthur Zimmermann to the German minister in Mexico City to offer German support for the Mexican recovery of Texas, New Mexico, and Arizona in case of war between Germany and the United States. Publication of this document in the American press on March 1, 1917, prepared all but a few ardent isolationists and some German-Americans for war on the Entente side. President Wilson's war message to Congress on April 2 led to a joint resolution of Congress, passed on April 6 by a vote of 465 to 56, to join the Entente as an "Associated Power."

The war had become a worldwide conflict. Moreover, the effort to hammer a way out of the stalemate inevitably drew the belligerents into more and more total war. The inhuman sufferings of the fighting front were soon followed by severe home-front privations and dislocations. The war of 1914 to 1918 is still justly called the Great War, if for no other reason than the profound changes it wrought in European society.

Suggestions for Further Reading

Cyril Falls, *The Great War, 1914–1918** (1959) gives the best brief account of military operations. A standard fuller military history is C. R. M. F. Cruttwell, *A History of the Great War, 1914–1918*, 2nd ed. (1936). Basil H. Liddell-Hart, *The Real War, 1914–1918** (1930), and Winston S. Churchill, *The World Crisis, 1911–1918*, 6 vols. (1923; one-volume abridgement, 1941) are absorbing accounts by participants.

For a larger perspective on the changing nature of war, see Cyril Falls, *A Hundred Years of War, 1850–1950** (1962), and Theodore Ropp, *War in the Modern World,** rev. ed. (1966). Quincy Wright, *A Study of War* (1942; abridged ed., 1964) makes fascinating browsing.

Maurice Hankey, *The Supreme Command,* 2 vols. (1961) publishes accounts of meetings of the British Committee of Imperial Defense. Gordon A. Craig and Fritz Fischer discuss German wartime strategic decisions in works cited in the bibliography for Chapter 2. Jere Clemens King, *Generals and Politi-*

cians (1951; reprint ed., 1971) treats civil–military relations in France.

The horrors endured by ordinary soldiers inspired a richer literature in the First World War than in the Second. Major war novels include Erich Maria Remarque, *All Quiet on the Western Front** (1927); Henri Barbusse, *Under Fire** (1917); Jules Romains, *Verdun* (1938); and Arnold Zweig, *The Case of Sergeant Grisha** (1928). Personal reminiscences of exceptional merit include Edmund Blunden, *Undertones of War* (1928); Robert Graves, *Goodbye to All That,** rev. ed. (1960); and e. e. cummings, *The Enormous Room** (1934).

There are a host of popular accounts of the war. Alistair Horne, *The Price of Glory** (1962) recounts the carnage at Verdun with indignation. Correlli Barnett, *The Swordbearers* (1964), and Barbara Tuchman, *The Guns of August** (1962) evaluate the military commanders on both sides in action. Richard M. Watt, *Dare Call it Treason* (1963) portrays the French Army mutinies of 1917.

THE IMPACT
OF TOTAL WAR

4

The Battle of the Marne proved that no one Great Power could finish off another at a single blow with the war technology of 1914. Yet the alternative of an immediate compromise peace remained unthinkable to all but a handful of European pacifists. The French had foreign troops on their soil; the Germans had tasted gain. After the Marne, the war could neither be won quickly nor ended quickly.

Those Europeans who thought about warfare before 1914 had been certain that advanced European societies could not support long wars. In a sense they were right. The societies could not support a long war *unchanged,* but they had to endure one anyway. The First World War became total war, or what the German General Erich Ludendorff later called "totalitarian war."[1] It left no aspect of European civilization untouched. It utterly transformed European governments, economies, and societies. "Everywhere in the world was heard the sound of things breaking," wrote a regretful liberal, the British author and diplomat

[1] Erich von Ludendorff, *The Nation at War,* trans. A. S. Rappoport (London, 1936), p. 9.

John Buchan. The war, said Trotsky, "was a furious pogrom of human culture."[2]

Total war worked its effects on several levels. Materially, total war demanded the marshaling of unprecedented quantities of young men, steel and explosives for them to hurl at one another, and a steady stream of basic supplies to support both. In political terms, since the material effort required allocating people and resources away from their accustomed uses, the state had to take on extensive new powers. All of this imposed such unequal burdens on the populations that the belligerent states had to find new ways to persuade people to accept sacrifices. They had to organize opinion too. Such concentration of energy and thought required nothing less than an unannounced revolution.

Adjusting to a War of Attrition

After the Marne, each side proceeded to wear the other down. A war of attrition among advanced industrial societies was something altogether outside historic experience, and in 1914 it remained to be seen how fully their large populations and vast productive capacity could be devoted to mutual destruction without leaving cities hungry and factories dark.

Every belligerent's advance planning for war had proved hopelessly inadequate. The British Army had expected to mobilize 100,000 men in the event of a European war; during the war they mobilized 3 million. France eventually called up 8 million men, or 62.7 percent of all males between eighteen and forty (about 20 percent of the total population). State budgets underwent the same sort of distortion. The French prewar budgets had amounted to about 5 billion francs per year by 1913. The French budget in 1918 was 190 billion francs. After the war, debt service alone—the interest paid to those who had bought war bonds—amounted to 7 billion francs. By that time, the purchasing power of the franc was only about one-sixth of what it had been before the war. With such fundamental matters as human employment and the value of money distorted beyond recognition, governments found their prewar precedents useless.

After the first two months of war, therefore, the belligerent governments were forced to begin the painful process of throwing away their prewar rule books, along with the preconceptions that lay behind them. The French, for example, had expected the civilian economy to more or less hold its breath while everyone who could carry a rifle was sent to meet the more numerous Germans in one decisive battle. They even closed down war plants in order to send their workers to the front. By the end of 1914, the unexpected rate of battlefield consumption and the prospect of a long war forced them to reopen the plants and to allocate men (and women) between the battle front and what began to be called

[2]John Buchan, *The King's Grace* (London, 1935), p. 161; Leon Trotsky, *Terrorism and Communism* (New York, 1921), p. 17.

the home front. The challenge of total war went beyond merely marshaling unprecedented quantities of men, money, and supplies. Whole civilian populations had to be kept fed, clothed, productive, and docile. Civilian production and consumption would have to be as minutely regulated as the army itself. A whole new range of human organization had to be conceived and put into operation.

Some of the belligerent states rose to this challenge. Others did not. Those that did not were states already divided by social and ethnic conflict, especially the multinational empires: Austria-Hungary, the Ottoman Empire, Tsarist Russia. Bureaucratic tradition, autocratic authority, large population and geographic size did not give these states the advantages one might have expected in a more traditional war. Success in the First World War depended more on industrial productivity—the ability to turn out masses of war matériel—and on the kind of internal cohesion and integration that equipped populations to endure the strains and accept the unequal privations of total war. While the empires showed that their authoritarian power was hollow, Great Britain rose best to the challenge, followed by republican France. In all fairness, it should be observed that Britain did not endure battles on its own soil. And it might be fairer still to call Britain least unsuccessful rather than most successful, for Britain never fully recovered from the effects of the First World War.

No belligerent state established the full reach of war government at one stroke. There was too much to be unlearned, and too many piecemeal expedients to be tried and rejected. No two belligerent states adapted in the same way, for the challenge laid bare their very different qualities and capacities.

War Governments: A Comparative Look

Great Britain

When the war began, Britain had been governed for eight years by the Liberal party. The Liberals had won the election of 1906 on a platform of free trade, and their commitment to a minimum of state interference in economic and social matters had been only slightly breached by the "peoples' budget" of 1909, with its income and inheritance taxes, and by the National Insurance Act of 1911. A more orthodox viewpoint was that of a laissez-faire liberal like Lord Runciman, a great shipowner and head of the Board of Trade, who said in 1914, "No government action can overcome economic laws, and any interference with those laws must end in disaster."[3] Harrods department store launched a popular slogan by placing a newspaper ad reading "Business as usual." Prime Minister Herbert Asquith, a cautious man whose initiative had much diminished

[3]A. J. P. Taylor, *English History, 1914–45* (Oxford, 1965), p. 15.

after eight years in office, left the various ministries to run things as they wished. The result was that Britain sent the largest volunteer army in modern history to France supported by uncoordinated administration at home.

The British government backed into wartime controls pragmatically, under the pressure of circumstances, without any clear decision of principle. Some resources had to be placed at once under government control. Britain's private railway companies were run by a government committee and guaranteed profits at the same rate as in 1913. Sugar, most of which had come from Germany and Austria before the war, was now traded exclusively by the government. Commodities that were left to free-market operations went up in price. The government then began surreptitiously to influence the wheat market, went on to direct control of food products, and by 1918 instituted food rationing.

Rent controls were imposed in Glasgow in 1915, where labor unrest was high, and gradually spread to the rest of the kingdom. In South Wales, where labor–management conflicts seemed insoluble, the government nationalized the coal mines for the duration of the war, guaranteeing prewar level of profits to the owners. The freetrader Reginald McKenna, Chancellor of the Exchequer in 1915, quietly introduced the "McKenna Duties" on automobiles, moving pictures, clocks, and other "luxury" imports—the first violation of the "holy writ of free trade" since repeal of the Corn Laws (grain tariff) in 1846—primarily to save shipping space and foreign exchange rather than to return Britain to protectionism.

The most pressing emergency was the production of a flood of munitions. Rumors that the campaign in France was being hampered by a shortage of shells shook confidence in the Liberal cabinet's capacity to run the war. Asquith sought to create a broader nonpartisan regime in May 1915 by bringing into the cabinet several Conservatives and the leader of the Labour party, Arthur Henderson—the first Labour parliamentarian to hold ministerial office in Britain. The major innovation of the new government was the creation in July 1915 of a Ministry of Munitions, under David Lloyd George.

Lloyd George, a native of the nonconformist radical mining country of South Wales, which has produced a number of dramatic political figures in modern British history, was the most striking British leader between Benjamin Disraeli and Winston Churchill. He brought his mercurial temperament, a boundless energy, a zest for political infighting, and a complete absence of any preconceived notions to an agency that would eventually extend its tentacles into every cranny of the economy. He was, as George Dangerfield said, a "one-man Welsh revolution."[4]

The business of spending millions of pounds quickly to get private

[4]George Dangerfield, *The Strange Death of Liberal England* (London, 1935), p. 19.

industry to produce war matériel led, necessarily, to control of profits, allocation of manpower and resources, and increasing regulation of the whole economy. Lloyd George did not hold back. In sheer size, his office grew from what had been the Army Contracts Office with 20 clerks in 1914 to a vast bureaucracy in 1918 of 65,000 clerks overseeing the work of 3 million men and women employed in munitions plants. The Ministry of Munitions made more important innovations than size, however. Lloyd George pushed through the Munitions of War Act in May 1915. It empowered the ministry to take over war plants directly in cases where the manufacturer refused the government's terms, which were: to limit profits, to resolve all labor disputes by arbitration, and to tie workers to essential jobs by forbidding the employment of any without a "leaving certificate" from the last employer. In practice if not in principle, the Ministry of Munitions moved the British government into as nearly total a planned and managed economy as technology could provide.

Conscription, the draft, was the government's major step into regulating private life—and death. Sufficient volunteers were available in the patriotic surge of 1914 and 1915, and indeed the British Army of 1 million men was the largest volunteer force in modern history. But volunteer service was both inequitable and insufficient for a situation in which a skilled worker might be more urgently needed in his factory than at the front. In January 1916, the government adopted compulsory military service. There was widespread opposition to this great leap in governmental power, even among fervent supporters of the war. The government provided for hearings, therefore, for those who objected on grounds of conscience. Eventually there were about 16,000 "conscientious objectors," all but about 1500 of whom accepted some form of alternate national service.

Compulsory military service opened up more jobs for women. There were already over 2 million poor women in the labor force. It was the independent wage-earning middle-class woman who created a real wartime breach with Victorian practice, and who sent the female labor force up to 3 million.

Lloyd George eventually replaced the cautious Asquith as prime minister in December 1916. Britain had found its war leader. This Welsh nonconformist from the radical wing of the Liberal party, who had bitterly opposed the Boer War and who had made England's greatest peacetime assault on the propertyholder's pocketbook with the peoples' budget of 1909, presided over Britain's evolution into a wartime omnicompetent state. In retrospect, it was a remarkably successful unplanned experiment in planning. Britain paid for more of the war effort by taxation (the income tax went up to an unprecedented 30 percent of income) than any other belligerent, and less by inflation. The sacrifices of war were probably borne less inequitably in Britain than in any other belligerent nation.

War government evolved in France in a similarly piecemeal fashion. As noted earlier, munitions plants had been closed down at the beginning of the war and their workers sent to the front in the expectation of a short conflict. Only after the Marne did it become apparent that one must fight and manufacture at the same time. France had a long tradition of compulsory military service; extending that principle to the home front was the first recognition of the necessities of total war.

The regulation of commodities followed more slowly. In October 1915, the government assumed authority to requisition grain at fixed prices, an authority extended in 1916 to sugar, eggs, and milk. In 1917, the Ministry of Food Supply was created, and finally, in June 1918, ration cards were issued for bread and sugar. Even agriculturally rich France had been forced to adopt the same kind of regulations as the food-importing island of Britain.

French war production suffered under special disabilities. The early German successes had cut off the richest industrial parts of the country. The ten occupied northern and eastern departments included nine of the seventeen French departments with over 40 percent of the population in industry. In those occupied parts, three-quarters of French coal and four-fifths of French iron and steel had been produced. That vast German bite into French wealth had two effects: it made a compromise peace all but inconceivable, and it made war government and supply that much more difficult. The French could not stop fighting, and yet they could not win without help.

In several respects, war government in France developed less successfully than in England. One problem was financing the war. Whereas the British had had an income tax since 1842, the French still bitterly opposed it. (Lloyd George had decisively defeated the House of Lords between 1909 and 1911 when they opposed funding social services with graduated income taxation.) The French parliament, dominated by small-town, small-property interests, had rejected income taxes in favor of sales taxes and government borrowing since the late nineteenth century. As a result, the French government managed to pay only one-fifth of the costs of war from 1914 to 1918 by taxation. To raise the rest, it sold war bonds and printed currency, two steps that prepared grave postwar economic burdens for the French: a crushing load of debt owed to French middle-class bondholders, and runaway inflation.

Civil–military relations also proved more troublesome in France than in England. There was never any doubt about civilian control in England, and when war government found its leader, it was in the person of a civilian and a radical democrat as well, Lloyd George. The French Army, as befits a major land power, had a stronger and more autonomous military tradition. Under the republic, the officer corps, strongly marked by conservative and even monarchist sympathies, had a tacit agreement with the republican government that they would leave each other alone. This worked fairly well, except when the Army tried to suppress a flagrant legal miscarriage, as in the Dreyfus Affair at the turn of the century. Even Frenchmen of impeccable republican convictions felt in 1914 that civilians should stand aside while the Army fought the war. When the commander in chief, General Joffre, assumed almost feudal authority over the national defense in the fall of 1914, it was understood that the national defense was something separate from the rest of the nation and that the emergency would soon be over. When, after the First Battle of the Marne, it became apparent that the war could be waged only by mobilizing the entire nation, the question of who was the ultimate authority became a thorny one.

That question was finally decided in favor of a civilian authority, in keeping with the French republican tradition. But not before a damaging sequence of squabbles had taken place the first three years of the war. The French parliament gradually reasserted its right to oversee the conduct of the war, through the army committees of the Senate and Chamber, and at the end of 1916, weary of Joffre's inability to break out of the post-Marne stalemate, a majority of deputies forced the government to sack him. The decline of military independence was accentuated when Joffre's successor, the ebullient General Robert Nivelle, failed to gain any ground with his widely heralded mass attack in May 1917. The Army mutinies that followed seemed to threaten collapse.

French war government finally found its leader at the end of 1917 in Georges Clemenceau. "War is too important to be left to generals," he said. Like Lloyd George, he not only was a civilian; he came from the left of center politically. A crusty old atheist democrat, trained as a doctor, Clemenceau had been a permanent one-man opposition in parliament for most of his life. He had already emerged as a tough administrator in his first prime ministry, from 1906 to 1909, when he used the Army to smash strikes. Now, in 1917, he brought that combination of surly toughness and left-wing nationalism in the French Jacobin tradition to the administration of the war. When asked in the parliament what his new government's program would be, he replied with four words instead of the usual long policy speech: "Je fais la guerre!" (I make war!) Despite that claim, Clemenceau's war government was more political than technical. He cracked down on defeatists, jailing or silencing those who dared speak for a compromise peace while Germans were still on French soil. Under the mantle of his authority, France moved into total war government, like the other belligerents.

Germany

German war government, by contrast with that in Britain and France, was consolidated under military authority. Germany's lack of self-sufficiency in food and in some strategic materials made organization especially urgent. The General Staff became the dominant force in war government, in keeping with the traditional autonomy of the German military under the sole command of the kaiser.

Two popular military heroes emerged as virtual dictators of the German war effort: General Paul von Hindenburg, as chief of the General Staff, and General Erich Ludendorff, as quartermaster-general (the traditional Prussian title of the deputy chief of staff). Hindenburg, a Junker aristocrat, and Ludendorff, one of the few commoners to reach the top of the Prussian officer corps, had become popular idols by winning the one outstanding victory of the first years of the war: the rout of the Russians in the battles of Tannenberg and the Masurian Lakes in the fall of 1914. After the bloody stalemate of Verdun in 1916 had discredited General Falkenhayn, Hindenburg and Ludendorff were put in charge by the kaiser on August 29, 1916. They emerged by 1918 more powerful than the kaiser himself.

What Ludendorff called "war socialism" *(Kriegssozialismus)* was already underway in 1916. Since the Schlieffen Plan had promised a quick knock-out blow of France and then Russia, there had been no prewar plans for organizing the economy and society for a long struggle. The German Army had about six months' supply of essential materials in 1914. Production was disrupted as skilled workers were called away to the Army. Faced with a long war and inadequate resources, Germany moved more completely than the other belligerents into organizing the home front.

The first major war agency drew on advanced business methods. Walther Rathenau, head of the German General Electric Company *(AEG, Allgemeine Elektrizitäts Gsellschaft)* was called to reorganize the Raw Materials Section of the Army staff. A prophet of technocracy as well as a successful businessman, Rathenau now had a chance to apply on a national scale his ideas of reconciling private ownership of business with economic planning. Rathenau grouped the companies in each branch of production into War Raw Materials Corporations, not unlike the cartels that some industries—coal, steel—had formed on their own before the war. Each corporation then bought raw materials and allocated them to the most efficient producers for the most necessary products. In practice, large concerns were likely to be favored over small ones (which did not displease an apostle of industrial efficiency like Rathenau), and, in the urgency of the moment, there was no way to limit exorbitant war profits. From the purely technical point of view, however, the German war machine was very effectively supplied when Rathenau handed over this agency to his successor, an army officer, in 1915.

The War Food Administration, founded in May 1916 under popular pressure, was far less successful. It did operate under extremely difficult conditions, for Germany had produced only 80 percent of its food supply before the war, and food production declined still further during the war because of shortages of farm workers, horses, and nitrogen for fertilizer. Hungry city dwellers demanded measures to compel peasants to relinquish their hoards or to stop the black market. In the winter of

1916/17 potatoes gave way to turnips as the stock food of the poor. The average caloric intake of Germans dropped to almost 1000 calories per day. Eventually, 750,000 Germans died of hunger. Scarcity of food and city–country antagonisms served to sharpen the sense of class cleavage and of burdens inequitably borne in wartime Germany.

When Hindenburg and Ludendorff took charge in August 1916 they adopted a system of total personnel mobilization. The Auxiliary Service Law of December 2, 1916, obliged all males between the ages of seventeen and sixty to work in the war economy. One motive, of course, was maximum production; another motive was to control the rising murmurs of discontent and the powerful leverage that the war was giving to labor. The guiding spirit of this project was General Wilhelm Groener, a military technocrat who had excelled in the organization of the railroads. Groener insisted that labor unions be brought into the regional boards that regulated employment. Although this innovation was highly distasteful to conservative industrialists, it permitted Groener to use the unions to help keep social peace while giving them for the first time a legitimate share in government regulation.

After the "turnip winter," the German government tried to reconcile the civilian population to its bitter sufferings. Much effort went into patriotic propaganda devices like the gigantic wooden statues of Field Marshal Hindenburg around which war bond rallies were held. But the gratification of military conquests on the stalemated western front was denied the German propagandists. Nor did it help much any more to

A gigantic wooden statue of Hindenburg erected in Berlin in September 1915 to aid the sale of war bonds.

talk openly about territorial gains in the Low Countries and Eastern Europe, and that vision of a German-dominated *Mitteleuropa* (Middle Europe) to which most German business and military leaders still clung. An increasing number of Germans wanted to be assured that they were suffering for something more than the privileges and advantages of a few. They were attracted to the possibilities of a German democracy and to "peace without annexations or contributions," a concept to which the new democratic regime in Russia after March 1917 gave much publicity.

Chancellor Bethmann-Hollweg tried to revive flagging spirits by getting Kaiser Wilhelm to promise an end to the hated three-class voting system in Prussia after the war. That step only angered Hindenberg and Ludendorff and did little to head off a growing movement in the German parliament for a statement rejecting any war aims of annexation on behalf of the German people. On July 14, 1917, Hindenburg and Ludendorff persuaded the kaiser to replace Chancellor Bethmann-Hollweg with a colorless bureaucrat who had never held high public office, Georg Michaelis. The decline of the civilian cabinet in the face of growing military authority was now obvious. Although the moderate parliamentary left (Social Democrats, Progressive party, Catholic Center) presented its "Peace Resolution" on July 19, 1917, this appeal for a "peace of understanding and reconciliation among peoples" had no effect on a government now wholly dominated by the annexationist German General Staff.

By 1918, Germany had moved far not only toward a fully militarized

Tsar Nicholas II holding an ikon, blessing Russian troops in 1915. Nicholas was the only European monarch who felt he had to assume direct military command himself.

war government but toward a highly bureaucratized war economy in which expert civil servants allocated resources and men and manipulated economic life, not always to the pleasure of industrialists and labor unions.

Russia

Imperial Russia, a genuine Great Power under the conditions of 1815, was soon overwhelmed by the challenges of total war. Such a war quickly revealed the disadvantages of being both backward and autocratic. Faced with crippling shortages of matériel from the beginning, the only possible Russian strategy was to swamp the enemy with sheer numbers. But only one soldier in four even had a rifle; the others were told to pick one up from the dead.[5] The shortage of Russian artillery shells was largely responsible for German advances in 1915, and for Brusilov's failure to hold the gains of his offensive into Austrian Galicia in the summer of 1916. Under these embittering conditions, to mobilize masses of men meant to radicalize them.

All the belligerents faced shortages, of course. In the Russian case, however, the creaking bureaucracy was incapable of taking steps toward more effective administration. Nicholas assumed personal command of the armed forces, for which he had neither training nor capacity. Domestic policies were left under the control of the tsarina, an ignorant,

[5]Nicholas V. Riasonovsky, *A History of Russia* (Oxford, 1963), p. 464.

high-strung German princess, and the Orthodox monk Rasputin, a peasant visionary given to Gargantuan excesses. The tsarina became dependent on Rasputin because she was convinced he could heal her hemophiliac son. Nicholas II and his coterie, unable to rule on their own, would not permit new strata to rule either.

Under such conditions, war agencies emerged parallel to the government or against it, rather than within it. The government itself lapsed into paralysis. While the military went its own way, well-meaning public figures tried to regulate the home front. The Union of Zemstvos and Towns, for example, a body of local government officials intended to look after refugees, assumed larger functions. Leading industrialists had to persuade the regime to let them form military–industrial committees.

It was impossible to mobilize allegiance in a country whose leaders still refused even to grant the vote to its middle class. The Duma (parliament) had been elected on a narrower and narrower franchise since its hopeful beginnings in 1905, and only 9500 of Moscow's 1.5 million residents could vote for their city council by 1914. The aged bureaucrat who served as prime minister, the seventy-five-year-old Ivan Goremykin, was incapable of grasping the necessity for internal concessions. "First of all," he told the Council of Ministers on September 2, 1915, "we must conclude the war instead of occupying oneself with reforms. There will be enough time for that after we chase out the Germans."[6] Such benighted government meant that discontent festered among privileged Russians and the educated as well as among workers, soldiers, and peasants. It was a group of aristocrats, including a royal prince, who murdered Rasputin. The conservatives and constitutional monarchists who dominated the Duma found themselves forced to oppose the tsar even to obtain effective administration of the war.

Austria-Hungary

The Habsburg Empire suffered more than any other belligerent from ethnic centrifugal forces. Of each one hundred soldiers mobilized by Austria-Hungary in August 1914, twenty-five spoke German as their mother tongue; twenty-three spoke Magyar (Hungarian); thirteen spoke Czech; nine, Serbo-Croat; eight, Polish; eight, Ukrainian; seven, Romanian; five, Slovak; three, Slovene; and one, Italian. As wartime propaganda heightened national self-consciousness and spread the idea of self-determination, the national minorities became restless. Britain, France, and even Germany could conciliate their populations with promises of expanded suffrage and a more democratic society, or by the integration of labor unions into government agencies, but the Habsburgs could not make concessions to ethnic separatists without dissolving the empire altogether.

The outpouring of dynastic loyalty in July and August 1914 had never been unanimous, and it proved ephemeral. The adversities of a long,

---

[6]Michael Cherniavsky, ed., *Prologue to Revolution. Notes of A. N. Iakhontov on the Secret Meetings of the Council of Ministers, 1915* (New York, 1967), pp. 6n, 226.

general war—so unlike the short, local war for which Austrian leaders had hoped—soon awakened the ethnic animosities that had preoccupied Austro-Hungarian politics since the late nineteenth century. Wartime passions only heightened the intransigence with which the dominant German and Magyar peoples had blocked any further linguistic or political decentralization in favor of Poles, Czechs, Romanians, or South Slavs. As a result, the General Staff could no longer send troops to any front with the assurance that Slavic soldiers, for example, would fight resolutely against Russians or Serbs.

Such ethnic complications only added to the troubles of a war government already hindered by dualism. The two halves of the Austro-Hungarian Empire competed for food and blocked the formation of efficient unitary wartime agencies. Nor was the traditional Habsburg bureaucracy an asset to war government. The new agencies thrown together pragmatically by the British, French, and Germans faced fewer entrenched rivalries. The Habsburg state was too decentralized to wage war effectively but not decentralized enough to satisfy its populations.

Low industrial productivity was another liability for the Habsburg lands. One unit had only enough uniforms for its soldiers in the front line; the men in reserve wore just underwear.[7] Unscrupulous contractors outfitted the Army with paper-soled boots. The allied blockade cut off essential imports. The reduction of the flour allowance in Vienna from 200 grams per day to 160 provoked a general strike in January 1918.

The Habsburg case shows how ineffective political autocracy was in waging total war. Since there was no way to mobilize public opinion without raising the nationalities issue, the Austrian prime minister, Count Karl Sturgkh, attempted to govern without it. Although the Hungarian parliament met during the war, the Austrian *Reichsrat* did not, for fear of giving a platform to dissident Social Democrats, Czechs, and Poles. The *Reischrat* building was converted into a military hospital. The Austrian parliament was finally convened in May 1917, after the young Social Democrat intellectual Fritz Adler had assassinated Count Strugkh in October 1916 with a cry of "Down with Absolutism! We want peace!" But it was too late. Separatist feelings had ripened beyond the point where Austria-Hungary could resolve the dilemma of finding popular support for war government by any means short of dissolving the empire itself.

When the old Emperor Franz Josef died at the age of eighty-seven in November 1916 after a reign of sixty-eight years, the last link holding these disparate peoples together snapped. His great-nephew and heir, Karl, understood that the war would destroy his dynasty. At the very end of 1916 he put out secret peace feelers through President Woodrow Wilson, the pope, and other possible mediators. The new Habsburg emperor's known wish for a compromise peace cost him the loyalty of

[7]C. A. Macartney, *The Hapsburg Empire, 1790–1918* (New York, 1969), p. 830.

the last of his faithful peoples, the ethnic Germans. They now looked to Berlin to carry the war on to the triumph of Germandom throughout central Europe. The Austro-Hungarian Empire withered from within before it was decisively beaten from without.

Italy

Unlike the other major belligerents who had entered the war in patriotic exaltation in August 1914, the Italian government entered the war late (May 1915) in a spirit of bargain rather than of crusade. King Victor Emmanuel III, Prime Minister Antonio Salandra, and Foreign Minister Sidney Sonnino joined the Entente side in the belief that war would be both short and advantageous. A noisy minority of nationalists, including futurist painter Filippo Marinetti, young syndicalist revolutionary Benito Mussolini, and poet Gabriele d'Annunzio, had demonstrated for war on the streets of Rome. They were convinced that violence would energize an Italy that seemed to slumber since the nineteenth-century battles for unification. "Friends, it is no longer time for talk but for action," d'Annunzio shouted to a crowd of 100,000 from a hotel balcony in Rome on May 12, 1915. "If it is a crime to incite citizens to violence, I shall boast of this crime."[8] The majority of Italians were never enthusiastic about the war, however. The two largest mass organizations in Italy, the Socialist party and the Catholic Church, opposed it. So did Italy's leading prewar centrist political leader, Giovanni Giolitti. There was no honeymoon period of national unity in Italy to mask the impact of war.

Italy organized to meet the demands of total war less successfully than the other Entente states, Britain and France. For one thing, Italy was no match industrially for the northern and western Great Powers. Shortages were especially difficult to deal with in a country whose south had never been well integrated into the national economy and society. No less than 38 percent of Italians were still illiterate in 1914, making efficient war government difficult to organize. Without effective governmental controls, the powerful distortions of war production and consumption affected Italians both harshly and with extreme inequity. Inflation reduced the real wages of workers in the war plants of Turin and Milan 27 percent by 1917. When campaigns went badly in the rough eastern Alps where the Italian armies fought the Austrians, Italian regional and social animosities turned into hard anger.

The Social Impact

No European society could attempt to channel all its resources into total war without undergoing profound change. At first glance, the intense common effort seemed likely to make European societies more uniform and egalitarian. Death itself was the greatest leveler. Every belligerent

[8]Quoted in Christopher Seton-Watson, *Italy from Liberalism to Fascism* (London, 1967), p. 446.

had some form of compulsory military service, and the European aristocracies probably lost a higher proportion of their sons in the hard-hit junior officer ranks than did the middle classes. Wartime scarcities made ostentation, idleness, and luxury bad form. In the euphoria of 1914 it was possible to believe that "warfare releases a devotion and an unconditional community of sacrifice"[9] that would transform each nation into a true family. The British Liberal leader Lloyd George rejoiced on September 19, 1914, that "all classes, high and low, are shedding themselves of selfishness. . . . It is bringing a new outlook to all classes. . . . We can see for the first time the fundamental things that matter in life, and that have been obscured from our vision by the tropical growth of prosperity."[10]

Clothing was a harbinger of a more homogeneous, simplified life style. During the war, dress became much more utilitarian and informal. Europeans would never again drape themselves in such a profusion of bustles, stays, trains, and plumes. Uniforms led the way. The bright blue and red prewar French infantry uniforms, which made such good targets for machine-gun fire in 1914, had not been changed during the first months of war because the General Staff was convinced that the war would be over before they could do so. Soon, however, every army was in utilitarian khaki. Meanwhile, women's skirts rose above the ankle for good.

The Status of Women

Women were integrated more fully into public life in the more advanced wartime regimes. Women undertook a variety of jobs previously held largely by men, such as clerical and secretarial work and teaching. They were also employed far more widely than before in industry. By 1918, 37.6 percent of the work force in the Krupp armaments firm in Germany was female. In England, the proportion of women workers rose strikingly in public transport (from 18,000 to 117,000 bus conductors and the like), banking (9500 to 63,700), and commerce (505,000 to 934,000).[11]

The war worked the most important changes among middle-class women. During and after the First World War, it became acceptable for young employed single middle-class women to have their own apartments, to go out without chaperones, and even to smoke in public. It was no longer imaginable to exclude women from the vote in Britain and in Germany after the war, and in 1919 Lady Astor was elected to the House of Commons, the first woman to be seated in a European parliament.[12]

[9]Max Weber quoted in Arthur B. Mitzman, *The Iron Cage* (New York, 1970), p. 211.
[10]David Lloyd George, *The Great War* (London, 1914), p. 14.
[11]Hajo Holborn, *A History of Modern Germany,* Vol. 3: *1840–1945* (New York, 1969), p. 461; Arthur Marwick, *Britain in the Century of Total War* (Boston, 1968), pp. 105ff. It was not until the Second World War that women were drafted for military service in Britain, however.
[12]Women had been permitted to join political parties and associations in Germany only since 1908.

Women workers in a German munitions factory during the First World War.

The Status of Organized Labor

The war also led to decisive changes in the power and legal status of labor unions. The right of workers to organize went back only a half-century on the Continent (1869 in north Germany; 1884 in France); up to 1914, employers struggled to keep union organizers out of their plants, and armed force was commonly used against strikers. But the almost universal rallying of workers to their national flags in 1914 opened the way for wider acceptance of unions, just as it did for the inclusion of reformist socialist politicians in wartime governments. The French socialists Marcel Sembat and Jules Guesde entered the Viviani government in August 1914; Arthur Henderson joined the Asquith cabinet in May 1915; John Hodge and George Barnes joined the Lloyd George cabinet in December 1916.

It was less by the parliamentary route than by the bureaucratic route, however, that organized labor was integrated into the most highly organized war governments. Only a short war was possible without union cooperation. When it became necessary to cajole longer hours and higher productivity out of war workers and to prevent free movement of skilled workers away from vital jobs, it became essential to consult with union leaders.

A bargain was struck in Britain, France, and Germany between unions and government. In general, unions accepted a temporary cessation of strikes and less favorable work rules in exchange for a *de facto* integration into government processes. In Britain, these arrangements were worked out in a conference at the Treasury Department in March 1915. Labor consented in the "Treasury Agreement"[13] to the proposal that war workers relax union restrictions on work rules and renounce strikes for the duration of the war in favor of arbitration; in return, labor representatives were named to the National Labour Advisory Committee, and the government undertook to control the industrialists' profits. Trade union integration went furthest in the German military-bureaucratic "war socialism." General Groener, over some opposition from conservative industrialists, forced the inclusion of union representatives in labor committees at the factory level and in regional food and labor committees. This "reform from above" brought greatly increased prestige and membership to the German trade unions, which grew from 967,000 in 1916 to 1,107,000 in 1917. At the end of the war, in the Stinnes-Legien Agreement between representatives of industry and labor, the first German official collective bargaining arrangements were concluded. France, too, followed up its wartime experience by giving legal force to collective bargaining in 1920. Labor leaders found, however, that the integration of unions into war government was a two-edged sword. They had purchased a public role for unions at the cost of having to act more often as the managers of labor than as the adversaries of capital. Many of the rank and file had rejected this bargain by 1918.

Social Cleavage

In some ways, the war was a leveler—as for women and for labor. But in other ways, the long war sharpened social cleavages and conflicts. One such cleavage was caused by the unequal apportionment of those who exposed themselves to the risks of war. Although total war meant total mobilization of human labor, not everyone was sent to the trenches. Skilled workers were more vitally needed in war plants. And some with connections managed to secure safe assignments at headquarters. It became clear after the war that two groups had paid the highest blood tax: unskilled young males and junior officers. French peasants made up a larger proportion of the war dead than of the general population. The casualty rate among British junior officers, often highly talented and motivated young men, was three times the overall casualty rate. Of the class of 1914 at Saint-Cyr, the French military academy, 63 percent did not survive the war. The survivors, whether mutilated or not, shared a blend of pride and bitterness that they had endured more than the lot of ordinary men. This "mystique of the trenches" created a resentful solidarity among front-line veterans, who felt a special mission to keep watch over the nations that they had saved.

The conflict of generations was also widened by the war. Veterans'

[13]The miners' unions rejected the Treasury Agreement; under the War Munitions Act of 1915, the mines were nationalized for the duration of the war.

disillusion fed on anger at the older generation that had sent them to the front. The villain of the greatest First World War novel, Erich Maria Remarque's *All Quiet on the Western Front,* was not the Allied enemy in the opposite trenches but the soldiers' earlier spiritual guides, such as the schoolteacher Kantorek, who had sent them off full of patriotic slogans.

> The first bombardment showed us our mistake, and under it the world as they had taught it to us broke in pieces.[14]

The Economic Impact

The malapportionment of wartime suffering was also felt in economic matters; at one end were those who profited from the war and at the other, those who suffered the very unequal effects of inflation.

War Profiteers

The possibilities for profit in war manufacture were enormous, and war profiteers were a public scandal. Fictional new rich, like Frederic Haverkamp, the manufacturer of shoddy boots in Jules Romains' *Verdun,* had numerous factual counterparts. It was rare, however, for governments to interfere with major firms, as happened when the German government prosecuted the Daimler motor car works for infringing war regulations.

More subtle was the way in which war government favored large, concentrated industries over smaller ones. On the Continent, especially, the cartelization of industry was substantially increased. In Germany, for example, Walther Rathenau's War Raw Materials Corporations allocated scarce materials to selected companies. Since the largest firms dominated these corporations, they were favored even beyond the natural stimulus of wartime boom profits. Nonessential firms, which tended to be small, were simply closed down when coal and other resources became too scarce. The war was also a stimulus toward grouping companies into larger firms. In 1916, the leading German chemical manufacturers pooled their resources to form the new combine that became the great postwar chemical giant, I. G. Farben.

The Effects of Inflation

Inflation worked the most pervasive economic and social effect of all. As war budgets rose to astronomical figures, war economies ran at white heat. Massive demand forced around-the-clock production of war matériel, causing shortages of many consumer goods. Virtually every able-bodied person was employed. This combination of high demand, scarcity, and full employment sent prices soaring, even in the least mismanaged war economies. No belligerent country avoided some

---

[14]Erich Maria Remarque, *All Quiet on the Western Front* (New York, 1966), p. 12.

degree of inflation. In Britain, a pound sterling bought in 1919 about a third of what it had bought in 1914.[15] French prices approximately doubled during the war, and worse inflation was yet to come in the 1920s. Inflation rates were even higher in the other belligerents; in Germany, as we shall see in Chapter 5, the mark simply ceased to have any value at all at the end of 1923.

The effects of inflation are unequal in that some suffer and some benefit. Skilled workers in strategic industries in Western Europe found that their wages just about kept up with prices, or even surged ahead of them. The unskilled and workers in nonstrategic industries lagged behind. Such disparities in wages among different industries stirred new animosities. Only in Britain did most workers' wages seem to have kept ahead of prices, with the average wage doubling while prices increased only about 75 percent.[16] On the Continent, wages also rose, but wage earners had less real purchasing power at the end of the war than at the beginning. The French cost of living stood in 1917 at an index figure of 180 (100 in 1914), while wages stood at only 170. German workers slipped a bit in real purchasing power, with workers in war industries faring far better than workers in the civilian sector. Even those wage-earning families whose standard of living kept pace with inflation suffered constant short-term grievances as they shopped for ever more expensive food.

The bitterest sufferers from inflation were those members of the middle class dependent on fixed incomes. The incomes of old people on pensions, of the marginal middle class living on small dividends or interest, and of many professional people remained about the same while prices doubled or tripled. Although such people fell into genuine material poverty, their sense of status continued intact. These "new poor" clung to a shabby gentility by repairing old clothes, eking out the food budget with rhubarb grown in the back garden, and giving up everything but the outward show of respectability. The middle class, wrote the English poet Stephen Spender, resembled dancers suspended in midair after the ballroom floor had been knocked away, "miraculously able to pretend that they were still dancing."[17]

Inflation did not just lower these peoples' standard of living; it radically changed their relative position in society. A host of clerks, lesser civil servants, teachers, clergymen, and small shopkeepers now earned less than many skilled laborers. Some members of the marginal middle class found this indignity harder to endure than reduced comforts and amenities. "I go in the gallery [inexpensive seat] to the cinema," complained an English country doctor's wife. "My charwoman goes in the stalls [best seat]."[18]

To make matters still more bitter for the "new poor," some great

[15]Taylor, p. 41.
[16]Arthur Marwick, *The Deluge* (London, 1965), p. 272.
[17]Stephen Spender, *World Within World* (London, 1951), p. 2.
[18]C. F. G. Masterman, *England After the War* (London, 1923), p. 105.

fortunes were built during the wartime and postwar inflation. Those able to borrow could repay their debts in devalued currency earned by the borrowed funds. Some industrialists expanded their plants under the twin stimuli of war contracts and borrowed capital; shortly after the war, the German entrepreneur Hugo Stinnes built an immense business empire by taking advantage of inflation.

The animosities and social divisions bred by the First World War rested less on the amount of wartime suffering than on its unevenness. The cry of "no more war" quickly led to a cry for basic changes in the economic, social, and intellectual system that had produced such a war and had apportioned its burdens.

The Impact on Internal Order

The patriotic fervor so widespread in 1914 suggested that war really did reduce internal conflict within belligerent nations, at least in the short run. That unified enthusiasm, however, was unable to survive long years of unequal privations and without hope of victory.

Strike Activity

One good measure of growing disaffection in the belligerent countries is strike figures. Strike activity had reached the highest levels in history throughout Europe in the years just before 1914. There had been over 1500 different work stoppages in France in 1910, the peak prewar year; more than 1 million British workmen had been on strike at some time or another in 1912; there had been more than 3000 work stoppages in Germany in 1910. Labor relations had been unusually tense in some

The Irish Easter Rebellion. Remains of a streetcar used as a barricade in Dublin, where Irish nationalists attempted to set up an independent republic in April 1916.

areas in the summer of 1914, with a bitter transport strike in Dublin, the "Red Week" of early June 1914 in Italy, and widespread strikes in St. Petersburg in July. Then, abruptly, there were hardly any strikes at all during the first year of war enthusiasm. Ten work stoppages involving 4159 people occurred in St. Petersburg during the rest of 1914. Only 98 work stoppages took place in France throughout 1915, and only 137 in Germany.

The revival of strike activity in 1916 shows that social peace was already wearing thin. Work stoppages and the number of people on strike in France quadrupled in 1916, as compared with 1915. The first major internal disorder in wartime Germany was a three-day walkout of 50,000 Berlin workers in May 1916 to protest the arrest of the pacifist Karl Liebknecht during an illegal May Day demonstration. Two regions of intense labor militancy became active in Britain: the mining areas of South Wales, and the shipbuilding areas along the Clyde River in Scotland downstream from Glasgow, where religious nonconformity, a sense of ethnic distinctness from the English, and a tight-knit worker community provided inhospitable terrain for war government. The South Wales and Clydeside workers rejected the compromises of their union leadership and went out on strikes led by grass-roots organizers at the plant level—shop stewards.

Ireland, where bitter controversy over Home Rule had been overtaken by the war, erupted in open revolution. Leaders of the Irish independence movement, Sinn Fein, with some aid from Germany, seized government buildings in Dublin on Easter day April 24, 1916. The British put down the Easter Rebellion in a week of bloody fighting and executed its leaders.

Liberal and Socialist War Critiques

Opposition to the war had been reduced in August 1914 to a few isolated dissenters. By 1916, organized oppositions began to work actively for a compromise peace.

Roughly speaking, there were two schools of opposition opinion in the belligerent countries: liberal and socialist. The liberal critique of the war rested on assumptions of nineteenth-century democratic internationalists like the Englishman John Bright (who had opposed the Crimean War in the 1850s), who had argued that wars resulted from the selfish ambitions of kings, aristocrats, and heads of states against the wishes of the peaceable mass of humanity. The liberal solution was twofold: the expansion of democratic control at home over foreign policy, and the replacement of "international anarchy"[19] with a system of international law. The main prewar monuments to this approach were the Hague conferences of 1899 and 1904, which drafted rules governing the conduct of warfare and the treatment of prisoners of war and set up the International Court of Arbitration.

[19]The phrase comes from G. Lowes Dickinson, a Cambridge political scientist and a prominent British pacifist.

Despite the blow given the liberals' assumptions by popular jingoism in 1914, the movement remained alive, especially in Britain. The Labour and Liberal politicians who had opposed war jointly formed the Union of Democratic Control in December 1914. Its members advocated an immediate negotiated peace, "open diplomacy" under watchful democratic eyes, and a "League of Nations"[20] to apply international law to the relations among sovereign states. In Germany, the coalition of Social Democratic, Progressive, and Center (Catholic) deputies in the *Reichstag* passed a resolution in July 1917 calling for a peace without annexations. They worked from assumptions similar to the British opposition, but with far less public impact.

The socialist critique of the war rested on Marxist theory, which attributes war to capitalist competition. It made no sense to Marxists to work for an end to the current war without also attempting to overthrow the economic system that, by their diagnosis, would cause others like it.

Marxist antiwar groups were stronger on the Continent than in Britain. The British Independent Labour party (ILP) of Ramsay Mac-Donald and Philip Snowden remained allied to Liberals in the Union of Democratic Control. In Germany, however, where the Social Democratic party (SPD) had unanimously voted for war credits in August 1914, eighteen dissidents left the party in December 1915 to form the Independent Socialist party (USPD), dedicated to an immediate negotiated peace and domestic revolution. It was more difficult for French socialists, on whose soil stood German troops, to break the *union sacrée* of 1914. Even so, by the time of the December 1916 national congress of the French Socialist party (SFIO), the party's pacifist wing had risen to almost equal strength with the faction devoted to supporting the war effort. Russian socialists had never taken part in war government, and a majority of Italian socialists opposed the war from the beginning.

These internationalist minorities naturally sought to restore their prewar foreign contacts. The old machinery of the socialist Second International,[21] however, was jammed by the antagonism between the prowar majorities of the French and German socialist parties. Socialists of neutral countries—Switzerland, Sweden, and, up to April 1915, Italy—worked together with Russian *émigrés* like Lenin in Switzerland and Trotsky in Paris to organize unofficial international socialist meetings. The first meeting of European socialists across the battle lines was the Zimmerwald Conference, in Switzerland, in September 1915. The group was small; one delegate commented wryly that all the internationalist socialists in Europe could be driven to the meeting place in four carriages.[22] Moreover, the delegates were irreconcilably divided between a majority (twenty-three votes) who wanted only to oppose annexationist war aims, and a minority (seven votes) who wanted to use the wartime tensions as a lever for revolution, or, as Lenin put it, to convert the war

---

[20]Another phrase coined by G. Lowes Dickinson.
[21]See Chapter 3, p. 77.
[22]Robert Wohl, *French Communism in the Making, 1914–24* (Stanford, Calif., 1966), p. 66.

into civil war. By the time the next conference met, at Kienthal in Switzerland in April 1916, the socialist antiwar movement had become far larger. Governments found it necessary to take notice and refuse passports to their citizens who planned to attend.

In 1917 war morale cracked wide open in all the belligerent countries. As the war approached its third anniversary without any sign of end, populations stirred restlessly. It was the year of the French Army mutinies, the "Peace Resolution" of the German *Reichstag,* the secret peace feelers of the Austro-Hungarian monarchy, the climax of agitation in the shop stewards' movement in Clydeside in Scotland. The Russian Revolution of 1917 was only the greatest of a whole series of shocks to the old regimes of 1914.[23]

Police Power

War governments responded to opposition with extensions of the police power. Authoritarian regimes like that of Tsarist Russia had always depended on the use of force and fear. But now even the parliamentary regimes felt required to expand police powers and embark on state control of public opinion.

Emergency police powers were given wide scope in England in August 1914 by the Defence of the Realm Act (DORA). DORA authorized the public authorities to arrest and punish dissidents under martial law if necessary. It was under this act that the leaders of the Irish Easter Rebellion of 1916 were executed. DORA, subsequently extended in later acts, also empowered the British authorities to suspend newspapers and to intervene in such sacrosanct aspects of an Englishman's private life as the use of lights at home, food consumption, and bar hours.

Police powers tended to grow as the war dragged on and as opposition to it increased. This trend was especially marked in France, where public authority had been relatively lenient at the beginning. The sharp rise of strikes, the Army mutinies in May and June of 1917, and increasing talk of a negotiated peace raised doubts whether the French war effort could go on. The selection of the tough prewar strikebreaker Georges Clemenceau as prime minister on November 16, 1917, signified that a majority of French political leaders wanted to continue the war even at the cost of less internal liberty. Clemenceau carried out that mandate. He cracked down ruthlessly on anyone suspected of supporting a compromise peace. Eugene Malvy, who as Minister of the Interior since 1914 had been lenient on suspects, was charged with treason and sentenced to five years' exile. Former Prime Minister Joseph Caillaux, who had publicly advocated a compromise peace, was imprisoned for two years awaiting trial on treason charges. Left-wing editor and deputy Paul Meunier was kept in jail for two years awaiting trial until his case was dismissed after the war. Others received long sentences, and some—notably Paul Bolo, editor of an antiwar newspaper believed to be

[23]See Chapter 5, pp. 126–42.

receiving German subsidies—were executed. After the war, many of these rather indiscriminate treason charges turned out to be the result of war hysteria or calculated political opportunism. They revealed the extent to which the wartime suspension of civil liberties could be accepted, even in libertarian France.

Control of Public Opinion

Expanded police powers extended also to the control of information and opinion. Its negative form, the censorship of newspapers and personal mail, was already established practice. Governments normally invoked the extra powers given them in an emergency to prevent disclosure of military secrets and the airing of opinions judged dangerous for the war effort. Positive forms of opinion control were a more genuine innovation of the First World War. All the belligerent governments resorted to what the French historian Elie Halévy later called "the organization of enthusiasm." The governments' efforts to influence their citizens' opin-

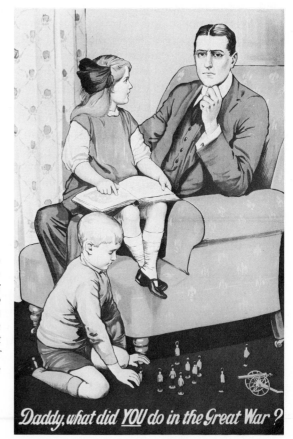

War propaganda. This British recruiting poster tried to arouse shame in able-bodied men who did not volunteer for military service.

Daddy, what did *YOU* do in the Great War?

ions was one sign for Halévy that the First World War had inaugurated an "era of tyrannies."[24]

At the beginning, governments hardly needed to fan public feeling. In the East End of London, for example, women organized "white feather" patrols to brand young men still in civilian clothes with a symbol of cowardice. Later, governments had to stimulate flagging enthusiasm. Wartime posters achieved a new level of effectiveness. Two British masterpieces helped put public pressure on young men to volunteer, before the imposition of the draft in England. In one of these, War Minister General Horatio Kitchener pointed directly at the viewer over the slogan, "Britain needs you." In another, a little girl asks her father, "Daddy, what did you do in the Great War?"

Clemenceau freely used his power as French prime minister to draft journalists or defer them in exchange for favorable news coverage. The German General Staff used labor leaders to run an "enlightenment program" in war plants. Late in the war, the German right adopted a more sophisticated tactic: they formed a new mass party, the Fatherland party, backed by secret Army funds and devoted to propaganda for war discipline and eventual territorial expansion for Germany. By 1918, the Fatherland party was larger than the Social Democratic party. German conservative nationalists were skillfully appropriating the mass party techniques invented by the left.

The Intellectual Impact

Four years of holocaust completely smashed the optimistic liberal-rationalist clichés of the average European of 1914. The most "advanced" quarter of the earth had redescended of its own volition into barbarism. Where was progress? where reason? The effect was to make the avant-garde criticisms and mockeries of pre-1914 Europe much more acceptable to the general population.

One can follow the loss of illusions and the emergence of a hard new anger in wartime poetry. Poets, like almost everyone else, had gone to war in 1914 believing in heroism. British poet Rupert Brooke exulted in the virile lessons of war:

> Now, God be thanked Who has matched us with His hour,
> And caught our youth, and wakened us from sleeping,
> With hand made sure, clear eye, and sharpened power,
> To turn, as swimmers into cleanness leaping,
> Glad from a world grown old and weary,
> Leave the sick hearts that honor could not move,
> And half-men, and their dirty songs and dreary,
> And all the little emptiness of love.[25]

[24]Elie Halévy, *The Era of Tyrannies,* trans. R. K. Webb (Garden City, N.Y., 1965), p. 266.
[25]Rupert Brooke, "1914. Peace," in *The Poetical Works of Rupert Brooke,* ed. Geoffrey Keynes (London, 1946), p. 19.

In France, Charles Péguy, a curious socialist mystic, wrote in 1913:

> Blessed are they who died in great battles
> Stretched out on the ground in the face of God . . .
> Blessed are they who died in a just war
> Blessed is the wheat that is ripe and the wheat
> that is gathered in sheaves.[26]

Both Rupert Brooke and Charles Péguy were killed in 1914, so one can only imagine the hardening and embittering impact of trench warfare on them. The British poet Wilfred Owen, who was not killed until 1918, was transformed from a rather pallid romantic versifier into a powerful denouncer of those who had sent young men off to war. In "Dulce et decorum est" (1917) he mocked "the old lie" that it was good to die for one's country, after giving a searing description of a gassed soldier coughing out his lungs. Another poem paraphrased the story of Abraham, ready to sacrifice his son Isaac on God's command. Unlike the biblical Abraham, however, Wilfred Owen's Abraham ignores the angel who directs him to "slay the lamb of pride instead."

> But the old man would not, and slew his son
> And half the seed of Europe, one by one.[27]

The anger of these soldier-poets was directed not against the enemy but against the fathers. The real enemy was the old society that had made it hard to avoid war, and the old values that had held that war "sharpened" a man rather than debased him. The First World War produced a whole literature of repudiation. Erich Maria Remarque's *All Quiet on the Western Front,* as noted earlier, made the patriotic school-teacher the real villain. *Eminent Victorians* (1918) by the British conscientious objector Lytton Strachey derided the whole preceding generation through belittling biographies of some of its leaders.

The war experience did not really produce new art forms or styles. It acted largely to make the harshest themes and the grimmest or most mocking forms of expression of prewar intellectual life seem more appropriate, and to foster experiments in opposition to the dominant values of contemporary Europe.

Prewar fascination with the absurd and the subconscious seemed much more timely after years of bloodletting. The dada movement elevated mockery to a minor art form with a series of shocking stunts designed to ridicule stuffy bourgeois culture. Dada (an ostentatiously meaningless name) was founded in Zurich in 1916 by the young Romanian poet Tristan Tzara and spread by the end of the war to Paris, Berlin, and New York. Dada artists enraged audiences by having ten

[26]Charles Péguy, "Blessed are. . . ," in *Basic Verities: Prose and Poetry,* trans. Ann Green and Julien Green (New York, 1943), pp. 275–77.
[27]Wilfred Owen, "Dulce et Decorum Est," in *The Collected Poems of Wilfred Owen,* ed. C. Day Lewis (New York, 1964), p. 55. "The old lie" refers to a verse from an ode by the Latin poet Horace, which Owen had learned at school: it is fitting and proper to die for one's country.

poets read their work simultaneously to the sound of bells, or by displaying a perfect copy of the *Mona Lisa* improved with a moustache. Marcel Duchamp entered a toilet bowl labeled "fountain" in a sculpture exhibit in New York in 1917. Beyond promoting mere pranks by comfortably bourgeois intellectuals, dada announced a serious goal of liberation from conformity and from the false aura of awe surrounding past art. It advocated the "necessary destruction" of the old world. "After the carnage, we keep only the hope of a purified humanity."[28]

Wartime experiences also prepared the way for the more important surrealist movement of the 1920s. André Breton, a young medical student assigned during the war to a psychiatric hospital in France, had ample opportunity to discover in shellshock cases the power of the unconscious and the importance of Freud's work. Fascinated by magic and dreams, Breton abandoned medicine to devote himself to a literature that would liberate the unconscious genius from the restraints not merely of bourgeois art styles but of "any control exercised by reason."[29] "We live still under the reign of logic," declared Breton. He sought to set free the inner genius by such devices as "automatic writing," in which one sets down words in free association. Breton began with dada but moved beyond it toward the founding of surrealism when he experimented with automatic writing in *Les Champs Magnétiques* (*Magnetic Fields,* 1920).

The early part of the war deeply gratified the fascination with speed, violence, and the machine of the Italian painters Filippo Marinetti, Umberto Boccioni, and others of the prewar futurist movement. Marinetti was arrested while demonstrating in the streets of Rome in favor of Italian entry into the war during the spring of 1915.

Although the leaders of these movements quarreled among themselves, they shared a resolute "modernist" contempt for all academic styles in the arts, a hatred for bourgeois culture (more violent in word than in deed), and a commitment to the free expression of individual genius. All these feelings were given an additional dosage of violence and anger by the horrors of the wartime experience.

A mood of desolation and emptiness prevailed at the end of a war in which such enormous sacrifice had accomplished so little. "My senses are charred," Wilfred Owen wrote to his fellow British poet Siegfried Sassoon on October 10, 1918, shortly before Owen was killed. A soldier next to him had been shot in the head, and the corpse had soaked Owen with its blood. "I shall feel again as soon as I dare, but now I must not."[30] Beneath the surface playfulness of dada lay a similar feeling of emptiness. Far from being mere nonsense, the surrealist Breton's automatic writing turned out to be a powerful evocation of desolation. The most famous single declaration of the spiritual emptiness felt by so many at

[28]Dada Manifesto (1918) in Maurice Nadeau, *Histoire du surréalisme* (Paris, 1964), Chapter 3.
[29]First Surrealist Manifesto (1924) in *Ibid.*
[30]Wilfred Owen, *Collected Letters* (Oxford, 1967), p. 581.

the end of the war was T. S. Eliot's poem "The Hollow Men" (1925). We know now that its despair was the product of personal difficulties, but its closing lines were immediately seized on to speak for the postwar generation:

> This is the way the world ends
> This is the way the world ends
> This is the way the world ends
> Not with a bang but a whimper.[31]

It was not yet clear at the end of the First World War where such wartime angers would be focused. If these intellectuals drifted into politics, it was bound to be antibourgeois politics. In the end, Marinetti went over to Mussolini, his fellow advocate of war for Italy in 1915. The surrealists André Breton and Louis Aragon thought that the Bolshevik Revolution in Russia was opening the way for the liberation of creative genius. They joined the new French Communist party. The reactions of young intellectuals to wartime experience showed that however widely they disagreed among themselves, they were likely to join whatever postwar movement seemed to cut with the sharpest knife.

[31]T. S. Eliot, "The Hollow Men," in *The Complete Poems and Plays* (New York, 1952), p. 59.

Suggestions for Further Reading

John Williams, *The Other Battleground: The Home Fronts, Britain, France, and Germany, 1914–1918* (1972) does not supplant Frank P. Chambers, *The War Behind the War, 1914–1918* (1939; reprint ed., 1972). The many volumes on the economic and social impact of the war in all the belligerent countries edited by James T. Shotwell for the Carnegie Endowment for International Peace in the 1920s are still in many instances the best material available. For example, nothing more recent on France has superseded the Pierre Renouvin volume in that series, *The Forms of War Government in France* (1925), and Arthur Fontaine, *French Industry During the War* (1926).

The indispensable study of German society and politics during the war is Gerald D. Feldman, *Army, Industry, and Labor in Germany, 1914–1918* (1966).

Arthur Marwick's anecdotal but absorbing *The Deluge** (1965) and *Britain in the Century of Total War* (1968) are useful for Britain. More analytical are the relevant parts of Samuel H. Beer, *British Politics in the Collectivist Age** (1967), and Bentley B. Gilbert, *British Social Policy, 1914–1939* (1970).

The historical context of Italy's decision to go to war is explored in John A. Thayer, *Italy and the Great War: Politics and Culture, 1870–1914* (1964).

For the wartime Habsburg Empire, refer to the works on the empire's break-up cited at the end of Chapter 5.

The essay of Elie Halévy, *The Era of Tyrannies** (1965), is indispensable for placing the First World War in broader historical perspective. See also the excellent articles assembled in Jack J. Roth, ed., *World War I: A Turning Point in Modern History** (1967), and René Albrecht-Carrié, ed., *The Meaning of the First World War** (1965).

REVOLUTION 1917–1920

5

By 1917, protracted war was producing revolutionary strains in all the belligerent countries. Every war regime faltered in 1917. Some of them, such as Clemenceau's France and the Germany of Hindenburg and Ludendorff, were able to cajole or force their peoples to endure another year of struggle. Others, most conspicuously Austria-Hungary and Russia, could no longer contain the pressures of war weariness, social conflict, and national separatism. The two Russian revolutions of 1917 were merely the most explosive examples of discontents that affected all of Europe. At one time or another between 1917 and 1920, the red flag flew from the Clydeside of western Scotland to Siberia. It remained flying only in Russia. Those nearly universal revolutionary pressures and their relatively localized success are the subject of this chapter.

Nicholas II shoveling snow in early 1918 in the park at Tsarskoe Selo, where the imperial family was interned. They were shot at Ekaterinburg on July 16, 1918.

The Russian Revolutions, 1917

Tsarist Russia was particularly vulnerable to worker unrest. As a newcomer to industrialization, its workers were peasant stock undergoing their first generation of factory discipline, the stage of greatest turbulence in every experience of industrialization. That turbulence, moreover, had unusual leverage, for Russian industry, stepping directly into the most advanced technological level, was highly concentrated in a few major cities. And the dark memories of the frustrated Revolution of 1905 poisoned Russian efforts at patriotic union.

Russia, like the other belligerents, might have survived worker discontent if the tsarist regime had enjoyed the support of any other major element of the population. But the middle classes and liberal aristocrats chafed at the revocation of even the minor democratic concessions of 1905; many of them still awaited Russia's 1789, the replacement of divine right autocracy by constitutional monarchy. Even conservative aristocrats were enraged at the bumbling and sycophancy that insulated the tsar and tsarina from efficient war government advisers. Finally, combat opened the eyes of the tsar's last naively faithful supporters, the peasantry. Russia went to war superior to its enemies in only one resource: sheer masses of men. The tsar threw the peasant mass of his people at German steel. Ill equipped and poorly led, the Russian soldiers underwent the most wasting campaigns of any army in the first years of the war. By the spring of 1917, Russia is estimated to have lost 6 to 8 million dead, wounded, or captured.[1] The tsar mobilized the mass of his subjects into uniform only to see them radicalized. Under such conditions, what needs explaining is how the regime survived as long as it did.

The "February Revolution"

Some historians have argued that the tsarist system was on the verge of revolution even in 1914, only to be granted two more years' respite by the injection of wartime patriotism. Others, to the contrary, feel that the dislocations and strains of war were fatal to a regime that might have limped along longer without war.[2] No one questions, however, that the first outburst in February 1917 came not from a planned revolution but from a spontaneous eruption of mass anger. Women began it, with demonstrations over the lack of bread and coal in the Russian capital of Petrograd[3] that began on March 8, 1917 (February 23 by the old Julian calendar still in use in Russia). The mass response to these demonstrations that welled up from a hungry and disgusted population took every political leader by surprise, even the socialists.

At first, these demonstrations seemed no more serious to the regime than similar unrest in other belligerent countries. The tsar ordered unquestioning repression. The death of forty demonstrators on March 11 when troops fired into a crowd simply solidified the people in their anger. The regime was fatally stricken when the troops sent to rout the demonstrators fraternized with them instead. Tsarist officials found that their ability to have orders obeyed simply evaporated.

Refusing an imperial order to disband, the Duma stepped into the vacuum and named a provisional government on March 12 from among its party leaders. The dominant group in this legislature, elected by increasingly restricted suffrage since its creation had been forced on the tsar in 1905, would have preferred a constitutional monarchy. But even such constitutional monarchists as Professor Pavel Miliukov, the new foreign minister, came to see that only a totally new regime had any chance of restoring public order. They persuaded the tsar to yield to the inevitable. He abdicated on March 12, naming Prince George Lvov, the Duma's choice, to be prime minister.[4] Prince Lvov was an ineffectual but

[1] William Henry Chamberlin, *The Russian Revolution,* Vol. 1 (New York, 1935), p. 65.
[2] Leopold Haimson has argued the first view most trenchantly; George F. Kennan may serve as an example of the second. See the bibliography at the end of this chapter for these and other perspectives.
[3] The Germanic name of St. Petersburg had been Russified at the beginning of the war.
[4] The tsar and the rest of the imperial family were subsequently put to death by their guards during the night of July 16, 1918, at Ekaterinburg, when it seemed likely that they might be rescued by counterrevolutionary troops.

respected constitutional monarchist who had headed the Union of Zemstvos and Towns.

Provisional Government and the Soviets

It was relatively easy to form a provisional government; to have its authority accepted and its orders obeyed was more difficult. The Provisional Government sprang from a legislature that had become less and less representative since its beginnings in the Revolution of 1905. In a country 80 percent peasant, it was a parliament of gentry, middle-class professional men, businessmen, and intellectuals. In essence, the Provisional Government's challenge was whether Russia's small liberal elite could succeed where the tsarist autocracy had failed: could it gird a backward and weary country to go on with the war effort?

That challenge was vastly complicated by the existence of another power in the land, the soviets. *Soviet* is simply the Russian word for council or committee. In 1917 the memory was still fresh of the St. Petersburg Soviet, the steering committee of militant workers formed to guide the general strike of 1905. A new Petrograd Soviet sprang into being at once in February 1917, led by workers' leaders who had already participated in a joint regulatory agency, the War Industries Committee. The executive committee of the Petrograd Soviet, receiving mass delegations and arguing all night about policy, became a kind of sounding board for mass feelings in the capital. More importantly, it issued its own orders and had some sway over hundreds of similar soviets springing up in army units, other factory towns, and even in the countryside. When an all-Russian congress of soviets met in Petrograd on April 11, it brought together delegates from 138 local soviets and soldiers' delegates from 7 armies, 13 rear units, and 26 front units.[5]

Whereas the Provisional Government was dominated by liberals, most soviet members were socialists of one school or another. One important current was composed of Social Democrats, Marxists who believed that a growing proletariat of industrial wage earners would eventually succeed in replacing privately owned factories, farms, and stores with collectivized production and distribution. Most Russian Social Democrats, heavily influenced by Western European parliamentary socialism, believed that backward Russia would not be ripe for socialism until industry had become as predominant in the Russian economy as it was already in Britain and Germany. In the meantime, they urged Russia along the path already taken by the West, convinced that if they helped the middle class achieve industrial growth and constitutional reform in Russia, the eventual socialist stage would be brought that much nearer. These reformist Social Democrats, known as Mensheviks, wanted to form a mass electoral socialist party on the Western model.

A vigorous but small faction of Russian Social Democrats, the Bol-

[5]Chamberlin, Vol. 1, p. 112.

sheviks,[6] agreed on orthodox Marxist goals but disagreed vehemently that electoral politics was the proper means to achieve them for Russia. Their exiled leader was Vladimir Ulianov (known by his underground name of Nikolai Lenin), a public school official's son who had been radicalized at the age of seventeen when his older brother was implicated in an assassination attempt on Tsar Alexander III and executed in 1887. Lenin dismissed parliamentary tactics as incompatible with revolutionary organization and discipline. He believed that even before the proletariat was ready, its "vanguard" should form a tightly disciplined party of dedicated professional revolutionaries, fit for surviving tsarist police methods and for seizing any revolutionary opportunity that presented itself.

The most numerous socialists in the soviets were not Marxist at all but agrarians who believed that Russian peasants should follow their own non-Western path to socialism by expropriating the great estates and establishing a rural democracy on the basis of traditional village councils. These Socialist Revolutionaries, or SR's, were as impatient as the Bolsheviks for immediate revolutionary social and economic change. Unlike Lenin, however, they placed their hopes in peasants rather than urban workers, they were skeptical of disciplined organizations, and they were attracted to tactics of individual violence.

The nine months between the "February Revolution" and the second revolution in November 1917 (October, by the Russian calendar) are often summarized as a competition between two potential governments—the gentry and professional men of the Provisional Government and the radical lawyers and journalists with their working-class following in the soviets. It is well to qualify this neat picture, however, by pointing out that even the soviets fell far behind the spontaneous urges of city crowds and landless peasants. The first land seizures began in March, and army desertions swelled from a trickle to a flood after the Provisional Government attempted one more military offensive, the Brusilov offensive of July 1917. One's sense of the revolution is complete only if one looks beneath the organizations struggling for power at the summit to see millions of Russian farm laborers taking over estates and hundreds of thousands of soldiers walking away from the front.

The Provisional Government was not completely without resources. It was immediately recognized and welcomed by the Western Allies who expected a new democratic regime (as in France in 1792) to fight more effectively than the decrepit tsardom. It had the support of the educated and skilled professional and business people. Its leaders were not without talent and idealism. They enacted such sweeping reforms as

---

[6]The word *Bolshevik* means simply "majority" in Russian. At a time when all Russian Social Democrats were either underground or in exile, the revolutionary faction had won a majority in a 1903 convention of exiles in Brussels and London. Subsequently, although the reformist minority (*Mensheviks*) of 1903 grew much larger after a Russian parliament was established in 1905, the two factions kept their original nicknames.

universal manhood suffrage and the eight-hour day. They established civil equality for all citizens: Jews were no longer required to live in the regions of the Ukraine and Poland called the "Pale of Settlement"; Polish independence was recognized. The Provisional Government promised that royal and monastic lands would be confiscated and redistributed. It summoned a constitutional convention to meet in the fall of 1917. Not least, it initially enjoyed explicit support from the soviets. Even Lenin, whose return from Switzerland in a sealed train was secretly arranged by the Germans in April 1917 in hopes of further impeding the Russian war effort, called Russia "the freest country in the world."[7]

Lenin's arrival at Petrograd's Finland Station, a favorite scene in modern Soviet iconography, opened a genuinely new phase of the revolution. Lenin's "April theses" (April 20, 1917) challenged the orthodox Marxist interpretation of the revolution. He argued that Russia was ripe to move at once beyond a bourgeois revolution toward socialism. Furthermore, Lenin presented a clear alternative program to the Provisional Government's mixture of democracy, eventual land reform, and continued war: immediate peace, land, and bread. He proposed to transfer "all power to the soviets," even though the Bolsheviks were still a minority in the councils.

From July 16 to 18, 1917, the Petrograd crowd, still inadequately fed and opposed to the renewed military offensive, rose against the Provisional Government. The demonstrations were spontaneous, but in order not to let the Bolsheviks be left behind, Lenin had to support them publicly. The Provisional Government still had enough military force to crush the demonstrators, killing 200 people, and Lenin had to flee to Finland disguised as a locomotive fireman. The July Days showed that Lenin's hope of overthrowing the Provisional Government was still premature.

Only four months later, however, in November 1917, the Provisional Government was swept away almost as easily as tsardom had been swept away the previous February, and with fewer casualties than in July. Although its composition had shifted steadily leftward, the Provisional Government never caught up with the leftward course of mass opinion. Those constitutional liberals around Pavel Miliukov who wanted Russia to claim all its territorial war aims, such as the Straits of Constantinople, went out in May. Prince Lvov resigned after the July Days. By the fall of 1917, there were ten socialist ministers and six nonsocialist ones, with Aleksandr Kerensky, the only man of even the moderate left in the first Provisional Government, now as prime minister. The Provisional Government's reforms always fell behind rising expectations. The promise that the constitutional convention would eventually redistribute royal and monastic lands, for example, had little allure when peasants were already seizing land for themselves.

[7]Quoted in Robert V. Daniels, *Red October: The Bolshevik Revolution of 1917* (New York, 1969), p. 4.

Aleksandr Kerensky, last head of the Provisional Government in Russia, studying a map shortly before the Bolshevik Revolution, November 1917.

Continuing the war, above all, caught the Provisional Government between two irreconcilable demands. On the one hand, a unilateral peace was unthinkable to most politically sophisticated Russians as long as German and Austrian troops stood ready to overrun Russian soil. Even a Bolshevik could agree that

> when an army faces an army, it would be the most insane policy to suggest to one of these armies to lay down its arms and go home. This would not be a policy of peace but a policy of slavery, which would be rejected with disgust by a free people.[8]

On the other hand, the Provisional Government had neither the skill nor the force to move enough men and matériel to wage war effectively. Lenin realized sooner than anyone else that merely to feed the population would require the Provisional Government to tamper with private property far more extensively than it was prepared to do. Caught in this vise, Kerensky ordered the offensive under General Brusilov in July, only to find it triggered the final dissolution of the Army. The Provisional Government could make neither peace nor war.

If parliamentary government could not solve Russia's problems in

[8]Lev Kamenev, in *Pravda*, March 17, 1917. See Edward Hallett Carr, *The Bolshevik Revolution, 1917–23*, Vol. 1 (London, 1950), p. 75.

1917, perhaps a military dictatorship could. That solution also was attempted and proven unworkable in 1917. General Lavr Kornilov tried to move troops into Petrograd to crush the rival power of the soviets in September. Kerensky's share in the "Kornilov affair" is probably forever clouded in mystery. The general's supporters asserted that it was Kerensky who asked for help; Kerensky claimed that his intentions had been misunderstood, and that he soon learned that Kornilov planned to sweep away democracy as well as the soviets. In any event, when Kornilov's troops began to move toward the capital, Kerensky turned for support to the left, his enemies of the July Days. He released some Bolsheviks from prison and distributed arms to volunteer units raised by the Petrograd Soviet, the "Red Guards." The refusal of prosoviet railroad workers to transport Kornilov's equipment and the fraternization of his troops with Red Guards prevented Kornilov from even reaching Petrograd.

Kerensky thus thwarted a military takeover, but at the price of making his Provisional Government dependent on the soviets. As the desire for peace at any price spread rapidly within the soviets in the fall of 1917, Kerensky was left carrying on the hated war without any reliable sources of support.

The "October Revolution"

When Lenin returned secretly from Finland on October 20, he believed that the situation had been transformed in two significant ways since July. Within Russia, his Bolshevik group had become a majority in the Petrograd and Moscow soviets. Outside Russia, reports of unrest in the German High Seas Fleet at Kiel convinced Lenin that a worldwide revolution was at hand. Lenin argued day and night to convince his fellow Bolshevik leaders that "we are on the threshold of a world proletarian revolution."[9] To let that moment pass, Lenin maintained, would be the ultimate betrayal of Europe's war-weary poor.

Lenin's eloquence met formidable opposition. He expected nothing else from the Mensheviks, who continued to support Kerensky against him. But there was substantial opposition even among Lenin's "old Bolshevik" colleagues. Lev Kamenev had been convinced by the bloody repression of the July Days that any Bolshevik insurrection would be premature. The Bolsheviks would be decimated and their historic chance lost. Their opportunity, argued Kamenev and other old Bolsheviks like Grigori Zinoviev, lay in awaiting the impending constitutional convention and fulfilling the role of militant opposition within a broader democratic regime. It would be wiser to grow within a democracy until the time was ripe than to attempt a premature coup and provoke counterrevolution. At the rate things were going, Kamenev contended, the time would be ripe soon.

[9]Quoted in Daniels, p. 60. Lenin does not seem to have known about the French Army mutinies of May and June 1917, which might have strengthened his case.

Away with these "constitutional illusions," Lenin retorted. With passionate conviction, he built up a majority within the Bolshevik Central Committee in favor of immediate insurrection against the Provisional Government, without waiting for the constitutional convention. He drew to his side Leon Trotsky, a brilliant young former Menshevik who had once opposed the "barracks regime" of the Bolshevik party organization, but who had been radicalized by opposition to the war. Other Bolsheviks acquiesced because they feared that Kerensky was about to make a preemptive move against the soviets. A number of younger, more militant agrarian revolutionaries (SR's), less committed to awaiting the historically ripe moment than many proper Marxists, also sided with Lenin.

This group turned the Petrograd Soviet into a base for Lenin's attempt to seize the central power. This was to be no spontaneous street demonstration by the hungry, as in February and in July. "Insurrection is an art,"[10] although it must have broad popular support to succeed. Lenin and Trotsky formed a Military Revolutionary Committee of the Petrograd Soviet on October 22 and 23 to plan the seizure of the principal government and communications centers of Petrograd.

The Bolshevik forces acted in the night of October 25 (November 9, new style). They had the support of most soldiers of the Petrograd garrison, who had been angered at Kerensky's attempts to send them to the front. The garrison's support meant easy Bolshevik access to weapons. The sailors of the naval base at Kronstadt, who had always been radical, moved the cruiser *Aurora* up the Neva River to command the Winter Palace, seat of the Provisional Government. Unable to raise military support from outside the city, the Provisional Government began to defend the Winter Palace with military school cadets and a unit of 140 young middle-class women that Kerensky had formed earlier in an effort to shame Russian men into military service. Late in the night, when the *Aurora* had fired a few rounds (mostly blanks), these forces melted away, and the Provisional Government collapsed almost without bloodshed. Kerensky escaped from the city, and when he was unable to muster enough troops to retake Petrograd, he went into hiding. Kerensky fled overseas in the summer of 1918.

The Bolshevik Regime

It still remained for Lenin and his supporters to extend their control over Petrograd to the rest of Russia. It was a formidable task, which was not complete until after three more years and a bloody civil war, exacerbated by foreign intervention. That was a much greater achievement than overthrowing the moribund Provisional Government. In a sense, power in Russia had been up for grabs for nearly a year. It had eluded the tsar, constitutional monarchists, democrats, and moderate

[10]Lenin, quoted in *Ibid.*, p. 53.

Bolsheviks march on the Winter Palace, headquarters of the Provisional Government, Petersburg, November 9, 1917.

socialists. Lenin deserves to be known as a consummate revolutionary tactician, but even more as a regime builder. He was the first Russian who managed to ride and govern the whirlwind unleashed in February 1917.

He accomplished this, to be sure, at enormous cost not only to his original program but to his people. He promised Russians peace, land, and bread. Under him, they had civil war, famine, and authoritarian rule by a single party. But almost alone among historical revolutionary leaders he succeeded in keeping permanently in power those whom the crest of revolution had carried to the top.

Lenin's "Peace, Land, and Bread"

Land redistribution was Lenin's major trump card. By any normal head count, the SR's, or agrarian revolutionaries, stood closest to the mass aspirations of the land-hungry Russian rural population. Lenin's first step was to appropriate the SR program, while avoiding their inner divisions over how to apply it. In principle, as a good Marxist, he declared the land nationalized and turned its further distribution over to local rural soviets, which were supposed to keep the large estates unified as "model farms." In practice, he simply gave free rein to the peasants

Lenin addressing a crowd in Moscow's Red Square on May Day, 1918.

who were already seizing the land. Thenceforth, Lenin's regime was invulnerable to any force that seemed likely to try to restore the old landlords.

The promise of peace was more difficult to realize than that of land, for a separate peace with Germany meant accepting such humiliating terms that even leading Bolsheviks like Trotsky and Nicolai Bukharin wanted to pursue a "revolutionary war." It also meant acquiescing to the secession from the former Russian Empire of many non-Russian peoples, for whom revolution implied national independence.

In order to obtain peace, the Bolshevik leaders accepted harsh German terms on March 15, 1918. The Treaty of Brest-Litovsk recognized German conquests and detached all of Poland, the Ukraine, Finland, and the Baltic provinces from Russia. Not until 1940 was Stalin, with Hitler's help, able to recover most of the 1914 frontier. For the moment, Lenin silenced his opposition by promising that the spreading world revolution would soon make this treaty obsolete.[11] But even this "revolutionary defeatism" did not bring peace to Russia, for anti-

[11]Lenin did unilaterally denounce the Treaty of Brest-Litovsk when revolution broke out in Germany in November 1918, but it was the successor states (the states that succeeded Austria-Hungary) and not Russia that gained the disputed ground at the Peace Conference. See Chapter 6, pp. 180–88.

Bolshevik Russians, aided by Allied troops, began to attack the Soviet regime in the summer of 1918.

The promise of bread proved the most difficult of all. Giving free rein to peasant land hunger meant, as Lenin's less pragmatic Marxist critics like Rosa Luxemburg perceived, creation of a mass of small landholders jealously guarding their crops from the city. Peasant hoarding, combined with the civil war that broke out in the summer of 1918, followed by poor harvests, led to years of food shortages and some periods of mass starvation, as in 1921.

The Establishment of a New Autocracy

The Bolshevik Revolution produced neither the wider European revolution that Lenin expected, nor the new day of liberty that many of his followers expected. We shall discuss that first surprise later in this chapter; the second surprise needs fuller discussion here.

During 1917, the Russian people "threw themselves into a veritable orgy of democracy, carrying it far beyond their Western mentors into practically every area of life. . . . Power cascaded down like water from a broken dam, to every town and province, to every village and regiment, to every mob and every committee that would receive it."[12] In addition

[12]Daniels, p. 4.

Famine in Russia, October 1921. Refugee children.

to the political councils, or soviets, that sprang up in Russian towns and villages, groups of soldiers formed committees in army units to elect their own officers, and groups of workers organized factory councils in the face of the frightened owners' attempts to lock them out.

This profusion of unplanned, often clumsy, grass-roots initiatives was replaced by centralized state administration under one party during 1918 and 1919 as the Bolsheviks consolidated their power. The soldiers' councils gave way to traditionally commanded troops. The factory councils gave way to centralized agencies and trade unions controlled from above. Loose association with the non-Russian border peoples was replaced by centralization under Russian domination thinly disguised as a federal state. This was the system known as War Communism that Lenin established in Russia by 1919.

Why did the promised liberty turn so quickly into authority after the Bolshevik Revolution? One standard answer has been the authoritarian character of Leninist political theory. From the time of the split in the Russian Social Democratic party in 1903, Lenin's followers were partisans of tightly disciplined party organization as opposed to those other Marxists who preferred to work more openly through a parliamentary party. The Leninist party's proven effectiveness in November 1917, and the necessity afterward of governing as a minority party, only heightened the importance of the party structure in Lenin's eyes.

The absence of any established tradition of self-government in Russia certainly hindered the germination of democratic institutions in 1918 and 1919. When the old autocracy was swept away, it exposed a void that the chattering profusion of local councils was ill-equipped to fill. Lenin's party was available to fill the vacuum.

The Bolsheviks never pretended to run their regime democratically. Universal suffrage in Russia under the conditions of 1917 could produce only some kind of rural small landholder majority. The Bolshevik regime was a dictatorship of the proletariat, or working class. If the Russian proletariat was still a minority, that anomaly would soon seem inconsequential when the world proletarian revolution spread from Russia to the more urban, industrialized states of Western Europe. Weighed against the possibility of the ultimate liberation of working people outside Russia, the necessity to govern against a majority in Russia seemed a small matter to Lenin and his followers.

Therefore the Bolsheviks dissolved the constitutional assembly after its first day, when that body summoned by the Provisional Government and eagerly awaited by Russian democrats finally met in January 1918. As expected, Russia's one historic exercise of universal suffrage had produced an agrarian majority. The constituent assembly contained 420 agrarian revolutionaries (SR's), as against 225 Bolsheviks. For a time, Lenin governed in coalition with the left wing of the SR's. They broke in June 1918. The left SR's, already opposed to the humiliating peace with Germany, resented Lenin's revival of central state administration. From that time on, Russia has been governed by authoritarian one-party rule.

There were also good pragmatic reasons for a new autocracy in Russia in 1918. One was the simple necessity to produce. Factory committees did not have the knowledge to revive production, nor always much interest in it. They resisted all outside efforts to coordinate their work with others. The intensely revolutionary railroad workers, for example, took over and operated the lines, but "for a long period set all external authority at defiance."[13] At issue was whether the new regime should limit itself to the coordination of the factory committees' local efforts or whether it should actually direct Russian industry in centralized fashion from above.

Lenin believed that the process of "trustification"[14] of industry, which capitalism had begun and which the war had intensified, must be carried through as the basis of a socialist economy. Each branch of industry, therefore, was not only nationalized but centralized into a single state trust. By the end of 1919, some ninety of these state trusts had been organized, all answering to a Supreme Council of National Economy at the top. The metallurgical industry, to take one example, was relatively easy to organize in this way since it had been highly concentrated before the war. By March 1918, it had been brought under a single state agency with a staff of 750, and its workers subjected to strict labor discipline through an official trade union. It did little good for partisans of the recent experiments in workers' control to object that "the masses are being cut off from living creative power in all branches of our national economy."[15] Lenin was determined that socialist production could only be built on centralized organization.

Civil War

Leninist authoritarianism was also a response to civil war. The Bolshevik regime had to fight for its life—against the armed opposition of anti-Bolshevik White Russian armies, against border nationalities that declared their independence from Russia, against the intervention of Allied troops, and against the passive resistance of the peasants who kept up a "green revolution" to counter the "red revolution" that requisitioned their grain to feed the cities. The Red Army was engaged in active fighting on every Russian border at some time between 1918 and the end of 1920. At times, Bolshevik authority was reduced to the old Russian heartland. In the end, the Bolshevik regime survived to establish its rule over all the former Russian Empire except the western lands lost to the new states of Poland, Czechoslovakia, Romania, and the Baltic States. But during the struggle the regime had been transformed into a bureaucratic, one-party, centralized state. And it emerged from the civil war deeply marked by hostility to the Allied powers that had actively supported its opponents.

[13]Carr, Vol. 2, p. 71.
[14]*Ibid.*, p. 176.
[15]*Ibid.*, p. 97.

During the Russian civil war, a group of White Russians hangs Bolshevik captives.

Allied intervention began as an attempt to keep the eastern front in action against the Germans. Even during the Kerensky period, as early as July 1917, the Western Allies sought ways to bolster the eastern front. The Bolsheviks' public quest for a separate peace after November 1917 was a serious blow to the British and French, who could never quite rid themselves of the suspicion that Lenin was a German agent. They foresaw the Germans moving all their troops to the west for a one-front, knock-out blow. Some Western policymakers maintained contact with the Bolsheviks at first, in the hope that they would eventually reject the harsh German terms and fight on. Bolshevik acceptance of the German terms at Brest-Litovsk in March 1918, however, strengthened the case in Britain and France for intervention. The decision was made in June 1918 when the Germans, now freed in the east, broke through the Allied trenches and advanced to within thirty-seven miles of Paris, the closest since the First Battle of the Marne.

The British and French sent about 24,000 men to the northern Russian ports of Murmansk and Archangel in June 1918 to secure Allied supplies, to prevent German and Bolshevik troops (still believed to be secret allies) from joining forces there, and "to make it safe for [anti-Bolshevik] Russian forces to come together in organized bodies in the north."[16] At about the same time, in Siberia, some 40,000 Czech troops (mostly former Austro-Hungarian soldiers captured by the

---

[16]President Wilson's instructions, quoted in George F. Kennan, *The Decision to Intervene*, Vol. 2 (Princeton, N.J., 1958), p. 418. At first reluctant, Wilson sent 5500 United States troops to join them only in September.

American soldiers in Vladivostok, 1918, marching in a parade organized to celebrate the arrival of the American expeditionary troops on Siberian soil.

Russians and now eager to fight on for Czech independence) revolted against the shaky local Bolshevik authorities and seized the Trans-Siberian Railroad in order to get out to the western front.

President Wilson, abruptly dropping his earlier reluctance to intervene in Russia, proposed a joint Japanese–American landing at Vladivostok to support the Czechs. The Japanese, who had stationed a few troops at Vladivostok as early as December 1917, now eagerly rushed in 72,000 more, far beyond the figures agreed on with Wilson. The American contingent there numbered about 7000. In addition, early in the winter of 1918/19 two British divisions were stationed on the oil-rich Russo-Turkish frontier, beyond the Caucasus, to hold the railroad line from Batum on the Black Sea to Baku on the Caspian. A French division, a French naval squadron, and a small Greek contingent were landed at Odessa, on the Black Sea coast of the Ukraine. In all, over 100,000 troops of fourteen countries—mostly Japanese, British, American, and French—were stationed at one time or another around the edges of Bolshevik territory.

The Allies' intention at first had been to keep the Germans from filling the vacuum left by the Bolsheviks' separate peace. The general armistice of November 11, 1918, made that purpose irrelevant, and the Allied forces that remained in Russia assumed a much more openly anti-Bolshevik function. Those forces were never very large or well equipped, and they never took direct combat roles in the developing Russian civil war. Nor were they ever united around any common Allied strategy in Russia. They gave moral and material encouragement to the anti-Bolshevik White Russian forces, however, and to secessionist border nationalities. Soviet Russians have always been taught—with much justification—that the Allied governments did their best to bring the Bolshevik experiment down.

Civil war raged in Russia for more than two years. The first serious threat to Lenin came from Siberia, where Bolshevik authority had never been established. In November 1918, Admiral Alexander Kolchak proclaimed himself "Supreme Ruler of Russia" in the western Siberian city of Omsk, and attacked westward, advancing almost to the Volga River by December. In the spring of 1919, the Red Army pushed Kolchak's forces back again.

The next serious threat came from the southeast, where the ethnically separate Ukrainians had gone their own way since November 1917. In mid-1919, General Anton Denikin advanced northward from the Black Sea, took all of the Ukraine, and threatened Moscow itself, while General Nicolai Judenich advanced eastward from the Baltic. Both were forced back in late 1919, and Commissar of War Leon Trotsky was able to turn again to Siberia where Admiral Kolchak's forces were defeated once more at the end of 1919. The admiral himself was captured and executed in February 1920.

The main threat in 1920 came from Poland. In the spring, the new Polish state set out to conquer parts of Lithuania, western White Russia, and the Ukraine that were not ethnically Polish but had belonged to the medieval Kingdom of Poland at its height. After initial Polish successes, a young Bolshevik commander, Michael Tukhachevsky, drove the Poles back to the very gates of Warsaw. For a moment, Lenin believed that his defeat of Poland might set off the long-awaited revolution in Western Europe on which his ultimate survival in Russia seemed to depend. Aided by French supplies and advisors, however, the Poles managed to push back their borders somewhat east of the ethnic frontier. The Peace of Riga in March 1921 established these borders, which remained until 1939.

Finally, at the end of 1920, Baron Peter Wrangel reactivated the southern front. Wrangel's defeat and the evacuation of about 100,000 anti-Bolshevik refugees from Odessa to Constantinople in Allied ships in November 1920 ended active military opposition to the Bolshevik regime.

The anti-Bolshevik armies failed in part because they took the offensive one by one, without any coordination. The Red Army, meanwhile, benefited from the talent for military organization revealed by Leon Trotsky. The Bolsheviks were aided by fighting on interior lines, and by the anti-Bolshevik's lack of popular appeal. Finally, their widespread passive resistance to Bolshevik control notwithstanding, Russian peasants were even less eager to help the Whites, who threatened to evict them from their new lands.

Early Bolshevik support for the independence of all the minority nationalities was a casualty of the civil war. The dissolution of the old Russian Empire into new revolutionary nations was acceptable to Lenin only on the premise of the worldwide revolution that he had believed was at hand. If a revolutionary regime survived only in Russia, the border nationalities became possible avenues for counterrevolution.

The Ukraine was a major lesson. In November 1917, the Ukrainian nationalists had taken the Bolshevik revolution as a signal to assume the home rule that the Provisional Government, no less than the tsars, had denied them. The Treaty of Brest-Litovsk in March 1918 detached the Ukraine from Russia and made it an independent state under German supervision. At the defeat of Germany in November 1918, a pro-Allied Menshevik socialist regime governed the still independent Ukraine, which now became a base for Allied anti-Bolshevik movements. When the Bolsheviks retook the Ukraine, first from General Denikin in 1919 and then from the Poles in 1920, there was no further Bolshevik tolerance for Ukrainian self-determination.

After winning the civil war, the Bolshevik regime also reestablished direct control over separatist areas in the Caucasus: Georgia, Russian Armenia, and Azerbaijan. In December 1922, the Union of Socialist Soviet Republics was organized as a federal but unitary state. Its constituent parts (Russia, White Russia, the Ukraine, Transcaucasia, and—after 1925—a number of smaller ethnic regions like Uzbekistan, Turkestan, and Kazakstan) possessed substantial autonomy on paper, but the real power lay in the victorious central regime in the new capital of Moscow.

Revolutionary Stirrings in Western Europe, 1917

The news from Russia rang like a fire bell through the other belligerent countries in 1917. Some observers, especially in France, believed for a time that a democratic Russia would fight with heightened patriotic energies, as the citizens of the French Republic had done after 1792. But for those disheartened Europeans who were witnessing the war enter its fourth winter, Russian developments made it possible to think seriously for the first time about a compromise peace. They also were an object lesson in how easily autocracy could be overthrown. In fact, the Russian experience suggested that peace would not be possible until regimes had been changed. Finally, the Russians called serious attention to the question of war aims. In November 1917 the Bolsheviks published the texts of secret treaties that the tsar had concluded in 1914 and 1915 providing for territorial gains for Russia and France in the event of victory. These revelations suggested that Europeans had been dying and starving for the dynastic or commercial advantages of the few.

As we have seen, all the belligerents' war efforts reached their nadir during 1917. In Italy, forty-one persons were killed during the summer in a bread riot in Turin. Both Pope Benedict XV and Italian socialists called for a compromise peace. When relief on the Russian front permitted, the Austrian Army gave the Italians their most stunning defeat of the war at Caporetto in October 1971. They threatened to break out into the Po Valley. Morale was saved from a complete collapse only by the Italian Army's ability finally to stop the Austrians on the Piave River, just north of Venice.

In France, the front-line armies themselves threatened to come apart in May and June 1917. After the Nivelle offensive[17] that spring had once more squandered thousands of lives in exchange for a few yards of terrain, reserve units refused to move up to the offensive. In addition to individual desertions, there were collective acts of mutiny. Some groups of soldiers commandeered trains and steamed for Paris. More than half of the 129 French divisions were affected, and 49 of them were probably unfit for action for several weeks. Although most of the agitation was directed specifically against the tactics of the mass offensive, the French General Staff was tempted to believe that repression of antiwar opinion was the best remedy for the mutinies.

The Germans were unaware that parts of the French line lay virtually open in May and June 1917, but even if they had known, they were preoccupied with problems of their own. Naval mutinies affected the German fleet during that same summer. Properly speaking, these were strikes over food and living conditions aboard the pent-up German fleet. German internal politics in the summer of 1917 were dominated by efforts to reassert parliamentary influence over war government and to renounce territorial aims in the July "Peace Resolution." The Germans' major ally, Austria-Hungary, was openly seeking a compromise peace in 1917.

Surmounting the 1917 slump required a mixture of force and persuasion from each war government. Public war weariness and Lenin's revelation of the secret treaties obliged the Allied governments to explain their war aims more clearly. Why, after all, should their populations sacrifice their property and their sons indefinitely for the rulers' glory or for secret territorial deals? Now that the United States had entered the war, President Woodrow Wilson took the Allied lead in explaining the better world of democracy, national independence, and permanent peace that the ultimate defeat of the Central Powers would make possible. As for France, less needed to be said about war aims as long as German troops remained deep in the country. Confident that the vocal advocates of a compromise peace would remain a minority, Clemenceau resolutely jailed his opponents and closed their newspapers after he assumed the prime ministry in November 1917. Even when a renewed German attack was expected in the spring of 1918, Clemenceau kept four cavalry divisions in reserve for possible internal use.

---

[17]See Chapter 3, p. 90.

The German solution to the unrest of 1917 was simultaneously autocratic and expansionist. With the support of the kaiser and of nationalist opinion, Generals Hindenburg and Ludendorff proposed to exploit Russian weakness in a final effort toward an expansionist victory. By straining every nerve, the Germans would be rewarded with territory to east and to west. At home, this meant silencing the parliamentary opposition that had renounced annexationist war aims in the summer of 1917. The kaiser's support was one element in the generals' success. By persuading him to replace Bethmann-Hollweg as chancellor with the inexperienced and docile Michaelis,[18] they reduced parliamentary majorities to a cipher. The other element in their success was the extent to which German centrists, even some of those who had voted for the "Peace Resolution," welcomed the major German gains in the east obtained in the Treaty of Brest-Litovsk, March 1918. The victory over Russia convinced most German leaders to support the generals' gamble on a final major offensive in the west in 1918.

General Ludendorff's all-out attack in the west in March 1918 came nearer to breaking through into a decisive war of movement than any campaign since the First Battle of the Marne. Highly conscious of the political dimension of modern warfare, Ludendorff struck at the British first, on the theory that the French would send their reserves to the British sector only reluctantly. Then if a gap opened between the two armies, he planned to strike for Paris. Five successive German offensives between March and July 1918 pushed the Allied front back nearly forty miles. German troops were at the Marne again, only thirty-five miles from Paris. But Ludendorff had never been able to open the decisive gap he sought. The Allies united their command under the French General Ferdinand Foch and drew heart from the American troops' arrival. It was the Allies who opened a hole in the overextended German line on July 18, in the Second Battle of the Marne. Having exhausted his reserves, Ludendorff could not prevent the initiative from passing for good into Allied hands. After July 1918 they advanced steadily toward the German frontier.

Ludendorff had made several serious errors. Determined to maintain enough troops in the east to hold the Germans' new territorial gains there, he failed to assemble a sufficient preponderance of force on the western front. He overestimated the exhausted Germans' willingness to support another whole-hearted effort for explicitly expansionist aims. He underestimated the psychic and material impact of United States participation (over 2 million men by August 1918). Above all, by staking everything on a decisive expansionist campaign, he ruled out the more modest alternative of a fall-back position on a defensive line to cover the German border during the negotiation of a compromise peace. When Ludendorff finally turned to a defensive strategy, no reserves of men or morale were left to support it.

[18]See Chapter 4, p. 106.

It was General Ludendorff himself who announced to his stunned government on September 29, 1918, that the German Army could not contain the Allied breakthrough and that the only way to defend German soil in the west was to make an immediate peace. In the next few weeks, he forced his incredulous government to ask President Wilson for a peace settlement based on the Fourteen Points, and then was dismissed by the kaiser when he refused to accept the conditions the Allies imposed. Since Ludendorff himself helped spread the legend after the war that the German Army had been "stabbed in the back" by revolutionaries at home, his initiatives in the first steps to an armistice must be emphasized.

Steps Toward Revolution

When President Wilson refused to deal with the "arbitrary power" that had ruled Germany up to 1918, Ludendorff supported the resurrection of the parliamentary form of government that he had pushed aside in 1917. It suited him that civilian authorities should bear the responsibilities of defeat. He is supposed to have said, "They [the parliamentarians] made this soup. Now let them eat it." In this way the first steps of a German revolution, a constitutional revolution, came down from above. Prince Max of Baden, a moderate member of one of the lesser German royal houses, was made chancellor. He accomplished at last the two reforms that German reformists had sought in vain under the prewar monarchy: the responsibility of the chancellor to a parliamentary majority instead of to the kaiser, and an end to the three-class voting system in the state of Prussia. But it was too late to head off with overdue reforms the anger and frustration of the German people.

The next step toward revolution in Germany came from below. It came this time from the armed forces. Ludendorff had changed his mind by late October in favor of continued fighting to hold the richest mining regions of Alsace-Lorraine. Although Ludendorff was forced out of the Army command by Prince Max, the kaiser aroused suspicions that he opposed an armistice by moving from Berlin to Army headquarters on October 29. When units of the German High Seas Fleet at Kiel were ordered to put to sea to engage the British in a last major battle, the crews mutinied. The sailors' refusal to obey orders spread to the naval base ashore at Kiel on November 4, where sailors' councils were formed. From there the movement spread to the formation of soldiers' and workers' councils in military supply depots and war plants. Ludendorff had led Germans to believe in March 1918 that one final effort could win the war. When another war winter loomed in October 1918, the last links of loyalty that had bound German soldiers and civilians to extraordinary sacrifices simply snapped.

In early November the mass movement for peace took on revolutionary proportions. The federal German Empire seemed about to tear apart when the Kingdom of Bavaria tried to negotiate a separate peace on November 7. The antiwar parliamentary socialist Kurt Eisner led workers and the army garrison in Munich in an uprising that expelled the last Wittelsbach king; he then opened peace negotiations with the Allies. On the morning of November 9 thousands of Berlin workers went into the streets to demonstrate for peace. When it proved impossible to find reliable troops to move against them, the senior Army commanders themselves—Generals Hindenburg and Groener, Ludendorff's successor—persuaded Wilhelm II to abdicate as king of Prussia and emperor of Germany before the collapse of all authority affected even the officers' ability to march their troops home.

The Socialist Struggle for Power

As in Russia a year earlier, the question in Germany on November 9, 1918, was who could pick up the pieces of a disintegrating nation. Along with the kaiser and the Army command, much of the German parliamentary center had been compromised by its support for a war of territorial expansion rather than defense in 1918. The most important organized opposition was the German Socialist party, and its leaders now stepped to the fore.

But which German socialists would prevail? The once highly organized German Social Democratic party (SPD) was passionately divided over all that had happened in August 1914 and after. A majority clung to its prewar reformist tendencies. They wanted to set up a parliamentary republic first, within which they believed social democracy would germinate. The SPD majority was deeply discredited on the left, however, by its support for war credits in 1914. The minority that had seceded in 1916 to form the Independent Social Democratic party (USPD) in support of immediate compromise peace was pulled in two ways in November 1918. Some members wanted to restore unity with the majority in this hour of peace and opportunity. Others were drawn to a small but militant antiparliamentary left, which demanded immediate social revolution through the soldiers', sailors', and workers' councils, on the Russian model. This movement, led by Karl Liebknecht and Rosa Luxemburg, called itself "Spartacus" after the Roman gladiator-revolutionary of the first century B.C.

The two tendencies produced two parallel authorities in Germany at the end of 1918. At 2:00 P.M. on November 9, Philip Scheidemann of the SPD majority proclaimed a parliamentary republic from a window of the *Reichstag* building. At 4:00 P.M., Karl Liebknecht declared a revolutionary socialist republic from a window of the royal palace, now held by delegations of the soldiers' and workers' councils. On one side emerged a provisional executive of six "peoples' commissars" elected by the Berlin soldiers' and workers' councils on November 10, but composed of majority SPD and reformist USPD leaders. Its dominant personality was Friedrich Ebert, a saddlemaker turned SPD functionary. A lifetime spent in the creation of the party's first paid permanent staff in the early

1900s predisposed Ebert to orderly administration. On the other side was the Spartacist following in the councils, who wanted to bypass a constitutional assembly and proceed directly to workers' control of a socialist state through the German equivalent of soviets.

This conflict of parallel authorities was resolved during the winter of 1918/19 in the opposite direction from the Russian case. In Russia, Lenin's Bolsheviks had come to control the Petrograd Soviet by the end of August 1917. The German soldiers' and workers' councils remained primarily in the hands of followers of the majority SPD. When an all-German congress of soldiers' and workers' councils was held in December 1918, only 10 of the 488 delegates were Spartacists. No less than the majority SPD leadership, the councils called for political democracy first. They supported the provisional executive's call for a constitutional assembly to be elected in January 1919.

As for the Spartacists, Rosa Luxemburg rejected Lenin's strategy of firm party control in favor of spontaneity in revolution and direct worker control after revolution. Thus the Spartacists deprived themselves of one of Lenin's decisive advantages—a disciplined party structure. More importantly, there was no massive popular ground swell to bolster the Spartacists. Ebert preempted the mass peace movement by concluding on November 11, 1918, the armistice that Prince Max had already prepared. No immense land-hungry mass was burning manor houses and seizing estates in Germany. Of Lenin's three great issues—peace, land, and bread—only bread was seriously lacking in Germany in the winter of 1918/19, and Ebert could blame that on the Allied blockade.

The Failure of the Social Revolution

During December 1918 and January 1919, the German social revolution was liquidated by two simultaneous processes: failure to seize power from below and repression from above. From below, militants among the soldiers' and workers' councils simply failed to take over the decisive political and economic institutions. The way in which the professional state administration and the traditional ruling families reestablished control of local government during the weeks following November 9, 1918, has been best studied in the old port city of Hamburg.[19] The councils attempted to govern the city, but in the very act of trying to revive administration they found they needed tax revenues. The old merchant families, which had long dominated the Hamburg Senate, offered the councils financial support in return for moderation. For lack of other leadership, the Hamburg soldiers' council fell into the hands of an energetic career officer. The reformist trade unions and SPD officials of Hamburg retained the loyalty of many workers. Thus normal administration revived in Hamburg. The same quiet evolution occurred

[19]Richard A. Comfort, *Revolutionary Hamburg: Labor Politics in the Early Weimar Republic* (Stanford, Calif., 1966).

in many German localities. Social and governmental structure had not dissolved in Germany as it had in Russia in 1917. Only very briefly was there any power vacuum at the grass-roots level.

From the top, the provisional executive repressed the Spartacists with the ferocity of sectarian warfare. Friedrich Ebert clearly feared the Spartacists and the radical minority in the soldiers' and workers' council movement more than he feared the German Empire's traditional state services and officer corps. During the few days when German institutions were genuinely malleable, Ebert turned his attention to restoring order instead of achieving basic social change. In a celebrated telephone conversation with General Groener on November 9, he agreed to leave intact the authority of the Imperial Officer Corps (all sworn to personal loyalty to the kaiser) in exchange for the High Command's help in controlling the soldiers' and workers' councils.

The decisive test came in early January 1919. When Ebert removed the Berlin police chief who had been installed by the councils, demonstrators began occupying public buildings. Karl Liebknecht and Rosa Luxemburg, who had just formed the German Communist party on December 30, 1918, incorporating the Spartacus movement and its supporters in the councils, felt they had to assume leadership, even though they feared that the time was not ripe for a seizure of power. Ebert was determined to crush these rivals to the reformist socialists' control. Having failed to set up an armed force directly loyal to the new regime, however, Ebert was obliged to rely on General Groener and the Imperial Officer Corps, and on groups of antirevolutionary volunteers known as *Freikorps* (free corps), which the officers had quietly formed to keep order while the regular Army was being demobilized. Although the SPD Minister of the Interior, Gustav Noske, was nominally in charge of keeping order, it was the *Freikorps,* steeped in front-fighters' brutality and animosity toward workers, who actually broke up the Spartacist demonstrations. Officers murdered Luxemburg and Liebknecht while transferring them from one prison to another.

Hundreds were killed in Berlin in this Spartacist uprising, and a thousand in a second revolt in March. Noske said, "Somebody has to be the bloodhound" and thus earned the epithet of "the bloodhound of Kiel." Ebert was secure, but at the price of the left's bitter resentment and of the surviving independence of the old Imperial Officer Corps.

Restoring administration also meant arresting provincial separatism. The revolutionary movement had gone furthest in the former Kingdom of Bavaria, which had never been fully reconciled to Prussian domination of the German Empire. When the new Bavarian socialist leader Kurt Eisner was assassinated in February 1919, his fellow reformist socialists were unable to hold the state together. During the week of April 7, 1919, members of a revolutionary workers' council and a group of intellectuals including the playwright Ernst Toller formed a communist republic in Munich. Again, Ebert in Berlin had no weapon

Revolution in Berlin.   ABOVE Spartacists firing from behind a makeshift barricade of rolls of newsprint, Berlin, January 1919.   BELOW The barracks of the elite Uhlan Guards surrender to members of the workers' and soldiers' council, November 1918. The sign reads, "Brothers! Don't Shoot!"

except the Army and the *Freikorps*. The destruction of the Munich communist republic by the *Freikorps* was savage. Although the majority socialists were restored to nominal power there, real power lay with the Army and *Freikorps*. Ebert was unable to keep Bavaria within the German republic without delivering it over to his own enemies.

On the surface, Germany had accomplished its democratic revolution. The constitutional assembly elected in January 1919 met in Weimar, a provincial capital far removed from Prussian pomp, to found a parliamentary republic that would replace the German Empire's narrow oligarchy with true popular sovereignty. The Weimar Republic seemed to embody the most carefully planned democratic institutions, including women's suffrage. But in his eagerness to restore normal government in 1918 and 1919, Ebert had allowed the traditional bureaucracy and Army and the oligarchy of great corporations and Prussian estates to survive untouched. The Weimar Constitution was applied to the old imperial society, without making significant structural changes in that society. And it had come into being over the bodies of some of its natural supporters. The republic also bore the stigma of having to accept a harsh peace from the Allies. The nationalists, who hated the Weimar Republic for that, had plenty of leverage thereafter with which to fight it. Only the most successful operation would save the Weimar Republic from its internal enemies.

The Dissolution of Austria-Hungary, 1918–19

The Habsburg Empire perished in the war it had provoked. The very nationalism that the imperial regime had tried to stifle by making war on Serbia in July 1914 was greatly magnified by the war, until by 1918 the various component peoples simply went their own way. The monarchy's authority evaporated. Within the borders of the old empire, the revolutionary impulses of the war's last days were largely absorbed in the enterprise of carving successor states out of the former ethnic parts.

After the disillusioning later history of these successor states, the victors of the First World War, and especially United States President Woodrow Wilson, have frequently been accused of sacrificing a useful federal system in the Danube basin to the principle of national self-determination. In reality, the old monarchy could no more have been put together again in 1918 than Humpty Dumpty. Even without the war, one wonders how much longer dynastic loyalty could have held that linguistic patchwork together. One of the more optimistic of the monarchy's recent historians thinks that "in 1914 the future of the monarchy was at best problematical."[20]

Those who believe the old empire was salvageable rest their case on dreams of greater federal autonomy. Habsburg federalists proposed to grant the most vocal unsatisfied minorities, the Czechs and South Slavs,

[20]C. A. Macartney, *The Hapsburg Empire, 1790–1918* (New York, 1969), p. 810.

the same local self-rule already enjoyed by the Germans of Austria, the Magyars of Hungary, and, to a more limited extent, the Poles of Galicia and the Croats with their own parliament (*Sabor*) in Hungary. Younger members of the Habsburg dynasty, notably the heir to the throne himself, Archduke Franz Ferdinand, were known to be sympathetic to this approach.

Evolution toward a federal solution was blocked, however. Neither Czechs nor South Slavs could be satisfied without lands taken from both halves of the dual monarchy, Austria and Hungary.[21] The Hungarians held a veto over any such compromises. Ever since the first "compromise" of 1867 had elevated the Kingdom of Hungary to parity with the Empire of Austria in a dual monarchy, no further compromise had been possible since it would have had to take place at the Magyars' expense. No new ethnic groups could be satisfied without alienating those already satisfied. Having moved toward a federal solution by becoming a dual monarchy, the Habsburgs were prevented from moving on to becoming a triple or quadruple one. Even if the Central Powers had won the First World War, the problem of absorbing more Poles from, say, Russian Poland into a new Habsburg Kingdom of Poland in a triple monarchy would have fatally unbalanced the empire's delicate ethnic standoff of 1914.[22]

It is difficult to avoid an air of fatality in any detailed account of the wartime evolution of the Habsburgs' subjects from federalist goals to goals of outright independence. Through 1916, it must be admitted, dynastic loyalties still showed astonishing vitality. Many Polish nationalists supported the Austro-Hungarian cause because they still thought that defeat of Tsarist Russia with its large Polish minority offered the best chance of reconstituting the Polish national state, as a Habsburg Kingdom of Poland. The Catholic Croats were loyal, and even the most advanced Czech nationalists were still either federalists or discreetly silent. The Czecho-Slovak National Council, set up in early 1915 in Paris by a professor from Prague, Thomas G. Masaryk, had as yet little direct influence at home. The same can be said for the Yugoslav Committee established in London in May 1915.

The Breakdown of Dynastic Loyalties

The first major change in the attitude of the Habsburg minorities followed the entry into the war of additional states whose ethnic brothers lived within the Austro-Hungarian realm. The Italian declaration of war on Austria-Hungary on May 23, 1915, and the Romanian declaration in August 1916, won two Habsburg minorities over to the Allied cause: the Italians along the Adriatic coast, and the Romanians of Transylvania. This meant that an Allied victory must now entail territorial losses for

[21]See maps, p. 53 and inside front cover.
[22]Lewis Namier, "The Downfall of the Habsburg Monarchy," in *Vanished Supremacies* (New York, 1958), p. 127.

Austria-Hungary. Then, at the end of 1916, Emperor Franz Josef died at the age of eighty-seven, snapping a personal link on which the empire depended. Even more influential was the Russian Revolution of February 1917. Now the Poles could perceive more hope for a revived national state on Allied terms than on German–Habsburg terms.

The Bolshevik "October Revolution" in 1917 had a mixed effect on Habsburg solidarity. In the short run, by taking the pressure off the eastern front, the Bolsheviks allowed the Austro-Hungarians to turn all their resources to defeating the Italians at Caporetto. In the long run, however, the Bolsheviks brought home to the war-weary Habsburg subjects how fragile an ancient autocracy was, and gave them an object lesson in self-determination.

War weariness in the Habsburg Empire, therefore, took the form of ethnic polarization. Not only did the minorities come to despair of Habsburg federalism, the dominant German and Hungarian nationalities became even less willing to grant concessions. The first meeting of the Austrian parliament (*Reichsrat*) on May 30, 1917, only gave a public forum to demands for extensive ethnic autonomy. The Czech and South Slav delegates called for "a federal state of free national states with equal rights."

When the imperial government tried to buy off secessionist feelings in 1918 with promises of cultural autonomy that might have been welcomed before 1914, it was too late. Furthermore, the last Habsburg struggles exposed the final flaw: the disaffection of the dominant nationalities, the Germans and Magyars. When the young Emperor Karl's secret peace feelers to the Allies were revealed to the world by Clemenceau in the spring of 1918, many German nationalists began to perceive that Habsburg dynastic interests (peace) diverged from German national interests (victory for Berlin). Magyar leaders became even more disaffected with a dynasty that threatened to buy off the minorities with concessions at Hungarian expense.

These developments show that the Allies were not the principal agents in the destruction of the Habsburg Empire. They hastened its dissolution, however, by propaganda for independence of subject peoples in 1918. During the early years of the war, allied to multinational and autocratic Russia, the British and French had said nothing about self-determination. The Russian Revolution, combined with American entry into the war, put democratic reform forward as a major Allied war aim. Woodrow Wilson favored some kind of federal solution for Austria-Hungary in his Fourteen Points speech given in January 1918; later the Allies supported the full independence of subject peoples. In June 1918, the United States promised the South Slavs "complete freedom," even though there were difficulties with Italian claims to the lands at the head of the Adriatic. During the summer, the Allies recognized the full sovereignty of the Polish and Czech national committees located in Paris.

The end came, militarily, in October 1918. An Allied army, mostly French, moving north from Greece forced Bulgaria out of the war at the end of September 1918. Bulgaria's request for an armistice on September 26 opened the Habsburg forces to a threat from the south. At the same time, the Italians began a new campaign at the end of October and defeated the Austrians at Vittorio Veneto. When the Habsburg regime asked for an armistice on November 4, much of its territory was already under the control of *de facto* Polish, Czech, and South Slav governments.

153

THE
DISSOLUTION
OF AUSTRIA-
HUNGARY,
1918–19

Nation-Building in the Successor States

Would national successions lead to social revolution? Eastern Europe, at the Soviet borders, was in chaos. Like Russia, much of Eastern Europe had a huge land-hungry peasantry. Seizure of the great estates seemed likely to provide revolutionary fuel. Starving urban workers and land-grabbing peasants might well mix the same brew as in the Russia of 1917.

In all the emerging successor states except one, however, Social Democrats and peasant (or agrarian) parties rather than Bolsheviks managed to harness these discontents. Potential class conflicts were neutralized among many Eastern European peoples by ethnic pride and by the excitement of creating or reviving a nation. Ethnic revival aroused strong emotions in the poor as well as in the educated middle classes of Eastern Europe, contrary to Karl Marx's assertion in 1848 that workers have no country. Socialist leaders were well aware before 1914 that international working-class solidarity faced exceptional obstacles in the Austro-Hungarian climate of sharpening ethnic identity. German skilled workers excluded Czechs from their trade unions in Bohemia, for example, while across the frontier in Polish-speaking parts of the German Empire, patriotic Polish workers withdrew from the SPD to form their own Polish Social Democratic party in 1903. The Austrian socialist intellectual Otto Bauer[23] warned that independence for every ethnic group, however small, was a retrograde step unless it followed the creation of an international socialist world economy. His views carried little weight with ordinary workers, however, among whom nationalism was a more vital loyalty than socialism. When the chance for ethnic self-determination came in 1918, workers danced in the streets of Prague, Warsaw, and Belgrade alongside the nationalist middle class.

Peasants, too, could submerge their revolutionary energies in nation-building in many parts of the Habsburg lands. In Czechoslovakia, for example, where the big landlords were mostly German in the Czech areas and mostly Hungarian in the Slovak areas, expropriation of estates seemed more a national than a class act.

[23]Otto Bauer's *Die Nationalitätenfrage und die Sozialdemokratie* (Vienna, 1907) was the most notable "Austro-Marxist" effort to find a place for nationalism within the Marxist values of world economic system and class loyalty.

The passions for change and reform in Eastern Europe were channeled mostly into the heady excitement of building new nations that would be reformist and democratic but not socially revolutionary. This was true of most of the successor states, whether they were new states (Czechoslovakia, Yugoslavia), expanded nineteenth-century states (Romania), or revived long-eclipsed states (Poland).

The major exception was Hungary, where national independence brought no satisfaction. The Magyar leaders decided in 1918 that they could better defend their historic borders as a separate state than as one subject to the frantic last-minute ethnic reorganization proposed by Emperor Karl. Hungarian independence thus began as a conservative reaction to preserve the Magyar predominance and the limited suffrage of the old Kingdom of Hungary. The wartime Magyar leaders declared their independence of all but the personal Habsburg tie on October 16. But they were unable to reach a separate armistice through President Wilson without internal reforms. On October 31, therefore, they handed over power to Prince Michael Karolyi, a maverick reformist aristocrat who had led the small wartime pacifist opposition. Karolyi declared Hungary an independent republic on November 16.

Prince Karolyi's October Republic rested on the calculation that a new, democratic Hungary that accepted the universal suffrage and minority language rights the old oligarchy had always resisted would be rewarded

A revolutionary demonstration in the streets of Budapest shortly before the establishment of the Budapest Soviet in March 1919.

by the Allies with retention of the historic Hungarian borders. That calculation was mistaken. The Allied commander in chief in southeastern Europe, the French General Franchet d'Esperey, did not prevent Hungary's new neighbors from seizing their ethnic areas. Romanian armies advanced into the rich grain-growing plain of Transylvania, where a majority of the peasants spoke Romanian. The Slovaks joined the new Czechoslovak state that had been proclaimed on October 21. The South Slavs of both Austria and Hungary proclaimed the new state of Yugoslavia on October 29.

Since the Allies, and particularly the French, who had the only Allied armed force in the area, favored Romania and Czechoslovakia as building blocks of the new Eastern Europe, Karolyi could not keep Hungary intact by dealing with the Allies. Instead, the Allies treated Karolyi's Hungary as a defeated enemy. When General Franchet d'Esperey ordered Hungarian troops on March 20, 1919, to withdraw behind a line that Hungarians feared would be the new border, Karolyi abandoned power. It was grasped by Béla Kun, a Hungarian journalist who had been in Moscow in 1917 and who returned now to lead the Hungarian Bolshevik movement. Kun managed to gain command of the rising tide of strikes and demonstrations in hungry Budapest during the spring of 1919. There was no other alternative to the left of Prince Karolyi, for the Hungarian Social Democrats had been a major component of the October Republic.

The Béla Kun Regime

Béla Kun's soviet regime governed in Budapest for 133 days, from March 20 to August 1, 1919. It was the only soviet regime of Eastern Europe between Berlin and Moscow and the longest-lived soviet government outside Russia. It controlled Budapest and those parts of the countryside not occupied by Romanian troops, the French, or the counterrevolutionary Hungarian movement that soon formed in southern Hungary under Allied protection.[24]

Kun attempted to proceed immediately to the establishment of socialism in Hungary, assisted by the Marxist philosopher Georg Lukacs as Minister of Culture and by earthier figures such as Tibor Szamuelly, Minister of the Interior, whose "Red Terror" produced about fifty deaths. Rumors of a much larger figure swept the Hungarian upper classes. Kun's decisive enemies in agrarian Hungary were not bourgeois, however, but peasants. Unlike the Russian soviet regime, the Budapest Soviet alienated the peasantry from the very beginning. Less pragmatic than Lenin, Kun nationalized the great estates rather than distribute them to small landholders. Furthermore, caught in the classic city–country conflict of any urban regime short of food, he paid for the crops he requisitioned in inflated paper currency. The countryside

[24]See Chapter 7, pp. 206–08.

155

THE
DISSOLUTION
OF AUSTRIA-
HUNGARY,
1918–19

responded with the traditional peasant reactions of hoarding and crop destruction. Kun was unable to deliver peace, land, or bread.

Some Hungarian patriots had supported Kun's regime, believing that Russian aid would help preserve Hungary's historic frontiers against the Allies. Kun's Russian gamble worked no better than Karolyi's Allied gamble. Lenin was occupied at home with civil war and Allied intervention. The Allies saw the Budapest Soviet as an unacceptable extension of Bolshevism westward, since it helped inspire the Munich Soviet, a revolutionary uprising in Austria, and widespread simultaneous strikes in Italy and France. When Kun rashly attacked the Romanians in July 1919, therefore, the Allies helped them roll over Hungary. They captured Budapest in early August 1919. Kun fled. Since the Social Democrats and constitutional republicans had been discredited earlier in the October Republic, Hungary was delivered over to the reactionary former commander in chief of the Austro-Hungarian Navy, Admiral Miklós Horthy. His "White Terror" took ten times as many lives as had Szamuelly's "Red Terror" in the preceding spring.[25]

Britain, France, Italy: The Unrest of 1919–20

The postwar revolutionary wave was not merely a matter of throwing out defeated regimes. Accumulated war weariness and social bitterness burst out in the victorious countries, too. Wartime resentments there were compounded by postwar unemployment as demobilization began. In Britain, the traditional "red" areas, especially the Clydeside area of Scotland, experimented with workers' councils under the wartime rebel shop steward leadership. British workers, led by Ernest Bevin's dockers, struck against ships carrying supplies to anti-Bolsheviks in Russia. In France, an extensive general strike on May 1, 1919, and a somewhat smaller one in May 1920 marked the historic high-water mark of the syndicalist tactic of sponsoring one great insurrectionary day. There was considerable labor militancy even in the United States, culminating in the Seattle general strike of 1920. Italy came close to real social dissolution in the months following war. It came closer perhaps even than Germany, where the revolutionary pressures were more easily channeled into mere constitutional democratization.

Postwar yearnings for fundamental change took more irrepressible form in Italy than in the other victor nations because, first of all, few Italians felt any sense of victory. Italy's limited territorial gains, compared with its wartime dreams of control over the whole Adriatic area and southern Asia Minor, seemed a poor recompense for the war's cost in men, effort, and material. Second, ineffective war government had sharpened social conflict in Italy. In a nation already divided between an industrial north and a virtually feudal south, social antagonisms were too raw to bear wartime pressures well. Third, Italy suffered the worst

[25]See Chapter 7, pp. 206–08.

inflation of any victor power. The cost of living quadrupled during the war, with wages trailing behind, and then doubled again in the two immediate postwar years. To make matters worse, wartime regimes had encouraged postwar hopes. Premier Antonio Salandra had promised in 1916 that returning veterans would receive land. At the war's end, three virulent protest movements—industrial strikes, agrarian land seizures, and nationalist demonstrations—carried Italy to the brink of revolution.

The strike movement of 1919 and 1920 exceeded anything in prior Italian experience. Whereas an average of 200,000 Italian workmen went out on strike each year in the immediate prewar decade, five times that many (about 1 million) went out on strike in 1919 and six times that many (about 1.2 million) in 1920. About 320 persons were killed in 140 clashes between police and demonstrators between April 1919 and September 1920.

One strike motive was support for the Soviet Union against Western intervention. A general strike was called for July 19 and 20, 1919, after the Italian government had extended diplomatic recognition to the White Russian regime of Admiral Kolchak. A more immediate spur was the rapid rise in the cost of living, which soon outran all wage settlements. Worker-elected factory councils, which had acquired a kind of unofficial existence under war government, now claimed a larger role in plant management and a future position as Italian soviets.

The northern industrial cities of Milan and Turin were the centers of worker militancy. At Milan, long negotiations over wages between factory owners and the leading metalworkers' union (FIOM) were sharpened by worker slowdowns. The exasperated employers locked the workers out of the Alfa-Romeo automobile works on August 30, 1920. In response, FIOM occupied all the factories in the Milan area, then in Turin, and eventually in fifty-nine cities. Some 500,000 strikers were involved. Factory councils maintained production in the plants as a demonstration of the soviet principle, under the intellectual leadership of Antonio Gramsci of Turin, the chief theoretician of communism in modern Italy.

The occupation of the factories in August and September 1920 was the end, rather than the beginning, of the workers' revolutionary wave in postwar Italy. Premier Giovanni Giolitti understood far more clearly than the factory owners that the workers did not know what to do next. He insisted on negotiation rather than the use of armed force. After three weeks, the workers, their *élan* broken, evacuated the factories on the basis of a quite traditional wage raise and an essentially meaningless recognition of the principle of workers' councils, which was soon forgotten.

Meanwhile, a wave of land seizures during 1919 frightened rural farm and estate owners. Wartime promises of land to veterans coincided with long-felt peasant resentments against the owners of uncultivated lands of great estates and hunting preserves. In the spring of 1919, bands of rural day laborers and sharecroppers simply occupied fallow lands in many parts of Italy, as they had done in many earlier periods of unrest. The innovation of 1919, however, was the degree of organized support that these land seizures received. Veterans' movements, radical Catholic movements (*Popolari*) in the south and in Lombardy and Tuscany, and socialist agricultural labor unions in the traditionally "red" rural areas around Bologna all provided organized support for rural militants. In some areas, the landless marched out to fallow lands with bands and banners to dig and plough, encouraged by legislative proposals to grant squatter's rights on uncultivated lands. Farm laborers were organized for wage settlements and for "estate councils," the counterpart of factory councils. Little land actually changed hands by force in the north, although some did in the center and south. In the north, however, many landowners found they could not hire farm labor except on the terms demanded by socialist and Catholic rural unions and peasant cooperatives.

The third kind of postwar direct-action movement was the nationalist seizure of territories claimed by Italy but denied it at the Peace Conference. With the disintegration of the Habsburg Empire, Italian troops had established themselves further east around the head of the Adriatic than wartime promises had provided for; notably, they occupied the port of Fiume (or Rijeka, as the Yugoslavs called it). The Peace Conference's orders for the withdrawal of Italian forces led to angry protests in Italy. The bombastic poet and war hero Gabriele D'Annunzio led 8000 volunteers, mostly war veterans, to seize the area in September 1919. While the Italian government played for time, D'Annunzio set up the "Republic of Carnero," which displayed many of the themes and postures of later fascism on a comic opera scale. Neither rhetoric nor appeals to Lenin and the Sinn Fein could save him, however, when the Italian government reached agreement with the Yugoslavs to make Fiume an international free city. Italian troops expelled D'Annunzio and his legionnaires in December 1920. But the incident established a lasting resentment among many veterans, and the precedent of nationalist direct action to trouble later Italian politics.

Postwar insurrectionary pressures were clearly diminishing in Italy by the fall of 1920. In retrospect, the impression of imminent revolution was misleading. It is true that the great majority of organized Italian socialists were committed to revolution and supported the position known as "maximalism": they refused any alliances with "bourgeois parties" and assumed a revolutionary posture, flying the red flag rather than the tricolor in areas they controlled and encouraging worker instransigence.[26] As good social democrats, however, they expected to gain political power by winning an electoral majority. Moreover, the socialist movement was divided among the "maximalists"; a "reformist" minority, powerful in the trade unions, that wanted to form alliances

[26]Under the guidance of the maximalists, led by Giacinto Serrati, the Italian Socialist party was the only major Western European socialist party to join the Third International en bloc in October 1919.

with liberals against the right; and a small abstentionist minority that wanted to have nothing to do with electoral politics. The maximalists, who controlled the party machinery, divorced themselves from the most widespread popular ground-swell movement for change by condemning the land seizures as a petty bourgeois movement toward small property. The land seizures, in their turn, were divided among socialist, radical Catholic (*Popolari*), and veterans' leadership.

With the collapse of the occupation of the factories in September 1920, dispirited workingmen dropped away from unions, whose membership declined rapidly. The beginnings of postwar unemployment further weakened the will and the bargaining position of what was left of organized labor. Electorally, Marxist parties fell away from their high point of November 1919 (156 seats out of 508 in the national legislature), losing 18 seats in the election of May 1921. The revolutionary surge had passed, but the panic it provoked in the Italian middle and upper classes had only begun, as we shall see in a subsequent chapter on the rise of fascism.

By late 1920, the tide of revolution was receding everywhere in Europe. In Germany in 1923 the socialist–communist coalition state governments in Saxony and Thuringia and an abortive uprising in Hamburg were only the last remnants of insurrection. Even before then, it was apparent that Soviet Russia, instead of becoming the trigger for revolution in the more advanced countries, as Marxists had anticipated, had survived alone as a socialist regime.

Aftermath and Results

Success and Failure: A Comparative Look

Why had the revolutionary pressures generated by the war produced a new regime in Russia and nowhere else? The question has not ceased to reverberate through the rest of this century. Marxists and counter-revolutionaries alike have based their plans since 1923 on their respective analyses of this unexpected turn of events.

A few conclusions seem obvious. Losing a major war proved fatal to every regime; indeed, no modern European state has survived even the loss of a minor war in which the population felt that national prestige was deeply involved.[27] However, the converse was not true. Being on the winning side was not enough to assure social stability, as Italy's postwar social explosion showed.

It appears that relatively homogenous societies in industrially advanced countries, with a tradition of democratic institutions, such as Britain and France, withstood the social pressures of total war far better than less homogeneous, less industrialized, more autocratic societies. Certainly revolutionary pressures were greater in southern and Eastern

[27]Consider the French Fourth Republic, overthrown in 1958 after losing Indochina and failing to hold Algeria.

Europe than in Western Europe. This observation has had profound repercussions among the theoreticians of revolution. Marxist thinkers, who had held earlier that socialist revolution could not succeed in a backward country like Russia without simultaneous revolution in Western Europe, had to admit in 1919 that revolution had broken out first in backward Russia, Hungary, and Bavaria. As Trotsky noted: "History has moved along the line of least resistance. The revolutionary epoch has made its incursion through the least barricaded gates."[28]

Even if revolutions begin at the "weak link" of established society, that still does not explain why some succeeded in the face of armed counterattack while others quickly collapsed.

Revolutionary pressures certainly carried further against autocratic regimes because there was a broader coalition of discontent. Governments that still denied elementary political liberties faced many layers of challenge, ranging from liberal aristocrats and middle-class liberals to socialists. The old regime in Russia was swept away in the first instance by all of these oppositions combined. The German monarchy, too, was destroyed by simultaneous democratic and social revolutions. The Germans stopped short at constitutional change, however, so still other factors must be sought to explain successful social revolution.

One of the most important preconditions of successful revolution was the existence of a land-hungry peasant mass. Most of industrially advanced Europe had few people on the land (as in England) or had many small family farms (as in France). When urban unrest appeared in such societies, the countryside was inert, if not actually hostile to workers' demands. That had been the lesson of nineteenth-century Western European revolutions, too. But where urban demonstrations have coincided with a tidal wave of land seizures of large estates, it has usually proved impossible to resist these twin forces. France in 1789, Russia in 1917, China in 1948, and Cuba in 1958 all vouch for this observation. The areas of strongest revolutionary stress after the First World War fit rather well, although not perfectly, with areas of simultaneous urban discontent and rural land seizures.

Among socialists, the land issue had been an awkward one. If the peasants were granted their own land, they then became small farmers and a bulwark of the *status quo,* as in France. That is the reason for Marx's bitter denunciation of peasant conservatism in 1848. Thereafter, socialists remained divided on the land question. Reformist socialists in small-farming areas, like Jean Jaurès in France and Georg von Vollmar in Bavaria, accepted the necessity of wooing small-family farmers as the only way to get rural votes; Rosa Luxemburg, by contrast, considered such tactics a sellout to rural propertyholding conservatism, and insisted on the goal of nationalizing rather than distributing land.

That debate had its echoes in the years 1917 to 1921. Lenin, always

---

[28]Leon Trotsky, "Reflections on the Course of the Proletarian Revolution," in Isaac Deutscher, *The Prophet Armed: Trotsky, 1879–1921* (New York, 1965), p. 455.

more concerned for power than dogmatic purity, officially "nationalized" the land but in fact acquiesced in its direct seizure by peasants. Thereafter, he was largely immune from any counterrevolutionary movement, however well armed or financed, that threatened to restore the old landlords' property. By contrast, the Budapest Soviet of Béla Kun attempted to transfer land directly from estates to state farms. His city-based regime foundered, in part, on peasant animosity to his orthodox socialist land policy.

Nationalism also affected revolutionary regimes' changes of survival. As a general rule, revolutionary regimes that offended national pride were quickly swept aside. In Hungary, both Prince Michael Karolyi and Béla Kun paid dearly for their inability to keep the Romanians from taking Transylvania. The Bavarian Soviet threatened to divide Germany into minor states. However those Eastern European successor states that gratified national feelings—Poland, Czechoslovakia, Romania, and Yugoslavia—satisfied their peoples' clamorings even without substantial social change or impressive economic success. The Russian case was more complicated, for the humiliating Treaty of Brest-Litovsk drove even some Bolsheviks into opposition. During the civil war, however, the Bolshevik regime drew added strength from its claim that Leon Trotsky's Red Army was effectively defending the national soil against foreign intervention.

The Third International and the Division of the European Left

Lenin remained convinced throughout 1920 that the Russian Revolution would trigger socialist revolutions in the more industrialized countries. He did his best to encourage them. In March 1919, optimistic over the situation in Hungary and Germany, he summoned the socialists of the world to Moscow to form a new global organization. It was called the Communist International, or Third International, to distinguish it from the prewar socialist leadership of the Second International (formed in 1889), which had, in Lenin's eyes, made fatal compromises with middle-class patriotism and parliamentarism.

The first response to Lenin's appeal among Western European socialists was enthusiastic. The thirst for renewed unity on the left was intense. The Second International was in general disrepute because of its failure to stop war in 1914 and because of the participation of many of its leaders in wartime governments. The first socialist regime in history held power in Russia, and Western European socialists were eager to prevent their governments from crushing it. If the great moment were really at hand, to hold back would be treasonous. The Italian, Norwegian, and Bulgarian socialist parties adhered en masse in 1919 to Lenin's new International, and the parties of Germany, France, and Britain sent sympathetic observers.

Lenin did not want general support or sympathy, however. He wanted committed followers who would emulate the Russian Bolsheviks by forcing revolution on the more cautious parliamentary socialists through the will and discipline of a minority party. Lenin set stringent conditions for admission to the Third International at its second congress in July 1920. Convinced that Russian success in the war with Poland would soon carry revolution into Germany, Lenin demanded that all candidate parties assent to Twenty-One Points. Would-be member parties must purge their reformist elements, restructure themselves "in the most centralized fashion," support the "Soviet Republics" (sic) in their fight against foreign intervention, prepare for a violent seizure of power, and fight by all possible means the rival power of reformist Social Democrats.

Lenin's provocative challenge and the Western European socialists' ambiguous response divided the European left permanently and passionately after 1920. The feasibility of revolution divided them. While Lenin was convinced that world revolution was at hand, many Western European socialists were reluctant to gamble away their previous gains for an uncertain outcome. The cost in liberty and in material comfort of a Leninist seizure of power also divided them. Up to 1914, the German SPD, with its elaborate legal organization, its massive electoral success, and its vision of widening human freedom, had been the preeminent model for other socialists. In 1917, Lenin had introduced a rival model, incompatible with the values of many Social Democrats but incontestably more successful than the SPD in seizing power. Most Social Democrats still preferred to achieve socialism under conditions that would not require dictatorship. Leninists accused them of sabotaging an historic opportunity. The breach remains intensely bitter to this day.

Every mass socialist movement outside Soviet Russia was split in 1920 and 1921. Lenin accepted no qualified adherence to the Twenty-One Points. He specified by name the reformist leaders whom each party must purge, along with their followers. The British Labour party and some powerful Social Democratic parties, such as the Austrian and the Swedish, lost only a fraction of their members to the Third International. After Lenin rejected the enthusiastic adherence of Serrati's Italian "maximalists" unless they would purge their own ranks of reformists, only about a third of them finally joined the new Italian Communist party in January 1921. On Christmas Day 1920 a majority of the French SFIO voted to accept the Twenty-One Points, taking the party machinery and newspaper (*Humanité*) with them. The old German SPD had been split over the war since 1914, but even that ardent Spartacist Rosa Luxemburg had questioned the applicability of Lenin's methods to Western Europe before her death. Only about a third of the Independent Social Democrats, the USPD, went over to the Third International in December 1920. The rest returned to the majority SPD fold or left the movement in disillusion.

Even these moderate successes of the Third International were further weakened as the revolutionary perspective faded in Western Europe after 1920. As the Russian leaders attempted to bring Western European Communist parties under tighter Bolshevik control from

Moscow in the 1920s, they discovered that Lenin had recruited enthusiasts for immediate revolution but not disciplined followers. The largest new Communist party in the West, in France, was filled with anarcho-syndicalists who had always opposed parliamentary socialism but who dropped away from communism as soon as its centralized governance became clear. The Norwegian Labour party, which had rushed eagerly into the Third International in 1919, withdrew in 1923. So there remained in the West minority Communist parties and larger Social Democratic parties, frozen in permanent opposition to each other around the issue of whether revolution had been possible in 1919 and 1920.

One more result of the revolutionary movements after 1917 became clear only later. Even as the revolutionary pressures subsided, a panicky reaction to them began. Many frightened middle-class Europeans began abandoning the nineteenth-century liberalism of their fathers for some stronger bulwarks against revolutionary socialism. We shall look more closely at those bulwarks in Chapter 7, after first examining the peace settlement of 1919.

Suggestions for Further Reading

William Henry Chamberlin, *The Russian Revolution,** 2 vols. (1935), the work of the *Christian Science Monitor*'s correspondent in Moscow, has still not been superseded for the grand sweep of events from 1917 to 1921.

Robert V. Daniels, *Red October** (1969) is the most carefully detailed narrative of the course of the second, Bolshevik, revolution. While Daniels attributes much to chance and accident, George Katkov, *Russia, 1917* (1967) emphasizes conspiracy and German aid to Lenin. The view that revolution was the product of Russian social conflict and political blockage is argued compellingly by Leopold Haimson, "The Problem of Social Stability in Urban Russia: 1905–1917," *Slavic Review*, Vol. 23, No. 4 (1964) and Vol. 24, No. 1 (1965).

The richest study of social and economic dissolution and reconstruction under the new regime is Edward Hallett Carr's series: *The Bolshevik Revolution, 1917–1923,** 3 vols. (1950–53); *The Interregnum* (1954); and *Socialism in One Country, 1924–1926,** 3 vols. (1958–64).

Among participants' accounts, the American John Reed's *Ten Days That Shook the World** (1919), and the hesitant Bolshevik N. N. Sukhanov's *The Russian Revolution, 1917* (1955) are justly famous. Aleksandr Kerensky argued tirelessly for the rest of his life, in such works as *Catastrophe: Kerensky's Own Story of the Revolution* (1927), that Russia's normal progress toward democracy had been perverted by the Bolsheviks.

Bertram D. Wolfe, *Three Who Made a Revolution** (1948) is the standard biography of Trotsky, Lenin, and Stalin up to 1914. Isaac Deutscher, *Trotsky,** 3 vols. (1954–65) is a disciple's masterpiece. Although more has been written about Lenin than about any other modern leader, there is no fully satisfactory biography. Among brief introductions, M. C. Morgan, *Lenin* (1971) is a warmly sympathetic account of the person. Robert Conquest, *V. I. Lenin** (1972) asks how Lenin's ideals produced such contrary results. Louis Fischer, *Life of Lenin** (1964) is the most useful of several full-scale popular biographies. Adam B. Ulam, *The Bolsheviks** (1955) treats both Lenin and the party.

Robert C. Tucker, *Stalin as Revolutionary, 1873–1929: A Study in History and Personality* (1973) examines the shaping of Stalin's character. Adam B. Ulam, *Stalin: The Man and*

His Era (1973) is the most comprehensive modern biography, although the brilliant polemic by an admirer of Trotsky, Isaac Deutscher's *Stalin: A Political Biography,** 2nd ed. (1967) is still important.

Paul Avrich, *Kronstadt 1921* (1970) is a gripping account of opposition to Bolshevik rule from the left. See also Robert V. Daniels, *The Conscience of the Revolution** (1960), and Oliver H. Radkey, *The Agrarian Foes of Bolshevism* (1958).

David Mitchell, *1919: Red Mirage* (1970), although sensationalized, has the merit of treating postwar unrest on a worldwide basis. Francis L. Carsten, *Revolution in Central Europe* (1972) is an authoritative study of Germany and Austria.

For the revolution in Germany, see A. J. Ryder, *The German Revolution of 1918* (1967); Richard A. Comfort, *Revolutionary Hamburg* (1966); Allan Mitchell, *Revolution in Bavaria* (1965); Werner T. Angress, *Stillborn Revolution: The Communist Bid for Power in Germany, 1921–1923* (1963; reprint ed., 1971); and Reinhard Rürüp, "Problems of the German Revolution, 1918–1919," *Journal of Contemporary History,* Vol. 3, No. 1 (January 1968).

The most significant soviet regime outside Russia is examined in Ivan Völgyes, ed., *Hungary in Revolution, 1918–1919: Nine Essays* (1971), and Rudolph Tökés, *Béla Kun* (1967).

Leo Valiani, *The End of Austria-Hungary* (1973) takes a close scholarly look at the diplomatic papers. See also Z. A. B. Zeman, *The Break-Up of the Habsburg Empire, 1914–1918* (1961), and the very thorough Arthur J. May, *The Passing of the Hapsburg Monarchy,* 2 vols. (1966). The essay by Lewis B. Namier, "The Downfall of the Habsburg Monarchy," reprinted in his *Vanished Supremacies** (1958) is as penetrating as when first written in 1920.

THE VERSAILLES
PEACE SETTLEMENT 6

It was not Lenin who drew the charter of postwar Europe: it was the remaining Allied powers. It was the Council of Four at the Paris Peace Conference, January to June 1919: President Woodrow Wilson of the United States; Premier Georges Clemenceau of France; Prime Minister David Lloyd George of Great Britain; Prime Minister Vittorio Emanuele Orlando of Italy; along with Count Seiki Terauchi of Japan, an Asian state now being recognized formally for the first time as a Great Power.

The delegates and their staffs who assembled in Paris in January 1919 gathered, as peace conferences had gathered before, for the victors to impose their will on the vanquished. In wide sectors of an attentive public, however, and among some of the most powerful delegations, there prevailed strong feelings that this peace should not be one-sided, like the vain, ephemeral treaties of the past. Europeans wanted to change the very basis of politics among states and within states so that there would never be another war. A total peace, many felt, was the only appropriate end to a total war.

Harold Nicolson, a young member of the British delegation, recalled later how optimistically he had gone to Paris. He had been sure that "he knew exactly what mistakes" the "misguided, the reactionary, the pathetic aristocrats" who had represented Britain in earlier conferences had made.

> We were journeying to Paris not merely to liquidate the war, but to found a New Order in Europe. We were preparing not peace only, but Eternal Peace. There was about us the halo of some divine mission.[1]

The Setting: Ideals, Interests, and Ideology

War Aims

Expectations about the peace had been strongly colored by wartime emotions. A long war was impossible without massive propaganda campaigns to rally the home fronts. The war willingness of Entente populations was first nurtured by stories of German aggression and atrocities in Belgium. In time, propagandists on both sides began to extoll the social reforms that victory would make possible. The German parliamentary opposition was mollified by promises to abolish the old three-class voting system[2] in Prussia. In Britain, H. G. Wells justified the war for liberals by calling it "the War that will end war."[3] War governments thus made an implicit bargain to win their populations' hearts: give all for victory, and a better world will follow.

By a series of steps, the war had shifted from a fight over national interests to a crusade for principles. At the beginning, it had been difficult to argue that the Entente, including Tsarist Russia, stood for democracy and progress against the Central Powers. But the first Russian Revolution of February 1917 allowed the Allied populations to believe that their side now represented democracy.

In October 1917, Lenin announced that Russia was leaving the war and called for all peoples to force their rulers to end a war whose aims were solely "to decide which of the strong and healthy nations should dominate the weak ones."[4] To reinforce these accusations of imperialist war aims, the new Commissar for Foreign Affairs, Leon Trotsky, got the keys and safe combinations to the deserted foreign ministry and published copies of the wartime secret treaties. In this way, European populations first learned what deals had been reached by secret diplomacy: that the Russians were fighting in order to annex Galicia from the

---

[1]Harold Nicolson, *Peacemaking, 1919* (London, 1935), p. 25.
[2]See Chapter 4, p. 106.
[3]Quoted in the *Daily News*, August 14, 1914. See also A. D. Lindsay, *The War to End War* (London, 1915).
[4]Vladimir I. Lenin, "Decree on Peace, October 26, 1917," in *Selected Works*, Vol. 6 (New York, 1936), p. 401.

Austrians and the Straits from the Turks; that the French had received Russian promises of support for its reconquest of Alsace-Lorraine; that Italy expected to expand around the head of the Adriatic Sea and into the Alps. Lacking other weapons, the Bolsheviks sought to get out of the war by exposing all nations' expansionist goals to their war-weary populations.

The "Fourteen Points"

President Wilson's Fourteen Points speech of January 8, 1918, was an attempt to recapture the propaganda initiative from Lenin. Wilson shifted the war aims debate away from Lenin's appeal for immediate peace to the good peace that could follow Allied victory. Speaking to the United States Congress in the traditional State of the Union address, Wilson outlined in "Fourteen Points" a lasting, just peace that would warrant persevering on to victory. Several declarations of principle later in 1918 completed the Wilsonian vision of eventual peace. Its basic principles were "open covenants of peace, openly arrived at" to replace secret diplomacy; freedom of commerce and trade; reduction of armaments; "readjustment" of colonial empires so that the interests of indigenous populations should have "equal weight" with those of the imperial powers; self-determination of peoples so that nations could have rulers of their choosing and frontiers corresponding as fully as possible to national lines; and, finally, the formation of a "general association of nations" to keep the peace and guarantee the safety of "great and small states alike."

United States President Woodrow Wilson (left) responds to the cheers of enthusiastic Parisians before the opening of the Peace Conference, 1919. On the right is French President Raymond Poincaré.

While some Europeans on both sides were ready to achieve Lenin's vision of immediate peace through revolution, a majority on the Allied side placed almost religious hopes in Wilson's vision of the just peace that could follow victory. In Britain, Wilson's ascendancy lent further influence to such liberal war critics as the Union of Democratic Control. Wilson's assumptions coincided with theirs: that democracies based on the nationality principle were more peaceable than autocracies; that diplomats would keep the peace if subjected to public scrutiny; and that if national aspirations were granted, there would be no future grounds for war. Wilson's views also made him a prophet elsewhere in Europe; he seemed to crystallize unformed but fervent hopes for a release from the old order that had produced the First World War. As Wilson toured parts of Europe on his way to Paris, he was thronged by adulatory crowds, especially in Italy. Most importantly, it was to Wilson that the Germans had turned for an armistice, which they asked to be based on the Fourteen Points. The liberal critique of the war emerged, then, as the dominant intellectual influence on the making of the peace.

It was impossible, of course, to draft peace terms purely on the basis of abstract ideas. The deliberations were powerfully shaped by three sets of pragmatic considerations: prior treaties and agreements that the Allies had made with one another and with other peoples during the war; the various national strategic and economic interests of the participating nations; and the containment of revolutionary regimes in central and Eastern Europe in the spring of 1919. In the end, the idealistic language of the peace treaties jarred badly with the interests and deals reflected in their actual terms.

Wartime Treaties and Promises

First came the wartime "secret treaties" to complicate the work of the peacemakers. As the war had settled into stalemate in the fall of 1914, the Allied governments had tried to solidify and enlarge their alliance by making secret promises. Partly to help prevent a Russian separate peace, Britain and France agreed in March and April 1915 that after an Allied victory Russia should control Constantinople and the Straits in return for Russian acceptance of British aims in Egypt and French aims in Alsace-Lorraine. The Treaty of London, signed on April 26, 1915, held out rich promises to Italy in exchange for Italian entry into the war on the Allied side. In the event of Allied victory, Italy was to receive the Alpine areas up the Brenner Pass, large sections of the islands and coastline at the head of the Adriatic Sea, the south coast of Turkey if the Ottoman Empire were divided up after the war, and expansion of Libya and other Italian African colonies. Shortly thereafter, Italy ended its neutrality and, denouncing its German–Austrian alliances that went back to 1882, declared war on Austria-Hungary. Romania had been brought into the war on the Allied side after the promise on August 18, 1916, of major expansion in the partly Romanian areas of Hungary, especially the rich plain of Transylvania. But since Romania had made a separate peace with Germany on May 7, 1918, these promises could be assumed to have lapsed.

During most of the war the Allies had threatened to amputate territory from the Central Powers but not to destroy them. At the end of the war, however, they also made promises to minority peoples within the great multinational empires on the other side, and contributed to the revolutionary pressures of nationalism within them.

The Poles were the first stateless people to receive public Allied support for postwar national independence. As long as Russia remained in the war on the Allied side, many Poles, such as the socialist-nationalist leader Josef Pilsudski, had seen more promise for statehood in a German victory. The Germans had announced in November 1916 their intention of making former Russian Poland an independent kingdom. When Russia left the war in the spring of 1918, however, the Allies made a unified Polish national state—comprised of German Poland, Austrian Poland, and Russian Poland—a public war aim. An "independent Poland" with access to the sea was Point 13 of Wilson's Fourteen Points of January 1918.

The Allies recognized the independence of other Habsburg subjects in the summer of 1918. The Czecho-Slovak National Council in Paris, benefiting from the anti-Bolshevik activities of the Czech Legion in Siberia, was recognized as a *de facto* government. Although the Allies declined to choose among the Serbian government in Belgrade, the Yugoslav Committee in London, and the Yugoslav National Council in Zagreb as official spokesmen for all South Slavs, they accepted the goal of a single South Slav state. By the end of October 1918, the Austro-Hungarian Empire had simply ceased to count outside the German and Hungarian areas, as the subject peoples took local administration into their own hands. Thus the Peace Conference was confronted in 1919 not only with Allied promises but with a series of *faits accomplis* by which the new nationalities had asserted their existence.

The peoples of another great multinational empire—Ottoman Turkey, which had been drawn into the war by German influence in November 1914—were the object of particularly vague and contradictory promises that returned to haunt the Peace Conference. One set of promises was the result of British efforts to encourage Arab separatism as a weapon against the Turks and a buffer around the Suez Canal. First, they supported guerrilla operations among the Bedouin along the Hijaz Railway in what is today Saudi Arabia.[5] British officials led one of the main Arab families, the Hashemites, to expect British support for an independent Arab kingdom in the Near East if the Arabs helped destroy the Ottoman Empire. Meanwhile, in the Sykes-Picot Agreement of May

---

[5]A highly romanticized account of this action by the British leader T. E. Lawrence was the source of a great postwar legend. See T. E. Lawrence, *The Seven Pillars of Wisdom* (London, 1935).

1916, British and French officials were dividing between themselves future colonial spheres of influence in the Near East that were in irreconcilable conflict with the very notion of an independent Arab state. By this understanding, the French were to have predominant influence in the northern coastal areas and their hinterland (Syria, the Lebanon) while the British were to exercise control in the Tigris-Euphrates Valley (present-day Iraq) and in the Jordan Valley (present-day Israel and Jordan). Finally, the British government agreed in the Balfour Declaration of November 1917 to "look with favor" on the creation of a Jewish "national home" in Palestine, thus encouraging Zionist hopes at potential variance with both other sets of understandings.

The bearers of all these wartime promises and aspirations attempted to cash them in at the Peace Conference that convened in Paris in January 1919. The national committees of Czechoslovakia and Poland, already recognized as governments, were there. So was Prince Faisal of the Hashemite family, with Colonel T. E. Lawrence, in order to argue for an Arab kingdom in the Middle East. Chaim Weizmann, a chemist from Manchester, lobbied for the Zionist ideal of a Jewish national homeland. W. E. B. DuBois organized the first Pan-African Congress on the fringes of the conference. But it was obvious that the secret treaties and the national hopes of the war years were going to meet with very unequal recognition at the Peace Conference. The Czechs, for example, had used their segment of the old Habsburg armed force and local bureaucracy to establish their own *de facto* state even before the armistice; the Arabs, by contrast, had only their dreams.

Even if victorious Great Powers had chosen to honor all their promises, it was not within their power to do so. Some of them were simply unfulfillable. There was no way, for example, to draw a Poland that was both ethnically predominantly Polish and still had access to the sea, as President Wilson had recommended. Some agreements, as in the case of the Middle East, were contradictory. Moreover, the earlier "secret treaties" with previously existing states dated from a time when the war was still being waged for dynastic and national interests. Those agreements shifted frontiers with cavalier disregard for ethnic line and popular self-determination. The emergence of the war aims issue as a major ingredient of propaganda for restless and war-weary peoples, and the intense popular longing for a change in world politics along the lines advocated in the liberal critique of the war, made this kind of territorial deal unacceptable. It was far more difficult in 1919 to bargain away tracts of land without regard to their inhabitants' feelings than it had been in 1915.

National Interests of the Great Powers

A second set of considerations that shaped the Peace Conference's work was the national and strategic self-interest of the principal victors. Georges Clemenceau, in particular, represented France with keen awareness that his people had borne the brunt of the Allied war effort and must bear the brunt of enforcing the peace terms on the continent of Europe. He was determined that the peace terms should favor French security.

The French understood only too well that their influence in 1918 as the main Continental Great Power was an artificial and transitory situation. They could not afford to revel in victory in 1918 as if it had been total and unambiguous. The French had nearly collapsed at home in May 1917 and on the front in July 1918. And in the longer run, they were haunted by the growing industrial and demographic imbalance between 60 million Germans and 40 million Frenchmen. The French predominance of 1918 rested on the simultaneous eclipse of Germany and Russia, a state of affairs virtually unprecedented in the history of Great Power rivalries in modern Europe. French troops provided the vast bulk of armed force not only on Germany's western frontier but in Eastern Europe as well. Theirs was the main force between Germany and Russia, and French military advisors assisted in the capitals of many Eastern European successor states. It was tempting to try to transform their temporary military superiority into a permanent system of dykes and barriers behind which the decline of Germany and Russia might become permanent.

A major thread running through the Peace Conference was Clemenceau's stubborn campaign for firm guarantees of French security. An even more intransigent French nationalist group on his right battled for detachment of the Rhineland from Germany so that the Rhine River could serve as a military frontier. But Clemenceau was able to assert his authority over this group, and in fact profited by its public opposition. By renouncing claims to a separate Rhineland, Clemenceau could refuse to make other concessions. French security interests remained a major criterion for deciding which of the various nationalities would be favored in the postwar system.

Clemenceau was not the only Great Power spokesman to press national interests forward at the conference. The French charged the British with wishing to revive Germany as a "balance" against the victorious French and as a trading partner. Indeed, there is some evidence to support the charge. British national interest seemed to lie in a self-enforcing nonpunitive peace and rapid economic revival. The British economist John Maynard Keynes stressed the economic importance of a healthy Germany to the European economy in his best-seller *The Economic Consequences of the Peace,* which was published the following year. David Lloyd George supported President Wilson in opposing the French plans for a separate Rhineland. The British also tried to obtain an active role in former German colonies in Africa and in the Middle Eastern territories "liberated" from the Ottoman Turks.

President Wilson did not hesitate to fight for United States interests. The Polish constituency in America provided him with good domestic political reasons for supporting Polish claims beyond their ethnic limits. And such Wilsonian principles as the "absolute freedom of navigations upon the seas . . . alike in peace and in war" of the Fourteen Points

French Premier Georges Clemenceau, United States President Woodrow Wilson, and British Prime Minister David Lloyd George (left to right) leave the Versailles Palace after signing the peace settlement, June 1919.

(Point 2) and removal of barriers to international trade (Point 3) were helpful to a rising commercial power. President Wilson also was forced by mounting Senate opposition to have a phrase inserted in the League of Nations Covenant (Article 21) explicitly asserting that the League did not supersede "regional understandings like the Monroe Doctrine."

Fear of Bolshevism

The third set of pragmatic considerations that influenced the Peace Conference was alarm about spreading revolution. This theme has received little attention in histories of the Peace Conference until relatively recently, when scholars like Arno Mayer began probing back to the 1917 to 1919 period for evidences of the beginnings of the Cold War.[6] The conference did, in fact, devote a lot of time and energy to the wave of revolutions apparently sweeping Europe in the spring of 1919, and to the question of how to deal with the new Soviet regime in Russia.

The German armies were not required at first to withdraw from former Russian territories in the east, even though the armistice terms demanded it. German troops remained in the Ukraine and in former Russian Poland until February 1919. They held some vital railroad lines

[6]Arno J. Mayer, *The Politics and Diplomacy of Peacemaking, Containment and Counterrevolution at Versailles, 1918–19* (New York, 1968).

in the Baltic region until the new governments of Estonia, Latvia, and Lithuania could assure their own stability in the summer of 1919. Thus, eight months after the armistice, a *Freikorps* of some 30,000 German volunteers under General Rüdiger von der Goltz was still on a war footing in the fluid borderlands of Eastern Europe, acting as *de facto* allies of the Western powers against the Bolsheviks.

This help did not win the Germans a role in the Versailles settlement as counterbalance to Russia. Instead, the Allies set up a *cordon sanitaire* of Eastern states whose function was to apply counterweight to both Germany and Soviet Russia. The new Poland spread beyond its ethnic frontiers to the east as well as to the west, especially after the French had helped Poland in the Russo-Polish War of 1920 and 1921. The new Czechoslovakia extended eastward to include Ruthenian people, closely related to Ukrainians; Romania acquired two ethnically related but mixed areas: Bessarabia from former Russian territory and Transylvania from Hungary. These new states were meant to keep both Bolsheviks and Germans bottled up within smaller frontiers.

The Peace Conference leaders' anti-Bolshevism was strong enough to make them forget their commitment to democracy in an emergency. In Hungary they acquiesced in the formation of a reactionary government as the most effective successor to Béla Kun's soviet experiment. Although it was Béla Kun himself who caused his own downfall by attacking the Romanian Army in Transylvania, the Allies imposed no effective restraint when the Romanians advanced into Budapest in August 1919 and expelled not only Kun but the moderate socialists who tried to govern after him. The Allies were willing to negotiate the Hungarian peace settlement with the Hungarian officers who took charge when the Romanians withdrew, men of the right without sympathy for any Wilsonian principle except anti-Bolshevism.

It will not do, of course, to make anti-Bolshevism the predominant motive in Paris. Four years of anti-German propaganda could not be forgotten in a moment, especially by the French. For many conservatives, the Bolsheviks' cardinal sin at first was helping Germany. In January 1919, the French *Action francaise* journalist Jacques Bainville rejoiced in the Spartacist uprising in Berlin, predicting that a soviet Germany would be weak and fragmented. Premier Clemenceau always waved away German warnings that a harsh peace would spread Bolshevism. Fear of Bolshevism did not win an easier peace for Germany nor produce a rapid thaw with the Germans as in 1947 to 1949.

The Settlement

The terms finally produced by the Peace Conference are known collectively as the Versailles Treaties, or the peace settlement of Paris. Actually, there were five separate treaties, one with each of the defeated states. Each bears the name of the palace near Paris where the formal signing ceremony took place. The first and most important was the <u>Treaty of Versailles, with Germany, signed on June 28, 1919,</u> in the Hall of Mirrors in that vast palace. Terms were reached with Austria in the Treaty of Saint Germain of September 10, 1919, and with Hungary in the Treaty of the Trianon on June 4, 1920, after the destruction of Béla Kun's Soviet regime. The Treaty of Neuilly with Bulgaria was signed on November 27, 1919. Last of all, delayed by the rise of a Turkish nationalist movement under Mustafa Kemal, was the Treaty of Sèvres with Turkey on August 10, 1920.

Instead of studying each treaty in detail, we shall look briefly at the terms as a whole, as they applied to Western and Eastern Europe. But

THE PEACE SETTLEMENTS IN EUROPE, 1919-1920

first we should consider the first major act of the conference, the
adoption of the League of Nations Covenant.

It was President Wilson who insisted that the first business of the
conference be the establishment of a permanent peacekeeping organization, a League of Nations. Considerable popular sentiment for basic
changes in the conduct of international relations stood behind this
proposal, and Wilson, the first president of the United States to visit
Europe while in office, invested all his personal prestige in it.

The principle of a League of Nations was unanimously adopted on
January 25, 1919. Drafting the exact terms of the League Covenant took
up much of the early months of that year. As finally adopted on April
28, the League of Nations Covenant created a General Assembly of all
member states[7] and a Council consisting of the five Great Powers plus
four other nations elected by the General Assembly. The League
members agreed to "respect and preserve" the territorial integrity of all
members—that is, to maintain the national boundaries as they existed
after the First World War. In case of disputes, the members of the
League bound themselves to submit to arbitration, judicial award, or
enquiry by the League Council, and they agreed not to go to war until
three months after such steps had been completed. If any League
member went to war in spite of these rules, the others were bound to
take "sanctions" against that member in the form of blockade or even
military action (Article 16). The League, however, was not sovereign. It
had no military force of its own, and it could not take action without
unanimous consent of the Council.

The League Covenant contained a number of other important
general provisions. The colonies and overseas territories of the defeated
nations were not awarded directly to the victors, as in the past, but
placed under the "tutelage" of the League, if they were "not yet able to
stand by themselves under the strenuous conditions of the modern
world" (Article 22). The "tutelage" was to be exercised by one of the
"advanced" nations under mandate from the League of Nations, to
which the mandatory power was supposed to report each year.

The Covenant set up three classes of mandates, graded according to
European conceptions of how "advanced" toward possible in-
dependence each territory was. Class A mandates were newly liberated
peoples expected to reach eventual independence, such as the non-
Turkish parts of the former Ottoman Empire. In a settlement closer to
the Sykes-Picot Agreement than to the British promises to the Arabs,
Syria and the Lebanon were mandated to France, the Tigris-Euphrates
Valley and Palestine to Britain. Class B mandates consisted of former
German colonies in Africa whose peoples were not expected to accede to

[7]Forty-two wartime allies and neutrals were invited to join at first. Germany was admitted
in 1926, and the Soviet Union joined in 1934.

independence within the foreseeable future, but which the treatymakers preferred not to have simply absorbed into the existing African empires. Most of Tanganyika (present-day Tanzania) was mandated to Britain, except for parts adjacent to the Congo, which Belgium was to administer. The West African areas of Togo and the Cameroons were divided between Britain and France as mandatory powers. Class C mandates consisted of former German possessions that were to pass directly under the laws of the mandatory power. South Africa obtained former German Southwest Africa under this provision, whose application is still hotly debated today. The German Pacific holdings north of the equator went to Japan; those south of the equator went to Australia and New Zealand.

Despite their obligation to administer these territories under League of Nations scrutiny, the mandatory powers tended to assimilate class B and class C mandates into the existing colonial system. Not one class A mandate had acceded to full independence twenty years later when the Second World War broke out, although Britain had extended a large measure of sovereignty to Iraq in 1932.

The League Covenant also called for general disarmament (Article 10). Further, the Minorities Commission of the conference promoted a series of treaties between the League and some member states with large national or religious minorities, guaranteeing those minorities protection against discrimination. An International Labor Office was established to report on conditions of work and wages. And a number of specialized agencies were created to deal with medical, humanitarian, and legal matters. In their modest way, these specialized agencies were the most lasting part of the League machinery.

As for its central function of peacekeeping machinery, the League of Nations was ambiguous from the beginning. It was torn between two irreconcilable conceptions. At one pole was the ideal of world government, empowered to keep its members from fighting among themselves, just as the federal government of the United States prevents fighting among the states. At the other extreme was Clemenceau's conception of an armed coalition of the victors designed to keep Germany permanently in check. The League as created fell somewhere in between. Its membership was too inclusive to act as a pro-French international policeman. Yet it was

MANDATES UNDER THE LEAGUE OF NATIONS

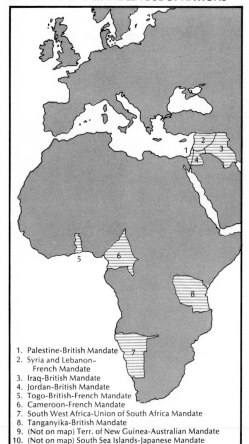

1. Palestine-British Mandate
2. Syria and Lebanon-
   French Mandate
3. Iraq-British Mandate
4. Jordan-British Mandate
5. Togo-British-French Mandate
6. Cameroon-French Mandate
7. South West Africa-Union of South Africa Mandate
8. Tanganyika-British Mandate
9. (Not on map) Terr. of New Guinea-Australian Mandate
10. (Not on map) South Sea Islands-Japanese Mandate

no world government. It remained a coalition of sovereign states. It was illusory to suppose that the nations of the world—some of which had just achieved statehood—would willingly delegate their sovereignty to a world body. Wilson himself, mindful of the eventual need for a Republican Senate to ratify the League Covenant along with the peace treaties, had no intention of giving up sovereignty. Before the League could act against an aggressor, the Council must first vote unanimously that aggression had been committed. Then member states must pledge forces to action in the League's name. In practice, the League could do only what all of its powerful members agreed to do.

Because the conference spent much of its early months drafting the covenant, more time was left for territorial settlements to be prejudiced by *faits accomplis.* Wilson was willing to make compromises in the territorial settlements to ensure the League's acceptance, however, for he believed that any faults in the treaties could be remedied later if the League were functioning properly.

The Western European Settlement

Wilson's Fourteen Points entered directly into the Franco-German settlement, for it was on their basis that Prince Max of Baden appealed for an armistice in October 1918. Only two points dealt with Western Europe specifically. Point 7 required that Belgium, the first victim, be "evacuated and restored." France, according to Point 8, should not only have its invaded territory freed and "restored," but the "wrong done to France in 1871" should be undone by the restoration to France of Alsace-Lorraine. The Western European settlement was more complicated than this, however, because of more pragmatic considerations.

The Attempt to Separate the Rhineland

The fact that Germany was militarily defeated, however late and unexpectedly, put the French Army in a position to shape the settlement by direct action. The armistice terms of November 11, 1918, drafted by the French inter-Allied commander in chief Marshal Ferdinand Foch with an eye for later, more permanent arrangements, authorized the Allied armies (largely French) to advance to the Rhine, to occupy three bridgeheads across it—at Mainz, Koblenz, and Cologne—and to establish a neutral zone on the other side of the Rhine.

Established on the Rhine, French officials worked directly to detach that area from Germany, although it is not clear with what authority they did so. They found some German Rhinelanders willing to cooperate. Hans Adam Dorten, former district attorney of Düsseldorf and spokesman for the Düsseldorf Industrialists' Club, prepared a Rhineland Constituent Assembly in February 1919. He had the support of some who thought they would be spared harsh peace terms, a few industrialists who wanted ties with France rather than with the socialist regime in Berlin or the soviet regime briefly in power in Bavaria, and Catholics who resented the domination of Protestant Prussia (including the young Catholic mayor of Cologne, Konrad Adenauer, who was to become West Germany's first chancellor thirty years later).

Marshal Foch went over Clemenceau's head to lobby in the conference for a separate Rhineland. But separatism was only a minority current in the German Rhineland, and Lloyd George and Wilson strenuously opposed a territorial settlement that threatened to create another cause for future revenge. The French delegate himself, Georges Clemenceau, overrode his determined military associate on this matter.

Territorial Changes

Actual territorial changes in Western Europe, therefore, were relatively limited. It was obvious that Alsace-Lorraine, which Louis XIV had conquered in the seventeenth century and which had remained French until the Germans took it in the Franco-Prussian War of 1870, would be returned wholly to France, despite some areas of Germanic dialect. The border communities of Eupen, Malmédy, and Moresnet were transferred to Belgium, the first victim in the west, although they were restored to Germany in 1926. Plebiscites were arranged for border areas taken from Denmark in 1864. The coal mines of the Saar, just across the border north of Lorraine, were placed in the possession of France for fifteen years as "compensation for the destruction of the coal mines in the north of France," after which the Saar population could vote on its national status. (It voted overwhelmingly to remain German when the plebiscite was held in 1935.) The territorial changes in the west left the map of Western Europe still recognizable to a European of 1914.

"Demilitarization" of Germany

Since France had failed to obtain the separation of the Rhineland, the conference tried to set up a physical barrier against future German military movement westward. The German territory west of the Rhine and a strip fifty kilometers wide (about thirty miles) on the east of the Rhine were demilitarized in perpetuity. German military forces would never be permitted to enter those parts of German soil. The "demilitarized zone" was intended to make a surprise German attack westward very difficult, while facilitating French movement east in case France wanted to rescue an Eastern ally. The Allied troops occupying the west bank of the Rhine would remain there for fifteen years. Furthermore, it was proposed that the United States and Great Britain extend treaties of guarantee to France by which they would aid France in the event of a German attack.

Beyond that, the settlement attempted to end Germany's military power. The German General Staff was dissolved. The German Navy was limited to no more than six battleships of 10,000 tons each, six light cruisers, and twelve destroyers. Germany was forbidden to manufacture or possess submarines, military aircraft, heavy artillery, tanks, and poison gas. The German Army was limited to 100,000 volunteers, required to serve for twelve years each so that Germany could not rebuild a large reserve of short-term recruits.

Reparations

A major extension beyond the Fourteen Points was the whole question of reparations. The devastation of northeastern France and other occupied areas, and the enormous debt run up by all the belligerents, made it tempting to try to get Germany to pay for reconstruction. Wilson's Fourteen Points had spoken in unclear terms of "restoring" the invaded parts of France and Belgium. When the Germans tried to make the Fourteen Points the basis of armistice negotiations in October 1918, the British and French, not overly enthusiastic about all of Wilson's aspirations, were willing to accept them only with the added demand

A British soldier patrols the Rhine, with the spires of Cologne Cathedral in the background. Allied forces were supposed to remain in occupation of the left bank of the Rhine for fifteen years after the signature of the Treaty of Versailles. The British evacuated the Cologne sector in December 1929. The Americans handed their sector (Koblenz) over to the French in January 1923. The French remained there and in their original sector (Mainz) until June 1930.

PASSING THE BUCK.

*The reparations problem, as seen by a
British cartoonist in 1923.*

that Germany make compensation "for all
damage done to the civilian population of
the Allies and their property by the aggression of Germany."[8]

In the "khaki election" of December
1918, Lloyd George demagogically promised the British public that the Germans
would pay for the war effort. French politicians went even further in assuring their
constituents that postwar taxes would not
have to be raised, since German reparations would pay for postwar reconstruction. These expectations placed reparations figures so much higher than the
German capacity to pay, however, that the
exact sum was not finally set until 1921.[9]
Although the other defeated nations were
also required to pay reparations, Germany
was expected to bear the lion's share. Reparations were to become a major focus of
antagonism against the way in which the Versailles settlement was
applied to Germany.

The Eastern European Settlement

Territorial Changes

While minor adjustments were being made in the ancient Franco-
German frontier in the west, the map of Eastern Europe was being
entirely redrawn. The Paris Peace Conference presided over the most
extensive revision of frontiers of modern European history except for
the Vienna Conference of 1815, and, unlike the Vienna settlement, it
enlarged the number of states in Europe instead of diminishing them.
The proud empires that had controlled Eastern Europe had been
destroyed. The German borders were pulled back hundreds of miles
westward, giving up much of Silesia and East Prussia. The Russian
border remained far to the east of the 1914 frontier, where Imperial
Germany had imposed it in the Treaty of Brest-Litovsk,[10] for the
Western Allies were happy to accept the anti-Bolshevik consequences of
German victory in the east. The Austro-Hungarian Empire disappeared
from the map altogether. New nation-states took the place of parts of
these three empires in the north and center: Finland, Latvia, Estonia,
Lithuania, Poland, Czechoslovakia, Austria, and Hungary. In the Bal-

[8]Memorandum of Observation by the Allied Governments, November 5, 1918.
[9]See Chapter 8, pp. 221–23.
[10]The Soviet regime subsequently improved its border slightly at the expense of Poland in
the Russo-Polish War of 1920 and 1921, and recovered most of the rest of tsarist
territories, roughly speaking, during the Second World War.

DESTRUCTION OF THE EMPIRES

RUSSIA

1914

SWEDEN — FINLAND — Baltic Sea — St. Petersburg — ESTONIA — LATVIA — Moscow — LITHUANIA — RUSSIA — GERMANY — POLAND — BESSARABIA — AUSTRIA-HUNGARY — ROMANIA — Black Sea — OTTOMAN EMPIRE — Adriatic Sea

1921

SWEDEN — FINLAND — Baltic Sea — Petrograd — ESTONIA — LATVIA — Moscow — EAST PRUSSIA — LITHUANIA — SOVIET RUSSIA — GERMANY — POLAND — UKRAINE Ceded at Brest-Litovsk, reoccupied in 1920 — CZECHOSLOVAKIA — HUNGARY — ROMANIA — YUGOSLAVIA — Black Sea — Adriatic Sea — BULGARIA

AUSTRO-HUNGARIAN EMPIRE IN 1914

Vienna • Budapest

AUSTRIA AND HUNGARY IN 1919

Vienna • Budapest

• Berlin

GERMANY IN 1914

Berlin •

GERMANY IN 1919

kans, Romania gained territory from Hungary, Russia, and Bulgaria, while Serbia—where the war had begun—became the root stock of a large new South Slav state, the Kingdom of Serbs, Croats, and Slovenes, later known as Yugoslavia.

The principle on which the makers of postwar Eastern Europe claimed to base their work was the self-determination of nations, as promised in President Wilson's Fourteen Points and subsequent statements. The practice did not always fit the principle. Even more than the Western European settlement, the postwar settlement in Eastern Europe was influenced by the national interests of the victors, prior commitments, *faits accomplis* by Eastern European national movements, and the noncommunist states' desire to keep Bolshevik Russia at bay.

Frontier Problems

The application of the principle of self-determination was complicated in Eastern Europe by the absence of neat ethnic frontiers. In the west, states had been consolidated prior to the appearance of mass nationalism. Their central governments had subsequently been able to impose a single language and national loyalty on the varied peoples within their borders through education and common experience. In Eastern Europe, national consciousness grew up in the nineteenth century around folk languages and dialects, at cross purposes with existing state frontiers or economic relations. Forming new states along national lines in Eastern Europe would have been easy if an ethnic or linguistic map had revealed sharp, unshaded borders. That state of affairs was rare enough along the relatively stable borders of Western Europe; it was rarer still in Eastern Europe. The "clearly recognizable lines of nationality" of President Wilson's Point 9 often clashed with the "historically established lines of allegiance and nationality" of Point 11.

The case of Teschen, a small mining area claimed by both the new Poland and the new Czechoslovakia, shows how intractable some border issues were. Although not part of Bohemia proper, Teschen had been ruled for 500 years by the kings of Bohemia. "Historically established lines of allegiance" suggested that it pass with Bohemia to the new Czechoslovakia. The 1910 census, however, reported that 56 percent of the inhabitants of Teschen were Polish-speaking; 26 percent, Czech-speaking; and 18 percent, German-speaking. The principle of national self-determination thus seemed to favor the Poles, even though ethnic and linguistic censuses were notoriously uncertain and somewhat arbitrarily assigned the speakers of intermediate Czech-Polish dialects to one side or the other. To introduce a third criterion, the Teschen area was economically linked to the banks and markets of Vienna. Vienna, however, was being reduced from an imperial capital and regional center to the overgrown capital city of the small nation of Austria.

Since history, language, and economic links gave conflicting answers to the question of Teschen's proper national identity, the solution was left to the traditional means of international politics: force or bargaining. The Versailles settlement split Teschen approximately in two, in a judgment of Solomon that satisfied no one. The Poles and Czechs fought over Teschen in 1919 and 1920. Later, in 1938, when the Czechs were preoccupied with German claims to German-speaking areas in Bohemia, the Poles simply stepped in and took the rest of Teschen by force.

The list of frontier problems in Eastern Europe complicated by national self-determination was endless. In much of Eastern Europe, cities and commercial and industrial life had developed under strong German influence. Local ethnic groups prevailed in the countryside. For example, industrial development in Silesia took place in the nineteenth century, after that part of Poland had been seized by Prussia in the eighteenth century. The entrepreneurs and merchants were German, and many Silesian Polish families were assimilated into German culture as they became miners or factory workers in new industry. The peasantry, however, remained Polish. How could Silesia's national identity be established in 1919? How could a homogeneous nation-state

EUROPEAN NATIONALITY PROBLEMS, 1919-1939

Polish
German
Russian
Serbian
Croatian
Slovenian
Bosnian
Macedonian
Bulgarian
Hungarian
Romanian
Albanian
Czechoslovakian

MILES
0   200

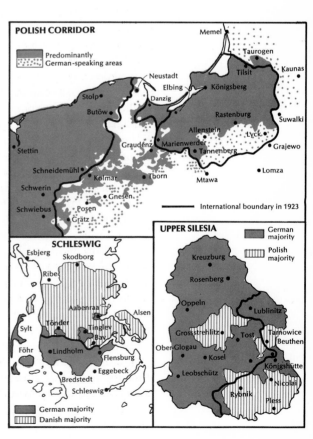

POLISH CORRIDOR

Predominantly German-speaking areas

International boundary in 1923

SCHLESWIG

German majority
Danish majority

UPPER SILESIA

German majority
Polish majority

be built on this urban–rural cultural and national division? A similar problem arose with the promise to Poland of access to the sea. The largely German port city of Danzig was imbedded in a region of Polish peasantry.

The task of recomposing Eastern Europe on the basis of a separate state for each nationality—so appealing from afar—revealed all sorts of ugly complications as the delegates to the Paris Peace Conference consulted their maps and listened to the experts and the spokesmen for the nationalities. An Eastern Europe of independent nations, drawn to the satisfaction of every claimant, was probably beyond human wisdom in 1919, even if the Versailles peacemakers had been totally free from any other kinds of considerations. Other considerations had a major influence on the settlement, however.

Discrimination among Nationalities

To begin, not all nationalities in Eastern Europe received equal recognition. Those whose national consciousness was reborn in the nineteenth century—Poles and Czechs—had already won strong emotional acceptance in Western Europe from the days of Chopin and the Czech poet Adam Mickiewicz in the 1840s. Others, such as the Croats or Slovaks, were only beginning to arrive at national or linguistic self-consciousness. Still others, such as the Slovenes, had hardly begun to claim to be a separate people. In any event, where would the process of atomization end if the speakers of every local dialect developed a fierce separatist consciousness?

The Eastern European nationalities also differed in the services they had performed for the Allies during the war. Although Poles had fought on both sides at the beginning, the fall of Tsarist Russia brought the strongest force, Marshal Josef Pilsudski's Polish Legion, into action against Germany at the end. Czechs taken prisoner on the Russian front formed a pro-Allied army in Russia in 1918. "Gallant Serbia" had been the Central Powers' first victim. Although independent Romania had joined the war on the Allied side in 1916, it was defeated and signed a separate peace in May 1918. Did Romania still deserve the advantages promised in 1916 by the Allies? On the other side of the ledger stood Austria and Hungary, which had made war against Serbia in the first place, and Bulgaria, whose king had dragged it reluctantly into the war on the Central Powers' side. Hungary was doubly damned by having formed a soviet in May 1919, at the very moment its borders were on the drafting boards in Paris.

France had the largest stake in discriminating among favored and disfavored nationalities in Eastern Europe. French diplomacy and armed forces were more active in Eastern Europe than those of any other Great Power. As the chief land power of the Continent, principal victim and principal rival of Germany, France desired strong allies on Germany's eastern frontiers. Such allies would permit the French to

Escorted by veterans of the Czech Legion that fought in Russia, Thomas Masaryk enters Prague in 1919 to assume the presidency of the Czechoslovakian republic.

continue their strategy of threatening a resurgent Germany with a two-front war. Since France's major Eastern ally since 1892, Russia, was now materially weak and politically hostile, French security planners built on maximum satisfaction for Poland, Czechoslovakia, Yugoslavia, and Romania. If these states were made as strong as possible, even at the expense of some valid nationality claims, French security needs would be doubly served, against Germany and against Bolshevik Russia.

With tacit Allied acceptance and even support, the favored Eastern European nationalities embarked in the closing days of the war on a round of "claim-jumping" in which they established a *de facto* military presence in disputed areas. On October 6, 1918, the South Slavs set up the National Committee of Croats, Slovenes, and Serbs to establish sovereignty in the former South Slavic areas of the Habsburg Empire. The Czech national committee set itself up in Prague as a government in October 1918; in January 1919 it was fighting with Polish forces over Teschen. The Poles, remembering the vast medieval Kingdom of Poland, attempted from 1919 to 1921 to conquer parts of Lithuania and the Ukraine to form a Great Confederation. The Romanians, who had taken Bessarabia from the Soviet Russians in 1918, went on in July 1919 to seize Transylvania from Hungary. Thus before the Peace Conference opened and while it sat, future boundaries were set by direct action in Eastern Europe, with Allied, and especially French, complicity.

At the conference, France took the lead in favoring a strong Poland, Czechoslovakia, Romania, and Yugoslavia. Clemenceau pressed for Polish expansion in Silesia and right up to the Baltic in a corridor of clearly Germanic population. Lloyd George, worried about creating future ethnic trouble spots, forced the conference to provide for plebiscites in Silesia and for the separate status of German-speaking Danzig as a free city. As for Czechoslovakia, the French supported the integral inclusion of historic Bohemia despite large numbers of Germans along the western border, and prevented any consideration of separate Czech and Slovak nations. The spokesman for Slovak separatism, the Catholic priest Father Andrej Hlinka, was hustled out of Paris by French police. The same treatment was accorded Stepan Radič, the spokesman for a separate Croatia instead of a great Yugoslavia. The largest possible Romanian claims were also supported at the conference.

The resulting map of Eastern Europe, therefore, was not an even-handed application of the principle of self-determination, even if such a thing had been possible. On the one hand were a large Poland, created at the expense not only of Germany and Russia but also of Lithuania; a large Czechoslovakia, including an extensive German minority; an enlarged Romania, which had grown at the expense of Russia and especially Hungary; and a large Yugoslavia of Serbs, Croats, and Slovenes, united mainly in opposition to Vienna. On the other hand were a truncated remnant of Hungary; the German remnant of Austria, forbidden to exercise its own national self-determination by joining Germany; and a diminished Bulgaria.

The Settlement Assessed

The peacemakers at Paris worked under the multiple disadvantages of high emotions, time pressure, and a fluid situation of daunting complexity. Their work has had its defenders. Its main outlines survived a second war and Russian domination of Eastern Europe, and it is difficult to deny the legitimacy of the new and revived Eastern European states without denying the very principle of national self-determination. As the American historian Paul Birdsall wrote in 1941, the Versailles settlement in Eastern Europe was "the closest approximation to an ethnographic map of Europe that had ever been achieved."[11] Nor can all the problems of interwar Eastern Europe be attributed to the peacemakers' work. Like all new nations, the successor states had to contend with inexperienced leaders and economic backwardness. But the Versailles settlement did replace the old problems of subject peoples within the Habsburg Empire with a whole Pandora's box of new problems. And it failed in its most immediate, practical test: a second global war grew out of Eastern European border disputes twenty years later.

One problem was that the whole settlement rested on the unprecedented and temporary eclipse of Germany and Russia. Neither of these acutely self-conscious peoples with traditions of power was about to accept the eastern frontiers. Marshal Hindenburg and others in Germany wanted to return to war when the annexations of German territory for Poland were announced; even those Germans in favor of

[11]Paul Birdsall, *Versailles Twenty Years After* (New York, 1941), p. 9.

accepting the Treaty of Versailles had reservations about the frontiers. Russia never accepted the loss of Bessarabia to Romania, which cut Russia off from the mouth of the Danube. These highly artificial geographic arrangements could subsist only if propped up from outside. Since Britain and the United States were unwilling to participate in direct action in Eastern Europe, France was left with a potential burden far beyond its capacities to handle, even in 1919.

Furthermore, the settlement left numerous local grievances on which a renascent Germany and Russia would be able to play. The nations of Eastern Europe were divided between the wars into *status quo* states and revisionist states. Poland, Czechoslovakia, Romania, and Yugoslavia looked to France to help maintain the *status quo.* Hungary, and to some degree Bulgaria, sought every avenue for change. Even after Béla Kun's collapse, no Hungarian regime could exist that failed to preach revision of the treaties. Admiral Miklós Horthy, Hungary's strong man between the wars, emerged from isolation first in 1927 with ties to Mussolini's Italy; eventually he looked to Hitler's Germany for help.

Another problem was that every one of the new states contained national minorities. Poland had its German minorities in the part of Silesia it eventually won in plebiscites. The minorities in Czechoslovakia were especially ominous. Nearly one-quarter of the population, 3 out of 13 million, was German,[12] mostly concentrated in the western border-land of Bohemia (the Sudetenland). The subordinate role of the Slovaks in the new state was another potential irritant. The new Czech president, Edouard Beneš, liked to claim that Czechoslovakia was an "Eastern European Switzerland," in which different language groups could live together in a progressive, democratic federal state. Potentially, the new Czechoslovakia was another Austria-Hungary in miniature. For a time, Czechoslovakia was the most democratic and prosperous of the new states. The depression and Hitler's agitation pulled the nationalities apart, however. After Hitler had annexed the German-speaking areas in 1938, the Slovaks went their own way to form a separate state in 1940. The Yugoslav peoples also separated during the Second World War. The Croats formed a separate state in 1941 under Hitler's protection.

One more problem was the effect of new national boundaries on the Eastern European economy. Old economic ties were broken by the profusion of new states, and new channels of trade and finance had to be opened. The Austro-Hungarian Empire, formerly a trading unity, was now seven units, each with its own frontiers, customs officers, and commercial regulations. For example, the Slovak iron miners, who had shipped their ore to Budapest under the old regime, now redirected their trade to Prague. These dislocations might have been temporary and the whole area might have once more functioned as an economic unit in prosperity, but the strains of new statehood were soon compounded by the first harbinger of depression in the late 1920s, the

[12]Elizabeth Wiskemann, *Czechs and Germans,* 2nd ed. (Oxford, 1967), p. 124.

decline of agricultural prices. The new states subsequently erected ever higher protectionist barriers against one another. Economists began to talk nostalgically about the economic benefits of the old empire as it became apparent that the prospect of a Danube basin free-trade area was receding from possibility.

There remained one final issue. The Wilsonian ideal of self-determination of peoples assumed that new nations would automatically be democratic, with freely elected governments resting on the will of the newly independent people. This proved a misplaced hope in Eastern Europe. Societies were poorly amalgamated. Most of the areas were still predominantly agricultural, with extensive estates and land-hungry peasants. Cities often contained large ethnic minorities, Germans and Jews. Only Czechoslovakia had a sizable industrial base and a fairly smoothly functioning middle-class democracy, at least among the dominant Czechs; elsewhere, the new republics fell into the hands of strong men or resurgent authoritarian monarchs, with the acquiescence of Western Allies more fearful of Bolshevism than eager for social reform.

At first sight, the Eastern European settlement seemed the fulfillment of nineteenth-century progressive hopes: national independence and internal democracy. But with respect both to frontiers and to internal regimes, the question was not whether they would change but when, and whether the pressures for change would plunge the rest of Europe into war again.

Suggestions for Further Reading

A good brief summary of the Paris Peace Conference, impregnated with Wilsonian hopes and disappointments, is Paul Birdsall, *Versailles Twenty Years After* (1941). The massive H. W. V. Temperley, ed., *History of the Peace Conference*, 6 vols. (1920–24) is still basic. It needs to be counterbalanced by the French perspective in André Tardieu, *The Truth About the Treaty* (1921), and by David Lloyd George, *The Truth About the Peace Treaties* (1938).

The proceedings themselves may be followed in Paul Mantoux, ed., *Proceedings of the Council of Four* (1964), and, more completely, in the notes of the secretary to the British delegation, Sir Maurice Hankey, published in U.S., Department of State, *Foreign Relations of the United States*, "The Paris Peace Conference, 1919," vols. 3–6 (1943–46).

Harold Nicolson, *Peacemaking, 1919,** new ed. (1945) remains the most evocative of participants' memoirs. John Maynard Keynes's criticism in *The Economic Consequences of the Peace** (1920) is criticized in turn by Étienne Mantoux, *The Carthaginian Peace* (1946).

Recent scholarship has emphasized the effect on the peace settlement of social tensions within states, and of fear of the spread of communist revolution. Arno J. Mayer, *The Political Origins of the New Diplomacy, 1917–1918** (1959) shows the impact on Allied propaganda and war aims of Lenin's peace proposals. Mayer's *The Politics and Diplomacy of Peacemaking* (1968) traces the theme of defense of the social order through 1919. For the politics of German acceptance of the terms, see Klaus Epstein, *Matthias Erzberger and the Dilemma of German Democracy* (1959). See also Harold I. Nelson, *Land and Power: British and Allied Diplomacy on Germany's Frontiers, 1916–1919* (1963).

F. P. Walters, *The League of Nations*, 2 vols. (1952) is the standard history.

The peace settlement in Eastern Europe is best approached in the works on the defeat of the Habsburg Empire cited at the end of Chapter 5. In addition, the following are useful: Ivo J. Lederer, *Yugoslavia at the Paris Peace Conference* (1964); opening sections of C. A. Macartney, *October Fifteenth: A History of Modern Hungary, 1929–1945*, 2 vols. (1957); and Hans Roos, *A History of Modern Poland* (1966).

7 REVOLUTION AGAINST REVOLUTION: FASCISM

The revolutionary wave in Europe after 1917 generated a counterrevolutionary response at once. But postwar counterrevolution did not mean the return to religion and to social deference with which nineteenth-century traditional conservatives had tried to meet revolutionary threats. There was a new name—*fascism*—and behind it, a new reality. Fascism put together mass movements, nationalism, antisocialism, and antiliberal values in largely unforeseen ways.

Mass politics had entered European history in the nineteenth century on the left. The values of nineteenth-century middle- and lower-middle-class Europeans tended to be liberal: they invested great hopes in the ballot box; in universal, secular, public education; and in the

Members of the new Fascist boys' movement, the Figli della Lupa *(Roman Wolf's Sons), parading with miniature rifles before Benito Mussolini on the twentieth anniversary of the Italian entry into the First World War, May 1935.*

self-determination of nations. In the 1890s, many working-class and lower–middle-class Europeans became attracted to the new socialist parties. Their electoral success enabled Karl Marx's collaborator and successor Friedrich Engels to believe in 1895 that "we shall conquer the greater part of the middle strata of society, petty bourgeois and small peasants, and grow into the decisive power in the land."[1] The broadening of citizen participation in politics, as the middle and lower classes expanded, seemed to promise an indefinite progression of European mass politics toward the left. Nineteenth-century conservatives, with some exceptions, had preferred a passive citizenry. A European familiar with the political landscape up to 1890, suddenly transplanted to a mass rally of the 1920s or 1930s in which an aroused crowd bayed its approval of a uniformed leader's harangue against socialists, intellectuals, foreigners, and Jews, might have believed himself on another planet.

With the advantages of hindsight, it is possible to see a number of ways in which fascism was prepared by late–nineteenth-century developments. We shall look back to these precursors later in this chapter. But first, to recapture the sense of newness and urgency with which fascist movements sprang up in the disorder of postwar Europe, it seems best to take a close look at the movement that provided the name, Italian

[1]Friedrich Engels' 1895 introduction to Karl Marx, *The Class Struggles in France, 1848–1850* (New York, 1964).

fascism, and at two important similar movements of the years 1919 to 1923 in Germany and Hungary.

Fascism in Italy   Many Italians were disillusioned at the close of the First World War by the costs of an inconclusive victory, and they bitterly confronted one another over social and national issues after the armistice.[2] The strikes and factory occupations of 1919 and 1920 and the land seizures of 1919 seemed to be leading toward an Italian socialist revolution. Meanwhile, Gabriele D'Annunzio's seizure of Fiume in 1919 proved to militant nationalists that they could shove aside a faltering state and get what they wanted by direct action. In that chaos was born Benito Mussolini's Fascist movement.

Mussolini: From Syndicalism to Fascism

When asked to define fascism, Mussolini liked to say, "I am Fascism." So it is appropriate to begin this discussion with a look at the leader himself. He was born in the traditionally volatile *Romagna* region northeast of Rome to a schoolteacher and an anarchist blacksmith, who named him after the Mexican revolutionary Benito Juarez. Unlike his German imitator Hitler, Mussolini had achieved some prewar status. He had become a leading figure on the Italian left before he was thirty. He became editor of the Socialist party newspaper *Avanti!* (*Forward!*) at the end of 1912, and quadrupled its readership to 100,000 over the next two years. In 1913 he was elected to the city council of Milan, Italy's largest industrial city.

By political persuasion and temperament, Mussolini was syndicalist rather than socialist. Syndicalism was an individualistic, antiauthoritarian movement of revolt endemic to rural artisans, agricultural laborers, railroad workers, and miners in France, Italy, and Spain. Syndicalists were bitterly hostile not only to parliamentary, reformist socialists but also to the Marxist strategy of attempting to take over the state. They wanted to dissolve the state, not take it over. Their strategy rested on bringing down the whole immoral world of property with one apocalyptic "great day," a mass general strike. Then they would replace the state, not with another authority as previous revolutionists had done from the Jacobins to the Leninists, but with a free community in which the only organizations would be workers' associations (*syndicats*) exchanging goods and services among themselves. Syndicalism's inchoate millenarian revolutionism was particularly deeply rooted in the *Romagna*, and as a student the young Mussolini further steeped himself in the French syndicalist George Sorel's cult of action, in a vulgarized Nietzschean exaltation of will, and in Bergsonian faith in intuition. It was actually easier for a syndicalist to pass to the far right than to subside into

---

[2]See Chapter 5, pp. 156–59.

moderation, and Mussolini never lost his impatient contempt for parliaments and his intransigent activism through a lifetime of political metamorphoses.

Mussolini was named editor of *Avanti!* in December 1912 when Italian syndicalists won control of the Italian Socialist party machinery from parliamentary socialists, some of whom had discredited themselves by supporting the Italian conquest of Libya. He was expelled from the party two years later, however, when in a characteristic about-face, he urged Italian entry into the First World War on the Allied side. Mussolini had become a "national syndicalist." His nationalism had grown during a period of political organizing in Italian-speaking areas of the Austrian Alps—the Trentino area that Italian nationalists called *Italia irredenta* (unredeemed Italy). Moreover, war seemed to his impatient temperament a more revolutionary state than passive neutrality. His new prowar newspaper, *Il Popolo d'Italia,* got money from France, although this seems to have come afterward as reward rather than beforehand as bribe, as sometimes alleged.

In 1918 Mussolini was one of millions of veterans finding their way in the dislocations of demobilization. Since he had seen some front-line service, and had been wounded accidentally but painfully when a howitzer shell went off prematurely in the barrel (he characteristically dramatized this as "forty-four wounds" by counting every fragment), his *Popolo d'Italia* had some claim to speak for veterans. With the peace settlement at hand, Mussolini joined the annexationist chorus, calling Italy a "proletarian nation" that must expropriate the colonies of rich nations. His social criticism reflected the veterans' bitterness at war profiteers, pacifists, and the comfortable. Mussolini thought that the floating mass of veterans could be harnessed to a movement that would be both left and nationalist.

> The bourgeois revolution of 1789—which was revolution and war in one—opened the gates of the world to the bourgeoisie. . . . The present revolution, which is also a war, seems to open the gates of the future to the masses, who have served their hard apprenticeship of blood and death in the trenches.[3]

Early Fascism

The first *fasci*[4] were formed on March 23, 1919, when Mussolini gathered 145 friends in an upstairs room in Milan. There were a number of old syndicalist faithful who had shared his prowar attitudes in 1914, to whom were added veterans especially oriented toward chauvinism and direct action, such as the former *arditi* (commandos). The Milan *arditi* had their headquarters in the home of the futurist

---

[3]*Il Popolo d'Italia,* March 1919, quoted in Christopher Seton-Watson, *Italy from Liberalism to Fascism, 1870–1925* (London, 1967), p. 517.
[4]*Fasci Italiani de Combattimento. Fascio* was simply a Latinate word for "bundle," or, by extension to politics, a closely knit band, unlike a party. Its usage had been largely left wing, as in the Sicilian anarchist *Fasci di combattimento* of 1894.

Benito Mussolini during a speech from the balcony of the Palazzo Venezia in Rome.

painter Filippo Marinetti, whose adulation of speed and violence helped set the intellectual tone.[5]

The fascist program, which was drafted by the prowar syndicalist Alceste De Ambris, mixed nationalism and social radicalism with impatient yearning to sweep away discredited prewar institutions. It demanded just Italian rewards for its victory—acquisition of *Italia irredenta* lands in the Alps and along the Dalmation coast. It also called for a constituent assembly, the vote for women, abolition of the Senate, a tax on capital, an eight-hour day in industry, workers' share in control of factories, confiscation of Church property, and a redistribution of land for peasants. The Italian Socialist party, from which Mussolini had been expelled in 1914, was attacked with a special loathing proper to a syndicalist renegade. Mussolini now joined nationalist war veterans in denouncing socialist moderation on Italian war aims as "renunciation," or betrayal of the soldiers.

Deeds spoke even louder than the caustic words of the *Popolo d'Italia.* Mussolini and Marinetti deliberately wrecked a socialist meeting at La Scala Opera House in Milan on January 11, 1919, and in April a group of *arditi* led by Marinetti sacked and burned the editorial offices of

[5]See Chapter 1, pp. 42–43, and Chapter 4, p. 123.

Avanti!. Still, Mussolini supported workers' demands at the grass roots and publicly backed several sit-down strikes in which the workers themselves carried on production. It was not yet clear in 1919 whether fascism was meant to be a rival to socialism on the left or its enemy on the right.

Early fascism's blend of radicalism and nationalism failed to gain many recruits in 1919. As an independent candidate for parliament from Milan in November 1919, running on a program that mixed antiliberalism and antisocialism with attacks on big business, Mussolini got fewer than 5000 votes out of 270,000. Less than 1000 members remained active in the *fasci* at the end of 1919.

Fascism's New Course

It was the near civil war of 1919 and 1920 that set fascism on a new course and made its fortunes. Mussolini found that his group's physical attacks on socialists aroused more interest and more support than his radical language. The strikes and land seizures of 1919 had created genuine panic among the factory- and landowners. The turning point came with the workers' occupation of factories in Turin and Milan in August and September 1920.[6] Although Prime Minister Giovanni Giolitti had successfully waited it out, so that the "factory council" movement burned itself out quickly, his unhurried calm had heightened the panicky owners' conviction that the liberal state could not save them. After the threat to their property had begun to subside, the owners of factories and land began to take matters into their own hands. To help them, they called on Mussolini's direct-action bands, the *squadristi*.

Mussolini had organized his *squadristi* in the supernationalistic Adriatic frontier territories. They saw their first action in Trieste in July 1920, where they sacked the headquarters of a Slovene nationalist association. It was a simple matter to switch from beating Slavs to beating socialists. Moreover, the *squadristi* received money from the landowners and industrialists for this purpose, as well as trucks and equipment from the Army. Through late 1920 and 1921, they exercised their war-learned brutalities on Italian socialists.

The *squadristi* were most active in the small towns and country villages of northeastern Italy, where local landowners used them to break up farm laborers' unions and cooperatives. Their "punitive expeditions" set off at night in borrowed trucks, manned by nationalist veterans, the unemployed, and sons of threatened landowners. At their destination, they beat socialist or left-Catholic organizers, often administering a near lethal dose of castor oil, or shaving off half a moustache. There were a few fatalities, but mostly the *squadristi* destroyed the offices or presses of their enemies. During the first six months of 1921, to take one period for which there are statistics, Mussolini's toughs destroyed twenty-five cooperative apartment houses, fifty-nine local labor clubhouses, eighty-

[6]See Chapter 5, p. 157.

five cooperatives, thirty-four headquarters of agricultural workers' unions, fifty-one political party headquarters, ten printing works, and six newspaper offices, mostly in rural north-central Italy.

Although Mussolini denied that the Fascists had become "watchdogs of capitalism," some of the economic radicals and revolutionary syndicalists of the first days dropped away, as did Marinetti. Their places were taken by a horde of frankly right-wing newcomers. Membership in the *fasci* mounted to 30,000 in 1920 and to ten times that, 300,000, by the end of 1922.

Governmental Crisis

Premier Giolitti tried to practice on the burgeoning Fascist movement the same coopting strategy that had worked with the reformist left in the course of his long parliamentary career. Giolitti believed that, like the factory occupations in 1920, fascism would lose its vehemence with time and experience. He drew Mussolini into an electoral coalition with his Liberal party and the Nationalists. In Italy's second postwar election on May 15, 1921, Giolitti's National Bloc won 105 seats out of a total of 535, of which Mussolini and the Fascists had 35. At first, Giolitti had reason to believe that he had tamed fascism and yoked it to his parliamentary coalition. Mussolini had already acceded to Giolitti's compromise over Fiume in 1920, and the Fascists had done nothing when Italian troops forced D'Annunzio's volunteers to give up the city. During 1921 Mussolini also made some attempt to curb the *squadristi*. That movement was almost beyond his control, however, and the local militants repeatedly forced Mussolini's hand by undertaking more raids.

At the same time, the parliamentary monarchy was proving incapable of governing postwar Italy. Postwar ministries had been unable to maintain law and order against either the revolutionary left or the vigilante right. The 1921 elections made things even worse by returning a parliament with no possible coherent majority. The center liberal and democratic parties had no majority by themselves. Socialists, with 123 seats, refused to participate in any bourgeois ministry. The most important newcomer on the Italian political scene was the left Catholic *Popolari* party of Don Luigi Sturzo, with 108 seats. But their demands for social reforms like land redistribution made coalition with Giolitti's Liberals impossible. And although some of Sturzo's followers were more radical than some socialists, the Church–state issue blocked any coalition between the *Popolari* and the anticlerical left. Giolitti, the personification of prewar centrist coalition politics, found no stable majority and left office in June 1921 for good at the age of seventy-eight.

For the next fourteen months, Italians endured a lingering governmental crisis, while postwar internal problems went unsolved. Demobilization and the end of wartime production had thrown Italy into economic depression. Rising unemployment and the defeats of 1919 and 1920 left Italian workers bitter and apathetic. Resentments seethed among returning veterans and a middle class pinched by inflation and fearful of revolution. Italians looking to the government for salvation saw only an unedifying round of fruitless coalition-mending among parliamentary factions. No government at all could be formed during the first three weeks of February 1922, the longest ministerial crisis up to that time in Italy. After August 1922, there was only a caretaker ministry under a colorless Giolitti lieutenant, Luigi Facta, who governed without a majority.

The *squadristi* helped make Italy ungovernable during 1922. Local Fascists in northeastern Italy had now developed their own momentum of "punitive expeditions." The local leaders, called *ras* after Ethiopian feudal chieftains, resented Mussolini's attempts to curb their activities from his seat in parliament. Encouraged by local conservatives and army commanders, they now took over entire towns, expelling socialist or Communist mayors and councils. In May 1922, Italo Balbo, one of the most brutal of the *ras,* mobilized 50,000 unemployed in a "fascist strike" that held the town hall of Ferrara for a week until the local prefect had promised to hire them all on public works projects. At the end of May, he did the same with the Communist city government of Bologna. In July, Fascists took over Rimini, Cremona, and Ravenna, and in August, briefly, Milan. By the early fall of 1922, Fascists had become the *de facto* local government in parts of northern Italy.

The concentration of early Fascist power in north-central and northeastern Italy (Emilia, Tuscany, *Romagna*) is significant. It follows rather closely the region of maximum revolutionary agitation and conservative backlash in 1919 and 1920, especially areas where land tenure was threatened, as in the Po Valley. Such workers' strongholds as Turin remained closed to Fascist influence, and the underdeveloped south was almost untouched by it. Where it was strong, however, fascism exposed the incapacity of the Italian government to have its orders carried out.

The "March on Rome"

Mussolini, struggling to remain in control of his followers, heightened the governmental crisis by talking vaguely but incessantly about a "march on Rome." He suggested that, just as the *squadristi* had marched on Bologna and other cities to clear out leftists, they would march on the capital to clear out incompetents. The Fascist Congress of October 1922 in Naples (the movement's first penetration of the south) went beyond talk. A high command of four Fascist leaders—*quadrumvirs* in the grandiose Latinisms that the movement relished—laid plans for three Fascist columns to converge on Rome during the night of October 27. The *quadrumvirs* themselves were a cross section of what Fascist personnel had become: Italo Balbo, former officer of Alpine troops and *ras* of Ferrara, stood for disgruntled veterans. Michele Bianchi had been a revolutionary syndicalist; he stood for fascism's roots in the antiparliamentary left. General Emilio De Bono came from the regular Army.

Cesare De Vecchi, the organizer of fascism in Piedmont, was an avowed monarchist who stood for fascism's more recent recruits among traditional conservatives disillusioned by parliamentary monarchy.

It was not by a "march on Rome," however, that Mussolini became prime minister of Italy on October 30. He arrived by Pullman car from Milan, after King Victor Emmanuel III had asked him to form a government in due constitutional form. The "march on Rome" was a threat, not a *coup d'état.* The threat exposed Prime Minister Luigi Facta's dependence on dubious Army support for survival. Rather than test that support, the king preferred to ask Mussolini himself to take over the task of maintaining order. The Fascist columns did not conquer Rome by force. Small, dispirited in a steady rain, and still apprehensive of the Army's reaction, they entered the city only after Mussolini had been legally invested with the office of prime minister.

How had this marginal agitator of 1919 become the head of the Italian government in October 1922? Mussolini's success was due partly to the absence of alternatives. A resolutely anti-Fascist government was possible only on condition that the socialists and the Catholic *Popolari* submerge their differences over religion. Only at the last minute, when it was too late, did the reformist socialists express a willingness to participate in an anti-Fascist coalition, but this act split their party. The governmental coalitions that were possible preferred to coopt Mussolini rather than block him. In October 1922, Giolitti was busy behind the scenes directing one more combination to include Fascists in a new ministry, but he offered Mussolini only a few seats, and he negotiated with pre-1914 slowness. Mussolini was encouraged to hold out for more by the fact that wartime Prime Minister Antonio Salandra was simultaneously bargaining with him to bring the Fascists into a more frankly conservative coalition.

Mussolini's bedraggled *squadristi* might have been kept out of Rome and Mussolini left waiting by his telephone in Milan on October 29, had Prime Minister Facta and the king acted resolutely against them. There is good reason to think that the Army would have obeyed an order by the king to disperse the *squadristi,* whatever the private feelings of many officers. The king bears a heavy responsibility for refusing to test the Army's obedience. Encouraged by the queen, and nervous about reports that his cousin the Duke of Aosta was maneuvering for the crown with Fascist support, Victor Emmanuel refused to countersign Facta's decree of martial law on the morning of October 29. Instead, he appealed directly to Mussolini, who was anxiously waiting in the Milan offices of his newspaper. Mussolini arrived in Rome the following morning, October 30, and began forming his ministry.

Technically, Mussolini had become the prime minister of Italy according to constitutional form. In another sense, however, Mussolini had come to power by force. He had helped to make normal government impossible in 1921 and 1922, until the political leaders of Italy bought him off. Moreover, he had made a violent antisocialist weapon available to those groups in Italy—industrialists, landowners, army officers, and police—who wanted to smash socialism at all cost. By the time the *squadristi* had seized a number of northern and central towns, it would have taken force to exclude the Fascists from power.

The Emergence of Personal Rule

It was not clear in October 1922, whether Mussolini would govern by force or whether he would be "transformed," according to Giolitti's term, into just another parliamentary coalition-monger.

Mussolini's appearance when he stepped from the train reflected that ambiguity. He was wearing the black shirt and trousers of a Fascist, combined with the white spats of a bourgeois. "Your Majesty," he said to the king, "will you forgive my attire? I come from the battlefields."[7] The new cabinet also reflected its mixed origins. It was a coalition of Fascists with the center and right. Although there were only four Fascists among fourteen ministers, the Fascists held the key posts. Mussolini himself was interior minister (who controls the national police in most European countries) as well as foreign minister and prime minister. Three other Fascists held the ministries of justice, liberated territories, and finance. There were even two reformist Social Democrats in the cabinet, and such eminent centrists as Salandra served the regime as representative to the League of Nations. Behind this coalition, however, stood the restless *squadristi,* who began to talk of a "second revolution."

[7]Laura Fermi, *Mussolini* (Chicago, 1961), p. 204.

Fascist blackshirts burn socialist literature following the "March on Rome," November 1922.

How this mixture of elements would sort itself out remained an open question for the next two years. By external appearances, Mussolini reassured those who hoped only for another bourgeois ministry that would be a bit firmer and more antirevolutionary than the last. He appeared in black cutaways in public and instituted no startling innovations. The brutal side showed only in the Corfu affair. When an Italian general and some officers inspecting the Greek–Albanian border were assassinated on Greek territory in August 1923, Mussolini bombarded the Greek island of Corfu and occupied it until the Greeks were forced to apologize and pay an indemnity. Elsewhere, Italian foreign policy gave the impression of moderation, especially when the differences with Yugoslavia over Fiume were settled by treaty in January 1924.

Internally, the major change was the Acerbo Election Law.[8] This election gimmick awarded two-thirds of the seats in the lower house of the parliament to the party that received the largest number of votes (provided it was over 25 percent) and then distributed the rest among the other parties by proportional representation. It was approved by 235 votes to 139 (mostly socialist and communist) in a Chamber that included only 35 Fascists. Clearly, the center and right parties still chose order over electoral democracy, even if the Fascists were the chief gainers. With the machinery of government in their hands, Mussolini's coalition slate won 374 out of 535 seats in the elections of April 1924, of whom 275 were Fascists. It was the last quasi-normal election in Italy for twenty years.

Another brutal act of *squadrismo* soon forced Mussolini to choose between personal rule or defeat. On June 10, 1924, an emerging young leader of the parliamentary socialists, Giacomo Matteotti, was abducted and murdered by five Fascist thugs on the payroll of Mussolini's press secretary, Cesare Rossi. Although there is some reason to think that Mussolini had not directly ordered the killing, Matteotti's murder brought into the open the major issue of whether Mussolini was capable of even controlling the violence he had unleased. Some centrist supporters of Mussolini broke with him, and the left opposition began to revive. For some months, Mussolini was disoriented and uncertain, exposing the vacillator under his tough mask.

Mussolini eventually saw that he must assume total power or lose the power he had. He spoke to the Chamber in a new, defiant mood on January 3, 1925: "We wish to make the nation fascist." At the same time, the militia was mobilized, a police crackdown was ordered on the growing liberal and socialist opposition, and restraints were removed from the *squadristi*. A series of decrees transformed Italy from a parliamentary monarchy into a one-party dictatorship. By the end of 1926, all parties except the Fascists had been dissolved, the death penalty, abolished in 1890, had been restored, controls had been imposed on the press and local government, and Mussolini was on his

[8]Named for its sponsor, the Fascist deputy Giacomo Acerbo.

way toward the "second revolution" for which his more impatient followers had clamored.

201

In Germany defeat had followed the military triumphs of the spring of 1918 with dizzying suddenness. The German Empire had been overthrown, the kaiser exiled, and a new republic created whose ability to protect German property, German values, and German borders was doubted by conservatives and nationalists. The victors were busy carving off great slices of former German territory. The German Communist party was preparing further revolutionary steps. The Allied blockade made food scarcer than ever in the months following the armistice. Prices and unemployment were rising. Humiliation, hunger, and fear were the daily companions of many Germans during 1919 and 1920.

It was under these conditions in 1920 that a demobilized corporal named Adolf Hitler joined a nationalistic workers' society that had been formed in Munich in January 1918 to support the war effort, and was now trying to unite demobilized veterans and working men in a nationalistic but economically radical program.

Postwar Antirevolutionary Activity

Munich had become a gathering spot for radical right fringe groups and angry nationalists by 1920. The revolutionary pendulum had swung farthest to the left in Munich with the Soviet Republic of April 1919, and then far to the right with that brief regime's destruction by the Army and General Franz X. von Epp's *Freikorps* in early May 1919. For the moment in 1920 the armed forces restored power to the moderate Social Democrats who had governed in Bavaria since November 1918. Many of the officers, however, had only contempt for the new republic, which was bowing to the Treaty of Versailles. The *Freikorps* were even more passionate and less disciplined in their hatred of it.

As noted earlier, the General Staff had created these volunteer units to help control Berlin in December 1918, with the acquiescence of Social Democrats like Friedrich Ebert and Gustav Noske who dominated the provisional government.[9] There was no difficulty finding *Freikorps* volunteers among the unemployed and among the swollen numbers of demobilized officers now adrift. The *Freikorps*' experience in putting down workers' uprisings in Berlin, Leipzig, and Munich in the spring of 1919 sharpened their antisocialist edge, and those who held the Baltic frontiers against the Russian Bolsheviks in 1919 and 1920 identified antisocialism with defense of the national territory. The *Freikorps* mixed together a poisonous brew of attitudes drawn from the young middle-class antibourgeois style of the prewar German hiking clubs (*Wandervö-*

[9]See Chapter 5, p. 148.

gel), the wartime hardening of the "front fighters," and the postwar crusade to save Germandom on the Baltic or in the streets of cities held by revolutionaries.

These armed enemies of the infant Weimar Republic could not destroy it by a frontal attack. They had tried to do so in the "Kapp *Putsch*" of March 1920. When the republic attempted to demobilize some of the *Freikorps* units, one unit, the Erhardt Brigade, which had helped "clean up" Munich in May 1919, rebelled and marched into Berlin wearing its swastika symbol. Powerful antirepublicans, such as General Walther von Lüttwitz and Wolfgang Kapp, a nationalist politician who had helped found the Fatherland party in 1917, hoped to use Erhardt's men to unseat the government. When the Army commander in chief, General Hans von Seeckt, refused to divide the Army by ordering it into action against the Erhardt Brigade, the government left Berlin to the mutineers. Kapp's attempt to form a new government failed, however, when career civil servants refused to carry out his orders and when the most widespread workers' general strike of modern German history paralyzed the economy. After four days, Kapp gave up, and the Weimar Republic resumed its functions in Berlin.

In Munich, meanwhile, the local army command finally pushed aside the Social Democratic Bavarian state government and installed a more amenable nationalist state government under Gustav von Kahr, a conservative supporter of Bavarian autonomy. In the climate of the early Weimar Republic, "autonomy" meant not carrying out the federal government's efforts to control the insurrectionary right in the early 1920s. Those efforts were meager enough, for the republic's leaders had chosen to leave the reconstruction of the German Army under the Versailles restrictions to General Seeckt, whose political "neutrality" in March 1920 had opened Berlin to the Erhardt Brigade. In Munich, the Army did not even pretend to be neutral.

The Emergence of Hitler

The army command in Munich set up political instruction programs to guard its soldiers against subversive propaganda. One of the instructors was Adolf Hitler, a demobilized corporal now adrift in Munich. Hitler was the son of an Austrian customs official, a moody, solitary youth who had spent his early twenties in Vienna failing to get into architecture school, soaking up the German nationalism and anti-Semitism of the Vienna crowd, and feeling sorry for himself. Gifts from his mother and eventually an inheritance kept him from real want, although he chose to describe his Vienna years later in his autobiography *Mein Kampf* (1925) as a misunderstood young artist's struggle against poverty and subversive anti-German ideas. The outbreak of the First World War found him in Munich, where he had emigrated to avoid the Austrian draft. In 1914 Hitler volunteered in the Bavarian Army. The war gave him the first real fulfillment of his life. As a runner carrying messages between the front and headquarters, he spent four years in some physical danger. He was awarded the Iron Cross, a rare award for a corporal. Blinded temporarily by gas in 1918, he experienced hallucinations during which he claimed to have received a mystical summons to save Germany.

The Second Army's Political Department in Munich ordered Hitler in 1920 to investigate the German Workers' party as an undercover agent. The party had been founded in Munich in January 1918 by a locksmith eager to win his fellow workers from socialism to nationalism. Hitler joined the movement with card number 555, came to dominate it, and eventually dropped his army job to spend full time with the party. He changed its name to National Socialist German Workers' (Nazi) party.[10] Under Hitler, the party took on new dynamism and drew many new members from the same sources as the *Freikorps*. He bought a newspaper, the *Völkischer Beobachter* (*Peoples' Observer*).[11] The party's paramilitary direct-action squad, the *Stürmabteilung* (SA.), or storm troopers, fought socialists in the streets and kept up the *Freikorps* tradition of the chosen band sworn to a single leader.

The Nazi Party

Hitler's new party was only one of the nationalist anti-Semitic direct-action groups that flourished in Germany in 1920. But it was more successful than the others. Hitler managed to recruit a social cross section, one of the hallmarks of a fascist movement. In addition to the small craftsmen with which the movement had begun, there was support from the highly placed and the wealthy. Hitler enjoyed support from politically minded army officers, such as Captain Ernst Röhm and Major General Epp, the *Freikorps* leader who had "liberated" Munich from the soviet in May 1919. Half the purchase money for the *Völkischer Beobachter* came from them, as well as useful protection and publicity. Other wealthy supporters were two women, Frau Bechstein (the piano-manufacturing family) and Frau Bruckmann (publishing), whom Hitler had met through Putzi Hanfstängl, a Harvard-educated art dealer's heir and Munich café intellectual. There were drifting veterans, such as Captain Hermann Göring, the much-decorated fighter pilot who had succeeded Baron Manfred von Richthoven as commander of Germany's most famous fighter squadron and who was now unemployed and taking drugs. And there were ethnic Germans from the lost eastern borderlands, such as Alfred Rosenberg from the Baltic.

The Nazi party's program was set forth in the Twenty-Five Points, adopted in February 1920 when the party was still a small movement of artisans and craftsmen. Its content was a mixture of ardent nationalism,

[10]NSDAP, *National-sozialistische Deutsche Arbeiterpartei.*
[11]The German adjective *völkisch* is imperfectly translated as "peoples'." It refers to one's own ethnic stock in both racial and cultural terms, a meaning developed in nineteenth-century German nationalist writing.

Hitler and his fellow conspirators in the Munich "beer hall Putsch" during their trial for high treason, February 24, 1924. General Erich Ludendorff is at the center next to Hitler, and Captain Ernst Röhm, commander of the SA., is second from right.

anti-Semitism, and anticapitalism. The program called for the abrogation of the Versailles Treaties and union with Austria in a Greater Germany, that is, a state larger than 1914 Germany. Jews were to be excluded from citizenship and office. The anticapitalism of the Twenty-Five Points, for which Hitler's predecessors in the German Workers' party were responsible, was not socialist in the sense of opposing private property or calling for socialist revolution. It was rather an assertion of the small man's grievances against his creditors and the rich. It called for abolition of unearned income, confiscation of war profits, nationalization of trusts, and regulation of the profits of large corporations. The Nazis proposed to "communalize" department stores in order to rent out their premises to groups of small tradespeople. They called for land reform, prevention of land speculation, and expropriation of land "for communal purposes."

The Twenty-Five Points were more noteworthy as an expression of lower–middle-class grievances than as a guide to later Nazi action. Once in power, a decade later, Hitler pursued quite different social policies. Even at the beginning, however, the Nazis put more stress on the techniques of mass mobilization than programs. Mass parades and assemblies may have entered European politics on the left, but the Nazis turned them into an art form in the service of nationalism, antisocialism and anti-Semitism. Uniforms, banners, and night rallies by torchlight touched many German emotions. The party openly mocked the Weimar Republic's efforts to control public order, as in the parade of 800 SA. men in Coburg in October 1922 in defiance of a ban on demonstrations.

The direct actions of the SA. in breaking up enemy meetings gratified hatreds directly or vicariously, and provided publicity even in the hostile parts of the press.

The "Beer Hall Putsch," 1923

The German political climate grew stormy again in 1923. The French had occupied the Ruhr, the Communist party attempted to take power in the states of Saxony and Thuringia, and the currency inflated out of sight. Despair and scorn for the Weimar Republic pushed a tide of support toward the Nazis. General Ludendorff, the First World War commander, now stood at Hitler's side at rallies. Buoyed by such support, Hitler decided to force the nationalist state government of Bavaria to serve as his base for overthrowing the Weimar Republic. Invading a meeting in the Munich *Bürgerbräukeller* (a large beer hall) on November 8, 1923, the Nazis seized the Bavarian Governor Gustav von Kahr and senior local army and police officials and forced them to pledge public support to Hitler's appeal for a national revolution. Although Kahr and the others repudiated Hitler as soon as they were set free, Captain Ernst Röhm and his SA. men succeeded in occupying the Bavarian War Ministry with the complicity of army officers. Hitler led a march on other government buildings on November 9, confident that the presence beside him of General Ludendorff would neutralize the army and police units guarding them. The army commanders in Bavaria

Hitler returns the salute of one of his followers during a Nazi parade in the town of Weimar, 1926. Party Secretary Rudolf Hess is just behind Hitler's left elbow, and Captain Hermann Goering is partly hidden by the saluting member of the SA. at the front of Hitler's Mercedes.

supported legal authority, however, and when Hitler and Ludendorff approached the government's barricades at the head of their column, the troops fired. Sixteen Nazis and three policemen were killed. Hitler was arrested, and although he made use of his trial as a public platform ("I wanted to become the destroyer of Marxism"), he was sent to prison.

During 1924, the Weimar Republic managed to stabilize itself, and the tensions and vigilantism of 1923 greatly diminished. Nazism seemed to be in decline. But the ingredients it contained were still latent in German society and values, ready to be summoned forth in the event of any future crisis.

Counterrevolution in Hungary

Hungary, too, was ripe for a mass, anti-Marxist, nationalist movement after the First World War. Proportionally, Hungary was the greatest territorial loser of the war. Once a ruling state lording it over minorities of Slovaks, Romanians, and South Slavs, Hungary was now a starving remnant barely one-third its prewar size. Three million Magyars were now themselves minority subjects in Romania, Yugoslavia, and Czechoslovakia. Every political movement, from Marxist to royalist, rejected the Treaty of the Trianon (Hungary's part of the Versailles settlement) and called for national restoration. Nearly every Hungarian was revisionist and nationalist. Their slogan was *Nem, nem, soha* (no, no, never) in response to Hungary's postwar status.

The British historian A. J. P. Taylor had some reason for calling Hungary "the first breeding ground of fascism."[12] Postwar events had poisoned liberal values in Hungary, for the October Republic of Prince Michael Karolyi,[13] even more than the Weimar Republic for German nationalists, spelled national humiliation and social disorder. The soviet regime set up in 1919 gave a nasty fright to the ruling gentry and aristocracy, who had always enjoyed the most one-sided land distribution in Europe outside of Romania and southern Spain.[14] The desperately land-hungry peasants hated "communists and gentlemen" equally.[15] A large uprooted and frightened mass of demobilized army officers and of Hungarian officials expelled from the lost two-thirds of the kingdom, further swelled by business and professional people bankrupted by territorial amputation and postwar economic dislocation, built up both anti-Semitic and anti-Marxist sentiments. They resented the extremely large role of Jews in Hungarian banking and commerce,[16] as well as Béla Kun's soviet regime.

[12]A. J. P. Taylor, "Introduction," in Michael Karolyi, *Memoirs. Faith Without Illusion* (New York, 1957), p. 7.
[13]See Chapter 5, pp. 154–55.
[14]C. A. Macartney, *The Hapsburg Empire, 1790–1918* (New York, 1969), pp. 713, 716. About 4000 great families owned about a third of the arable land in prewar Hungary.
[15]Istvan Deak, "Hungary," in Hans Rogger and Eugen Weber, eds., *The European Right* (Los Angeles, 1965), p. 385.
[16]"In 1910, 21.8% of salaried employees in industry, 54.0% of self-employed traders, and 85.0% of the self-employed persons in banking and finance were Jews." (*Ibid.*, p. 368.)

Postwar Hungary was formed in counterrevolution. Even during the October Republic of 1918, before Kun's 133-day soviet regime, demobilized officers and uprooted civil servants were forming secret societies devoted to replacing Western ideas with "Hungarianism," a vague mixture of racist and hierarchical social ideas expressed in romantic neomedieval language. The town of Szeged, on the southern border and behind the protection of French armies, was the center of these movements. From here sprang the "circle of the twelve captains," antiliberal young army officers who furnished part of the interwar Hungarian leadership. They soon formed such underground activist groups as the Awakening Hungarians or the EZSZ (Etelköz Association), which claimed to be an imitation of early Hungarian tribal society, complete with an oath to seven tribal chiefs and commitment to "a great, Christian, and racially pure Hungary."

The most eminent personnage at Szeged was Admiral Miklós Horthy, the last commander in chief of the Austro-Hungarian Navy. But the most dynamic figure was one of the "twelve captains," Captain Gyula Gömbös, who organized a volunteer anti-Bolshevik army under Horthy's command. Gömbös, born to a schoolteacher and a farmer's daughter in a German-speaking district, stood outside the gentry families that had traditionally ruled Hungary, and even outside a fully Hungarian cultural inheritance. He compensated for this, however, by the vehemence of his opposition to the Versailles settlement, his devotion to Hungarian cultural revival, and his attacks on Marxism as "a destructive heresy foisted on simple workers by self-seeking international Jews."[17]

Gömbös was already calling himself a national socialist in 1919: national, in his determination to restore Hungarian values and frontiers to what he imagined was their historic right; socialist, in his proposal to expropriate international financiers to make jobs for Hungarian workers and expropriate great estates to give land to Hungarian peasants. Unlike the Hungarian gentry, Gömbös had no use for the Habsburg ruling house. He was later to block all attempts to restore Austro-Hungarian Emperor Karl as king of Hungary during the 1920s, and when he became prime minister in 1932, Gömbös formed the first cabinet in modern Hungarian history that contained no aristocrats. Gömbös' Party of Racial Defense became a rallying point

[17]Quoted in Eugen Weber, *The Varieties of Fascism* (New York, 1964), p. 90.

Admiral Miklós Horthy, regent of Hungary, 1919–44.

for demobilized junior officers, angry nationalists, and anti-Semitic lower-level civil servants and businessmen. He drew inspiration after 1922 from Mussolini's platform style and was in touch with Hitler as early as 1923.

Another Hungarian counterrevolutionary center in 1919 was Vienna, where an anti-Bolshevik Committee was formed under Count Istvan Bethlen, a great landowner from the Calvinist aristocracy of eastern Hungary. Bethlen spoke for a more aristocratic, tolerant, and cultivated milieu of great landowners who were more sympathetic than Gömbös to the limited parliamentary traditions of the late–nineteenth-century ruling families of Hungary.

From these two counterrevolutionary centers—Szeged and Vienna— came the forces that occupied Budapest after the Romanians had driven Béla Kun out on August 1, 1919. The retaking of Budapest was accompanied by a "white terror" that took the lives of 2000 persons more or less indiscriminately identified as socialists or Jews. Admiral Horthy began a landlocked second career as "regent" of a Hungarian monarchy whose throne was vacant.

The predominant influence at first lay with the "racialist dynamism and the anti-Red fury" of Szeged secret societies and young "captains." By 1921, however, the social fever had diminished. Horthy made Count Bethlen prime minister. Although the Bethlen regime was free from the more strident anti-Semitism and mysticism of the Szeged officers, it tried to restore gentry rule. Bethlen reduced eligible voters to 27 percent of the population, for example, and restored public balloting in the rural precincts so that landlords could know how their peasants voted. He permitted labor unions to function again in cities, but this bargain forbade them to try to organize agricultural workers. A form of oligarchic parliamentarism thus took over from the Szeged groups for the rest of the 1920s.

A Closer Look at Fascism

The three groups examined above—Italian fascism, German National Socialism, and Hungarian counterrevolutionary movements—were not the only popular, violence-prone, antiliberal, and anti-Marxist movements active in Europe at the end of the war. There were many smaller, less successful examples. The Frenchman Georges Valois broke with the monarchist Catholic *Action française* after the war in search of a more radical nationalism and antiparliamentarianism with which to draw French workers away from Marx. His *Faisceau* was an attempt to adapt the Italian *fascio,* or band of brothers, directly to French conditions. A longer lasting French movement was *Jeunesses patriotes* (Patriotic Youth), a direct-action squad of nationalist students and veterans, founded in 1924 by the champagne manufacturer Pierre Taittinger. The Romanian student Corneliu Codreanu's National-Christian Socialism movement of 1920 was devoted to strikebreaking, the disruption of liberal professors' classes, and a campaign to restrict the number of Jews in Romanian universities and professions. Such movements were widespread, novel, and important. What did they stand for, and how did they come about?

The Meaning of Fascism

Fascism was not simply the far right. The terms *right* and *left* were first applied to politics during the French Revolution.[18] They belong to the political vocabulary of nineteenth-century struggles over popular sovereignty, individual liberties, and property. With fascist movements, we find ourselves in a strange landscape where familiar signposts like *right* and *left* did not give very precise directions.

Much about the early fascist movements seemed insurrectionary and hostile to traditional rightist conservatism. Like the left, fascism was a mass movement. Its marching ranks wearing identically colored shirts, its plebeian leaders full of contempt for kings and aristocrats, its strident rallies, and its appeals to action were worlds away from the hereditary hierarchies and deferential, passive lower orders that traditional conservatives longed for. No one would mistake Captain Gömbös for the polished Count Bethlen, or Mussolini for an Italian aristocrat or wealthy industrialist. Many fascists were hostile to the Church (although less so in Romania and Hungary).

Early fascist platforms called their movements "national syndicalist" or "national socialist," and leveled bitter attacks on international capitalism, department stores, banks, and, in some cases, on large land holdings. They recruited former syndicalists who hated the Socialist party, young bourgeois who hated their parents' generation, veterans who hated those who had sent them to war and then not provided them with jobs, intellectuals who hated modern mass culture, and desperate marginal shopkeepers and professional people. Because all of them wanted sweeping, violent changes, it has been tempting to consider fascists revolutionaries. "National Socialism," wrote Hermann Rauschning, a former Nazi leader in Danzig who broke with the party, "is an unquestionably genuine revolutionary movement in the sense of the 'mass rising' dreamed of by Anarchists and Communists."[19] This revolution was aimless, Rauschning thought, except in terms of grasping and consolidating power, but it was no less destructive of the *status quo.*

On the one hand, the anticapitalist and antibourgeois rhetoric would appear to make the fascists opposed to the right. On the other hand, all fascist movements without exception saw Marxism as the enemy and flabby liberalism as the enemy's main accomplice. Fascist violence was directed against socialist and left-Catholic parties and unions and against ethnic "enemies." The regimes that fascists wished to overthrow were

[18]In the converted riding stable used for the National Assembly of 1789, seats were arranged in the shape of a fan, rather than facing each other as in the chapel long used by the British parliament. The French king's supporters fell into the habit of sitting on the speaker's right, his opponents on the speaker's left.

[19]Hermann Rauschning, *Revolution of Nihilism* (New York, 1939), p. 19.

the ineffective liberal or reformist regimes that they judged inadequate to maintain national power, jobs, and order.

Anticapitalist and antibourgeois rhetoric, moreover, was not universal to fascist movements, and it was always a selective anticapitalism they preached. Their grievances were those of a middle class squeezed by inflation and caught between growing capitalist corporations and growing trade unions. When they called for the nationalization of the banks to which they were indebted, to "break the capital-interest yoke" (Point 11 of the Nazi Twenty-Five Points), they wanted easy credit and low interest for their small businesses, not socialism. When they called for the nationalization of the trusts whose competition threatened them, they wanted to protect small property, not abolish property. Their call for an organized economy meant the dissolution of independent trade unions, not the end of free enterprise. Despite the antibourgeois rhetoric of some of its intellectuals, fascism wanted a revolution to protect the middle class, not to install the proletariat in power. "Things must change if they are going to remain the same," says one of the characters in Giuseppe de Lampedusa's novel of Sicilian society, *The Leopard* (1956).

In any event, fascist rhetoric was much less important than fascist practice. The one fascist movement to gain power in the 1920s, Italian fascism, did so with the aid and complicity of traditional conservatives. Once in power, it forgot its early rhetoric and came to terms with king, aristocracy, Church, and business (as we shall see in more detail in Chapter 9). German National Socialism made similar alliances to reach power. To claim as have some Marxists that fascism was merely a device created by capitalists for the dual purpose of beating back Marxism and organizing a chaotic world economy is to underestimate the popular roots of fascist movements.[20] But it is difficult to deny that fascists and traditional conservatives often struck up fruitful alliances. Fascism belongs on the right clearly enough, but it was a new right.

The proper placement of fascism on a right–left scale is further complicated by its claim to cut across class lines. Fascists promised to cancel out the class struggle in a fervent national reconciliation. That was one of its appeals to the traditional right. That claim was not altogether spurious. Although the middle class provided the most recruits, fascism did indeed attract some workers, mostly those outside the pervasive socialist culture of the European working class: patriotic antisocialists, the youthful unemployed, and the unorganized poor in areas like Eastern Europe and southern Italy, where the poor had never received the attentions of a mass movement.

In some ways youth distinguishes fascism better than does class or political ideology. Fascism tapped the rebellious rejection of the young outsiders of a generation that had come of age in the trenches of war or in the street demonstrations and unemployment lines of the immediate

[20]Serious Marxist interpreters of fascism have avoided this error. See Daniel Guérin, *Fascism and Big Business* (New York, 1939).

postwar days. Mussolini's *squadristi* marched off singing *Giovinezza* (Youth). Captain Gömbös was thirty-three in 1920; Codreanu was twenty; Hitler thirty-one.

Fascism leaves behind the nineteenth-century world in which middle- and lower–middle-class Europeans were usually liberal. In times of emergency like economic depression, national defeat, or inadequate access to political redress, middle-class Europeans had tended to polarize toward the left, as in the revolutions of 1848. In fascist movements, lower–middle-class Europeans moved toward a radical antisocialist, antiliberal authoritarianism. They found wanting the predominantly liberal or socialist values of their fathers. This is the larger historical transformation that students of fascism must examine.

The Roots of Fascism

Although fascism in its fully developed form burst on the world only after the shocks of the First World War and the Bolshevik Revolution, it is possible to discern a number of ways in which the terrain had been prepared in the late nineteenth century.

A first step was some conservatives' acceptance of mass politics. As early as the 1850s, activist authoritarians like the French Emperor Napoleon III and the German Chancellor Otto von Bismarck adopted universal manhood suffrage as a tactic for recruiting mass support over the heads of the upper-class liberal parliamentary opposition.

The Catholic Church, too, began to make its peace with anticlerical liberals who were sufficiently antisocialist. In the days of Pope Pius IX (1846–78), the main enemies of the Church had been the new, militantly anticlerical French Republic, which took public education out of the Church's hands in the 1880s, and the new, unified Kingdom of Italy, which had seized Church lands in 1870. Pope Leo XIII (1878–1903) nudged French Catholics toward acceptance of the French Third Republic in the 1890s. Leo's successor, Pius X (1904–14), made an even more conspicuous departure in 1904 when he authorized Italian Catholics to vote in cases where their ballots could block a socialist candidate. It was the first Italian election since 1870 in which Catholics had been permitted by the Church to take part. The clerical issue was not dead, as a bitter squabble over separation of Church and state in France in 1905 proved. But it was one of the nineteenth-century divisions whose significance was becoming eclipsed by the growing power of socialism. By the end of the nineteenth century, many European conservatives preferred to adapt to mass politics rather than follow the traditional conservative aim of trying to keep the masses out of politics.

This tactic made sense, of course, only if mass support for conservative interests was forthcoming. There were signs at the end of the nineteenth century of the exhaustion of liberalism as the organizer of the European middle and lower middle classes. On the political level, as socialist parties began winning substantial numbers of parliamentary seats through manhood suffrage in the 1890s,[21] some middle-class Europeans began having second thoughts about the efficacy of parliamentary democracy. On the economic level, many middle-class Europeans felt no love for a laissez-faire, free-market economy that pinched them between increasingly organized capitalists and increasingly organized labor. Small property, the individual shop or craft, had been the chief lower–middle-class route to independence. But such property came under permanent pressure in the late nineteenth century: small shops suffered from the competition of new forms of retailing through chains and department stores; craftsmen suffered from industrial competition. These pressures were intensified during periods of cyclical business depression in the 1880s and early 1890s.

The resentments of small businessmen and craftsmen could not be expressed very well through existing parties, either Marxist or liberal. Liberal political economists still resisted state intervention in the economy. Marxists opposed all private property in production and commerce, while advocating continued industrialization as the necessary preparation for the next stage of socialist, collectivized abundance. Middle-class opponents of laissez-faire capitalism were groping confusedly before the war for some "middle way" or "third way,"[22] neither liberal nor Marxist. Only something new seemed able to protect small property from both big business and big labor. That was the kind of new formula that Charles Maurras was already putting together in the *Action française* movement of the early 1900s. One of his precocious campaigns, for example, attacked a dairy chain that threatened the livelihood of small grocers.

While the independent lower middle class slowly and painfully contracted in Europe before the First World War, the salaried lower middle class grew rapidly, providing another potential mass clientele for fascism. Karl Marx had expected industrial progress to produce an ever-larger proletariat. Instead, the proportion of factory workers in northern and Western Europe leveled off at around one-third of the total populations in the 1890s. Although the absolute numbers of industrial workers continued to increase, their relative numbers were kept down by enormous increases in the lower middle class, or what has been called workers in the tertiary sector of the economy: white-collar employees, clerical workers, workers in sales and distribution, and lesser civil servants. These groups have constituted the fastest growing segment of the population of industrialized and urbanized European countries in the twentieth century. Although they worked for wages like any factory worker, many white-collar employees clung to some sign of middle-class respectability. The German or Austrian petty civil servant,

[21]The number of French socialist deputies increased from twelve to forty-one in the election of 1893; the German Social Democratic party's voters grew from 763,128 in 1887 to 3,010,771 in 1903, or from 10.1 percent to 31.7 percent of the total vote.
[22]These phrases recur in the political discussions of the 1920s and 1930s. See Chapter 11, pp. 317–18.

black suit worn shiny at the elbows, briefcase containing only a lunchtime salami, is, like many caricatures, close to reality. This new middle class supported democracy as long as it promised them security or progress. In a crisis, however, they were terrified of dropping into the proletariat. Although many of them hated their bosses, they hesitated to become socialist, which meant accepting proletarian status. The European lower middle class had supplied mass recruits for the revolutionary barricades of 1848; they supplied even more mass recruits for the fascist right in the twentieth century.

The exhaustion of liberalism was apparent also on the intellectual plane before the war. This did not mean the victory of liberalism's old enemies. By the end of the nineteenth century, traditional conservatives' challenge to liberalism in the name of faith and the divine right of hereditary authority was no longer taken very seriously. The important change was a dissipation of liberal confidence in human progress and the universality of human reason within liberalism's former stronghold, the educated middle class. An earlier chapter examined the many levels—the visual arts, philosophy, psychology, and science—in which nineteenth-century liberal assumptions were being challenged.[23] Some of the challengers themselves, such as the futurist painter Marinetti, joined enthusiastically and directly into the action and the contempt for liberal values that Mussolini's fascism offered. Other Europeans were prepared more subtly and indirectly for fascism by the disintegration of the familiar liberal intellectual universe. Some felt a sense of foreboding at the century's end. Some felt revulsion at the ugliness of urban, industrial society, at the shrill destructiveness of intellectuals, and at the bland optimism of unthinking philistines. They were frightened by a feeling that Europe was decadent. The fear of decadence easily turned into a cosmic historical pessimism. Maurras' Frenchmen could measure the decline of their nation's power under the flabby Third Republic; Italians looked back to a vanished Roman Empire; Georg von Schönerer's Austrian-Germans saw their people being swallowed up in a sea of Slavs and Jews. One remedy appeared to be the kind of national revival in which racial purity, mass fervor, and authoritarian rule somehow reinforced one another.

The generous nationalism of the early nineteenth century, which envisioned the self-determining nations as a future happy family, had become much more closed and exclusive in the late nineteenth century. At the same time, the concept of race gained greater currency. Liberal intellectuals had put uppermost those qualities of all humanity that united people across the artificial barriers of title and rank, but the explorers, travelers, geographers, and anthropologists of expanding nineteenth-century Europe rediscovered humanity's diversity, most of which they attributed to race. Racial thinking spread among less-educated Europeans in the form of anti-Semitism. Efforts by the Russian

[23]See Chapter 1, pp. 39–44.

tsars to "Russify" all their minorities after the 1880s helped stimulate popular passions against the Jews concentrated in the Pale of western Russia and Poland, to which they were restricted by law. Pogroms, attacks on Jewish shops and settlements, caused thousands of deaths after the 1880s; the most vicious single pogrom before the war was the murder of over 300 Jews in Odessa in October 1905 while the authorities stood by. The emigration of Orthodox Jews from Russia aroused antagonism to these outsiders in Western Europe in the 1890s. Medieval Christian hostility to Jews was now reinforced by notions of racial difference and the fear that Jews weakened the homogeneity of any nation that harbored them.

All the ingredients of fascism were thus present before 1914. The First World War was a catalyst of fascism rather than its creator. In a number of different ways at once, the war experience magnified and fused these disparate elements. The war so discredited the entire prewar European dispensation, particularly among the young, that the search for a "new way" took on new urgency among all those unwilling to accept the Soviet model for change. The war also revealed depths of human evil and irrationality that confirmed the prewar critique of liberal assumptions.

The war multiplied by many times fascism's potential clientele. A whole generation had gone off to war, and some of these young men had returned hardened and embittered with the "front fighter" mentality of those who had been through the "steel bath" of the First World War. Italo Balbo, Mussolini's future associate, recalled that

> when I returned from the war—just like so many others—I hated politics and politicians, who, in my opinion, had betrayed the hopes of soldiers, reducing Italy to a shameful peace and to a systematic humiliation Italians who maintained the cult of heroes. To struggle, to fight in order to return to the land of Giolitti, who made a merchandise of every ideal? No. Rather deny everything, destroy everything, in order to renew everything from the foundations.[24]

These veterans, unassimilable into peacetime drudgery, sought ways to keep alive the hard, pure masculine camaraderie of the trenches. By themselves they would have merely created marginal street gangs. A mass clientele was provided, however, by wartime social change: dislocations threatened the status of whole masses of formerly secure members of the middle class. The workers' rise frightened the status conscious, and the enormous impetus given to industrial concentration by total war frightened the small businessman. But the major engine of dislocation for the middle classes was inflation.

Wartime price rises did not stop in 1918. In France, after a brief postwar stabilization, the franc fell on international exchanges during the years 1924 to 1926 to a fraction of its prewar value. When the franc was stabilized in 1928 at one-fifth of its prewar international exchange

---

[24]Quoted in Herman Finer, *Mussolini's Italy* (London, 1935), p. 139.

value, the French middle class, whose savings were now worth only twenty centimes for every prewar franc saved, felt they had paid a disproportionate share of war damages. Inflation was still worse in Italy, and far worse in the truncated remnants of Austria-Hungary. In Austria, in July 1919, it cost about 2500 crowns to buy a month's supply of food for a family of four; in July 1922, it cost 297,000 crowns.[25] In Germany, the currency simply ceased to buy anything in the runaway inflation of 1923. Anyone with a fixed income was reduced to charity, and the underpinnings of middle-class independence—savings, investments, and annuities—were simply wiped out.

The final catalyst to fascism was the threat of revolutionary socialism. A map of emerging fascism fits the map of revolutionary emergency in 1919 and 1920 fairly well, although not perfectly. Some Europeans still put their faith in traditional conservatism. After the intense labor strife of 1917 to 1920 in Spain, a military dictatorship under General Primo de Rivera governed the country in conventional authoritarian fashion, under the ultimate authority of King Alfonso XIII. The Portuguese Republic was overthrown in 1926 by a military junta without any clear program except disgust with party politics. The victor nations of Britain and France resolved their postwar problems within their existing parliamentary framework. By 1923, only one European nation—Italy— had a regime of the new style, and although some other Europeans imitated the uniforms, the colored shirts, the rhetoric, and the tone of fascism, it was not certain how widely it would spread.

Fascism remained available, however, for future emergencies. If faced with disintegration of the economy in depression or inflation, disintegration of the culture in modern decadence, and disintegration of the nation in class struggle, frightened Europeans might well turn to a forcible integration of economy, culture, and classes within a fascist state.

[25]Charles A. Gulick, *Austria from Habsburg to Hitler,* Vol. 1 (Los Angeles, 1948), p. 153.

Suggestions for Further Reading

A good starting point is the narrative of Francis L. Carsten, *The Rise of Fascism** (1967). There are excellent studies of right-wing movements, in the broader sense, in various European countries in Hans Rogger and Eugen Weber, eds., *The European Right** (1965).

The Fascist takeover in Italy is the subject of two excellent accounts: Angelo Tasca, *The Rise of Italian Fascism, 1918–1922* (1938), the work of an ex-Communist exile, and Adrian Lyttelton, *The Seizure of Power: Fascism in Italy, 1919–1929* (1973).

There is no entirely satisfactory biography of Mussolini in English. Ivone Kirkpatrick, *Mussolini: A Study in Power* (1964) is fullest on politics and diplomacy; Laura Fermi, *Mussolini** (1961) is still the most reliable of the more personal accounts. Gaudens Megaro, *Mussolini in the Making* (1938) is still useful for the early years.

The most authoritative summation of the Nazi experience in Germany is Karl-Dietrich Bracher, *The German Dictatorship** (1970). A. J. Nicholls, *Weimar and the Rise of Hitler** (1968) provides a solid brief introduction and bibliography. In addition to Dietrich Orlow, *The History of the Nazi Party*, 2 vols. (1969–73), Jeremy Noakes, *The Nazi Party in Lower Saxony, 1921–1933* (1971) shows how the party began and developed in one region. Harold J. Gordon, *Hitler and the Beer Hall Putsch** (1972) explains how Hitler gained ascendancy over all other nationalist leaders in the early 1920s. Allan Bullock,

Hitler: A Study in Tyranny,* 2nd ed. (1962) is still the most successful biographer at weaving the life into the larger historical context, but there is much interesting detail in Joachim Fest, *Hitler* (1974), and Werner Maser, *Hitler: Legend, Myth, and Reality* (1973).

The best introduction to fascism in Hungary is the relevant portion of C. A. Macartney, *October Fifteenth: A History of Modern Hungary, 1929–1945*, 2 vols. (1957).

A number of works attempt to provide a general interpretation of fascism. Eugen Weber, *The Varieties of Fascism** (1964), enriched by an excellent selection of fascist texts, stresses its ideological and revolutionary aspects. John Weiss, *The Fascist Tradition** (1967) emphasizes fascism's links to traditional conservative elites. Ernst Nolte, *Three Faces of Fascism** (1968) probes for fascism's roots in the exhaustion of liberal, universalist values in modern Europe. Stuart J. Woolf, ed., *The Nature of Fascism** (1968) contains a number of important articles.

Fritz Stern, *The Politics of Cultural Despair** (1961); George L. Mosse, *The Crisis of German Ideology** (1964); and Peter G. J. Pulzer, *The Rise of Political Anti-Semitism in Germany and Austria** (1964) all discuss some of the cultural precursors of National Socialism. A. James Gregor, *The Ideology of Fascism: The Rationale of Totalitarianism* (1969) provides a valuable description of fascist programs, although taking them too literally as a guide to understanding fascist policies.

THE VERSAILLES
SYSTEM
IN PRACTICE
THE 1920s

8

The Paris peace settlement did not take instant effect at the treaty-signing ceremony on June 28, 1919, in the Hall of Mirrors at Versailles.[1] A number of complicated steps were required to implement the treaties. Plebiscites had been promised in two areas of mixed population on Germany's new borders: Danish–German Schleswig-Holstein and Polish–German Upper Silesia. The disarmament of the defeated Central Powers had to be completed, and their remaining armed forces inspected. A final reparations sum had to be fixed. The League of Nations had to be set up.

[1]Strictly speaking, only the Treaty of Versailles between Germany and the Allies was signed that day. The Treaty of St. Germain with Austria was signed on September 10, the Treaty of Neuilly with Bulgaria on November 27, the Treaty of the Trianon with Hungary on June 4, 1920, and the Treaty of Sèvres with Turkey on August 10. The treaties are referred to collectively in this chapter as the Paris peace settlement or the Versailles settlement.

To complicate matters further, the peoples of Eastern Europe continued to fight over their new frontiers. Even after settlement of the Polish–Russian War in 1921, Polish irregulars held the city of Vilna, which the Peace Conference had awarded to Lithuania. Poles also fought with Czechs over Teschen until July 1920, and they contested the outcome of the plebiscite in Upper Silesia. Austrians and Hungarians fought over the Burgenland, a border area near Vienna, until late in 1921. Yugoslavia claimed the Adriatic port of Fiume, which was occupied by Italian volunteers in contravention of the Peace Conference's decision. A Turkish nationalist movement under the army officer Mustapha Kemal (later known as Ataturk) rejected the treaty terms that the sultan had accepted, overthrew the sultan, defeated a Greek army supported by the Allies, and won control over all of Anatolia by 1923.

The letter of the treaties, therefore, often mattered less than the ways in which they were interpreted and enforced. The treaties themselves were ambiguous. According to one possible interpretation, they were meant to produce open dealings and free trade among satisfied nation-states. According to another quite legitimate reading, they perpetuated the *status quo* of 1919 under the watchful eyes of the wartime alliance. The second interpretation tended to predominate as the peace settlement was put into effect. For one thing, the treaties were not self-enforcing. The German government accepted the Treaty of Versailles in June 1919 under protest only when the Allies threatened to renew the war. To most Germans, the peace settlement was a *Diktat,* and not a freely negotiated agreement. Only a continued application of force could keep Germany and Russia in the state of subordination to which defeat and revolution had reduced them. France was the nation most eager to perpetuate the *status quo* of 1919, and it was the nation with the largest armed force available on the European Continent to do so.

The first five years after the Peace Conference were years of coercion in which France, supported less and less willingly by its wartime allies, attempted to preserve its 1919 eminence by force. After 1924, the weary French and Germans accepted a degree of accommodation, and there followed five years of conciliation.

The Years of Coercion, 1919–24

The stage was set for the years of coercion by the election of conservative and nationalist majorities in the principal Allied countries. The exultation of victory, combined with fears of revolution at home, hardened public spirits. In the United States in November 1918, Woodrow Wilson's Democrats lost both houses of Congress to Republicans increasingly distrustful of entangling alliances in Europe. Having failed to involve the Republican leadership sufficiently in his personal diplomacy in Paris, Wilson faced powerful opposition when he returned. The Senate refused to ratify the Treaty of Versailles and the League Covenant without reservations that Wilson would not accept. In the course of taking his case before the American people in a whistle-stop tour in September 1919, Wilson was incapacitated by a stroke. The American return to political isolationism was confirmed by the election of the Republican Warren G. Harding as president in November 1920. British Prime Minister David Lloyd George had enlarged his wartime coalition in the "khaki election" of December 1918, but the "hang the kaiser" nationalism of that election was soon transformed in British public opinion into a reluctance to be drawn into Continental entanglements by a vindictive France. Even before a Tory majority was elected in 1922, the British government had declined to enter into a defensive treaty with France.

These developments left France in effective charge of the European Continent. And in no other country was the set toward conservatism and nationalism more pronounced than in the French elections of November 1919. The new Chamber of Deputies, the most conservative since 1871, contained so many war veterans that it was dubbed the "horizon blue chamber," in reference to the color of army dress uniforms. Until the next election in 1924, the French parliament supported policies of traditional national interest, military strength, and alliance diplomacy.

Both the parliamentary majority and a military command with enhanced political influence helped formulate these policies, but it is Prime Minister Raymond Poincaré (1922–24) who has come to personify their spirit. A strong-willed lawyer from the traditionally nationalist French Lorraine, Poincaré was said to "know everything and understand nothing."[2] He construed the treaties with a strict legalism, backed with the natural force of his character. Poincaré brought unusual prestige to his task, for he had been president of France from 1913 to 1920.

French Hegemony

The 1920s was the decade of French hegemony in Europe. France had the most powerful land army in the world. Its forces not only occupied the German Rhineland; they were also stationed in Eastern Europe and (briefly) in Russia. Since the League of Nations excluded the defeated powers from membership, that institution conformed more closely to the French concept of a perpetuated wartime alliance than to the Wilsonian concept of a world parliament. Moreover, detailed supervision of the treaties' application rested less on the League than on the Conference of Ambassadors, the "Big Four" Ambassadors in Paris, a kind of institutional offspring of the Peace Conference.

French dominance was almost devoid of confidence, however. Its fragility was apparent to all. Victory had been possible in 1918 only with Allied aid, and at a cost in men and matériel that could never be spent a second time. Soon Germany would again produce more steel and babies than France. In place of the Franco-Russian Alliance, the main prop of French security since 1892, there was now a cluster of shaky and squabbling successor states in Eastern Europe.

[2]This popular jibe contrasted him to his main political rival of the 1920s, Aristide Briand, who "understood everything and knew nothing."

On the western front, the United States and Britain had left France the sole guarantor of its own security. The failure of the United States Senate to ratify the Treaty of Versailles also meant the lapse of the simultaneous treaties that provided for automatic United States and British aid in case of German attack. French leaders felt betrayed, for they had moderated their demands on Germany at the Peace Conference in return for this promise of future outside support. Although the French government tried to negotiate a substitute treaty of mutual defense with Britain alone during 1921 and 1922, the negotiators were unable to agree on how automatic British support of the French along the Rhine should be, for British public opinion was increasingly fearful of being drawn into another war by French bellicosity. As for European frontiers further east, no British government would make any commitments at all until 1939.

French governments after 1919 attempted to make up for the deficiencies of their country's position by two lines of conduct. They tried single-handedly to apply the punitive features of the Versailles Treaties with punctilious rigor. And they cultivated their system of alliances in Eastern Europe to maintain the pre-1914 strategy of threatening Germany with a two-front war.

Those new states in Eastern Europe that France had favored in the Peace Conference became the links in a chain of alliances meant to reinforce the League and the Versailles system with more traditional diplomacy. Three states that had everything to lose by a revival of Hungary and Germany—Czechoslovakia, Romania, and Yugoslavia—formed the Little Entente in 1920 and 1921. France later concluded military alliances with them and strengthened their mutual economic and cultural ties. Poland was the other essential nation in the new French alliance system. Even though Poland was divided from Czechoslovakia by the dispute over Teschen, it had the most to lose by German and Russian revival. French officers had helped the Poles stave off Soviet armies in 1920, and French diplomats helped Poland obtain generous settlements of the outstanding border questions: the main mining and industrial areas of Upper Silesia from Germany, and the city of Vilna from Lithuania. In 1921, Poland and France concluded a treaty of mutual assistance in which each promised to aid the other in case of attack.

This network of alliances was a poor substitute for the pre-1914 Franco-Russian Alliance. The only successor state with a strong industrial base was Czechoslovakia. The Little Entente was really directed more against Hungary than against Germany. And Poland and Romania had more to lose by Russian revival than by German revival. The eastern alliances actually complicated France's interwar foreign policy more than they strengthened it.

Another consequence of France's revival of alliance politics was the encouragement of a counteralliance among the outsider nations. The

Treaty of Rapallo in 1922 between Weimar Germany and Soviet Russia
was the first major step outside the Versailles political order. It came as a
bombshell. While the European states, including Germany and Russia,
were meeting at Genoa to discuss world economic problems and the
Western nations' desire to get the Soviet Union to repay the tsarist debts
to them, German Foreign Minister Walther Rathenau and Russian
Foreign Minister George Chicherin slipped off to nearby Rapallo and
signed a treaty establishing diplomatic relations and promising not to
make any economic demands on one another. There were no secret
military clauses, but soon thereafter General Hans von Seeckt was
working out secret arms manufacture and training arrangements for
German soldiers in the Soviet Union. One of the basic recurring patterns
of interwar European alignments had been created: France and the
Little Entente on one side, Germany and the Soviet Union on the other.

The Reparations Issue

The thorniest conflict raised by the Versailles settlement was the
reparations issue. It had long been normal practice for victors to impose
a punitive fine on the loser, sheer financial booty without moral
connotations. After Napoleon's final defeat in 1815, the victors had
levied an indemnity of 700 million francs, about half the French annual
budget in peacetime; it was paid off in five years. After the Franco-
German war in 1871, France had been obliged to pay 5 billion francs to
Germany; that took only four years. The reparations required of
Germany after the First World War were not only far beyond any
amount imagined before; they came clothed in a language of moral
recrimination. "The aggression of Germany and her allies" had caused
the war, asserted the famous Article 231 of the Treaty of Versailles, and
so Germany should "make compensation for all damage done to the
civilian population of the Allied and Associated Powers and to their
property" (Article 232).

A hard-headed political calculation lay behind this demand. None of
the belligerent states had paid for all the costs of the war by taxation.
They had borrowed immense sums by selling bonds on which interest
had to be paid after the war. They had also issued floods of additional
currency to cover wartime budget deficits. The resulting inflation meant
that the bondholders would eventually be paid back in money that
bought less. A state might even default on its bonds, although that would
make it more difficult to borrow again. Either inflation or default meant
that the middle-class purchasers of war bonds would end up paying for
the war by losing their investment. Governments hesitated to antagonize
the bondholders to that extent. In addition, vast sums were needed to
reconstruct destroyed buildings, railroads, and bridges, and to restore
shell-strewn farmland to productivity. No government would find it easy
to raise taxes to pay for all that.

The final difficulty was war debts. Both Britain and France owed large sums to the United States, while France owed additional war debts to Britain. Although the United States advocated a moderate reparations settlement (without actually participating in the work of the Reparations Commission), it adamantly refused throughout the 1920s to consider waiving any part of these war debts. Without collecting reparations from Germany, however, Britain and France could hardly pay what they owed the United States.

The Peace Conference had been unable to agree on a reparations figure low enough for the Germans or high enough for the British and French. It left that problem to the Reparations Commission. In the meantime, Germany was supposed to start paying a preliminary 1 billion marks, plus deliveries of coal to compensate the French for mines that were flooded during the German retreat. The Reparations Commission, consisting of representatives of Britain, France, Belgium, Italy, and Serbia, labored through seven conferences in various European resorts before finally agreeing in April 1921 on the sum of 132 billion gold marks ($33 billion), payable in yearly installments of 2.5 billion gold marks. A French economist has calculated that this total sum represented about two-and-a-half times the prewar German national income.[3] Payments would continue late into the twentieth century.

No German government believed it could accept such a burden on future generations and survive, but neither could a French government that failed to collect reparations survive. In March 1921, even before the final bill had been presented, French troops were sent to occupy three cities in the Ruhr industrial area—Düsseldorf, Ruhrort, and Duisburg—when it was charged that the Germans had fallen behind in deliveries in kind.

The payments posed enormous problems. Even assuming German willingness to pay, it was not simply a matter of raising the necessary sum each year by taxes or borrowing. The money had to be transferred into foreign currencies: that is, the German government had to buy the necessary francs or pounds for marks. The total amount of foreign exchange needed each year amounted to about 65 percent of the entire annual exports of prewar Germany.[4] One solution was for Germany to earn much more foreign exchange by increasing its exports, but the Allies did not intend to finance reparations by buying German exports. Another partial solution was to pay a larger proportion in kind, and in fact the brilliant German Jewish industrialist and technocrat Foreign Minister Walther Rathenau worked out such an agreement in 1922. French industrialists disliked payments in kind, however, and Rathenau was assassinated soon after by German anti-Semitic nationalists for making such a concession. The solution adopted was to haggle and wrangle while the mark declined in value. Germany's runaway inflation

[3]Alfred Sauvy, *Histoire économique de la France entre les deux guerres,* Vol. 2 (Paris, 1965), p. 142.
[4]*Ibid.,* p. 143.

had begun long before the first reparations payments were made, the result of wartime deficit spending, continued easy credit after the war, and the speculative purchase of gold and foreign exchange by wealthy Germans. Rather than adopt the internal austerity measures that might have stablized the mark, German bankers and government financial experts blamed inflation solely on the effect of reparations payments. In this way they used the sufferings of inflation victims to bring further pressure on the Allies.

The Occupation of the Ruhr, 1923

When Poincaré assumed the prime ministry of France in January 1922, he decided to crack down on reparations. In early 1923, he announced that the Germans were in default in payments in kind. The default— 55,000 out of 200,000 telephone poles—was trivial in itself. It provided a pretext, however, for cutting through the red tape of years of moratoriums, partial payments, and international study commissions. Poincaré occupied the Ruhr with troops.

Poincaré's original intention had, in fact, been more limited. He had sent a "technical control commission" (MICUM) to the offices of the German Coal Syndicate in Essen, guarded by an armed force (two French divisions and a small Belgian detachment), to see to the strict delivery of coal. But an armed mission sent into hostile territory even on a limited technical errand easily grew into outright military occupation. The German Coal Syndicate abandoned Essen, and the German government ordered the German residents there to practice passive resistance, which left Ruhr industry and transportation at a standstill. The French eventually had to send in thousands of engineers and railroad men, as well as five divisions (plus a Belgian division), to run the coal mines and railroads. In this way, France actually received German coal from the Ruhr in 1923. Poincaré achieved his aim: payments in kind were extracted. But the price paid, in broader terms, far outweighed that victory. Poincaré won the battle over reparations and lost the war.

One cost was the paroxysm of anger and disorder that shook Germany in the last half of 1923. Although most residents of the Ruhr obeyed the order of passive resistance, there were acts of sabotage and clashes; in the most serious of these, thirteen Germans were killed. The mark plummeted to become worthless paper. The German Communist party revived in the Ruhr and took power in coalition governments in the states of Saxony and Thuringia. Hitler entered the German political scene with his abortive Munich "beer hall" *Putsch.*

Another cost was open opposition to French policy on the part of its allies. British opinion, in particular, had drifted away from the vengefulness of the "khaki election" of 1918. John Maynard Keynes's best-seller *The Economic Consequences of the Peace* (1920) argued that French vindictiveness was damaging the European economy. The French, in turn, charged the British with a balance of power shift toward Germany in search of richer markets. It was the Ruhr occupation that made these bitter undercurrents public. The British delegate to the Reparations Commission, Sir John Bradbury, referring to the German deficit in delivering telephone poles, proclaimed that wood had not been put to such a use in international affairs since the Trojan horse. The British conspicuously failed to take part in the occupation. The Belgians did send token forces, and Mussolini's Italy gave Poincaré at least moral support. But it was clear that if France wanted to extract its pound of flesh from Germany by force, it would have to do it alone.

A more direct cost was financial. Although the French proceeds in coal were said to be larger than the cost of the expedition, the operation's expense set off another round of inflation in France. The franc had already lost much of its prewar purchasing power during the war. Now it lost even more. When financial stability was finally restored in 1928, the franc was worth about one-fifth of its prewar international value and about one-quarter of its prewar purchasing power. The Frenchmen who had prewar savings or who had bought war bonds came to belive that they had paid for the war after all, with the loss of their savings.

"Hands off the Ruhr!" This poster illustrates the adoption of nationalist themes by the German far left during the French occupation of the Ruhr in 1923.

The French occupation of the Ruhr produced a mutual exhaustion out of which emerged a more conciliatory European diplomacy. The French proved that they could not coerce Germany alone; the Germans proved that passive resistance demanded a kind of self-immolation. Out of this negative balance grew a normalization of European international relations in the later 1920s.

Electoral Shifts in Britain and France

A new mood was reflected in the elections of 1923 and 1924. When the British Conservative party was defeated in the general elections of December 9, 1923, Labour emerged for the first time ahead of the Liberals as the larger party of the opposition. So the first British Labour government was formed with Ramsay MacDonald as prime minister and foreign minister. It represented the triumph of the wartime liberal opposition that had been defeated in the jingoistic election of 1918. In the new ministry were parliamentary leaders of the wartime pacifist opposition, such as MacDonald himself, and nine members of the Union of Democratic Control.[5] The government committed itself explicitly to "a policy of International Cooperation through a strengthened and enlarged League of Nations; the settlement of disputes by conciliation and judicial arbitration; . . . and disarmament, the only security of the nations."[6]

In France, the elections of May 11, 1924, were a direct repudiation of Poincaré's coercive policy toward Germany. A "left alliance" (*cartel des gauches*) of the moderate left (Radicals) and parliamentary socialists replaced the "horizon blue" majority of 1919 in parliament. Edouard Herriot became premier and foreign minister. Herriot was leader of the Radical party, which was no longer "radical" by then, but a center-left party opposed to big government, militarism, and clericalism.

While international relations was not the only issue in these elections,[7] it was a prominent one. Both governments rested on liberal–socialist coalitions that found it easier to act in foreign policy than in domestic affairs. Both began with conspicuous symbolic acts abroad. MacDonald and Herriot extended their nations' diplomatic recognition to the Soviet Union, and Herriot, gratifying his anticlerical backers, withdrew the French ambassador from the Vatican City. More fundamentally, the two men appeared eager to set European international affairs off on a new footing, beginning with Germany and the reparations crisis.

Germany's Policy of "Fulfillment"

From the German side, too, came conciliatory signals. By late summer 1923, passive resistance in the Ruhr had gone as far as it could. As the mark lost its last vestiges of public confidence, it took more and more of

[5]See Chapter 4, p. 118.
[6]Labour party platform, 1923, quoted in Charles L. Mowat, *Britain Between the Wars* (London, 1955), p. 180.
[7]For domestic aspects of the British and French elections, see Chapter 9, pp. 244–53.

them to buy anything. Prices leaped higher almost by the hour in a spiraling inflation quite unlike anything known before. A wholesale item that cost 100 marks in July 1922 cost 74,787 marks in July 1923 and, just a month later, in August 1923, 944,041 marks. Two thousand printing presses ran night and day to provide new banknotes.[8] Separatism had revived in the western German borderlands, and the two political extremes—communism and Nazism—gained increasing numbers of adherents. In August 1923, therefore, a "Great Coalition" government, including all the major republican parties, from Social Democrats on the left to the Peoples' party on the center-right, was formed under Gustav Stresemann.

Gustav Stresemann became the outstanding figure in German politics and in European diplomacy until his death in 1929. Although Stresemann's own government lasted only three months (August to November 1923), it was a decisive "hundred days" during which he ordered an end to passive resistance, issued a stable new German currency, blocked a communist uprising in Hamburg and the Hitler *Putsch* in Munich, and made overtures for an understanding with France. Stresemann became foreign minister in the next government and held that position until his death nearly six years later.

Stresemann launched Germany on a policy of "fulfillment" (*Erfüllung*). He attempted to negotiate gradual changes in the Versailles system while carrying out its provisions. His new German foreign policy has received varying assessments. At the time, and even more in retrospect when Germany was under Hitler, Stresemann seemed the very model of international conciliation. He was awarded the Nobel Peace Prize in 1926. After the Second World War, however, the discovery of his private papers produced a harsh reassessment from the newly victorious Allies. It was clear that even though Stresemann was willing to live with Germany's west frontiers, he never accepted the eastern frontiers. One key document discovered after the war was a secret memorandum of September 7, 1925, to the exiled crown prince of Prussia, in which Stresemann set out a kind of timetable for dismantling the Versailles system. First, resolution of the reparations issue. Then, the protection of Germans outside the national frontiers. Finally, the rectification of the eastern borders: regaining Danzig, the Polish Corridor, and parts of Upper Silesia; revising the frontier with Czechoslovakia; and perhaps eventually uniting with Austria. Stresemann thought all this could be achieved by cautious but ever more forceful steps. "First we must get the throttler from our throat"; then Germany could seek more active goals by "being crafty" (*finassieren*).

Stresemann never had time to carry out his grand design, but his private papers reveal him as a determined revisionist who sought many of the changes that Hitler achieved in the late 1930s, including expansion beyond Germany's 1914 borders in the east. Any comparison with Hitler must, of course, stress the total absence in Stresemann of

[8]Gustav Stolper, *The German Economy: 1870 to the Present,* 2nd ed. (New York, 1967), p.85.

At the height of the 1923 inflation in Germany, bank notes quickly became worthless. ABOVE A street vender sells apples for 300 billion marks per half pound. BELOW Old bank notes are collected for pulping, along with old rags (Lumpen) and bones (Knochen).

territorial aims outside German-speaking areas, of overt racialist doctrines, or of Hitler's evident need to display force in his victories.

The Dawes Plan

Stresemann's first priority was reparations. That, after all, was the immediate issue behind the Ruhr crisis of 1923 that brought him to power. By November 1923, Poincaré himself was willing to accept the appointment of an international commission to review the whole question and to move reparations from the realm of moral censure to the more realistic realm of economic capacity. Charles G. Dawes, an American financier and later vice president of the United States under Calvin Coolidge, headed a commission that produced a new plan for reparations in London in July and August 1924.

The Dawes Plan was meant to put reparations on a businesslike footing. To begin, German payments must be based not on Allied moral indignation or even on Allied reconstruction needs but on German capacity to pay. The funds were to be raised in Germany by new taxes and by income from the railroads, which were placed under international supervision. The transfer of the marks into foreign currencies was to be carefully regulated in order to avoid damaging the mark on international exchanges. Finally, the Dawes Plan recognized the need for a respite. Payments were to begin at a low level, assisted at first by foreign loans (the "Dawes loans"). Only by 1928 and 1929 would the payments reach the full 2.5 billion marks per year. Then another settlement must be agreed on, for the Dawes Commission had refused to set any total figure. In practice, the Dawes Plan worked very smoothly. The new German currency was firmly stabilized, and foreign loans flowed in to the reviving German business community to such a point that they far outweighed the reparations payments going out.[9]

Conciliatory Diplomacy: The Geneva Protocol and Locarno

In the new climate of 1924, Ramsay MacDonald and Edouard Herriot attempted to change the whole spirit of European diplomacy. European affairs had been run by a coalition of victors; they wanted to replace that with a family of nations. They began to work for the entry of both Germany and the Soviet Union into the League of Nations. Beyond that, they attempted to give the League of Nations a stronger role.

One difficulty with the League was the vagueness of its procedures for collective action against an aggressor. In practice, it was almost impossible to agree on a sufficiently unambiguous definition of aggression. MacDonald and Herriot proposed an arbitration device, by which any power involved in a dispute that refused arbitration would automatically be named the aggressor and be subject to sanctions by other members of

---

[9]Foreign investments in Germany in the late 1920s totaled 23 billion gold marks; reparations payments by Germany totaled 7.5 billion gold marks. (Pierre Renouvin, *Les Crises du XXe siècle*, Vol. 1 [Paris, 1957], p. 257.)

the League. This project, known as the Geneva Protocol, was the last significant attempt between the wars to replace traditional power politics with some kind of legal procedure for the resolution of international disputes. The proposed arbitration machinery was probably unworkable. It was never even tested, however. The Conservatives who returned to power in Britain in new elections in September 1924 rejected the idea of an international arbitration device.

Although the domestic shift to the left had been temporary, the desire for more conciliatory relations with Germany remained. This attitude prevailed with both the British Conservative foreign minister, Austen Chamberlain, and the French foreign minister who replaced Herriot in April 1925, Aristide Briand. Once a young radical lawyer, Briand had drifted to the political center when he became prime minister (for the first of seven times) in 1909. In international relations, however, he emerged after 1921 as the foremost partisan of the view that French concessions to Germany would produce a "moral disarmament" on the German side. Where Poincaré was dry and legalistic, Briand was warm and effusive, and his emotional speeches at the League of Nations in the late 1920s won him a worldwide reputation as a man of conciliation. Actually, since he had to retain the confidence of a nationalist parliament, in private negotiation he generally conceded very little. Remaining in the French Foreign Ministry from April 1925 until his death in January 1932, Briand served as the French counterpart to Stresemann and the personification on the French side of the new spirit of international amity.

Into the vacuum that followed the demise of the Geneva Protocol, Stresemann introduced a very simple proposal: a mutual French–German agreement not to violate the Rhine frontier. Briand took up the proposal with alacrity. Together with Foreign Minister Chamberlain, after long months of negotiation, they met at the Swiss resort of Locarno, on Lake Maggiore, in October 1925 and concluded the Locarno Agreements, which launched a new era of European international relaxation.

The heart of the Locarno Agree-

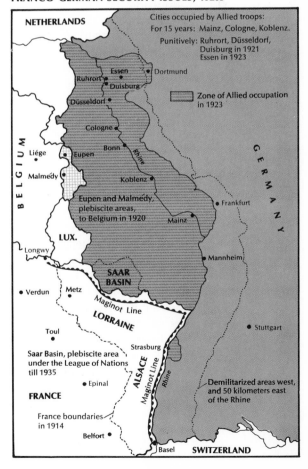

FRANCO-GERMAN SECURITY ISSUES, 1920s

Cities occupied by Allied troops:
For 15 years: Mainz, Cologne, Koblenz.
Punitively: Ruhrort, Düsseldorf, Duisburg in 1921 Essen in 1923

Zone of Allied occupation in 1923

NETHERLANDS

Essen · Dortmund
Ruhrort · Duisburg
Düsseldorf

Cologne

BELGIUM

Liége · Bonn · Rhine
Eupen
Malmédy · Koblenz

Eupen and Malmédy, plebiscite areas, to Belgium in 1920

GERMANY

· Frankfurt

Mainz

· Mannheim

LUX.

Longwy

SAAR BASIN

· Verdun · Metz

Maginot Line

LORRAINE

Toul

Strasburg

Saar Basin, plebiscite area under the League of Nations till 1935

· Epinal

FRANCE

France boundaries in 1914

Belfort ·

Basel SWITZERLAND

· Stuttgart

ALSACE

Maginot Line

Rhine

Demilitarized areas west, and 50 kilometers east of the Rhine

ments was a Franco-German promise to maintain the Rhine frontier as the Treaty of Versailles had settled it. France and Germany recognized their common border as legitimate. Britain and Italy promised to intervene if either France or Germany tried to send an army across that frontier, or if Germany sent troops into the demilitarized areas of the Rhineland. The German eastern frontiers were not guaranteed in the same way. To make that omission less threatening, Germany subsequently signed arbitration treaties with Poland and Czechoslovakia. And just to make sure, France strengthened its ties with the Little Entente states by making even more binding treaties of mutual assistance among them in case of a German attack.

Each participant yielded something and gained something in the Locarno Agreements. Germany renounced any attempt to regain Alsace-Lorraine by force, or to remilitarize the Rhineland unilaterally. Those acts were far beyond Germany's military capacity for years to come anyway, given the embryonic state of its clandestine rearmament. In return, Stresemann won separation of the issue of the eastern frontiers from the western, was assured of French support for German admission to the League of Nations (1926), and obtained French acquiescence to an early withdrawal of occupation troops from the Rhineland (1930), which effectively ended French efforts to detach that area from Germany.

France renounced the possibility of direct armed intervention in Germany, as had been attempted several times from 1920 to 1923. Those efforts had proven counterproductive anyway, as had French efforts to promote separatist sentiment in the Rhineland. In addition, the troops that were supposed to occupy the Rhineland until 1935 were to leave in 1930, and the French accepted Germany as an equal diplomatic interlocutor, as symbolized by its entry into the League. Briand also tacitly accepted a less settled status for the eastern frontiers. Of course, as long as the Rhineland remained empty of German troops in perpetuity, as was explicitly stated in the Locarno Agreements, France could still bring an effective threat to bear on Germany from the west in case Poland or Czechoslovakia were menaced.

Britain renounced its isolation and participated for the first time since 1919 in a Continental guarantee. That pledge was limited to Western Europe, however, and it applied equally to Germany and to France, so that the British public, exasperated by French intransigence, would have less fear of being dragged into a war by France. Thus Locarno relieved the French pressures for a British treaty of assistance that both Briand and Poincaré had sought in vain.

The most significant feature of the Locarno Agreements was the spirit of hope they had awakened in Europe. When the accords were concluded, on October 16, 1925,

Austen Chamberlain, the British Foreign Secretary, trembled and wept with joy, as did the French Foreign Minister, Aristide Briand. Benito Mussolini

A summit meeting in 1928: the architects of Franco-German rapprochement, Aristide Briand and Gustav Stresemann, meet in the Hotel Splendide in Lugano with the British foreign minister, Sir Austen Chamberlain. Zaleski of Poland and Adatci of Japan (hidden) are at the left; Chamberlain is at the center facing the camera. Briand is in profile at the right. Scialoia of Italy is seen from behind, partly obscuring Stresemann.

kissed Mrs. Chamberlain's hands. Bands played, members of the assembled crowd danced in the square. . . . The next day the headlines in the New York *Times* read, "France and Germany Ban War Forever," and those in the London *Times* declared, "Peace at Last."[10]

When the German delegates took their seats for the first time in the League of Nations in March 1926, Briand welcomed them with one of those orations that made his reputation as the "apostle of peace."

France and Germany are working together now for peace. . . . Down with cannons, machine guns, rifles; down the mourning veils. Make way for conciliation, arbitration, peace.

The League Assembly responded with a "delirious ovation."[11] It was for that spirit, rather than for the concrete terms of the agreements, that the three foreign ministers—Stresemann, Briand, and Chamberlain—were jointly awarded the Nobel Peace Prize in 1926.

In this heady mood, the major European states, the United States, and Japan concluded the Kellogg-Briand Pact on August 27, 1928.[12] The signatories promised to "renounce war as an instrument of national

[10]Jon Jacobson, *Locarno Diplomacy: Germany and the West, 1925–29* (Princeton, N.J., 1972), p. 3.
[11]Jacques Chastenet, *Les Années d'illusions* (Paris, 1960), p. 157.
[12]Frank B. Kellogg was the United States Secretary of State.

policy," although no means of enforcing this promise were included in the pact.

On closer inspection, the Locarno spirit was far too optimistic. It rested on a transient balance struck briefly between French and German force. France had publicly revealed its inability to coerce Germany alone. Britain had publicly revealed its unwillingness to help France do so. Germany's clandestine rearmament had hardly begun, despite some Soviet assistance, yet any clear-sighted person could foresee the disparity of potential force between 60 million Germans and 40 million Frenchmen. Everything depended on Briand's gamble that concessions would disarm the Germans "morally," and that moderation would reconcile them to Versailles where force had failed.

Those hopes were not realized. The follow-up after Locarno was slow and grudging, for Briand was under constant pressure from his centrist majority. Moreover, Briand was a careless diplomat who promised more in his generous oratory than he could actually deliver. Stresemann, for his part, was never able to persuade German nationalists that the French concessions really amounted to anything, compared with the immense humiliation of Versailles.

When the temporary reparations arrangements of the Dawes Plan expired in 1929, a storm of German nationalist opposition arose over the successor plan worked out by the American businessman Owen D. Young. The Young Plan removed Allied tutelage from the German economy, but it provided for continued reparations payments far into the century. The howl of resentment over the Young Plan helped revive the Nazi party in the summer of 1929, even before the onset of the depression.

The Disarmament Issue

The Locarno spirit did not suffice to make disarmament possible. The League of Nations Covenant, borrowing the exact language of Wilson's Fourteen Points (Point 4), had called for "the reduction of national armaments to the lowest point consistent with national safety" (Article 8). The Treaty of Versailles had stripped Germany of armed force as a "first step" toward a general reduction of armaments; Germany had promised to observe those limitations on the understanding that other states would also disarm. The World Disarmament Conference promised in 1919 was not seriously prepared for until 1927 and did not actually meet until February 1932, when it was already far too late. In the meantime, no government had felt confident enough of its national security to entrust its survival to anything except its own armed force.

With respect to land armies, the basic problems were the inequality of the German potential force and the French force, and the difficulty of verifying any artificial ceiling placed on German military power. The experience of German clandestine rearmament in the 1920s had shown that outside inspection teams could do very little to impose artificial limitations of armaments on a recalcitrant government that is backed by its public. The Allied Control Commission filed two long reports, one on January 5, 1925, and the other on January 31, 1927, stating that Germany "had never disarmed, had never had the intention of disarming, and for seven years had done everything in her power to deceive" the foreign inspectors.

Even if one accepts the later opinion of the British strategist Major Basil H. Liddell-Hart that the practical effects of German clandestine rearmament were "overrated,"[13] and that well into the 1930s the German Army was no match for the French, the long-term implications were clear then. The view from Paris was that Germany would eventually gravitate back toward a position of equality or better with the French, and given the resentments bred by Versailles, it would attack as soon as the chances of success became more or less even. French fears were greatly magnified by solitude; neither the United States nor Britain had been willing to conclude a bilateral defense pact with France. The French believed that general disarmament would make Germany more likely, not less, to commit aggression. As a result, France continued to spend a higher percentage of its national income on armaments in the late 1920s than any other European state except Soviet Russia.[14] Even the moderate left leader Edouard Herriot said on January 28, 1925:

> Remember that France has constantly to discuss peace with a dagger an inch away from her heart. Let us away with this dagger.[15]

Beginning in 1929, successive French governments, from right to moderate left, appropriated huge sums for the construction of the Maginot Line, a vast network of underground fortresses and armored turrets whose overlapped fields of fire were impassable to anything known in 1918. When completed at the end of 1935, the Maginot Line extended along the Franco-German frontier from the Swiss border north to the Ardennes Forest, at the Franco-Belgian border, and public opinion was urging the government, against military advice, to extend this steel womb all the way to the English Channel.

From 1927 until 1932 the Disarmament Preparatory Commission worked on preliminary drafts for an agreement. The German demands centered on equality of armament, which in practice meant leveling upward. When a Soviet delegate joined the commission in 1928, he urged the immediate liquidation of all armed forces. All Allied proposals foundered on unstated French assumptions that French survival depended on having a larger ground force than Germany. It was as the

---

[13]Basil H. Liddell-Hart, *The German Generals Talk* (New York, 1948), pp. 13–14.
[14]Figures for 1929: Russian military expenditures, 5.3 percent of national income; French, 4.5 percent; Italian, 4.4 percent; Japanese, 4.3 percent; British, 2.5 percent; American, 1.1 percent; German, 1 percent. When all states' military expenditures soared in the 1930s, France slipped to fifth place. (Quincy Wright, *A Study of War* [Chicago, 1941], pp. 670–71.)
[15]Quoted in Royal Institute of Internal Affairs, *Survey of International Affairs, 1925*, Vol. 2 (London, 1926), p. 15.

Spanish diplomat Salvador de Madariaga said in his parable of the disarmament conference of the animals: the lion proposed the abolition of all weapons except claws and teeth; the eagle, all weapons except beaks and talons; and so on.

When the World Disarmament Conference actually opened in Geneva in February 1932, the moment for agreement had long passed. The opening day of the conference was postponed by news of the Japanese bombing of Shanghai. The German delegation left the conference between July and September 1932 until the French accepted the principle of equality within a system of collective security. Hitler's delegate left the conference for good in October 1934. Indeed, as long as no larger sovereignty than the nation-state functioned in Europe, and as long as each state subordinated disarmament to its own definition of "the lowest point consistent with national safety," it is difficult to imagine any effective reduction of armaments in Europe by treaty.

There was some decline in the proportion of the national income devoted to armaments in the 1920s as compared with 1914 in all the Great Powers except the United States and Japan.[16] But it had much more to do with internal budgetary restraints than with international negotiation. And after the depression of 1929, armaments expenditure would depend primarily on whether a state tried to balance the budget, as in Britain and France, or engaged heavily in deficit spending, as in Germany, Italy, and, under conditions of total economic isolation, the Soviet Union.

Naval disarmament offered more hopeful signs of progress in the 1920s than disarmament of land forces. That was because naval forces were easier to inspect, the conferences were held sooner after the end of the war, and the Franco-German conflict was less directly involved. The Washington Naval Conference of 1921 and 1922 managed to agree on ratios of tonnage in capital ships (battleships, aircraft carriers) among the five main naval powers as follows: the United States and Britain, 5; Japan, 3; France and Italy, 1.75. But the conference failed to deal with smaller ships, such as submarines, destroyers, and cruisers. When that effort was made at Geneva in 1927, it uncovered heated controversy between Britain and the United States and between France and Italy; neither Britain nor France accepted parity in cruisers with its Washington Naval Conference partner. A final attempt to settle naval force limits at the London Naval Conference of 1930 did produce agreed ratios for all types of ships on the part of Britain, the United States, and Japan (France and Italy refused to be bound by any such agreements), but the overriding importance of national self-reliance was made clear in the famous "Escalator Clause": any nation that felt threatened by a nonsignatory power could unilaterally go beyond the agreed limits. In the world of 1930 and after, all nations felt threatened, and the whole enterprise of disarmament by conference failed by trying to alleviate symptoms rather than fundamental causes of that insecurity.

[16]Wright, pp. 670–71.

The more ardent Wilsonians of 1919 had hoped to replace the prewar methods of professional diplomats, working in secrecy and answerable only to kings or prime ministers, with the "open covenants of peace, openly arrived at" of President Wilson's Fourteen Points. "After that, there shall be no private international understandings of any kind but diplomacy shall proceed always frankly and in the public view" (Point 1). No postwar leader, including Wilson, conducted his relations with other national leaders in this way. Nevertheless, the way in which the European states dealt with one another and with the rest of the world differed substantially from prewar diplomacy.

Public Involvement

Although statesmen continued to negotiate in secret, foreign affairs became a more and more public matter between the wars. Before 1914 it was still uncommon for foreign relations to become a major political issue in peacetime.[17] Occasionally political oppositions formed around foreign and colonial policy, as they did in Britain during the Boer War (1899–1902) and in France at the time of the secret diplomacy of the second Moroccan crisis of 1911, but executive branches remained in full control of foreign policy. Even in parliamentary systems, the deputies' powers of review of treaties was incomplete. No one believed, for example, that a parliament could declare a past treaty invalid. As often as not, the executive powers themselves injected issues of foreign and colonial grandeur into partisan politics in order to strengthen their position. The German Chancellor Bernhard von Bülow won an enlarged government majority in the so-called Hottentot election of 1907. Bülow appealed for unlimited executive freedom to conduct foreign policy and colonial expansion among the African Hottentots or anywhere else the government chose, without the "unendurable meddling"[18] of parliament. As Bülow hoped, his patriotic appeals helped reduce the anticolonial Social Democrats' representation from eighty-one seats to forty-three.

The passions of the First World War aroused public sensitivity and emotion concerning foreign policy. During the last year of the war, Wilson and Lenin heightened expectations with a propaganda duel about war aims and programs for reordering the world. The great gathering of world leaders in Paris in 1919 made the ensuing world system seem more man-made and less a natural inheritance than before. Thus the subsequent disillusions about that system brought blame to political leaders, and elections turned more and more frequently on foreign policy issues. Aristide Briand lost office as prime minister and

---

[17]One exception was the Turkish slaughter of rebellious Bulgarians in 1876 and the ensuing war between Russia and Turkey, which involved British public emotions for the first time in daily newspaper accounts of a distant war. The word *jingoism* entered the language from a British patriotic song of 1878: "We don't want to fight, but, by jingo, if we do, we've got the men, we've got the ships, we've got the money too."

[18]Quoted in Carl E. Schorske, *German Social Democracy, 1905–17* (Cambridge, Mass., 1955), p. 60.

foreign minister in 1922 for seeming too compliant toward England, and was narrowly limited after Locarno in the concessions he could offer Germany. The elections of 1924 turned partly on foreign affairs in both France and England. Hitler's immediate predecessors struggled to win electoral support through foreign policy successes. In 1935, to look a decade ahead, British and French governments fell because they seemed to acquiesce in the Italian conquest of Ethiopia, and in the late 1930s the reaction to Hitler's expansionism was the dominant preoccupation of politics. Sustained public emotional involvement in foreign policy was not the guarantee of peace that the Wilsonians had expected, for public opinion turned out to be more jingoistic than rulers had been, and weak governments catered to that jingoism.

One major reason for public emotion over foreign relations was economic. Almost every European was touched in his pocket by international affairs in ways that seemed to him all the more frightening for being uncontrollable and beyond comprehension. Most Frenchmen knew that the catastrophic inflation of the franc in the 1920s was somehow tied to war debts to America and the failure of Germany to pay full reparations. Most Germans felt that the implacable Allied victors had somehow destroyed the mark in 1923. Most Englishmen were aware of the fact that the great coal and textile industries, the foundations of the British Empire, were somehow worth less in the postwar world and that Britain was now in debt to its offspring America. Popular emotions were closely tied to foreign affairs after 1918 because the purchasing

The defeated people suffered intensely from hunger and cold in the winter of 1918/19. The Austrians cut down the Vienna Woods for fuel, and the middle class as well as the poor were reduced to carrying firewood.

power of one's money and the value of one's property were now more buffeted about by international fluctuations and influences than ever before.

The Communist Threat

Foreign relations took on a more ideological tone, too, now that the communist movement controlled the machinery of a state. World Communist parties intervened in interstate relations on two levels: through traditional diplomacy and through revolutionary parties. As a sovereign state, the Soviet Union sought normal diplomatic relations with other states after the expected world revolution had failed to materialize. The Weimar Republic was the first major state to exchange ambassadors with the Soviet Union, at Rapallo, in 1922. Britain and France and most other countries followed suit in 1924.[19] The Japanese evacuated their last holdings in Siberia in 1925 and recognized the new regime. As the British Liberal politician Lloyd George said, one trades even with cannibals. Leaders on both sides recognized that even though the Bolshevik Revolution stood little chance in the 1920s of spreading outside Russia, the Communist party was in firm control there. The Soviet Union practiced its conventional interstate diplomacy in the 1920s under George Chicherin, a veteran tsarist diplomat but a Menshevik, or reformist socialist, by conviction.

Simultaneously, however, the Soviet Union was the major force in the Comintern,[20] the global organization of pro-Soviet Marxist parties formed by Lenin in 1919 in the expectation of imminent world revolution and led through the 1920s by the old Bolshevik Gregory Zinoviev. Agents of the Comintern worked within foreign states to strengthen communist internal opposition. The Comintern's influence over Soviet foreign policy diminished through the 1920s as the exercise of state power in Russia and the protection of the homeland of communism came to prevail over the promotion of world revolution. Nevertheless, the noncommunist states' relations with the Soviet Union were always complicated by this ambiguous dual diplomacy. Allegations of Comintern activity in Britain brought about defeat of the Labour party in 1924 and suspension of diplomatic relations with the Soviet Union. The British election of 1924 revealed how sensitive an issue the unofficial foreign activities of Communist parties remained.

Diplomatic Machinery

European diplomacy had been transformed, since 1914, by greater and more sustained public involvement in foreign affairs, by economic complications, and by the existence of a new communist state in their

---

[19] The United States did not exchange ambassadors with the Soviet Union until after the election of Franklin D. Roosevelt in 1932, although there had been aid missions during the famine of 1921 and 1922, and some United States firms had negotiated contracts with the Soviet government.

[20] The Communist International, or Third International. See Chapter 5, pp. 161–63.

midst. But the basic techniques of interstate relations were not changed. The League of Nations did not provide effective machinery for resolving international disputes by organized international consultations and sanctions. The League had never been intended to have sovereign authority over its member states. While the League was effective in facilitating agreements in the 1920s in cases where the Great Powers concurred anyway, it could not coerce any major state against that state's will. This handicap was not immediately apparent in the calmer years after Locarno, and Geneva appeared to be bustling with preparations for disarmament, with the settlement of minor disputes, and with the tasks of the social agencies. The League's inability to do anything about the Japanese invasion of Manchuria in 1931 dealt the League its first conspicuous public humiliation, however, and it was one from which it did not recover.

Between the wars, sovereign states still dealt with sovereign states in Europe and in the wider world. Without a higher authority to appeal to, there was no way to adjudicate disputes other than by some mixture of bargaining and force. The main difference was that there were far more players in this game than before 1914. That meant international relations were less under the control of the former Great Powers of Europe than before. European diplomats struggled to adapt to a world filled with many more active sovereign states, some of which—notably the United States and Japan—could affect European lives more profoundly than Europeans could affect them. The new nation-states of Eastern Europe generated no fewer conflicts and problems than the old dynasties they replaced. Germany and Russia were both bound to reclaim some of their temporarily eclipsed power, and there was no effective machinery for making that process a smooth one. Thus European international relations under the Versailles system were at least as unstable as before 1914.

Suggestions for Further Reading

The removal of the last restrictions on British and French archives for the 1920s has made obsolete much earlier work on European diplomacy and interstate relations after Versailles. Among older works that retain their importance, E. H. Carr, *The Twenty Years' Crisis,** rev. ed. (1946) is a suggestive comparison of different styles of diplomacy by a convinced internationalist. Arnold Wolfers, *Britain and France Between Two Wars* (1940) remains a lucid account of those two countries' differing priorities, as does W. M. Jordan, *Britain, France, and the German Question* (1943). The annual volumes published by the Royal Institute of International Affairs in London provide interesting contemporary accounts of each year's main developments in international relations.

Jon Jacobson, *Locarno Diplomacy* (1972) shows, on the basis of new research in British and German archives, how little Locarno resolved conflicts of interest among the European states. Even without access to French archives, it provides the best account of Briand in action. Other important new work on France includes Judith M. Hughes, *To The Maginot Line: The Politics of French Military Preparations in the 1920s* (1971), which shows that French soldiers and politicians approached the insuperable problems of preserving French hegemony with much the same inadequate solutions, and Piotr S. Wandycz, *France and her Eastern Allies* (1962). Hans Gatzke, ed., *European Diplomacy Between Two World Wars, 1918–1939** (1972) samples recent scholarship. German foreign policy in the 1920s is virtually synonymous with the career of Gustav Stresemann. See Hans W. Gatzke, *Stresemann and the Rearmament of Germany** (1954). German–Russian relations in the 1920s are the subject of Gerald Freund, *Unholy Alliance* (1957), and Gustav Hilger and Alfred G. Meyer, *The Incompatible Allies: German–Soviet Relations, 1918–1941* (1953).

On the Russian side, Adam B. Ulam, *Expansion and Coexistence: The History of Soviet Foreign Policy, 1917–1967** (1968) is now the most authoritative of a number of works.

Alan Cassels, *Mussolini's Early Diplomacy* (1970) is the most useful study of Italian foreign policy in the 1920s.

David Felix, *Walther Rathenau and the Weimar Republic: The Politics of Reparations* (1971) has not entirely supplanted J. W. Wheeler-Bennett, *The Wreck of Reparations* (1933).

9 "NORMALCY": EUROPE IN THE 1920s

Only in the mid-1920s could Europeans begin to feel "the full sunshine of peace."[1] Then tensions relaxed, and a period of calm and prosperity followed in the late 1920s. Internationally, the bitter confrontations of the early years of the decade, such as the French occupation of the Ruhr, were replaced by the Locarno spirit. In domestic politics, the surges of both revolution and counterrevolution subsided, and the parliamentary states settled down into the alternation of more moderate left and right. Wartime controls were disbanded, and reconstruction began to cover up the outward signs of war. In Western Europe, at least, booming prosperity carried production figures higher than anything known up to 1914. The war's loosening of social restraints, compounded by the indulgence of deferred desires, lent these boom years of the late 1920s a glitter of brash vulgarity.

[1] Robert Graves and Alan Hodge, *The Long Week-End: A Social History of Great Britain, 1918–39* (London, 1940), p. 113.

United States President Warren Harding's term for this period was a "return to normalcy." But what was "normal" for Europe after four years of total war, followed by another four years of postwar turmoil? The moderate center-left and center-right coalitions that dominated public life in Western European parliamentary regimes in the late 1920s revived the values of late–nineteenth-century liberalism: broadened parliamentary democracy, individual liberties, and a market economy based on private enterprise and operating under a bare minimum of state intervention. Since the liberal Western states, Britain and France, had won the war, had restrained revolution, and had then recovered the highest living standards in Europe, those values tended to seem "normal" to many Europeans in the late 1920s. The question still to be answered was how adequately these "normal" nineteenth-century liberal values fit the postwar world.

Neoliberal Economics: Dismantling War Government

No one expected to maintain the fever-pitch effort or the stringent controls of war government indefinitely. Once military demobilization had been completed and internal order was assured, the various war boards and regulations began to be dissolved. By 1922, outside the Soviet Union, wartime agencies had been almost entirely dismantled. Liberal values held that economic and social decisions are best made in a free market, and "normalcy" meant the fullest possible return to that state of affairs. European liberals thought of wartime economic management as distasteful emergency expedients. "We want to get on with our business," said the British Tory Lord Inchcape, and

> not spend our time arguing with Government clerks, dancing attendance at the Board of Trade, appearing before committees, wheedling Consuls for permission to import what we need, throwing open our books, bills, and invoices to inspectors from Whitehall, and going through all the worry and expense to justify every transaction . . . to some official inquisitor.[2]

Even in states with the least tradition of state intervention, however, it was clear that the old world could not be fully restored. One small but revealing example was the passport. In 1914, Europeans had traveled freely throughout the Continent except in the Russian and Ottoman empires. After 1918, all European states required travelers to carry passports.

Restoring a pure laissez-faire economy would have been even more difficult than restoring unrestricted travel, for no European economy had been left to the free play of market forces even before 1914. All European states except that preeminent trading nation, Britain, had protected domestic industry by tariffs or other trade restrictions after the 1880s. Internally, governments had intervened to protect firms

[2]Paul Barton Johnson, *Land Fit for Heroes: The Planning of British Reconstruction, 1916–19* (Chicago, 1968), p. 451.

against their workers, and had been far more vigilant against combinations of workers than against combinations of employers. Virtually all governments had begun to supervise working hours and conditions and to support health- and retirement-insurance plans. In Britain, Lloyd George had promised a postwar "land fit for heroes." How could this promise be kept by letting everything seek its own level?

In fact, no European liberal proposed to restore a mythical pure laissez-faire economy in Europe, nor would either businessmen or organized labor have accepted such aims. The liberals hoped to restore as much as possible of the economic freedom that businessmen had enjoyed before the war within a world financial, trading, and banking system resembling that of 1914. The clearest sign of these intentions was the reestablishment of the international gold standard, first in England in 1925 and subsequently in most European states outside the Soviet Union.

But even in its most booming prosperity the European economy of the late 1920s could only be a distorted imitation of that of 1914. For one thing, the war had vastly increased the scale and power of organizations in the economy. Business cartels, already present before the war, had emerged vastly strengthened by war government, especially on the Continent. In the 1920s, international cartels regulated the sales of iron, steel, oil, chemicals, and other major industrial products in Europe. At the same time, labor unions enrolled a higher proportion of industrial workers than before the war, and they had participated in centralized economic decisions under war government. Under such conditions, a liberal economic policy amounted to arbitrating among powerful organized interests.

The international economy was also permanently changed by the effects of war. The reinstitution of the gold standard did not restore a smoothly functioning medium of international trade. Postwar inflation had made currencies fluctuate wildly in relation to one another, and speculators stood ready to profit by these swings and to accentuate them by large purchases and sales of currency. Above all, the burden of reparations and war debts interfered with international trade and exchange. Germany owed money to Britain and France; France owed money to Britain and the United States; Britain owed money to the United States. United States loans to Germany in the late 1920s made the whole circuit possible. If anything happened to the economy of the United States, the whole delicate structure of the neoliberal international payments system would come tumbling down.

Neoliberal Politics: Broadening Parliamentary Democracy

Normalcy in politics meant a hastening of the late–nineteenth-century march toward universal suffrage, parliamentary regimes, and republics.

For the first time in Europe, republics became the rule rather than the exception. Before the war, only one Great Power, France, had been a republic. War and revolution swept away three great hereditary thrones (the Hohenzollern, the Habsburg, and the Romanov) as well as some minor ones, such as the royal families of Bavaria and Greece. After the war, only Great Britain and Italy, among major states, remained monarchies. Most monarchies were now small states, as in the Low Countries and Scandinavia. Only one of the new Eastern European successor states was a monarchy: Yugoslavia.

The creation of new regimes provided a field day for constitutionmakers. New constitutions drew heavily on the examples of the Allied powers; they often combined French parliamentary structures with a popularly elected president on the American model. The most important state to draft a new parliamentary constitution was Germany. The Weimar Constitution of August 1919 was supposed to distill the best legal scholarship and experience in the workings of parliamentary systems. Drafted by a liberal Berlin law professor, Hugo Preuss, assisted by sociologist Max Weber and others, the Weimar Constitution was meant to move German politics firmly onto a democratic path and at the same time strengthen the central power over the individual German states. A president, popularly elected to serve seven years, designated the chancellor, whose cabinet must have the support of a majority in the popularly elected chamber (*Reichstag*). An upper house (*Reichsrat*) of delegates of the states could delay but not block legislation. In order to provide the most mathematically equal weighting to each citizen's vote, the Weimar drafters experimented with proportional representation, by which every political party received seats in the legislature in proportion to its popular vote.

The vote was significantly widened in the postwar constitutions. Wartime pressures had forced even the German Empire to promise in 1917 to end the Prussian three-class voting system. More women received voting rights in Europe just after the First World War than in any other comparable period until the next wave of new constitutions in 1946. Before the war, women in Europe had been permitted to vote only in Finland (1906) and Norway (1913).[3] In 1918, Britain introduced virtually universal manhood suffrage and the vote for women over thirty; other women were enfranchised in 1928. In the same postwar period, women got the vote in Weimar Germany, three successor states (Poland, Czechoslovakia, and Austria), the Low Countries, and Scandinavia. Women could not yet vote in Italy, Switzerland, France, or Spain. And women occupied important political roles between the wars only in Britain and the Soviet Union.

The leveling effects of the war were apparent in postwar politics. Socialist parties, including some members of genuine working-class background, shared power in the parliamentary democracies. The new president of Weimar Germany, Social Democrat Friedrich Ebert, had

[3]Women could also vote in New Zealand (1893), Australia (1902), and twelve western states of the United States before 1914. See M. N. Duffy, *The Emancipation of Women* (Oxford, 1967), pp. 44–45.

been a saddlemaker's apprentice. The first British Labour government members of 1924 debated heatedly among themselves about the proper clothing to wear for the ritual call on King George V. Eventually they decided on the traditional tailcoats. One war later, the Labour leaders of 1945 were to call on George VI in street clothes.

The three major parliamentary democracies of Western Europe— Britain, France, and Germany—settled into centrist coalitions by the mid-1920s. During the late 1920s, these regimes gave an outward impression of governmental stability and consensus.

Postwar normalcy meant not only the attempt to restore liberal politics and economics in northern and Western Europe but the urge to spread them to the rest of the Continent. Parliamentary institutions could not be effectively transplanted to Eastern and southern European areas, however, where large parts of the population were illiterate peasants and where nationalities clashed.

Britain

The highly personal government of wartime leader David Lloyd George had continued after the armistice, fortified by the "khaki election" of December 1918. But in late 1922 Conservative party leaders, confident of their strength in the country and chafing under Lloyd George's one-man rule and taste for governmental activism, withdrew from the coalition that had lasted since 1916. The collapse of Lloyd George's personal majority marked a return to more traditional party politics in Britain.

A Three-Way Party System

As the election of November 1922 showed, however, British party politics no longer resembled the nineteenth-century alternation of Liberals and Conservatives. While the Conservatives won their largest majority in this century, the balance of political power shifted, and Labour emerged as the second most powerful party of the kingdom. The Liberal party, the proud successor of eighteenth-century Whigs and nineteenth-century reformers like Grey, Peel, and Gladstone, slipped to third place.[4] For the moment, since many British voters were doubtful of Labour's capacity to govern, the Liberal party held on to a balancing third of the electorate. The British parliamentary system, which had evolved in the rivalry of two parties, functioned as a three-party system throughout the interwar period.

On one level, the Liberal decline could be attributed to the vagaries of politics. The Liberal party had split twice in two generations: once in the 1890s over the question of Irish independence, and again between followers of Asquith and Lloyd George during the First World War. On

---

[4]Electoral results, November 1922: Conservative—345 seats; Labour—142 seats; Liberal—117 seats.

a more profound level, however, the Liberal decline suggested that the party's values of political democracy and economic laissez faire offered a diminishing prospect of coping with the social and economic challenges Britain had confronted since 1914. The British economy's nineteenth-century staples, coal and textiles, were no longer very profitable, and much of its cushion of foreign investment had been liquidated during the war. Social expectations had been raised by the experiment of war government, while the British capacity to earn had been deeply eroded. The Liberal party was destined to shrink to a mere splinter by the 1940s, one war later.

The Conservative ministers who followed Lloyd George from 1922 to 1924 wanted Britain to "get on with its own work, with the minimum of interference at home and of disturbance abroad."[5] This was a reasonable program for normalcy. The major innovation of the postwar Conservatives was their full commitment as a party to protective tariffs, in recognition of British industry's diminished competitive advantage in the postwar world. Some individual Conservatives had advocated special trade privileges for the empire before 1914, and wartime trade controls had set a precedent. But when Conservatives chose to fight the elections of 1923 on the issue of tariff protection, it was the first time since 1846 that a major British party had advocated peacetime tariffs in an election. In the hostile economic jungle of the postwar world, Conservatives had abandoned the trade principles of most nineteenth-century British leaders. Both Liberals and Labour supported free trade, however, and their majority in the elections of December 1923 provided an unambiguous mandate for it.[6] A return to free trade could also be considered a vote for normalcy, since Britain's nineteenth-century economic supremacy had been bound up with it.

The First Labour Government, 1924

Although Labour had reinforced its position as the largest party of the opposition, neither the Liberal party nor Labour enjoyed a majority of its own after the election. Instead of joining in a coalition, the Liberal party leader, former Prime Minister Asquith, decided to allow the Labour party its first taste of governing responsibility—and perhaps enough leeway to discredit itself. Thus the Labour leader Ramsay MacDonald was able to form the first nominally socialist government in Britain in January 1924.

Some Englishmen feared the nationalization of "everything including women"[7] from a Labour government. Some hoped for a revolutionary socialist regime. MacDonald's government fulfilled neither the fears nor the hopes aroused at its beginning. Although MacDonald had helped

[5]Electoral program of Prime Minister Bonar Law, 1922, quoted in A. J. P. Taylor, *English History, 1914–45* (Oxford, 1965), p. 196.
[6]Electoral results, December 1923: Conservative—258; Labour—191; Liberal—158.
[7]Graves and Hodge, p. 76.

found the more radical Independent Labour party in the 1890s and had been among the handful of outspoken British pacifists during the First World War, he had no intention of trying to impose socialism on Britain. Nor had he the power to do so. His government depended on Liberal votes for its majority. His cabinet included a number of recruits from the Liberal party, but only one of the wartime radicals from the Clydeside industrial area, John Wheatley. The Wheatley Housing Act, which launched the construction of municipal housing at controlled rents, was the one genuine domestic innovation of the period. Aside from that first peacetime experiment in business–government cooperation and social planning, the MacDonald government did more to adapt politicans of genuine working-class background (MacDonald himself was the son of a Scottist sharecropper) to the mainstream of British politics than vice versa. "It's a lum hat (top hat) government like a' the rest," one disillusioned British workman is supposed to have said.

The MacDonald government was more a reaffirmation of economic liberalism and the continued dismantling of wartime controls than a turn to the left. No doubt this was what most of the electorate wanted, and MacDonald effectively established the legitimacy of Labour as a governing party and enormously widened access to the British political elite. That was no mean achievement.

In any event, the first Labour government was brief. It fell ten months later over personal matters: "Gentleman Mac" had been accused of accepting an expensive limousine and of shelving the prosecution of a communist newspaper. In the ensuing election of October 1924, the Conservatives focused on the alleged dangerous radicalism of Mac-Donald's foreign policy, including the government's recognition of the Soviet Union. The conservative press produced a letter from Comintern Chairman Gregory Zinoviev advising British Communists on ways to undermine British capitalism. MacDonald was accused of being dangerously "soft" on subversive activities. The Zinoviev Letter is now known to have been forged by a Polish anti-Bolshevik, although the British editors who used it probably thought it was genuine. It was enough to help defeat Labour, although the Liberal party suffered even more heavily in the climate of political polarization that the letter created.

Return to Conservative "Normalcy"

The election of 1924 brought back to power the Conservative leader Stanley Baldwin, who personified the British version of normalcy in the late 1920s. Baldwin was a cabinet member from 1924 to 1937, except for the period of the second Labour government (1929–31), and prime minister during 1923, 1924 to 1929, and 1935 to 1937, one of the longest spans of political power in modern British history.

Stanley Baldwin went to some pains to present himself as moderate rather than conservative. Photographers and cartoonists pictured him as a prosperous yeoman of Old England, a ruddy-faced taciturn man

walking the fields and admiring his pigs, puffing a pipe, waving aside
intellectuals, and speaking a bluff, frank common sense. He was the first
British prime minister to address cabinet members by their first names,
and the first to make effective political use of the radio. He prided
himself on good relations with Labour. He helped establish a pragmatic,
middle-class style in the British Conservative party that supplanted
forever the aristocratic manner of the previous generation of Tory
leaders, such as Lord Salisbury and Lord Curzon, who is said to have
called Baldwin "a man of the utmost insignificance." On closer inspection, Baldwin turns out to have been a shrewd parliamentary tactician
and a man of quite fixed economic orthodoxy. The wealthy son of a steel
manufacturer, he helped steer England back to a hollow reconstruction
of pre-1914 financial and business arrangements.

The most noteworthy single step in British neoliberalism was the
return to the international gold standard. The two fixed poles of
nineteenth-century world trade had been the free interchangeability of
all major currencies with gold and the role of London as world financial
capital. But the gold standard had been suspended by wartime currency
controls, while London had been separated from part of its clientele,
disrupted by the war effort, and permanently weakened by the loss of
British investment overseas during the war. To the economically orthodox, return to the gold standard and the revival of London went hand in
hand.

Winston Churchill, Baldwin's Chancellor of the Exchequer, announced the end of the wartime suspension of the gold standard in his
budget speech of April 1925. Henceforth, the pound was freely convertible anywhere in the world to gold. It was not a classic gold standard,
for gold coins no longer circulated freely in domestic transactions in
England. But it gave the illusion that the old world was restored and that
the last of the war's effects had vanished.

Britain's return to the gold standard probably hampered the nation's
search for renewed prosperity in the late 1920s. For one thing, it made
British goods more expensive on the world market, since Churchill had
insisted on returning to 1914 exchange rates, which overvalued the
pound in relation to the dollar.[8] A more fundamental criticism was that
whereas the prewar free exchange of pounds for gold had rested on a
large British surplus in international accounts and large gold holdings,
the postwar London gold market rested on a weakened economy. Gold
was supplemented by holdings of reserves in foreign exchange, such as
marks or dollars, which could be quickly withdrawn in case of trouble.
That fragile system came crashing down from 1929 to 1931, damaging
the British economy far more severely than a less grandiose financial
restoration in 1925 would have.

Normalcy did nothing for the British workingman's standard of living

---

[8]In *The Economic Consequences of Mr. Churchill* (1925), John Maynard Keynes charged that
the pound was overvalued by 10 percent as compared with 1914. In fact, British exports
never returned to the 1914 level in the 1920s.

in the 1920s, or for the very high level of chronic unemployment that persisted between the wars. The basic adjustments that Britain had to make to a changed place in the world economy were made more difficult by the high price of British goods abroad on the gold standard. The mainstays of the British export trade were stagnating industries like coal and textiles. British exports never made up for the wartime loss of overseas investments, and unemployment in Britain never dropped below a shocking 10 percent throughout the interwar period, even in the most prosperous years of the late 1920s. Stanley Baldwin's solution to Britain's economic troubles was nothing if not frank. "All the workers in this country," he said in a speech on July 30, 1925, "have got to take reductions in wages to help put industry on its feet."[9]

The coal industry provided the most serious challenge to Baldwin's hope for Britain's return to normalcy. Rich coal mines close to the sea had been a major stimulus to British commercial and industrial preeminence in the nineteenth century, and the mines were still the largest single employer in Britain. In the 1920s, however, there was a world glut of coal. The British mines competed especially poorly, for their markets had been interrupted during the war, their equipment was outdated,

[9]Quoted in Taylor, p. 239.

Opponents of the General Strike of May 1926 in England organized makeshift transportation to get to work.

and their management was fragmented among many marginal companies. The mineowners believed that wage cuts were their only way back to the world market; the miners adamantly refused to work for less than they had been receiving.[10] A government-appointed commission, headed by Herbert Samuel, tried unsuccessfully to persuade the mineowners to rationalize, consolidate, and modernize their mines in return for government assistance in negotiating lower wages. When negotiations deadlocked, the miners went out on strike at the beginning of May 1926.

The miners' grievances were the principal fuel for the General Strike of 1926, the tensest moment of class conflict in modern Britain between the "hands off Russia" strikes of 1919 and 1920 and the energy crisis of the winter of 1973/74. The striking miners were joined by very nearly all organized labor in the fullest demonstration of union solidarity in British history. Close to 4 million workers were out on the peak day, May 13. The general council of the Trades Union Congress (TUC) accepted a compromise after nine days (government enforcement of the modernization advocated in the Samuel report in exchange for any lowering of wages), but some of the rank and file continued the strike. Many miners were starved back to work, at lower wages, only six months later.

The British General Strike of 1926, in retrospect, seems an end rather than a beginning. Its leaders had intended all along to use the strike as a lever for negotiation, not as a revolutionary step. The TUC even used the term *national strike* rather than the old syndicalist term *general strike,* with its intimations of replacing the state by workers' associations. Unlike the strikes in the Clydeside area just after the war, there was no mention during the 1926 strike of soviets or strike committees assuming governmental functions. Although there were some acts of violence on both sides as well as organized strikebreaking by the government and by university students, there were no deaths. All this gives the lie to hysterical fears of "microbes of Bolshevism" published in the conservative press at the time, and to dire predictions by hard-liner Winston Churchill that the strike could "only end in the overthrow of Parliamentary Government or its decisive victory."[11]

The results of the General Strike, on the government side, were a new law in 1927 outlawing sympathy strikes and the rupture of trade and diplomatic relations with the Soviet Union, which some Conservatives accused of having contributed relief funds to the miners. On the Trade Union Congress side, the British union movement eventually recovered its losses in funds and membership; its commitment to collective bargaining within the existing British social system was actually strengthened. At the level of the individual miners and their families, the bitterness and suffering had no chronicler.

[10] The least skilled mineworkers in the hardest hit region were asked to accept a wage cut from 78s per week to 45s 10d (from about $19 to about $12 at current exchange rates), with hours cut to six per day.
[11] Quoted in Charles L. Mowat, *Britain Between the Wars, 1918–40* (London, 1955), p. 319.

In the later 1920s, Britain appeared peaceful and prosperous. But the external trappings of normalcy barely concealed the inadequate adjustment Britain had made to its diminished world economic position.

France

After the Poincaré government's hard line toward Germany had been discredited by the occupation of the Ruhr, the French electorate gave a majority to a moderate left coalition in the elections of May 1924. The *cartel des gauches* was an electoral alliance of the two main parliamentary left parties in France, Radicals and reformist Socialists.

The Cartel des Gauches

This coalition bears close examination, for it provides the key to the apparent labyrinth of Third Republic politics in interwar France. American readers, used to a more cautious political vocabulary, are likely to be misled by the flaming labels given Latin parties. The French Radical party was the lineal descendant of genuine radicals of the 1860s Second Empire: partisans of universal suffrage, parliamentary primacy over the executive, free universal secondary education, the disestablishment of the Catholic Church, and the replacement of professional armies by militia. Although some Radicals had favored an income tax in the 1890s, the party generally disapproved of state intervention in the economy. By 1905, with the separation of Church and state in France, the Radical program had been virtually fulfilled. The Radical party remained as the main political expression of the "little man" in France: anticlerical, egalitarian in political terms, laissez faire in economic terms, sentimental about the French Revolution, ready to rally to the defense of the republic threatened by bishops, generals, or aristocrats. (All European Catholic countries had similar anticlerical, democratic, small-property parties).

The other half of the *cartel des gauches* was the French Socialist party (SFIO, or French Section of the [Second] Workers' International). This was the remnant of French parliamentary socialism left when a majority of Socialists voted in 1920 to join the Third International (Comintern). The SFIO was well on its way back to becoming the other main parliamentary party on the French left by 1924. Although nominally committed to Marxist socialism and the eventual workers' revolution, the SFIO placed a high value on the survival of the parliamentary republic as a first step toward these goals. French Socialists were willing to cooperate at election time with the Radicals in order to prevent a split in the moderate left vote, but they were unwilling to take part in a "bourgeois" government until they had an electoral majority of their own and could enact socialist laws.

The basis of the alliance, then, was defense of the Third Republic against clerical or monarchist enemies on the right, not a common social policy. It was a 1924 reincarnation of the Radical–Socialist alliance that had formed at the turn of the century (1899–1905) over the Dreyfus Affair, when it seemed that clericals and army officers were willing to violate the constitution rather than admit that a military court had erred in sentencing the Jewish Captain Alfred Dreyfus on a trumped-up charge of treason. Such an alliance worked best at election time, when the danger of splitting the left vote was uppermost in the politicians' minds. Both Radicals and Socialists promised to support whichever of their condidates was ahead in a run-off.[12] This practice of "republican discipline" returned reformist left majorities to parliament in three of the five French elections between the wars (1924, 1932, and 1936).

Once elected, however, Radical and SFIO deputies had trouble cooperating in a positive governmental program. They could agree on political liberties, freer education, anticlericalism, and antimilitarism. But if economic issues arose, the Radicals' small-property bias clashed fundamentally with the SFIO's Marxism. Between elections, therefore, the pivotal Radical party tended to turn back toward center coalitions. The resulting incoherency of majorities was a major ingredient of what the American political scientist Stanley Hoffmann has called the "stalemate" of the Third Republic, an immobile political system that was the counterpart of the cautious economy and low birth rate that prevailed in France.

The election of the *cartel des gauches* in May 1924 permits us to see this political stalemate at work. The new prime minister was Edouard Herriot, leader of the Radical party between the wars and the personification of the nonsocialist left in the later Third Republic. Herriot was a man of good qualities, a humanist *littérateur* (he wrote a number of books, including biographies of Beethoven and Madame De Staël), active in providing municipal social services when he was mayor of Lyons, genuinely concerned about political liberties, a consummate parliamentary bargainer; his enormous physical bulk testified to his pleasure in the cafés and restaurants of Lyons and Paris.

Herriot's accomplishments as French premier (June 1924–April 1925) are a guide to the areas in which the *cartel des gauches* was capable of decisive action. We have already seen Herriot's contribution to international conciliation, along with Ramsay MacDonald and Gustav Stresemann in 1924.[13] He extended French diplomatic recognition to the Soviet Union and withdrew it from Vatican City. French laws removing clerical influence from the public schools were extended to Alsace-Lorraine (which had not been part of France when those laws were passed in the 1880s). Steps were taken toward democratizing the elitist French public high schools. Antimilitarism, anticlericalism, enlargement

[12]French electoral practice, as is proper in a multiparty political system, provides for a run-off in the likely event that no candidate gets 50 percent or more of the votes in the first election.
[13]See Chapter 8, pp. 225–29.

of individual opportunity through education: that was the common ground on which French Radicals and Socialists felt happy.[14]

Unfortunately, the major problems faced by the *cartel des gauches* were economic and financial. France had expected to pay its war debts with German reparations. German reparations were also expected to cover the enormous costs of postwar reconstruction, which were causing the French budget to continue to run at a deficit. Herriot's liquidation of the Ruhr occupation, however, showed that France was probably never going to squeeze much money out of Germany. Inflation had run rampant since the end of wartime economic controls. French conservatives, distrustful of Herriot, lost confidence in the international value of the franc. Holders of francs began selling them for gold and other currencies, creating a "run on the franc." At the same time, the financial community and the Bank of France put pressure on Herriot to balance the budget. Eventually the Bank of France refused to lend current operating sums to the government.

Herriot and the Radical party always claimed that conservative financiers had erected a "wall of money" against the republic. It was typical Radical rhetoric, the "little man's" suspicion of great economic powers. There is no doubt that conservative hostility to Herriot contributed to the run on the franc. But the real problem lay in the French people's years of refusal to support the expenses of war and reconstruction by taxation, and in the Radicals' horror of state regulation. As in Britain in 1924, the move to the left meant less governmental intervention, not more. Wartime controls were an unpleasant memory. Aside from creating steeper income taxes, the French Socialists had no interest in government intervention within capitalism. The Radicals preferred to let the economy regulate itself. So Herriot held back from the higher taxes and currency control that might have helped stabilize the franc.

Following Herriot's fall in April 1925, there were seven ministries within fifteen months. While the Radicals felt their way toward a more centrist coalition without the Socialists, inflation soared, and the franc declined on the world's money markets to about one-tenth of its prewar value.

Poincaré: Return to "Normalcy"

France finally found its normalcy of the late 1920s in the austere person of Raymond Poincaré. Poincaré, repudiated in 1924 for occupying the Ruhr, returned in 1926 as a kind of national financial savior. His personal probity and dour legalism provided a kind of emotional reassurance to a people frightened at seeing their savings evaporate in a never-ending inflationary spiral. Even before Poincaré did anything, investors begun buying francs back, and the recovery began. Mostly by that emotional reassurance, and in part by the traditional conservative

---

[14]The SFIO did not hold cabinet positions in this "bourgeois" government but contributed essential votes to its parliamentary majority.

remedies of governmental parsimony and careful management, Poincaré was able to nurse the franc back to one-fifth of its prewar international value in 1928. At that point he returned to the international gold standard. The "Napoleon franc" had endured unchanged from 1807 to 1914 as a firm economic rock on which the French middle class built in serenity. Then it had been shaken by the war and destroyed by postwar inflation. Now that it was replaced by the "Poincaré franc" in 1928, the middle class could begin to glimpse the revival of a stable world. The war had been paid for out of their savings, however, and even during the historic high level of prosperity reached in 1929, there remained tender spots on French middle-class consciousness. The franc must never be touched again. And France must never again embark on another war, so costly in gold and blood.

The Poincaré government, one of the longest "reigns" of any Third Republic premier (July 1926–July 1929), symbolizes the French version of the late 1920s normalcy. The presence of Aristide Briand, the man of Locarno, at the Foreign Ministry assured that Poincaré's hard line of 1922 to 1924 had been replaced by conciliation and the end of dangerous foreign confrontations. At home, the return to the gold standard and balanced budgets seemed a reassuring reappearance of the economic verities. Wartime controls and scarcities and postwar turmoil seemed things of the past.

Weimar Germany

The Weimar Republic was, outwardly, a dramatic departure for Germany. The very decision to draft the new constitution during the summer of 1919 in Weimar, the town of Goethe, rather than in Berlin, was itself a powerful symbolic gesture. Berlin had been the garrison city of the Hohenzollern kings of Prussia; it had become the Red city of Rosa Luxemburg, Karl Liebknecht, and the Spartacists. At Weimar, the liberal ideals of the nineteenth century seemed to reach belated fulfillment. These ideals had been deflected in Germany during the 1860s and 1870s, when a majority of German liberals overlooked Chancellor Bismarck's subversion of the parliamentary system in their enthusiasm for German unification and military victories. A German liberal like the historian Friedrich Meinecke could now hope that in the regime created at Weimar the German "men of culture" (*Kulturmenschen*) had won the upper hand over the German "men of power" (*Machtmenschen*) at long last.[15]

Burdens of the Weimar Republic

The Weimar Republic was burdened from the beginning by almost crushing liabilities. The constitution no doubt had its faults; the proportional representation system, for example, magnified the country's

[15]Friedrich Meinecke, *The German Catastrophe*, trans. Sidney B. Fay (Cambridge, Mass., 1950), pp. 27–29.

divisions in a multiparty parliament. But a reasonably harmonious national community can govern itself well, despite all sorts of flawed constitutional arrangements. The Weimar regime faced far more fundamental problems. It was indelibly imprinted for many Germans with the stain of defeat, for it was the regime that had accepted the *Diktat* of Versailles in the summer of 1919. It was the product of a revolution in which (in the eyes of many German nationalists) the left had first stabbed the German Army in the back by undermining it with revolution in November 1918, and had then been rewarded with political power. At the same time, the incomplete character of the German revolution of 1918 and 1919[16] had left most of the Weimar Republic's enemies intact: the officer corps, the aristocracy, leaders of powerful business cartels, nationalist and monarchist movements unreconciled to the overthrow of the Imperial regime.

Organizations had grown larger and more influential at all levels of public life in Germany during the war. The cartels of German heavy industry, while not in agreement among themselves on everything, worked together against Weimar labor policies. Trade unions, with increased membership, dealt directly with business. The traditional two legislative houses and cabinet of ministers set up by the Weimar Constitution could never adequately control these organizations. Moreover, the Weimar Republic lacked deeply rooted values on which to build, since it had not germinated naturally out of a successful middle-class resistance to authority during the previous generations. "The authoritarian state had fallen into eclipse, but the wonted traditions, attitudes, and institutions that had been formed in reference to it gradually resumed their accustomed sway."[17]

To make matters worse, the Weimar Republic was forced to assume responsiblity for allocating the material burdens of a lost war. Even the victorious nations had trouble taxing their populations for the costs of reconstruction and of increased social services. Efforts of the Weimar Republic to institute broader progressive income taxes were doubly resented because, as nationalists charged, some of the money went to pay hated reparations to the Allies.

The Weimar Republic, then, passed through exceptional turmoil and class antagonism up through 1923. Even after it had crushed its own revolutionary left in January through May 1919, accepted the Treaty of Versailles unconditionally under threat of invasion in June 1919, and survived the occupation of Berlin by *Freikorps* in the Kapp *Putsch* of March 1920,[18] the new German republic had to face still more conflicts. The details of the peace settlement, applied under duress, continually opened raw wounds. French troops occupied Ruhr cities in the spring of 1919 and again in March 1921 to enforce their interpretation of the treaties; meanwhile conflict over implementation of the border settle-

---

[16]See Chapter 5, pp. 147–50.
[17]Leonard Krieger, *The German Idea of Freedom* (Boston, 1957), p. 465.
[18]See Chapter 7, p. 202.

ments in Silesia and Schleswig-Holstein continued until 1922. Workers in the Ruhr, with the support of Spartacists, went out on insurrectionary strikes in the spring of 1920. The purchasing power of the German mark lost ground steadily. The nationalist state government of Bavaria went its own way, protecting and encouraging the remnants of the *Freikorps* and militant nationalist groups like Hitler's German National Socialist Workers' party. Assassinations punctuated political life. Mathias Erzberger, leader of the Catholic Center party, who had proposed the Peace Resolution of 1917, had taken part in accepting the Versailles settlement, and had proposed progressive income taxation, was murdered by a nationalist in August 1921. Walther Rathenau, who as foreign minister in 1922 had tried to negotiate a compromise reparations settlement, was murdered in June 1922. At this point, the worst was still to come—the occupation of the Ruhr in 1923, and total collapse of the mark.

Eventually, in the late 1920s, the Weimar Republic settled into relatively stable years. Even then, however, parliamentary government never had the wide acceptance it enjoyed in England or France, nor did the Weimar institutions work in the ways their creators had expected. Weimar Germany was a nation in which military and economic organizations held vast power outside parliamentary control and in which liberal values had no deep historical legitimacy.

The "Weimar Coalition"

No coherent political majority emerged to deal with these manifold problems within the Weimar constitutional machinery. The "Weimar Coalition" of Social Democrats, Democrats, and Center party members that had written the constitution might have been expected to run the government. These parties had received about two-thirds of the votes when the constituent assembly was elected in January 1919, and that assembly had prudently extended its life as the first parliament of the Weimar Republic after the constitution had been adopted. Social Democrat Friedrich Ebert had been named first president of the republic (1919–25) by the constitutional assembly. When the "Weimar Coalition" was tested in the first parliamentary elections in June 1920, however, its popular vote fell to about 40 percent.

Each party of the "Weimar Coalition" was precluded in some fundamental way from serving as the basis of a broad parliamentary majority. The Social Democrats proclaimed themselves a Marxist workers' party, but they had been stained with workers' blood when they prevented the constitutional revolution of 1918 and 1919 from turning into a social revolution. The Democratic party remained a small group of liberal intellectuals around Hugo Preuss, the drafter of the Weimar Constitution, most of whose potential middle-class following still preferred nationalist success to liberal principle. The Center party was a Catholic confessional group rather than either a class party or an ideological party; its following ranged from constitutionalists like Mathias Erzber-

President Friedrich Ebert of Germany reviews police forces on the fifth anniversary of the Weimar Constitution, August 1924.

ger to conservatives. Although the "Weimar Coalition" parties came close to winning an electoral majority in 1928, they never again after the election of June 1920 could run by themselves the machinery they had created.

Every Weimar government after 1920 was able to form a majority only by drawing some support from elements of the center and right that were at best provisionally tolerant of the Weimar Constitution. The new People's party, based on former National Liberals with close ties to business and led by Gustav Stresemann, captured about 15 percent of the electorate in 1920. So did the German National People's party (DNVP), a regrouping of nationalists and monarchists. The People's party accepted the parliamentary republic as Germany's most feasible instrument for regaining world power. The DNVP's acceptance of parliamentary participation was far more conditional than that of the People's party. They participated only in order to work for a more authoritarian system. In times of crisis, the Communists and Nationalists (DNVP) drew even more support away from the fragmented center. At such times, the Weimar center resembled a candle burning at both ends.

President Ebert, nothing if not a scrupulous observer of the constitution, made no attempt to assure the continued power of his Social Democrats in the face of the poor electoral results but instead chose new chancellors from the moderate center of the legislature. Even so, the trend was not so much toward the middle parties as it was toward nonparty rule by technicians. After two brief ministries of the Catholic Center party had failed either to reach a more satisfactory settlement with the Versailles powers or to stop the galloping inflation that was reducing the mark to worthless paper, the head of the Hamburg-America shipping line, Wilhelm Cuno, was asked to form a government of nonparty technical experts in November 1922. Cuno was not even a member of the *Reichstag.* The pattern was established of turning to presidential authority and technical expertise to fill the void of a parliamentary majority.

Another pattern was set in that the chief preoccupations of the regime were foreign and economic. The possibility of internal changes that would liberalize German social institutions like the Army, the civil service, and universities to match the new democratic constitution had vanished with the election of June 1920, if not earlier. German governments henceforth succeeded or failed according to their success in coping with foreign affairs and the economy.

These two issues came to the crisis point in 1923, the year of the French occupation of the Ruhr and the collapse of the mark. In that year the Weimar Republic faced its gravest challenge of the decade. Chancellor Cuno's policy of passive resistance against the French in the Ruhr only helped bring the economy to a standstill. Both Communists and nationalists battled the French and made a hero of Leo Schlageter, a young *Freikorps* veteran executed by the French for having sabotaged a rail line near Düsseldorf. Encouraged by rising strike activity and widespread dissatisfaction with the soaring cost of living, the German Communist party attempted a revolutionary uprising in October. Popular militia, or "proletarian hundreds," were recruited in the states of Saxony and Thuringia where dissident Social Democrats brought Communists into the state government. At the other extreme, Adolf Hitler, taking a lesson from Mussolini, attempted to launch a nationalist revolution in Munich with the beer hall *Putsch.* German central authority was imperiled at the same time as the mark lost its power to buy anything; the very fabric of life seemed to be coming apart.

The "Great Coalition"

In March 1920, the Kapp *Putsch* had been thwarted by a general strike of the trade unions, and political authority had been restored by the "Weimar Coalition." In late 1923, by contrast, the republic was saved by three conservatives, who worked principally outside the parliamentary framework and who remained dominant figures in the stable Weimar regime of the later 1920s: the political leader Gustav Stresemann, the German Army commander General Hans von Seeckt, and the financial expert Hjalmar Schacht.

The dominant political figure was Gustav Stresemann. Stresemann was a saloonkeeper's son who had succeeded in business and in centrist politics under the empire. A supporter of German expansion during the war, Stresemann was deeply shocked by the revolution of 1918 and skeptical of the new republic. But his humble origins, his realism, and his taste for stability made him even more hostile to the aristocrats and officers of the intransigent right. Offended by the nationalist follies of the Kapp *Putsch* and the assassinations of Erzberger and Rathenau, Stresemann gradually brought his People's party into positive support of the Weimar Constitution as a lesser evil. Contemporaries called him a *Vernunftrepublikaner*, a republican of the mind but not of the heart.

In the crisis of August 1923, Stresemann was able to piece together a parliamentary majority committed to saving the Weimar Republic from both the right and the left. He joined the People's party to the "Weimar Coalition" of Social Democrats, Democrats, and Center party to form the "Great Coalition."[19] Stresemann's Great Coalition (August–November 1923) was as decisive to preserving the Weimar Constitution within Germany as his subsequent career as foreign minister was decisive in establishing a climate of international conciliation.[20] But the inclusion of such contradictory parties in the Great Coalition was a source of weakness as well as strength. When Stresemann proved far more resolute in expelling the Communist ministers from the state governments of Saxony and Thuringia than in forcing the nationalist state government of Bavaria to apply the law to the far right, at least until Hitler's beer hall *Putsch* on November 8, the Social Democrats went into opposition for the first time. Centrist coalitions governed Germany for the next four years without them. Stresemann had saved the republic, but he had helped take it permanently out of the hands of the "Weimar Coalition."

It was to General Hans von Seeckt, rather than to parliament, that Stresemann had to turn to beat back the insurrectionary movements on the political extremes. Seeckt, commander of the German Army from 1920 to 1926, had worked more or less within the Versailles limitations to make his 100,000-man force a unified, high-quality body of potential future leaders, even more socially conservative and insulated from government control than the old Imperial Army.[21] Seeckt's highest values were the unity of the German state and the unity of the Army. He was willing to use the Army to defend the republic as long as the republic promoted those two values. The Communist–Social Democrat state governments formed in October in Saxony and Thuringia threatened central government authority as well as property. The local army commander acted to defend both when he occupied the two state capitals (Dresden and Weimar) and deposed the state governments in

[19]See Chapter 8, p. 226.
[20]See Chapter 8, pp. 226–32.
[21]Almost every other officer in the Weimar officer corps was the son of an officer, compared with every fourth in the Imperial Officer Corps; one officer in five was a nobleman in 1920, one in four in 1932. There were fewer Social Democrats in the small Weimar Army than there had been in the Imperial Army. (Hajo Holborn, *A History of Modern Germany, 1840–1945* [New York, 1969], pp. 586–87.)

October and November. To meet the threat of Bavarian separatism posed by Hitler's Munich *Putsch,* Seeckt was entrusted with full dictatorial power on November 8 under Article 48 of the constitution, the emergency presidential power article. Fortunately for Seeckt, the local Bavarian conservatives crushed the *Putsch* without the need for using federal army force against Hitler's most famous accomplice, the world war hero General Ludendorff. At the same time, police and navy units crushed the last Communist uprising of Weimar Germany, in the port city of Hamburg, on October 23. The republic had been saved but at the price of greater centralization and a more autonomous Army.

The other emergency that Stresemann had to deal with was runaway inflation. On November 12, Stresemann appointed the banker and economist Hjalmar Horace Greeley Schacht as currency commissioner. Schacht simply started over with a new currency, the *Rentenmark,* each of which was worth 1 trillion marks. The "miracle of the *Rentenmark*," for which Schacht took full credit, consisted in two achievements that were as much psychological as economic. Because not enough gold and foreign exchange were deposited in German banks to back the new currency Schacht backed it with an unexchangeable medium, a mortgage on all the land, industries, and commerce of Germany. Then he kept the new currency stable by stringently limiting the amount available for the government to spend and for firms to borrow. When the Dawes Plan loans began to flow into Germany in 1924, Schacht was able to shift to a gold-based currency, the *Reichsmark,* which remained stable until the Great Depression.

It has been said that "the Inflation was the real German Revolution."[22] Unlike the political revolution of 1918 and 1919, it changed economic and social relationships. It reduced many middle-class people to scrubbing their own floors. Such people would follow any savior in the event of another economic crisis. Schacht's tight new deflationary economy forced marginal enterprises out of business. Only large firms that rationalized and modernized production profited by the German economic boom of the late 1920s. New cartels and trusts were formed. The United Steel combine (*Vereinigte Stahlwerke,* 1926), which grouped many of the coal, iron, and steel interests, produced about one-half of German steel. The great Krupp empire produced most of the rest. The chemical and dye trust (*Interessengemeinschaft Farbenindustrie A.g.,* or I. G. Farben, 1925) was the largest corporation on the European Continent.

Thus the Weimar Republic emerged from the brink of destruction in 1923 into a period of calm. Politically, it continued to move to the right. When President Ebert died in 1925, the old Social Democrat was replaced by the Prussian war hero Field Marshal Paul von Hindenburg. Other presidential candidates together received more than a majority of votes, but the Communist candidate, Ernst Thälmann, drew off decisive votes from the centrist republican candidate, Wilhelm Marx, a striking

[22]Godfrey Scheele, *The Weimar Republic* (London, 1946), p. 77.

instance of the consequences of a divided left. Government majorities stepped one more notch to the right in 1927 by including members of the German Nationalist party (DNVP), whose press and local leaders continued to call for the replacement of the republic by either a king or a dictator. The left gained in the 1928 elections, but the new Social Democratic chancellor, Hermann Müller, could govern only with a "Great Coalition."

With the economy booming, the political fever chart did fall. The assassinations of the early period now ceased, and the paramilitary street gangs of angry veterans and authoritarians were less conspicuous. Following his failed *Putsch* Hitler sat in Landsberg prison writing his political credo, *Mein Kampf* (1925). Individual liberties were more or less assured, and Berlin rivaled Paris as a cosmopolitan center of artistic experimentation. The Weimar Republic was surviving, but its parliamentary façade barely concealed an autonomous, authoritarian officer corps, dominant big business combines, and a technocratic civil service with no real commitment to political liberties. If the parliamentary regime failed in either foreign or economic affairs, these powerful bodies would shove it aside in favor of something more effective.

Eastern Europe

The new states of Eastern Europe, like Germany, were the scene of constitutionmaking on the liberal model after the First World War. Strong liberal influence was only to be expected. The new regimes were the product of three simultaneous liberal victories: the victory of the Western parliamentary powers—Great Britain and France—over the autocratic Central Powers; the victory of national patriotic movements over the multinational dynasties of Germany, Austria-Hungary, and Russia; and the victory of middle- and upper-class interests over the Bolshevik movement in Eastern Europe in 1919 and 1920.

National independence went hand in hand with parliamentary democracy in the political climate of the 1920s. The new states (Austria, Poland, Czechoslovakia) were republics, with the exception of Yugoslavia, or the Kingdom of Serbs, Croats, and Slovenes as it was known until 1929. The preexisting kingdoms of Romania and Bulgaria adopted new parliamentary constitutions in the early 1920s, while Hungary remained a regency without a king, and Greece became a republic in 1924. The new constitutions drew largely on French, British, and American political practice. Manhood suffrage was far more widespread than before; the limited suffrage of Hungary was the major exception.

It seemed, on paper at least, that the decade of the 1920s was the high point of political democracy in Eastern Europe. Liberal politics and economics, however, were being transplanted into alien soil. Western parliamentary systems had evolved gradually through long and painful conflicts between divine right monarchy and gentry allied with a large, growing middle class. In Eastern Europe, by contrast, liberal values had been espoused by nationalist intellectuals without a broad social base.

There was no substantial middle class in Eastern Europe. The region
was overwhelmingly rural almost everywhere. Commercial and professional people in many parts of Eastern Europe, such as Poland,
Hungary, and Romania, were often German or Jewish and hence on
uneasy terms with the national movements that had created the successor states. Only among the Czechs was there a large, national middle
class with liberal traditions.

The problems of new states further complicated matters for the infant
parliamentary systems of Eastern Europe. Indigenous leadership was
inexperienced, and the great majority of the rural population had never
been drawn into sustained involvement in national political life. As much
as three-quarters of the population was still illiterate in parts of the
Balkans. Under these conditions, politics was bound to remain the
preserve of a few. The inclusion of obligatory voting in some new
Eastern European consitutions was less an expression of advanced ideas
of political participation than of fears of a passive citizenry.

Economic dislocation imposed another severe burden. New frontiers
abruptly cut off many Eastern Europeans from the cities with which they
had customarily traded. There was massive demand for land reform and
for the development of basic transportation resources. Inflation was
nearly as disastrous as in Germany. Under such conditions, laissez-faire
economics made no sense.

The liberal experiments in Eastern Europe had to come to terms with
two fundamental features of the region: rural predominance and ethnic
diversity. Regimes have stood or fallen in Eastern Europe during much
of the first half of the twentieth century by their handling of the issues of
agriculture and nationality.

The Problem of Rural Predominance

Most Eastern Europeans still worked on the land at the end of the war.
The proportion of the total population engaged directly in farming or
herding reached almost 80 percent in Bulgaria and Yugoslavia; it was
over 60 percent in Romania, Poland, and Hungary. The agrarian
proportion fell only to half in the region's most industrialized state,
Czechoslovakia. (At the same time, by contrast, that proportion was less
than 20 percent in Britain.) Moreover, as has been noted, much of the
land was owned by great landlords. Latifundia (huge estates) dominated
the countryside in Poland, Hungary, and Romania to a degree matched
only in southern Spain in the Europe of 1920. Since there were few
urban or industrial outlets for a growing population, massive underem-
ployment and land hunger festered among the mounting number of day
laborers and subsistence farmers on small holdings.

Direct, violent peasant action seemed likely. An assault by Romanian
peasants on manor houses and Jewish moneylenders in 1907, the
bloodiest peasant uprising in modern European history, had been a first

warning. Its suppression had cost 10,000 peasant lives. The massive land seizures of the Russian peasantry in 1917 and 1918 set an almost irresistible example nearby. Eastern European rulers knew that some form of land redistribution was almost inevitable in the early 1920s; the main question was what form it would take.

Béla Kun's Budapest Soviet had proposed revolutionary land redistribution in the spring of 1919, but Kun's orthodox insistence on land collectivization had less appeal to the Eastern European peasantry than Lenin's more flexible acquiescence in land redistribution among individual peasants. In any event, a revolutionary solution had been blocked by the crushing of Béla Kun's regime in the summer of 1919. Henceforth Eastern European land reform was in the hands of the middle- and upper-class leaders of the successor states. Their approach to land reform, supported by liberal intellectuals and a few progressive landlords as well as many peasants, aimed at a substantial increase in the number of independent family farms. This would be accomplished by redistributing to family farmers expropriated crown lands and foreign estates and excess land purchased from estates above a maximum permissible size.

Every Eastern European successor state redistributed some land in this fashion in the early 1920s. The change was fairly substantial in Czechoslovakia and Romania, where the landlords were mostly foreign. In Romania, by 1930, only 7.4 percent of the land, compared with 40 percent in 1920, remained in estates over 1250 acres.[23] Bulgaria was unique in having widespread small holdings and almost no aristocracy to begin with, but it broadened its family farm base still further under the agrarian regime of Alexander Stamboliski (1919–23).[24] Stamboliski set an upper limit of seventy-five acres on Bulgarian rural property holdings, and by 1934 only 1 percent of the country's farms and 6 percent of its total land area were in units larger than seventy-five acres.[25] Elsewhere, land reform was much more grudging. In many cases, newly independent peasants, heavily mortgaged and suffering declining agricultural prices in the later 1920s, sold out again to larger landlords. The Radziwill estates in Poland still amounted to 200,000 acres in 1937. Nor did mere redistribution solve basic rural problems of overpopulation and inefficient farming methods.

Manhood suffrage in predominantly rural countries opened up political opportunities for farmers' parties. Agrarian, peasant, or smallholders' parties (to use the most common names), dedicated to serving the interests of the small landowner, held a major position in the parliaments of Eastern Europe, whereas they were largely absent from Western European party systems. A Smallholders' party emerged in the first Hungarian elections in 1919 as the largest single party, although it

[23]Robert Lee Wolff, *The Balkans in Our Time* (New York, 1967), p. 163.
[24]See below, p. 263.
[25]Joseph Rothschild, *The Communist Party of Bulgaria* (New York, 1959), p. 90.

was eventually overshadowed by the counterrevolutionary elements discussed in Chapter 7. The Peasant party of Wincenty Witos dominated Polish ministries between 1923 and 1926. Stepan Radič of the Croatian Peasant party was a powerful politician of the Yugoslav region of Croatia during the 1920s. But the most striking peasant leader was Alexander Stamboliski, head of the Bulgarian Peasant Union.

Stamboliski ran Bulgaria as a virtual agrarian dictatorship from 1919 until his assassination in 1923. He loathed the urban middle-class "parasites" who kept the peasants in debt, and he had contempt for industrial workers who, he belived, were narrowed by repetitious mechanical work.

> I don't like these workers with the narrow ideas of the West; they have little culture. . . . With peasants it is different—In the peasant are the seeds of a fully developed human personality. . . . The experience of the peasant assures him an incontestable advantage over the worker for nature, who is his master, took it upon herself to round off his education.[26]

Convinced that productivity, virtue, and wisdom reside close to the soil, Stamboliski looked forward to a peasant democracy in which bankers and bureaucrats would disappear.

Stamboliski was the only Eastern European peasant politican who almost had the power to bring such a democracy about. The Bulgarian rural mass gave him close to an absolute majority—112 seats out of 236 in the *Sobranie,* or Bulgarian parliament. The Communist party, also strong in the villages, was second with 50 seats. In addition to imposing an upper limit of seventy-five acres on rural property holdings and making it difficult for city dwellers to own rural property, Stamboliski slanted taxation heavily against urban middle-class taxpayers and placed tight controls on law and banking. His private army of Orange Guards beat up his enemies and broke strikes. He founded a "Green International" to unify individual peasant interests throughout Eastern Europe against the collectivist "Red International."

Stamboliski came to a brutal end in the style of his own Orange Guards' forays. He had frightened the urban middle class, offended both nationalists and Communists by siding with the Allies in international matters, and antagonized the Macedonian minority by accepting good neighborly relations with Yugoslavia. While the Communists stood aside, Stamboliski was overthrown by a reserve officers' *coup* in 1923. He was then captured by a Macedonian terrorist band, who cut off his hands before beheading him.

The Bulgarian experience suggested that even the most uniform peasant population in Eastern Europe could not govern a state in opposition to the towns and the Army. The peasant parties had sufficient numbers to complicate parliamentary life, but not enough strength to provide a coherent political program. They were unified

[26]Quoted in *Ibid.,* p. 87.

only by a vague antiurban populism, the notion that cities corrupt and that peasants should liberate themselves from the domination of bankers and merchants. Beyond that, they were pulled in contradictory directions. Some peasant leaders, like the Croatian populist Stepan Radič, favored radical agrarian reform and joined the Third International. Others, like Stamboliski, defended small landholders against Marxist collectivists. This lack of political cohesiveness reflected the conflicting interests of rural populations, divided among landless laborers, owners of dwarf plots, family farmers, and landlords. Moreover, peasant politicians were often inexperienced; they were soon tempted to conform with the style of urban politicians, for which their constituents then despised them. The peasant parties of Eastern Europe deprived urban liberal politicians of a governing majority without providing a workable. alternative.

Even more fundamentally, the strength of Eastern European peasant parties, it could be argued, made it more difficult to overcome social backwardness. In the long run, one could imagine a prosperous Eastern Europe built either on efficient, highly productive agriculture, as in Denmark, or on the absorption of excess rural population in growing industry. What Eastern Europe got in the 1920s was a dense population that remained on the land, a plethora of inefficient small farms, and slow industrialization. All the Eastern European countries were especially vulnerable later, during the Great Depression, when world farm prices dropped, and their main livelihood was destroyed.

The Problem of National Minorities

The other major problem in governing the successor states in the 1920s was unresolved national aspirations. The defeated states, especially Hungary, chafed in resentment. The victor states contained large unassimilated ethnic minorities, the price paid for the construction of a large Czechoslovakia, Romania, and Poland in 1918 and 1919.

The South Slavs are a striking example of the fate of new parliamentary regimes confronted with intractable nationality divisions. None of the component parts of the Kingdom of Serbs, Croats, and Slovenes was large enough to dominate the others, nor could they cooperate without friction. After the defeat of their common Habsburg enemy, the Serbs (Orthodox religion, Serbo-Croatian language, Cyrillic alphabet), Croats (Catholic religion, Serbo-Croation language, Roman alphabet), and Slovenes (Catholic religion, Slovenian language, Roman alphabet) found little to unite them. The new kingdom's decentralized federal system exaggerated the divisions. Since the Croatian leader Stepan Radič had turned to the Third International, separatism was overlaid with a Bolshevik threat. King Alexander abolished the constitution in January 1929, replaced the ethnically based federal districts with a centralized authority, and renamed the kingdom Yugoslavia, thereby "solving" in one blow the problems of revolution, local separatism, and governmental instability.

Many other Eastern European states had already gone the same authoritarian route. King Boris of Bulgaria named a conservative politician to run that country by police power after the murder of Stamboliski in 1923. Prince Carol of Romania, who had lived in voluntary exile since 1925, returned in 1930 to resume the throne and active rule. Most striking of all was the military *coup* by which Marshal Josef Pilsudski took over the Polish government from the agrarian Prime Minister Witos in May 1926.

The Polish constitution of 1921 had vested power in a cabinet responsible to a parliamentary majority. But that majority was so fragmented among no less than fifty-nine parties (including thirty-three groups representing ethnic minorities) that fourteen ministries succeeded one another in the eight years between November 1918 and May 1926. Witos' agrarians and the urban liberal groups, who had the most to gain by the success of a parliamentary regime, could form no coherent center. Without effective administration, the Polish economy had difficulty adjusting to unity. Silesians who had traded with Berlin, Galicians who had traded with Vienna, and eastern Poles who had been oriented toward Russian economic life redirected their economic activities slowly and painfully around Warsaw.

The parliamentary regime gradually fell into popular contempt. Marshal Pilsudski, an old patriot-socialist who had led Polish legions against the Russians in the First World War, had the support of both the trade unions and the Army in his *coup* in May 1926. After assuming power, Pilsudski founded a single national movement, the Nonpartisan Bloc for Cooperation with the Government. Its function was to promote the national "moral renovation" (*sanacja*) that had been so lacking in the squabbling of parties.

In new nations that desperately needed unity and administrative stability, the parliamentary regimes of the 1920s had won a reputation for inefficiency, corruption, and factious divisiveness. Parliamentary institutions that survived the 1920s were replaced by authoritarian regimes during the 1930s. Only Czechoslovakia functioned smoothly as a parliamentary republic throughout the interwar period. The Czechs, alone among Eastern European peoples, had a substantial indigenous middle class and a highly developed liberal tradition. Having inherited an important part of the industrial base of the old Austrian Empire, Czechoslovakia experienced less maladjustment and inflation while establishing economic life within the new borders than did the other successor states. The Czechs had managed to sidetrack the grievances of the Slovak and German minorities within a centralized administration. Above it all presided the person of Thomas Masaryk. Until his death in 1935, Masaryk held together a parliamentary center of reformist socialists, agrarians, and Catholics by the sheer force of his character, in what the French historian Maurice Baumont has called a "dictatorship of respect."[27]

The Iberian Peninsula

As in Eastern Europe, lackluster parliamentary regimes in both Spain and Portugal could not survive the 1920s. Like Eastern Europeans, the Iberian populations were overwhelmingly rural, predominantly illiterate, still deeply anchored in traditional village routines, and powerfully influenced by local landlords and clergy. Agriculture was inefficient as well. For example, although three-quarters of the Portuguese people lived in the countryside, Portugal had trouble producing a sufficient basic bread supply.

The Iberian countries differed in important ways from Eastern Europe, of course, but not in ways conducive to the success of liberal institutions. Instead of being new successor states struggling to launch an administration and an economy within new frontiers, Spain and Portugal were old decayed empires struggling with entrenched political clienteles and a top-heavy bureaucracy. The Catholic Church was far more pervasive in Spain and Portugal than was any one clergy in Eastern Europe outside of Catholic Poland, but the Iberian populations were not thereby any more homogeneous. Urban–rural antagonisms, conflicts of interest between a small landholding north and a latifundist south, and especially bitter cultural divisions among Basques, Catalans, and the dominant Aragon-Castille heartland of Spain obstructed formation of the basic consensus necessary for functioning electoral politics. Finally, neither the parliamentary monarchy of Spain nor the Portuguese Republic of 1910 enjoyed even the brief euphoria of nation-building with which the successor states began. Liberal institutions had been implanted in the Iberian Peninsula in the late nineteenth century on the model of dominant northwestern Europe. They bore the blame for wartime and postwar dislocations, whether the regime remained neutral in the war, as did Spain, or participated in it, as did Portugal on the Allied side after 1916. During the 1920s, both countries slipped back into the nineteenth-century tradition of military *pronunciamientos* (revolts). Officer groups took over both governments with promises of social order and regeneration.

In Spain, the industrial boom and inflation accompanying the First World War had magnified social tensions in the principal industrial areas, culturally distinct Catalonia (Barcelona), and the Basque region. The strikes that began in 1917 and continued from 1919 to 1923 combined familiar ingredients of church-burning, calls for Catalan antonomy, and the rhetoric of revolutionary general strikes, which talked more of obtaining power than ameliorating working conditions.

[27]Maurice Baumont, *La Faillite de la paix: de Rethondes à Stresa* (Paris, 1951), p. 439.

Their scale, however, was unprecedented, and they were accompanied by anarchist peasant risings in the south. Soviet influence was much in evidence; one peasant leader in Andalusia changed his name from Cordon to Cordoniev. Colonial defeats in 1921 by Moroccan guerrillas were simply the last straw for Spain, long haunted by the decline of its empire. With the approval of King Alfonso XIII, General Miguel Primo de Rivera led a military *coup* in September 1923.

Primo de Rivera swept away the "old politicians," whom he blamed with simplistic military bluntness for Spain's decline, and set up a one-man rule that lasted until 1930. Primo was no mere Spanish reactionary, however. He established arbitration committees of labor and management, in which some reformist trade unions took part. He surrounded himself with technical experts committed to economic modernization and he greatly expanded Spanish road and electrical systems. *La Dictadura* was a modernizing dictatorship, determined to bring labor into peaceful participation with the more progressive sectors of the economy. But Primo de Rivera made enemies among reactionaries and big business as well as among republicans and the intransigent left. When the Spanish economy began to suffer from the depression in 1930, King Alfonso XIII withdrew his confidence rather than go down with a failing military junta. Primo went into exile in France in January 1930 and died there shortly thereafter.

The Portuguese Republic of 1910 had never achieved either political stability or financial probity. Since its political base was a relatively narrow stratum of free-thinking commercial and professional people in the cities of Lisbon and Porto, and since its chief accomplishment was anticlericalism (separation of Church and state, legalization of divorce, an end to the educational monopoly of the Catholic University of Coimbra), the republic depended on the passivity of the rural population and the acquiescence of the bureaucracy and the Army. Participation in the First World War on the British side (where most of Portugal's trade was transacted), ran the country deeply into debt, setting off a disastrous inflation that damaged the republic's own supporters the most. General strikes were declared in 1919, 1920, and 1921, but by the mid-1920s an eight-hour day was widespread, and workers' purchasing power no lower than it had been in 1914. By then, bitterness was most widespread in the middle classes. Upper civil servants (including army officers) found that inflation and government economies had eroded their real purchasing power to half what it had been in 1914.

These conditions were easy to blame on the republic's constitution of 1911, which gave primacy to a parliament whose inner circle of liberal politicians traded cabinet seats among themselves. Portugal had no less than forty-five ministries during the sixteen years following the overthrow of the monarchy in 1910, and fifteen elections (in which nearly half the electorate did not bother to participate).

Opposition to the republic was centered in the Army and among Catholic professors at Coimbra, who were deeply influenced by the "integral nationalism" of the French publicist Charles Maurras.[28] In 1926, the countryside remained passive while a group of officers overthrew the republic. By 1928, an ascetic professor of economics at Coimbra, Antonio de Oliveira Salazar, had emerged as the strong man of the regime; he was the only person capable of balancing Portugal's precarious finances. First as Minister of Finance and after 1932 as premier, Salazar dominated the government until he was incapacitated by a stroke in 1968. His dictatorship was the most hermetically closed and longest-lived clerical authoritarian regime of modern Europe.

Fascist Italy In his rebound from momentary immobility after the murder of Matteotti, Mussolini had gone on in 1925 and 1926 to lay the basis for a one-party dictatorship in Italy. There were two ways open to him. He could initiate the "second revolution" called for by the more radical Fascists; or he could make his peace with the principal nonparliamentary institutions of conservative Italy—monarchy, Church, and Army. The first route involved an ill-defined program of sweeping away all the worn-out institutions of pre-Fascist Italy, including the monarchy.

[28]See Chapter 1, p. 38.

Mussolini and Cardinal Gasparri, Papal Secretary of State (fourth from left) sign the Lateran Pact on February 11, 1929, making peace after fifty-nine years of conflict between the papacy and the Italian state and establishing the pope as temporal ruler of Vatican City.

The old governing elites of Italy would be replaced wholesale with *squadristi,* the angry young anticlerical, antisocialist veterans who had ejected the town governments from northern cities in 1922. When Roberto Farinacci, an ex-socialist railwayman and toughest of the *squadristi,* who had become boss (*ras*) of Cremona when the Fascists took the town over in 1922, became Fascist party secretary in February 1925, it looked as though Mussolini was headed down that route.

In April 1926, however, Mussolini removed Farinacci from office. Thereafter, he quietly reduced the power of the Fascists who had helped bring him to power, and he made his peace with the *status quo.* The most striking step was his pact with the Catholic Church. The Church had never recognized united Italy after that secular state had seized papal lands in the 1860s. In the Lateran Pact of 1929 Mussolini's Italy recognized papal sovereignty in miniature in Vatican City and made other concessions (such as agreeing to abolish divorce except under the most stringent conditions) that not even the most conservative leader of pre-Fascist Italy could have made. In return, the papacy declared its differences with the Italian state at an end and urged the faithful to support the regime.

In the late 1920s, Fascist Italy slipped into a normalcy of its own. The state continued to be a one-party dictatorship, but it ruled in partnership with the institutions and groups that had brought the Fascists to power in 1922. Non-Fascist elements—the monarchy, the Church, the Army— retained their autonomous authority. Big business achieved a form of unofficial self-regulation under the developing corporatist system.[29] All these elements accepted Mussolini's political rule, and the Fascist stage effects that went with it, as long as Mussolini was able to assure internal order and prosperity.

Revolutionary Russia in a Stabilized World

The civil war was over in Russia by the end of 1920, when Trotsky's Red Army defeated the last two counterrevolutionary offensives: the Polish campaign (October 1920), and the campaign of Baron Peter Wrangel in the Crimea (November 1920). Sheer survival in the face of internal and external opposition had been an extraordinary achievement for the Bolshevik regime. The country was in desperate straits, however.

Challenges to the Bolshevik Regime

In 1921 industrial output was down to about one-fifth of what it had been in 1913. The temporary expedient of War Communism, which had called for full collectivization of productive capacity, could not help get production started again amidst the wreckage of war. The most important obstacles were lack of raw materials, transportation chaos, and

[29]See Chapter 11, pp. 333–35 for a fuller discussion of corporatism in practice.

the absence of technical and managerial skills. War Communism even made conditions far worse in the countryside. Forced requisitions had provoked the age-old peasant reactions of hoarding, consuming at home, and the willful destruction of livestock. Drought was added to these problems. Between 1913 and 1921 Russia had been transformed from a major exporter of grain to a country that could not feed itself.

The cities stood half-empty in 1921. Massive starvation, epidemics of typhus, and fighting took more lives between 1918 and 1921—perhaps 20 million—than losses in the First World War and the relatively bloodless 1917 revolution put together. One Bolshevik declared in 1921 that the economic collapse was "unparalleled in the history of humanity."[30]

Most alarming for the Bolsheviks was the massive disaffection that began to spread among their most enthusiastic supporters. Peasant bands defied authority. There were 118 peasant disorders in February 1921 alone. At the end of February, a strike wave swept Petrograd. Opposition came to a head on March 1 with an uprising of sailors at the Kronstadt naval base in Petrograd harbor; this was the very unit whose guns had covered the Bolshevik seizure of the Winter Palace in October 1917. The Kronstadt sailors proclaimed a "third revolution"[31] of "freely elected soviets" against the "commissarocracy" of Lenin's War Communism. The Kronstadt rising was crushed by a 35,000-man Red Army force, but at the cost of immense loss of life. Moreover, the danger signals could not be ignored. The revolt had been spontaneous, even though some anti-Bolshevik exiles had tried unsuccessfuly to aid it once it had broken out. Similar resentments were expressed in the underground Workers' Truth movement. As a leading Bolshevik, Nikolai Bukharin, said in March 1921, "Now the Republic hangs by a hair."[32]

Lenin responded to these challenges in March 1921 by replacing War Communism with the New Economic Policy (NEP). Under NEP, grain requisitions were replaced by fixed payments to the state, and peasants were eventually allowed to market their surpluses freely. About 75 percent of retail trade, as well as a large number of small craft enterprises, slipped back into private hands. The state, however, retained what Lenin called the "commanding heights" of the economy: heavy industry, wholesale commerce, banking, and transport. During 1922, the revived market and a good growing season produced enough food, and normal life became possible in Russia.

It was at this point, in May 1922, that Lenin suffered the first of a series of strokes; in January 1924 he died. No clear line of succession had been provided for. The ensuing struggle for power was not merely a personal rivalry for ascendancy over party and country. The most

---

[30]Quoted in Paul Avrich, *Kronstadt 1921* (Princeton, N.J., 1970), p. 8.
[31]The "bourgeois" revolution of February 1917 had been the first, and the Bolshevik Revolution of October 1917 was the second.
[32]Stephen F. Cohen, *Bukharin and the Bolshevik Revolution* (New York, 1973), p. 106.

fundamental and vital issues of how to build the first socialist regime in history were at stake. What would the new regime be like and what would be its first normal steps, now that the crisis out of which it had been born had lost its immediacy?

The situation facing the Russian Bolsheviks at Lenin's death was one for which neither Marxist theory nor practical experience had prepared them. There was no sign of the workers' revolution in more advanced countries that all Russian Marxists deemed essential for the survival of socialism in backward Russia. The last spark of postwar disorder in Europe flickered out with the crushing of the Hamburg uprising of October 1923. The Russian Bolshevik regime would have to adapt to a world in which capitalism had stabilized itself, around liberal institutions in advanced northern and Western Europe and under authoritarian regimes in more agrarian Eastern and southern Europe. Under these conditions, could the Russian Bolsheviks progress toward "socialism in one country," and in a largely preindustrial country at that?

The "Industrialization Debate"

The Bolsheviks believed that progress toward socialism was possible only through the development of a large base of industrial workers in a country like Russia, or through the support of companion Communist regimes in countries that already had such a base. Since further revolution abroad seemed precluded after 1923, the problem was how to build a large industrial base in their own country.

A "left" group, led by War Commissar Leon Trotsky joined later by Comintern chairman Gregory Zinoviev and Lev Kamenev, chairman of the Moscow Soviet, proposed a return to the "heroic" stance of 1917 both at home and abroad. Abroad, the left group wanted to continue revolutionary pressures; they would carry these pressures into Asia if Europe proved totally unresponsive. At home, they held that the "dictatorship of industry" was the only possible route to socialism. This meant squeezing a maximum of development capital out of the one Russian group capable of producing excess wealth—the peasantry.

Before 1914, agricultural export had been the chief earner of foreign exchange, and Tsarist Russian industrial development had been built, in a sense, on peasant backs.[33] The left proposed to continue to pump the surplus productive capacity of the peasants into industrial growth by setting food prices low and the prices of manufactured goods high, spread apart like the blades of a scissors. During the early years of NEP, peasants had complained of a "scissors crisis" of just this sort; the Bolshevik left wanted to continue and even accentuate that pressure. The left strategy consisted of self-financing rapid industrialization by wringing wealth out of the great majority of Russians, the farmers who had benefited from the land redistribution of 1917 and 1918, especially

[33]Grain composed 62 percent of Russian exports in 1900.

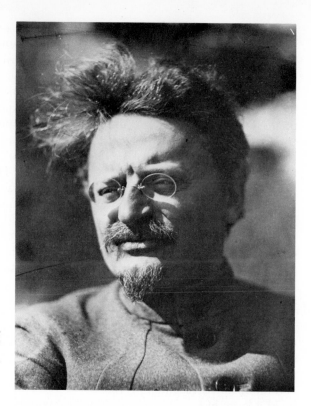

*Leon Trotsky, organizer of the
Red Army, as he appeared
in the early 1920s.*

the middle-class farmers, or "kulaks," who now threatened to create a
powerful agrarian middle class.

A "right" group, led by Nikolai Bukharin, argued that socialist
industrialization with the cooperation of a satisfied peasantry was not
only possible but preferable. Like the left, Bukharin thought that Russia
must industrialize to develop socialism and that the resources must come
from within. Unlike the left, he thought that those resources would be
generated much more quickly if peasants producing for the market were
allowed to profit and thus swell their own purchasing power for
industrial goods. After all, Bukharin argued, peasants were "the huge
majority on our planet."[34] If Bolshevik Russia showed the way to
cooperation between peasants and industrial workers, socialism could
bypass the stabilized West and spread naturally through the rest of the
world. Bukharin had endured exile like the others; nevertheless, he
maintained an open manner and a preference for conciliation that his
admirers believe could have produced a socialist but uncoercive state in
Russia.

Neither side in the great "industrialization debate" of the 1920s
advocated returning to a bourgeois regime and a multiparty govern-

[34]Cohen, p. 168.

ment to await the inevitable ripening of a revolutionary proletariat in Russia or elsewhere. Both sides were determined to dig in and defend socialism in Russia from being reabsorbed into the prosperous liberal economic sphere of the West. Both saw the necessity of financing Russian industrialization from within. Those decisions made political dictatorship necessary, regardless of whether the Bolshevik left or right won the day.

The Consolidation of Political Dictatorship

Only a minority of Russians were urban wage earners; only a minority of these workers were convinced and reliable Bolsheviks. For example, in the Smolensk District, a rural region in western Russia with a population of about 2.3 million, there were only 5416 Communist party members, mostly in the city of Smolensk itself.[35] Under such conditions, the regime could survive only through firm bureaucratic control, under the sole political direction of the Communist party. The "dictatorship of the proletariat" would have to be exercised on the proletariat's behalf by a minority party.

Lenin never had any doubts about the necessity for one-party rule during postrevolutionary consolidation. In 1919 he had written that the soviets, "which according to their program were organs of government by the workers, are in fact only organs of government for the workers by the most advanced sections of the proletariat, but not by the working masses themselves."[36] It could not be otherwise in Lenin's opinion, as long as the mass of workers had not acquired a communist culture. In the meantime, "the Party's proletarian policy is not made by the rank and file, but by the immense and undivided authority of the tiny section that might be called the Party's Old Guard."[37]

Up to 1921 civil war and revival of production had required the Bolshevik leaders to adopt a high degree of bureaucratic centralization. The loosening of market controls for small enterprises under NEP, however, did not lead to the loosening of political control. Lenin had made the decision in March and April 1921 to forbid the existence of factions in the party and to give the party's Central Committee the power to exclude those who publicly opposed the committee's policy. Thus the relaxations of NEP did nothing to restore any of the free communitarian self-government that the soviet movement had seemed to promise at the beginning.

Toward the end of his life Lenin began to worry about the nature of party rule. He spoke about the danger of that handful of "the best Communists" being submerged in the "alien culture" of a mass of shortsighted bureaucrats.

[35]Merle Fainsod, *Smolensk Under Soviet Rule* (Cambridge, Mass., 1958), pp. 17, 44.
[36]Moshe Lewin, *Lenin's Last Struggle* (New York, 1968), p. 6.
[37]*Ibid.,* p. 12.

Take the case of Moscow: 4,700 Communist leaders and an enormous mass of bureaucrats. Who is leading and who is being led? I very much doubt if it can be said that the Communists are leading. I think it can be said that they are being led.[38]

As long as Lenin lived, his personal ascendancy kept power in the hands of the Old Bolsheviks who made up the party's Central Committee. After his death, however, the full-time administrative personnel of the party—the Political Bureau (Politburo) of the Central Committee and its permanent Secretariat—gradually assumed more and more control over running the state.

The Rise of Stalin

This tendency favored the rise of Josef Stalin, the party secretary since 1922 and perhaps the only Old Bolshevik of truly lower-class origin. Stalin was born Josef Djugashvili, the son of a shoemaker and the grandson of serfs, in the trans-Caucasus province of Georgia. After dropping out of theological seminary, he was drawn into the Bolshevik movement around 1900 and undertook such clandestine activities as bank raids for party funds. It was then that he adopted his underground name, which means "man of steel." Hardened in tsarist prisons and Siberian exile, Stalin had none of the broader culture of his colleagues, most of whom had passed years of exile in Western Europe. There is no certain proof to the allegations that he had acted as a double agent for the tsarist secret police. What is certain is that Stalin's strategic position as party secretary, coupled with his toughness, coincided with the growing ascendancy of a hard new generation of officials who had been bred not in the exile movements of the Old Bolsheviks but in the struggles since 1917. Easily overriding the warnings against his "rudeness" and rigidity contained in Lenin's testament, Stalin seized the initiative.

Stalin sided firmly with Bukharin in the "industrialization debate." The NEP concessions to peasant trade were broadened, and agricultural production rose again toward 1913 levels. As the left Bolsheviks lost vote after vote in the Central Committee, they were expelled one by one from positions of power. Trotsky, who had created and exhorted the Red Army, was removed from the War Commissariat in 1925. Zinoviev was dismissed as Comintern chairman after the failure of a communist uprising Bulgaria in 1925 whose main accomplishment was the dynamiting of Sofia Cathedral. The Old Bolsheviks' bases of independent authority, such as Kamenev's control of the Moscow party organization and Zinoviev's in Petrograd (renamed Leningrad after Lenin's death), were gradually replaced by centralized party control. The Fifteenth Party Congress in December 1927 finally condemned all "deviation from the Party line" as decided by Stalin. In 1929 Trotsky was forced into

[38] *Ibid.*, p. 10.

exile, where he wrote about "the revolution betrayed" and the "substitution" of party for proletariat. Stalin had emerged as the preeminent leader of Soviet Russia. Russia had become, said one disgruntled Old Bolshevik, "the dictatorship of the Secretariat."[39]

The Soviet Union thus adjusted to a nonrevolutionary world in the late 1920s and stabilized around a combination of NEP economics and one-party bureaucratic political control. It was a period of some material improvement, although industrial production and livestock breeding renamed below 1913 levels. The literacy rate rose rapidly, and the excitement of creating a new regime released powerful literary and artistic energies. Under Minister of Culture Anatole Lunacharsky, there was a brilliant period of expression in architecture, theater, and poetry. The great beneficiaries of the period were 100 million peasants, whose 25 million family farms were more numerous and freer than ever before or since in Russian history. The questions raised in the "industrialization debate" remained, however. Could the Soviet Union avoid stagnation if its economy continued to be dominated by small peasantry?

By comparison with the past and with what was to come, Europe in the late 1920s seemed stable and prosperous. Northern and Western Europe flourished, and even Eastern Europe's economies improved. When the British historian A. J. P. Taylor referred to the late 1920s in his country as "the years of gold,"[40] however, his definition was two-edged. The international gold standard had been restored, but the rest of the nineteenth-century liberal vision had not automatically returned with it. Unemployment, for example, never dropped below 10 percent. Much of the gold of those years was the dross of garish pleasure-seeking in the "roaring twenties."

The attempt to restore or expand liberal Europe on the Continent had been only a qualified success. Parliamentary systems had not worked in Eastern and southern Europe, where agrarians predominated and nationalities clashed. Even the prosperous populations of France and Germany were scarred by their recent experiences with inflation: their loyalties to neoliberal regimes would last only as long as they assured economic stability.

For the moment, many Europeans could afford to sing and dance to the new American jazz and enjoy the novelties of the movies and more widespread automobiles. It was a neoliberal illusion, however, to believe that the relative prosperity of the late 1920s could endure simply by letting things alone. The Great Depression was to bring that illusion to an end.

A Fragile Stability: Neoliberalism Assessed

[39]Boris Souvarine, quoted in Cohen, p. 214.
[40]Taylor, pp. 227ff.

Suggestions for Further Reading

A good recent introduction to interwar Europe, with an excellent bibliography, is Raymond J. Sontag, *A Broken World, 1919–1939** (1971).

Two works discuss wartime hopes for change and their frustration in the return to the social and economic *status quo* in postwar Western Europe: Paul B. Johnson, *Land Fit for Heroes: The Planning of British Reconstruction, 1916–1919* (1968), and Charles S. Maier, *Recasting Bourgeois Europe: Stabilization in France, Italy, and Germany in the Decade After World War I* (1974).

In addition to the national histories recommended at the end of Chapter 1, the following works deal with individual European states between the wars: Charles Loch Mowat, *Britain Between the Wars** (1955); A. J. P. Taylor, *England, 1914–1945** (1965); and Alfred F. Havighurst, *Twentieth Century Britain,** rev. ed. (1966). Robert Graves and Alan Hodge, *The Long Week-End** (1940) recall everyday life and popular fads between the wars with irony and zest. Barbara C. Malament, "Baldwin Re-Restored?" *Journal of Modern History*, Vol. 44, No. 1 (March 1972) is a useful introduction to conflicting assessments of Stanley Baldwin. D. E. Moggridge, *The Return to Gold** (1969) is important, and the works of Marwick, Beer, and Gilbert cited at the end of Chapter 4 are also useful for the 1920s.

Nathanael Greene, *From Versailles to Vichy** (1970) is an excellent brief introduction to interwar France. Rudolph Binion, *Defeated Leaders* (1960) examines the workings of the Third Republic through biographies of three politicians too strong-willed to succeed.

In addition to the Nicholls work cited on page 216, see the analysis of Arthur Rosen-

berg, *A History of the German Republic* (1936), the work of an exile sympathetic to social democracy, and the more detailed narrative of Erich Eyck, *A History of the Weimar Republic,** 2 vols. (1962–63). S. William Halperin, *Germany Tried Democracy** (1965) is still useful. The Weimar Republic has been well served by biographers. See Klaus Epstein, *Matthias Erzberger and the Dilemma of German Democracy* (1959); Henry A. Turner, Jr., *Stresemann and the Politics of the Weimar Republic** (1963); and David Felix, *Walther Rathenau and the Weimar Republic: The Politics of Reparations* (1971). The republic's relationship with the officer corps is studied in Francis L. Carsten, *The Reichswehr and Politics, 1919–1933** (1966), and Gaines Post, Jr., *The Civil–Military Fabric of Weimar Foreign Policy* (1973).

The Fascist regime in Italy after its stabilization is assessed in Edward R. Tannenbaum, *The Fascist Experience: Italian Society and Culture, 1922–1945* (1972), and the less analytical Max Gallo, *Mussolini's Italy: Twenty Years of the Fascist Era* (1973). There is a useful collection of articles and thoughtful bibliographical advice in Roland Sarti, ed., *The Ax Within** (1974). None of these works entirely supplants the keen contemporary observations of Gaetano Salvemini, *Under the Axe of Fascism* (1938), and Herman S. Finer, *Mussolini's Italy,** 2nd ed. (1935). Harry Fornari, *Mussolini's Gadfly: Roberto Farinacci* (1971) is the best biography of a Fascist stalwart.

Karl J. Newman, *European Democracy Between the Wars* (1971) examines the failure of parliamentary institutions in the new states of Eastern Europe. The most enlightening case study of a return to authoritarianism in Eastern Europe in the 1920s is Joseph Rothschild, *Pilsudski's Coup d'Etat* (1966). Peter F. Sugar and Ivo Lederer, eds., *Nationalism in Eastern Europe* (1971) contains interesting studies of each state.

The general history of Eastern Europe is recounted in C. A. Macartney and A. W. Palmer, *Independent Eastern Europe** (1962); Hugh Seton-Watson, *Eastern Europe Between the Wars,** 2nd ed. (1967); and Robert L. Wolff, *The Balkans in Our Time** (1967). Joseph Rothschild, *East Central Europe Between the Two Wars* (1974) is the latest survey.

Klemens von Klemperer, *Ignaz Seipel: Christian Statesman in a Time of Crisis* (1972) is important for Austria in the 1920s. There is rich detail in Charles A. Gulick, *From Habsburg to Hitler*, 2 vols. (1948). The indispensable work on interwar Hungary is C. A. Macartney, *October Fifteenth: A History of Modern Hungary, 1929–1945*, 2 vols. (1957). Hans Roos, *A History of Modern Poland* (1966) is the most balanced brief survey. Vincent S. Mamatey and Radomír Luža, eds., *A History of the Czechoslovak Republic, 1918–1948* (1973) is the best introduction. See also the later sections of Elizabeth Wiskemann, *Czechs and Germans,* 2nd ed. (1967), and Vera Olivova, *The Doomed Democracy: Czechoslovakia in a Disrupted Europe, 1918–1938* (1972).

Henry S. Roberts, *Rumania: The Political Problems of an Agrarian State* (1951) is illuminating. The most powerful agrarian populist of Eastern Europe in the 1920s, Alexander Stambolisky, is discussed in Chapters 5 and 6 of Joseph Rothschild, *The Communist Party of Bulgaria* (1959). See also Cyril E. Black, "Bulgaria in Historical Perspective," in L. A. Dellin, ed., *Bulgaria* (1957).

In addition to many of the works on Russia cited at the end of Chapter 5, Stephen F. Cohen, *Bukharin and the Bolshevik Revolution: A Political Biography, 1888–1938* (1973) is essential for the 1920s. Moshe Lewin, *Lenin's Last Struggle** (1968) presents the beginnings of the struggle for leadership after Lenin. The standard works on the beginnings of one-party rule in Russia are Leonard Schapiro, *The Origins of Communist Autocracy* (1955) and *The Communist Party of the Soviet Union*, rev. ed. (1971). Merle Fainsod, *Smolensk Under Soviet Rule** (1958) uses local party archives captured by the Germans during the Second World War to provide an exceptionally clear picture of Communist administration in one district.

Fernand Léger, The City, *1919.*

MASS CULTURE AND HIGH CULTURE BETWEEN THE WARS

10

The 1920s summon up images of the brilliant triumph of modernism in the arts: Picasso painting in Paris and Kandinsky in Weimar; Stravinsky composing in Paris and Schoenberg in Vienna; the functionalist buildings of Gropius and Le Corbusier. Closer inspection shows that the vigorous new generation of the 1920s was only working out the results of the great prewar shift in high cultural values.[1] The primary achievement of these artists in the interwar years was to bring the avant-garde of prewar Europe into the cultural mainstream. The more significant and profound changes were taking place in popular culture. It was the mass transmission of commercialized popular entertainment that most radically transformed the culture of Europeans between the wars.

---

[1]See Chapter 1, pp. 39–44.

Mass Culture: The Age of Radio and Movies

Two new forms of communication in the 1920s enabled the famous and the powerful to address millions of persons at once for the first time: radio and motion pictures. In one bound, Europeans left behind an era when a person could speak to groups only if they were within physical earshot. Even the massive propaganda efforts during the war had been largely limited to the printed word, to the artistry of posters, or to the voices of speakers physically present. Not until the end of the war were the possibilities of movie newsreels being realized; radio was still at the stage of occasional broadcasts by amateurs.

The Technological Basis for Mass Media

Public radio broadcasting was made possible by a quickening stream of nineteenth-century inventions in communications. The first major step had been the telegraph, which permitted virtually instantaneous transmission of coded messages wherever lines had been strung. With the opening of a line from England to Australia in 1872, the telegraph net was almost worldwide. At the same time, the early telephone permitted voice transmission along lines. Rapid communications acquired real flexibility, however, only with liberation from transmission wires. In 1901, an Italian engineer, Guglielmo Marconi, managed to send messages by "wireless" radio waves from England to Canada. Subsequent improvements, especially the development of the vacuum tube in the United States after 1906, made it possible to transmit the human voice instead of just coded messages reliably by wireless.

So far, these transmissions had linked individuals. The major breakthrough of the 1920s was the assembly of a mass audience for instantaneous communication. The first radio broadcasts were one-time transmissions, such as the concert by soprano Nellie Melba from London on June 16, 1920, or the report of the United States presidential election results from Pittsburgh, which scooped the press in November 1920. During 1921 and 1922, permanent broadcasting facilities were established in the United States, Europe, and Japan, and receiving sets began to be mass produced. The Age of Radio was at hand. When the BBC (British Broadcasting Corporation) was reorganized as a public corporation in 1926, there were 2,178,259 radio receivers in the United Kingdom. At the end of the 1930s, there were 9 million—nearly three out of every four British households. By 1938 Germany had more than 9 million receivers; France, more than 4 million sets; Russia, 4.5 million sets (for a much larger population); and Czechoslovakia, Sweden, and the Netherlands each had more than 1 million sets.[2]

An imposing radio set now jostled with the piano and the potted Aspidistra plant for a conspicuous place in every middle-class living room, and the European consumer boasted of the number of his set's

---

[2]Asa Briggs, *The History of Broadcasting in the United Kingdom* (Oxford, 1961–70), Vol. 1, p. 12; Vol. 2, p. 6; Vol. 3, p. 737. Italy and Belgium followed with slightly less than 1 million receivers in 1938.

tubes in the same vein as he boasted of the cylinders of his car. Radio sets began to spread to working-class homes as well. In the 1930s, the cheapest German set, which the propaganda-conscious Nazi regime encouraged its people to buy, cost thirty-five marks, or about one week's average wage.[3] After furniture and a bicycle, a radio was the next major purchase for many a settled working-class family in Europe.

The technical basis for motion pictures had been developed in the 1890s as an adjunct to vaudeville and music hall entertainment. The early short action and trick reels soon gave way to multireel films with a story line. *The Great Train Robbery* (1903), one of the first films with a plot, lasted a full eight minutes and enjoyed tremendous success. The Italian-made *Quo Vadis* (1912) ran for two hours, and the way was open for the cinema to draw on the theatrical tradition as a conscious art form. But motion pictures did not become the nearly universal public entertainment until after the war. By the end of the 1930s, 40 percent of all British adults went to the movies once a week; 25 percent went twice a week. British attendance in 1937 was running at a rate of 20 million persons a week in a country of 50 million. It reached a peak of 31 million a week in 1946 before giving ground to television.[4] Figures were much the same on the Continent.

The Creation of Mass Audiences

Radio and motion pictures created simultaneous mass audiences on a national and even international scale for the first time. One would have to go back to the invention of movable type to find a threshold of equivalent importance in the transmission of culture. The mass audience in itself was not a total novelty, strictly speaking, thanks to the spread of literacy and cheap printing in the nineteenth century. Alfred Harmsworth, later Lord Northcliffe, had begun a commercial revolution in the newspaper industry in the 1890s by selling his papers at or below cost and shifting his revenues from sales to income from advertisements. He found that businesses were willing to pay large sums to buy display advertisements designed to appeal to a mass readership. His *Evening News* and *Daily Mail* were the first half-penny papers in London and the first in Europe to reach the unprecedented circulation figure of 500,000.

The spread of newspapers beyond the elite was a gradual process, however. Only after 1910 did more than half the adult British population read one of the Sunday papers, which generally emphasized reports of crimes, sports, and sensational fiction. More than half read a daily paper only after 1920.[5] Continental newspapers between the wars reached, if anything, a more traditionally elite audience. Prestigious dailies like the Paris *Le Temps* preferred to draw revenue from secret

[3]Richard Grunberger, *The Twelve-Year Reich* (New York, 1971), p. 401.
[4]Noreen Branson and Margot Heinemann, *Britain in the Nineteen Thirties* (New York, 1971), p. 251; and Raymond Williams, *Communications*, 2nd ed. (London, 1966), p. 29.
[5]Williams, pp. 23–24, 32.

government funds than from large display advertising. By contrast, radio and the movies very rapidly became majority pastimes. Moreover, radio and the movies, unlike the printed word, could provide a mass audience with the immediate impact of experience. Early audiences shrank back as the speeding locomotive approached the bound heroine in *The Perils of Pauline* with the same involuntary reaction shown by later audiences as they gripped their seats during the roller coaster ride in the first of the "three-dimensional" (3-D) films of the 1950s.

The Political Uses of Radio and Movies

Political figures turned to the radio early, and it was quickly apparent that some of them were much more effective at the microphone than others. The learned discourses carefully drafted by nineteenth-century parliamentarians had far less impact over a radio than they had in a room full of other parliamentarians, or read the next day in the *Journal des débats.* At the radio microphone, two very different styles proved to be successful. The friendly, simple chat was perfected by the stolid British Conservative leader Stanley Baldwin, who managed to project old-

"All Germany listens to the Führer on the people's radio set." Governments quickly learned the power of radio, and the Nazi regime subsidized the production of inexpensive receivers like the one in this poster.

fashioned rural common sense as if speaking "with his feet on your fender" (fireside). Baldwin was more effective on the radio than the greater public orators of the time like Lloyd George, whose rhetoric seemed strained without the face and hands in view. The other style that worked on radio was the impassioned harangue that hammered away on a few simple slogans, as perfected by Mussolini and Hitler. Although Hitler did not neglect dramatic personal appearances, where he materialized quickly in an airplane or a high-powered Mercedes, he was so convinced of the importance of radio that he delivered no less than fifty radio speeches during his first year in power. His propaganda minister, Josef Goebbels, also a master of the fevered radio harangue, lent state support to the production of inexpensive radios and organized group listening in youth camps, factories, and barracks. As a result, Germany seems to have had the densest radio coverage in Europe: 16 million out of 23 million households were equipped with radios by 1942. Britain came in second place. Because Italy had far fewer radios it was a less fruitful terrain for Mussolini, but he used radio effectively and organized group listening. Among the high points of political radio between the wars were Mussolini's broadcast announcements on October 2, 1935, that he had decided to invade Ethiopia and on May 9, 1936, proclaiming victory. Mussolini's broadcasts were punctuated over the radio by the braying of hundreds of thousands of people who were below his balcony:

> Officers! Non-commissioned officers! Soldiers of all the armed forces of the state in Africa and Italy! Blackshirts of the Revolution! Italians in the Fatherland and in the world! Listen!
> With the decisions that in a few moments you will learn . . . a great event is accomplished: Today, 9 May, of the fourteenth year of the Fascist era, the fate of Ethiopia is sealed. . . .
> The Italian people has created the empire with its blood. It will fecundate it with its work and defend it against anyone with its arms.
> Will you be worthy of it? (Crowd: "Yes!")[6]

Radio thus reduced the effectiveness of traditional oratory and increased the effectiveness of both personality and of ritual in European politics.

Politicians also quickly realized the propaganda potential of movies. The fascist regimes carefully controlled the content of newsreels, although newsreels in all countries were characterized by the stentorian voice, the simplified sentiment, the short take, and the emphasis on individual exploits (whether in sports or war) and on "human interest." Hitler engaged a young woman filmmaker, Leni Riefenstahl, to film the Nazi party rally at Nuremberg in 1934 and the 1936 Olympics. In the film of the party rally, *The Triumph of the Will* (1934), aerial views of Nuremberg through steeply banked cumulus clouds then close in on stunning shots of tight ranks of marchers and ceremonial ritual; it remains a stirring and troubling visual experience.

[6]Laura Fermi, *Mussolini* (Chicago, 1961), p. 327.

The central political problem was who should control the mass media. Radio broadcasting required some kind of international regulation, if only to prevent several broadcasters from interrupting one another on the same frequency. Beyond that essential technical coordination, three basic forms of control developed. The United States, Latin America, and Japan left broadcasting entirely in the hands of companies whose revenue came from advertisements. No European state, liberal or collectivist, accepted sole commercial sponsorship. In the 1920s most Continental states, including France and Weimar Germany as well as Fascist Italy and Communist Russia, placed radio broadcasting under some form of direct government control. A third form of control was represented by the BBC, a public monopoly run by its own board and financed by an annual license fee paid by each radio owner. The first general director of the BBC, the strong-minded Scotsman John Reith, firmly established the dual tradition of intellectual uplift and political neutrality that made the BBC the most independent of all noncommercial radio systems. Although the BBC was sometimes accused of blandness, it successfully avoided the major pitfalls of the other systems: the crass commercialism of the American pattern, and the abuses of government propaganda in the Continental pattern. The way each nation controlled radio was doubly important, for the even more pervasive medium of television settled naturally into the same patterns after 1945.[7]

Except for the subsidized party-oriented films of the Nazi and fascist regimes and the Soviet Union's tight control over all films, motion pictures were an almost entirely commercial proposition. Indeed, most films shown in Europe between the wars were not only commercial products; they were American. Although French and Italian filmmakers had led the way before 1914 in producing long features, their momentum had been halted during the war because the nitrocellulose used for film was needed for explosives. This pause allowed United States filmmakers to dominate the industry with their silent films in the 1920s. The coming of "talkies" at the end of the decade tended to limit the audiences to single-language groups and give Continental filmmakers a new impetus in the 1930s. The British government, however, felt obliged to impose quotas of home-produced films on British movie houses when American films had absorbed 90 percent of the market.

Newspapers were commercially controlled in most of Europe, outside the party press of Nazi Germany, Fascist Italy, and the Soviet Union.[8] Newspapers were also changing in character and falling into the hands

---

[7]No European radio system conformed absolutely to one pattern of control. French national radio accepted advertising until 1935, and even after that French listeners could hear commercial radio from Luxemburg and Monaco. The British government authorized an independent (commercial) television network in 1955.

[8]Party newspapers, especially on the left, competed with the blander commercial dailies in the liberal states. Large "nonpolitical" commercial dailies survived in Germany and Italy. Only the Soviet Union had a party press monopoly.

of large press empires. European dailies continued the commercial revolution begun in England by Lord Northcliffe in the 1890s. Between the wars, major dailies like the *Daily Express* and the *Petit Parisien* reached circulation figures of around 2 million through the formula of extensive advertising and low price per copy.

The Role of Advertising

Radio, the movies, and the popular press made it possible to inundate whole populations with skillful and aggressive commercial salesmanship to a degree hardly imagined before 1914. Advertising was an ancient medium, and it had grown rapidly with the development of large newspaper displays after the 1890s. Between the wars, however, it grew so dramatically in size and in kind as to dwarf what had gone before.

Most great daily newspapers between the wars drew from one-half to three-quarters of their revenues from advertising.[9] To entice the advertisers, publishers had to keep circulation high by pandering to popular tastes for sports, crime reporting, and sentimental fiction as well as simplified, chauvinist news coverage. In each major city, two or three large sensationalist dailies, usually owned by one of the large press empires, dominated the advertising market and forced smaller papers out of business. Sometimes a serious newspaper like the London *Times* (circulation, 225,000) survived by promising advertisers access to the most educated and influential minority. On the Continent, where the commercial evolution was less advanced, some dailies like the Paris *Le Temps* preserved an old-fashioned seriousness without display advertising by receiving secret subsidies from its own and foreign governments hoping to obtain favorable news coverage. Radio gave advertising a whole new dimension. Professional advertising agencies learned to apply psychology to taste-shaping. Total advertising expenditure grew prodigiously. In England, it expanded from about £26 million per year before the war to more than three times that figure in 1938, £96 million, or close to 2 percent of the national income,[10] far more than was spent on either scientific research or the fine arts. At its best, advertising drew on good modern design and helped elevate the taste of popular culture. At its worst, European advertising encouraged frivolous buying by those who could not afford it; and in the case of untested medicines, it could be positively dangerous.

Popular mass culture went hand in hand with the leisure to enjoy it. When the nineteenth century ended, leisure time was still for the most part the preserve of the wealthy. Second- and third-generation business families had only recently emerged from the abstemious habits and long

The New Leisure

[9]Williams, p. 27.
[10]Ralph Harris and Arthur Selden, *Advertising and the Public* (London, 1962), pp. 39–42. The proportion of national income spent on advertising was slightly higher in the United States than in Britain, and slightly lower on the Continent.

working hours needed to accumulate capital at the beginnings of industrialization. By the 1890s, many factory workers were working only a ten-hour day, although rural workers still stumbled from sleep to toil and back to sleep according to the rhythms of the sun, just as most factory workers had done in the early stages of the Industrial Revolution. A few workers, such as miners in France, enjoyed eight-hour work days even before 1914. At the end of the First World War, the eight-hour day became quite general for office and factory workers in northern and Western Europe. In 1936 the French government set the work week at forty hours. For the first time in the history of work, men and women wage earners had as many waking hours for their own amusement as they spent on the job.

Early legislation limiting working hours had usually been intended to preserve the health and productivity of the worker. After the war, a new conception of leisure as a positive human right made itself widely felt. The healthy fulfillment of each citizen's individual qualities in leisure-time recreation began to be a concern of governments.

Along with the forty-hour work week, the French government provided in 1936 for two weeks' vacation with pay for all employees of firms larger than family shops. In August 1936, then, millions of ordinary Frenchmen found themselves blinking their eyes unaccustomed to midday sunshine, with two weeks free to be used as they wished, without having to be sick or injured to receive time off. Many French workers could not afford to go anywhere at that time, but the way was open for the human tide of campers, cyclists, hikers, and tourists who now inundate the beaches and mountains of Europe.

Organized Recreation

Totalitarian regimes were not satisfied merely to leave their citizens the rich delight of free time. Every moment must be filled with useful—and nonpolitical—activity. "Their leisure hours were a danger-spot for the whole nation,"[11] wrote an Italian Fascist spokesman of his fellow citizens in 1925. In that year, the Fascist regime swallowed up every autonomous leisure-time organization, from mandolin societies to football clubs, into a vast national recreation agency: the *Operaio Nazionale Dopolavoro*.

The *Dopolavoro* (afterwork) was charged with organizing the supposed willfully individualistic Italian workers in mass recreational activities that would make them docile citizens and good soldiers. Zealous officials published statistics showing how many million Italians had been marched to museums, parks, beaches, operas, and sports matches each year, to the point where a scornful refugee, Gaetano Salvemini, predicted that

> the number of kisses exchanged under the auspices of the Dopolavoro . . . will soon be counted, and the staggering total will be attributed to the genius of Mussolini.[12]

[11]Quoted in Gaetano Salvemini, *Under the Axe of Fascism* (New York, 1936), p. 334.
[12]*Ibid.*

In soberer fact, only about 2 million out of 12 million Italian workers could be persuaded or coerced into joining *Dopolavoro* activities, and rural and village workers were inevitably less accessible to a distant bureaucracy. In many areas of southern Italy, however, the *Dopolavoro* was the first agency to step between the villagers and their virtually feudal superiors. Fascist recreation was one of the first steps toward a fuller mobilization of Italian citizens into modern mass culture.

After 1933 Hilter copied the *Dopolavoro* in his *Kraft durch Freude* (strength through joy) movement. Although workers' cruises to Madeira and Norway were widely publicized, only about one worker out of twenty actually enjoyed such a privilege. But the regime did invest great sums in promoting and organizing sports and mass recreation in ways designed to spread enthusiasm and inculcate discipline and induce workers to forget that real wages were lower than in 1929.

The Soviet state also assumed responsibility for leisure-time activities. The *Komsomol* (Young Communist League) organized summer camps and promoted sports, and the regime turned the villas and hunting lodges of the aristocracy into vacation centers. In practice, however, the enormous strains of rapid land collectivization and factory development after 1929 left little surplus of either resources or free time for widespread leisure and recreation.

"Strength Through Joy," the Nazi recreation agency, gave wide publicity to the special vacations it provided for a few chosen workers, such as this cruise to Madeira in 1935.

Professional sports was the leisure-time activity that most Europeans enjoyed between the wars. Games like association football (soccer) had been transformed from spontaneous play into systematic contests in the nineteenth century, with formal rules and a network of permanent teams (The Football Association in England, 1854). Lower-class professional players began to succeed middle- and upper-class amateurs in public sports contests. Association football spread to the Continent and to Latin America before the First World War, in conscious imitation of the British: the football team in Milano even used the English name of its own town in its team title, A. C. Milan. The game became a mass spectator sport in the twentieth century, and the establishment of World Cup contests in 1930 sharpened the nationalist fervor that surrounded it.

The 1920s and 1930s were the great era of stadium-building both in Europe and in the United States. Whereas the first modern stadiums, such as the one built in Athens in 1896, had held 50,000 to 60,000 spectators, the great football stadiums built after 1918 held crowds approaching the size of the armies at Waterloo. The Lenin Stadium in Moscow held 103,000; Wembley Stadium in north London, 126,000. The great stadium built in Berlin for the 1936 Olympics held 140,000, and the *Sportspalast* built the following year in Nuremberg held 225,000. The biggest stadium in the world was the Strahav Stadium in Prague (1934), designed for gymnastics and track meets, which could hold 240,000 spectators.

The enormous sums bet on association football were some measure of the public's infatuation with the game. It is estimated that the total wagered in the football pools in England in the 1934/35 season was about £20 million (nearly $100 million at current exchange rates), and that the figure doubled in 1936; extra postmen had to be put on duty in working-class neighborhoods every Monday and Tuesday, when the wagers for the following weekend's matches were sent in.[13] The amount bet on horse racing was still bigger. These mass-attended sports far outweighed in popularity the more traditional upper-class amateur sports of Rugby football, tennis, and cricket.

Bicycle racing was always more fanatically popular on the Continent than in England. Following the bicycle craze of the 1890s when the machine was new, a number of celebrated long-distance bicycle races absorbed vast advertising money and popular enthusiasm between the wars. The Tour de France, a bicycle race that attracted Belgian and Italian cyclists as well as French, went on for ten days or so. The Berlin bicycle race tied up the city for six days.

[13]Robert Graves and Alan Hodge, *The Long Week-End: A Social History of Great Britain, 1918–39* (London, 1940), pp. 383–84.

With leisure, travel also became more accessible to masses of people. Great technical breakthroughs revolutionized the pace of travel. Most important was the conquest of air. Once the basic techniques of flight had been mastered, progress was very rapid. The Wright brothers had kept a heavier-than-air machine aloft for three minutes across the dunes at Kitty Hawk, North Carolina, in 1903. Just six years later the Frenchman Louis Blériot flew across the English Channel in thirty-seven minutes. Military use of aircraft during the war enormously increased both speed and distance, so that at the war's end Europe and the world were ready for civilian air travel.

In 1919 the British flyers John Alcock and Arthur Brown first flew the Atlantic nonstop,[14] and in the same year the first regular international airmail service was begun, linking Paris and London. Passenger service followed almost at once. By 1934 an Englishman could reach Australia in four days by air, a trip that took weeks by ship. The only comparable acceleration in travel had been the application of steam to travel in the 1830 to 1870 period.[15] Air travel was even more liberating, however, for air passengers (and bombers) could reach any point on earth across both geographical and political frontiers without the need for a continuous path or waterway.

Only the wealthy or adventurous traveled by air between the wars, of course. But the average traveler could now supplement the train with buses and private cars. Many traveled by bicycle. Hiking, too, became very widespread among European youth in the 1930s. Germany, with its long tradition of scouting and hiking in the prewar *Wandervogel* movement, was the center of knapsack traveling among the young. This was combined with the cult of outdoor toughness that the Nazi regime liked to contrast with liberal, bourgeois flabbiness. Every year several young Germans fell to their deaths on the sheer north wall of the Eigerwand in Switzerland trying to prove themselves and their ideology against the mountain. The knapsacking cult was not limited to Germany. The young hostels movement was created in France in the 1930s and spread elsewhere. Even some Frenchmen equated tramping youth with an antiliberal toughening: "The France of camping out will vanquish the France of the *apéritif* and the Party Congress," wrote the right-wing novelist Drieu La Rochelle in 1937.[16]

However they traveled and under whatever ideological sign, ordinary Europeans had much more chance of moving about than their fathers

[14]The significance of Lindbergh's exploit of 1927, surrounded by much more publicity, was that he made the flight alone.
[15]The opening of the United States transcontinental railroad in 1869 cut travel time across the United States from four weeks by horse to four days, a thirty-fold reduction in time. Propeller-driven airliners cut train time in the 1940s only about ten-fold.
[16]*L'Emancipation nationale,* August 20, 1937.

and grandfathers. The business of catering to leisure had been completely transformed. Lavish nineteenth-century resorts like the mountain springs of Marienbad, Bad Godesberg, and Vichy, where the wealthy gathered to "take the waters," were being jostled by more plebeian holiday camps. Crowds built up on beaches like the one at Brighton, where the prince regent had first popularized sea bathing in the 1820s. The giant liners that took first-class passengers across the Atlantic in the comfort of a luxury hotel now passed *Kraft durch Freude* ships on their way to Madeira and *Dopolavoro* cruises to Majorca. The ease with which news, styles, and people traveled around the earth had much to do with the increasing similarity of popular culture after 1918.

The Effects of Mass Culture and Leisure

The cumulative effects of mass leisure and a newly self-confident and economically powerful popular culture are still a subject of debate. One major effect clearly was to increase the homogeneity of national populations, a process that had begun in the nineteenth century. The popular press and radio transmitted the tastes and spoken accents of Paris or Berlin or London or Rome to the remotest villages of the Auvergne or Bavaria or Northumberland or Calabria. Deep-rooted local culture began to be replaced by a national culture; in turn, national ways of life were influenced more and more by an international consumer culture. The heroine of Thomas Hardy's novel *Tess of the D'Urbervilles* (1891) had felt as though moving from one valley to another was the equivalent of changing countries; the time was not too distant when only the elderly would retain traces of local accents and customs.

The process of homogeneity was hastened by cheaper, more uniform manufactured clothing. Europeans of the 1920s were perhaps the last generation whose class status and even employment could be told at a glance by dress. Rayon, the first widely used synthetic fabric, was already becoming a commonplace during the 1920s.[17] Rayon blurred the ancient line between those who could afford silk and those who could not.

Some observers felt that more homogeneous populations were a sign of fruitful egalitarianism. If the visible marks of class—the blue smock, the cloth cap, the different accent—were diminished, might not the old "two nations" about which Disraeli had commented in the 1840s at last be merging into that single body of citizens about which democrats had dreamed since the French Revolution?

Some of the techniques used to mobilize the classes and local minorities into a common citizenry, however, aroused worries about manipula-

---

[17]The word *rayon* was first used in 1924. First commercial production began in 1891, but remained small until the First World War. British production grew twenty-five fold between 1913 and 1929.

tion. Youth groups, organized recreation, and the pageantry of parades and rallies were only the most spectacular examples of the ways by which totalitarian governments attempted to mold citizens according to a type. The techniques of mass political manipulation were also developed in liberal states. An early example was the Budget League in England in 1909, a group established to arouse public opinion in favor of Lloyd George's Liberal party budget reforms. It was a pioneer in the use of press releases, mass meetings, and publicity in British politics.[18] Organized opinionmaking during the war vastly increased each government's experience in manipulating its citizenry. It seems likely that the vast machinery of persuasion set up by advertisers and promoters in the popular culture also worked to mold a citizenry that was prepared to march to a single command. That command might not come from a government; it might come from a sponsor commanding the public to buy a new product, or it might come from a deep popular emotion, such as anti-Semitism. Many Europeans focused concern about their manipulability on an evil conveniently labeled "Americanization," for much of the content of popular entertainment—jazz, escapist movies—came from the United States, and the techniques of advertising and publicity seemed more highly developed there.[19]

A more homogeneous citizenry meant the disappearance of an older, more localized, orally transmitted popular culture. To some cultivated Europeans, that culture seemed vastly superior to the commercial mass culture, with its appeal to the lowest common denominator and its artificially stimulated wants and curiosities. Richard Hoggart, a British intellectual of working-class origin, has reflected with some bitterness on the disappearance of the values of his grandparents' generation between the wars:

> The world of club-singing is being gradually replaced by that of typical radio dance-music and crooning, television cabaret and commercial-radio variety. The uniform national type which the popular papers help to produce is writ even larger in the uniform international type which the firm studios of Hollywood present. The old forms of class culture are in danger of being replaced by a poorer kind of classless, or by what I was led earlier to describe as "graceless," culture, and this is to be regretted.[20]

Other European intellectuals were more worried about mass culture's inroads on elite values than on the old customs. There had always been "popular culture," of course, as long as there had been ballads, folk dances, and tales handed down outside schools and the literary world. Highly educated Europeans had generally ignored it, for it made few converts outside its own class. What was frightening to these intellectuals was the material power and dynamism of the new mass culture and its ability to wean away with facile pleasures the elite young who were

[18]Cameron Hazelhurst, "Asquith as Prime Minister," *English Historical Review,* Vol. 85, No. 336 (July 1970).
[19]See, for example, Georges Duhamel, *America the Menace* (Boston, 1931).
[20]Richard Hoggart, *The Uses of Literacy* (London, 1957), p. 280.

supposed to carry on the arts and sciences. Who would learn Greek and mathematics, and who would advance physics if middle-class European students joined the masses at the movies? The young Jean-Paul Sartre and his mother slipped off to the movies despite his scholarly grandfather's displeasure.

> We blindly entered a century without tradition, a century that was to contrast strongly with the others by its bad manners, and the new art (the cinema), the art of the common man, foreshadowed our barbarism. Born in a den of thieves, officially classified as a travelling show, it had popular ways that shocked serious people. It was an amusement for women and children.[21]

The Spanish philosophy professor José Ortega y Gasset provided one of the most widely read warnings against mass culture in *The Revolt of the Masses* (1930). Already predisposed by the pessimism of the Spanish Generation of 1898 to reflect on Spain's decadence and decline, Ortega was convinced that European civilization, that fragile creation of exceptional men, would be trampled by "mass men," self-satisfied enjoyers of life unwilling either to master civilized creativity themselves or to submit to those who were civilized. Although he was a self-professed "democrat" and an opponent of both fascism and Bolshevism, Ortega spoke for many who intimated that they would accept strong measures to preserve elite culture from the brute force of mass commercial culture.

Oswald Spengler put some of the same concerns into a more specifically German context in a best-seller of 1919, *The Decline of the West.* Spengler's book is best remembered for its view of the inevitable rise and fall of cultures. In keeping with a tradition of German nationalist writing, Spengler feared that "Culture" (deep-rooted German traditions as distinct from those of Western Europe) was being overwhelmed by "Civilization" (the more cosmopolitan, commercialized mass culture that Spengler identified with liberal Western Europe). Spengler foresaw an emerging "World City," a faceless, cosmopolitan anthill within which the national Cultures (including the virile, spiritual values of Germanness) would be submerged and lost. One can recognize a form of attack on mass culture here, distorted by the passions of Germany's defeat in 1918 and by the nationalist assertion of the distinctness and superiority of German traditions. Down the road that Spengler took was an intellectual acceptance of dictatorship if dictatorship was necessary to save German values from cosmopolitan mass values.

There were several problems with this point of view. One was that ordinary Europeans, left to their own choices, enthusiastically embraced the new popular culture. Radio, movies, and the popular styles flourished mightily. The other problem was that the high culture itself was abandoning tradition with alacrity and embarking in the 1920s on a period of rich and raucous experiment.

[21]Jean-Paul Sartre, *The Words* (New York, 1966), p. 118.

On the surface, 1920s culture has a reputation for glitter, brash vitality, and novelty. Indeed, there was a wide variety of artistic and literary events whose main common ingredient was a strenuous effort to be new: the first performance in Berlin in 1925 of the opera *Wozzeck,* Alban Berg's powerful union of serial music and expressionist drama; the triumph of the opening night of Bertolt Brecht and Kurt Weill's jazz play *The Threepenny Opera* (Berlin, 1928); Darius Milhaud's Negro ballet *La Création du Monde* (Paris, 1923), with sets by the cubist painter Fernand Léger; the extraordinary assemblage of talent, including Walter Gropius and Paul Klee, teaching and designing at the Bauhaus in Weimar.

The high culture of the 1920s did not innovate, however, in basic aesthetic terms. The artistic leaders in that decade simply continued to work out the implications of the great aesthetic revolution of the turn of the century. More importantly, they brought the isolated experiments of the pre-1914 avant-garde into the mainstream of acceptance. In Peter Gay's terms, the prewar "outsiders" had become "insiders."[22]

How did the prewar avant-garde culture become acceptable, even fashionable, in the 1920s? First, the horrors of global war had somehow made the language of primitivism, subjective irrationality, and violence far more appropriate to an interpretation of the world. Second, the revolutionary impulse at the war's end heightened impatience with the *status quo,* in the arts as elsewhere. "There is a new spirit,"[23] said the young Swiss architect and city planner Le Corbusier in 1923. We need a "revision of values: if there is no revolution in architecture, there will be social revolution."[24] Third, young people, caught up in a generation conflict at the end of the war, had a strong sense of their mission to reject and reshape the values of their elders, who had put them in the trenches. Finally, the prosperity of the 1920s revived as enemies and targets "all those who long for a return to philistinism and the glorious time when it was only necessary to make money and accompany a decent digestion with a pious upward glance."[25]

The twentieth century has preserved a basic aesthetic unity. An explanation for that is apparent when one contemplates the long lives of the great pre-1914 pioneers: the *Fauve* painter Henri Matisse lived productively until 1954; Picasso until 1973; the musical pioneer Igor Stravinsky lived until 1972 actively composing almost to the end. Among the founders of functionalist architecture, Le Corbusier lived until 1965; Walter Gropius and Ludwig Mies van der Rohe until 1969. No wonder their successors seemed to be mostly derivative, the lesser practitioners of arts invented by more formidable predecessors. No wonder that most of the artistic idioms of the 1920s still seem modern fifty years later.

[22]Peter Gay, *Weimar Culture: The Outsider as Insider* (New York, 1968).
[23]C. E. Jeannerret-Gris (Le Corbusier), *Towards a New Architecture* (London, 1931), p. 89.
[24]*Ibid.,* pp. 227–29.
[25]Harry Kessler, *In the Twenties, The Diaries of Harry Kessler* (New York, 1971), p. 267.

High Culture Between the Wars

Interior, Savoie House (1929), showing the clean, functional lines of Le Corbusier's architecture.

Experimental Aesthetic Values

A few experimental painters had already renounced before 1914 the aesthetic assignment of the Renaissance—to portray nature and human nature—and were establishing new aesthetic values. Most postwar painters took up these values, which indeed were still being worked out in the third quarter of the twentieth century. As Paul Klee, one of the more articulate of painters, put it in lectures at the Bauhaus in 1923, artists no longer attached "such intense importance to natural form . . . but more value to the powers that do the forming." Klee imagined a dialogue with one of those tiresome laymen who "always looks for his favorite subject" in a picture:

> Layman: "But that isn't a bit like uncle." The artist, if his nerve is disciplined, thinks to himself: "To Hell with uncle. I must get on with my building. This new brick is a little too heavy and to my mind puts too much

weight on the left. I must add a good-sized counterweight to the right to restore the equilibrium."[26]

The artist "must distort," insisted Klee, "for therein is nature reborn."[27]

In his emphasis on "building" a painting and on "composition," Klee continued, like many interwar painters, the prewar cubists' fascination with form and structure. The Dutch painter Piet Mondrian was less playful than Klee in his shapes and balances; his explorations of pure form, simplified and reduced to basic elements, were severely two-dimensional.

Purified, simplified form for its own sake was a new aesthetic basis for other arts as well. The musical avant-garde had partially broken with key and harmony before 1914. Then, in 1924, the Viennese composer Arnold Schoenberg published a piano suite in which he perfected an altogether different musical idiom: the twelve-tone or serial system, in which the composer arranged twelve tones in a series that then became the building block of the composition instead of a conventional scale. Together with his pupils Alban Berg and Anton Webern, Schoenberg took music into whole new realms, although few of their contemporaries could follow these innovators with pleasure.

Many architects completed the prewar rejection of ornament in favor of a severe architecture subordinated to functional needs and the aesthetics of simple mass and balance. Le Corbusier turned for guidance to the engineer, whose only aesthetic was thought to be the natural harmony derived from smooth, simple utility. "The Engineer's aesthetic and Architecture are two things that march together and follow one from the other."[28] After praising the functional elegance of grain silos, automobiles, airplanes, and other machines, Le Corbusier insisted that "a house is a machine for living in."[29] He designed mass-produced houses of reinforced concrete with long horizontal windows and flexible interior spaces to express the functional simplicity with which people should live. Cities, he said, should be towers among gardens and playing fields, with living, playing, and transportation carried on at different levels.[30]

A machine aesthetic permeated a number of artistic fields in the 1920s. Arthur Honegger's railroad composition, *Pacific 231* (1924), is only the most celebrated of a number of efforts to enrich the musical vocabulary with industrial sounds, most of which are simply dated curiosities today. Some painters, like the Frenchman Fernand Léger, applied cubism to the exploration of industrial shapes. More important than these superficial influences on mere subject matter was the discovery of a fundamental kinship between the simple elegance of a

[26]Paul Klee, *On Modern Art* (London, 1948), p. 19.
[27]*Ibid.*, p. 29.
[28]Le Corbusier, p. 1.
[29]*Ibid.*, p. 15.
[30]*Ibid.*, p. 57.

machine and artistic expression. Members of the Bauhaus community tried to bring good design to everyday objects like furniture and household utensils. They wanted to unite aesthetics and material considerations into a "social art" whose combination of beauty and efficiency would restore wholeness to everyday life.

Functionalism, good social organization, and delight in purified form, then, were aesthetic values carried forward in the 1920s from the prewar avant-garde. Another major taproot of modernism was the expression of feeling, heightened if necessary by distortion, emphatic techniques, harsh flat colors, and morbid subject matter. The *Fauves* had replaced modeling with flat, bright color for shock effect as early as 1905 in Paris; the German expressionists applied their neo-Gothic morbidity, distortion, and heightened emotion to all the arts before 1914.[31] The expression of heightened feeling and emotion by artistic distortion was still a major characteristic of modernism in the 1920s.

The theater and the new art of motion pictures lent themselves particularly well to expressionist purposes. Films were ideally suited to a powerful evocation of horror and mystery through calculated distortion, as was proved by the masterpiece of German expressionist filmmaking, *The Cabinet of Dr. Caligari* (1919). A high point of expressionist drama was Alban Berg's opera *Wozzeck*—a melodramatic tale of a soldier driven to murder his mistress by a mysterious inner terror heightened by the taunts of others about her unfaithfulness.

New Concerns

Whether clarity of form or power of expression was their main purpose, the modern artistic movements of the 1920s shared a number of new concerns. All the intellectual leaders rejected "art," in the sense of traditional or learned techniques invested with exaggerated awe by a social elite. The modern arts were intensely personal acts of self-expression, and those who cared to respond did so on their own emotional terms. With few exceptions, the modern artists "did" rather than "talked." They were better at denouncing dead tradition and the philistines than at explaining what they wanted to do. Their creations would have to speak for themselves.

All the interwar art forms plunged yet deeper into the subjectivity that had appeared before the war. War and revolution heightened Europeans' fascination with the human unconscious, sometimes in very direct ways. We have already seen how his work with shellshocked soldiers in 1917 had awakened André Breton's curiosity about expressions of deep unconscious feelings in the arts.[32] His surrealist movement (1924) tried automatic writing, in which the author was supposed to produce whatever words were suggested by some mysterious inner prompting. It glorified the "divine madness" of those reaches of the unconscious that

[31]See Chapter 1, pp. 41–42.
[32]See Chapter 4, p. 123.

Scene from The Cabinet of Dr. Caligari, *a striking example of expressionist filmmaking in Germany.*

the arts had hitherto ignored. Later, surrealist painters, such as the Belgian René Magritte and the Spaniard Salvador Dalí, placed highly realistic details in grotesque imaginary landscapes, in playful yet disturbing explorations of the depths of the human psyche.

In addition to Breton's surrealist writing, other new literary techniques reflected the growing interest in the unconscious. Marcel Proust probed the workings of memory and of social status in the multivolume novel *A la recherche du temps perdu (Remembrance of Things Past)*. Although his first volume had gone unnoticed in 1913, the next volume won a major French literary prize in 1921. And there was the "stream of consciousness" technique, by which the reader is brought directly into the mind of a character with all his disconnected ramblings, free association of banalities and profundities, and suggestive, half-understood allusions. The most masterful of the "stream of consciousness" writers was the Irish exile James Joyce, whose *Ulysses* was published in 1922.

Sigmund Freud, perhaps the single most influential thinker in interwar intellectual life, made Europeans aware of the unconscious. Freud had established his two principal points before the war: that our conscious reasoning is to some extent rationalization of unconscious desires and conflicts; and that sexuality is the main formative element in human personality, even in infancy. Freud continued to refine his work after the war, adding the famous three-fold analysis of the personality: the id, or unconscious; the ego, or drive for self-preservation; and the superego, or Freudian equivalent of conscience. Freud also undertook after the war an interpretation of human history and society. In *Civilization and Its Discontents* (1929) he argued that some form of sexual repression was a necessary concomitant of group living and cultural

Pablo Picasso, Igor Stravinsky, *1920.*

development. The overall thrust of Freud's writing was somewhat pessimisitic and determinist, strongly suggesting that every individual's personality elements were at war with one another and with the surrounding culture. The best one could hope for was a certain mitigation of the pain by psychoanalytically assisted "adjustment."

Freud's scientific influence spread after the war because of wartime experiences with the treatment of battlefield emotional disorders. Outside Freud's Vienna, important centers of psychoanalysis grew up in Berlin, London, and New York. His influence among ordinary people, however, was of a different kind, for his name became associated with a prurient exploitation of youthful postwar hedonism. The notions that sexual repression was harmful and that salvation came through free sexual expression were closer to Freud's heretical student Wilhelm Reich than to the master himself. Freud did not know whether to be angry or amused when the Hollywood producer Sam Goldwyn offered him $100,000 in 1925 to serve as consultant for a series of films on the variants of love.[33]

Human sexuality was treated far more explicitly and centrally in the arts after the war than before. Even the late–nineteenth-century naturalistic French novelist, Emile Zola, whose sexual frankness had resulted in censorship and lawsuits, had described lust and sexual violence as merely unpleasant and discrete aspects of human ugliness. For some interwar writers, sexuality was not only more pervasive but more sanctified; it was an expression of humanity's most fundamental energies and passions. The British novelist D. H. Lawrence frankly reveled in the pagan enjoyment of instinct. His novels contrasted the effete, repressed upper classes with vigorous primitives who "thought with their blood."

The vitality of primitive creative instincts was accepted without argument by most interwar artists. The whole point of self-expression in the arts was to bypass the thin-blooded conformism of learned art and the academies. Just as Picasso and Matisse had found inspiration in

[33]Ernest Jones, *The Life and Work of Sigmund Freud,* ed. and abridged Lionel Trilling and Stephen Marcus (London, 1961), p. 566.

Marc Chagall, Solitude, *1933.*

primitive African masks in 1905 and the German expressionist Ludwig Kirchner in statues from the Pacific in 1904, the interwar artists continued to look for sources of primitive vigor and certainty, whether in their own unconscious, in the work of children, or in the arts of the happily "uncivilized" peoples of the world. Study of primitive art in ethnographic museums or through travel had become an essential part of a painter's experience; Kandinsky referred to the "shattering impression that the ethnographic museum made on me."[34]

The search for primitive roots was especially pronounced among the Russian exiles who contributed so much to Western European intellectual life after 1917. The composer Stravinsky turned away from the lush romanticism of his first compositions toward simplicity, clarity, and ritual. His *Weddings* (*Les noces,* 1923) recalled folk rituals in music of great strength and hypnotic repetition; in subsequent revisions he made his orchestration leaner and purer as if in a continuing effort to return to the simplest verity. The painter Marc Chagall created his own fanciful world of the people of his native village in the Jewish Pale of Russia.

On any scale—imagination, individuality, or vigor—the postwar years rank among the most brilliantly expressive. To understand cultural climates with some realism, however, we need to know more about their settings.

The Settings of Interwar Culture

Sophisticated cultural expressions were restricted, for the most part, to large cities. Two European cities stood out for the brilliance of their cultural life: Paris and (until 1933) Berlin. Paris had attracted an international artist community since the 1890s, when it had been the freest republican capital in the world and the center of intense experimentation in the visual arts: Picasso had come from Spain, Van Gogh from Holland, Sergei Diaghilev from Russia, among others. Paris, then, was a natural setting for the flowering of avant-garde art. After 1918, Americans joined the European artists, and the introduction of jazz, together with the new spare literary style of American expatriate writers like Hemingway, marked the first time that the United States had been a contributor to rather than a borrower of European cultural expression.

Berlin was different. Its cultural flowering followed a revolution, so that the triumph of new forms of expression was accompanied by the entry of the prewar "outsiders" into positions of influence and authority. They found jobs and patrons under the Weimar Republic. The architect Gropius and the painters Klee and Kandinsky, among others, taught at the state-subsidized Bauhaus; Alban Berg found a wealthy patron, Alma Mahler Werfel, to pay for producing his opera *Wozzeck.* The prewar experimenters thus found a stage and a voice. But the revolution that brought the Weimar Republic into being ultimately failed, and the old

[34]Quoted in Frank Whitford, *Expressionism* (London, 1970), p. 180.

conformities were soon powerful again. The experience of having once been "outsiders" and the tenuousness of their victory gave Berlin artists a stridency and combativeness that fit well with the political and economic uncertainties of the time.

Social Status of Artists

As in the late nineteenth century, most artists and intellectuals were bourgeois. And as in the late nineteenth century, they were rebels against their own upbringing. Nothing had diminished their scorn for middle-class values and their rage at authority and stupidity. Some of their artistic expressions took the form of playful mockery. Klee's *Twittering Machine* (1922) revealed both his delight in pure form and his pleasure in ridiculing the sanctimoniousness of "serious art." The French composers who called themselves "The Six" drew on the musical games and foolery of their master, Erik Satie. The predominant tone, however, especially in Berlin, was an insecure, angry scorn. Count Harry Kessler wondered why his friend George Grosz devoted "his art exclu-

Paul Klee, Twittering Machine, *1922.*

sively to the depiction of the repulsiveness of bourgeois philistinism." Kessler decided that Grosz was a wounded idealist whose sensitivity had been turned "outrageously brutal" by his "fanatical hatred" for everything in modern German life that was authoritarian, crassly materialist, and self-satisfied.[35]

There were signs of change in the class position of artists after the war. A few working-class painters and writers achieved major successes in the arts, which now required less training: D. H. Lawrence, from a coal mining family of the English Midlands, is a major example.

The Search for a Mass Audience

Artists reached out for popular audiences after the First World War. Few artists accepted the notion of the arts as ornament for royal or ecclesiastical patrons, or even as delectation for a narrow circle of sophisticated initiates, in the manner of some late–nineteenth-century aesthetes. To attract a wider audience some interwar artists drew enthusiastically on popular culture, not only on disappearing folk culture as in Chagall's paintings or Stravinsky's compositions, but on the new mass culture. Kurt Weill, at first a struggling composer of difficult chamber music, eventually found his metier in composing jazz rhythms and spare, angular, bittersweet music for Bertolt Brecht's antibourgeois satires *The Threepenny Opera,* and *The Rise and Fall of the City of Mahagonny* (1930). Francis Poulenc, best-known of the French "Six," also worked jazz into much of his lean antiromantic composition of the 1920s. And, of course, film was rapidly seized on for artistic experimentation.

The more radical among postwar artists regarded the arts as a medium for transforming society. Even before the war, the first expressionists had established a group studio in the poorest neighborhood of Dresden rather than set up the customary individual studios in middle-class neighborhoods or in the country: "As youth, we carry the future with us, and want to establish the freedom of life and movement in opposition to the entrenched older forces."[36] George Grosz, a savagely antibourgeois artist, told a friend in 1919 that he wanted to become "the German Hogarth, deliberately realistic and didactic; to preach, improve, and reform. . . . He loathes painting and the pointlessness of painting as practiced so far."[37] The Bauhaus in Germany was a high point of using the arts as instruments for transforming society. Its classes, according to Walter Gropius, "would enable the coming generation to achieve the reunion of all forms of creative work and become the architects of a new civilization."[38]

[35]Kessler, p. 64.
[36]*Die Brücke* Manifesto, 1905.
[37]Kessler, p. 64.
[38]Quoted in Gay, p. 99.

The theater lent itself especially well to the efforts of postwar artists to affect a vast popular audience. Berlin, with its rich dramatic tradition and its state-supported theaters, was a center of stage experimentation designed to involve a wider audience in the theatrical experience. The director Max Reinhardt transformed the plays of Aeschylus and Shakespeare into stunning displays using revolving stages and spectacular lighting. Reinhardt abolished the curtain and the old naturalistic sets in order to bring the audience more intimately into the spectacle. More political was Leopold Jessner, a Social Democratic director designated by the new Weimar regime to run the Berlin State Theater. His 1919 production of Schiller's *William Tell* presented the tyrant Gessler as a German general with rouged cheeks and covered with medals; Tell himself was depicted as a thinly disguised defender of the German revolution of 1918. Most radical of all was Erwin Piscator, who began his Berlin career as a director by presenting plays to workers on picket lines during the 1918 and 1919 strikes. Piscator expected to find a large proletarian audience for experimental drama with a strong political message heightened by techniques like newsreels and slides interspersed with the play and fast-moving short scenes on a stage free of naturalistic sets. According to his widow, Piscator meant to present "plays of active protest, a deliberate J'Accuse; a reportage and montage; a warning, history marching on; political satire, morality plays and court trials, purposefully shocking."[39] Piscator had Walter Gropius design a flexible theater-in-the-round for his concept of total theater, but he never managed to raise the money to build it.

The possibility of creating a new humanity through cultural revolution seemed greatest in Russia. Leon Trotsky predicted in 1923 that under communism

> man will become immeasurably stronger, wiser, and subtler; his body will become more harmonized, his movements more rhythmic, his voice more musical. The forms of life will become dynamically dramatic. The average human type will rise to the heights of an Aristotle, a Goethe, or a Marx. And above this range new peaks will rise.[40]

Trotsky and Lenin, both men of broad cultivation, dismissed the attempts of some Bolsheviks to sweep away everything except proletarian culture. Although a number of intellectuals chose exile, those that remained were forbidden only overt opposition. Many of them were stimulated to rich creativity in the relatively open atmosphere of the 1920s. Sergei Eisenstein developed stunning camera techniques in his epic films of the Bolshevik Revolution. Vladimir Tatlin developed a "constructivist" architecture that rejected surface ornament in favor of functional buildings, garden cities, and monuments derived from the

[39]Quoted in Otto Freidrich, *Before the Deluge: A Portrait of Berlin in the 1920s* (New York, 1972), p. 255.
[40]Leon Trotsky, *Literature and Revolution* (New York, 1957), p. 256.

industrial forms he thought appropriate to a socialist society. The poet Vladimir Mayakovsky declaimed rough-hewn verses that exalted the revolution.

> Fall in and prepare to march!
> No time now to talk or trifle.
> Silence, you orators!
> The word is with you,
> Comrade Rifle!
> We have lived long enough by laws
> Of which Adam and Eve made the draft.
> Stable history's poor old horse!
> Left!
> Left!
> Left![41]

The Russian theater experienced a golden age like that of Weimar Berlin. While Konstantin Stanislavsky continued to train his actors at the Moscow Art Theater in the method of close psychological identification with their parts, his pupil Vsevelod Meyerhold carried out an "October revolution of the theater" with stylized sets and actors trained in mechanical gestures. He arranged seats freely in his theater and issued tickets at random to soldiers and workers. As late as 1929, Meyerhold was allowed to produce a play as critical of the Soviet bureaucracy as Mayakovsky's *The Bedbug* (1928).

Whether in Paris, Berlin, or Moscow, the postwar artists' and intellectuals' desire to assemble a mass audience and transform it was doomed to frustration. The artists would do everything to spread their message except renounce individual self-expression in favor of the weary, traditional aesthetics that mass taste still preferred. There is a pathetic note in Klee's concession in his 1923 Bauhaus lectures. All that was lacking in the community begun at the Bauhaus, Klee said, was an audience: "We seek a people."[42]

The Academic and Scholarly Worlds

The modern arts not only found no mass audience between the wars; they had little effect on the academic and learned worlds. Higher education was relatively unchanged by the postwar revolutionary urges, at least outside the Soviet Union. Education beyond elementary school was still directed to a small elite carefully selected on the basis of excellence in classical education. In France, the superb *lycées* (public high schools) required fees until 1930; the prestigious British "public schools" were in fact costly private institutions, while the inferior public secondary schools required fees of all but a few winners of scholarships. Even where secondary schools were free, as were the *Gymnasia* of Weimar Germany, admission was limited to those who had excelled in written

[41]Vladimir Mayakovsky, "Left March," trans. C. M. Bowra, in C. M. Bowra, ed., *Second Book of Russian Verse* (London, 1948), p. 131.
[42]Klee, p. 55.

and oral examinations on classical subjects. Admission was by merit, of course, but lower-class children were deprived of the home environment needed for scholarly excellence in the classics. The day of widespread, free secondary education was far in the future, one of the basic social changes of the post-1945 reconstruction.

Beyond the elite secondary schools, the universities were an even more confined world of specialists. In the French *lycée* system, more than half the students—already a small elite—were expected to fail the rigorous *baccalauréat* examinations that gave entry to universities and professional schools. The struggle to replace Latin and Greek with modern languages and philosophy was already underway at the universities, but technical education was still considered inferior in European school systems. It was outside class, and partly in protest against their narrow classical education, that secondary school and university students associated themselves with the new art forms. No wonder the modern artists looked for popular audiences and appropriated elements of popular culture. They scorned the academic world, which more than returned that scorn.

As knowledge increased, the learned world fragmented more and more into specialization. That community of craftsmen sought by the Bauhaus no longer resembled the reality of learned specialists in the sciences and scholarly professions.

The prewar revolution in physics begun by Rutherford, Bohr, Planck, and Einstein was carried further between the wars. The indeterminacy theory (1926–27) of the German physicist Werner Heisenberg completed the overthrow of classical physics. Heisenberg's predecessors had shown that atomic structure was based on force fields or electric charges rather than on particles of matter, but they had tended to argue, by analogy with the Newtonian solar system, that subatomic elements were organized within the atom somewhat like planets around a sun. Heisenberg found that the location of any particular electron could be predicted only within a range of probabilities, and was, hence, indeterminate.

Only a handful of Europeans were capable of really understanding these theories. Indeed the difficulty that readers—and writers—of textbooks encounter in trying to make sense of the enormously subtle mathematical language of modern physics is a reminder of the increasingly closed compartments into which knowledge became divided in the twentieth century. No single scientific thinker or doctrine between the wars had as much impact on public attitudes as Charles Darwin, for instance, had had in the late nineteenth century. Albert Einstein was clearly the nearest parallel after 1918, but Einstein had more notoriety than genuine cultural influence.

Einstein's special theory of relativity (1905) had suggested that gravity has an effect on light waves in space; since the speed of light is constant, that effect could be true only if space and time were relative to each observer's place in a universe of flux. When a solar eclipse in 1919 enabled British astronomers to verify that light waves were indeed affected by gravitational fields, headlines proclaimed that the "relativity" of time and space had been proven. Einstein's name became a household word, much to the bemusement of that modest, self-deprecating scientist. "Relativism" came to lend a supposed scientific support to subjectivism in other areas of culture between the wars. Popularizers of science like Sir Arthur Eddington, whose *Nature of the Physical Universe* (1930) was widely read, suggested that physics no longer conflicted with spiritual beliefs.

As for the scientists themselves, the area of Heisenbergian uncertainty within the application of hypotheses to experimental cases in atomic physics did not lessen their sense that each successive hypothesis came nearer to explaining every aspect of the universe in terms of scientific knowledge. The early–twentieth-century revolution in physics quietly prepared the way for the next generation's revolutions in the study of crystals, solid state physics, high-energy particles, and the living cell.

The other fields of scholarly knowledge were no more clearly understood outside a narrow circle of specialists. The gap between popular Freudianism and psychoanalysis has already been noted. Major advances made in other areas of study had little popular impact. Sociology had been established as an academic discipline only at the end of the nineteenth century. It was profoundly influenced by the German Max Weber, who wanted to supplement (but not replace) Marx's emphasis on economic causation in social development with other kinds of social force—the growth of bureaucracy, religion, and what he called "charismatic leadership." The assumptions and field techniques of the young science of anthropology were decisively influenced by Bronislaw Malinowski, a Polish scholar working in England.

Philosophy developed in divergent directions in England and on the Continent. English philosophy, under the influence of the Viennese Ludwig Wittgenstein, moved toward a rejection of speculation on metaphysical issues in favor of the careful logical analysis of concrete statements. On the Continent, the German philosophers Martin Heidegger and Edmund Husserl developed a difficult philosophy of direct experience in which problems of anxiety, human responsibility, and the nature of existence were the center of concern. It is difficult to suggest the range of scholarly vitality of interwar Europe because of the growing isolation of each specialty.

These very different worlds—the artistic, the academic, and the scholarly—went their ways between the wars, with mass culture affecting them only in the case of a few notorious individuals. The artistic world in particular found notoriety enough with its scandalous novelties, but not the new popular base that many artists had hoped to find. Hence the feverish experimentation of the 1920s was highly vulnerable to its enemies.

The experimental arts did not fail to arouse savage antagonism. They were connected, especially in Germany, with the revolution of 1918 and the installation of "democrats, Jews, and other outsiders"[43] in cultural and academic realms heretofore reserved for an older elite. Worse still, the new arts and sciences positively gloried in trampling on established values. Many of the more celebrated opening nights, particularly in Berlin, were occasions for fistfights between the supporters of the new arts and nationalist, traditionalist action squads. There were two irreconcilable conceptions of the cultural life: on the one hand, the sacred duty of self-expression to the limits of one's creativity; on the other hand, the arts as a heritage of values that must be transmitted to the otherwise unruly young.

One of the roots of fascism was the panic among many traditionalist Europeans at what they feared was a tidal wave of degeneracy and decadence in the arts and sciences. When the Hungarian officers destroyed Béla Kun's Budapest Soviet in August 1919, one of their first acts was to close down the offices of Freud's most active disciple, Sandor Ferenczi. The Nazis in Germany specialized in breaking up artistic performances that seemed to threaten the German state or the racial purity of traditional *Kultur*. The objects of their displeasure ranged from the film based on Remarque's novel *All Quiet on the Western Front* to expressionist plays to psychoanalysis. In 1929, the Nazi pseudophilosopher Alfred Rosenberg founded the Militant League for German Culture. In and out of power, the Nazis won supporters by promising "to substitute a 'German' art and an eternal art" for the international "modern art" that tried to "reduce art to the level of fashions in dress, with the motto 'Every year something fresh'—Impressionism, Futurism, Cubism, perhaps also Dadaism." That was the crowd-pleasing mockery used effectively by a one-time architecture student, Adolf Hitler. As he dedicated the House of Culture in Berlin on July 18, 1937, containing an exhibition of "decadent" art presented for public ridicule, Hitler made these further remarks:

> As in politics, so in German art-life: we are determined to make a clean sweep of phrases. Ability is the necessary qualification if an artist wishes his work to be exhibited here. . . . The influence of Jews was paramount and through their control of the press they were able to intimidate those who desired to champion "the normal sound intelligence and instinct of men." . . . From the pictures sent in for exhibition it is clear that there really are men who on principle feel meadows to be blue, the heavens green, clouds sulphur yellow—or as they perhaps prefer to say, "experience" them thus. I need not ask whether they really do see or feel things in this way, but in the name of the German people I have only to prevent these pitiable unfortunates who clearly suffer from defects of vision from attempting with

[43]The phrase is Gustav Meyer's, a Jewish historian who failed to get a post as professor in Germany until the republic was established. See Gay, p. 88.

violence to persuade contemporaries by their chatter that these faults of observation are indeed realities, or from presenting them as "Art." . . . The artist does not create for the artist; he creates for the people and we will see to it that henceforth the people will be called in to judge its art. . . . The people regarded this art as the outcome of an impudent or unashamed arrogance or of a simply shocking lack of skill . . . which might have been produced by untalented children of from eight to ten years old . . . this art-stammer . . . which might have been made by a man of the Stone Age.[44]

Nazi Germany was not the only society in which the arts were subordinated to the inculcation of "useful" social values in the 1930s. As Stalin consolidated his grip on the Soviet Union in the late 1920s, the heady artistic experimentation of the early years of the decade became suspect as an excess of bourgeois individualism. Stanislavsky was removed as director of the Moscow Art Theater in 1928, and Anatole Lunacharsky was dismissed as Commissar of Education in 1929. Mayakovsky, tormented by personal troubles as well as disillusioned by the regime, committed suicide in 1930. Eisenstein was ordered to change his film *The General Line* in the same year. Meyerhold disappeared in the purges of the late 1930s. All writers were required to join the National Union of Writers in 1934. At the same time, the party congress approved the doctrine that all art should express "socialist realism," a numbing conformity to nineteenth-century pictorial style that would be devoted to the propaganda services of the regime.

No one has explained why both Hitler and Stalin tried to impose commonplace nineteenth-century art styles on their subjects in what professed to be revolutionary regimes. But it is clear that the burst of artistic and scientific energies of the 1920s had not won the popular support that might have saved them from persecution in the 1930s.

[44]Quoted in George L. Mosse, *Nazi Culture* (New York, 1966), pp. 11–15.

Suggestions for Further Reading

Raymond Williams, *Communications*, 2nd ed. (1966) is a stimulating introduction. The same author's *The Long Revolution* (1961) examines cultural changes produced by mass schooling and mass communications in England.

The most comprehensive study of mass communications in any European state is Asa Briggs, *The History of Broadcasting in the United Kingdom*, 3 vols. (1961–70).

Robert Graves and Alan Hodge, *The Long Week-End* * (1940) is a lively look at British popular culture between the wars. José Ortega y Gasset, *The Revolt of the Masses* * (1932) is the classic alert against the mass dilution of high culture. Michael R. Marrus, ed., *The Emergence of Leisure* (1974) breaks new ground.

The most penetrating work on the social and political context of culture in any interwar European state is Peter Gay, *Weimar Culture: The Outsider as Insider* (1968). See also the informative studies of French social thinkers between the wars in H. Stuart Hughes, *The Obstructed Path: French Social Thought in the Years of Desperation, 1930–1960* * (1968).

Ernest Jones, *The Life and Work of Sigmund Freud*, abridged ed. (1961) is a compelling biography. See also Henri F. Ellenberger, *The Discovery of the Unconscious* (1970).

Ronald W. Clark, *Einstein: The Life and Times* * (1971) is the latest comprehensive biography.

For thoughtful guides to the abundant literature on the arts and sciences in Europe between the wars, see the bibliographies in Oron J. Hale, *The Great Illusion, 1900–1914* * (1971), and Raymond J. Sontag, *A Broken World, 1919–1939* (1971).

11

DEPRESSION POLITICS 1929–1936

In the late 1920s, many Europeans had expected a future of peace and broadening prosperity. After 1929, however, millions of them could not find work, even though they might be strong and skillful. Millions of them were in want, while the factories that could produce what they needed lay idle. Some went hungry, while farmers destroyed crops they could not sell. Maddened by their impotence in the face of these absurdities, most Europeans were sunk in despair or swept by rage. These were some of the effects of the Great Depression.

A depression is a prolonged slowdown in buying and selling. Businesses are unable to sell all they produce. Stocks pile up, despite price-cutting by competitors. Firms fire some of their workers or go out of business. Since the unemployed, in turn, can buy nothing, sales decline still further. More firms close, and banks that have lent them money can no longer cover all their deposits. Savings are swept away in bank failures. The sufferings are uneven. As prices fall, those who still have jobs or who spend cash reserves can live comfortably. For the rest, there is demoralizing helplessness. Businessmen go bankrupt; professional people lose their clients; millions of salaried people lose their jobs and can find no way to support themselves and their families.

Europeans had known depression before 1929. But never before had there been unemployment on such a great scale, or so deep a business decline. Nor had European leaders seemed so helpless. The depression of 1929 completely outran previous experience. The American economist Wesley Clair Mitchell, in a classic work on the business cycle, had written that depressed economics normally begin to recover in the first or second year because lower prices encourage more buying.[1] Two years after the crash of 1929, however, the European economies were still plummeting downward. At the same time that the public was coming to expect more of governments, government performance had never been more ineffectual.

At the worst point of the Great Depression, in 1932, one Englishman in four was on the dole, while two Germans out of five were unemployed. There were over 6 million unemployed in Germany in 1932, about 12 million in the United States. Industrial production dropped by 47 percent in the United States between 1929 and 1932, by 44 percent in Germany, and by 37 percent in all the advanced industrial states of the world, excluding the Soviet Union.[2]

These statistics tell little about the depression's impact on individual people. For that, we must turn to the arts. The 1930s were a brilliant period for mordant social criticism in novels, essays, and the theater (painting, among the visual arts, had largely relinquished the role of social criticism to photography and film). There was a notable shift of emphasis away from the private self-expression of the 1920s toward expression of social concerns. The fiction, essays and drama of the 1930s often speak with the authentic voices of the angry and bewildered during the depression. For the wounds of the depression were not merely physical want. They were the psychic wounds of humiliating helplessness among strong men unable to provide for their families; there were sharpened and polarized social antagonisms and the search for a savior. All these concerns permeate the art forms of the 1930s.

The waitress Jenny, in *The Threepenny Opera* (1928) of the German playwright Bertolt Brecht and the composer Kurt Weill, has a bitter daydream: a "pirate ship with fifty cannon" comes into the harbor, and she dreams that the pirate chief asks her whom she wants killed. Jenny orders all the townsmen killed and goes off with the pirates. In real life, however, she is still waiting on tables and scrubbing floors. There are satirical attacks on the depersonalizing machine in films like René Clair's *A nous la liberté* (1931) and Charlie Chaplin's *Modern Times* (1936). There is the desperate jobless sales clerk in the German novelist Hans Fallada's

---

[1] Wesley Clair Mitchell, *The Business Cycle* (New York, 1913).
[2] Wilhelm Grotkopf, *Die Grosse Krise* (Düsseldorf, 1954), p. 15.

British miners looking for work. The queue at the Labour Exchange in Wigan.

Little Man, What Now? (1932). The British writer George Orwell reflects on life and social distinctions in an English coal mining town. At one point, Orwell describes the "scramble for coal" in which poor families glean fragments of coal from the mine tailings.

> That scene stays in my mind as one of my pictures of Lancashire: the dumpy, shawled women, with their sacking aprons and their heavy black clogs, kneeling in the cindery mud and the bitter wind searching for tiny chips of coal. . . . In winter they are almost desperate for fuel; it is more important almost than food. Meanwhile, all round, as far as the eye can see are the slag-heaps and hoisting gear of collieries, and not one of those collieries can sell all the coal it is capable of producing.[3]

That very juxtaposition of poor people in desperate material want and companies unable to sell the goods they produced aroused profound questioning in Europe. The very values that had seemed the formula for success in the 1920s now seemed touched with a curse. National self-determination had appeared a lofty ideal, but it had helped cut Europe up into economically inefficient units. The end of wartime regulation had been welcomed as a return to normalcy, but it had left the European economy a jungle. Return to gold had seemed a self-evident improvement, but it had kept prices and unemployment high.

 It was the whole nineteenth-century liberal ideal of a self-regulating market economy that went bankrupt in 1929. Those ideas came to be regarded as not only absurd but positively evil after 1929. No regime could survive that could not provide its citizens with a way to earn a living. This concrete problem made the depression a "crisis of liberalism." The search for something better dominated European affairs in

[3]George Orwell, *The Road to Wigan Pier* (London, 1937), p. 95.

the 1930s and challenged Europe as profoundly as world war had done.
Whoever could solve the economic riddles of the 1930s would have
Europe at his feet.

The Great Depression is commonly traced back to the collapse of the
New York stock market in October 1929, with its repercussions in
international finance. Well before the crash, however, there were signs
of a downturn in domestic economies. It is probably helpful at this point
to make a distinction between two aspects of the depression: domestic
economic difficulty and the international financial panic set off by Wall
Street in 1929. Within the European countries, there was a slowing down
of buying and selling before 1929, beginning with a depressed market
for agricultural goods and coal and later extending into all commodities
as the depression deepened. After 1929 an international banking and
currency crisis affected banks' holdings of gold and foreign currencies
and nations' abilities to maintain the international value of their currencies.

The two matters were closely interrelated, of course, and to separate
them, even for purposes of discussion, is somewhat artificial. For
example, rapid withdrawal of American capital from Germany in 1929
had much to do with the business slowdown there; in turn, the
weakening business activity within each of the countries undermined the
solvency of banks and national currencies, especially in agrarian Eastern
Europe. The point of separating these two aspects is to observe that it
was the international side of the depression that governments set out to
remedy, rather than attempting to stimulate the domestic economy.
Indeed, those governments that threw their budgets into deficit in the
effort to create new jobs or assist the unemployed promptly provoked
international speculation against their own currencies.

Domestic Crisis

Like an earlier long depression in the 1880s, when American and
Russian wheat first appeared on world markets and pushed farm
incomes down in Europe, the Great Depression began with declining
agriculture in the mid-1920s. The First World War had encouraged a
large increase in farm production. In response to high wartime prices,
about 33 million additional acres had been put to the plow in the United
States, Canada, Argentina, and Australia. After the war, this acreage
produced more grain than existing markets could easily absorb. Furthermore, by 1930 it cost 60 percent less to ship wheat from Vancouver
to the mouth of the Rhine than it cost to move wheat by rail from
Budapest to Berlin. The world agricultural price index, at 226 in 1919,
dropped to 134 by 1929.

Because agrarian parties were important to the politics of the succes-

**The Origins and
Course of the
Great Depression**

sor states in Eastern Europe, the farmers' plight quickly translated itself into political instability. Moreover, each of the numerous small states in Eastern Europe had already begun before 1929 to shut out foreign agricultural competition. The resort to tariffs in central Europe was the first major flight from liberal economic ideals. Germany restored farm tariffs in 1925; the Czechs renounced their agreement to buy Hungarian wheat in 1929; and so on. The former free-trade area of the Habsburg Empire was by now a collection of small, competing economic units.

The calamities befalling European agriculture also afflicted coal mining between the wars. Coal had been the fuel of the early Industrial Revolution. England, in particular, had built an empire partly on the export of coal. After the war, however, coal sales were never again as profitable as before 1914. The war relocated trade patterns, some of them toward the United States. And the global demand for coal rose more slowly after the war, due in part to competing new sources of power: oil and hydroelectricity. British coal never recovered its prewar position, and that helps explain why unemployment in Britain never fell below 10 percent of the work force between the wars. The coal industry, like agriculture, was in depression even before 1929.

International Financial Crisis

The international financial arrangements of Europe after the First World War constituted a house of cards. Like the prewar system, the international finance system artificially reconstructed after the war could be criticized for its tacit acceptance of business cycles as regulating devices. But the postwar system contained three additional flaws. First, it restored to the British pound its prewar role as the main international currency of exchange, at a time when the British economy no longer had its prewar power. Second, there was the distorting effect of reparations. The Germans were expected to pay large sums to France, Britain, and Belgium until the end of the twentieth century outside the normal exchanges of commerce; since 1924, the Germans had made reparations payments by borrowing from the United States. Finally, there was the question of the war debts that France and Belgium owed Britain, and all three owed the United States. A major feature of these arrangements was the close dependence of the whole financial structure on United States bank loans to Germany. Under the Dawes Plan, the equivalent of 25 billion marks went into Germany in the form of American purchases of municipal bonds or loans to industry, while about 8 billion marks had come out as reparations.

In 1928 and 1929, however, American credit was pulled out of Germany and attracted back to the higher profits available in the booming New York stock market. The German credit structure was badly shaken by this shift of funds. Then, after the New York market crashed in October 1929, many American speculators who were caught short quickly pulled the rest of their capital out of Germany and other

European investments. In this way, the depressing effect of the Wall Street slump was transmitted to Europe. That effect was compounded by the sharp decline in United States purchases from Europe after October 1929.

The international position of German and central European banks was seriously weakened by the withdrawal of foreign funds, mostly American, in the years following the Wall Street crash. In the first seven months of 1931, 2 billion marks were pulled out of Germany alone by American and British creditors, who needed the money at home or were losing confidence in the safety of their German investments.

The news on May 11, 1931, that the most powerful bank in Vienna, the *Credit-Anstalt,* had gone broke triggered a four months' international financial crisis that ended only when the British pound was devalued and untied from gold the following September. It was to be expected that the first major bank failure of the European depression should occur in Vienna. All the elements of depression converged there: the long decline in Eastern European farm incomes; the erection of trade and financial barriers. The financial establishments of Vienna, once a regional capital, had been forced to constrict their fields of activity more and more to tiny Austria.

Efforts by other European financial centers to prop up the *Credit-Anstalt* did not succeed. Individual investors and speculators withdrew their funds from Austrian banks as quickly as possible to avoid losing them, and moved them from country to country looking for safety. This began an epidemic of bank runs wherever rumors suggested that currencies were about to be devalued or banks to fail. The situation was further complicated by international rivalries and pressure politics. The French, for example, did not help the *Credit-Anstalt* at first because they were trying to bring pressure on Austria to block a proposed German–Austrian customs union, which the French regarded as a violation of the Treaty of Versailles.

The crisis in Austria cast suspicion next on the stability of the closely related German banks. When a decline appeared in the German government's weekly statement of foreign exchange and gold reserves in early July 1931, a run on the mark was set off. German and foreign holders of large quantities of marks tried to sell them for gold or for what they believed to be safer currencies before it was too late. The moratorium on all payments of foreign debts (reparations and war debts) announced by United States President Herbert Hoover on July 6 was not able to stem the tide. In August, Germany was forced to "freeze" foreign credits, that is, refuse to transfer marks held by foreigners into foreign currencies.

London now remained the largest free gold market in Europe, and speculators eager for the safety of gold tried to sell as many pounds for gold in London as possible. British banks were obliged to sell gold to anyone with pounds who wanted to buy gold, but they had been seriously weakened by the "freezing" of that part of their assets that had been deposited in Germany and Austria. When it became impossible to sell any more gold without calling the value of the pound into question, the British government was forced on September 19, 1931, to "go off the gold standard" and refuse to sell gold freely for pounds. The postwar effort to reestablish a world international banking system based on gold had collapsed forever.

Losses suffered in this series of international banking collapses pushed business activity down even further in the various domestic economies. Furthermore, the adoption of currency restrictions and the absence of any one standard of exchange made foreign trade much more complicated and uncertain. By 1932, the European economies were limping along at half or a little more of their 1929 level of activity.

Depression Remedies

The Great Depression confronted European leaders with their greatest challenge since the First World War. There were several different remedies available in contemporary economic thought. They had different political constituencies and proposed to lay the burdens on different shoulders. But no remedy could claim final wisdom, for this was a totally new experience.

Liberal Economics

Classical, or orthodox, liberal economics was the conventional wisdom. In this view, the root problem was malfunction of the international monetary system. Solutions, therefore, must deal with the international monetary system. If a country's currency came under speculative pressure, the way to stop a "run" on the currency was to balance the government's budget, thereby proving to the world the solidity and responsibility of its economy. Currency fluctuations reflected loss of confidence, the classical liberals believed, and they were best cured by restoring confidence among the bankers, financiers, and speculators of the world. To shut oneself off from the international money market would simply make everyone poorer. The second part of the classical remedy concerned world trade. A declining economy was best revived by becoming more competitive in world markets. One good way to become more competitive was to cut prices by lowering wages. This was to the ultimate benefit of workers, so ran the classical argument, for one could sell more and thus eventually put more workers to work.

These solutions were called "deflation": lowering government expenditures to balance the budget and lowering the costs of products in order to sell more. A government that intervened to keep wages high, by maintaining unemployment benefits and running a budgetary deficit, only made matters worse by preserving inefficient sectors of the economy and pricing itself out of the world market. The healthiest cure came out of market self-adjustment. Thus the classicists subordinated immediate domestic welfare to the imperatives of international monetary stability.

The classical liberal economics had many supporters in 1929. It was the position of a majority of bankers, professional economists, academics, and government experts. Most politicians shared the same assumptions in a less scholarly form. These views served the interests of exporters, bondholders, and other powerful business leaders. Tradition also favored this view, for no government up to 1931 had ever regulated foreign currency transactions during peacetime.

The classicists faced one overwhelming difficulty, however. A brief deflation might be politically possible, but to cut government expenditure and to lower wages for a long period would raise a growing howl of misery. The howl would be all the more insistent since the experiments of war government had made people familiar with the possibilities of government social action. A long-term deflation was probably possible only if governments were allowed to stifle dissent. Deflation, in other words, required authoritarian rule. Thus the liberal economic solution worked only with illiberal politics.

Socialist Economics

Socialists, like liberals, saw the depression as a result of overproduction. But they drew the opposite conclusion. What was produced could not be consumed under capitalism because the profit system skimmed off the value that workers created, leaving them with a subsistence wage. Hence, underconsumption. The only meaningful solution was massive change in the ownership of factories and farms. Once the workers owned the means of production and received the full value of their labor, they would be able to buy more, and there could be no such thing as overproduction. From such a perspective, the technicalities of world monetary exchanges were irrelevant nuisances. The only solution to depression, socialists argued, was to end the capitalist system with its inherent contradictions.

The socialists were not remotely ready to seize power. Indeed, the effect of unemployment was to weaken unions, diminish organized militancy, and lessen the effect of the strike weapon. A subtler disadvantage was that socialists had never given much thought to short-term partial remedies, so that where reformist socialists shared power (as in Germany and England), they had nothing to offer except, perhaps, tax reform. The British Labour party, in fact, was militantly orthodox in its immediate economic solutions.

New Economic Solutions

Yet another strand of social thought was the attempt to find a "middle way" between discredited liberalism and Marxism. Like the liberals, seekers for this middle way wanted to preserve the property relations of capitalism. But they regarded the liberal global monetary system and the self-regulated market economy as hopeless anachronisms. Like socialists, they thought the heart of the problem was underconsumption, and they put domestic welfare ahead of international monetary stability. Their ultimate aim, however, was to maintain existing property, not abolish it. Their first priority was to revive the domestic economy, if necessary by a radical dose of state intervention of the sort pioneered during the First World War. If the budget deficits incurred in subsidizing full employment unleashed the international speculators against one's currency, then it would be necessary to impose currency restrictions. A country should secede from the world economy, if necessary, and develop a planned, managed prosperity within a closed national economy.

Partisans of the "middle way" formed no school, professed no orthodoxy, and followed no one leader. We refer here to those varied and desperate Europeans who rejected both liberal capitalism and international socialism, and whose quest for solutions led them to two fundamental points agreed on by most innovators in the 1930s: economies must be planned to some degree and prosperity managed, and depression solutions must be national rather than international. The most famous "middle way" thinker in the Anglo-Saxon world was the British economist John Maynard Keynes, whose major innovations in consumer-based state economic management are discussed more fully later in this chapter. Some heretical socialists also reacted to the depression with a similar emphasis on planning and on national solutions. The Belgian Henri de Man and the French neosocialist Marcel Déat advocated thoroughgoing economic planning in cooperation with the middle class, and within national units. The depression turned these socialists into "national socialists."

A "middle way" much favored by businessmen was corporatism. Corporatists proposed to organize each branch of the economy into a nationwide corporation empowered to settle prices, restrict production to meet demand, and deal with labor relations. Some corporatists proposed to include workers' representatives alongside management in these planning bodies, on the theory that the "class struggle" would be submerged in the common interest shared by capital and labor in the prosperity of each branch of industry. Other corporatists wished to elevate existing cartels and trusts into national agencies, thus, in effect, turning the economy over to regulation by organized business. The ideas of corporatism predated the depression, but the corporatist experiments of Mussolini aroused considerable interest among European businessmen, and they will be considered more closely in the discussion of the depression in Italy.

The Call for "Return to the Soil"

One last social nostrum was revived by the depression. Some publicists and intellectuals, mostly innocent of economics, proposed a "return to the soil." A number of European thinkers had long found the city immoral; after 1929, they added that it was unworkable. A stable, healthy society could be restored only where people produced true wealth from the soil or at the workbench, instead of making transient, speculative wealth from the stock market. Such nostalgic cries helped discredit the existing regimes in Europe, but while the proponents of a return to the soil helped fascism to come to power in some countries, they were unable to impose their views on fascist regimes once in power.

This was the range of intellectual perspectives available to the European governments as they tried to come to grips with the depression.

319

DEPRESSION
POLITICS
IN THE
LIBERAL
STATES

The Scandinavian Countries

Only the Scandinavian countries won comparatively high marks in the 1930s for coping with the depression without either stagnation or dictatorship. Naturally the Scandinavian economy, highly dependent on foreign trade, suffered severely in the depression, and unemployment exceeded 20 percent for a time. But the difficulties were mitigated to some degree by a homogeneous population, rich resources in dairy products, fisheries, and iron ore, the absence of international conflicts, and coherent political majorities. Reformist Social Democratic parties came to power in Denmark (1929), Sweden (1933), and Norway (1935) and governed, sometimes with coalition support from farmers' parties and liberals, for the next forty years. Scandinavian Social Democrats were able to build on deeply rooted traditions of public social service and a strong cooperative movement.

In Sweden, to take the largest and most prosperous example, cooperatives expanded in the 1930s until about half the population belonged to some consumer or producer cooperative association. No businesses were nationalized, but cooperatives enlarged their share of the market by buying in bulk and offering low prices until they accounted for 12 percent of retail trade. Producer cooperatives affected only about 2 percent of production, but advocates of the cooperative movement maintain that private producers kept prices low for fear of stimulating further inroads by cooperatives. Social services were greatly expanded in the 1930s into such areas as free prenatal care, social insurance, and garden cities. Sweden was not exempt from difficulties with high tax rates and growing rates of alcoholism and divorce. But the Swedish economy returned to predepression levels sooner than most; by 1939 Sweden enjoyed a greater rise in real wages since 1900 than any other European country.

Britain

For reasons quite unconnected with the onset of the depression, Britain's second Labour government (May 1929–August 1931) was in power when the crisis came. But that did not presage any attempt to remedy the depression by redistribution of property. Both Prime Minister Ramsay MacDonald and Chancellor of the Exchequer Philip Snowden were reformist to the core and thus opposed to immediate collectivization by force. And although the Labour party had emerged as the largest British party for the first time in the elections of May 1929, it did not have an absolute majority.[4] The government depended on Liberal votes.

The main problem, however, was that Labour spokesmen had no intellectual alternative to classical liberal economics in the short run. All economic thought had gone into future major changes, not into immediate remedies within the existing system. Moreover, planning seemed an affront to Labour's sacred free trade, a prop to the existing system, and a step toward authoritarianism.

The new Chancellor of the Exchequer was one of the genuine proletarians who set the British Labour party apart from the more intellectual middle-class socialist leaders of the Continent. Politically, Philip Snowden came from the left of his party; he had been a pacifist during the First World War. But Snowden, the son of a weaver, was steeped in a devout chapel-going puritanism and defense of free trade against Tory protectionist schemes. Completely lacking any economic training, Snowden was convinced that government's main economic precepts should be thrift and probity. He identified free trade with

[4]Labour—287 seats; Conservative—261 seats; Liberal—59 seats.

Sharp divisions in social class were evident in Britain during the depression years. Here, local boys watch two Eton students outside Lords cricket grounds in London, at the 1937 Eton v. Harrow match.

cheap bread for the poor. Crippled in a childhood bicycle accident, Snowden had transcended both pain and poverty in a long climb up the ranks of the Labour party. His pinched, intense face gave some clue to the evangelical fervor with which he held to the economic virtues.

When the economy began to falter in late 1929, Snowden and the cabinet increased public works and unemployment benefits, while bringing the budget into balance with a steeper income tax. The rise in government spending and the decline in tax receipts caused by unemployment, however, created an unbridgeable gap between the two sides of the government's ledgers. Since Liberal votes prevented further tax increases, Snowden had to borrow, that is, sell bonds, in order to maintain unemployment benefits.

The banking crisis in London in July 1931 fed on the lack of confidence that bankers and investors felt for a Labour government. They brought pressure on the government to reduce unemployment benefits in order to keep the budget in balance. When the Bank of England sought to stem the run on the pound by borrowing from Paris and New York, the American investment firm of J. P. Morgan and Company replied that it could not lend any more to the Bank of England unless the Labour government cut its expenditures.

Morgan's answer on August 23 put the choice very clearly between those measures that would improve domestic living standards and those that would save the pound. Saving the pound meant cutting unemployment relief. MacDonald and Snowden accepted the classical diagnosis and prepared a 10-percent cut in the "dole." About half the cabinet refused to go along, however, and the second and last interwar Labour government resigned on August 24.

It was replaced by the National Government (1931–35), a nonparty coalition of leading individuals joined to remedy the depression crisis by deflation. Ramsay MacDonald retained the post of prime minister, flanked now by Conservative leader Stanley Baldwin. Labour opinion thereafter regarded "Gentleman Mac" as a traitor, along with Philip Snowden, who also remained in the cabinet.

Investors and speculators continued to sell pounds for gold, despite the cut in relief. Indeed, the government's efforts to reduce costs only made things worse. Sailors demonstrated against pay cuts in the British home fleet at Invergordon, Scotland, in what became known as the "Invergordon Mutiny." Because "mutiny" in the British fleet sounded like Gibraltar sinking, the run on the pound became an unstemmable flood. On September 19, 1931, the National Government took Britain off the international gold standard. Individuals were no longer permitted to buy gold for pounds. Furthermore, the pound was allowed to sink about a third in international exchange value.

The National Government's backing now became frankly conservative. The elections of October 27, 1931, gave the Tories over 60 percent of the vote, the highest majority in British electoral history, and ushered in an era of Conservative predominance that was to last until 1945.

321

DEPRESSION
POLITICS
IN THE
LIBERAL
STATES

Having lost its battle to save the pound on the world market, the National Government might have been expected to take bold action to stimulate employment, but it did not. Devaluation of the pound, of course, made British goods cheaper on the world market for a time. Housing construction was spurred by lower costs and by Labour's Wheatley Act of 1924 and a slum clearance act of the 1930s. Several very advanced steel mills were also constructed in this period. By and large, however, the National Government followed a policy of protectionism and cutting back production. Protective tariffs, defeated so roundly at the polls in the 1920s, became government policy for the first time in peacetime in nearly a century. The Import Duties Act of 1932 imposed a 10-percent duty on all goods except those produced in the empire ("imperial preference") and a few free items. Factory owners were allowed to replace competition with planned production levels in order to keep prices up. The Labour government had already accepted this expedient for the outdated and vastly overextended British coal industry; under the National Government, restrictive practices became generalized in such ailing traditional industries as shipbuilding and iron and steel. Thus the British economy slowly revived in the 1930s more by a gradual turn in the business cycle, aided by devaluation and *de facto* cartelization, than by any significant rise in production or decline in unemployment. In retrospect, the existing British party structure simply failed to provide alternatives to classical depression remedies. Those few people with valid theoretical or practical alternatives to offer were outsiders. Sir Oswald Mosley, a wealthy thirty-three-year-old convert to Labour who had a minor office but major ambitions in the Labour cabinet, produced a memorandum in the spring of 1930 that attracted attention in the party left. Mosley assigned first priority to alleviating unemployment and then let other policy matters fall into place around a "living wage policy." Unemployment would be ended by increasing purchasing power, permitting earlier retirement on good pensions, and forcing up productivity. This required public planning and management of production, as well as deficit spending. Those departures from accepted government practice would shock investors and speculators, of course, so the British economy would have to be insulated from international financial pressures; that is, it must be national rather than international. These heresies left older and more orthodox Labour leaders like Chancellor of

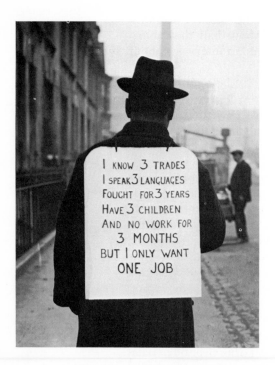

A middle-class victim of unemployment in Britain, 1930.

the Exchequer Snowden aghast. Mosley's rejection by Labour leaders in 1930 points up the inability of that generation to tear itself free from the perspectives of classical economists.

The better known outsider was John Maynard Keynes. When the depression struck, the Cambridge economist was only beginning to refine his new doctrine, which was published in 1936 as *General Theory of Employment, Interest, and Money*. Keynes, too, gave top priority to a solution to unemployment. But unlike that impatient pragmatist Mosley, Keynes's major contribution was to provide a whole new theoretical framework within which to refute classical remedies. The orthodox looked on unemployment as the result of overproduction; from such a perspective, raising wages would only make conditions worse. Keynes argued that the level of unemployment depended less on overproduction than on insufficient demand. Demand could be increased by increasing the money supply, stimulating production by public works, and making society's distribution of wealth more equal. Such policies, of course, demanded a high level of government intervention and were incompatible with international financial practices as they existed. Keynes's impact was destined to be overwhelming on the Second World War generation; it was minimal during the depression.

Still other outsiders advocated the nationalization of all or part of British productive capacity. Some of them, like G. D. H. Cole, an Oxford professor of politics and historian of the labor movement, were on the intellectual fringes of the Labour party. The intellectuals had little influence, however, with the Labour party leadership or with the rank and file, mostly trade union members.

In short, none of the advocates of planning or nationalization had any organized political force behind them. The intellectual perspectives of those who had such force—Labour, Liberal, and Conservative—allowed them to contemplate no way of dealing with the depression except to leave Britain in stagnation through the 1930s.

France

The depression came late to France. For the first two years, Paris remained a haven for gold, which had fled from German and British banking systems. French social commentators praised their country's cautious, small firms and numerous independent peasants who had avoided the boom and bust of more dynamic economies. By 1932, however, the French economy had settled into a deep slump that then lasted longer than elsewhere. Even in 1938, French production was not back to 1929 levels.

The depression was never the cataclysm in France that it was elsewhere. There was no spectacular run on the franc, no awesome crash of world role as in the British devaluation of 1931; the regime was not swept away as it was in Germany. Official unemployment figures never exceeded about 600,000. That figure greatly understated the reality,

323

DEPRESSION
POLITICS
IN THE
LIBERAL
STATES

however, for it did not reflect the many Frenchmen underemployed on family farms or in small firms. In any case, the depression in France was a slow, demoralizing rot rather than a major upheaval.

Several conditions made it worse than it might have been. French public opinion resisted with a passion any governmental tampering with the international value of the franc. Even within classical economics, a timely devaluation of the franc would have helped stimulate exports. But French small savers and investors had been so traumatized by the inflation of 1924 to 1928 that they clung fervently to the Poincaré franc. No French politician was willing to incur public wrath by touching it in the 1930s. That devaluation in a depression was altogether different from inflation made no difference to public opinion.

More adventurous economic policies were even farther from political feasibility than devaluation. There was no possible majority support for a planned or managed economy. Most French socialists rejected planning under existing property relationships as a mere prop to capitalism and an authoritarian step backward. Only a minority of socialists were more interested in reviving production than in equalizing distribution in the economy; they recognized that planning required working within a national framework insulated from the world economy by tariffs and currency control. Some of these minority socialists seceded to form a new neosocialist party in 1933, whose most conspicuous leader was Marcel Déat. Déat, like Oswald Mosley, was to follow the implications of his heresy all the way to national socialism.

On the right, among businessmen, industrialists, high civil servants, and professors of law, there was great enthusiasm for corporatism. But it was the center-left that won both the 1932 and 1936 elections. And even though the Radical party drifted back toward the center after elections, especially on economic issues, the Radicals did not support the corporatists' proposal that organized business regulate the economy. Like the small peasants and shopkeepers whom they represented, the Radicals believed only in applying their personal economic values of thrift and prudence to the state: spend no more than you take in, and put the savings in a sock. Thus the French Third Republic dealt with the depression under conditions of entrenched economic orthodoxy.

Governmental instability tended to compound the effects of the depression. As in the inflation years of the mid-1920s, economic emergency made the French party system incoherent. The parliamentary elections of 1932 were won by a center-left coalition similar to the *cartel des gauches* of 1924 (Radicals, SFIO, and smaller reformist parties). Once again the two main partners—Radicals and Socialists—found their incompatibilities widened by an economic challenge. It had been effective during the election to stress unifying issues like Catholic and military threats to the republic. But as the depression deepened after 1932, divisive matters such as whether the state should intervene in the economy were brought to the top of the agenda.

The premier who emerged from the electoral victory of 1932 was that stalwart leader of the French Radical party, Edouard Herriot.[5] Herriot was thrust into a situation for which his broad literary background and parliamentary skills had not prepared him. French investors and speculators, prejudiced against even a moderate left victory in 1932, sold francs for gold in expectation of a decline in the international value of the franc. It was a self-fulfilling prophecy; the franc declined. Unwilling to invoke currency controls, Herriot could do little but try to balance the budget and to display confidence by continuing to pay war debts to the United States. That gesture cost him his parliamentary majority. Herriot was followed by five governments in the next fourteen months. Meanwhile, the economy drifted downward.

By 1934 the Radicals had drawn away from their Socialist election partners over economic policy, and a Radical-center coalition was the only possible majority. Premier Pierre Laval (June 1935–January 1936) vigorously applied classical deflationary measures during this period. Laval was an innkeeper's son from the southern hill country of the Auvergne who had worked his way up by combining politics, business, and a law practice. After winning his first major case, the defense of some workmen charged with blowing up a power line, Laval won election to parliament from a Paris suburb as a socialist. Once in politics, however, he gravitated to the center and became wealthy by canny investments helped along, it was suspected, by political influence.

Laval had the superb self-confidence of a self-made man, without any economic knowledge. Deciding that the budget had to be balanced in a declining economy, Laval ruthlessly cut wages paid by the state by 10 percent and tried to roll back wages paid by private industry. To ease the wage earners' lot, he also tried to reduce rents and prices. But while Laval deserved very high marks for vigor, he earned low marks for results. The deflationary remedy of 1935 further slowed the French economy at a time when other countries were beginning to revive. It also swung the electorate sharply to the left for the elections of 1936.

The elections of May 1936 brought to power the Popular Front, an electoral coalition of the left that included the Communist party for the first time in French history, as well as those more habitual electoral allies, the Radicals and Socialists. Because the startling innovation of Communist participation in reformist parliamentary politics resulted more from Stalin's desire for alliances against Hitler than from the depression, the Popular Front is discussed more fully in a subsequent chapter on the antifascist alliances of the 1930s.[6] But Premier Léon Blum (June 1936–June 1937) must be included in this consideration of depression politics, for of all Western European parliamentary leaders he made the boldest attempt to find an alternative to deflation within the context of a

325

DEPRESSION
POLITICS
IN THE
LIBERAL
STATES

---

[5]See Chapter 9, pp. 251–52.
[6]See Chapter 13, pp. 381–89.

middle-class democracy. Reversing the wage-cutting of his predecessors, Blum tried to remedy the depression by an increase in general purchasing power.

Leader of the French Socialist party (SFIO) since 1920, Léon Blum became premier of France in 1936 in an atmosphere of mingled jubilation and panic. The Popular Front's electoral victory was accompanied by the most massive work stoppage between 1919 and 1920 and 1947 and 1948, a general strike surpassed only once in French history, in May and June 1968. In retrospect, we know that the workmen and department store clerks who occupied the premises and sometimes danced in them were celebrating Blum's victory. The strikes were a grass-roots release of steam after years of pent-up resentment at deflationary wage cuts; they were not a concerted effort to expropriate property. Trade union leaders struggled to channel the movement into traditional wages and hours negotiations. At the time, however, it looked very much like revolution to French conservatives already unsettled at the prospect of France's first Jewish, socialist premier.

In one way, that climate helped Blum accomplish major changes quickly. The terrified French manufacturers' association turned to Blum as to their only port in the storm. In an all-night session at his official residence, Blum brought the manufacturers' association and the trade union leaders together on a settlement providing raises of up to 15 percent, as well as belated recognition by employers of workers' rights to join unions without being fired and of the right of unions to negotiate collective contracts on behalf of their members. In the next few days, Blum pushed through parliament a forty-hour week and two-week vacations with pay for all salaried employees except those of the smallest shops. Finally, he increased public spending, particularly in armaments.

In other ways, the crisis atmosphere made the Popular Front's economic life more difficult. French savers and investors had learned under the *cartel des gauches* in 1924 and 1925 to associate left governments with financial instability. They were especially adamant against a devaluation of the franc, a perfectly orthodox measure that would have stimulated French exports. Even though Blum promised publicly not to devalue and refrained from alarming the business community by imposing monetary controls, large-scale speculation against the franc set in. Eventually, the government was forced to devalue twice under heavy international pressure. Blum thus lost middle-class support at home without gaining any of the trade benefits that an early voluntary devaluation might have achieved.

In the end, Blum's government did not succeed in reviving the depressed French economy. The forty-hour week, designed in part to spread employment more widely, was interpreted rigidly to mean that plants operated only forty hours a week on one shift. Wages were raised more for social reasons than as a Keynesian increase in purchasing power, and they were insufficient to stimulate declining demand. By 1938 French industrial production was still below that of 1929.

Weimar Germany

327

DEPRESSION
POLITICS
IN THE
LIBERAL
STATES

The depression swept the British Labour party out of power until 1945, and it reduced the French Third Republic to its weakest and most divided condition since its founding. In Germany, the depression brought the whole Weimar Republic down.

The German republic had entered the crisis with a socialist chancellor, Hermann Müller, an old trade union leader and socialist from the prewar years. Müller had governed since 1928 at the head of the Great Coalition, a parliamentary majority composed of no less than five parties ranging from right to left. Such a spread of parties had been unavoidable. No coherent socialist majority was possible while Social Democrats and Communists continued to be so bitterly divided by the split of 1917 to 1919; no coherent nationalist majority was possible while the moderate parties remained committed to the republic and to at least partial "fulfillment" of the Versailles settlement.

As long as the major issues remained foreign policy and the survival of the republic, the Great Coalition could find reason to cooperate in a program of international "fulfillment." When the central issues became economic, there was no common ground. The urgent appearance of economic issues in late 1929 pulled the Great Coalition's majority apart.

The precise issue on which the Great Coalition splintered was a classic example of depression alternatives: should unemployment benefits be reduced in order to balance the budget? Or should they be maintained or increased in order to keep up purchasing power? The economic decline of late 1929 hit Germany quickly and sharply, and the fund for unemployment benefits was soon exhausted. The options were to support unemployment benefits from other government sources (such as the *Osthilfe,* the relief fund for Prussian agriculture), or to raise more taxes, or to reduce unemployment benefits. The first two of these options were politically impossible: President Hindenburg was deeply committed to the *Osthilfe,* and the German people would not support a tax increase. When the German government approached the New York investment bank of Dillon, Read for a loan to cover immediate governing expenses, they were told that American lenders could have no confidence in a government that did not balance its budget. Since the German economy desperately needed to reassure its American creditors (who were withdrawing funds anyway in the aftermath of the crash in New York), the government decided to balance the budget by reducing unemployment benefits. This decision angered the German trade unions, which forced the Social Democratic deputies to withdraw their support from the government. Müller's government resigned on March 27, 1930. One could argue that the Weimar Republic's parliamentary system actually ceased to function at that point. Henceforth there was no way to build a majority around any one depression remedy: deficit spending or classical budget-balancing.

For nearly the next three years, Germany was governed without any

A soup kitchen for the unemployed in Berlin, 1930.

parliamentary majority. President Hindenburg used the authority granted by the Weimar Constitution (Article 48) to govern by decree in case of emergency. During most of that time (March 1930–June 1932), Hindenburg conferred his powers on Heinrich Brüning as chancellor.

Brüning was a conservative Catholic who had served as executive secretary to the German Catholic trade union organization. That administrative experience commended him to Hindenburg, as did Brüning's reserve officer commission. For over two years the cold, precise administrator was able to persuade the aged field marshal to legitimize his actions by use of Article 48.

Brüning, who never doubted the validity of classical economic liberalism, used presidential powers for two interlocking policies. First, he attempted to cure the domestic economic crisis by deflation: he took vigorous government action to cut prices, wages, and state expenditure in order to stem the flight of foreign capital from Germany. A series of decrees cut civil servants' salaries by 12 to 16 percent, reduced unemployment benefits twice, and ordered wages lowered to the level of January 1, 1927. Although Brüning tried to compensate by ordering a lowering of rents and prices, it was of course easier for the government to roll back wages than prices.

The second half of Brüning's strategy was dramatic foreign success. Since deflation was painful to all except creditors, the chancellor hoped to assuage public discontent and undercut rising nationalist competition by bringing off two striking diplomatic moves. He planned a customs union with Austria (a country forbidden by the Versailles settlement to form any kind of political tie with Germany) and he campaigned for German parity in armaments.

The net result of Brüning's twin strategy was the opposite of his hopes. The vigorous government deflationary efforts only accentuated the economic downturn. Unemployment figures soared until they reached 6 million in 1932. Abroad, both of his grandstand plays were frustrated. France, in what was to be its last vigorous defense of the Versailles terms, fought the Austro-German customs union as a violation of the treaty. The Bank of France brought pressure to bear by witholding assistance to Viennese banks, thereby helping to permit the collapse of the *Credit-Anstalt* in May 1931 and setting off the European banking crisis.[7] Nor would France hear of arms parity for Germany just at the moment when the European disarmament conference was about to open.

Without dramatic foreign successes, of course, Brüning was more and more dependent on presidential decree powers to carry out an unpopular domestic policy. Nevertheless, he hoped to return from presidential to parliamentary government. Strongly antisocialist, Brüning saw more hope in wooing the nationalists (including the growing National Socialists) into a new parliamentary majority than in trying to revive a Great Coalition that included the Social Democrats.

[7]It is no longer certain that the French actually made things worse by withdrawing funds from the *Credit-Anstalt*, as is usually charged.

329

DEPRESSION
POLITICS
IN THE
LIBERAL
STATES

Unemployed Germans without enough money for a room pay a few pennies for several hours' sleep "on the line" in a Hamburg flophouse.

Believing a new nationalist majority could be elected, Brüning dissolved the dormant *Reichstag* in September 1930 and called for new elections. The result made parliamentary government even less possible. The anger and frustration generated by the depression had strongly polarized the electorate. The Nazi party was the most spectacular gainer, jumping from 12 seats to 107. Communists also gained at the expense of Social Democrats. Except for Brüning's own Catholic Center party, all the moderate and liberal parties lost to the extremes. Most disquieting of all, Nazism and communism were particularly attractive to new and young voters. Brüning had proven that the Weimar Constitution was incapable, even under presidential emergency authority, of success either at home or abroad.

Brüning himself, a stiff, formal man in public, was incapable of building a following. The British novelist Christopher Isherwood has described the chancellor at a public meeting:

> His gestures were sharp and admonitory; his spectacles gleamed emotion in the limelight. His voice quivered with dry academic passion.[8]

"Every week," wrote Isherwood, "there were new emergency decrees. Brüning's weary episcopal voice issued commands to the shopkeepers and was not obeyed."[9] In June 1932, President Hindenburg, at the age of eighty-three, easily influenced by gossip from his immediate associates, abruptly withdrew his support from Brüning, whom he now suddenly suspected of dangerous radicalism because the chancellor wished to investigate reported fraud in the administration of *Osthilfe* funds.

Baron Franz von Papen, a Catholic aristocrat with close friends in the president's own circle, became the new chancellor. Papen's efforts to appropriate the Nazi following belong to the next chapter. Under Papen, however, the Weimar Republic unquestionably became an authoritarian state without pretense of constitutional rule. Parliamentary government in Germany was destroyed by its inability to deal with the depression several years before Hitler came to power.

Depression Politics in the Authoritarian States

Nazi Germany

After Adolf Hitler assumed power in Germany in January 1933,[10] the new Nazi regime adopted economic policies totally different from the deflation of Brüning. The external effects seemed nothing less than a miracle. Germany was transformed from the country hardest hit by the depression in 1932 to the frightening giant of 1938. Unemployment dropped from 6 million in 1932 to 164,000 by 1936. After 1936, Germany imported foreign labor to fill a manpower shortage.

This economic "miracle" was accomplished by policies as far removed

---

[8]Christopher Isherwood, *Berlin Stories* (London, 1935), p. 85.
[9]*Ibid.*, p. 88.
[10]Hitler's assumption of power and his new regime are treated in Chapter 12, pp. 344–54.

from the return-to-the-soil jargon of Nazi intellectuals as they were from the nostrums of classical liberalism. There were basically three interrelated steps: a vast public investment stimulated production; the market mechanism of setting prices, wages, and allocating materials had then to be replaced by universal controls to avoid inflation; and the German economy was sealed off from the world banking and monetary system to insulate the mark from international speculation. Hjalmar Schacht, who had restored the German currency on neoliberal lines in 1923 and 1924, now adjusted his thinking to become chief financial and economic planner of a managed economy closer to the economic control of the First World War than to any liberal model.

331

DEPRESSION
POLITICS
IN THE
AUTHORITARIAN
STATES

The first step was a great surge of government expenditure. Since rearmament was still theoretically forbidden under the Treaty of Versailles, the most conspicuous early project was a network of four-lane superhighways, the *Autobahnen*. After open rearmament began in 1935, military spending rose to 60 percent of the budget by 1938, or 21 percent of the gross national product.[11]

In a free-market situation, this full-throttle rearmament would have triggered another inflation. Building on the precedents of the war, the government organized all branches of industry and agriculture into cartels, set prices, regulated wages through officials of the Labor Ministry (trustees of labor), and allocated raw materials according to a Four-Year Plan. Owners were no longer free to make individual business decisions, but to many that seemed a small price to pay for order and prosperity. Furthermore, labor unions were dissolved and wage disputes handled by civil servants.

A major obstacle to such measures in a liberal economy was their expected effect on the country's currency abroad and on foreign trade. The Nazi solution was autarky, or economic self-sufficiency. Foreign trade had fallen sharply anyway as a result of the depression, and the partisans of autarky were happy to leave it at about a third of the 1928 and 1929 level, even in 1938.[12] Instead of depending on imports, the German economy was supposed to become self-sufficient in agriculture and invent synthetic substitutes for materials it could not produce.

Major steps toward isolating the German economy were taken in 1936 with the announcement of the second Four-Year Plan. Schacht, who had wanted to expand foreign trade now that the economy was reviving, was replaced by Hermann Goering, head of the Air Force. The Reich began to produce several very expensive synthetics: Buna, which cost seven times as much as natural rubber, and synthetic oil. Steel was also produced expensively with low-quality coal in the Hermann Goering factory.

The dynamism of the German economy by 1938 was an object of fear

[11]These rates of military spending were comparable to those of the United States in the late 1960s, but they were unprecedented in peacetime before the 1930s.
[12]Gustav Stolper, *The German Economy: 1870 to the Present,* 2nd ed. (New York, 1967), pp. 144–45.

and wonder in the struggling liberal countries. Unlike them, Germany had full employment, growth, and stability—at the price of individual liberties. It had smashed trade unions and organized the economy into universal cartels. As in liberal capitalism, owners of farms and factories continued to own them, although they had renounced some liberty of economic decision (including the unwanted liberty to make wrong economic decisions). Unlike the situation in liberal capitalism, however, the owners were subject to a planned and managed economy, in which they contended with civil servants for predominance. Some observers tended to lump this experiment with communism as two faces of a single totalitarianism, but it must be remembered that in Hitler's Germany there was no social displacement of owners of farms and factories.

Who profited from the new German dynamism? By 1938, the real purchasing power of German wage earners had risen to the levels of 1913 and 1929, years of maximum pre-Nazi prosperity. Deprived of the strike weapon, however, German workers failed to keep pace with the enormous growth in national production. Compared with 1929, wages and salaries made up a smaller share of the national product; profits in trade and industry a larger share.[13] Even so, after the Weimar nightmare, most German wage earners were reconciled by full employment and nationalist excitement.

Small farmers and the middle class, who had supported the Nazis most enthusiastically, continued their long slow decline in the face of bigger enterprises. Production was oriented away from consumer goods, and savings were funneled off into the great enterprises of the regime. For example, small savers poured 285 million marks into advance down-payments on Ferdinand Porsche's brilliantly designed cheap "peoples' car," only to find when Volkswagens began to roll off the assembly line in 1939 that they all went to the Army. But most middle-class Germans were too enthusiastic over the destruction of socialism and over revived German power to object.

Big business leaders grumbled at having to share the costs of such expensive projects as the Hermann Goering steel mill, and some great speculative fortunes were lost. Huge industries like the Krupp armament works and I. G. Farben chemicals, into whose growth the nation's energies and savings were channeled, were clearly the principal gainers from the Nazi economic miracle.

The most important decisions affecting the Nazi economic system were not taken solely on their economic merits, however. The political aims of the regime took precedence over mere economic efficacy. The decision to seek autarky was motivated in large part by the desire to overcome the material shortages that had condemned the German Empire during the war. That decision forced the German people to pay

[13]David Schoenbaum, *Hitler's Social Revolution: Class and Status in Nazi Germany, 1933–39* (New York, 1967), p. 97.

for expensive substitutes and to consume lower quality goods (such as ersatz coffee). The drive for autarky may also have made territorial expansion more attractive to the Nazi leaders, who coveted the wheat and oil of Eastern Europe. For those political aims the German people were eventually to pay very highly indeed.

333

DEPRESSION
POLITICS
IN THE
AUTHORITARIAN
STATES

Corporatist Italy

Despite the serious difficulties of modern industry in the north of Italy, the depression gave the appearance of being less cataclysmic in Italy than in other countries. Unemployment was easily concealed in Italy's backward south and in its numerous small shops. Immense publicity was given to "progressive" projects like the draining of the Pontine Marshes for settlement,[14] and to the famous trains that ran on time. And Italy seemed to be free of social discontent. The system that was alleged to produce these combined boons of progress, efficiency, and order was called corporatism. Since corporatism was widely praised and imitated in the 1930s, it deserves more than passing mention here.

Corporatism was not Mussolini's idea. Intellectually, it derived from several attempts in the late nineteenth century to discover a solution to worker misery that would be neither liberal nor Marxist. Catholic social thinkers made one such attempt. They contrasted the atomized city world, easily whipped up into artifical class alignments by demagogues, with an organic society in which natural groupings, such as families, villages, or crafts, lived and worked in harmony. Pope Leo XIII's encyclical *Rerum Novarum* (1891) castigated liberal capitalism for its impersonal financial ties and its heartless exploitation, proposing instead the application of Christian charity to the economy and a revival of organic social groups.

Another intellectual root was syndicalism, the revolutionary labor union movement that was powerful in southern Europe. The syndicalists' basic unit of action was the *syndicat,* or labor union, organized by factory or village rather than by craft. When the "great day" of the revolutionary general strike came, each *syndicat* would simply seize its factory or village. Together they would abolish the state. Thereafter, the workers would run things themselves, with the *syndicats* as the only remaining organizations in a free society.

Despite their profound differences, Catholic organic social thought and revolutionary syndicalism had some elements in common. Both distrusted parliamentary and electoral action; both preferred local "natural" groupings to the centralized bureaucratic state. People from both traditions would be able to cooperate in an anti-Marxist, antiparliamentarian reconstruction of the social order.

Corporatism had pragmatic roots as well as intellectual ones. Cartels

---

[14]Only 19,000 families were actually settled there.

were widely used in highly concentrated industries for bringing a whole branch of production together to limit free competition in the marketplace. The experience of managed economies during the war, while too bureaucratic for most industrialists' tastes in good times, revealed the possibilities of regulation as a remedy for distorted economies in bad times.

Drawing from all these sources, corporatists proposed to regroup each branch of industry, agriculture, and commerce in its own syndicate, or corporation. Each of these could then regulate its own affairs: allocating resources, dividing up the market, rationalizing production, and replacing the liberal free market with planned, managed economic activity. The main questions, of course, were who would run the corporations and whom their decisions would favor. The answers to those questions were not immediately apparent when Mussolini assumed office in 1922.

One of Mussolini's first associates was the ex-syndicalist Edmondo Rossoni, an IWW (International Workers of the World) organizer among Italian immigrants in New York before he joined Mussolini. Rossoni began to apply corporatism as a form of updated syndicalism: workers and managers would cooperate in the new corporations around a goal of higher productivity. Expanded production, rather than a revolutionary redistribution of property, now seemed to Rossoni the solution to poverty. Businessmen could agree with that, but they were alarmed by the way Rossoni promised a direct role in economic management to active new worker associations. By 1924, Mussolini had removed Rossoni from influence.

Businessmen and big landowners had contributed money to Mussolini, and the *Duce* had apparently promised a group of industrialists headed by Alberto Pirelli, the tire manufacturer, before the March on Rome in 1922, that he meant to "reestablish discipline particularly within the factories and that no outlandish experiments would be carried out."[15] By the late 1920s it was clear that Mussolini intended to develop the same kind of pragmatic working relations with industrial and agricultural leaders as he was establishing with other traditional Italian power blocs: king, Army, and papacy. The Fascist regime talked less and less of corporatism while quietly shifting economic influence from Fascist ideologues like Rossoni and from state agencies to the Italian businessmen's association, the General Confederation of Italian Industry (CGII).

When Italian businesses began to suffer after 1929, however, Mussolini devised on paper a system of economic organization called corporatist for public effect. The National Council of Corporations was set up in 1930, within which twenty-two different branches of industry and trade were organized into "corporations" by 1934. The replacement of the Chamber of Deputies with the Chamber of Corporations in 1938

[15]Roland Sarti, *Fascism and the Industrial Leadership in Italy, 1919–40* (Berkeley, Calif., 1971), p. 37.

was designed to transfer representation from the discredited liberal system of elected citizens to spokesmen for economic interests. Although Fascist propaganda talked much about the harmonization of "natural" interests within corporatism, the whole machinery was in fact staffed by the CGII. Workers were not only excluded from these organizations but had long since lost the right to strike.

335

DEPRESSION
POLITICS
IN THE
AUTHORITARIAN
STATES

The most lasting monument to what corporatism meant in practice in fascist Italy was the IRI (Institute for Industrial Reconstruction). When some important Italian businesses approached bankruptcy as the depression worsened, the IRI was established in January 1933 to lend them money. By the time the IRI was made permanent in 1937, the government owned a controlling interest in Italian steel, heavy machinery, shipping, electricity, and telephones. In this way, the Fascist regime rescued unprofitable sectors of the Italian economy by what amounted to partial nationalization. Even then, however, civil servants had little role in so-called corporatism. Organized business continued to manage the cartelized economy very much on its own terms. Wages remained low, and production failed to gain very much. Fascism permitted Italian businessmen to ride out the depression freed from meddling bureaucracy, independent trade unions, and responsibility for unprofitable sectors of the economy.

The Soviet Union

By 1928, the Bukharin policy of slow, steady economic growth based on the productivity of a satisfied small peasantry had yielded disappointing results.[16] The decline of world agricultural prices lowered the value of grain, Russia's main commodity, and the world's first socialist state was in danger of becoming economically becalmed in a sea of 25 million small family farms. Now all-powerful at the head of the Russian Communist party and freed from the left opposition of the earlier 1920s, Stalin turned on Bukharin and adopted the left's economic policy of stimulating industry through the profits extracted from collectivized farms.

Stalin's first intention was to collectivize only the farms of the wealthier kulaks, the larger farmers who employed wage labor and accounted for perhaps 14 percent of Russia's farms. The collectivization was widely resisted, however. Whole rural communities, including the poorest peasants, responded with the traditional weapons of hoarding crops and slaughtering livestock. In reaction to this unexpectedly strong resistance, and convinced by the Wall Street crash that the era of "capitalist stabilization" had ended, Stalin and his party bureaucracy sharply escalated their program. Close to half of all peasant households—10 million families—were forced into collectives by March 1930. When agricultural production subsequently dropped to nothing, Stalin called a temporary halt on the grounds that Russia was "dizzy with success," but

[16]See Chapter 9, p. 272.

there was no way to proceed but forward. By 1934, the 25 million family farms had been combined into 250,000 collectives. Not only was grain production far lower than in 1928, but the slaughter of livestock was so widespread that 1928 levels in meat production were recovered only in the 1950s, a quarter century later. Stalin himself admitted years later to British Prime Minister Winston Churchill that 10 million peasants died in the artificially imposed famine of 1932 and 1933,[17] and the figure may have been higher.

Soon after the collectivization of farms was under way, Stalin launched the first of what was to be a series of Five Year Plans to stimulate Soviet industrial production. The First Five Year Plan, to run from October 1928 through 1933, was the most important internal decision of Stalin's career. It was a virtual economic revolution, this time from above, and it sealed Russia off from the influences at work in the rest of Europe during the depression years. Since the wealth necessary for the crash program could come only from expropriating a resisting peasantry, the plan engendered a far harsher authoritarian control than anything seen in the relatively open late 1920s. The Soviet example offered rapid industrial growth and full employment at a time when capitalist Europe could offer neither, but it did so at the price of renewed starvation, tens of millions of deaths, and eventually an unspeakably harsh system of labor camps and political purges.

The economic changes in Russia after 1929 constituted a profounder revolution than that of 1917. The ancient ways of Russian village life, where the vast bulk of the population still lived, were completely transformed. The Soviet Union was on its way to becoming an urban, industrial nation within one generation. It is incorrect to suppose that Russia had no significant industry before the Five Year Plans began; Russia stood fifth in world production in 1929. Only thirty years later, however, it stood second, behind the United States. The wealth skimmed off the land by requisition from the rural collectives was poured into the construction of factories, dams, and entire new cities. By 1937, heavy industrial production had increased by three to six times (depending on whose statistics are used) since 1928. A new city such as Magnitogorsk could grow from a population of zero to 250,000 in a few years. The Soviet Union advanced from fifteenth to third place in the production of electrical power during the time of the first three Five Year Plans (1929–41). Regardless of whether one accepts the Soviet figures of an annual growth rate of 20 percent a year in overall production or the more cautious Western figures of 14 percent a year, the effects were astonishing to a world sunk in depression.

Stalin's "great change" was possible only because the party bureaucracy had been strengthened under his sole command. That iron rule was made even more necessary by the chaos that accompanied forced

[17]Winston Churchill, *History of the Second World War: The Hinge of Fate* (London, 1950), p. 498.

A group of kulaks (peasants prosperous enough to employ others) is deported from a Russian village during the first stages of land collectivization, 1930. The banners read, "The kulak class must be eliminated."

collectivization and the discipline needed in new industry. Factory workers were no longer permitted to change jobs. A regime of low wages, speeded up production, and steeply differentiated piece rates in industry was sweetened by propaganda and praise for sacrifice for the new socialist state. Aleksey Stakhanov, a coal miner in the Donetz Basin who exceeded his quota by 1400 percent in 1935, became a model for other workers to emulate. "Stakhanovites" were paid in praise rather than in consumer goods, however, and the Soviet economy under the Five Year Plans bore no relation to a consumer economy on Keynesian lines.

The rigors of forced collectivization and industrialization were harsh enough in themselves. Even harsher was the treatment of peasant resisters, industrial misfits and saboteurs, and political opponents, who swelled the populations of forced labor camps in Siberia in the early 1930s. But the worst was yet to come in the great purges of 1936 to 1938, a product of Stalin's own suspicious temperament coupled with his drive for sole control of decisionmaking.

Until 1934, the weight of political repression had fallen on old tsarist personnel and those who obstructed the new course. At the end of 1934, the Communist party secretary in Leningrad, Sergei Kirov, was assassinated, and the left opposition was officially accused of the act. Revelations in the de-Stalinization speech by Nikita Khrushchev in 1956 make it appear likely that Stalin himself arranged Kirov's execution in order to remove a troublesome new rival. In any case, the assassination was followed by an ascending spiral of denunciations and arrests as virtually the entire remaining Old Bolshevik leadership, as well as all those suspected of supporting it, was decimated. The most astonishing aspect of the great purge was the series of show trials in which many Bolshevik leaders confessed to various crimes of treason before being shot. The left opposition leaders Kamenev and Zinoviev were tried in 1936; sixteen other eminent Bolsheviks in 1937, including Marshal Mikhail Tukhachevsky, who had defeated the Poles in 1920; and another twenty-one including Bukharin in 1938.

At lower levels, an orgy of denunciation and spy-mania engulfed the party, the state apparatus, and ordinary citizens. The purge was particularly severe among senior army officers, diplomats, and others who could be shown to have had foreign contacts (including contacts with foreign communists). It is likely that 8 million Russians, including many party members, perished in the great purge. Tens of millions more were sent to Siberia, that world of prisoners and outcasts that the novelist Aleksandr Solzhenitsyn (who was later one of them) has described as "the mysterious and terrible country of 'Gulag' . . . with its own social system, its written and unwritten laws, its population, its customs, its rulers, and its subjects."[18]

The poisoning of Soviet Russian life by the purges of the late 1930s has aroused passionate controversy. For some sympathetic Western observers at the time, the Old Bolsheviks' confessions proved that the Soviet experiment was indeed under fascist and capitalist attack and was forced to depart from ordinary judicial measures in order to protect itself. It seems likely today that the confessions were extorted, if not by physical torture, at least by promises to spare the wives and children of the accused. Other Western observers concluded that despotism had always been inherent in Lenin's concept of a vanguard party exercising dictatorship in the name of a backward proletariat. Still other Westerners, such as George Kennan, attributed the purges to Stalin's own paranoia.

The most interesting debate about Stalinist rule has raged within the Soviet Union. Nikita Khrushchev opened a Pandora's box of criticisms of Stalin at the Twentieth Party Congress in 1956. The Soviet historian Roy Medvedev has argued that Lenin's imperfect but promising beginning was perverted by Stalinism, a personal aberration that built on elements present in party rule but was not inevitable. Solzhenitsyn came to believe that Lenin had erred fatally in trying to create socialism in an underindustrialized country, and that Stalin simply "followed in Lenin's footsteps."[19]

Whatever its proper explanation, the Stalinist blood bath made the Soviet economic achievement considerably less attractive after 1936. The British Labour party intellectuals Beatrice and Sidney Webb had referred to the Soviet Union in the early 1930s as "a new civilization." A

---

[18]Aleksandr Solzhenitsyn, *The Gulag Archipelago, 1918–1956,* trans. Thomas P. Whitney (New York, 1974), as described by the Soviet historian Roy Medvedev in the *New York Times,* February 7, 1974, p. 10.

[19]*Ibid.*

later Western journalist called the 1930s Russia's "new iron age."[20] It was that, in two senses of the term: an extraordinary achievement in heavy industrial production and a descent into barbarism.

Conclusion

Governments dealt with the challenges of the depression with widely varying success. The authoritarian regimes expanded their industrial power and kept order despite low wages. The liberal regimes sank ever deeper into unemployment as they tried deflation and lapsed into internal social conflict. Liberal politics and liberal economics were completely discredited. From the vantage point of the bread lines and soup kitchens of London, Paris, or republican Berlin, either Communist Russia or Fascist Italy looked like greener pastures, according to one's predilection. Then when Nazi Germany grew into the industrial and military giant of the Continent by the mid-1930s, the comparative impression of decadent liberalism and burgeoning authoritarianism grew much stronger.

The British novelist E. M. Forster summed up the air of doubt and lassitude felt in the major liberal states with the title of his volume of essays, *Two Cheers for Democracy.* The liberal states were deprived by their depression remedies of both the material and moral means and will to oppose the dictators resolutely. In the 1930s, fascism seemed the wave of the future.

[20]William Henry Chamberlin, *Russia's Iron Age* (Boston, 1934).

Suggestions for Further Reading

An excellent introduction to the Great Depression in Europe is Chapter 6 of David S. Landes, *The Unbound Prometheus** (1969). W. Arthur Lewis, *Economic Survey, 1919–1939** (1949) provides a nontechnical description of European economic fluctuations. Charles P. Kindleberger, *The World in Depression, 1929–1939** (1973) argues that the absence of any one guiding economic power, as Britain had been before 1914, made the slump longer and deeper than it need have been. Goronwy Rees, *The Great Slump: Capitalism in Crisis, 1929–1933* (1971) is a popularized account. See also Roy Harrod, *The Life of John Maynard Keynes*, 2nd ed. (1952). The *Journal of Contemporary History*, Vol. 4, No. 4 (October 1969) is devoted entirely to the depression. The best book on depression politics in any one country is Robert Skidelsky, *Politicians and the Slump* (1967), a critical evaluation of the Labour government of 1929 to 1931. Works by Marwick, Beer, and Gilbert cited at the end of Chapter 4 are also important for the depression years. Noreen Branson and Margot Heinemann, *Britain in the Nineteen Thirties* (1971) portrays the bleak everyday life of the poor. George Orwell, *The Road to Wigan Pier** (1937) is a justly famous essay on a coal-mining town during the depression by a middle-class intellectual acutely aware of his temptation to condescend.

In the absence of any specialized work in English on the depression in France, see the relevant portions of Joel Colton, *Léon Blum: Humanist in Politics* (1966).

German economic and social problems are explored in Alexander Gerschenkron, *Bread and Democracy in Germany* (1943); Edward W. Bennett, *Germany and the Diplomacy of the Financial Crisis, 1931* (1962); and Arthur Schweitzer, *Big Business in the Third Reich* (1964). Gustav Stolper, *The German Economy: 1870 to the Present*, 2nd ed. (1967) is a good recent survey. David Schoenbaum *Hitler's Social Revolution** (1967) shows whom Hitler's depression remedies benefitted. Most authoritative on the position of labor after 1933 is T. W. Mason, "Labour in the Third Reich, 1933–1939," *Past and Present*, No. 33 (April 1966). Hans Fallada, *Little Man, What Now?*(1933), and Christopher Isherwood, *Berlin Stories**(1935) are among the most enduring depression fiction, one employing pathos, the other satire to portray Berlin just before Hitler.

Italian corporatism in action is effectively summarized in H. Stuart Hughes, *The United States and Italy*, 2nd ed. (1965). Roland Sarti, *Fascism and the Industrial Leadership in Italy, 1919–1940* (1971) is important.

Marquis Childs' admiring *Sweden, The Middle Way** (1936) is a classic study of the cooperative movement in Scandinavia.

The Russian decision to industrialize rapidly out of the surplus of collectivized agriculture is explored in Alexander Erlich, *The Soviet Industrialization Debate* (1960), and, with a wealth of illustrative detail, in Edward Hallett Carr and R. W. Davies, *Foundations of a Planned Economy, 1926–1929*, 2 vols. (1969–72). There are important essays in Alexander Gerschenkron, *Economic Backwardness in Historical Perspective* (1962).

The effect of collectivization on the Russian peasantry is assessed in Moshe Lewin, *Russian Peasants and Soviet Power* (1968). For collectivization in detail in one region, see Merle Fainsod, *Smolensk Under Soviet Rule** (1958).

The most authoritative history of Stalin's purges is Robert Conquest, *The Great Terror: Stalin's Purge of the Thirties** (1968). Interesting documents are published in Robert C. Tucker and Stephen F. Cohen, eds., *The Great Purge Trials* (1965). The most penetrating criticism of Stalin's dictatorship to emerge from a dissident Soviet citizen is Roy Medvedev, *Let History Judge: The Origins and Consequences of Stalinism** (1972). See also the poignant memoirs of a survivor of the camps, Nadezhda Mandelstam, *Hope Against Hope* (1970).

Fascist propaganda on a grandiose scale: National Socialist units

THE SPREAD OF FASCISM: THE AUTHORITARIAN 1930s

12

Make way for the "new man, the fascist man, the man of the twentieth century." "We are the pioneers that head the column of the future."[1] For a time, these claims by young fascists of the 1930s seemed on the verge of fulfillment. Whereas in the 1920s only one regime,

[1]Corneliu Codreanu and Anton Adriaan Mussert, Romanian and Dutch fascists.

at a consecration ceremony in Luitpoldhain, 1933.

Italy, had called itself fascist, in the 1930s it was joined by Nazi Germany, and clerical regimes influenced by fascism ruled in Austria, Portugal, and, after 1939, Spain. The trend toward authoritarian regimes in Eastern Europe was completed in the 1930s (with the exception of Czechoslovakia). There was a time in 1934 when it looked as if fascist movements would overthrow the French Republic. Small but vociferous fascist movements were active in Britain, the Low Countries, and Scandinavia. Although not all these movements or regimes adopted the irreligion, the guided economies, the anti-Semitism, and the unbridled dynamism of Italian fascism and German Nazism, much of the political tone and style of the 1930s were influenced by apparent fascist successes.

Fascism seemed the wave of the future; the liberal regimes, by contrast, seemed old and tired. Liberal Europe, complained the Austrian socialist leader Otto Bauer, was "betwitched" by the apparent mechanical efficiency of fascist states where "the trains ran on time."[2]

[2]Otto Bauer, *Zwischen zwei Weltkriegen?* (Bratislava, 1936), p. 135.

The Revival of Nazism, 1929–32

Even before the great crash of 1929, the Nazi party had begun to reemerge from its mid-1920s obscurity. The passions aroused by debate over the Young Plan (1928–29), which set reparations payments over many years to come, gave Hitler his best platform since the French occupation of the Ruhr in 1923. It was the depression of 1929, however, that really opened the way for Hitler by reviving fear of revolution and exposing the fecklessness of the Weimar Republic.

As we have seen, the deteriorating economy had made a parliamentary majority impossible in the Weimar Republic after March 1930.[3] The *Reichstag* election of September 14, 1930, only proved how radically the electorate had been polarized: Nazis increased their seats from 12 to 107, and the German Communist party rose from 54 to 77 seats. These processes continued in the *Reichstag* election of July 1932, when the Nazis replaced the Social Democrats as the largest party in Germany by winning 230 seats.

Hitler's mass electoral following provides a rough guide to the social dislocations of depression-ridden Germany. Hitler's supporters included declining small farmers, distressed shopkeepers, minor civil servants suffering from wage cuts, embittered nationalists, and frightened conservatives seeking some strong medicine against Germany's apparently headlong rush into an atomized, rootless, disorderly society.

The Nazis scored their greatest successes in Protestant agricultural areas. Schleswig-Holstein, a region of small independent diary and beef cattle farmers, was the only German state to give Hitler's party an absolute majority before the Nazis took power. Farmers there had become violently hostile to the Weimar regime. The tariff of 1925 had failed to protect them against frozen meat imports from the British Empire, while it had made imported feed grains more expensive.[4] When the world agricultural depression began around 1927, the number of farms and herds seized for unpaid debts rose sharply, victims of "interest slavery." The Schleswig-Holstein farmers' alienation was fostered by ethnic resentments, for their area had been added to the Prussian state by the war of 1866. To complete the picture, the farmers were worried that their way of life was being swallowed up by a faceless, godless, urban society that seemed to dominate the Weimar Republic, and especially the Social-Democratic Prussian state with its great decadent city of Berlin. Convinced that traditional political leaders already enmeshed in Weimar republican arrangements could do nothing to alleviate their predicament, the Schleswig-Holstein farmers flocked first to a local peasant party strongly impregnated with national socialist attitudes, and eventually to the National Socialist party itself. This local example of small independent farmers switching precipitously from

---

[3]See Chapter 11, p. 327.
[4]A British firm received a concession for a frozen meat importing facility at Altona, near Hamburg, in the 1920s.

middle-class Weimar parties to Nazism is only the most conspicuous case, and the one most fully studied.[5] Similar cases could be found among other Protestant small farmers, equally maddened by debt, concern for a vanishing way of life, and resentment of workers, unions, and cities.

No constituency in Germany gave the Nazis less than 20 percent of the vote in July 1932. This included the cities, even though Social Democratic political machines were powerfully entrenched there.[6] The independent lower middle class—retail merchants, artisans, lower civil servants, and those on the bottom rungs of the independent professions—was the urban group most susceptible to Nazi recruitment. In their view, the Weimar Republic neglected them. Whereas the workers had their unions and welfare legislation, the lower middle class felt isolated and vulnerable to the depression. The Marxist parties had no appeal to these Germans, who clung to their middle-class status. The established upper-class elites excited their envy or resentment more than their admiration. For the threadbare *petit bourgeois,* the National Socialists' two-pronged attack on socialism and big finance touched responsive chords.

At the end of Hans Fallada's novel *Little Man, What Now?* (1932), it is not clear whether the protagonist will turn to the far left or far right after losing his job with a heartless department store. This new proletarian's bitter sense of loss of status is complete when he is elbowed off the street by callous bourgeois on the way home. Since the Marxist parties appealed only to those ready to accept working-class status, Nazism was the only protest movement open to the desperate of every other social class. Hence its growth from 2.6 percent of the vote in 1928 to 18.3 percent in September 1930, and again to 37.3 percent in July 1932.

It was primarily Hitler's mass electoral following among Germany's rural and urban lower middle class that drew the German elite to him. At first, Hitler had seemed boorish and offensive to many upper-class Germans. But he was much less threatening to them than the Marxists, and after his vote-getting capacity had been demonstrated, Germany's leaders rushed to try to enlist that power for their own purposes.

German intellectual leaders had already helped prepare the way. As early as the Napoleonic Wars, nationalist professors tried to arouse patriotic pride in the distinctiveness of German *Kultur* from the invaders' values of liberty, equality, and fraternity. During the nineteenth century anti-Semitism and intellectual rejection of Western liberal rationalism grew more pervasive. At the beginning of the twentieth century, a mood of cultural pessimism was widespread among German intellectuals. They called for a redeemer who would save German blood, soil, and idealism from the corruptions of ugly factory cities, flabby bourgeois, and rootless aliens. Although few major German intellectuals

[5]Rudolf Heberle, *From Democracy to Nazism. A Regional Case Study of Political Parties in Germany* (1945; reprint ed., Baton Rouge, La., 1970).
[6]The lowest votes were in Berlin, Catholic Cologne, and rural Catholic lower Bavaria.

actually gave the uncouth Nazis their personal support during the movement's growth, they had helped make Nazi propaganda themes acceptable.

Business leaders also helped with money and useful contacts. Fritz Thyssen, heir to the powerful *Vereinigte Stahlwerke,* gave Hitler 100,000 gold marks in 1923. After Hitler's electoral success in 1930 aroused greater interest in him, prestigious big business groups such as the Düsseldorf Industry Club helped confer respectability on him by inviting him to speak. On such occasions Hitler stressed his movement's antisocialism and disavowed the anticapitalist rhetoric of some of his associates. It is not true, however, that German big business paid for Hitler's success. Hitler was chronically short of funds, and most big business leaders contributed more readily to a wide range of more traditional centrist and conservative politicians. Their decisive contribution came in January 1933 when they supported Hitler's entry into the government on the understanding that the government would be dominated by traditional conservatives.

The older nationalist movements tried hard to attract Hitler into their ranks. They had more money than Hitler, but he had the backing of the masses. Hoping to make Hitler a vassal rather than a rival, Alfred Hugenburg, a former Krupp director who became head of the German National People's party (DNVP) in 1928, attempted to make common cause with Hitler in the fight over the Young Plan in 1929.

Chancellor Brüning himself also tried to enlist Hitler's support. He needed it, for his deflationary depression remedies had made widespread enemies. Brüning's economic policies made it impossible for him to form any parliamentary majority with the existing parties. He did not want to work with the Social Democrats and, in any event, could not have ruled through them alone. He had to govern either by presidential decree or by finding some new form of mass backing. Deflation, in other words, could be carried out only by force or cajolery: Hitler's mass following and his shock troops were vital to either attempt.

Buoyed by their ascending influence, Hitler and his followers added all they could to the atmosphere of crisis in which they flourished. They gave an impression of tough vigor unmatched by anyone except the much less numerous German Communists, and an impression of anti-Marxist violence far beyond that of any other force on the right. The brown-shirted SA. (stormtroopers, *Stürmabteilungen*) held mass rallies, broke up leftist protest demonstrations and offices, and fought pitched battles in the streets with the Social Democrats' own direct-action squads. In one small town, the subject of William Sheridan Allen's *The Nazi Seizure of Power: The Experience of a Single German Town* (1965),[7] there were no less than thirty-seven political street fights between 1930 and 1933, of which four were general melees. This figure does not

[7]Allen's "Thalberg" was actually Nordheim, a small railroad town in northwestern Germany.

include the number of times that political rallies were forbidden without leading to violence, or the number of times that the state police had to be called in to supplement the local force. The atmosphere of incipient chaos led many conservative Germans to blame the unemployed for causing the disorder, the left for encouraging it, and the Weimar Republic for failing to prevent it. For such persons, Hitler's strong-arm tactics offered the satisfaction of bringing all three to heel.

The End of Weimar: Presidential Government, 1930–33

Parliamentary government had ceased to function normally according to the Weimar Constitution with the collapse of Chancellor Hermann Müller's majority on March 27, 1930. It was not clear for some time what would replace it.

One possibility was a pure socialist ministry. The Social Democrats, after all, remained the largest German party in Weimar's third legislature, having won about 30 percent of the popular vote in 1928; together with the German Communist party, Marxists had received just over 40 percent of the popular vote (compared with the Nazis' 2.6 percent). This possibility was only theoretical, however. Socialists and Communists had been bitterly divided since 1917. Moreover, a minority cabinet had to depend on the president's power to promulgate laws directly without a parliamentary majority in case of emergency. And since the death of the moderate Social Democratic President Friedrich Ebert in 1925, the president had been the far more conservative Marshal Paul von Hindenburg.

A second possibility was renewed recourse to elections to produce a coherent majority of left, center, or right. The German public did, in fact, endure a veritable orgy of balloting between 1930 and 1933: three *Reichstag* elections (September 1930, July 1932, November 1932) and a two-stage presidential election (March 1932), plus many state elections. No coherent majority emerged in the crosscurrents of depression politics and national politics, although Nazis replaced Social Democrats as the largest single party in July 1932, and the moderate parties nearly vanished. In the meantime, many Germans simply became disillusioned with the electoral process.

The course actually followed after March 1930 was a compromise that pleased no one. While continuing to seek a majority in frequent elections, a series of conservative chancellors who had President Hindenburg's personal confidence exercised presidential government, calling on the president to countersign their decrees under Article 48. Three chancellors in turn governed this way between 1930 and January 1933: Heinrich Brüning (March 1930–July 1932); Baron Franz von Papen (July–December 1932); and General Kurt von Schleicher (December 1932–January 1933). This situation obviously gave a great deal of power to the aging and impressionable field marshal. German history from 1930 to 1933 is a story of personal intrigue for the president's confidence. And it is a story that helps explain how far from inevitable was Hitler's accession to the office of chancellor and how large was the immediate responsibility of a handful of men.

Chancellor Brüning, as we have seen, was forced back on the president's support after his only electoral effort, the *Reichstag* elections of September 14, 1930, gave the Nazis the opportunity to display their popular appeal. Although the Social Democrats offered not to oppose the government, in a noble but self-defeating gesture of loyalty to the Weimar system, Brüning's recent memoirs make it clear that he wanted above all to draw the Nazi following into a new Catholic-nationalist majority.[8] Fearful of further elections, however, he continued his twin program of deflation at home and intransigence abroad with the president's support. The failure of both left him totally dependent on Hindenburg's friendship, and the old man's opinions were increasingly subject to influence from a few close associates. They persuaded him in May 1932 to replace Brüning with someone better able to harness the Nazi movement to conservative purposes.

Hindenburg then named as chancellor Baron Franz von Papen, a Catholic nobleman of good social connections and deeply conservative convictions. Papen put together a "ministry of barons" (senior army officers and top civil servants) that moved the government even further from parliamentary leadership. Papen began his ministry with two acts of conspicuous favor to the far right. On June 16 he cancelled a ban on the Nazi SA. that Brüning had imposed in April, thereby restoring to Hitler the possibility of mastering the street. In the ensuing brawls between Nazi and left demonstrators, 82 people were killed and 400 seriously wounded in Prussia alone during six weeks.[9] The disorder gave Papen the excuse to destroy the last remaining stronghold of the democratic left. On July 20, drawing on presidential emergency powers, Papen expelled the duly-elected Social Democratic state government of Prussia from office and put the state police under Army orders. Then Papen called a new *Reichstag* election for July 31, 1932. Nazi support grew from 18 to 37 percent of the popular vote.

Hitler now made a direct bid to President Hindenburg for office. The interview went badly. Hindenburg later remarked that Hitler was an odd sort who might be fit for, at most, the Ministry of Posts.[10] Angered by the old man's brusque discourtesy, Hitler insisted on the office of chancellor or nothing. Papen believed that he could electioneer the Nazis to death and then draw their following into his own machine. The elections of November 6, 1932, seemed to confirm his strategy. The Nazis were left exhausted and deeply in debt as they suffered their first electoral decline (from 37 percent to 33 percent). Papen, however, still had no parliamentary majority to show for his efforts.

[8]Heinrich Brüning, *Memoiren, 1918–34* (Stuttgart, 1970), p. 461.
[9]Alan Bullock, *Hitler, A Study in Tyranny,* 2nd ed. (New York, 1962), p. 213.
[10]*Ibid.,* p. 187.

*The new German
Chancellor, Adolf
Hitler, Vice Chan-
cellor Franz von
Papan (left), and
Propaganda Chief
Josef Goebbels
(right) at a youth
ceremony in May
1933.*

Here personal intrigue reached its most decisive point. Papen proposed a frank counterrevolution, using the president's powers to replace
the Weimar Constitution with a new authoritarian regime. But General
Kurt von Schleicher, Hindenburg's closest military associate, convinced
the president that the Army would not support such a step toward civil
war. Schleicher proposed one more try at a parliamentary majority in
which he would detach the "left" Nazi Gregor Strasser and his following
from Hitler and form a coalition extending all the way to trade union
officials on the left: it would be a last echo of the Army–union
cooperation under military government from 1916 to 1918.[11] Schleicher

[11]See Chapter 4, pp. 105, 113.

formed a government on December 2, 1932, and started to work on this byzantine coalition.

The outraged Papen was able to rally a group of his own—all of Schleicher's enemies. Hitler, worried by the apparent downturn of his fortunes since the November elections and eager to halt the defection of Strasser, now expressed his willingness to enter a coalition rather than rule alone. Prominent businessmen, upset at Schleicher's efforts to bring trade unionists into the government, increased their financial contributions to the debt-ridden Nazis. When Schleicher's scheme came apart as trade unionists and moderate party leaders refused to participate, Papen's new coalition was ready. He proposed that Hitler be made chancellor, Papen himself vice chancellor, and the nationalist leader Hugenburg Minister of Finance, a combination too full of mutual distrust to have come together unless threatened with exclusion by Schleicher.

Hindenburg was persuaded that the Papen plan might achieve what successive chancellors had sought since 1930. A Hitler-Papen-Hugenburg coalition government offered a chance to obtain a parliamentary majority excluding the Social Democrats and Communists, to keep the Nazis in line by absorbing their leaders within a reassuring conservative coalition, and to escape from the improvisation of presidential government. On January 30, 1933, Hindenburg received Hitler and made him chancellor of the German Reich.

Responsibilities for bringing Hitler to power are widely shared. The voters who awarded him the largest proportion of electoral strength gave him his basic leverage. When that electoral strength failed to reach absolute majority and began to recede in November 1932, however, President Hindenburg and the intriguers around him saved Hitler in the effort to harness Nazi street and electoral power to their own purposes. Prominent businessmen paid the Nazi party's debts in December 1932; they and other conservatives worked for any coalition that would keep the Marxists out of office.

Although at least 63 percent of the electorate voted for non-Nazi parties through November 1932, the opposition failed to make use of its majority position. The moderate parties were more willing to form coalitions with the Nazis than with the Marxists. The German Communists, convinced that Hitler

A Nazi electoral poster: "Women! Millions of men are without work. Millions of children are without a future. Save the German family! Vote for Adolf Hitler!"

represented the last stage of dying capitalism, actually cooperated with
the Nazis in a recall petition against the Social Democratic Prussian state
government in the spring of 1932 and in a Berlin transit strike in
November. They reserved their bitterest enmity for the Social Democrats, whom they called "social fascists" for being content to practice
politics as usual in times of crisis. Social Democrats, in fact, did just that.
Whereas they had thwarted the Kapp *Putsch* of 1920 with massive strike
movements, they made no similar effort against such flagrant illegalities
as Papen's expulsion of the Prussian state government in July 1932.

Hitler neither seized power nor was brought to power by some
inevitable working out of German history. He was given a temporary
prominence by large numbers of voters, brought into office by a
backstairs conspiracy, and, finally, acquiesced in by the majority of
average non-Nazi citizens.

Revolution After Power, 1933–39

What did it mean to have Adolf Hitler as chancellor of the German
Reich? The conservative politicians, senior officers, and high bureaucrats around Hindenburg thought they had at last escaped from
improvised presidential government by making use of Hitler's mass
following. Hitler, in turn, expected to make use of the office to
consolidate his still limited power. Hitler's interpretation proved correct.
If there was a Nazi revolution, it took place after he had become
chancellor, not before.

Hitler's first step was to heighten the impression that a communist
conspiracy was at work and that only the Nazis could deal with it
effectively. The burning of the *Reichstag* building in Berlin on February
23, 1933, provided the opportunity. It is no longer thought that the
Nazis hired the mentally retarded young Dutch Communist, Marinus
van der Lubbe, who set the fires.[12] The Nazis really believed that a
communist uprising was at hand. Much of the German public shared
that hysteria and raised no objection to the mass arrests and show trial of
Communist leaders that followed. A decree of Feburary 28 suspended
individual civil liberties (for good, as it turned out) "as a defensive
measure against Communist acts of violence."

Hitler's backers within the Establishment had hoped that he could
provide a way out from the electoral deadlock that had dogged German
politics since 1930. But even with all the resources of the state at their
command, as well as the calculated violence of the SA., Hitler's candidates could not obtain an absolute majority of the votes. In the elections
of March 5, 1933, the Nazis won 288 seats, just short of 44 percent of the

[12]Fritz Tobias, *The Reichstag Fire,* trans. Arnold J. Pomeranz (New York, 1963) argues that
van der Lubbe did in fact burn down the *Reichstag* building on his own, a conclusion
supported by the latest investigation, Hans Mommsen, "The Reichstag Fire and its Political
Consequences," in Hajo Holborn, ed., *Republic to Reich: The Making of the Nazi Revolution*
(New York, 1972).

*Hitler with the aging
President Hindenburg
at Hindenburg's country
estate, 1934.*

popular vote. The Catholic Center held firm, and the Social Democrats
and Communists shared almost a third of the popular vote. The
electoral route had still not given anyone an unquestioned mandate.

Hitler then proposed an enabling act empowering him as chancellor
to promulgate laws on his own authority for the next four years. The
Nazis, Hugenberg's Nationalists, and the Catholic Center party provided
the necessary two-thirds vote for this change in the constitution. Only
the Social Democrats, twelve of whose deputies were already in prison,
voted against the proposal; the Communist deputies were all in prison
already. That vote of 441 to 92, on March 23, 1933, freed Hitler from
the presidential countersignature as well as from the *Reichstag,* while in
the nation at large, the impression of impending communist revolution
freed Hitler from any genuine opposition from German moderates. The
stage was set for Hitler to grasp all the reins of power.

There followed a process that German historians call *Gleichschaltung,* a
useful word without an exact English equivalent that means "leveling" or
"bringing into line." Step by step, all public agencies and all entrenched
bodies that had formally enjoyed great autonomy in Germany—Army,

churches, bureaucratic corps—were brought into line over the following four years by a mixture of threat and reward.

Hitler never bothered to replace the Weimar Constitution with a Nazi charter. Nevertheless, he made decisive changes in German public order. Various parties were either outlawed (Communists, Socialists) or persuaded to dissolve (Center, Nationalists) until on July 14, 1933, the National Socialist party was declared the only legal party. The political autonomy of the federal states, which even Bismarck had not dared touch, was curtailed by appointing *Statthalters* to replace elected governments and by abolishing the German upper house or *Reichsrat,* which had represented the states. Thus Germany became a centralized rather than a federal state for the first time. Finally, with the death of President Hindenburg in August 1934, Hitler assumed that office and eliminated any possible rivalry from above.

Racial laws put Nazi anti-Semitism into effect. As early as April 1933, all "non-Aryan" members of the civil service were excluded from public office. The far-reaching Nuremberg Decrees of September 1935 deprived Jews of citizenship and forbade intermarriage with Aryans. Quotas were set in the professions. Following the assassination of a German diplomat in Paris by a Jew in November 1938, the Nazis took a number of harsh measures designed to force Jews to sell or abandon their property and emigrate. SA. men smashed 7500 Jewish store fronts throughout Germany during the night of November 9, the *Kristallnacht* (night of broken glass). In addition to being forbidden to collect any insurance on the damage, the German Jews were assessed a fine of 1 billion marks, and 20,000 of them were herded into concentration camps.

Hitler also tried to turn the churches into instruments of state policy. The Protestant churches, attended by many Hitler supporters and lacking any single center as a focus for opposition, were particularly susceptible to Nazi influence. The various state-supported Lutheran churches were united into a single German Evangelical Church under governmental authority; opposition leaders, such as Pastor Martin Niemöller, were imprisoned. The Catholic Church, unified and led from abroad, was less subject to Nazi control. But it was eager enough to safeguard the Catholic school system in Germany to sign a concordat with Germany in July 1933 forbidding priests to take part in politics and giving the Nazi regime a say in naming bishops.

The diplomatic corps and the Army were among the last German groups to be brought into line. When Foreign Minister Baron Konstantin von Neurath became sixty-five years old in February 1938, he was replaced by a party stalwart, Joachim von Ribbentrop, marking the party's intrusion into a corps traditionally reserved for career diplomats. At the same time leaders of the Army—General Werner von Blomberg (Minister of War) and General Werner von Fritsch (chief of staff)—were removed under spurious accusations of sexual irregularities.

Finally, as we have seen, the German economy was whipped into intense activity by public-works and rearmament projects managed by a highly organized corporatism.[13] Despite Nazi propaganda favoring peasants and craftsmen, Germany had more great industrial concerns and more crowded cities by 1939, and fewer small farmers and artisans, than in 1933.

This revolution after power was not the "second revolution" that some Nazi ideologues had hoped for at the beginning. Gottfried Feder had wanted to curb big business in favor of small business. Ernst Röhm had wanted to sweep away the old elites and replace them with new Nazi men; in particular, he wanted to replace the officer corps with a mass army based on his SA. Brown Shirts. Even as he brought German institutions into line with the party, however, Hitler also brought party mavericks into line with the real sources of power: big business, bureaucracy, and the Army. He did this by murder. During the chilling "night of the long knives," on June 30, 1934, hand-picked squads raided homes and apartments and took several hundred people off to their deaths: Röhm and much of the SA. leadership; Schleicher, who had tried to block the way in 1932; and the old-line Nazi, Gregor Strasser, who had wanted to accept a cabinet post from Schleicher. Thereafter, Hitler had no opposition within the party.

As for opposition from the general citizenry, it was effectively muted. Opposition still smacked of communism, and the penalties were severe. Above all, Hitler's mounting economic and strategic successes stilled criticism.

By 1939, Germany had been transformed from a pariah into the state most feared in Europe. But Hitler's *Gleichschaltung* had not really turned Germany into one well-oiled war machine. It is now known that the regime was kept running in many cases by carefully nurtured rivalries. The party encroached on the domain of professional civil servants; the Army resented Hitler's growing private armed force, the *Schutzstaffel,* or SS.; and so on. The capstone of *Gleichschaltung,* therefore, was the creation of an outward impression of monolithic efficiency through Joseph Goebbels' propaganda services and the efforts of an increasingly arbitrary police.

Clerical Authoritarianism

The antiliberal swing of the 1930s took on a special tone in Catholic Europe. It was no accident that only the Catholic Center party, among moderate constitutional parties of the Weimar Republic, retained its electorate during the polarizing elections of 1930 to 1933. European Catholics, who had for the most part never accepted the individualistic, anticlerical tenets of nineteenth-century liberalism, had their own forms of antiliberal politics to which Catholic electors remained loyal after 1929 as before.

[13]See Chapter 11, pp. 330–33.

In the late nineteenth century, the Catholic Church had struggled to defend itself against the effects of liberalism: the idea of separation of Church and state; the individualist notion that each man is master of his own conscience; the replacement of priests with laymen as schoolteachers when education became free, public, and compulsory. It was Republican France and the new constitutional monarchy of Italy that transgressed most actively in these regards: Italy had conquered Rome and the Papal States in 1870; France had made education both public and secular in the 1880s and had separated Church and state in 1905.

The mainstream of Catholic social and political thought, therefore, remained hostile to constitutional liberalism and individualism. Even Pope Leo XIII, who was finally willing to permit French and Italian Catholics to participate in republican electoral politics, supported a hierarchical, organic view of social rights and obligations in *Rerum Novarum* (1891), the Catholic Church's first formal pronouncement "on the condition of workers." In the ordered hierarchy of a good society, according to Leo XIII, each level enjoys rights and exercises duties commensurate with its station. Workers owe their employers respect and obedience; employers owe their workers respect and humane treatment. Some more radical Catholic social thinkers attacked capitalism itself for its callous disregard for workers. But they did not think private property should be abolished. It should be purified by a moral regeneration in which Christian employers would treat their employees as wards.

The depression encouraged the revival of Catholic criticisms of unbridled liberal capitalism. In his encyclical *Quadragesimo Anno* (1931),[14] Pope Pius XI outlined a model economic and social system in accord with "the natural law, or rather, God's will manifested by it." Property is legitimate, he argued, and "man is born to labor as the bird to fly." But capital had grasped "excessive advantages," leaving the workers a "bare minimum" under the "Liberalistic tenets of the so-called Manchester School." Worse still, free competition had produced "immense power and despotic economic domination . . . concentrated in the hands of a few." Capital and labor alike must be subordinated to the good of the whole community. Free competition must be limited, workers must receive a "just wage" sufficient to "overcome" the proletarian condition, and owners should receive a "just share only of the fruits of production."

The pope admitted that only the state could perform this work of social reconstruction. The best system, he thought, was corporatism. The state should grant virtual monopoly status to "Syndical or corporative organizations" that included representatives of workers and employers in the same trade or profession. These then would direct all matters of common interest; strikes and lockouts would be forbidden.

[14]The official English title reads, in part, "Encyclical letter . . . on Reconstructing the Social Order and Perfecting it Conformably to the Precepts of the Gospel." The opening Latin words *Quadragesimo anno* refer to the fortieth anniversary of Leo XIII's social encyclical *Rerum Novarum* (1891).

The advantages were "peaceful collaboration of the classes, repression of socialist organizations and efforts," and defense of "the peace and tranquility of human society . . . against the forces of revolution."

Followers of Pope Pius XI's socioeconomic views insisted on their distance from Hitlerian National Socialism. They rejected Nazism's atheism, its cult of action for its own sake, its frank acceptance of state power. They longed for an organic society in which "natural" groupings would run society in harmony and without great extremes of wealth and poverty. Like Nazism, however, they subordinated individuals to the good of the whole and pointed to socialism as the main enemy. They helped pave the way to acceptability for authoritarian regimes in Catholic countries.

fundamental contradiction — ? subordination of indivic. + protecting against repression, poverty etc., valuing respecting employer + employee

Portugal: Salazar

The Portuguese Republic had been swept away by a military coup in 1926, before the depression; it had lasted only sixteen years. Antonio Oliveira Salazar, the military junta's Finance Minister, emerged as the strong man of the regime in the 1930s. He was content to leave the presidency to generals, but as premier (1932–69) he actually ran Portugal in his own style.

Salazar was a Catholic Integralist.[15] As such, he considered the rights of individuals subordinate to the needs of the group, and longed for a hierarchical society in which each person knew his place and kept it. Commitment to stable order, deep philosophic doubt about the possibility of human progress, and piety marked Salazar's regime.

Salazar had abandoned theological seminary for the study of economics. As a student leader of young conservatives at the University of Coimbra he drew his values from Charles Maurras' *Action française* movement. He entered the government in 1928 when as Professor of Economics at the University of Coimbra he was called on to get the new military junta out of financial difficulties. Salazar was a strictly orthodox economist. A balanced budget was sacrosanct to him. He simply cut spending to fit income, paid off the national debt, and froze Portugal for twenty years in an almost immobile state of economic backwardness. In 1934 the total value of industrial production in Portugal was only one-fifth that of agriculture. It was not until the first Development Plan of 1953 to 1958 that Salazar actively promoted industrial development, with its concomitant need for outside capital and its risks of social disorder.

Politically, the New State (*Estado Nôvo*) sought the same immobilism. The Constitution of 1933 retained the nonparty Chamber together with the Chamber of Corporations, but no opposition candidates were permitted, and the premier was responsible only to the president. Strikes were forbidden; married women were not permitted to hold jobs. This regime kept Portugal politically somnolent until an opposition

---

[15]See Chapter 11, p. 333.

candidate ran for president in 1958. In 1959, Salazar abolished presidential elections.

In the 1930s, the regime took on some of the external trappings of fascism. An obligatory youth movement, the green-shirted *Mocidade Portuguêsa,* enrolled all youth from seven to fourteen. The paramilitary Portuguese Legion used the Roman salute. Tight censorship and strict police control restricted civil liberties in the name of order.

At root, however, Salazar's regime was more conservative than fascist. Salazar himself, an austere bachelor, shunned public appearances and did nothing to mobilize fervent masses. He quietly broke the National Syndicalist movement that attempted to found a more dogmatic fascist party in 1933 and 1934. Salazar chose immobility rather than adventure, safety rather than dynamism. In his quest for security, he even sacrificed economic growth for the preservation of Integralist Christian corporatist values and a stable society.

Christian Social Austria: Dollfuss and Schuschnigg

Post-Versailles Austria was a hydrocephalous monster. Its huge head, the former Habsburg Imperial capital of Vienna with its 2 million worldly inhabitants, was mismatched with the tiny body of the German parts of the former empire, some 4 million upper Austrians, mostly alpine farmers. The one solution longed for by almost every Austrian in 1919, union (*Anschluss*) with Germany, was forbidden by the Treaty of

General Oscar Carmona, Portuguese chief of state, and Premier Antonio Salazar, the real power of the regime, view a parade of the new Legiao Portuguêsa *in 1937.*

Saint Germain, Austria's part of the peace settlement. Economic activity within cramped new borders got underway only with the support of substantial Allied loans, which forced the Austrian state budget to stringent economies. Under such conditions, it is hardly surprising that parliamentary politics never worked in the infant Austrian Republic.

Austrian politics in the 1920s was a deadlock between two irreconcilable forces. A formidably solid Social Democratic party, fortified with its own armed paramilitary force (*Schutzbund*), governed Vienna. Less weakened by the Socialist–Communist split than most Western Marxist parties, the Austrian Social Democrats remained both large and intransigent during the 1920s under the leadership of the scholarly Otto Bauer. Austria's loose federal structure gave the party large powers in Vienna, where it created an elaborate social-welfare program including immense public housing projects like the 1500-family Karl-Marx-Hof. Arrayed on the anti-Marxist side was the Christian Social party, which united most of the Catholic population of the rest of Austria, fearful and hostile to "Red Vienna." It was led by an austere priest and professor of theology, Father Ignaz Seipel, who struck outside observers as a figure transplanted from the Counter-Reformation.[16] Also on the anti-Marxist side was another paramilitary force, the Home Guard (*Heimwehr*), a loose collection of local militias formed just after the First World War to fight against revolution and against possible incursions from neighboring successor states. Neither the Social Democrats nor the Christian Social party could capture more than about 45 percent of the votes, although Father Seipel managed to govern for most of the time between 1923 and 1927, with the aid of Protestant anti-Marxists and the Peasant party. At best, the two antagonistic blocs eyed each other sullenly. At worst, they fought it out. On the Black Friday of July 15, 1927, demonstrations got out of hand in Vienna: the Hall of Justice was burned, and eighty-seven persons were killed during uncontrolled police revenge.

This unpromising situation was seriously aggravated by two additional factors after 1930. The shaky Austrian economy was especially susceptible to the depression. As has been noted, the failure of the great Vienna bank, the *Credit-Anstalt,* unleashed the European banking crisis of the summer of 1931. Further, anti-Marxist activists were increasingly swallowed up in a burgeoning Nazi movement spreading from Bavaria. With the parliament deadlocked in an almost even split, some kind of authoritarian regime seemed inevitable. The issue became an international one in Austria, because no solution was possible without outside help. The Nazis sought help from Hitler; the Christian Social party turned to Mussolini.

The Christian Social dictatorship of Chancellor Engelbert Dollfuss (1933–34) combined a Catholic, corporatist authoritarianism at home with a foreign policy of independence from Germany supported by Italy. Dollfuss, whose small stature (4′11″) was more than compensated

[16]French wits called him "Autrichelieu" (The Austrian Richelieu).

for by his rashness, thought he could govern by "a single party, whose common bases will be the defense of Austrian independence and the corporative organization of the State."[17]

Dollfuss dissolved the deadlocked parliament in March 1933. Then he began to construct a new regime, which he claimed would be the first in the world based on the 1931 papal encyclical *Quadragesimo Anno.* Only a single party, the Fatherland Front, was allowed to function. Dollfuss reduced the independence of the Social Democratic city government of Vienna, and placed restrictions on socialist newspapers and organizations. The death penalty, abolished in 1919, was restored. The *Heimwehr* provided shock troops for the regime. The government was openly anti-Semitic. A concordat gave the Catholic Church the major role in public education. The new constitution, finally issued in May 1934, replaced "exaggerated parliamentarism" with a series of corporative councils, most of whose members were appointed.

The Social Democratic party found its activities more and more constricted. Finally, determined not to repeat the German Social Democrats' passivity in the face of Hitler, the Austrian left acted. After *Heimwehr* units had invaded a Social Democratic headquarters in Linz and seized some weapons, the Social Democrats decided to call out the *Schutzbund* in Vienna and begin a general strike. Dollfuss retaliated with military force, including an artillery shelling of the Karl-Marx-Hof apartment complex on February 12, 1934. That day 193 civilians were killed and 128 among the government forces. The Social Democratic newspapers and organizations were then outlawed.

Dollfuss insisted that his regime was not fascist. To guard against being swallowed up in an atheist, statist German dictatorship, the Christian Social regime even forbade Nazi party activities in Austria. In March 1934 Dollfuss negotiated an alliance with Mussolini and with Julius Gömbös, the authoritarian prime minister of Hungary, to aid him in this policy. When a Nazi band assassinated Dollfuss on July 25, 1934, and attempted to install a Nazi regime, Italian armed forces on maneuvers in the Alps gathered at the Brenner Pass while loyal *Heimwehr* units regained control for Dollfuss' associate, Kurt Schuschnigg. In many ways, Austria under Dollfuss and his successor Schuschnigg (1934–37) bore resemblances to Nazi Germany during the same period. Their sharpest difference was the Austrian regime's commitment to separate existence. The clerical authoritarian Austrians, aided by the Fascist Mussolini, thus administered a far more striking blow to Hitler in 1934 than did any of the liberal states at any time during the 1930s.

Spain: Franco and the Falange

The military revolt against the legal government of Republican Spain in 1936 and the subsequent three-year civil war are discussed in Chapter 13, on the Popular Front era. But this account of the European turn

[17]Quoted by French Minister to Austria Gabriel Puaux, September 15, 1933. *Documents diplomatiques français, 1932–39,* 1re série, Vol. 4, p. 367.

toward authoritarianism in the 1930s is not complete without a brief look at Franco's Spain.

The military dictatorship of General Francisco Franco (1939–) was the only interwar authoritarian regime to take power by military conquest. Franco and his followers invaded Spain from Spanish Morocco in July 1936. With the support of most of the professional Army and the acquiescence of conservatives and most of the clergy, they fought their way across Spain until the republican forces were finally defeated in 1939.

Unlike Hitler and Mussolini, therefore, Franco did not owe any of his power in Spain to a mass fascist movement. The *Falange,* a fascist-styled group founded by José Antonio Primo de Rivera, the son of the "dictator" of 1923 to 1930, contributed little to Franco's success and assumed only a marginal role in the new regime. Franco was a pragmatically conservative professional officer, bitterly opposed to the republic's anti-militarism, its incipient socialism, and the leeway it gave Catalan separatism. He prided order above dogmatic reaction. The new regime favored landlords, businessmen, and the clergy without being as dependent on any of them as they were dependent on it. Like Salazar, Franco chose immobilism rather than expansion and so survived the Second World War.

Fascism in Eastern Europe

Conditions were ripe for fascism in Eastern Europe in the 1930s. Ethnic antagonisms in each country remained virulent. Unsatisfied national minorities—Germans in the Polish Corridor and in the Czech Sudetenland, Slovaks in eastern Czechoslovakia, Croats in northwestern Yugoslavia—turned naturally to those arch enemies of the Versailles settlement, Hitler and Mussolini. Dominant national groups, threatened by internal secession movements, looked around for authoritarian routes to national unity.

Since Eastern Europe was heavily agricultural, the worldwide collapse of farm prices in the late 1920s drove government and citizens to bankruptcy. Bankers and merchants foreclosed on family farms. Because nowhere else in the world did Jews compose so high a proportion of bankers and merchants, anti-Semitism became a convenient shorthand for rural resentments against cities and against "the modern world." The land-hungry Eastern European peasants, attracted to Lenin a decade earlier, looked to new saviors after witnessing the results of Stalin's forcible land collectivization.

Eastern European parliamentary regimes offered no solution to these catastrophes. Their agrarian parties were composed of large and medium-sized landowners, and their liberal parties were based on urban professionals. Parliamentarism came to seem an alien implantation. Some Eastern Europeans rediscovered the charms of more or less fictitious "historic" traditions of authoritarian rule and ethnic purity.

All these encouragements to fascism were reinforced by a profound shift in Great Power positions in Eastern Europe in the 1930s. On every level—economic, military, and cultural—the French preeminence of the 1920s gave way to rising Italian and German influence. Successor states that had absorbed Russian soil in 1918 looked for stronger anti-Soviet bulwarks than the French Army, entrenched behind its Maginot Line. And the German economic boom after 1933 shifted the focus of Eastern European trade and finance from the sagging French economy.

Hungary and Bulgaria

It was only to be expected that the main losers of the Versailles settlement—Hungary and Bulgaria—would be drawn to the most vigorous anti-Versailles powers. Hungary, too, had experienced Bolshevik revolution in 1919; and among its bankers and merchants was an especially high proportion of Jews on whom rural resentment was focused. Admiral Miklós Horthy, who had guided the counterrevolutionary victory in Hungary in 1919, continued to rule as "regent" through the Second World War. The upper-class parliamentarism of the 1920s vanished, however, with the appointment of General Julius Gömbös—an admirer of Mussolini and Hitler—as an authoritarian prime minister (1932–36). He strengthened ties with Mussolini and established an alliance with Dollfuss. An overtly fascist movement, the Arrow Cross, advocated more violent solutions, but Hungary remained in the hands of the counterrevolutionary traditionalists when Gömbös died in 1936.

The same was true of Bulgaria. Under King Boris III there was virtual authoritarian rule after 1934, when the parliament was dispensed with altogether for several years. But Boris successfully blocked more radical right movements, such as IMRO, the Macedonian nationalist-terrorist organization.

Romania

A surprising development was the appearance of the most original, spectacular, and successful of the interwar fascist movements in Eastern Europe in a "victor" state, Romania. This was Corneliu Codreanu's Legion of the Archangel Michael and its strong-arm squad, the Iron Guard.

Even though Romania had been doubled in size and power by the Versailles settlement, that fact did not solve pressing internal problems. The nation was four-fifths peasant, suffering from vast rural overpopulation on tiny family plots. The merchant and professional classes were very largely Jewish; in Bucharest, anti-Semites claimed, 11,000 out of 14,000 employees of banks and commercial establishments were Jewish. Peasants in debt clearly thought of their creditors or of large landholding syndicates as Jewish. Romania's expansion had exposed the state to new perils, for it had acquired the mouth of the Danube (Bessarabia) from Russia, which had not recognized this cession. Hence, even though there was no internal Marxist threat (the Communist party was very small after the first years, and in 1937 socialists received only 0.8 percent of the vote), the external Marxist threat was very real. Finally, there was no effective political solution to any of these difficulties. When universal suffrage was first introduced in Romania in 1919, it was natural to assume that a peasant party would receive an automatic majority. In fact, the prewar elite managed to hold on through the Liberal party, which was in power for ten of the sixteen years after the First World War. And even when the Agrarian party spent some years in power, it could not solve Romania's problems. Meanwhile, the depression was beginning to affect farm prices. Romanians with grievances were forced to look outside the political system for redress.

Codreanu, son of a schoolteacher, managed to harness these discontents in an extraordinary movement. He began by organizing students, an alienated group without enough jobs to look forward to: their main demand was the imposition of quotas on Jewish admissions to the universities. The other main component was discontented, small family farmers, mostly in the poorest areas of northeastern Romania (Moldavia) where the middle class was almost exclusively Jewish and which earlier politicians had ignored. He welded these two groups together around religion, anti-Semitism, and hatred of cities and modern liberal society. Codreanu's legion was the most outwardly religious of all fascist movements: legionnaries, led by Orthodox clergy carrying ikons, were sent into remote villages with songs and costumes to win rural converts. Codreanu himself wore traditional Moldavian peasant dress.

The Iron Guard was a religious fraternity organized in cells (nests) whose members had sworn a blood oath to poverty, duty, and, if need be, murder on behalf of a purified Romania. Codreanu had begun his party activity with the assassination of a local police official. Political murder became virtually a way of life for the Iron Guard. Eleven public officials were killed by legionnaries in the 1930s.

Codreanu's party was no mere fringe movement. Its 16 percent of the popular vote in 1937 made it the third largest party behind the Liberals and Agrarians. Rather than continue with parliamentary government, however, King Carol II tried to beat the legion at its own game. In 1938 he suspended the constitution, imposed authoritarian rule, and jailed the legion's leaders. Codreanu and others were "killed while trying to escape," according to the official account.

The king's experiment failed, partly because Romania's problems in the 1930s were insoluble. A more immediate reason for failure was the country's vulnerability to a whole ring of neighbors (Russia, Bulgaria, Hungary) that had lost territory to Romania in the Versailles settlement of 1919. When Hitler and Stalin met in August 1939 to outline a new partition of Eastern Europe, there was no power to which Romania could turn to defend its swollen 1919 frontiers. A year later, after Hitler's defeat of Poland and France, the Russians demanded and received not only Bessarabia but other territories that had never been Russian. In September 1940, under German and Italian pressure, the Romanians had to give up much of Transylvania to Hungary and return to Bulgaria territories won in 1913. Altogether, Romania lost one-third of its territory. King Carol was forced to abdicate.

Codreanu's surviving colleagues in the Iron Guard finally came to power in September 1940. General Ion Antonescu, a professional officer with Iron Guard sympathies, ruled as "conducator" (the Romanian equivalent of *Führer*) with the aid of Horia Sima, Codreanu's successor as guard chief. The guard, pressing for a "second revolution," committed mass murders of Jews and imprisoned former political leaders. But since Hitler and Antonescu wanted order more than fervor at this point, the Iron Guard was crushed in three days of violent fighting in Bucharest in January 1941. Thereafter, Antonescu ruled as an outright military dictator without the ideological backing of fascist support.

The Iron Guard was the only fascist movement in Eastern Europe that actually ruled without direct German occupation, and its regime only lasted four months. Considering the virulence of Eastern European fascism, its relative failure may seem surprising. The social structure was partly to blame. In Eastern Europe, fascist movements drew on a massive distressed peasantry but only a rather small distressed middle class, and it was the older elites that remained in power. That is the chief reason for the fascists' relative lack of success. Even before 1929, Eastern European states had turned to authoritarian officers or revived monarchies. Thus, the work of "saving society" had already been performed by conservatives before the fascist revival of the 1930s. The Eastern European fascist movements appeared late on the scene, often as rivals or even enemies of more traditional authoritarian regimes. To the end, therefore, these fascist movements retained an anti-Establishment tone; scholars who have specialized in the study of Eastern European peasant fascism, such as as Eugen Weber, stress its revolutionary character. By and large, Eastern European fascisms remained sectarian minorities.

Fascist Minorities in Western Europe

Fascism also remained a minority movement in the deeply rooted constitutional regimes of Western Europe. Even there, however, it colored and influenced the more moderate center-right groups struggling to keep their supporters.

France

France had the most vigorous fascist minority in Western Europe. That was to be expected for a number of reasons. First, Frenchmen had become conscious as early as the 1890s of their country's decline from the greatest world power of the seventeenth century to the stagnant and sometimes unedifying Third Republic. Those who blamed the decline on bourgeois values and the rise of the left had already rallied to Charles

Maurras' *Action française* before the First World War.[18] The ambiguity of France's victory in 1918 contributed to the sense of decline. It had been possible only with powerful allies, and, even then, at a cost that could never be repeated without fatally weakening the French population. Second, the French middle class had suffered severely from inflation, and France was preeminently a nation of small, independent proprietors. Finally, in a country with a rich revolutionary tradition, the overwhelming commitment of French industrial workers to militant Marxism seemed a threat both to the wealthy and to many small, independent Frenchmen, nominally partisans of the "Great Revolution" of 1789. Under these conditions, movements that promised national revival, order, economic stability, and authority were endemic in French political life between the wars. They were relatively inconspicuous when things went well for the republic; when things went badly, they became a serious alternative.

Three developments transformed French fascism from a fringe movement to a serious mass movement in the 1930s. The republic proved totally incapable of dealing with the depression, and Germany slipped out from under the Versailles chains to become an even greater menace than in 1914. Veterans who charged that the republic had lost in useless palaver what the soldiers had won in the trenches joined their rage with that of the unemployed and those whose salaries or pensions had been cut by classical depression remedies.[19] Finally, the inclusion of Communists with the more moderate left in a new Popular Front electoral alliance in 1936, coupled with the spontaneous sit-down strike that accompanied the Popular Front's electoral victory, sent a wave of fear through French conservatives.

The largest of the new movements, claiming nearly 1 million members, was the *Croix de feu*,[20] headed by a retired colonel with monarchist connections, François de la Rocque. Much smaller but more outspokenly profascist was the *Parti populaire français* of Jacques Doriot, former leader of the French Communist youth movement. When Doriot was expelled from the Communist party in 1934 for premature espousal of a Popular Front strategy, he ricocheted across the political spectrum. A magnetic personality, Doriot was so deeply entrenched as mayor of the working-class Paris suburb of Saint-Denis that he brought that following over with him into anti-communist authoritarian nationalism, which also attracted ardent middle-class reactionaries disillusioned with the rather lackluster de la Rocque. Another French fascist movement derived from the French left grew out of a youthful revolt against the financial orthodoxy of the French Socialist party (SFIO). Marcel Déat and other reformist socialists broke with the SFIO in 1932 over their desire to

[18]See Chapter 1, p. 38.
[19]See Chapter 10, pp. 323–25.
[20]The name comes from its origins as a veterans' movement restricted to soldiers who had won the *Croix de guerre* under fire; that is, front-line veterans. It has nothing to do with the "fiery cross" of the Ku Klux Klan.

participate in a bourgeois government. Déat then went on to preach a nationalist rather than internationalist socialist solution to the depression in his neo-socialist movement. In addition, there emerged a number of anti-Semitic groups and right-wing action squads, such as the blue-shirted *Solidarité française* financed by the perfume manufacturer François Coty. All these movements called themselves leagues, to distinguish themselves clearly from "corrupt" electoral parties.

The climax of French fascism between the wars came the night of February 6, 1934, when a number of right-wing leagues combined in a massive demonstration against the Chamber of Deputies. The immediate pretext was a moral crusade against the part played by some of the deputies in the Stavisky Affair, a case involving cover-up of fraud by a promoter, Alexander Stavisky. But behind that crusade lay the pent-up exasperation of veterans, nationalists, sufferers in the depression, and all those who associated France's troubles in the 1930s with inadequate public authority. Premier Edouard Daladier called out armed police to keep the crowd out of the parliament buildings, and in the ensuing fight thousands were injured and twelve persons were killed, the bloodiest internal conflict in France between the mutinies of May 1917 and the liberation of 1944. Daladier resigned the next day, even though he still had a majority of votes in parliament. A former president of the republic, Gaston Doumergue, put together a nonparty cabinet of national unity, ranging from Radicals on the left to the parliamentary right and including such extraparliamentary figures as Marshal Pétain as Minister of War. Thus the fascist leagues had been able to shift the government from the moderate left to a nonparty emergency regime.

In the long run, however, French fascists were unable to gain power by their own devices. Although their tone became much more shrill after the left electoral successes of May 1936 and the subsequent strike wave, they were clearly on the defensive and unable (or unwilling) to take action when the Popular Front government outlawed all direct-action leagues in June 1936. Since the scheduled elections of 1940 were overtaken by the war, it is impossible to give any precise measure of the electoral support for the legal parties that de la Rocque and Doriot created after suppression of their leagues. All that can be said is that the French fascist critique of the Third Republic's inefficacy and decadence helped sweep away the republic and all its works after the defeat of June 1940, and it strongly colored the French regime that replaced the republic after the armistice.

Why did French fascism remain a minority movement in the 1930s? Nationalists were too traditionally anti-German to copy German models for French revival. And France had, after all, been nominally victorious in the First World War and therefore less disastrously affected by subsequent economic disasters than Germany. French grandeur continued to be associated with the revolutionary traditions of 1789, rather than with the conservative opposition to them. Finally, the division of the

French fascist movements and the absence of any one exceptional leader made coordinated efforts difficult. The riots of February 6, 1934, helped arouse the old cry of republican defense more fully than any event since the Dreyfus Affair, and the French fascist leagues never achieved another such peak of activity until the German occupation in June 1940.

Britain

The only significant fascist movement in interwar Britain grew out of the frustrations of the depression, which hit Britain more disastrously than any other nation except Germany and the United States. While unemployment was reaching 20 percent of the labor force, no party had any convincing solution to offer.

The Labour government's rejection of Sir Oswald Mosley's bold and original plans for stimulating purchasing power[21] in 1930 convinced Mosley that the Labour party was a bunch of worthless weaklings, "a Salvation Army that took to its heels on the day of Judgment." He endeavored to transcend the existing party deadlock by founding the New party in March 1931, but this effort only convinced him that any parliamentary combination was a hopeless instrument for radical change. The New party won no seats in the election of September 1931, and its original recruits of young Labour leftists (John Strachey, Aneurin Bevan) soon quit in protest over Mosley's hiring of strong-arm squads to protect him from hostile Labourites and his anti-Soviet attitude.

In October 1932, Mosley founded the British Union of Fascists (BUF). His starting point, as always, was a bold and decisive remedy for unemployment. That led him to other far-reaching proposals. A "living wage policy" was impossible, of course, with the "old gang of present parliamentarism," left and right. Mosley proposed a "modern" regime "capable of rising to new tasks,"[22] in which a Chamber of Corporations would manage the economy, and a parliament, composed of representatives of various economic interests, would have only consultative powers. The king would name the prime minister after consultation with a National Council of Fascists; the prime minister's work would be ratified by plebiscites every five years. Mosley turned current economic priorities upside down, giving domestic measures against unemployment precedence over concern for international financial stability. Hence he attacked "international finance capital" and talked of nationalizing the banks. Although he opposed the international capitalists of London, he based his hopes for British economic revival on "national" capitalism, which, he insisted, had common interests with the workingman. Both would benefit by Britain's turning its back on Europe and developing the empire under a system of imperial preference. With this last proposal, Mosley resembled the proempire right of prewar days. But his political

---

[21]See Chapter 11, p. 322.
[22]Oswald Mosley, *Greater Britain* (London, 1932), pp. 16. 156.

techniques had not been seen in Britain before. BUF mass meetings were marked by black-shirted guards and floodlit black flags. Mosley insisted on the "dynamic" and "modern" character of fascism.

The high point of Mosley's popularity came in 1934, when the *Daily Mail* published an editorial headlined, "Hurrah for the Blackshirts!"[23] Party membership was estimated to reach 20,000. Mosley's only genuine mass following, however, emerged in the proletarian East End of London, where he struck a responsive chord with his contempt for parliamentary Labour and, later, with his anti-Semitism. His Black Shirts switched from beating up Labour party members to beating up unassimilated Eastern European Jews who had settled in the East End of London before the war.

These tactics produced widespread revulsion in England, and in 1936 the Tory government outlawed uniformed groups and tightened police measures against parades and rallies. But the BUF's decline after 1934 stemmed from more fundamental causes. Tory electoral victories in 1931 and 1935 reassured most British conservatives that Stanley Bald-

[23] *Daily Mail,* January 8, 1934.

Sir Oswald Mosley inspects a British Union of Fascists unit in London, October 1936.

win was safeguard enough, as did the quite undeserved revival of prosperity that Britain enjoyed under Baldwin. Britain had not suffered military defeat, and parliamentary government was closely associated with British images of national greatness. Mosley's BUF had been founded before Hitler came to power, and growing anti-German sentiment lessened his appeal to the British middle class. After 1936, Mosley, a declining star at the age of thirty-eight, was reduced to Jew-baiting in the East End of London, a scurrilous end for a man of his brilliant but wayward talents. In the end, the far right was less successful in interwar Britain than it had been in a previous crisis, the battle over Irish Home Rule from 1910 to 1914.

British fascism is an interesting phenomenon, not only because of Mosley's stature (he was one of few European fascist leaders who achieved eminence before becoming fascist) but also because its original motive force was economic crisis rather than cultural despair or military defeat. Above all, British fascism revealed the vigor of reaction against liberal parliamentarism and free-trade capitalism in the 1930s, even in their homeland. Although the overtly fascist BUF became a marginal sect, the traditional parties were also subtly drawn away from liberal values. They accepted the necessity of protective tariffs, state-regulated business cartels, and other types of public economic management that had still been anathema ten years earlier.

The Low Countries and Scandinavia

Flemish resentment against the French-speaking Walloons' dominance of binational Belgium was by far the most active unresolved nationality issue in Continental Western Europe between the wars. It was only natural that Flemish nationalists, for whom the established Belgian parties (Catholic, Liberal, Socialist) offered no redress, should turn in the 1930s to antiparliamentary mass movements with fascist trappings. Various Flemish movements united to form the *Vlaamsch Nationaal Verbond* (Flemish National Union) in 1933, led by a former schoolmaster, Staf de Clercq, and supported in part by German money. The VNV had a genuine mass following in rural Flemish districts; it received 13 percent of the vote in the four northern provinces in 1936 and 15 percent in 1939. Its main rival was the fervent uniformed squad of young men known as *Verdinasos* or *Dinasos* (a contraction of *Verbond van Dietsche Nationaalsolidaristen,* Band of Dutch-speaking National Solidarists) led by a young lawyer, Joris Van Severen, with special appeal to veterans and students. Van Severen advocated the reunion of all Flemish (Dutch) peoples in modern Holland, Belgium, and Luxemburg in an expanded Netherlands as powerful as that of the seventeenth century.

The most successful antiparliamentary mass movement in the Low Countries—indeed, perhaps the biggest for a brief time in all Western Europe—was not based on nationalist resentments, however, Léon

Degrelle's Rexist movement in Belgium tapped a protean ground swell of disgust with parliamentary politics in 1935 and 1936 and seemed capable, for a moment, of replacing the old parties with one new mass party. Degrelle emerged as a militant in the Belgian Catholic Youth Movement; he was in charge of its publishing house, called "Rex" (after *Christus Rex,* Christ the King). In November 1935, at the age of twenty-nine, he launched a campaign to displace the stuffy leadership of the Catholic party, as well as of the Liberal and Socialist parties. Promising to sweep clean with a "new broom," Degrelle unleashed a kind of emotional binge against slack and corrupt parliamentarism. His followers demonstrated with brooms in front of party headquarters, and they packed political rallies shouting "Rex vaincra" (Rex will win).

The movement mobilized crowds in a way unknown to staid Belgian parliamentary politics. Its Catholic, monarchist, corporative authoritarianism owed much to Degrelle's former idol, Charles Maurras. His followers were the young, the previously apolitical, and a host of rural and small-town folk easily aroused against "high finance," corrupt cities, and Marxism ("Rex or Moscow" was a leading slogan). Although the depression was passing, its ravages were clearly a factor in Rexist popularity. Mussolini sent secret funds to the Rexists and allowed Degrelle to use Italian radio beamed to Belgium.

The elections of May 1936 gave Rexist candidates 11.5 percent of the total vote (21 out of 202 seats). Votes ran as high as 29 percent in rural French-speaking districts, but Degrelle also had some following in the Flemish districts of northern Belgium. The showdown came in a parliamentary by-election in early 1937 in which Degrelle himself was a candidate. He proclaimed that if he won his seat, a general election would then have to be called. The existing parties united around Prime Minister Paul Van Zeeland as the opposition candidate. After the Catholic primate of Belgium condemned Rexism as a "danger for the country and for the Church," Degrelle was held to 20 percent of the vote against Van Zeeland's 80 percent. This broke the spell, for a movement whose main asset was the promise of a victorious new style of politics could not survive any interruption of its climb. Brief as its heyday was, however, Rexism revealed how deep was the inarticulate frustration with parliamentary regimes in postdepression Western Europe.

In Protestant Holland, fascism was a more secular affair than Degrelle's Catholic Integralism, but there were common themes of authority, anti-Marxism, national regeneration, and the "new man." The immediate spur to Dutch fascism was a naval mutiny aboard the warship *Seven Provinces* in Dutch Indonesia in 1931. Profiting by this shock to the social and imperial order, a waterworks engineer, Anton Adriaan Mussert, founded the National-Socialist League (NSB). Mussert received almost 8 percent of the vote in elections of April 1935, with the proportion reaching 20 percent in Protestant small-farming areas in the southwest. The NSB was then the fifth largest party in Holland. The stability of Dutch parliamentary monarchy, recovery from the depression, and growing fears of Nazi Germany hurt Mussert's movement, and in spite of the slogan "Mussert or Moscow" his electoral toll dropped in 1937.

Even relatively stable Scandinavia had its fascist movements, although there, too, they remained noisy minorities. The most conspicuous of these was the Norwegian movement of Vidkun Quisling, whose last name became a synonym for collaboration after the German occupation of Norway in 1940. Quisling was a professional army officer (like Franco, Mosley, and the Hungarian Julius Gömbös). As Norwegian military attaché to St. Petersburg, he had actually witnessed the Bolshevik Revolution and its aftermath, when he participated in international food relief in the Crimea. After entering Norwegian politics in the Agrarian party, Quisling became Defense Minister in 1931, a position that he lost in a controversy surrounding his use of troops against strikers. Quisling then founded the *Nasjonal Samling* (National League) in May 1933. His following remained small, for Norway had no sensitive nationality problem, and Quisling's efforts to generate excitement over recovering Greenland and Iceland from Denmark remained fruitless. Furthermore, even though the Norwegian Socialists had been the only Scandinavian Socialist party to join the Third International in 1919, the Norwegian left posed no revolutionary threat in the 1930s. The special stamp of Quisling's fascism, beyond a vague anti-Marxism and ritual attacks on "Anglo-Jewish finance capital," was the leader's taste for evoking ancient Norse grandeur and Nordic racial solidarity. The movement was important mainly for assembling those elements on which wartime collaboration after 1940 could be built.

The Appeal of Fascism

At the very onset of the depression, before Hitler came to power, the Scottish writer and diplomat John Buchan looked back gloomily at the decline of parliamentary institutions and the breakdown of creeds in the twentieth century: "But for the bold experiment of Fascism, the decade has not been fruitful of constructive statesmanship."[24] During the 1930s, similar doubts expressed about the European liberal tradition swelled to a roar.

Fascism caught up the refugees from a liberal system that no longer appeared to work. Liberalism seemed to provide neither a living nor security. Some of these ideological refugees could turn to Marxism, but that step required one to identify with the proletariat and to accept the Soviet Union as a model. Thus, Marxism's growth in the 1930s had inherent limits. Fascism offered something to every kind of discontent; indeed, its very denial of class was one of its major assets. To the threatened elites, the authority of fascism offered an immediate end to class struggles and a managed economy without ruinous competition. To a desperate lower middle class, fascism offered security and a chance

[24]John Buchan, *The King's Grace* (London, 1929).

to bring organized labor to heel. To embittered nationalists, it offered national unity and glory. To the jobless, it offered jobs.

It will not do, of course, to assess fascism's appeal solely in terms of economic and social interest. In ways still only partly understood, fascism offered all sorts of individual psychological gratifications: for some, the reassurance of belonging; for some, the thrill of vicarious brutality.[25] Most people, no doubt, merely acquiesced.

At bottom, the authoritarian regimes seemed simply to work better than liberal regimes in the 1930s. The appeals of success were, of course, completely discredited by fascism's military defeats in 1945. The outer trappings of fascism have therefore fallen into disrepute. That does not preclude the possibility, however, of similar future reactions by a frightened and insecure middle class.

[25]See "L'enfance d'un chef," Jean-Paul Sartre's short story of a self-doubting adolescent boy who enjoys the tough pose of a fascist youth gang. Jean-Paul Sartre, *Le Mur* (Paris, 1939), pp. 145–241.

Suggestions for Further Reading

Most of the works on Hitler and National Socialism cited at the end of Chapter 7 are also essential for the Nazi seizure of power.

Excellent articles on the collapse of Weimar and the Nazi ascent to power have been collected in Henry Ashby Turner, ed., *Nazism and the Third Reich** (1973); Fritz Stern, ed., *The Path to Dictatorship** (1967); Anthony Nicholls and Erich Matthias, eds., *East German Democracy and the Triumph of Hitler** (1972); and Hajo Holborn, ed., *Republic to Reich** (1972).

Two illuminating local studies of the Nazi assumption of power are William Sheridan Allen, *The Nazi Seizure of Power: The Experience of a Single German Town** (1965), and Rudolf Heberle's study of Schleswig-Holstein, *From Democracy to Nazism** (1945; reprint ed.,1970).

David Schoenbaum, *Hitler's Social Revolution** (1967) argues that Nazi policies favored urbanization and industrial concentration at the expense of the lower middle classes, which had afforded the most fervent party following. Arthur Schweitzer, *Big Business in the Third Reich* (1964), and T. W. Mason, "Labour in the Third Reich, 1933–1939," *Past and Present,* No. 33 (April 1966) are best on their respective subjects. Richard Grunberger, *The Twelve-Year Reich: A Social History of Nazi Germany** (1971) is more anecdotal.

Nazi–Army relations are dealt with in John W. Wheeler-Bennett, *Nemesis of Power: The German Army in Politics, 1918-1945,** 2nd ed. (1964), and in relevant portions of Gordon A. Craig, *The Politics of the Prussian Army, 1640–1945** (1964). For Nazi efforts to bring professional diplomats into line, see Paul Seabury, *The Wilhelmstrasse: A Study of German Diplomats Under the Nazi Regime* (1954).

John S. Conway, *The Nazi Persecution of the Churches* (1968), and Guenter Lewy, *The Catholic Church and Nazi Germany* (1964) are the most satisfactory of many works on the churches under Nazism.

The most thorough analysis of arbitrary police powers under Nazism is Helmut Krausnick *et al.*, *Anatomy of the SS State* (1968), a series of reports compiled for the trial of the Auschwitz concentration camp staff. See also the more popularized Heinz Höhne, *The Order of the Death's Head** (1970). Eugen Kogon, *The Theory and Practice of Hell** (1950) is a survivor's reflection upon the camps.

Karl A. Schleunes, *The Twisted Road to Auschwitz* (1970) shows that Nazi racial policies developed gradually and by improvisation. Hannah Arendt, *Eichmann in Jerusalem: A Report on the Banality of Evil** (1963) is the most vivid evocation of the workings of the final solution. See also Gerald Reitlinger, *The Final Solution*, 2nd ed. (1968), and Raul Hilberg, *The Destruction of the European Jews,** rev. ed. (1967).

The works cited at the end of Chapter 7 are most useful also for Italy in the 1930s.

J. W. D. Trythall, *El Caudillo* (1970) is the most balanced of several biographies of Franco, with the fullest discussion of recent years. Stanley Payne, *The Falange** (1961) makes clear how little influence the party exerted in the new regime.

The best starting point for fascism elsewhere is the chapters on individual states in Hans Rogger and Eugen Weber, eds., *The European Right** (1966), and in Stuart J. Woolf, ed., *European Fascism** (1968). In particular, the article on Portugal by H. Martins in the Woolf volume is the most lucid assessment of the Salazar regime in print. One may also refer to the general history of Portugal cited at the end of Chapter 1; to James E. Duffy, *Portugal in Africa** (1963); and to the most usable of the biographies, Hugh Kay, *Salazar and Modern Portugal* (1970).

On Austrian clerical authoritarianism, in addition to the works of Klemperer and Gulick cited at the end of Chapter 9, see Alfred H. Diamant, *Austrian Catholics and the First Republic* (1960).

The general works on Eastern Europe cited at the end of Chapter 9 all discuss fascist movements there. Nicholas M. Nagy-Talavera, *The Greenshirts and the Others: A History of Fascism in Hungary and Rumania*

(1970) is a vividly detailed study. See also the articles in Peter F. Sugar, ed., *Native Fascism in the Successor States* (1971). Eugen Weber, "The Men of the Archangel," in Walter Laqueur and George Mosse, eds., *International Fascism, 1920–1945** (1966) is a revealing study of where Romanian fascists recruited their rank and file following.

René Rémond, *The Right Wing in France*, 2nd ed. (1969) argues that French conservatives left no room for a true fascism to develop in France. The most perceptive short treatment is Robert Soucy, "The Nature of Fascism in France," in Laqueur and Mosse.

Sir Oswald Mosley is most clearly understood in the article by Robert Skidelsky in the Woolf volume cited above. Colin Cross, *The Fascists in Britain* (1961) provides an inside view by a postwar sympathizer.

A good brief account of Dutch fascism is Lawrence D. Stokes, "Anton Mussert and the NSB, 1931–1945," *History*, Vol. 56, No. 188 (October 1971). For Vidkun Quisling, see Paul M. Hayes, *Quisling: The Career and Political Ideas of Vidkun Quisling* (1972). Ralph Hewins, *Quisling: Prophet Without Honor* (1965) takes Quisling's frictions with Hitler as proof of patriotism. For fascism elsewhere in Scandinavia and the Low Countries, see the appropriate articles in Woolf and in Rogger and Weber.

Alistair Hamilton, *The Appeal of Fascism: A Study of The Intellectuals and Fascism* (1968) surveys many literary and artistic figures drawn to fascism between the wars. George Mosse is more analytical in "The Intellectuals and Fascism," in Laqueur and Mosse.

THE EUROPEAN LEFT IN THE POPULAR FRONT ERA, 1934–1939

13

In 1933, Daniel Guérin, a young French left intellectual, toured Germany by bicycle gathering material for articles in the French socialist newspaper, *Le populaire.* He reported what he saw in a mood of mingled fear and awe:

> By bicycle, across Germany, I pedaled as though through a ruined city, and I drew up the bleak inventory. The worker colossus, Social Democracy, Communist Party, unions with millions of members, collapsed or were swept away like a house of cards. Their banners, newspapers, posters, and books burned on bonfires in the town squares. Their members peopled concentration camps. Their sumptuous headquarters flew the swastika. I was present at a twilight of the gods.[1]

[1]Daniel Guérin, *Front populaire: révolution manquée,* 2nd ed. (Paris, 1970), p. 57.

After the destruction of socialism in Italy, Germany, and Austria, where would the fascists strike next? Would the democracies of Europe and European socialist parties and trade unions be picked off one by one by fascism's apparently inexorable advance? Did fascism's opponents hate each other more than they feared fascism? The anxious search for answers to these questions produced the Popular Front of the 1930s.

The Popular Front was an alliance of Marxists and democrats against a common fascist enemy. It rested on two fundamental assumptions: that fascism was so urgent a threat that impeding its advance took precedence over everything else; and that the best means of blocking fascism was a broad coalition around the defense of political liberties rather than a narrow coalition around revolutionary goals—that is, numbers counted more than unanimity on goals. In order to agree on those assumptions, the diverse elements of the European left had to make major changes in outlook and strategy. Marxists had to subordinate their social program to the defense of middle-class democracies; democrats had to suspend their distrust of Marxists. Within the Marxist camp, Social Democrats and Communists had to forget fifteen years of bitter recriminations over blame for the failure of Western revolutions from 1917 to 1920. No wonder such an alliance was awkward, slow, and difficult to achieve.

A Popular Front had been unthinkable in the 1920s, when the possibility of social revolution had been the uppermost issue for the European left. It became unthinkable again later during the Cold War. The Popular Front was possible only in the 1930s and the resistance years during the Second World War, for it was a child of the depression and of the fears aroused by the conquests of Hitler and Mussolini. Even then, Popular Front coalitions were successfully formed only here and there in nonfascist Europe: in France, Spain, and among German and Italian exiles.

For the participants, the Popular Front was an experience of fervent commitment: "the 1848 of the 20th century."[2] It meant the reconciliation of the left, divided since 1917. It meant a possible turn of the tide against fascism, and a chance to do something other than wring hands as Hitler and Mussolini advanced. For committed revolutionaries, however, the Popular Front meant selling out to another flabby political alliance. For conservatives and many frightened democrats, the Popular Front meant opening the doors of Western Europe to communism. Those controversies lay at the center of public life and intellectual activity in the liberal regimes of the 1930s. They gave that decade much of its character of passionate engagement in a struggle to determine whether democrats, Marxists, or fascists would control the world.

[2]Stephen Spender, *World Within World* (London, 1951), p. 187.

The Popular Front was a grass-roots enthusiasm before the organized parties worked their way around to accepting it. Its first signs appeared in France in February 1934. During the night of February 6, the powerful antiparliamentary leagues fought with police in what looked then like an attempt to overthrow the French Republic. That night, French Communists also demonstrated against the bourgeois republic—separately but in parallel fashion. A significant shift took place during the next few days, however. Paris sections of the Communist party agreed to take part—although still separately—in a great parade against fascism organized by noncommunist trade unions and the main parties of the parliamentary left, Socialists and Radicals (middle-class democrats). As the two columns turned together into a broad avenue in the Paris suburb of Vincennes, they fused, with shouts of "Unity! Unity!" At the head of what now became a single column, the Communist leader

From "Class Against Class" to Popular Front

A street scene in Paris during the right-wing demonstrations of February 6, 1934.

Maurice Thorez linked arms with the Socialist leader Léon Blum and the recently deposed Radical premier, Edouard Daladier. Hundreds of thousands of Parisians remembered that day of February 12 as one of reconciliation and a new beginning for the French Republic.

But there remained a period of difficult transition before the Communist, Socialist, and democratic party leaders of France and the rest of nonfascist Europe could overcome years of mutual animosity.

The Communist Policy of "Class Against Class", 1928–34

Communist parties had to make the largest leap to accept a Popular Front coalition, for they had been ordered at the Sixth Comintern Congress (1928) into a position of hardened intransigence against reformist socialists. Like most of Stalin's major decisions, this one remains wrapped in some obscurity. It was probably partly a reaction to foreign disappointments. During the period of liberal and capitalist stabilization after 1924, the dwindling Communist parties of the world had accepted some degree of cooperation with the reformist left in Western Europe and with nationalist movements in the Third World. This tactic had not been very fruitful. In Britain, for example, Communist support for the General Strike of 1926 had done nothing to improve the party's marginal position there. It had only helped prod the Conservatives into breaking diplomatic and trade relations with the Soviet Union in 1927. Far more damaging was the fiasco of cooperation with the nationalist Kuomintang party in its attacks on Western capitalist concessions in China. Stalin was deeply shaken when nationalist General Chiang Kai-shek turned on the Chinese Communists and their Russian advisors in April 1927 and massacred a large number of them, driving the rest into the interior.

Stalin's decision also conformed to the sharp left turn of Russian internal policy. It was illogical to permit Communists abroad to accommodate themselves to capitalist stabilization at a time when the Russian population was straining to carry out a "second revolution" of collectivization and industrialization.[3] Some of Stalin's critics have accused him of forcing foreign Communists into the same "ultraleftism" out of "meaningless mimicry,"[4] without regard for local parties' tactical needs. It seems likely that Stalin knew little about foreign Communist parties and cared only for their perfect conformity to Russian requirements.

Comintern intransigence reflected Stalin's assertion in December 1927 that capitalism was entering a "third period,"[5] a time of sharpened contradictions and intensified disorder. The world depression of 1929 added plausibility to the view that the overthrow of capitalism was once more possible. In that case, workers must not be sidetracked into the

[3]See Chapter 11, pp. 335–39.
[4]Isaac Deutscher, *Stalin: A Political Biography,* 2nd ed. (New York, 1967), p. 404. This compelling biography is strongly colored by sympathy for Trotsky.
[5]The revolutionary years of 1917 to 1923 were alleged to form a "first period," followed by a "second period" of capitalist stabilization in the mid-1920s.

defense of democracy. According to the Comintern view, democracy and fascism were merely different forms of a single reality, bourgeois governments devoted to the defense of property and the rescue of capitalism. Indeed, the Western democracies were singled out as Soviet Russia's most dangerous enemies. Italy was still the only example of a fascist state. Britain and France had been the creators of the Versailles system, the promoters of armed intervention in Russia in 1919 and 1920, and the chief bulwark of capitalist stabilization. There is some evidence that Stalin feared renewed military intervention by Britain and France in the late 1920s.

In the Comintern perspective, the proper course for workers in the "third period" was heightened class struggle, aligning all workers against all members of the middle class, whether democrats or fascists, in an attitude of "class against class." Stalin viewed the efforts of Western European Social Democrats to defend democracy as treason to the workers' cause. Social Democrats, he claimed, were propping up capitalism and lulling workers into nonrevolutionary stances in a revolutionary time. "Objectively," Stalin had written in 1924, "Social Democracy is the moderate wing of fascism. . . . They are not antipodes but twins."[6] It was a position to which he returned after 1928. Social Democrats and reformist trade unions were the principal support of bourgeois democracy and the principal obstacle to the overthrow of capitalism. They must be destroyed.

In the French elections of 1928, for example, Communists competed with Socialists for established Socialist seats. The Communist leader Jacques Duclos defeated Socialist leader Léon Blum for the Paris seat Blum had held since 1920. French Socialists could complain that "class against class" cost them twenty-two seats (including the seat of Karl Marx's grandson Jean Longuet) in cases in which a Socialist had been leading in the first ballot only to have a Communist remain in the run-off and throw the election to a united right-wing candidacy.[7] The French Communist poet Louis Aragon gave the clearest literary expression of "class against class" politics in his poem *Red Front* (1931):

> Fire on Léon Blum . . .
> Fire on the trained bears of social democracy[8]

In Germany, Hitler's ascent was but one more confirmation for Stalin that capitalism was grasping for desperate remedies. The correct policy for German Communists, from Stalin's point of view in 1932 and 1933, was to heighten the tension, help widen political polarization, attack Social Democrats as "social fascists," and count on the next swing of the pendulum to bring revolution. That analysis was not shaken by Hitler's success in taking power in 1933, for Communists could believe that the

[6]Deutscher, pp. 406–07.
[7]Georges Lefranc, *Le Mouvement socialiste sous la IIIe République* (Paris, 1963), p. 275.
[8]Louis Aragon, "Red Front," in Maurice Nadeau, *History of Surrealism*, trans. Richard Howard (New York, 1965), p. 288.

pendulum would swing again. Stalin was not totally wrong. Communism did succeed Nazism in at least part of Germany, but Stalin had not expected that process to take twelve painful years and a world war.

Germany was important to Russian national interests, whoever its leader. Since the Treaty of Rapallo in 1922, a revisionist Germany had been Russia's natural ally against the Versailles victors. Therefore Stalin did not renounce the Russo-German pact of neutrality and friendship of 1926 when Hitler came to power. Indeed, he renewed it in May 1933, and so became the first ruler to conclude a diplomatic agreement with Hitler. The secret training and arms production in Russia for the German Army continued through 1934. Behind a smoke screen of hostile rhetoric, the two states maintained practical working relations. As late as the Seventeenth Communist Party Congress in January 1934, Stalin was still stating publicly that "fascism is not the issue," that the Soviet Union enjoyed the "best relations" with Italy, and that the Soviet Union was still an opponent of the Versailles settlement. Dimitri Manuilski, the party secretary-general, told the conference that "the destruction of Social Democracy is one of the most essential conditions for hastening the growth of the revolutionary crisis."[9]

Reversal of Comintern Policy, 1934

The change came some time in the late spring of 1934. For several months there had been straws in the wind. Soviet diplomats expressed great concern to Western diplomats in late 1933 about Japanese expansion in Manchuria, a sign that Stalin was beginning to worry about a two-front war. In late 1933 and early 1934 the Soviet government made inquiries about French technical assistance to the Soviet Air Force, and in early 1934 about possible Soviet membership in the League of Nations. By June 1934, a united front with democrats had become the official policy of the French Communist party, obviously with official approval from Moscow.

Stalin's reassessment was a sweeping one. He renounced revolution as a real possibility in the rest of Europe. Defense of the Soviet state took precedence over class warfare abroad, and the chief threat to the Soviet state was clearly a resurgent Germany. The democracies, in this changed perspective, became the most promising military allies in case of war with Germany. The democracies' crisis was no longer something to foster, and the Social Democrats or reformist Socialists were no longer "social fascists." Stalin's aim was now to seek the widest possible alliance against Germany, on pragmatic military grounds.

In September 1934, the Soviet Union joined the League of Nations. Later in 1934, the Soviet foreign minister, Maxim Litvinov, was one of the main proponents of an "eastern Locarno," a multinational guarantee of Germany's Versailles frontiers in the east to match the guarantees of

---

[9]*Rundschau,* the Comintern newspaper, February 20, 1934, quoted in Julius Braunthal, *History of the International,* Vol. 2 (London, 1967), p. 423.

the western frontiers settled in 1925. When that project was thwarted by German and Polish opposition, the Soviet Union concluded mutual security treaties with France and Czechoslovakia in which each partner promised to help the other in case of German attack. The new policy was made official at the Seventh World Congress of the Communist International (Comintern) in Moscow in the summer of 1935. The delegates were told that the main task of workers was to unite in defense of democracy against fascism.

At the time of the signing of the Franco-Soviet Pact in May 1935, Stalin himself gave a striking confirmation of the Popular Front. French Foreign Minister Pierre Laval returned from Moscow authorized to announce that Stalin "understood and fully supported" French policies of national defense. This constituted a communist accolade to the French Army, chief bulwark of Versailles, against whose appropriations French Communists had voted since the party's creation. Stalin's statement served notice that the Popular Front was at bottom a military alliance against Hitler and that all dreams of social progress evoked by the reunion of the European lefts must take second place.

Because of its military nature, Stalin meant for the Popular Front to extend as far as possible into the democratic center. There had been united fronts between socialists and Communists before; this was to be a "peoples' front," including middle-class democrats (liberal and Radical parties) and even conservatives[10] who where willing to lend active opposition to fascism.

The Liberal Reaction

The Popular Front idea divided democrats in Western Europe. There was virtually no sympathy for it among British Liberals, or even among British Labour. On the Continent, many erstwhile political liberals disapproved of an alliance including Communists. Most of those Continental democrats who responded warmly to the idea were members of Radical parties.

Radical parties were no longer radical, in any contemporary sense, in interwar Europe. They had been radically committed to the nineteenth-century struggles for universal suffrage, universal free public schools, separation of Church and state, and curbs on professional armies. Vigorous anticlericalism kept them militant after their other goals had been achieved, so that Radical parties flourished far longer with a keener sense of left identification in Catholic countries (France during the Dreyfus Affair, Italy under Giolitti, Spain) than among Protestant liberals in England or Germany. In social and economic terms, Radicals were defenders of the independent small man: shopkeepers, family farmers, village lawyers, and schoolteachers. They were in fundamental disagreement with Marxists over property: while Marxists wanted to

---

[10]The French Communist leader Maurice Thorez, in a speech on April 17, 1936, extended a fraternal hand to Catholics, war veterans, and all those "oppressed by the same cares" who wanted to "save the country from ruin."

replace private property with collective property, Radicals wanted to give every citizen a chance to own property. But since the Popular Front muted these social questions, the issues that aroused the Radicals' traditional libertarianism came to the fore in the face of fascism. Against Mussolini, Hitler, and their allies, Radicals rallied to their ingrained individualism and the defense of freedom of thought and expression.

Radicalism was dead in Italy, but Radicals in France and Spain responded to the fascist advance by reviving the cry they used against kings and churches: "no enemies to the left." Although Edouard Herriot and Edouard Daladier battled for control of the French Radical party in the "war of the two Edouards," they agreed in seeing the new fascist leagues as the revival of the old enemy: counterrevolution, powerful priests and officers, and the authoritarian state. Moreover, the sufferings of French small property owners during the depression had heightened many Radicals' willingness to accept vigorous, if limited, social reforms. Similar attitudes were found in Spain, where Manuel Azaña, president of the Madrid literary club (the *Ateneo*), journalist, militant anticlerical, and proponent of civilian control over the military, was to be the Popular Front prime minister. Such democrats responded readily to the Communist proposal of a broad alliance against fascism that played down social questions.

The Socialist Reaction

Without the Socialists, the Communist–Radical understanding would be meaningless. But the bitterness between Socialists and Communists was not easy to overcome. There were both old and new wounds: the ancient reformist-revolutionist quarrel, the resentment against those who had carried Socialists over to national patriotism in 1914, the antagonisms created during the splits of 1919 to 1921, and the policy of "class against class" after 1928.

While Communists had accused Socialists of not being revolutionary enough, Socialists had accused Communists of introducing an alien and retrograde authoritarianism into the advanced socialist movements of the west. Communist attacks on German Social Democrats as "social fascists" had been the last straw. The Austrian Social Democrat Friedrich Adler, leader of the Second (Socialist) International, accused Communists of regarding the destruction of democracy as a condition for achieving socialism and following tactics "which led to the hell of fascism" because they felt that "the only way to the socialist paradise leads through this hell."[11] Socialists were also reluctant to agree to a common program that included so little social change. They wanted to be reassured of the Popular Front's commitment to social reforms, and, even more, of the willingness of Communists to cooperate with the

---

[11]Quoted in Braunthal, Vol. 2, p. 399. Friedrich Adler was not necessarily always opposed to violent action; he had personally assassinated the Austrian Minister of the Interior, Karl Stürgkh, in 1916.

existing socialist leadership. Socialists could well be skeptical of united fronts, which heretofore had often meant uniting from the base—drawing off the socialist following from its leaders, or "plucking the socialist goose" (*plumer la volaille*), as the phrase went. In the end, however, the emergency presented by fascist advances and grass-roots enthusiasm for the Popular Front overcame many socialist leaders' hesitations.

Popular Fronts were not created everywhere in democratic Europe. In general, they were formed where the fascist threat seemed paramount, as among the German and Italian exiles, and where large Marxist parties coexisted with anticlerical Radicals, as in Catholic France and Spain. In England, Labour was not only anticommunist but anti-Liberal after the disastrous coalitions of 1924 and 1929 to 1931. The few left-wing Labour intellectuals who advocated a Popular Front alliance with the tiny Communist party found no following among the trade union rank and file. The strong Social Democratic parties of the Low Countries and Scandinavia expressed little interest in reconciliation with small Communist parties there. In Sweden, Social Democrats had governed on their own since 1931, and in Norway since 1935. The only Communist party surviving in Eastern Europe, the Czech Communist party, had not been accepted by the pronational Social Democrats because of its opposition to the very principle of a Czechoslovak state up to 1935.

Where Popular Front coalitions were successfully established, they released a fervent enthusiasm among politicians, rank and file, and intellectuals. Popular Front supporters believed that at last the natural numbers of antifascists would exert their due weight. The painful divisions of the European left seemed healed, and at last something constructive could be done to stop the advancing fascist monster.

The Popular Front in France

France was a logical place for the most prominent Popular Front experiment. The antiparliamentary demonstrations of February 6, 1934, had made it seem that France was next on the fascist list. Drawn up on the other side were the Socialists and Communists, the two largest Marxist parties remaining in Western Europe after the destruction of those in Italy, Germany, and Austria. While part of the French middle class saw in fascism the only way to both grandeur and safety, several features of the French political tradition made many middle-class Frenchmen sympathetic to a Popular Front. The French had fought a great popular war against the kings of Europe under Jacobin[12] leadership in 1793; many Frenchmen responded emotionally to a new Jacobin appeal against a new form of counterrevolution. In the Jacobin tradition, a Frenchman could be both left and nationalist in the defense of

---

[12]The revolutionary democrats in France during the French Revolution were called Jacobins because they held their meetings in the Jacobin friars' convent.

republican liberties. Anticlericalism also kept many middle-class French-men receptive to the left. More immediately, Pierre Laval's conservative deflationary depression remedies of 1935[13] turned many a French pensioner, war veteran, and lower civil servant toward the left. In France, the Marxist parties could win middle-class allies by stressing nationalism, defense of political liberties, and economic revival.

Even so, a Popular Front was difficult to construct. The negotiations were nearly wrecked at the very beginning, in June 1934, when French Socialists demanded a Communist promise to refrain from attacking their leaders, a legacy of fifteen years of fratricidal conflict. The French Socialists also wanted a Popular Front program of immediate social changes, including some nationalization of industry and more steeply graduated taxes. Communists and Radicals alike, although for different reasons, insisted on a minimum program emphasizing the defense of political liberties against fascism. In the end, the rising specter of mass support for Colonel de la Rocque's protofascist *Croix de feu,* which threatened to become the largest French party by the time of the elections of 1936, overrode all hesitations. The Popular Front alliance was sealed with a Bastille Day parade on July 14, 1935, in which the Socialist, Communist, and Radical leaders—Léon Blum, Maurice Thorez, and Edouard Daladier—linked arms before more than 1 million jubilant Parisians in the traditional setting of Jacobin unity, the *Place de la Bastille.*

The Formation of Léon Blum's Government

The election of May 1936 was the most important in interwar France. The Popular Front candidates won a small increase in total votes (57 percent, compared with 54 percent for the same parties separately in 1932) but an overwhelming victory in parliamentary seats: 386 out of 608, a gain of 40 seats since 1932. Few French voters had changed their minds; the two-stage electoral system simply favored the most united coalition. Communists and Socialists had not competed with one another in the run-off as they had before. The parliamentary strength of the Popular Front was, therefore, far greater than its actual electoral strength, a disproportion that led to exaggerated fears on the right, exaggerated expectations on the left, and exaggerated disappointment within the Popular Front over what accomplishments were eventually possible.

The elections also produced a realignment within the French left. Communist seats increased from eleven to seventy-two, the most important advance the party made in France until the first elections after the liberation in 1945. The Radicals, who had formed the largest party in France before the First World War, now fell behind the Socialists for

[13]See Chapter 11, p. 325.

the first time. They began to have second thoughts about the Popular Front even before the electoral coalition became a governing coalition.

Since the French Socialist party emerged as the leading party of the victorious coalition, its leader, Léon Blum, became premier of France on June 5, 1936; he was the first Socialist and the first Jew to hold that office.

Blum, the son of a prosperous Parisian wholesaler of silk ribbon, had distinguished himself in two careers before turning to politics. In his twenties, at the turn of the century, he was already a prominent avant-garde literary critic and essayist. He also spent a quarter century as a legal expert in the *Conseil d'état,* France's highest court of administrative law, where citizens' disputes with government agencies were adjudicated. The Dreyfus Affair drew him into socialist politics, along with so many other intellectuals of his generation. But Blum could not imagine socialism without political liberty. When the majority of French socialists joined Lenin's Third International in 1920, Blum led the minority who refused to accept the Bolshevik formulas of strict party discipline and membership purges. Blum's party recovered to become the largest French party by 1936, and Blum himself assumed the mantle of Jean Jaurès as the leading French democratic socialist of the first half of this century.

This slender, ascetic, refined intellectual seemed something of an anomaly as head of a working-class party. Blum's reedy voice spelled out all the theoretical pros and cons of each policy with the elegance he had once displayed in his avant-garde essays and the analytical rigor he had employed in his legal briefs. He never swayed audiences in the manner of the ebullient Jaurès. Blum was villified and beloved in his own time. The right attacked him as a "subtle Talmudist" who had no business governing an "ancient Gallo-Roman" people."[14] Nationalist demonstrators beat him in the street in February 1936; in his seventies, he survived a German concentration camp. On his own left, he was accused of insufficient revolutionary will. Blum nonetheless won a devoted following by his earnest commitment to humanitarian ideals and the open honesty with which he evaluated in public his agonizing choices.

The 1936 election seemed to promise a new direction in European affairs. At a time when no democracy had worked well since 1929, a major European state had turned resolutely toward a left coalition committed to parliamentary practice. Europeans watched the results to see whether the democracies had discovered a new lease on life.

The French New Deal

Blum's year in power, from June 1936 to June 1937, is sometimes referred to as the French New Deal. Blum did not have the electoral support, the fixed term of office, the broad executive powers, or the

[14]The Catholic nationalist Xavier Vallat in the Chamber of Deputies, June 5, 1936.

comparative freedom from international complications enjoyed by President Franklin D. Roosevelt. Like Roosevelt's New Deal, however, it was a time when a major democratic regime seemed to be capable of making a fresh start.

The French Popular Front faced problems in three major areas: social reform, the economy, and the rising tide of fascism. Blum's first acts dealt with an immediate crisis bordering on civil war rather than with the application of a long-term program.

Blum took office amid exalted hopes and exaggerated fears. Over 2 million French workers were out on strike—or rather *in,* for the tactic of sit-down strikes or factory occupations spread like a grass fire, beyond any capacity of the union leadership to control it. At the other political pole, another 2 million Frenchmen belonged to extraparliamentary leagues like the *Croix de feu.* Even the moderately conservative press, such as the staid *Le Temps,* referred to the Popular front as "revolutionary" despite its quite modest program.

To bring the strike movement to an end, Blum met all night with terrified industrialists and trade union leaders in his official residence, the Matignon Palace, on June 7 to arbitrate a new package of wages and working conditions. The Matignon Agreements recognized collective bargaining, the right of labor to organize, and the necessity for a substantial wage increase. Then the union leaders and the Communist party leader Maurice Thorez persuaded the strikers to go back to work. At the time of the strike the exiled Russian revolutionary Leon Trotsky had been sure that "the French Revolution had begun." Thorez, however, told the last strikers on June 11 that while it was important to know how to lead a strike, "we must also know how to end one." The Popular Front began by restoring a slightly reformed *status quo.*

Extensive change in the French social system was not part of the Popular Front's mandate. The coalition depended on muting social questions in order to form the largest possible antifascist alliance. Léon Blum, with his characteristically scrupulous distinctions, reminded his socialist followers that the Popular Front was an "exercise of power within the framework of existing institutions and . . . the present constitution"[15] rather than a revolutionary "conquest of power" in which existing institutions ceased to be legitimate.

Nevertheless, expectations ran exceedingly high. Many Frenchmen could believe, with the leader of the Socialist party's more intransigent wing, Marceau Pivert, that "everything is possible." The rush of legislation in the Popular Front government's first weeks produced some measures that changed the lives of millions of Frenchmen and that no subsequent government, even under German occupation in the Second World War, dared repeal. Most important of these was the two-week vacation with pay for employees of all except purely family enterprises. With this act the French government first recognized leisure as a basic

---

[15]Joel Colton, *Leon Blum: Humanist in Politics* (New York, 1966), p. 70.

France, mass strikes of May and June 1936. The placard identifies the boss as "one of the thieves."

social need; the massive movement of French families to the sea and the mountains in August remains the most substantial monument to Blum's humanitarian vision. Blum's government also intervened more directly in labor–management relations than any of its predecessors. In addition to the Matignon Agreements of June 1936, a new law was passed on June 24 promoting collective bargaining and providing for the election of workers' representatives in larger factories. Blum also gave three minor cabinet posts to women, the first to hold political office in France. Although they were limited in scope, the Popular Front's social reforms constituted its most lasting contribution.

Blum's government dealt less successfully with the depression. His policy of replacing deflation with "reflation" and stimulating the economy by increased purchasing power[16] was clearly one that current Keynesian economists would approve of. In application, however, these remedies were vitiated by awkward circumstances, internal resistance, and the government's own mistakes. The forty-hour week, however desirable in social terms, was applied in ways that reduced production. Exports continued to fall, for French prices rose faster than production,

[16]See Chapter 11, pp. 325–26.

and Blum hesitated to take the one measure that would most stimulate exports—devaluation of the franc—because of popular sensitivity about monetary fluctuations. As the French balance of payments worsened, French investors and speculators—no friends of the Popular Front under any circumstances—started a flow of francs out of the country by buying gold and foreign currencies. Eventually these pressures forced the government to devalue the franc twice, in September 1936 and in May 1938, under conditions that brought no gain in foreign trade. By 1938, production was still lower than the level of 1929, and price rises had absorbed the wage gains of the summer of 1936.

The fight against fascism was the Popular Front's chief reason for existence; yet it became its chief obstacle to survival. Blum's government, less committed to a balanced budget than its predecessors, began the first significant rearmament of France against the German menace. A left government that strengthened the Army remained a left government in conservative eyes, however. In a curious reversal of foreign policy, many conservatives began to regard Hitler as a bulwark against communism and a war to stop Hitler as "Stalin's War," which would simultaneously let the Russians into Europe and unleash revolution at home, as in 1917. Polarization in French foreign affairs made every potential ally politically unacceptable to some important section of French opinion.

The only plausible counterweight to a revived Germany was Russia, even in its weakened economic condition as a result of forced collectivization. Indeed, the old Franco-Russian Alliance of 1892 to 1917 began to be revived before Blum came to power, when Laval visited Stalin and signed an agreement of mutual defense in May 1935. When that treaty came before parliament for confirmation in February 1936, however, bitter opposition nearly defeated it. Blum did nothing with this treaty, claiming later that the Army had been opposed to it. The only other potential counterweight to Germany, Fascist Italy, had already broken irrevocably with the democracies in 1935 over the Ethiopian War,[17] although the French right never ceased blaming Blum for not trying to reopen contacts with Mussolini. The Eastern European states, the basis of France's alliance system against Germany in the 1920s, were drifting into the more dynamic German economic orbit; in any case, the French Army was incapable of coming to the aid of a successor state after Germany reoccupied the Rhineland in March 1936. After that event, the Belgians ended their defensive arrangements with the French in the summer of 1936 and declared their neutrality. The Popular Front had set out to oppose Hitler's spread by military and diplomatic means, but it was left with a partly disaffected Army and a single ally, Britain, which, in turn, was committed to a policy of noninterference on the Continent.

The antifascist stance of the Popular Front was challenged in its very first days by the outbreak of the Spanish Civil War. Blum had hardly

[17]See Chapter 14, pp. 408–11.

begun his most active first weeks of domestic reform when word came that dissident generals and the Spanish Moroccan Legion had rebelled against the Spanish Republican government on July 18, 1936. Spain had also been governed by a Popular Front coalition since February, and Blum was eager to aid a sister regime. The situation seemed straightforward. A legitimate Spanish government was asking for French arms in order to defeat a military uprising, and France had every reason to want to avoid facing yet another fascist regime on a third frontier.

In fact, Blum had to pick his way through a mine field of problems. His own moderate coalition partners, the Radicals, threatened to bring down the coalition if France accepted active military involvement in Spain. The British government warned it would stand aside if France were drawn into a war over Spain. Given the power of fascist leagues in France, Blum was afraid that direct French participation in the Spanish struggle would spread civil war to France.

Fearful of the consequences of all-out war, Blum gambled on the hope that Republican Spain would survive if Germany and Italy were prevented from aiding the insurgents. He cooperated with England and other European states in setting up a Non-Intervention Commission to prevent outside assistance to either side. The result was a leaky blockade through which the Spanish government received less aid (mostly from the Soviet Union) than the Spanish insurgents received from Germany and Italy. Blum was faced with total war in Spain anyway, and an impossible position at home. Conservatives accused the government of tolerating clandestine aid to Spanish "Reds" and predicted the spread of civil war to France; the left of the Popular Front demonstrated in favor of more aid to Spain. During a clash between a right-wing league and Communist demonstrators in the Paris suburb of Clichy on March 16, 1937, police killed six Popular Front supporters. The regime seemed to be devouring its own children. The Popular Front, formed to combat fascism, found itself curbing those who wanted to fight fascism in Spain.

Financial strains had already forced Blum to declare a "pause" in February 1937. In an effort to persuade rather than coerce French financiers and industrialists, he restored the free market in gold, appointed a group of orthodox financial advisors, and announced an end to wage raises until the economy could catch its breath. As real wages lost ground again in the spring of 1937, and as discontent among the Popular Front's left over nonintervention in Spain grew, Blum was caught in precisely the situation that he had warned against when defining the concept of "exercise of power." He had committed the French Socialists to the responsibilities of office without being able to avoid compromise policies that were abhorrent to the party's rank and file. When the Senate refused in June 1937 to vote full powers to Blum to deal with the worsening economic situation, Blum took the occasion to resign.

Technically, the French Popular Front coalition continued to hold office until November 1938 under more moderate Radical leaders, with another brief Blum ministry in the spring of 1938. But the original spirit had vanished in that first winter. The French New Deal was both brief and profoundly disillusioning to its supporters.

Blum's Popular Front Assessed

Blum's achievements in office have been the subject of intense controversy. Those who believe that the great strikes of May and June 1936 created an unanticipated revolutionary situation blame Blum for adhering to the limited reforms contained in the Popular Front electoral program. They feel he let slip a historic opportunity to carry through major changes in the distribution of wealth and the power of private corporations in the economy. Blum's defenders accept his evaluation that the situation permitted only a socialist "exercise of power" within capitalism and not a "conquest of power." They see the strike wave as a surface effervescence without any deep drive toward collectivization; the workers had not even tried to operate the factories by worker committees as in Italy in 1920. French society, based on widespread family farms and numerous independent enterprises, was fundamentally stable. The broad French middle class, together with the Army and the bureaucracy, would have offered formidable resistance to any attempt to use a mere electoral plurality as a mandate for major changes in the economic system. Considering the basic stability of French society, Blum's social reforms were as much as could be achieved.

Even if one accepts Blum's prudently restricted view of his mandate,

Premier Léon Blum addresses a rally in Paris on Bastille Day (July 14), 1936, soon after the Popular Front came to power. At the extreme right of the picture, the French Communist leader Maurice Thorez (with hat in front of him) and Radical leader Edouard Daladier, to his right, occupy the front row.

did he exercise power skillfully? It is arguable that even the limited Popular Front program gave Blum the power to deal with current problems more resolutely than he did. Vigorous actions, such as an immediate devaluation of the franc and strict controls on the exchange of francs into gold and foreign currencies, would probably have strengthened the economic situation. Direct aid to the legitimate government in Spain might have prevented the victory of another anti-democratic regime on France's southern flank. Blum himself argued later that aid to Republican Spain risked setting off a similar civil war in France. Possibly so. But his effort to reassure French conservatives by exercising moderation was his greatest failure. The French right reacted as bitterly as if Blum had actually tried to make the major changes his left urged him to make.

Spain was the only other European country in which a Popular Front coalition held power. A Popular Front coalition won the elections of February 1936 and tried to defend the newly founded Second Republic against the insurgent generals who rose against it in July 1936.

Spain: Republic, Revolution, and Civil War

The Creation of the Second Republic

The Second Spanish Republic (1931–39) was not created by a revolution; it simply filled a vacuum. The authoritarian regime of General Primo de Rivera (1923–30) had not made the monarchy any stronger.

When municipal elections in April 1931 revealed widespread disaffection for the monarchy, King Alfonso XIII left the country rather than risk a struggle in which he was not sure of military and police support.

Into the vacuum rushed a number of competing claimants for power. These claimants were far more diverse than those in France, for Spain was a far less homogeneous country. At the top, there were an entrenched aristocracy, a deeply conservative Catholic hierarchy, an Army still smarting from its defeats by the United States in 1898 and by Moroccan tribesmen in 1921, an ancient tradition of political bossism, and intellectuals brooding over Spain's long decline from the sixteenth century. At the bottom was a poverty-stricken and largely illiterate population. Most of Spain was agricultural. Small peasant plots predominated in northern Spain, whereas in southern Spain (Andalusia) less than 2 percent of the population owned 66.5 percent of the land.[18] Spain was not wholly preindustrial, however. There were two very vigorous islands of industrial activity. Catalonia, with its great industrial city of Barcelona, was Spain's most economically advanced area. The Basque country in the north contained the leading coal and iron mining areas. Since both of these regions had separate languages and a strong sense of cultural distinctness, industry only aggravated Spain's lack of national integration.

It was not easy to find an electoral majority capable of speaking for such diverse interests. Nevertheless, when King Alfonso XIII left in 1931, a coalition of democrats and reformist socialists provided Spain with a parliamentary consitution modeled on the French and Weimar examples (at a time when both countries were having trouble coping with depression strains themselves). A single chamber (*Cortés*) elected by all adult men and women held the preponderant power in this "republic of workers of all catagories." The president's powers were carefully limited, in reaction against Primo de Rivera and Alfonso XIII.

Political Phases of the Republic

The short-lived Spanish Republic passed through three distinct political periods. An anticlerical, antimilitarist intellectual, Manuel Azaña, was prime minister during the "red biennium," from October 1931 until just before the elections of November 1933. Those elections gave 40 percent of the seats to conservatives and only 20 percent to the various lefts (the anarchists had counseled abstention), and so a center-right coalition governed during the "black biennium" (1934–36). A Popular Front coalition then won control of the legislature in the elections of February 1936.

Quite independently of these political phases, massive extraparliamentary currents carried Spain along beyond the control of politicians. Submerged popular resentments broke to the surface of public life.

[18]Edward E. Malefakis, *Agrarian Reform and Peasant Revolution in Spain: Origins of the Civil War* (New Haven, Conn., 1970), p. 29.

Anticlericalism was manifested in the burning of two dozen churches and convents in May 1931 and some scattered ones later.[19] Agrarian rebellion, expressed since the 1880s in a popular anarchism as distrustful of parliamentary reform as it was hostile to the landlords, led to land seizures and communal uprisings among Andalusian farm laborers. Fearful conservatives grew increasingly willing to accept some authoritarian solution to disorder. It is probably fair to say that none of the successive governments of the republic after 1931, including the Popular Front, ever managed to contain all these forces.

The first phase of the republic (1931–33) was most important for the enemies it made. Prime Minister Azaña's majority was radical in the late–nineteenth-century European meaning of the word: it considered universal suffrage and education to be the most important reforms, and the Catholic Church and professional officers to be the most important threats to democracy. The Jesuit order was dissolved, the liberty of religious orders to engage in teaching and in business was sharply curtailed, and Catholic private schools were ordered closed by the beginning of the school year of 1933. Divorce was permitted for the first time in Spain. Azaña took steps to reduce the surplus of officers in the Spanish Army, cut military service to one year, and abolish the Army staff college—the pride and joy of Spain's most rapidly rising young general, Francisco Franco. Catalonia received a large measure of provincial autonomy. Land reform was the most obvious social need. The Azaña government forced through a law for the redistribution of some of the largest tracts of uncultivated latifundia, but the legal provisions were so complicated that only about 40,000 peasants were resettled, many of them only temporarily.[20] While social unrest continued to rise, Catholics and many officers aligned themselves against the republic.

What Spanish republicans call the "black biennium" began with conservative victories at the polls in November 1933. For over two years, governments were headed by a coalition of centrist republicans who depended for their majority on the CEDA (Confederation of Autonomous Right Parties), a new Catholic party that was now the largest Spanish party. José María Gil Robles, the young dynamic CEDA leader, refused to recognize that the republic had any legitimacy except as "the regime of the moment." When several CEDA deputies were given cabinet posts in October 1934, the miners of the Basque region of Asturias revolted to protest this threat to the republic, as well as their depression sufferings. Spanish Moroccan Foreign Legionnaires, under General Franco, suppressed the Austurias resistance. The clerical associates of Gil Robles proceeded to undo much of Azaña's anticlerical and antimilitarist legislation; they restored the death penalty, abolished Catalonian autonomy, and stopped coeducation in state schools.

[19]Terrified Catholics believed that hundreds of churches had been burned and tombs desecrated. On this controversial issue, I have accepted the figures of Gabriel Jackson, *The Spanish Republic and The Civil War, 1931–39* (Princeton, N.J., 1965), p. 33.
[20]Malefakis, p. 281.

General Francisco Franco takes the oath as Supreme Head of the insurgent "Nationalist Government" in Burgos, in northern Spain, which he made his capital in October 1936.

From the end of 1934, the Spanish government maintained an official "state of alarm," which permitted the suspension of civil liberties. Thousands of Spaniards were in prison; thousands more contemplated direct action. As the elections of February 1936 approached, Spaniards increasingly classified themselves according to hatreds. Each camp nourished its own horror stories: nuns raped by miners; miners tortured by Foreign Legionnaires. Those who felt that a revolution had already begun in the anarchist villages of Andalusia, in the mines of Asturias, and in separatist Catalonia, threw their support to conservatives, or to Franco's Foreign Legionnaires, or to José Antonio Primo de Rivera's *Falange*. Those who believed that clericals and reactionaries had goaded peasants and miners to desperate action in order to repress them brutally prepared a massive electoral turn-out for the Popular Front.

The Spanish Popular Front resembled the French one only in general outline: an antifascist electoral coalition of democrats, socialists, and the revolutionary left. As such, it conformed to a larger European pattern. Adapted to Spanish conditions, however, the Popular Front was transformed. It faced a domestic political spectrum far more polarized than in any northern European country. And the mix of the various lefts was quite unique. The Communist party was a marginal movement in Spain, with 20,000 members; it won only sixteen seats in 1936. The heart of the Spanish left was anarchist and syndicalist. The peasants' anarchist counterculture, with its own tradition of uprisings and village communes, was intractable to organization or control by formal parties. The largest unions were syndicalist, fervent believers in general strike tactics and skeptical of parliamentary action. In 1936, the Spanish Socialists, under the leadership of the genuinely proletarian stonecutter Francisco Largo Caballero, rushed toward the left to keep up with the rank and file unionists. Even more than in France, Popular Front in Spain consisted of the combined efforts of democrats and Communists to subject Socialists, syndicalists, and anarchists to political discipline in the name of a worldwide struggle against fascism.

Manuel Azaña again became prime minister after the Popular Front electoral victory of February 1936 (the anarchists had voted this time). The Popular Front's efforts seem petty against the forces that began to move then. Despite energetic land reform that resulted in the settlement of 111,000 peasants on new lands in three months, peasants ceased to work for their landlords and began seizing lands in the most extensive strike wave in Spanish history.[21] During the same spring, senior army officers drew up plans to seize power. In a private plane lent by a British admirer, Franco flew to Morocco from the Canary Islands, where Azaña had exiled him. The generals gave the signal to invade from Spanish Morocco on July 18, 1936, and with the aid of transport planes lent by

[21]*Ibid.*, p. 365.

British cartoonist David Low took a skeptical view of Franco's independence of his Axis supporters in 1939, when Britain and France were considering recognizing the new Spanish regime. Here Franco tells Chamberlain and Daladier, "Honest, Mister, there's nobody here but us Spaniards."

Mussolini, began ferrying Foreign Legionnaires across the Straits of Gibraltar to Andalusia. The Spanish Civil War had begun.

The Civil War

It took three years and more than 500,000 deaths[22] for the insurgents to fight their way to conquest of a brutalized Spain. Neither side was strong enough to carry a speedy victory, nor weak enough to lose heart early. The insurgents could rely on most of the Army, on money and arms and men from Italy and Germany, and on broad middle- and upper-class backing in the agricultural areas of Spain. They began with a solid foothold in Andalusia and along the Portuguese frontier to the province of Galicia in northwestern Spain. The Popular Front's assets included a good part of the Spanish Air Force and Navy, volunteers from abroad, aid from the Soviet Union and Mexico, and mass support in the industrial areas, the capital, and the east coast. The insurgents could feed themselves and mount massive military campaigns; the Popular Front could produce more goods and rely on more of the population, but it had to improvise its military actions.

The focus of the first year of fighting was the capital city, Madrid. The insurgents advanced on the city with a formidable military force in four columns and expected help from a "fifth column" of sympathizers within the city. A makeshift but fervent Popular Front force unex-

[22]Jackson, p. 539.

Refugees from the Spanish Civil War crossing into France at a Pyrenees mountain pass, 1938.

THE SPANISH CIVIL WAR, 1936-1939

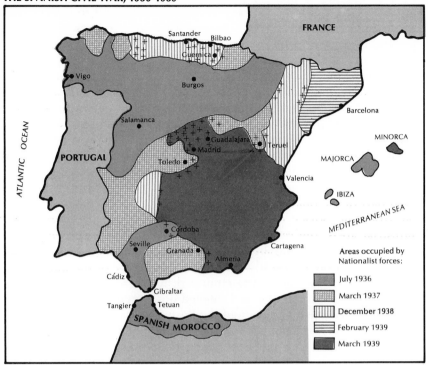

pectedly held Madrid, however, showing what a determined popular militia could do in an urban setting.

The insurgents then drew on fascist Europe for help. The Anglo-French Non-Intervention Commission kept more foreign aid from the government than from the insurgents. Between December 1936 and April 1937, the Italians sent 100,000 troops (70,000 Italians and 30,000 North African colonial soldiers) to Spain. In November 1936 the Germans sent the Condor Legion air units, manned by about 6000 men, along with some artillery and tanks. Even so, the insurgents still could not succeed in driving on Madrid. When an Italian tank division was decimated by republican planes in mountain passes at Guadalajara in March 1937, the Italian CTV (Corps of Voluntary Troops) was renamed *¿Cuándo Te Vas?* (When are you leaving?) by jubilant Spanish republicans.

Organizing the Popular Front for war posed a choice between spontaneity and discipline. The passions and necessities of war pushed the republic rapidly to the left, but would the anarcho-syndicalist left or the Communist left call the tune? The syndicalist workers of Catalonia, once more grasping provincial autonomy, seized factories and ran them by workers' committees, and set up rural cooperatives. The syndicalist POUM (*Partido Obrero de Unificación Marxista,* Unified Marxist Workers' Party) insisted it was initiating the libertarian society of the future. The

Communists called these steps "infantile leftism," quoting Lenin, and argued that hasty internal social changes would rupture the common front against fascism. They charged that the workers' committees produced less war matériel than the previous owners.

The Communists won, not only because war production put a greater premium on efficiency than on liberty, but also because the Soviet Union provided the only substantial outside aid to the republic. The Russians sent about 400 trucks, 50 planes, 100 tanks, 400 pilots and tank drivers, and a number of senior military advisors before "nonintervention" agreements closed the ports in late 1936. As Russian advisers increased in influence, the Communist party in Spain ceased to be a marginal element of the Spanish left; it became a mass party for the first time. Communist opposition to hasty social change made itself felt. In August 1937, for example, public worship was restored in the republican zones. Far more importantly, the Communist-dominated police in Catalonia arrested the POUM leaders and closed its offices in June 1937.[23] The Communists made some headway in imposing dicipline on the Popular Front, but it must be asked whether they did not also kill its spirit.

In the meantime, the better-equipped insurgents turned away from Madrid after the first year and nibbled at the republic's other strongholds. First they pierced through the Basque areas to the Bay of Biscay, causing British businessmen with extensive mining and banking interests there to wish to do business with Franco. Then they cut the republican areas in half by following the Ebro River down to the Mediterranean coast in late 1938. After that, it was only a mopping-up process. As thousands of refugees streamed into France from Catalonia, the European democracies debated whether to recognize the Franco regime. They did so in February 1939. With the fall of Madrid on March 28, the civil war came to an end.

The Spanish Civil War had been fought with passionate intensity on both sides. The Popular Front's efforts caught the imagination of intellectuals and the left throughout the world; some 40,000 volunteers came to aid the Spanish Republic at one time or another. From the insurgent side, the operation was partly a reenactment of the wars of unification of the fifteenth and sixteenth centuries, with aristocratic Castile reconquering the Catalonians and Andalusians, and partly a transplant of colonial war methods to the homeland, with the Spanish Legionnaires' cry of ¡Viva la muerte! (Long live death!). In its brutality, the Civil War was a foretaste of the Second World War, as exemplified by the Condor Legion's bombing of the Basque market town of Guernica on market day, April 26, 1937. In its exaltation, it was a last crusade, burning out most of the fervor before the more dogged great war to come.

[23]The best known English-language memoir of the Spanish Civil War, the British volunteer George Orwell's *Homage to Catalonia* (London, 1938), takes its tone of bitter disillusionment from his personal friendship with POUM leaders and his rage at Stalin's destruction of the POUM's revolutionary experiments.

The depression and the rise of fascism turned European intellectual life away from the self-expression of the 1920s to the social activism of the 1930s. A few intellectuals were drawn to the camaraderie, the action, and the "defense of Western values" against decadence promised by fascism. The vast majority of European writers and artists, however, enlisted in the enthusiasms of the Popular Front. Even painting, the most thoroughly private of the arts in the 1920s, produced important works of antifascist propaganda, such as Picasso's *Guernica* (1937).

The manifest bankruptcy of liberalism in the 1930s sent some intellectuals searching for new values. The only possible movement, according to the British writer Stephen Spender, was "forward from liberalism." Spender argued that while nineteenth-century liberalism at its best had represented an "active will toward political justice,"[24] that same goal could now only be pursued within communism. He was willing to accept the necessity of fighting and of temporary coercion in order to reach a new classless society in which the highest goals of forerunners like John Stuart Mill could be truly realized. Spender believed the arts would be more creative in such a society. A half-educated democracy evolved out of contemporary liberalism would produce only the "mob rule of tastelessness." Spender clearly shared Trotsky's prediction of 1937 that "the average human type will rise to the heights of an Aristotle, a Goethe, or a Marx."[25] As intellectuals seeking the best route to personal liberty and artistic creativity, Spender and his like were drawn to an alliance with communism in the 1930s rather than to a conversion to it.

Others became true converts. One should not take too literally the self-criticism of ex-converts like Arthur Koestler, who later attributed communism's appeal to intellectuals of the 1930s to a psychological craving for a disciple–master relationship, and to the deep satisfaction afforded by a closed system with unassailable answers to all questions.[26] Nevertheless, discipline and self-sacrifice clearly attracted some sensitive younger middle-class intellectuals who rejected the condescension and self-indulgence of their elders' individualistic games of protest in the 1920s, such as surrealism. A young French philosophy student, Paul Nizan, for example, found in the Communist party "a framework of order, duty, and discipline within which the individual could channel his sense of revolt while avoiding self-love."[27]

The Popular Front posed problems, of course, for its intellectual admirers. One problem was the manifest coercion and drab conformity of the Soviet Union in the 1930s, to which was added the international reaction to the purge trials. Spender could mitigate his doubts about these matters by arguing that the Russian experience had been per-

[24]Stephen Spender, *Forward from Liberalism* (London, 1937), p. 189.
[25]See Chapter 10, p. 303.
[26]See, for example, Arthur Koestler's contribution to the collection of statements of renunciation of communism, Richard Crossman, ed., *The God that Failed* (New York, 1959).
[27]David Caute, *Communism and the French Intellectuals, 1914–1960* (New York, 1964), p. 95.

verted by its difficult birth and encircling enemies, not by innate faults. Another problem was the justification of violence. But after the fate suffered by the passive German left in 1933, it became easier to renounce the pacifism of the postwar generation. As the crusade against fascism in Spain took shape, the possibility of sharing in a just war proved to be a positive attraction to intellectuals.

The Spanish Civil War drew intellectuals into active commitment as did no other twentieth-century crisis. Robert Graves thought that no foreign issue had so divided educated British opinion since the French Revolution.[28] The division, however, was one-sided. A poll taken in England in 1937 turned up only five British intellectuals publicly in favor of the insurgents (including Evelyn Waugh and the South African poet Roy Campbell). Another sixteen (including T. S. Eliot and Ezra Pound) were neutral, and a round one hundred were in favor of the Spanish Republic. A number of scholars and writers left their desks to fight in Spain, impelled by an emotional commitment unknown to either world war. The First World War had been fought under dehumanized conditions by blind masses; the Second was fought at a distance by machines. It seemed that the Spanish Civil War was fought by individual heroes, especially among volunteers on the republican side who were drawn by the illusion of doing something direct and personal to defeat fascism. The volunteers included a number of remarkable individuals: the French novelist André Malraux, who flew fighter planes for the Popular Front; John Cornford, Charles Darwin's great-grandson, a brilliant student at Cambridge and a communist organizer, who died in Spain on his twenty-first birthday; the Cambridge scientist J. B. S. Haldane and his wife, who were first drawn in by the enlistment of their sixteen-year-old son in the International Brigade and who eventually became leading British Communists. Whether communist or not, the intellectuals among the international volunteers were torn between spontaneity and discipline, between the critical nuances of intellectual judgment and the clear commitment of action. Not a few of them emerged disillusioned. In André Malraux' Spanish war novel, *Man's Hope* (1937), the "lyric illusion" with which the volunteers began is slowly eroded by the increasing mechanization of the war and doubts that the victory of either side will make much difference in social justice. At the end, "the age of parties" has arrived.

> What worries me the most is to see how much, in any war, each one takes after his enemy, whether he wants to or not.[29]

The European Left After the Popular Front

The Popular Front was dead before 1939. In Spain, it had been conquered by a military insurrection. In France, the alliance came apart from within. The Radical party, disquieted by Socialist and Communist

---

[28]Robert Graves and Alan Hodge, *The Long Week-End: A Social History of Great Britain, 1918–39* (London, 1940), p. 337.
[29]André Malraux, *L'Espoir* (Paris, 1963), p. 494.

gains in the 1936 election, was the first partner of the French coalition to grow dubious. The Communist party, which had no cabinet seat except a hypothetical "ministry of the masses," criticized the government bitterly for its inaction in Spain and its economic failures. The Socialists, committed by the "exercise of power" to the compromises and disillusionments of office, suffered more and more from internal rifts. The Popular Front alliance was officially dissolved when Radicals joined a more conservative government in November 1938, but its spirit had been broken long before that.

It is easy to see, in retrospect, that the Popular Front had been an incongruous alliance. Its common demoninator was antifascism. But how best to oppose fascism aroused passionate discord. Military preparedness, one obvious solution, flew in the face of the left's traditional pacifism. The other taproot of the Popular Front was the depression, and in this case there was no broader consensus about remedies. Piecemeal reforms seemed worse than nothing to revolutionaries, while a Marxist remedy promised to drive away the middle class and all hopes of a majority.

The divisions left by the Popular Front seemed to doom the left in its familiar Western European forms, democratic and socialist, to a position of permanent minority status. One of the partners, however, made striking gains. In France, the Communist party consolidated the hold it had established among factory workers at the end of the nineteenth century, and extended it among farm laborers and intellectuals. Since 1936 the French Communist party has never fallen below a level of 15 percent of the electorate. Its very gains, however, increased doubts and reservations among the other Popular Front partners, parliamentary socialists and democrats. Moreover, Marxism had come close to exhausting its potential recruiting ground. Contrary to Marx's own expectations, it was not workers but clerks and lower civil servants who had become the fastest growing elements of the European populations. Marxism appealed forthrightly to one class, the working class, which turned out to have leveled off at about one-third of the population. Marxism was to hold on very effectively to its recruits in Western Europe, but at the cost of becoming an isolated enclave in European political life. After the Popular Front, a party capable of being both proletarian and majoritarian began to seem a contradiction in terms.

These developments were to be interrupted by the Second World War. For a time, the Popular Front was revived in the resistance movements of occupied Europe. In the long run, however, the problems raised by the Popular Front have still not been worked out today. Are electoral majorities of the left that are both democratic and social-reformist increasingly unworkable in industrialized Europe? Does the political future lie with other majorities?

In the short run, the Popular Front left a quite disproportionate legacy of fear among conservatives. Many Europeans began to prefer fascism to communism: "Better Hitler than Blum." Although conservatives had traditionally supported national glory and national defense, they feared being dragged into "Stalin's War" by the antifascist crusade of the left.

As for Stalin himself, he could well judge by 1938 that the Popular Front had done nothing to insure the safety of the Soviet Union. It had produced no reliable military allies on Germany's western frontier. The purge trials that reached their peak in 1936 and 1937 were one sign of Stalin's deepening distrust of outside influences. Among the Soviet leaders who disappeared were all those who had served in Spain.

Hitler had a freer hand than ever by 1938. The Popular Front had left Britain and France cool to each other and the Soviet Union cool to both. The remaining democratic countries were worried about the internal expansion of Marxism and fearful that a renewed war would plunge them into revolution. The disillusioned Austrian exile Arthur Koestler could later describe the Popular Front, "with drums and fanfares, advancing from defeat to defeat."[30]

[30]Arthur Koestler, *The Invisible Writing* (London, 1954), p. 188.

Suggestions for Further Reading

Many of the general works on the European left cited at the end of Chapter 1 contain important discussions of the Popular Front era. See also Franz Borkenau, *World Communism: A History of the Communist International** (1962), the work of a disillusioned former Comintern official.

Joel Colton's warmly sympathetic treatment of Blum, *Léon Blum: Humanist in Politics* (1966) is a good introduction to the French Popular Front. There are good accounts of all the participant parties: Daniel R. Brower, *The New Jacobins* (1968); Annie Kriegel's superb *The French Communists: Profile of a People* (1972); Peter Larmour, *The French Radical Party in the 1930s* (1964); and Nathanael Greene, *Crisis and Decline: The French Socialist Party in the Popular Front Era* (1969).

Gerald Brenan, *The Spanish Labyrinth,** 2nd ed. (1960) is the essential introduction to the atmosphere of the 1930s in Spain. Gabriel Jackson, *The Spanish Republic and the Civil War, 1931–1939** (1965), written from a perspective sympathetic to the moderate left, is the most comprehensive account. Burnett Bolloten, *The Grand Camouflage: The Spanish Civil War and Revolution, 1936–1939*, rev. ed. (1968) blames the Spanish left for the first resort to illegality and for subservience to the Comintern. So, more cautiously, does Richard A. H. Robinson, *The Origins of Franco's Spain: The Right, The Republic, and the Revolution, 1931–1936* (1971), a study of the moderate right. Edward E. Malefakis, *Agrarian Reform and Peasant Revolution in Spain: Origins of the Civil War* (1970), the best work on Spanish rural society, concludes that neither reformists nor revolutionaries had an answer to Spain's agarian crisis. Hugh Thomas, *The Spanish Civil War,** rev. ed. (1965) remains the most spirited account of the war itself. Pierre Broué and Emile Témime, *The Revolution and the Civil War in Spain* (1972) are sympathetic to the social experiments and ideals of the Spanish left during the war. Stanley G. Payne, *The Spanish Revolution** (1970) is a more balanced scholarly synthesis.

For intellectual reactions to the Popular Front and the Spanish Civil War, see relevant parts of David Caute, *Communism and the French Intellectuals, 1914–1960* (1964) and *The Fellow Travellers* (1973). Peter Stansky and William Abrahams, *Journey to the Frontier: Two Roads to the Spanish Civil War** (1966) is the moving story of two British students killed in Spain. Ernest Hemingway, *For Whom the Bell Tolls** (1940) is the classic novel of the war, and Arthur Koestler, *Arrow in the Blue** (1952) and *The Invisible Writing** (1954) are the classic memoirs of a 1930s intellectual. The most exact accounting of foreign participation on both sides is Robert H. Whealey, "Foreign Intervention in the Spanish Civil War," in Raymond Carr, ed., *The Republic and the Civil War in Spain* (1971). Verle B. Johnston, *Legions of Babel* (1967) examines the international brigades.

14

THE VERSAILLES SYSTEM DISMANTLED: EXPANSION AND APPEASEMENT 1933–1939

The Versailles system, still largely intact in 1929, had been virtually swept away by 1939. It was not a self-enforcing system. The attempt to fence in a truncated Germany could last no longer than Germany's neighbors were willing and able to maintain that fence by force. Before the outbreak of the Second World War on September 3, 1939, Germany had already made substantial territorial gains in the east, extending far beyond its 1914 frontiers in Austria and parts of Czechoslovakia. The dismantling of Versailles had two complementary aspects: increasingly militant German pressures on the one hand, and a divided and demoralized First World War victor coalition on the other.

There was no overnight change in German foreign policy when Hitler became chancellor of the German Reich on January 30, 1933. For the moment, Hitler reserved his lightning thrusts for the internal work of *Gleichschaltung:* bringing German institutions into line. He was still an upstart, uncertain of his power. The vice chancellor, Franz von Papen, expected to dominate the government. Marshal Hindenburg remained president. Bureaucracy, Army, church, professional diplomats all remained what American political scientist Karl Friedrich has called "islands of separateness," which would be brought under Hitler's control only gradually.

Although Foreign Minister Konstantin von Neurath assured foreign diplomats in February 1933 that the presence of old-line officials like himself in the new government was a guarantee that "no experiments in foreign policy were to be tried," and that "Hitler was proving reasonable,"[1] that did not mean that a majority of Germans did not desire revision of the Treaty of Versailles. When Hitler's campaign for revision reached demonic intensity in 1938 and 1939, traditional career officials, far from restraining him, for the most part fell into line. Even Hitler's predecessors, Stresemann and Brüning, had worked for revisions of the Versailles settlement; the Army had quietly circumvented its provisions by clandestine training and arms manufacture in the Soviet Union; neither had admitted the legitimacy of the eastern frontiers of 1919. But in 1933 the French Army was still clearly master of the field, despite the beginnings of secret German rearmament; the depression had affected Germany far more disastrously than France.

Hitler's first steps, therefore, were cautious. When he withdrew from the League of Nations and the Disarmament Conference in October 1933, it was only after astutely proposing measures of general disarmament that proved the other powers were unwilling to disarm down to the German level. His vigorous campaign for a pro-German plebiscite in the Saar in January 1935[2] was accompanied by a promise that he had no other claims on France, thus seeming to renounce Alsace-Lorraine. He concluded a mutual pact of nonaggression with Poland in January 1934, a state that he had vowed in *Mein Kampf* to destroy. He continued to renew agreements with the Soviet Union until 1935. Up until 1936, Hitler portrayed himself in public speeches as a veteran of the trenches who hated war above all things.

what about militarism of Nazism?

Setback in Austria

Impatient violence showed only in Hitler's early dealings with Austria, his birthplace. An *Anschluss* (unification) between Germany and German-speaking Austria had been blocked before 1918 by the inclusion of

[1]Quoted in Jürgen Gehl, *Austria, Germany, and the Anschluss, 1931–38* (Oxford, 1963), p. 90.

[2]In 1920 this rich coal region had been placed under French administration for fifteen years, after which the population would decide whether to be part of France or Germany. It voted overwhelmingly in 1935 to be restored to Germany.

Chancellor Englebert Dollfuss addressing a large group in Vienna, October 29, 1933, gathered in the Gross Mugl to demonstrate faith in the government.

Austria in the multinational Habsburg Empire. Now that the empire was broken up, Hitler was determined to bring Austria into the Reich. The main obstacles were Article 80 of the Treaty of Versailles and the Christian Social authoritarian regime of Engelbert Dollfuss, which was creating a new sense of separate identity for Austrians.[3] Hitler could assume, however, that his western opponents had no love for Dollfuss, who had shelled the Austrian Social Democrats into submission in February 1934. Moreover, the Austrian branch of the Nazi party was growing rapidly among Austrians who wanted union with a revived Greater Germany. Even so, Hitler seems to have meant to rely on indirect means. In May 1934 he closed off German tourist traffic to Austria, a serious blow to the Austrian economy, and permitted his ministers to talk openly about Austria's future destiny as part of Germany. He acquiesced in a *coup* planned by the Austrian Nazis, who misled him about their support in the Austrian Army. On July 25, 1934, a Nazi band seized the chancellery and radio stations in Vienna. In the ensuing scuffle, Chancellor Dollfuss was shot and left to bleed to death on the sofa in his office.

As it turned out, it was not the western Allies but Mussolini who gave Hitler the severest foreign setback of the 1930s. Mussolini had a large stake in Austrian independence, an important element in Italian influence in the Danube basin. He mobilized 100,000 men on the Brenner Pass while the Italian-supported *Heimwehr* recovered domestic control

[3]See Chapter 12, pp. 357–59.

for Dollfuss' successor, Kurt Schuschnigg. Hitler was obliged to disavow the failed Austrian *coup* and agree to the separation of the Austrian and German sections of the Nazi party. The *Anschluss* seemed postponed indefinitely.

First Renunciation of Treaty Provisions

Hitler's first major unilateral renunciation of provisions of the Versailles Treaties came only after two years in power. In the first of his famous Saturday pronouncements, on March 9, 1935, Hitler announced the formation of a German Air Force. A week later he declared that Germany was reinstituting the draft to form an army of thirty-six divisions (500,000 men).

The reaction of the Allies was hostile but muted, for they had not fulfilled the Versailles disarmament provisions either. The British and French prime ministers met with Mussolini at the Italian lakeside resort of Stresa, the highest-ranking international assemblage since the Versailles conference itself. The "Stresa Front's" agreement to use military force if necessary to maintain the existing political structure of Europe seemed the beginning of a powerful anti-Hitler alliance. But Mussolini was already chasing after an African empire in Ethiopia, and a few months after Stresa, in June 1935, the British and German governments announced a naval agreement whereby the Germans could rebuild a fleet up to one-third the size of the British Navy. It was clear that no one was prepared to enforce the letter of the Versailles system; the way was open to whatever new arrangements could be worked out by pressure and negotiation.

The Remilitarization of the Rhineland, March 1936

On the morning of March 7, 1936, Hitler sent a division of 10,000 men to the Rhine and a battalion of about 1000 men across the river in each of three places: Düsseldorf, Cologne, and Mainz. That act remilitarized the Rhineland. It thereby broke down the most important security barrier that the Versailles system had erected on Germany's western frontier.

The Treaty of Versailles forbade Germany to place any soldiers or military installations in a broad band of German territory: all land west of the Rhine, and a strip fifty kilometers (thirty miles) wide along the east bank of the Rhine. That highly artificial restriction on German sovereignty served two purposes: to expose any German military build-up against France at an early stage, and to permit easy French invasion of Germany in case the Germans attacked France's allies in the east. The remilitarization of the Rhineland was a crucial turning point in the European power shift of the 1930s from the Allies to Germany, and in the march toward the Second World War. Perhaps the most familiar cliché about interwar European international relations is that the Allies missed their best chance of stopping Hitler by decisive action at this point.

The Allies faced two alternatives. On the one hand, they could admit Germany's sovereign right to move troops anywhere within its frontiers and thus quietly abandon an unusual and outdated security arrangement. After all, the few troops that Hitler had moved into the Rhineland were clearly not intended to invade any foreign territory. As the London *Times* commented, the Germans were only "going into their own back garden." In fact, in the preceding months, British and French diplomats secretly discussed this alternative, although it was rather a different matter to negotiate such a relaxation mutually than to accede to a unilateral act of defiance.

On the other hand, the Allies had abundant justification for immediate armed counteraction. Article 44 of the Treaty of Versailles had made clear this provision's importance, declaring that any violation of the demilitarized Rhineland "in any manner" was a hostile act. In the Locarno Pact of 1925[4] Germany had explicitly accepted these terms once again, and recognized the Allies' right to maintain them by force, if necessary, as an "exercise of the legitimate right of self defense." France had sufficient legal authority to act, alone or with the other signatories of Locarno.

There was some political justification for a French reaction, too, since the demilitarized Rhineland had itself been a lesser substitute for French plans for a separate state there. The French had accepted a compromise only when promised an Anglo-American mutual defense treaty, which had never materialized. Once the Rhineland barrier was down and German troops stood on the frontiers of Alsace-Lorraine, nothing would be left of the military security arrangements of 1919. With these considerations in mind, French Prime Minister Albert Sarrault made a ringing declaration on French radio on March 8 that "we will not let Strasbourg[5] fall within German cannon range." French military staffs began planning the seizure of the Saar and Luxembourg as a "bargaining counter," and, alternatively, planned for a military operation deep into the Rhineland.

In the end, France merely lodged a protest with the League of Nations. There were technical obstacles to a military riposte: the French Army had been reorganized in a fashion that required it to move all at once, including mobilization of reserves, or not at all. There was no striking force for immediate, limited action. Even if there had been, however, the political obstacles were even greater. Mobilization of reserves would have been political suicide in March 1936, the eve of elections. The Ruhr occupation of 1923 had not been an encouraging precedent. Moreover, France was in the trough of the depression: austerity budgets limited military preparation and the economy's effects on morale were severe. Morale was further reduced by the "hollow

---

[4]See Chapter 8, pp. 228–32.
[5]The capital of newly regained Alsace.

German infantry crossing the Rhine on the Hohenzollern Bridge at Cologne, March 7, 1936. This act, and similar crossings by small detachments at Mainz and Düsseldorf, signaled Hitler's repudiation of the clause of the Treaty of Versailles that demilitarized in perpetuity the left bank of the Rhine.

years," the years beginning in 1936 when the reduced birth rate of 1917 and 1918 produced only half as many draftable eighteen-year-olds as usual. It was a time to reflect on the human wastage of war. The Versailles structure had been designed to block an all-out German onslaught by war. Few in France were ready to wage war over a largely symbolic German troop movement within Germany.

Even fewer in Britain were ready to support an active French response. Since 1919 British governments had consistently opposed the more vigorous French security measures. British public opinion, still influenced by John Maynard Keynes's *The Economic Consequences of the Peace* (1920), tended to regard the French as militaristic and unreasonable. The French have frequently charged that Britain vetoed the necessary action in 1936. It is clear now that the decision not to act was made in Paris, but the certainty of Britain's opposition made that decision easier to make.

In retrospect, the popular cliché of the last, lost opportunity in 1936 to stop Hitler can be seen to rest on several false assumptions. One assumption is that the token German forces had orders to withdraw at the slightest sign of opposition, a notion based on the testimony of General Alfred Jodl at the postwar Nuremberg trials. A closer look at captured German documents shows that the units had orders to resist. Another assumption is that the German opposition to Hitler would have overthrown him from within at his first serious setback, but this seems doubtful in view of the German populations' patriotic response to later crises. A French riposte would probably have led to significant fighting, in which the French would have been labeled the more conspicuous aggressor. What would the French have done after seizing parts of German territory, which they had the physical power to do? Would internal opposition have been stronger on the Allied side than on the German side?

All these legitimate speculations call for serious thought about the use of force in maintaining a treaty system over long periods, particularly when some parties to the treaty have significant doubts about its legitimacy. It has been common to draw lessons from the Rhineland crisis of 1936 about the virtues of early force against challengers to the *status quo.* The character of Hitler and his later triumphs have made it easier to defend this case than it perhaps should be. The Rhineland crisis needs careful thought in a wider perspective, one that would consider the validity of the Versailles arrangements, the precedent of the Ruhr invasion of 1923, and their share in Hitler's coming to power. The case for 1936 as a "lost opportunity" to overthrow him by force from outside remains unproven.

Italy Shifts Sides

Despite Italian conflicts of interest with the French and British in the Mediterranean, Fascist Italy remained, at least until 1935, in an anti-German coalition. Well into the 1930s Mussolini's main foreign policy interest had centered on the old nationalist dreams of succeeding the Habsburgs in the Danube basin and around the head of the Adriatic Sea. These ambitions made Germany the principal rival. As leader of the prowar socialists in 1915, the young Mussolini had helped push Italy into war against Germany. Mussolini had supported the French occupation of the Ruhr in 1923, had been one of the guarantors of the Locarno Agreements in 1925, and during the attempted takeover of Austria in July 1934 had administered the only international public humiliation to Hitler of the whole interwar period. As late as April 1935, he was host to the Allied conference at Stresa protesting German rearmament. By the beginning of the Rhineland crisis of March 1936, however, he had moved out of the German containment camp for good.

The Ethiopian Conquest

Dreams of imperial expansion in Africa were the main reason for this policy shift. Mussolini became his own foreign minister in 1932 and replaced career diplomats with Fascists in important foreign policy posts. At first there was a burst of activity in the European area. In June 1933 Mussolini initiated the Four-Power Pact, an attempt to establish a directorate ruling European affairs in which Italy would share an equal role with Britain, France, and Germany. The Four-Power Pact never really led to anything, and growing German vigor in the north suggested doubts about future Italian possibilities on the Continent. Furthermore,

Before a huge portrait of Mussolini, Italian troops celebrate in Taranto shortly before sailing for Ethiopia.

the Fascist regime was undergoing an internal crisis of confidence in 1933 and 1934. A new generation of Italians was coming of age without direct experience of the "heroic" days of 1923. The aging Fascist leadership seemed to them to offer little more than the liberal parliamentary monarchy it had replaced ten years earlier. The depression affected Italian employment and morale far more than appeared on the official façade. Corporatism was revealed more and more clearly to be self-regulation by subsidized big business. Without an effective social program and without some means of recruiting youth, fascism's best way out was grandeur.

In late 1933 or early 1934, Mussolini began to study the possibility of taking Ethiopia. Ethiopia was both a logical and an emotional choice: it lay inland from Italy's East African possessions of Eritrea and Italian Somaliland, it was the one major African region still uncontrolled by Europeans, and it was the scene of an Italian defeat in 1896 (Adowa) that Italian nationalists would delight in avenging. The attempted Nazi *coup* in Austria in July 1934 seems to have convinced Mussolini that he must act quickly before the start of a new European war. By August

1934, foreign diplomats in Italy were already reporting the beginning of military preparations.[6]

A skirmish between Italian and Ethiopian soliders at Walwal—a desert waterhole in disputed frontier territory—in December 1934 served as the public pretext for Mussolini's planned invasion. Intense European diplomatic bargaining among Italy, France, and Britain only convinced Mussolini that he would meet no effective European obstruction. Italian troops invaded Ethiopia in October 1935. Although the Ethiopian troops fought more stubbornly than anyone in Italy had anticipated, they were no match for Italian aircraft and poison gas. King Victor Emmanuel II was proclaimed emperor of Ethiopia in May 1936.

Breach with the West

Mussolini seems to have expected to mend his fences with Britain and France after conquering Ethiopia, but that conquest's repercussions were much too violent for that. When Ethiopian Emperor Haile Selassie appealed to the League of Nations for help in October 1935, he became a heroic symbol to European democratic opinion. It was forgotten that Ethiopia had been admitted to the League in 1923 only on Italian insistence, and that Britain and France had voted against entry because slavery was still practiced there. Athough a powerful groundswell of democratic opinion urged active League sanctions against Italy in 1935, diplomatic prudence suggested that Mussolini should not be permanently lost as a potential ally against Hitler. In the end, Britain and France settled somewhere between the two policies and suffered the disadvantages of both. They pursued what the British Foreign Minister Sir Samuel Hoare called "a double line of approach."[7] In an effort to take some action without actually antagonizing Italy, the League adopted an arms embargo and a limitation on loans and credits to Italy and imports from Italy. That was enough to arouse patriotic resentment in Italy without taking the one step—stopping shipments of oil to Italy—that would actually have hampered the campaign in Ethiopia.

Meanwhile, diplomats tried to arrange a solution behind the scenes that would recognize a predominant Italian role in Ethiopia without condoning outright Italian conquest. The French and British foreign ministers, Pierre Laval and Sir Samuel Hoare, drafted a plan in December 1935 to end the fighting on these terms, only to have it leak out to an outraged public opinion, especially in Britain where Hoare's public career was ended. Italian preponderance in Ethiopia was attained by arms rather than by negotiation, and the breach between Britain and France and Mussolini was never healed.

That breach was widened in July 1936 when Mussolini supplied essential military assistance to Francisco Franco's revolt against the Spanish Republic. Eventually 70,000 Italian "volunteers" were fighting

[6]*Foreign Relations of the United States, 1934,* Vol. 2, p. 754, quoted in George W. Baer, *The Coming of the Italian-Ethiopian War* (Cambridge, Mass., 1967), p. 42.
[7]Samuel Hoare, *Nine Troubled Years* (London, 1953), p. 168.

for Franco. It was now the turn of French public opinion to become inflamed, for a fascist Spain would nearly complete the ring of hostile dictatorships around republican France.

Mussolini solidified his new alignment by sending his foreign minister, Count Galeazzo Ciano, to visit Hitler in October 1936. On November 1, 1936, Mussolini first referred publicly to a Rome–Berlin "Axis" as the new focus of European alignments.

Alliance Patterns

Mussolini's shift in 1935 and 1936 had grave consequences for Europe. It threatened France with a two-front war, and it aligned European powers on the basis of ideology rather than of interest. Since it was still possible that Mussolini might return to an anti-German coalition, the hope of winning him back by concessions continued to tempt some British and French leaders until 1940. From 1935 on, in effect, two patterns of anti-Hitler alliance competed for attention and became increasingly incompatible. Western conservatives tried to revive the "Stresa Front" with Italy, or even Mussolini's project of a four-power directorate: a coalition of the conservative powers of Europe, both dictatorships and republics, perhaps even including Germany, to settle Europe's affairs among themselves. The other pattern was an alliance with the Soviet Union as the only force capable of bringing serious pressure on Germany.

British and French leaders engaged in both these patterns of anti-Hitler alliances at various times after 1936. The British, in particular, offered concessions to Mussolini: the "Gentleman's Agreement" to respect the *status quo* in the Mediterranean and the Red Sea in 1937 and 1938, and a recognition of Italy's empire in Ethiopia in 1939. The pattern of alliance with the Soviet Union seemed to have the upper hand during the Popular Front ministries in France in 1936 and 1937, and briefly in the spring of 1938, when the French government resumed aid to the Spanish republicans. But the two patterns were too strongly ideological to be either combined or pursued to the end. An alliance with Italy seemed to sanction fascism; with Russia, communism. No simultaneous alliance was possible with both, and any one set of alliances against Hitler was too divisive to be acceptable.

As for Mussolini, he clung more and more to the Axis. Although he told Hitler he could not engage in a European war before 1943, he allowed himself to be drawn into a military pact with Germany in May 1939, the "Pact of Steel."

Hitler's Designs in the East

Hitler's moves of 1935 and 1936 had essentially aimed to restore full sovereignty within the German frontiers of 1919 through rearmament and remilitarization of the Rhineland. The next moves, those of 1938 and 1939, changed the frontiers of 1919 in Austria, Czechoslovakia, and

Poland. These far more ambitious steps took the Third Reich not only back to the 1914 eastern frontiers of the Second Reich but beyond them, and even beyond the areas of ethnic German settlement. What led Hitler to take these steps?

Ideological Motives

Hitler had talked about expanding the German frontiers all his adult life. *Mein Kampf* (1925–26)[8] had made clear a set of racial ideals that were to govern his choices to the end. He had never intended a mere return to the eastern frontiers of 1914, the undeclared aim of his Weimar predecessors, Stresemann and Brüning. Hitler intended to assemble the whole German *Volk*[9] in one nation, including his homeland Austria and the other Germanic parts of the former Habsburg Empire. Beyond that, he meant to give the German *Volk* sufficient "living space" (*Lebensraum*), which could be taken from inferior peoples to the east. Renouncing the Second Reich's interests in the west and in colonial empire, Hitler intended his Third Reich to establish good relations with "Germanic" Britain, leave France isolated, and turn to a vast agrarian settlement project in Poland and the Ukraine.

The program outlined in *Mein Kampf* was not carried out in detail, of course. The agreement with Britain proved impossible, and Hitler did indeed return to western conquests and to overseas colonial projects. But he never abandoned the ideological priorities; they were responsible for his subsequent choice of the fatal attack on Russia in 1941 rather than a much more fruitful Mediterranean strategy.

Economic Considerations

Another interpretation of Hitler's actions in 1938 and 1939 rests on economic considerations. The brilliant Nazi success in restoring full employment by 1935 was based on massive public spending, sealing the German currency off from international fluctuations, and maintaining low wages by political authority. The major problem in the mid-1930s was what to do next. The recurrence of either inflation or domestic disorder would destroy the regime, and it was not certain that simply continuing those early economic measures indefinitely could avoid one or both disasters.

The chief architect of Germany's economic "miracle" after 1933, Finance Minister Hjalmar Schacht, thought that German economic isolation was impossible in the long run. The only way to overcome Germany's basic raw material shortages was by reviving foreign trade, which was feasible within the improved economic circumstances of 1936. *Reich Marshal* Hermann Goering, however, advocated a policy of au-

---

[8]An autobiographical work, *Mein Kampf* was written in prison after the Munich *Putsch.* Hitler wrote another book in 1928 on foreign policy, which remained unpublished until 1961.
[9]People, in a racial sense.

tarky, or economic self-sufficiency. Goering's views prevailed, and he was named head of the Four Year Plan organization in September 1936 to develop self-sufficiency. The decision for autarky committed Germany to developing low-grade ores and expensive substitutes for oil and rubber. Under these conditions, economic prosperity and social stability may have seemed possible only through territorial expansion: to obtain the oil and wheat of Eastern Europe, and to instill pride in the glory of conquest. The case is not proven, but it may well be that the economic decisions of 1936 and 1937 forced Hitler to undertake an aggressive foreign policy in order to avoid domestic difficulties.

According to yet another interpretation of Nazi aims, Hitler was simply a master pragmatist, seizing opportunities as they presented themselves. Such an opportunity was clearly at hand at the beginning of 1938. Italian involvement in Ethiopia freed Hitler from his main rival in Austria; the way was open for another attempt at *Anschluss.*

After Chancellor Dollfuss' murder in the failed *coup* of 1934, his associate and successor Kurt Schuschnigg attempted to keep Austria independent by balancing off rival forces. On the one hand was the home militia (*Heimwehr*) under Prince Ernst Rüdiger von Starhemberg, Mussolini's main support in Austria. On the other hand was the Austrian Nazi party, temporarily set back by its failure in July 1934. Germany's growing strength and the desire of many Austrians to escape from the petty nationhood left to them by the Versailles settlement soon revived the illegal Austrian branch of the Nazi party. When it became apparent that Italian interests had shifted elsewhere with the conquest of Ethiopia, Schuschnigg was forced to contend with the Austrian Nazis without outside help. At the end of 1937, he tried to divide the pro-*Anschluss* forces by bringing one of their more law-abiding leaders, Artur von Seyss-Inquart, into the government, while cracking down on the illegal Nazi organization in Austria.

These steps provide the background for the famous meeting between Hitler and Schuschnigg on February 12, 1938, at Berchtesgaden, Hitler's alpine retreat. On the basis of Schuschnigg's own account of the three-hour browbeating he received from Hitler, it was long assumed that Hitler was treacherously preparing armed force behind Schuschnigg's back. In fact, Hitler decided to send German troops into Austria only several weeks later, in a spur-of-the-moment decision that lends weight to the opportunistic interpretation of Hitler's expansionist moves. At Berchtesgaden, Hitler had assumed he was making sufficient progress through indirect pressure: Schuschnigg agreed to appoint the pro-*Anschluss* Seyss-Inquart to the vital position of Minister of the Interior, with its control of the police.

Hitler decided on armed action when Schuschnigg suddenly announced on March 9 that he would put the question of Austrian independence to a plebiscite on the following Sunday, March 13. If a majority of Austrians voted for independence, Hitler's hopes for *Anschluss* by indirect means would suffer another long postponement. The next day, March 10, Hitler ordered troops to prepare for movement into Austria. Late on March 11 he gave the signal to move. By then, Schuschnigg had agreed to cancel the plebiscite, but Goering engineered a fictitious request for German intervention "to preserve order" from the new Minister of the Interior, Seyss-Inquart. At the same time Mussolini assured Hitler that he now had no objections to *Anschluss.* Hitler's response over the telephone to the German ambassador in Rome shows his nervous excitement and relief:

PRINCE PHILIP OF HESSE I have just come back from the Palazzo
    Venezia. The duce accepted the whole thing in a very friendly manner.
    He sends you his regards. . . .
HITLER Then please tell Mussolini I will never forget him for this.
HESSE Yes.
HITLER Never, never, never, whatever happens. . . . As soon as the Aus-
    trian affair is settled, I shall be ready to go with him, through thick and
    thin, no matter what happens.
HESSE Yes, my Führer.
HITLER Listen, I shall make any agreement—I am no longer in fear of the
    terrible position which would have existed militarily in case we had got
    into a conflict. You may tell him that I thank him ever so much; never,
    never shall I forget.
HESSE Yes, my Führer.
HITLER I will never forget, whatever may happen. If he should ever need
    any help or be in any danger, he can be convinced that I shall stick by
    him, whatever may happen, even if the whole world were against him.
HESSE Yes, my Führer.[10]

At dawn on March 12, German troops marched into Austria. Hitler
received a tumultuous welcome in his hometown, Linz, and in Vienna,
the city of his student days. Although much of the German equipment
broke down along the highway to Vienna, there was no time or resources
for an opposition to form. Abroad, it was accepted that the *Anschluss* was
probably supported by a majority of Austrians, which made it a belated
exercise in Wilsonian self-determination. No European power was
prepared to use force against a *fait accompli,* and a popular one at that.
Hitler's Germany had expanded into territory that had never been part
of the old Reich. Germany was now a nation of 80 million people.

Czechoslovakia and Appeasement, 1938

After the *Anschluss,* Germany's other eastern frontiers were called into
question. Hitler had acquired a new sense of assurance. German-
speaking populations in Czechoslovakia and Poland began to clamor for
protection. Europe passed through one border crisis after another for
eighteen months until the Second World War began on September 3,
1939.

Czechoslovakia's Precarious Position

Czechoslovakia was now in a very exposed position. On the map,
Czechoslovakia looked very much like a man with his head in a lion's
jaws. The ring of mountain defenses on the German border could now
be turned from the south through Austria. Worse still, the new state
suffered from nationality problems. The large Czechoslovak state
created in 1919 with French support was not so much a triumph of
self-determination for Czechs as it was something analogous to the

---

[10]Quoted in Alan Bullock, *Hitler: A Study in Tyranny,* 2nd ed. (New York, 1962), p. 432.

Habsburg Empire writ small. Alongside 7.25 million Czechs were 5 million Slovaks, not all of whom were reconciled to union with dominant Czechs; 750,000 Magyars, 500,000 Ruthenians, and 90,000 Poles remained conscious of linguistic and cultural distinctness. And some 3.25 million Germans lived in the Sudetenland, along the western border. It was from the Sudetenland that Georg von Schönerer had come, the founder of the pan-German movement that had influenced Hitler as a drifting youth in Vienna.[11] Although a law in 1920 permitted the use of minority languages in schools and law courts where a minority surpassed 20 percent of the population, there continued to be much resentment over the language of schooling and over alleged discrimination against minorities in the public services. To make matters worse, the depression hit hardest in German-speaking cities. The overall unemployment rate was about 25 percent, but Germans complained that they were laid off before Czechs. Czechoslovakia had seemed the most successful democracy among the Eastern European successor states, but depression and resurgent nationalism began to threaten its very existence. Small wonder that President Eduard Beneš and the dominant Czech parties were adamant against the idea of plebiscites among the other nationalities. Any concession seemed likely to open the floodgates of massive secession.

Czechoslovakia was made of flammable material, and Hitler blew vigorously on the sparks. He encouraged the nationalist demonstrations led by Konrad Henlein, a physical education teacher in a German-language high school in the Sudetenland, who had emerged as the leading spokesman of the German people there. Soon after the *Anschluss,* Hitler received Henlein at Berchtesgaden and encouraged him to escalate his demands steadily beyond whatever the Czechs were willing to accept. "We must always demand so much that we can never be satisfied."[12]

Appeasement Policy

Rising tensions in Czechoslovakia made some dramatic new German gain there likely. We must now look closely at the British and French responses to this prospect, for their solution to the Czech crisis was the high point of the policy known as "appeasement." The errors of appeasement at that time were so firmly impressed on those leaders who reached adulthood in the 1930s that they spent the 1950s and 1960s reacting in the opposite fashion to international crises: for example, Anthony Eden against the Egyptians at Suez in 1956; American policymakers against the Viet Cong in 1965. Since it has been the most influential negative lesson for a whole generation of Western leaders, it is important to understand appeasement in the 1930s.

One notion to dismiss is that the appeasers of Hitler in Britain and

[11]See Chapter 1, p. 38.
[12]*Documents on German Foreign Policy, 1933–45,* Series D, Vol. 2, No. 107, pp. 197–98.

France were sympathetic to Hitler's ideas or methods. The dominant figure in the appeasement policy was Neville Chamberlain, who succeeded Stanley Baldwin as prime minister and foreign minister of England in May 1937. Chamberlain came from the progressive wing of the Conservative party, from a tradition of municipal social services in Birmingham where both he and his father had been mayor. As Minister of Health in 1931, he was the strongest Tory spokesman for positive government measures of social welfare and an ancestor of the welfare-state Tories of the following generation. He occupied the other extreme of the party from men like Winston Churchill, who was much more interested in world grandeur and not unsympathetic to Franco and Mussolini. Chamberlain's letters to his sister, the best guide to his way of thinking, are full of a fastidious distaste for Hitler and Nazism, befitting a rather austere Unitarian reformer: "Is it not positively horrible to think that the fate of hundreds of millions of persons depends on one man, and he is half mad."[13]

Appeasement was neither a policy of drift nor an absence of policy. Chamberlain, in particular, was an activist in foreign policy. A post-Wilsonian idealist who distrusted professional diplomats, he was convinced by his own successes in labor–management relations that he could do better himself with face-to-face contact. In addition to his own "summit diplomacy," Chamberlain was inclined to rely on other amateurs, such as the shipping magnate Lord Runciman, for delicate diplomatic missions.

Appeasement was Chamberlain's energetic and calculated effort to locate the sources of Germany's frustrations and then to "remove the danger spots one by one"[14] by bargaining instead of letting them spin out of control, as in 1914. *To appease,* before 1938, was simply a noncontroversial verb meaning "to lessen friction and conflict." In that sense, the policy led by Chamberlain and accepted by the French had its reasonable side. Only later, after that policy had failed to keep Europe from plunging once more into war, did the word become an epithet.

Appeasement rested on a number of assumptions. Perhaps its basic foundation was the conviction among the survivors of the First World War that Europe could not survive another such bloodletting. Every French town had its *monument aux morts* with its long list of the dead; no British village was without its war memorial. Even tiny villages displayed prodigious lists of casualties. Mutilated war veterans were conspicuous reminders, as was the arrival of the "hollow years" in the 1930s. Added to this were science fiction conceptions of the next war, with its aerial bombardments and poison gas. Millions of deaths were predicted, and imaginations ran riot about the fate of London or Paris as larger Guernicas. Or Berlin: even German populations had to be reassured in the late 1930s that they were safe from aerial bombardment.[15] On the

[13]Quoted in Keith Feiling, *The Life of Neville Chamberlain* (London, 1946), p. 357.
[14]Quoted in *Ibid.,* p. 351.
[15]*Illustrierter Beobachter,* August 24, 1939, pp. 1316–18.

Allied side, a growing consciousness of inferiority in armaments made hearts sink even lower at the prospect of war.

Appeasement rested, further, on several less explicit suppositions. Nazism, the appeasers believed, was a political disease caused by the Versailles Treaties. Once the worst irritants were removed, the fever and swelling would go down. Many British, in particular, accepted the validity of some of the German grievances at the hands of an arrogant and bellicose France in 1919. Although the German tone was truculent, the changes demanded up through 1938 did not extend beyond the apparently enthusiastic union of German-speaking peoples in Eastern Europe; the most shocking internal excesses were still to come (the smashing of Jewish shops in the *Kristallnacht* of November 1938, for example). The appeasers assumed that Hitler would prefer a peaceable negotiation of issues to forcible settlement, and that he would raise only a finite number of such issues. Chamberlain, therefore, tried to explain to Hitler that he could win substantial revision of the Versailles system by negotiation if he would just lower his voice.

Finally, and least explicitly of all, appeasement rested on domestic considerations of internal order. At the most elementary level, the appeasers assumed that a new war would lead to another round of revolutions like those of 1917. They had no stomach for another bout with the social tensions of total war. Regardless of how distasteful his manners or his regime were, Hitler was a barrier to Bolshevik expansion into central Europe. Two of Chamberlain's associates—Lord Halifax and Sir Horace Wilson—praised Hitler to his face in 1938 for his "great services" to the defense of European civilization from the Bolsheviks. Geoffrey Dawson, editor of the most authoritative conservative newspaper in England, the London *Times,* was "certainly influenced," says his biographer, "by the thought that Nazi Germany served as a barrier to the spread of Communism."[16] Chamberlain's predecessor Stanley Baldwin said, "If Hitler moves east, I shall not break my heart."[17]

The curious effect of these assumptions was to align the proponents of military action and the proponents of peace in the Western democracies in 1938 and 1939 in unexpected camps. The proponents of military action sympathized with Léon Blum's Popular Front in France, considered the possibility of a more active alliance with the Soviet Union, and favored more vigorous aid to Republican Spain. They drew on traditionally pacifist elements of the European left. The proponents of appeasement hoped to woo Mussolini away from the Axis, and offered substantial concessions to Hitler in the effort to avoid a war that could only benefit the revolutionary left. They began to regard a war to block Hitler as "Stalin's War." They drew on elements of the traditional admirers of armies and empires. This exchange of traditional foreign policy preferences helped to make any concerted policy toward Hitler on the part of Britain and France nationally divisive.

[16]Christopher Thorne, *The Approach of War, 1938–39* (London, 1967), pp. 14–15.
[17]Robert Keith Middlemas and John Barnes, *Baldwin* (London, 1969), p. 947.

Working from the presumptions underlying appeasement, Neville Chamberlain set out even before the *Anschluss* to replace Stanley Baldwin's passivity with an active policy of finding and resolving conflicts with Hitler before they could become crises. He took the initiative, not waiting for Hitler's thrusts. In November 1937, he sent Lord Halifax to attend a fox hunt with *Reich Marshal* Goering, whose many titles included that of Master of the German Hunt. Halifax's mission was to assure the German leaders privately about "questions arising out of the Versailles settlement which were capable of causing trouble if they were unwisely settled—Danzig, Austria, Czechoslovakia—: on all these matters we were not necessarily concerned to stand for the status quo as of today, but we were very much concerned to secure the avoidance of such treatment of them as would be likely to cause trouble."[18] In other words, the British government was ready to negotiate adjustments in Germany's eastern frontiers if the changes could be carried out peaceably.

The British government did not change this approach after the *Anschluss* and in the spring of 1938 when pressures began to build around Czechoslovakia. French Premier Léon Blum, whose government was already bound to Czechoslovakia by the mutual defense treaty of 1924, proposed in March 1938 that Britain and France issue a joint statement guaranteeing the existing Czech borders. But the British government continued to refuse any commitments east of the Rhine, as it had done since 1919. Lord Halifax, now foreign minister, gave the reply: "Quite frankly, the moment is unfavorable, and our plans, both for offence and defence, are not sufficiently advanced."[19] After Blum left office again in April 1938, his successors—Prime Minister Edouard Daladier and Foreign Minister Georges Bonnet—left foreign policy initiatives to Chamberlain.

Build-up of the Czechoslovak Crisis

Technically speaking, the quarrel was an internal matter between the Czechoslovak government and its German-speaking minority in the Sudetenland. Konrad Henlein presented an ambitious list of demands in April 1938. The Karlsbad program, as it was called, demanded internal autonomy for German-speaking areas, reparations to the German minority for all their sufferings since 1918, and full liberty for Germans to express "the ideology of Germans." The Czechoslovak government countered with plans to liberalize the Nationalities Statute of 1920 to some degree. A war scare over the weekend of May 20 and 21, however, showed how easily these internal tensions might bring all the principal states of Europe into conflict. Claiming that the Germans were amassing troops on the frontier, the Czechoslovaks mobilized their Army on May 20. The French and Russian governments publicly affirmed their treaty

[18]Quoted in A. L. Rowse, *Appeasement* (London, 1961), p. 65.
[19]*Documents on British Foreign Policy, 1919–1939,* Series 3, Vol. 1, No. 107, p. 87.

September 30, 1938: Neville Chamberlain returns to London after signing the Munich settlement. Chamberlain is reading the terms over the BBC on arrival at Heston Airport.

commitments to Czechoslovakia, and Lord Halifax warned that Britain could not be guaranteed to stand aside if the Germans intervened in Czechoslovakia. Hitler was forced to deny publicly any aggressive intentions toward the Czechs.

After the war scare, positions hardened on all sides. Hitler seems to have decided not only to get his revenge on the Czechs but to do so by force, regardless of the possibilities of negotiation that might arise. He issued military orders on May 30 stating his "unalterable intention to smash Czechoslovakia by military action in the near future," whenever "a convenient apparent excuse and adequate political justification"[20] could be found. Czech President Beneš stiffened his resolve not to yield to German force. The Allies, and particularly Neville Chamberlain, resolved not to be led to the brink of war again by Czechoslovak intransigence. A senior British diplomat in Berlin suggested to a German official that if the German government would confidentially make known its wishes in the Sudetenland, the British government would force the Czechs to accept them.[21] When Czechoslovak concessions to the German minority were slow, the British ambassador to

[20]*Documents on German Foreign Policy, 1933–45,* Series D, Vol. 2, No. 221, p. 358.
[21]*Ibid.,* No. 151.

Germany, Sir Neville Henderson, thought in July 1938 that it was time for the Czechs to get "a real twist of the screw."[22]

Tension mounted sharply again in September 1938. Following an impassioned speech by Hitler at the Nuremberg Party Rally on September 12, rioting broke out in the Sudetenland, whereupon the Czechoslovak government declared martial law. Henlein fled into Germany and organized a *Freikorps* for raids across the border. Signs increased of a German armed intervention. At the end of September, it seemed so certain that war would break out that armed forces were being mobilized in Britain and France, and schoolchildren were being evacuated from London.

The Munich Settlement

Neville Chamberlain now took the initiative to force a solution on Czechoslovakia that would satisfy Hitler and thus avert war. Boarding an airplane for the first time in his sixty-nine years, the British prime minister flew to Germany three times in fourteen days: to Hitler's mountain retreat at Berchtesgaden on September 15, to the Rhine resort town of Godesberg on September 22, and then to Munich on September 29. There it was agreed to buy Hitler off with immediate transfer of the Sudetenland from Czechoslovakia to Germany. The whole negotiation is known as the Munich settlement—virtually a synonym for appeasement.

At Berchtesgaden on September 15 Hitler delivered a tirade on alleged Czechoslovak atrocities against Germans in the Sudetenland. Chamberlain believed that only a border adjustment could prevent war. He accepted "the principle of the detachment of the Sudeten areas"—more than the mere autonomy Konrad Henlein had demanded a few months earlier, and more than Hitler had publicly demanded up to that time.

Chamberlain and French Premier Daladier then had to force President Beneš to accept this territorial cession. It was this task that engendered the guilt feelings that afterward clung to the Munich settlement in the west. Beneš held out until 5:00 P.M. on September 21, yielding only after the British and French governments had threatened to abandon Czechoslovakia to its fate. Thinking the crisis was over, Chamberlain flew to Godesberg to give Hitler the news on September 22. Chamberlain had not yet grasped that Hitler really did not want a peaceful compromise, even one that granted all his territorial demands. He was astonished at Hitler's reply to his good news: "Das geht nicht mehr." (That won't do any more.) The proposed cession of the Sudetenland must now take place within three days, and German troops must enter the ceded areas at once.

Chamberlain returned to London believing that his mission had failed. The British fleet was mobilized on September 27; French troops manned the newly completed Maginot Line for the first time. Trenches

[22]*Documents on British Foreign Policy*, Series 3, Vol. 1, No. 512, p. 590.

were dug and gas masks issued in London. For a few days horrified Europeans expected at any moment to hear the first bombs fall on their cities.

Frantic last-minute negotiations continued nevertheless. Mussolini proposed a four-power conference.[23] Although Hitler later claimed he was defrauded of his march into Prague, he agreed to negotiate the details of the Sudetenland cession rather than take it by force. Hitler's letter agreeing to discuss the matter once again was delivered while Chamberlain was addressing the House of Commons at 8:30 P.M. on September 28 about this "horrible, incredible" situation that had arisen "because of a quarrel in a faraway country between people of whom we know nothing."

At Munich on September 29 Hitler obtained almost everything he had demanded in his ultimatum to Chamberlain at Godesberg. The Sudetenland was transferred to Germany, of which it had never been part. All parts of that area with populations more than 50 percent German were transferred at once. Plebiscites were to be held in other parts with large German minorities (they were not, in fact, ever held). In addition to 2,825,000 Germans, some 800,000 Czechs were thus forcibly shifted into Germany in what claimed to be an exercise in national self-determination. Hitler agreed to respect the sovereignty of the rest of Czechoslovakia. Both Chamberlain and Daladier were mobbed by deliriously joyful crowds on their return. In the very short run, the Munich settlement was a success. There was no war in September 1938.

[23]Britain, France, Germany, and Italy. Czechoslovakia and the Soviet Union were excluded from the Munich Conference.

Silent citizens of Prague watch German troops enter the city on March 15, 1939, as Hitler assumed a protectorate over Bohemia-Moravia in violation of the Munich settlement of six months before.

In the longer run, the Munich settlement accomplished none of the goals that the appeasement policy had been intended to achieve. It did not preserve the rest of Czechoslovakia. Poland and Hungary demanded and received areas that contained their fellow nationals; then, exploiting unrest among Slovaks who showed renewed interest in separation from the Czechs, Hitler himself broke the agreement six months later. German troops moved into Prague on March 15, 1939. The Czech areas became the "Protectorate of Bohemia-Moravia," and the Slovak areas were set up as an independent nation. In the long run, settlement did not prevent war either. It further divided a potential anti-Hitler alliance by excluding the Soviet Union from an active role in the Czechoslovak crisis. The Munich settlement has had virtually no defenders, either on moral or pragmatic grounds.

The Alternative of War

The alternative to appeasement in 1938 was to stand ready to support Czechoslovakia by military force. France was bound to come to the Czechs' aid by a 1924 treaty, part of the French security system in Eastern Europe. The Soviet Union was bound by a 1935 treaty to come to the Czechs' aid if the French did so: If the Czechs held firm and went to war to retain the German-speaking Sudetenland, the play of alliances would bring France and then the Soviet Union into a widening European conflict against Germany. In short, the alternative was a preventive war against Hitler by France and perhaps Britain, alongside the Soviet Union, to preserve one of the national anomalies of the Versailles system.

The heart of the matter was what the Soviets meant to do. Here, there is much less evidence available about Russian intentions than about German intentions. Soviet Foreign Minister Maxim Litvinov stated publicly as early as March 17, 1938, that his country was ready to "participate in collective actions" to "stop the further development of aggression." On September 2, Litvinov proposed an appeal to the League of Nations and a joint British–French–Soviet "statement of intention" to protect Czechoslovakia. One major problem with Soviet military intervention was that Soviet troops or aircraft would have to pass over Polish or Romanian soil to enter Czechoslovakia. Although Poland was adamantly opposed to the passage of Soviet forces, there is some evidence that the Romanian government was willing to allow Soviet passage if the League of Nations voted for sanctions against Germany. Another problem was that the Soviet purge trials were in the process of eliminating more than half of the Soviet officer corps. There is no evidence that the Russians prepared any force to aid the Czechs.

What is clear is that the British and French governments wanted no part of a war fought alongside the Soviet Union. Western suspicion of Communist intentions in European affairs was at its height after two years of the Spanish Civil War. After the Soviet proposal of March 17,

Lord Halifax wrote the British ambassador in France that "we did not think it had any great value."[24] Chamberlain referred to the Soviet Union as that "more than half Asian" nation. The French government was eager to avoid a situation in which its treaty obligations would come into effect. For both Western governments, almost any concession was preferable to "Stalin's War."

Since the Second World War, there has been much speculation that if the other European states had supported Czechoslovakia in 1938, the German opposition to Hitler would have overthrown him. The appeal of this possibility is evident: it rests on the chance that Czechoslovakia could have been defended without war, that Hitler could have been removed from within, and that the Soviet Union would not have been brought into the heart of Europe by the Second World War, if only Britain and France had shown more courage in September 1938. Indeed, many German generals were alarmed by the prospect of war in 1938, a war for which they expected to be ready only in 1943. The chief of the General Staff, General Ludwig Beck, even resigned over the Czech crisis. But since other generals took no action, most of our knowledge of their intentions rests on postwar memoirs. Even if we accept their recollected intentions at face value, their chances of rallying many other German officers and bureaucrats to disobedience during a time of international crisis were extremely small. In any event, the appeasers were sure at the time that they would have had to fight to keep the Sudetenland Czech, and that they refused to do.

It may well be that an effort to save Czechoslovakia by force in September 1938 would have divided the Western powers and the Soviet Union more than it would have divided Germany. Revulsion against another war spread not only among the fearful conservatives but among the traditionally pacifist left. Even Léon Blum had to admit his "sense of deliverance."[25] A vast majority of Western Europeans backed appeasement in September 1938.

The appeasement policy failed both to save the rest of Czechoslovakia and to avoid war in the 1930s. That point is obvious to everyone now. All the assumptions were wrong in Hitler's case. That does not mean, of course, that the appeasers' basic aim of locating grievances and attempting to negotiate them rather than respond automatically by force to every challenge to the *status quo* should not be applied to other cases and at other times.

The Polish Crisis, 1939: Descent into War

It was soon clear that Poland was next. No other part of the eastern settlement of 1919 was as offensive to German public opinion as the Polish frontiers. The Polish Corridor cut East Prussia off from the rest of Germany; Danzig, a free city under League of Nations supervision, was mostly German in population; and Poland controlled German minorities

---

[24]*Documents on British Foreign Policy, 1919–1939,* Series 3, Vol. 1, No. 109, p. 88.
[25]Quoted in *Le populaire,* October 1, 1938.

in rich Silesia. In the spring of 1939, German Foreign Minister Joachim von Ribbentrop demanded that Poland return Danzig to Germany and permit a road–rail route across the corridor; in exchange Germany would offer some form of common defense against the Soviet Union. Hitler seems at this stage to have expected mere readjustments of the Polish–German frontiers without war, although Hitler's style of alternating between reason and force makes his intentions at any one point difficult to fathom. The Polish government of Colonel Josef Beck was ready to profit by Hitler's aggressions when it could; for example, Poland had seized the disputed area of Teschen from the Czechs soon after Munich. But Beck intended to balance between Germany and the Soviet Union rather than commit Poland to the protection of either giant neighbor.

Appeasement Abandoned

The decisive change came from England and France. Angered and disillusioned that the Munich settlement had been mocked by Germany's dismemberment of the rest of Czechoslovakia in March 1939 and alarmed by strident German propaganda attacks on Poland, Neville Chamberlain announced publicly in the House of Commons on March 31 that England and France would bring Poland "all the support in their power" if Polish independence were "clearly threatened." Here was the firm Continental commitment that the British had resisted since 1919. The British government had extended to Poland the guarantee denied the more easily defended Czechoslovakia a year earlier. Neville Chamberlain himself had abandoned appeasement.

This Anglo-French guarantee to Poland has become a hotly disputed step in the path to the Second World War. According to the conventional wisdom, the Western democracies should have done this from the first. But the guarantee raises legitimate questions. Some Polish–German frontier adjustment was not unreasonable. Did a righteously indignant Chamberlain, enraged by the results of the Munich settlement, seek to save face by blocking any chance for a second Munich over Poland, at the cost of leaving unexplored the possibility for negotiated settlement? Did he inject a new rigidity into European affairs?

Did he commit Europe to a global war by deciding that it was inevitable, with the same evangelical fervor with which he had earlier decided that all problems were negotiable? Was the guarantee a "provocative"[26] act that only hardened Polish obstinacy and goaded Hitler into a forceful solution he had not wanted?

One's feelings about a lost opportunity for negotiation over Danzig in 1939 depend on one's sense of Hitler's intentions. Whatever his interest in a negotiated settlement earlier, by the end of May 1939 Hitler had clearly decided that "successes can no longer be attained without the

---

[26]Basil H. Liddell-Hart, *Memoirs*, Vol. 2 (London 1965), pp. 214, 217, 255. These questions were first raised in vigorous form in A. J. P. Taylor, *The Origins of the Second World War* (London, 1961), Chapters 10 and 11.

shedding of blood. . . . There is no question of sparing Poland and we are left with the decision: to attack Poland at the first suitable opportunity. . . . There will be war."[27] The war he seems to have wanted, however, was meant to be both local and short. For that purpose he needed to divide Poland from its Anglo-French guarantors. By claiming in public to want only Danzig and the right of German transit across the corridor, he hoped to make the Poles appear the intransigent party and raise resentment against them in London and Paris. Then he could deal with Poland alone, without a general war.

Hitler could still believe that the Anglo-French guarantee was not serious. The British Army was unprepared. A groundswell of French opinion did not want to "die for Danzig." Above all, what force could Britain and France actually bring to bear on the defense of distant Poland? As tension mounted over Danzig in 1939, third parties became the crucial actors on each side: the Soviet Union and Italy.

The Nazi-Soviet Pact

The Anglo-French guarantee to Poland could not be implemented effectively without Soviet help. The French could attack western Germany, of course, but they would have little time to act before Poland had been defeated—even assuming there was anyone in France who wanted to make such an attack in 1939. A Soviet alliance was the obvious way to confront Hitler with the two-front menace of 1914. Chamberlain and the British government were not very enthusiastic, however. In addition to feeling a basic distaste for the Soviet regime, they were suspicious of Stalin's motives (was he trying to get Hitler involved in a war in the west?) and doubtful of the capability of his recently purged officer corps. Might not an alliance with Stalin make war more likely than less? Nevertheless, the British and French governments did negotiate all spring and summer with the Soviets over a possible three-power security treaty. On August 22, 1939, however, like a bombshell, came the astonishing announcement that German Foreign Minister Ribbentrop was in Moscow to sign an agreement: the Nazi-Soviet Pact.

The British and French governments have frequently been accused of throwing away potential Soviet help against Hitler, out of ideological distaste or even a scheme to encourage Hitler to move east. They settled the Czech affair without Soviet participation at Munich in September 1938; they rejected Soviet Foreign Minister Litvinov's proposals for a three-power treaty in April 1939; they sent minor figures by slow boat to negotiate in Moscow. There were genuine difficulties, however. Soviet troops could not attack Hitler without crossing Poland or Romania, neither of which was willing to negotiate rights of passage. The British and French refused to impose Soviet entry rights on Poland and Romania, and they were suspicious that Stalin meant to use rights to

---

[27]*Documents on German Foreign Policy, 1933–45*, Series D, Vol. 6, No. 433, pp. 574–80.

combat "indirect aggression" as a pretext for taking over the Baltic States (Latvia, Estonia, Lithuania). At bottom, however, the decisive fact in the signing of a Nazi-Soviet Pact was that Hitler could offer something to Stalin that the Western democracies could not.

German–Soviet contacts (not counting the military arrangements of the early years) went back to the revival of economic negotiations at the beginning of 1939. The Soviet economic negotiator dropped some broad hints to the Germans in April, and Stalin removed his "pro-League" Foreign Minister Litvinov in May. Hitler decided at the end of May to explore the possibility of obtaining Soviet neutrality.

The negotiations began in earnest only when the urgent tone of German communications to Russia in August 1939 made the Russians aware that the Germans were going to invade Poland. With that knowledge, Stalin's choice was clear. To join the Allies meant going to war over Poland; Hitler offered neutrality. Furthermore, Hitler offered the Soviets the opportunity of expansion in the Baltic region, eastern Poland, and Bessarabia. Stalin could also calculate that if an eventual clash with Germany came, he might be better able to fend it off later. In short, the Allies offered "war without gain"; Hitler offered "gain without war."[28] Stalin made the obvious opportunistic choice in the Nazi-Soviet Pact.

The Nazi-Soviet Pact in itself was simply an agreement for each side to remain neutral in case the other became involved in a war with other nations. Attached to it, however, was a secret protocol agreeing to the division of Eastern Europe into spheres of influence. "In the event of a territorial and political rearrangement," Soviet Russia was to get Finland, the Baltic States of Estonia and Latvia, the eastern part of Poland, and Bessarabia, the area east of the Danube mouth that had gone to Romania in 1918. Germany would get the rest of Poland and Lithuania.

Hitler now hastened his invasion plans. Assured of a free hand from Stalin, Hitler needed only Mussolini's support to make his short war absolutely safe. Mussolini, however, thought that war would strain his faltering regime and regretfully told Hitler that he would have to stand aside. At the same time, Chamberlain ostentatiously ratified the Anglo-Polish guarantee on August 25. Eager to avoid Sir Edward Grey's error of failing to let Germany know in 1914 what England would do if Belgium were invaded, Chamberlain repeated his public announcement that England would declare war if Polish independence were threatened. Hitler drew back for five days, seeming to go along with Mussolini's efforts to mediate. He was probably still convinced that Chamberlain was bluffing. Indeed, he was correct in judging the sinking hearts with which the British and French contemplated war. Although the German armies marched into Poland on September 1, the British and French did not declare war until September 3. Europeans entered the Second World War reluctantly, without any of the enthusiasm of 1914.

[28]Thorne, p. 137.

The Origins of the Second World War

There has been much less dispute about causes of the Second World War than the First. The war of September 1939 has been almost universally considered Hitler's war, far more the willful act of one man than an overcharged diplomatic-military economic system spinning out of control as in 1914.

In the case of the Second World War the historians have generally agreed with the propagandists. Twenty years after 1914, "revisionist" historians in the Allied countries had thoroughly discredited the Allied propagandists' version of sole German war guilt. That debate about 1914 forced attention away from personal and national "guilt" toward underlying problems of alliance diplomacy, economic rivalry, popular nationalism, and uncontrolled military planning.

Twenty years after 1939, only one "revisionist" account of the outbreak of the Second World War had appeared in the Allied countries,[29] and it has not yet been followed by a serious sequel. Moreover, that "revisionist" work actually focused the debate even more clearly on the leaders' personalities and decisions. Opening the German archives produced more evidence of Hitler's personal role; as for German survivors and historians, they have been delighted to unload all responsibility on a single set of shoulders. It may well be that Hitler's own cravings for violent solutions were the indispensable "proximate cause" of the war: no Hitler, no war.

There is a larger view, however, according to which both wars reflect fundamental shortcomings of a brilliant but flawed civilization that could not settle its differences without periodic blood baths. Nothing in the 1919 settlement had changed the basic division of Europe (and the world) into separate sovereign states that recognized no higher authority than national interest. Experiments with a League of Nations and a more public diplomacy had proved no more successful in averting war than the binding alliance systems and the secret dynastic diplomacy of the years before 1914; if anything, they were less successful. Some would argue that until the state system is replaced by a world government, there can be no lasting peace. Even that solution, however, assuming that it has the remotest chance of realization, leaves the way open for civil war or local conflicts.

Neither had the efforts at Versailles to recognize national aspirations and spread democracy in Europe impeded the resort to war. Indeed, the very conception of national or ethnic separateness lay at the root of the Eastern European border quarrels that Hitler had exploited. And democratic regimes reflected popular passions for triumph and revenge no less readily than authoritarian ones. Despite the manifest failure of a policy of recognizing ever more independent nation-states to create a stable Europe between the wars, the same pattern continued to spread in the world after 1945.

[29]Taylor.

Hitler visits tearful civilians in Poland after the German invasion, September 1939. The German propaganda office described them as members of the German minority weeping "tears of deliverance."

Some would argue that economic failure was the fundamental reason for Europe's return to war in 1939. Clearly the depression of the 1930s, the most severe Europe had ever endured, had much to do with Hitler's ascent to power and the inability of his neighbors to stop him. Marxists would put the case more fundamentally: the depression was inevitable to a ripe capitalist system at some point, and that when domestic profit rates began to fall, the capitalist powers would eventually go to war over the spoils of the rest of the world. That interpretation of war, however, is clouded by the possibility that Marxist states (for example, the Soviet Union and China) could well go to war among themselves.

It may be that no human groups have altogether avoided war for long. The novelty of the European experience may be not its near suicide twice in twenty-five years on the battlefield, but the spreading belief in Europe since 1914 that war is unnatural and avoidable.

Suggestions for Further Reading

Thirty-five years after the event, there has been less fundamental debate over the origins of the Second World War than over the First. The most important challenge to orthodoxy has been A. J. P. Taylor, *Origins of the Second World War,* 2nd ed. (1963), who argued that Hitler's designs did not differ fundamentally from those of Bismarck and Stresemann, and that the British and French bore some share of the responsibility for the resort to general war over Poland. The passionate controversy aroused by Taylor's work may be followed in William Roger Louis, ed., *The Origins of the Second World War: A. J. P. Taylor and His Critics** (1972). Another important article not included by Louis is T. W. Mason, "Some Origins of the Second World War," *Past and Present*, No. 29 (December 1964).

Keith Eubank, *The Origins of World War II** (1969) is a good brief introduction to the general subject. Laurence Lafore, *The End of Glory: An Interpretation of the Origins of World War II** (1970) is readable and suggestive and contains a perceptive review of other books on the subject. Pierre Renouvin, *World War II and its Origins: International Relations, 1929–1945* (1969) is a careful scholarly survey. Christopher Thorne, *The Approach of War, 1938–1939** (1967) lucidly recounts the final crisis.

Gerhard L. Weinberg, *The Foreign Policy of Hitler's Germany: Diplomatic Revolution in Europe, 1933–1936* (1970) is the most authoritative treatment of any phase of Hitler's foreign policy. E. M. Robertson, *Hitler's Pre-War Policy and Military Plans, 1933–1939* (1963), and Norman Rich, *Hitler's War Aims* (1973) weigh ideology against improvisation in Hitler's moves. The essays on individual statesmen in Gordon A. Craig and Felix Gilbert, eds., *The Diplomats, 1918–1939**

(1953) are still valuable. F. S. Northedge, *The Troubled Giant* (1966) takes a critical view of British foreign policy between the wars. Adam B. Ulam, *Expansion and Coexistence: The History of Soviet Foreign Policy, 1917–1967** (1968) is the starting point for consideration of Soviet foreign policy.

For the Ethiopian War, see George W. Baer, *The Coming of the Italian-Ethiopian War* (1967), and Angelo del Boca, *The Ethiopian War, 1935–1941* (1969).

Jürgen Gehl, *Austria, Germany, and the Anschluss* (1963) stresses international factors and Hitler's last-minute improvisation. Dieter Wagner and Gerhard Tomkowitz, *Anschluss: The Week Hitler Seized Vienna* (1971) is a vivid narrative.

Among many accounts of the Munich accords, Keith Eubank, *Munich** (1963; reprint ed., 1965) is up-to-date and judicious. John W. Wheeler-Bennett, *Munich: Prologue to Tragedy* (1948) is still important.

The Nazi-Soviet Pact is the subject of many works. In addition to the Hilger and Meyer book cited at the end of Chapter 8, see Gerhard L. Weinberg, *Germany and the Soviet Union* (1954). James E. McSherry, *Stalin, Hitler, and Europe*, vol. 1: *The Origins of World War II, 1933–1939* (1968) depicts Stalin somewhat too one-dimensionally as the consummate manipulator. The difficulties of earlier Soviet relations with the West are recalled in William E. Scott, *Alliance Against Hitler: The Origins of the Franco-Soviet Pact* (1962).

Martin Gilbert and Richard Gott, *The Appeasers* (1963) is a stern indictment. More sympathetic views are examined by D. C. Watt, "Appeasement: The Rise of a Revisionist School?" *Political Quarterly*, Vol. 36, No. 2 (April 1965). Keith Feiling, *The Life of Neville Chamberlain* (1946) contains revealing personal correspondence. For the other side, see Neville Thompson, *The Anti-Appeasers* (1971).

A Panzer unit moves up on the eastern front, 1941. Troops and supplies are motorized in order to keep up with the Mark III tank, at right. In Blitzkrieg, Panzer units supported by Stuka dive bombers broke through enemy defenses, followed by slower moving horse-drawn units to consolidate the gain.

HITLER'S EUROPE: CONQUEST, COLLABORATION, AND RESISTANCE 1939–1942

15

Hitler was genuinely surprised when his war against Poland turned out to be a general European war. But he was not overly alarmed. His Third Reich seemed to have solved the problem that had destroyed Kaiser Wilhelm II's Second Reich: how to expand in Europe without facing a two-front war. His armies were overwhelmingly superior to the Poles. The only potential rival to the east, the Soviet Union, was ready to join him in the spoils. His western enemies were obviously reluctant to fight. Free to reverse the timing forced on his 1914 predecessors, Hitler could deal with Poland first, and then move the bulk of his forces west to deal with France at his leisure, if that was even necessary. Hitler wrote to Mussolini on August 26, 1939:

> As Germany, thanks to her agreement with Russia, will have all her forces free in the East after the defeat of Poland . . . I do not shrink from solving the Eastern question even at the risk of complications in the West.[1]

[1]Quoted in Alan Bullock, *Hitler: A Study in Tyranny,* 2nd ed. (New York, 1962), p. 538.

The Nature of the Conflict in 1939

The success of Hitler's calculation depended on speed. He had not solved his predecessors' problem of insufficient resources for a long war of attrition. Germany's efforts toward self-sufficiency through exploiting low-grade German iron ores and producing ersatz rubber and oil had only narrowed the gap. For any extended war, Germany would be dependent on iron ore from Sweden, oil from Romania and the Soviet Union, and grain from the east. Diplomacy might keep these resources flowing for a time, but their supply remained uncertain for a long war. To win, Hitler must win quickly.

German Army logistics experts, fearful of another long war, thought that Germany must shift over its entire productive capacity for war matériel, a process that could not be completed before 1943. Hitler decided instead on a strategy of *Blitzkrieg* (lightning war). By simply stockpiling enough supplies and armaments for one decisive strike against a surprised enemy, he thought he could not only win his immediate objectives but capture enough supplies and armaments to make up for his losses. This approach had the added advantage of sparing German civilians the pains (and the resentments) of a war economy. Hitler had decided simply to sidestep Germany's economic shortcomings, not solve them from within.

Germany entered war in 1939, therefore, superbly equipped for rapid thrusts but quite unprepared for an extended war. There was no long-range bomber in the German arsenal. The German Navy had only fifty-seven submarines, of which just twenty-two were designated for the high seas.[2] This deliberate renunciation of what had been Germany's chief maritime weapon after 1917 was a sign that Hitler did not expect war with Britain. Although rationing and wage-price controls were instituted, the German economy put no more resources into war production in 1939 and 1940 than it had in the years 1936 to 1939. Consumer goods continued to be produced, superhighways built (not always for strategic purposes), and as late as 1942, marble was still being imported for Hitler's grandiose building projects in Berlin.

Hitler's combined enemies were his superior in both numbers and resources. Poland, France, and Britain together had 120 million people to Hitler's 80 million. They held undisputed control of the seas and, with them, access to the world's strategic resources. Despite the Neutrality Acts of the United States, Franklin Roosevelt's "cash and carry" policy (sale of goods to any belligerent who could pay cash and transport them from American shores) gave France and Britain a virtual monopoly of American productive capacity, unlike the situation under American neutrality between 1914 and 1917. The Allies could defeat Hitler, then, under two conditions: if they could stave off that first lightning thrust, and then proceed gradually to choke off the German economy by blockade and peripheral encirclement. No other strategies were open to the Allies. Their depression remedies had prevented the construction of

[2]Henri Michel, *La Seconde guerre mondiale* (Paris, 1968), p. 17.

powerful offensive forces, and public opinion would make a preemptive strike difficult, even if they had been equipped for one. Everything depended on the effectiveness of their defensive preparations and on their material and emotional readiness to sustain another prolonged war.

The Allies were not hopelessly ill-equipped for their strategic position. The French Navy alone was far larger than the German; the British and French navies together could control both the Atlantic and the Mediterranean. The British were more advanced in heavy bomber design, and their light Mosquito bomber, so fast that it could dispense with defensive armament, could reach Berlin. On the ground, the French Maginot Line effectively closed the Rhine frontier from Switzerland to the Ardennes hills, at the French–Belgian border; indeed the Germans never overran it directly.

Taking the defensive position imposed grave disadvantages on the Allies. Although France and Britain had excellent prototypes of fighter aircraft and tanks, they had not put the latest models into mass production for fear of stockpiling equipment that might become obsolete before a war began. And they had to cover all fronts, not knowing where the Axis would strike. Graver still was the problem of morale. Hitler also belonged to the generation of the First World War, and he had reason to judge that the Allied populations would not support the one strategy open to them, another long war of attrition. Especially not after several tastes of *Blitzkrieg*.

In sharp contrast to the naive enthusiams of 1914, the European populations of 1939 faced war with deepening gloom. Even in Germany, crowds watched in stony silence as the troops passed by. Europeans had grown to expect that the next war would involve massive bombing of cities and use of poison gas. There had been foretastes of the one in Spain and the other in Ethiopia.

Psychological warfare contributed to this sense of alarm. On the battlefield, *Blitzkrieg* made calculated use of surprise and terror. The *Stuka* dive bomber, although rather slow and vulnerable, was equipped with sirens to terrify opposing ground forces. The Germans parachuted mannequins behind enemy lines to great effect. Their use of commandos dressed in Polish and Dutch uniforms lent credence to exaggerated rumors of fifth columns. On the home front, both sides managed their own populations' opinions with great care and aimed propaganda broadcasts at the opposing populations.

The terrors aroused by the prospect of war in 1939 were closely tied to the general expectations that science and technology would dominate it. In fact, however, the war began with weapons that were recognizable derivatives of those of 1918. The only important exception was radar, a British invention that had decisive influence in the air war of 1940. In technological matters, the advantage lay less with conceptions of *Blitzkrieg*, which depended on stockpiled weapons, than with the long sustained efforts, the larger resources, and the total war economies of the Allies. Anti-Semitism probably set German science back. Although the Berlin chemist Otto Hahn was the first to achieve fission of a uranium nucleus in 1939, his chief assistant, the brilliant woman physicist Lise Meitner, and other leading Jewish scientists were forced into exile, where they helped the Allies develop atomic weapons. But the chief blame for the stagnation of German nuclear physics was the government's decision to invest in missile technology instead. The same decision explains the German failure to exploit their scientists' development of the world's first jet aircraft, the Messerschmidt 262, at the very end of the war.

When the war began in 1939, it was not clear who would win. It was clear, however, that the war would wreak even more terror and havoc on European civilians than the last one.

War in the East, 1939–40

Blitzkrieg *in Poland*

The Polish campaign of September 1939 provided Europe's first good look at *Blitzkrieg*. Propaganda helped open the way. Hitler proclaimed the terrible sufferings of Germans who had been forced to live "under a people of inferior cultural value."[3] At the end of August, he staged a mock raid on a German frontier post by SS. troops disguised in Polish uniforms; they left a dead concentration camp inmate in a German uniform as proof of Polish "aggression." Even as his armies assembled Hitler dangled hopes of negotiation, which persuaded the British and French to force the Poles to postpone mobilization for another twenty-four hours. At dawn on September 1, German forces invaded Poland.

The main weapon was the *Panzer* division. It was not so much the numerical superiority of Germany's sixty-three divisions to Poland's forty as it was the presence of six *Panzer* divisions that completely disrupted the Polish defenses. A *Panzer* division was a self-contained striking force led by 300 or so tanks and accompanied by supporting forces and supplies capable of moving along at the same speed. A screen of fighter aircraft flew overhead, while *Stuka* dive bombers demoralized and destroyed opposition just ahead of the tanks. After the *Panzers* had secured an opening in the enemy defenses, they moved on, leaving behind more conventional units with horse-drawn equipment to hold the newly gained ground. The flat, open Polish terrain was ideal for fast tank warfare.

Although Britain and France were explicitly committed to come to Poland's defense immediately by air and by the sixteenth day with ground troops, there was only a minor French advance into the Saar on September 8. Further attacks were cancelled when it had obviously become too late to help. Without foreign aid, it was only a matter of time for Poland to give way. Despite vigorous efforts to reassemble a

[3]Bullock, pp. 551–52.

shattered defense, Warsaw fell on September 27, and the last Polish holdouts surrendered on October 2.

Russian Gains in Eastern Europe, 1940

Stalin was no less surprised than anyone else by the speed of the German advance in Eastern Europe. Nervous about German armies reaching the Soviet frontiers and anxious to assure his share of territory as promised by the secret protocol of August 24,[4] he rushed troops west into Poland on September 17. In the end he gained more territory than the Germans. A division of territory was arranged in a second Ribbentrop visit to Moscow at the end of September, and Germany and Russia again shared a common border, as they had from 1815 to 1914.[5]

No doubt Stalin found this an opportune moment to improve his western defensive frontiers. He concluded treaties of mutual assistance with Latvia, Estonia, and Lithuania, with the right to station Soviet troops in the latter country. (Lithuania had grasped the opportunity to reannex Vilna, taken by the Poles in 1920.)

Stalin then demanded that the Finns give up the Vyborg area, at the

[4]See Chapter 14, pp. 426–27.
[5]Stalin rejected Hitler's original plan of a rump client state around Warsaw.

Polish cavalry preparing to face the Nazi Panzers.

head of the Gulf of Finland, where the frontier was only twenty miles from Leningrad. When negotiations proved fruitless, the Soviets renounced their 1932 nonaggression pact with Finland and, without declaring war, invaded Finland on November 30, 1939. The ensuing "winter war" was surprisingly difficult for the Russians. The rest of the world (including Mussolini, bitterly affronted by the Nazi-Soviet Pact, which threatened Italy's Balkan interests) cheered for the "brave little Finns," while the Russians lost more casualties than there were troops in the Finnish Army. The poor Russian performance confirmed Western suspicions that the Soviet Army had been fatally weakened by the purges. By concentrating overwhelming force, the Soviets were finally able to force the Finns to surrender Vyborg on March 12, 1940.

Stalin recouped most of the rest of Russia's 1917 losses in the summer of 1940, while Hitler was preoccupied in the west. He seized the three Baltic States—Latvia, Estonia, and Lithuania—in June and incorporated them in August as member republics of the Soviet Union. On June 26, Stalin demanded that Romania cede Bessarabia, which had been Russian before the First World War, and Bukovina, which had not. By these steps, Russia had gained more than it had lost in 1917 at the mouth of the Danube, had recovered a large portion of former tsarist territory in Poland, and had advanced beyond tsarist frontiers in Finland.[6] Stalin may have anticipated an eventual break with Hitler, for which his defensive position was now improved. For the moment, however, he fulfilled the terms of the Nazi-Soviet Pact scrupulously, supplying Germany with vitally needed materials, especially oil and grain.

War in the West, 1940

When Hitler publicly offered peace to Britain and France on October 6, 1939, Chamberlain and Daladier did not even inquire about the terms, although there were numerous partisans of a compromise settlement in both countries. In any event, Hitler had already ordered plans drawn up for action in the west. An immediate campaign was delayed by the onset of autumn, so a period of waiting ensued, cynically known as the "phony war," during which the French and British troops lost whatever fighting edge they might have had.

While waiting, the French and British governments discussed possible offensive strategies. They believed a direct preemptive assault across the Rhine was impossible both materially and politically (no one wanted to provoke the bombing of Paris and London); attrition and encirclement seemed more appropriate to the Allied position. A blockade was set up against Germany, although the Soviet Union and Italy (which still imported British coal, as the British hoped to keep Mussolini neutral) were gigantic leaks in the system. Other plans were directed with more

---

[6]Finland had been an autonomous grand duchy under the Russian tsar from 1809 to 1917.

alacrity against Hitler's Soviet ally than against Hitler himself. The French considered opening a Balkan front and bombing the Russian oil fields in the Caucasus. During the Russo-Finnish "winter war," an Anglo-French force was prepared to help the Finns. After the Finns were beaten, this plan was shifted to efforts to cut off the main summer route for shipment of Swedish iron ore to Germany along the coast of Norway.

Hitler forestalled this plan with his second lightning stroke of the war, a daring seizure of Denmark and Norway on April 9, 1940. Denmark fell in a few hours, with thirteen Danish casualties. There was more serious resistance to the thinly stretched German parachutists and sea-borne troops in Norway, however. The Franco-British forces that had been prepared for action there landed in the north (Narvik) in an attempt to help push the Germans back out. The great German western offensive of May 10 cut this effort short.

The Fall of France

The German attack on France and the Low Countries that began May 10 followed a daring but risky plan worked out by General Fritz Erich von Manstein, perhaps the most brilliant German tactician of the war. Instead of following the 1914 Schlieffen Plan route through coastal Belgium and Holland, Manstein proposed to thrust the main striking force—ten *Panzer* divisions—through the deeply wooded Ardennes hills to come out at the weakest point in the French defense system, at Sedan, north of the end of the Maginot Line. The French had believed the terrain was too rough for a major attack at this point.

The French and British had anticipated a repetition of the Schlieffen Plan. They planned to move their most modern units north into Belgium and Holland to confront the Germans as far away as possible from the French industrial zones of the northeast. But since Belgium and Holland remained adamantly neutral for fear of provoking a German attack, this complicated move and the junction with Belgian and Dutch defense lines could begin only after a German invasion. The Allied manuever, in the French historian Henri Michel's fine metaphor, was like a great tree pulling up its roots, making it all the easier to topple. Furthermore, it showed that the Franco-British sense of the pace of mechanized warfare was hopelessly out of step with the speed of *Panzer* divisions. They expected to move whole armies more than one hundred miles north to head off German armies that had already begun to move with a shorter distance to cover.

General Guderian's ten *Panzer* divisions drove through the Ardennes as scheduled, over a road system so narrow that one army "head" had reached the Meuse River while its "tail" stretched back east of the Rhine. What followed was a brilliant exercise in *Blitzkrieg*. Since the Ardennes offensive was not preceded by a long artillery barrage as in the First World War, the French continued for three days to think that the

On the beach at Dunkirk, May 30, 1940, troops of the retreating British Expeditionary Force await evacuation by a flotilla of small boats.

simultaneous advance of a conventional German army into Belgium was the main attack. By May 13, two days ahead of schedule, Guderian had burst out into open country at Sedan and was driving across to the North Sea, threatening to cut off the cream of the Allied forces in Belgium.

The chief risk in Manstein's plan was that the fast *Panzer* divisions would extend a long salient out across northern France that could then be cut off by simultaneous Allied attacks from north and south before the slower regular German troops had had a chance to fill in. That was indeed the plan of the Allied commander in chief, the French General Maurice Gamelin, and of his successor after May 19, General Maxime Weygand. There were moments of panic at German headquarters when General Guderian ignored orders to consolidate and instead plunged ahead, leaving a vacuum behind.

The fall of France is to be understood in the failure to pinch off Guderian's exposed salient in northern France immediately after May 13. Here was an opportunity for another Battle of the Marne, and the justification for arguing that Hitler's victory in France was not a foregone conclusion.

The French defeat has commonly been attributed to a combination of insufficient matériel and poor morale. In fact, the 94 French divisions, plus 10 British, 8 Dutch, and 22 Belgian divisions, were not hopelessly mismatched against Germany's 134 divisions. The Allies were superior in artillery, and they had about an equal number of tanks, a few of which were technically superior to the German tanks. Their most damaging shortages were in communications, antiaircraft artillery, and planes.

The Allies' chief problem was in the way their forces were used. Basing their strategy on lessons learned in winning the First World War, the French, in particular, tended to distribute their tanks among infantry units rather than organize armored divisions. The one British and four French armored divisions that were created (one under Colonel Charles de Gaulle, the main French proponent of tank warfare) were spread out in line defense by the high command, in accordance with good 1914 tactics, rather than massed for attack.

Another major problem was time. The Allies never adjusted to the new pace of war. Without adequate communications, it was impossible to plan the point of attack and then assemble units there before the opportunity to strike had passed. The Battle of France from the French side was a bit like one of those nightmares of slow-motion emergency in which one knows exactly what needs to be done but moves with agonizing slowness.

A final serious problem was Allied disunity. As noted, the Dutch and Belgians refused to run the risk of joint preparations before the German invasion actually began. The British Expeditionary Force under Lord Gort, fearful of being encircled in Belgium, began falling back toward the Channel ports rather than help cut off Guderian's salient to the south, an action that the French have never forgiven.

Under these conditions, the planned simultaneous counterattack from north and south on the *Panzer* salient produced only some uncoordinated local attacks. The Germans reached the North Sea at Dunkirk at the end of May, cutting off the best Allied units to the north. A heroic armada of small boats helped the British Navy evacuate 200,000 British and 130,000 French troops from Dunkirk in the first days of June, but they had to leave all their equipment on the beach.

After this, there was little chance left for the French to reorganize a new defense against a German move southward into the heart of France. Prime Minister Paul Reynaud and others wanted to fight on, with British help, and evacuate the government to North Africa if necessary. But a growing peace movement formed around First World War hero Marshal Pétain, joined by the commander in chief himself, General Weygand. They argued that social revolution might break out in France without some remaining civil and military authority, that the French had suffered all they could, and that the British had abandoned them at Dunkirk. Pétain formed a new government on June 16 and negotiated an armistice. It provided that only northern France and the coast would be occupied, while the French government agreed to demobilize, to keep its citizens from continuing any acts of war against Germany at home or abroad, and to "collaborate" with the German occupying authority. France, the greatest military power on the Continent only twenty years before, had been reduced to surrender in a bare six weeks.

The Battle of Britain

The French armistice left the British alone and exposed. The British Isles were defended only by the disarmed remnant of the Expeditionary Force taken off the beaches at Dunkirk, veterans armed with hunting shotguns who were hastily assembled as a home guard, the Navy, and the still untried Royal Air Force. Germany faced them with eighty divisions on the Channel coast and an opening on the Atlantic for its submarines. After what he had done to the better prepared French, Hitler expected the British to come to terms.

Instead, the British rallied to the leadership of Winston Churchill, who replaced Chamberlain as prime minister on May 10. Churchill, a brilliant but wayward man whose impetuous rashness ill-fitted him for peacetime politics, now found the words and the attitudes to unite his country around a supreme war effort. When the French request for an armistice became known on June 18, Churchill said that Britain would fight on, "if necessary alone, if necessary for years," so that if the British Empire lasted a thousand years, men would still say, "this was their finest hour." He stirred pride in going on alone, relishing "the honor to be the sole champion of the liberties of all of Europe," when "we stood alone and all the world wondered." He aimed at nothing less than "victory— victory at all costs . . . victory, however long and hard the road may be," even though the cost would be unremitting "blood, toil, tears, and sweat."[7]

In fact, the cost was to turn out to be nothing less than the empire and Britain's world role, for the logic of Churchill's (and Hitler's) policy of

---

[7]Churchill speeches in the House of Commons, May 13, June 18, and November 5, 1940.

Londoners spending the night in a subway station during the blitz, *October 1940.*

war to the finish eventually shifted the decisive role to two emerging superpowers outside Europe: the United States and the Soviet Union. In that larger sense, Churchill was a failure. More immediately, however, the resolution, verve, and style with which he mobilized Britain for the supreme effort made him one of the giants of the century. His policy certainly reflected public opinion in 1940. When the Independent Labour party proposed peace negotiations in December 1940, the House of Commons rejected the idea 341 to 4. The British braced for Hitler's onslaught with an almost exhilarated determination.

British intransigence left Hitler with several options. One was a frontal assault on Britain, the last western holdout. This is what the German Army and Air Force expected. A second option was an oblique strategy of encirclement. Axis forces could control the western Mediterranean and North Africa via Gibralter, exploiting the cooperation of Franco and Pétain; or they could control the eastern Mediterranean and Suez via the Balkans or Italian Lybia. Either way, the British stood to lose their empire, their oil, and their morale. This choice, supported by Admiral Erich Raeder and the German Navy, seems in retrospect to have been Hitler's best chance of winning outright hegemony in Western Europe. The third possibility was a return to *Lebensraum,* expansion in the east. No one except Hitler thought seriously about this choice, for although the oil and grain of Eastern Europe would become essential in a long

British shoppers carry on in blitzed *London, September 1940. Note the orderly queue and the Cockney orange-seller's defiant sign.*

war, to attack the Soviet Union without first reducing Britain was to choose deliberately a two-front war.

Hitler's astounding successes in May and June 1940 left him genuinely undecided about the next step; throughout the summer and fall of 1940, he kept all these possibilities alive. At the beginning, however, he went ahead with plans for the first of the options outlined above.

Frontal assault on the British Isles, against the superior British Navy, required air superiority at the very least. Indeed, encouraged by *Reich Marshal* Goering, commander of the Air Force, Hitler seems to have believed that he could break the British will by air attacks alone. While the German Navy gathered landing craft on the Channel coast, the *Luftwaffe* began the Battle of Britain. This contest for control of the skies over England became the greatest air battle of the war. The Germans could reach southeastern England with light bombers and fighter cover from airfields in France. If the Germans had continued their initial policy of bombing British airfields, they might have won local control of the air. Instead, they switched on September 7, 1940, to bombing London. This had come about after one German pilot had bombed London, against orders, on August 24. When the British began night bombing of German cities on August 25, Hitler and Goering let the desire for vengeance triumph over sound tactics.

London was bombed every night from September 7 to November 2. Although 15,000 people died in London in these raids and although thousands of buildings including the House of Commons were destroyed, the London population bedded down in cellars and subway stations and stoically endured their sufferings. Well before November, however, a decisive point had been passed. British radar and superior communications, the excellent Spitfire and Hurricane fighter aircraft, and the advantage of fighting close to home bases allowed the Royal Air Force to inflict a heavy margin of loss on the Germans. While London soaked up bombs, British aircraft factories increased their output. On September 17, 1940, Hitler postponed the invasion for the winter—and in fact, for good. The British could not yet know that the danger of invasion had passed, for the bombing went on into 1941. But Hitler had already changed his mind.

In October and November Hitler toyed with the second option, encirclement. He visited Franco and Pétain. Both wanted neutrality, but Pétain's France, war weary and embittered by Churchill's first war measures (the British bombarded the French Mediterranean Fleet on July 3 and 4, killing over 1200 French sailors, to keep it out of German hands) was eager for cooperation with Germany in a new Continental system. The French price was a generous peace settlement, which had no appeal to Hitler. At the same time, alarmed by Stalin's moves in June 1940, he began to study possible German moves east.

War in the East, 1941–42

On December 18, 1940, Hitler issued orders for the preparation of Operation Barbarossa, the invasion of the Soviet Union. That decision may have been the turning point of the war, Hitler's fatal mistake. He voluntarily chose a two-front war, insisting that Russia must be defeated even before Britain. Hitler evidently expected that the Communist regime would crack under pressure and that he could capture all the oil and grain he needed for a long war.

Blitzkrieg *in the Balkans*

The attack on the Soviet Union was preceded by one more stunning display of *Blitzkrieg,* this time in the Balkans. Mussolini, who had entered the war in the last stages of the French campaign (June 10, 1940), showed his independence by invading Greece in October 1940. The Greeks not only pushed the Italian forces back into Albania, but brought in a British force the following March. Hitler was forced to come to Mussolini's rescue to prevent his proposed invasion of the Soviet Union from being threatened by an Allied front on the Balkan flank. When the Yugoslav government agreed to assist Hitler and Mussolini, a military revolt in that country overthrew the regime, and the new government prepared to side with the Allies. German armies struck southward on April 6, overrunning both Yugoslavia and Greece and seizing the island of Crete in a daring paratroop operation on May 20.

At the same time, the Germans sent weapons to an Arab nationalist

Moscow women digging antitank trenches outside the city as the Russians prepare to defend the capital against approaching German forces, summer 1941.

rebellion in Iraq, where the British had reestablished bases in their former mandated territory. German use of the Vichy French colony of Syria as a staging area for supporting the Iraqi rebels obliged the thinly stretched British to occupy Syria as well in June 1941, aided by Free French forces. Hitler also sent General Erwin Rommel's tank force to Lybia to reinforce the Italians there. If Hitler had continued his conquest of the eastern Mediterranean along these lines in the summer of 1941, the British Empire might well have been cut in two at Suez. Instead, he persisted with Operation Barbarossa.

Attack on the Soviet Union

Hitler attacked the Soviet Union in the early hours of June 22, 1941, with his most massive force so far—175 divisions.[8] It was the mightiest operation of his career.

At first, Hitler seemed justified in his gamble on speedy success in Russia. Things looked dark indeed for the Soviet Union in the first months. Unlike the situation in 1914, the Germans were not preoccupied with another front in the west. Only Britain remained at war with Hitler there, and British resources were fully devoted to defending the home island and the life line to India. Moreover, the Russians were unprepared. Perhaps, as Khrushchev charged in 1956, Stalin had failed to fortify his frontier in order to avoid provoking Hitler. He may have

[8]He had pitted 134 divisions against the French, British, Belgians, and Dutch in May 1940.

clung to the hope (not unlike Neville Chamberlain in 1938) that Hitler would be satisfied with his acquisition of most of Poland in 1940. Whatever his reasons, Stalin had scrupulously kept up his side of the Nazi-Soviet Pact, delivering grain and oil to the very last. He had also disregarded several Allied warnings of an imminent German attack.

The German attack of June 22 threw the unprepared Soviet forces into total confusion. Instead of withdrawing to some defensible line, the Soviet command lost masses of troops in piecemeal defense. Furthermore, civilians in some areas—notably the Ukraine—welcomed the Germans as liberators. It had been only ten years since the rural rebellions against collectivization, and only four years since the liquidation of over half the officer corps in the purges. Stalin himself did not even speak on the radio for two weeks. While the rest of the government evacuated Moscow, he remained for a last-ditch defense of the capital. During the anti-Stalin revisionism of the late 1950s, Marshal Georgi Zhukov claimed that Stalin actually expected defeat. By November 1941, Hitler had penetrated deeper into Russia than had Napoleon: to the outskirts of Leningrad in the north, into the very suburbs of Moscow in the center, and to the Don River in the south.

Hitler had not, however, achieved the lightning victory essential to his plans. The logic of *Blitzkrieg* required the smaller, less well-supplied Germany to defeat the Soviet Union at once, without lapsing into a long war of attrition favorable to the larger combatant. By November 1941 the Germans had reached deep into the vast Russian spaces without managing to grasp a vital organ. The German troops, unequipped for winter fighting, were now dangerously overextended. Time, space, winter, and the natural weight of Soviet resources were on Stalin's side.

The first Russian counteroffensive at the end of November 1941 recaptured the city of Rostov-on-Don. This was a major psychological victory, for it was the first conspicuous German military reversal on the ground since the war had begun in September 1939. Then, in December, General Zhukov counterattacked in front of Moscow. Since the shivering German armies had no prepared fall-back line, Marshal Gerd von Rundstedt and General Wilhelm von Leeb advised Hitler to withdraw German troops all the way to the Polish frontier to avoid a winter encirclement.[9] Hitler accepted only limited withdrawals. The ability of the German soldiers to cling to their advanced positions fortified his contempt for his generals and his rejection of tactical retreats.

Soviet survival during that first winter was the eastern front's equivalent to the Battle of Britain in the west. *Blitzkrieg* had failed, and the Russians had forced Hitler to face a long war against an opponent with greater long-term productive capacity. The German threat was far from ended, however. There followed two more German summer advances, succeeded by Russian winter recoveries. The great German advance of

[9]Basil H. Liddell-Hart, *The Other Side of the Hill* (London, 1951), p. 203.

the summer of 1942, focused this time on the south, penetrated even deeper than in 1941. German armies reached the Volga River at Stalingrad, in the foothills of the Caucasus Mountains. In late 1942, they held more Russian soil than any other foreign army in modern history.

Hitler's "New Order"

At the end of 1942, Hitler had put together by conquest and by alliance a Continental empire without parallel in European history. The directly occupied areas extended from the Atlantic coast of France, the Low Countries, and Norway east to Leningrad, the approaches to Moscow, the Volga River, and deep into the Caucasus region, approaching the Caspian Sea. From Norway and Denmark in the north, the directly occupied areas extended south through the Balkans to Greece and Crete, while a German army helped the Italians in Lybia in an attempt to overrun the Suez Canal.

Around the rim of these directly occupied areas lay a ring of more or less cooperative or allied states. Italy, having abandoned Danubian interests for Abyssinian ones, had been publicly allied with Germany since November 1936 and a belligerent since June 10, 1940. Admiral Miklós Horthy's Hungary had been gratified by the acquisition in 1939 and 1940 of much of the disputed territories lost in 1918 to its new neighbors—Czechoslovakia, Yugoslavia, and Romania. Romania, under General Ion Antonescu, tried to make up for losing Transylvania to Hungary by joining Hitler's attack on the Soviet Union, hoping to reacquire the areas east of the Danube lost to Russia in 1940, and more. Independent Slovakia and Croatia had been established for grateful minorities in what had been Czechoslovakia and Yugoslavia. Marshal Karl Gustav Mannerheim's Finland received German help against another possible Soviet attack. In Western Europe, the French regime of Marshal Pétain controlled the unoccupied southern third of France and most of the French African empire in a state of cooperative neutrality. Spain was friendly, even though Franco had refused to help the Germans take Gibraltar in 1940. Sweden was officially neutral, but 10 million tons of Swedish iron ore supplied the German war machine each year. Only Switzerland and Portugal (doctrinally sympathetic to Germany but economically tied to England) were genuinely neutral in Continental Europe in late 1942.

A "New Order" began to take shape in Europe. At a minimum, the New Order meant an expanded Germany surrounded by a common market of client states, forming a Great Economic Unit (*Grosswirtschaftsraum*) in which German economic influence would supplant Anglo-French economic influence. The German frontiers were restored to the 1914 borders in the west (chiefly by reannexing Alsace-Lorraine from France) and extended beyond them in the east (Austria, Bohemia-Moravia, part of Poland). In the wake of the armies, German industrialists completed their economic conquest of Eastern Europe and the

Balkans, obtaining former French shares in Balkan mining concerns, the great Czech Skoda armaments factories, and control of Romanian oil. German farmers were settled on "abandoned" farms in Poland and northeastern France, and eventual massive settlement of German farmers was planned in Russia. Jewish businesses and art collections were confiscated.

At a maximum, the New Order meant fulfilling the fantastic dreams spun around Hitler's table late at night, when the old German conceptions of *Mitteleuropa* and expansion to the east were raised to new heights by success and overt racial doctrines. There was talk of absorbing the Low Countries or of reviving ancient Brittany and Burgundy at the expense of France. As for the Soviet Union: "This Russian desert, we shall populate it. . . . We'll take away its character of an Asiatic steppe,

HITLER'S EUROPE, 1942

Legend:
- Occupied by the Axis
- Allied with Germany
- Hitler's Greater Germany

we'll Europeanize it. . . . There's only one duty: to Germanize this country by the immigration of Germans and to look upon the natives as Redskins."[10]

Nazi War Economy

In early 1942 Hitler's Europe began to feel the economic effects of the shift from *Blitzkrieg* to a long war of attrition. The Nazi economy of the late 1930s had already devoted a higher proportion of the national budget to strategic and military purposes than any other state in peacetime.[11] According to *Blitzkrieg* tactics, accumulated resources would make possible short, sharp thrusts that would, in turn, recover their costs in booty. It would not be necessary to divert more resources away from the civilian economy. At the beginning of 1942, Germany was far less mobilized than Britain. Consumer goods production was still only 3 percent below peacetime levels; as late as April 1942, most German armaments factories still operated on only one shift a day.

Two developments in December 1941 forced Germany to mobilize more systematically for war in early 1942: the Russian campaign bogged down, and the United States entered the war. Fritz Todt, Minister of Armaments and Munitions, began setting up centralized machinery for allocating more resources to the war effort in the spring of 1942. After Todt's death in an airplane crash, his more famous successor, Albert Speer, managed to more than triple German armaments production between the spring of 1942 and July 1944. German populations began to know privation then, as well as a mounting rhythm of Allied bombing raids. Even so, the German civilian economy was never as fully subordinated to the war effort as the British. German women, for example, were not mobilized for war work on any significant scale, whereas British women were.

Increased war efforts forced the Nazi system to reveal its very essence. The early ideological commitment to defense of the small farmer and shopkeeper (long observed mostly in the breach) was now cast to the winds. Under Albert Speer's Central Planning Committee, staffed by business executives from the great companies and cartels, war resources and labor were allocated to the largest and most efficient plants. Industry, agriculture, and retail trade were all concentrated in far fewer hands. Occupation policy began to be shaped more and more by race ideology.

Occupation Policy

The apportionment of burdens in the New Order rested on the Nazi concept of Germans as the "master race" and others, especially Jews,

---

[10]*Hitler's Table Talk, 1941–44* (London, 1953), pp. 68–69. Conversation of October 17, 1941.

[11]The military and strategic spending of the United States and the Soviet Union during the Cold War was to reach roughly the same proportions of the national budget as the German spending did then.

Slavs, and Mediterranean peoples, as inferior. Hitler's Europe could be self-sustaining in a long war if enough resources were squeezed out of subject peoples. Huge financial contributions were exacted from the occupied nations in the guise of "occupation costs." France, for example, paid about 58 percent of its government receipts to Germany during the war. Within the occupied countries, the Germans also collected raw materials, melted down statues and church bells for scrap, and requisitioned vast quantities of food. Occupied peoples were explicitly meant to have less to eat than Germans.

The treatment of Poles showed racially inspired occupation policy in action. A decree of October 26, 1939, subjected all Polish men and women from eighteen to sixty years of age to "compulsory public labor." By 1942, more than 1 million of them had been brought to Germany to work on farms, in mines, and in heavy construction. While their lands were settled by German farmers, Polish workers in Germany were maintained at a bare subsistence level, forced to wear a violet *P* on their clothes, and segregated from social contacts with Germans. Editorials exhorted Germans to treat the Poles as "inferior to each German comrade on his farm or in his factory. Be just, as Germans have always been, but never forget that you are a member of the master race!"[12] The penalty for Polish men who had sexual relations with German women was death.

After June 1941, Russian prisoners of war became the main source for German heavy labor. But only about 1 out of 5 million Russian prisoners survived the war.[13] Their very high death rate forced the Germans to start drawing labor from the western occupied areas, mainly the Low Countries and France, in 1942. Late in the war, the largest national contingent among foreign workers in Germany was French.

The treatment of occupied peoples varied enormously, according to a mixture of racial prejudice and opportunity. The treatment of Slavic peoples was particularly harsh. Even though the Germans could have won Ukrainian allies by restoring family farms there, German desires for immediate deliveries of grain and future settlement led to self-defeating brutalities.[14] Despite the eagerness of many Frenchmen to end their long conflict with Germany, the Germans refused offers of cooperation from this "mongrelized" people and treated collaborationist France no less harshly than the fully occupied areas of Western Europe. Nordic occupied people like the Dutch and Norwegians, workers and farmers in Bohemia-Moravia, and farmers in the dairy regions of Denmark, had a relatively easy time of it at first. But the screws tightened everywhere after 1942. Many Europeans suffered severe shortages of food, clothing, and shelter, in addition to the humiliation of defeat and the grief of separated relatives.

[12]William L. Shirer, *Berlin Diary* (New York, 1941), p. 513.
[13]Edward L. Homze, *Foreign Labor in Nazi Germany* (Princeton, N.J., 1967), p. 83.
[14]"In the face of these tasks," said Erich Koch, German governor [*Gauleiter*] of the Ukraine, "feeding of the civilian population [in the Ukraine] is a matter of the utmost indifference." (Alexander Dallin, *German Rule in Russia, 1941–45: A Study in Occupation Policies* [New York, 1957], p. 345.)

Contrary to Western impressions at the time, the Nazi war machine was not a monolith of perfect efficiency. Below the single authority of Hitler, agencies and cliques competed for power and influence. Among these rival factions the agencies of police and terror became increasingly powerful. Chief among these was the black-shirted paramilitary party force, the SS. (*Schutzstaffeln*) of Heinrich Himmler, which became a virtual "state within a state." The SS. did not limit itself to filling and running the network of concentration camps. It recruited front-line fighting units, the *Waffen-SS.* It even competed with German businessmen, for whom some SS. leaders still felt the anticapitalist contempt characteristic of early Nazism, in setting up business enterprises in occupied Russia. The SS., with its cult of blood, seemed to be the ultimate expression of the Nazi system under pressure.

As the SS. grew in power, racial doctrines became more compelling than military need or economic advantage. After 1941, some "inferior" peoples—Jews, gypsies, Jehovah's Witnesses—were condemned to outright extermination rather than forced labor. At a time when manpower and transportation for the German war effort were critically short, the Nazis chose to move thousands of trainloads of "undesirable" Europeans to extermination camps.

Nazi officers oversee Dutch Jews being loaded aboard freight cars for shipment to extermination camps.

At first, the Nazi leaders had worked for the mass emigration of Jews from German-dominated Europe. After the *Anschluss* of 1938 a young SS. officer, Adolf Eichmann, distinguished himself by devising a profitable system of selling emigration papers to wealthy Austrian Jews, with part of the proceeds going to cover the costs of expelling the rest. By 1941, extermination had replaced emigration, for it was feared that "natural selection" under hardship would produce "the germ cell of a new Jewish reconstruction" to menace German hegemony in the future.[15] In the spring of 1942 mass extermination centers were set up in Poland, where Jews from all over Europe were brought. They were stripped and herded into what they thought were shower rooms, but the nozzles poured out lethal gas instead of water. The corpses were then incinerated. Valuable byproducts, such as hair and gold teeth, were carefully saved. Industrialized mass murder mounted at a steady pace until by 1945 6 million Jews had been killed, two-thirds of the Jewish population of prewar Europe.

Collaboration

Ideological Collaboration

Hitler's New Order was able to draw on the cooperation of a number of non-Germans in the occupied areas of Europe. The most conspicuous of these were ideological collaborators who sympathized with fascist doctrines: profascist intellectuals, and leaders of prewar fascist groups. For some intellectuals, such as the French novelists Pierre Drieu la Rochelle and Robert Brasillach, the defeat of the "decadent" democratic regime of their own country was little enough price to pay for a "virile" dynamic new Europe. Some of the prewar fascist leaders outside Germany looked forward to leading roles in the new Europe. For others, however, nationalism was still important, and a few even resisted the German occupation.

The ideological collaborators were more noisy than important. It was primarily Hitler who limited them to a minor role. He always preferred to work through local bureaucrats or generals in occupied Europe than to strike an alliance with foreign fascist leaders who might have pretensions about partnership and who could not always keep order. Thus he dealt with Marshal Pétain in France rather than with the French fascists (some of whom later fought in the resistance); with Admiral Horthy in Hungary rather than with the Arrow-Cross leader Ferenc Szálasy, who came to power only in October 1944, when the Russians were already pouring into Hungary; with General Antonescu in Romania, who crushed the fascist Iron Guard in 1941. The Dutch fascist leader Anton Adriaan Mussert was given only a figurehead role in 1942;

[15]Reinhard Heydrich, deputy chief of the SS., at the Wannsee Conference of January 1942, quoted in Karl D. Bracher, *The German Dictatorship*, trans. Jean Steinberg (New York, 1970), p. 427.

the Norwegian fascist Vidkun Quisling was shunted aside by German military commanders in April 1940 and assumed mere shadow power in February 1942.

Ideological collaboration received an important boost with Hitler's invasion of the Soviet Union on June 22, 1941. From that point on, anticommunism was Hitler's most telling propaganda device. Hitler's propaganda chief Joseph Goebbels could argue that whatever discomforts occupied Europe might be suffering under Hitler would be worse if the Russians conquered Europe. From this perspective, Hitler was the last remaining bulwark against Bolshevism, and the Allies' bullheaded insistence on invading Europe from the west was only helping Stalin. Eventually some 500,000 non-German Europeans fought the Russians in the volunteer foreign divisions of the *Waffen-SS*. East Europeans, such as Baltic peoples and Croatians fighting for their national independence, made up the largest number, but there were also 50,000 Dutchmen, 40,000 Belgians (about evenly divided between Flemish and French-speaking Walloons), 20,000 Frenchmen, about 6000 Danes, and another 6000 Norwegians.[16] Behind these volunteers stood millions of less committed Europeans who nevertheless shared the same basic priorities: some kind of accommodation with the New Europe, whose harshest phase would end with a German-imposed peace, rather than an Allied victory that would let the Russians in.

Collaboration for National and Economic Interests

The New Europe appealed to interests as well as ideology. The stepchild nationalities of 1918 at last had a chance to reshuffle the map of Eastern Europe. Hungary retrieved Transylvania from Romania and regained other borderlands from what had been Czechoslovakia and Yugoslavia. Admiral Horthy sent troops to assist the German conquest of Russia. Romania contributed thirty divisions to the invasion of Russia, hoping to make up east of the Danube and even in the Crimea the equivalent of what had been lost to Hungary. Two peoples who did not achieve statehood in 1918—Slovaks and Croats—now had their revenge against the formerly dominant Czechs and Serbs. The Slovak national leader, Father Andrej Hlinka, had been denied a hearing at Versailles; his successor, Monsignor Joseph Tiso (the Slovak Peoples' party was strongly Catholic) now headed an independent Slovakia. Ante Pavelić, who had led the Croat liberation movement (*Ustasha*) from exile in Italy since 1929, now headed an independent Croatia and applied the *Ustasha*'s terrorist methods to the Serbian remnant of former Yugoslavia.

Hitler's Europe served economic as well as national interests. Some industrialists outside Germany received lucrative orders for war matériel, especially after 1943 when Albert Speer reversed the policy of

---

[16]George H. Stein, *The Waffen-SS* (Ithaca, N.Y., 1966), pp. 138–39. Not all volunteers volunteered "voluntarily"; some foreign labor in Germany enlisted in the *Waffen-SS*. as a lesser evil, and some Eastern Europeans were more or less forcibly recruited.

bringing labor to the Reich in favor of dispersing production throughout occupied Europe. The new French aluminum industry, for example, produced more under the German occupation than before the war (although most French industries did less well). These industrialists were also liberated from the trade union movement, and some among them dreamed of a postwar Europe fully cartelized and united against the rising American giant. French industrialist François Lehideux, for example, the Vichy French Minister of Industrial Production and nephew of the automobile magnate Louis Renault, tried to plan a postwar Franco-German-Italian automaking giant that would dominate the world market, in opposition to the "American bloc."

Some farmers also prospered in a world desperately short of food, especially in such highly productive dairy regions as Normandy, Denmark, and parts of Bohemia-Moravia. Since the official food ration was little above starvation level, a vast black market sprang up for items like eggs and cheese, which were almost literally worth their weight in gold.

Passive Acquiescence

The true mass basis of collaboration was mere passive acquiescence. Some peoples, of course, had no choice. For Poles or Ukrainians, the occupation was so harsh that any voluntary impulse to seek a place in Hitler's New Europe was soon crushed. Occupied peoples who could lead more normal lives faced more ambiguous choices.

France had the most uncertain choices of all, which makes it the most interesting case for discovering who collaborated and who did not. Loyalties were uniquely divided in France after 1940 between two claimants to legitimate authority: the collaborationist French regime of Marshal Pétain in Vichy[17] and the Free French in London under General Charles de Gaulle. Other occupied peoples had less difficulty deciding where legitimate authority lay. The Dutch Queen Wilhelmina and the Dutch government in exile in London had the support of most of their people; so did the Norwegian ministers in exile in London under King Haakon VII. Although the Belgian cabinet went to London, King Leopold elected to declare himself a prisoner with his Army and ceased all governmental function. The Danish regime stayed in place, and the seventy-year-old King Christian X, a popular monarch of simple tastes, rode out in the streets of Copenhagen daily on his bicycle. Whatever their location, these governments had two features in common: they kept legitimacy intact; and they refused to legislate under German force, limiting their activity to basic administrative services.

In France, legitimacy was not only divided; the Vichy regime actively tried to replace the Third Republic with a corporative, authoritarian state. Underlying the French division was the intensity of social conflict in prewar France over the Popular Front, the bitter discredit into which

---

[17]Vichy is a health resort in the south-central mountains of France where the French government was located "temporarily" during the war.

the Third Republic had been thrown by losing the war, and the yearning of many Frenchmen to be spared another blood bath like that of the First World War, when their sufferings had been the most severe in Europe. Under the aged Marshal Pétain, the hero of the First World War battle of Verdun, Vichy France tried to reach a compromise peace with Hitler and to make a place for itself in the New Europe. Conservative leaders, out of power between the wars, attempted to create a "National Revival" even while German troops still occupied the northern half of France. They abolished parliament and trade unions, passed anti-Semitic legislation, favored the Catholic Church, and set up a corporative economic system operated, in practice, by executives of big companies. For French conservatives, the German defeat of the Third Republic was a choice opportunity to reverse what they regarded as fifty years of democratic "decadence."

A majority of Frenchmen agreed, or at least acquiesced. They trusted Marshal Pétain as a national hero and were relieved to be out of the war. General de Gaulle's Free French, by contrast, seemed to offer only renewed fighting (for England's profit, it appeared) and, after 1941, indirect help for Stalin and his French Communist minions. The normal course in France, at least through 1942, was to carry out "business as usual." Was this collaboration? Did delivering the mail or teaching

Marshal Philippe Pétain, chief of state of the collaborationist French state at Vichy, left, took France out of the war and tried to earn a place in Hitler's Europe. Here he meets Reich Marshal Hermann Goering at a small railroad station near the border of the occupied zone of France, December 1, 1941.

school in Pétain's regime constitute aid to France's German enemies? After the war, the treason trials of the liberation held that collaboration consisted of going out of one's way to help the occupying power, such as holding a policymaking position or exceeding mere duty in helping the Germans. On these terms, about 38,000 Frenchmen were imprisoned after the war for collaboration, over 700 were executed, and nearly 50,000 were deprived of voting rights.[18] But others who had acquiesced provided the climate in which more active support of Hitler's Europe became legitimized. By choosing to participate in the New Europe, the Vichy regime had tainted the most everyday acts of its citizens with *de facto* collaboration.

As Hitler's chances of victory waned, many Europeans gained renewed hope in an Allied victory. Many others, however, still feared the social consequences of renewed fighting in the west, which could only bring Stalin into Europe. By this logic, many Europeans not overtly sympathetic to fascism continued to wish for a compromise peace until 1944.

Resistance

Nazi domination confronted Hitler's opponents in Europe with a fundamental question: should they suffer in resignation, or should they take action against unjust authority? Action posed both practical and ethical problems. What action was possible against a tyranny both limitless and popular? What responsibility did each individual bear for opposing evil in the world, and for the kind of acts with which he opposed it? In the absence of any lawful forms of dissent, was it justifiable to commit criminal acts—even to kill people—in the name of a higher morality?

There were compelling reasons for acquiescence, the easiest and commonest course. First, resistance was dangerous. Second, the full brutality of German occuaption was not revealed all at once, particularly in Western Europe, Bohemia-Moravia, and Scandinavia, where the early occupation was comparatively mild. Third, many could feel no hope of change until after the war's turning point. Fourth, the Nazis' most bestial acts had no precedent, so that millions of Jews, for example, had gone passively to their deaths, unaware of their destiny. Finally, even when these horrors began to be known, those Europeans less immediately threatened felt strong inhibitions against violent acts in the name of a higher morality. Had not the Nazis themselves justified their attacks on Weimar legality in just this way? Might not a violent resistance simply replace tyranny with anarchy?

In spite of all these reasons, resistance movements appeared in occupied Europe, and even in Germany itself. Active resisters were those who committed overt acts punishable by the authorities, and not those

[18]Peter Novick, *The Resistance vs. Vichy* (New York, 1968), p. 404. A greater portion of the population was punished in Holland, Belgium, and Norway than in France.

who expressed mere disapproval, or dissented silently, or even practiced passive resistance. Overt acts ran a wide gamut, from writing or distributing subversive tracts and scrawling antiregime slogans on walls, through gathering intelligence information for the Allies and sheltering enemies of the regime, to outright acts of sabotage and assassination. All such acts required a decision to break the law. Most of them required endangering one's family and running personal risks of death or, even worse, torture. A resister had to renounce comfort, routine, safety, and even conventional morality. That is why active resisters were few, and why they were often misfits: young, single people without attachments; enemies of the regime who had no choice; old street fighters from both nationalist and revolutionary ranks.

Few in number, often isolated, and harassed by a vigilant and merciless authority, the European resisters rarely had direct military significance. But they captured the world's imagination with their bravery. The men and women who underwent danger together in the name of a new Europe after Hitler created a special fraternity, one that frequently threw together prewar opponents like priests and Communists. Their intellectual leaders helped shape postwar Europe and raised major moral issues about individual responsibility and the legitimacy of opposition to unjust authority.

Resistance Outside Germany

The European resistance varied greatly in time and place. In the early days of the war, there was neither hope nor (except in Poland) unbearable provocation. The early resistance leaders were mostly conservatives, nationalists, and officers like the Free French leader Charles de Gaulle. Their conception of the resistance was gathering intelligence for the Allies and preparing clandestine forces to assist an eventual Allied landing in Europe. As long as the Nazi-Soviet Pact remained in force, European Communists, with the strongest underground organization in Europe, were devoted to pacifism rather than resistance. The Comintern's instructions ordered European workers to take no part in this "imperialist war." To be sure, the party regarded Hitler and his collaborators as evil. But in a return to the "class against class" intransigence of 1928 to 1934, it argued that Hitler's enemies, the city of London and its vassals, were identical to Hitler in class terms. Workers would not benefit by the victory of either. "Neither cholera nor the plague," read illegal Communist handbills in occupied Paris in early 1941: that is, neither Pétain nor de Gaulle, neither Hitler nor Churchill. Down with the imperialist war. Frenchmen should not die for the capitalists. French Soviets to power. Long live peace.[19] Workers in Europe were urged to establish good relations with German workers and with the neutral Soviet Union, and to work for immediate peace. This position was intensely uncomfortable for many European Communists,

[19]A. Rossi (Angelo Tasca), *La Guerre des papillons* (Paris, 1954), pp. 37–53 and appendices.

both then and since. The party subsequently has been able to point with pride to some workers who disobeyed its orders, such as the French coal miners who struck in May 1941.

The first major turning point in the European resistance, then, came with the German invasion of the Soviet Union on June 22, 1941. The European Communist underground immediately swung with relief and enthusiasm into direct action against Hitler. There was a sudden rise in sabotage and assassination in the occupied countries. Well organized and manned by dedicated and committed fighters, the Communist movement was better prepared, both materially and morally, than other groups to attract the most vigorous and active resisters. The European resistance now became a renewed Popular Front: a coalition of all antifascists in a satisfying unity of action for national liberation. As the French Communist poet Louis Aragon wrote with relief, "My party has given me back the French flag."[20]

The second major turning point is less precisely dated but no less significant. In late 1942 and early 1943 the possibility of German defeat became apparent; simultaneously, the Germans began extorting much more from the occupied areas. This was a particularly striking shift for Western Europe, which up to that time had suffered more in pride than in body. But now young men began to be drafted in France, Holland, and Belgium to work in German factories. Food rations were diminished. Massive deportation of Jews from Western Europe to the crematoria began in the summer of 1942, the first issue on which the Catholic clergy in Western Europe took a public position against the occupation authorities. At this point, the French *maquis*[21] appeared: resistance encampments in remote areas peopled by those who were fleeing the labor draft or deportation; they lived on local support while preparing to aid an Allied invasion. Thus, at the beginning of 1943, there was an increase in both hope and anger, along with wider community acceptance of resistance acts. The European resistance had acquired a mass base.

Resistance was not uniform throughout occupied Europe, of course. Its strength depended on opportunity and the extent of animosity. Temptations to acquiesce to the Germans were greater in relatively comfortable occupied areas like Denmark and Bohem-

"The hour is coming." A crude but effective resistance sticker on a wall in Belgium, as D-Day drew near.

[20]Louis Aragon, "Du poète à son parti," in Claude Roy, ed., *Aragon* (Paris, 1962), p. 164.
[21]*Maquis* is a Corsican word for scrubby Mediterranean hillside brush in which outlaws hid, and, by extension, the bands of outlaws themselves.

ia-Moravia, or in half-occupied France. Resistance was also weak in states at the other extreme, like Poland, whose citizens were threatened with annihilation. The open terrain in Poland, moreover, could not protect the resistance fighters as did the French central hills, the Alps, and the mountains of Yugoslavia. The most suitable areas for resistance lay between the extremes, in places where hope was possible and shelter available.

Resistance also varied with the legal sanction given it by legitimate governments. Governments in exile that were recognized by almost all their citizens as legitimate and that fought alongside the British justified internal resistance in their own countries; the Dutch and Norwegian monarchs and governments in London were examples. In France, by contrast, the existence of rival regimes claiming legitimacy made the right path much more difficult to find. Almost all French people longed to be delivered from the harsh German occupation. But it was not until the Allied invasion of June 1944 had proved capable of driving the Germans out rapidly without another stalemate trench campaign as in 1914 to 1918 that a majority of the French decided that General de Gaulle's path of armed liberation was more promising than Marshal Pétain's path of negotiated cooperation. Before then, postwar figures suggest that about 2 percent of French adults took the heroic risks required of active resistance; perhaps as many as 10 percent read the clandestine press. At least that many fervently supported the Pétain regime to the end.[22]

Resistance Within Germany

Resistance within Germany faced special hazards and limitations. Resistance in the occupied countries could appeal to nationalism as well as to moral principle and self-interest. The German resistance, by contrast, was accused of stabbing its country in the back, especially after the war began. Strong national traditions of political discipline were reinforced by the genuine mass fervor aroused by Hitler's successes. A hostile public opinion exposed the German resisters more relentlessly to the attention of the police and SS. than in the occupied countries.

The German resistance was also deeply fragmented among mutually hostile groups on the left and right. They were without a goal of national liberation to unite them and without a strong common liberal tradition. The left had a potential mass following, but no means of penetrating the Army or bureaucracy. The conservative resistance had some chance of recruiting elements of the Army and bureaucracy, but no mass following.

A majority of Germans had voted against Hitler as late as March 1933, and some continued to oppose him. The left—Social Democrats, Communists, and trade unions—formed the largest potential opposition. But

[22]Robert O. Paxton, *Vichy France: Old Guard and New Order, 1940–44* (New York, 1972), p. 294.

the German left missed its last opportunity for concerted action in 1932 and 1933. Social Democrats and trade unionists remained committed to legal means against even lawless opponents; Communists clung to the belief that Hitler's destruction of the Weimar Republic only brought a German "Red October" that much closer; and the two factions regarded each other as the principal enemy. The German left's institutions were closed down in the first weeks of the regime and its leaders arrested or driven underground and abroad. Prison or death awaited anyone who attempted to reorganize socialist parties or trade unions. The great mass of Germans, including some workers, were "Nazified" by the economic and international successes of the regime. Eventually, the Social Democrats and Communists formed some important resistance movements, such as the "Red Orchestra" group rounded up in August 1942. The Nazi regime kept the German left under constant surveillance, however, and the main measure of what might have become a mass left opposition was the hundreds of thousands of Germans held after 1933 in the concentration camps.

The churches were the next most important potential source of resistance in Germany. Although German Protestants were too fragmented and too imbued with the Lutheran tradition of state loyalty to offer concerted opposition, Nazi efforts to found a new "German Christian" church—the "SA. of Jesus Christ"—produced a Protestant opposition in the Confessional Church, led by such men as Pastor Martin Niemöller, former U-boat captain in the First World War and opponent of the Weimar Republic. The Catholic Church concluded a concordat with Hitler in 1933 in which it agreed to abolish the Center party and abstain from political action in exchange for the survival of parochial schools and parish organizations. By 1937, the papacy and the German clerical hierarchy had expressed open opposition to particular features of the regime, including its militant secularism and the policy of euthanasia.[23] Notwithstanding the courageous opposition of many Christians, the churches worked more for their own autonomy within the regime than for an end to the regime.

Some conservatives remained opposed to the Nazi regime on religious or humanitarian principles. Generally, they retreated into private disgruntlement, or they formed secret discussion groups, such as Count Helmut von Moltke's Kreisau Circle, which laid plans for an integrated new Europe without international rivalries after others should have brought about Hitler's end. The possibility of losing a war, however, galvanized some of the military and bureaucratic opposition into action.

One high point of this opposition was 1938, when it seemed as though Hitler was driving a still unprepared Germany into war with both Russia and the West. It has been asserted since the war that Hitler's military and bureaucratic opponents planned to overthrow him at the moment he attempted to declare war. The chief of staff, General Ludwig Beck, did

[23]See the 1937 papal encyclical *Mit brennender Sorge* (With Burning Concern).

in fact resign in August 1938 in disagreement with Hitler's ambitions. But the postwar claim of some German officers and high civil servants that Neville Chamberlain's concessions at Munich undercut and neutralized their plan to overthrow Hitler must be regarded with some caution. When war did break out, under more favorable circumstances, in September 1939, patriotic reflexes overrode any significant opposition from Army or bureaucratic quarters. Furthermore, the conservative opposition had no mass following; it remained elitist and authoritarian, a continuation, in some ways, of the anti-Weimar movements of the 1920s. The final obstruction to their action was the narrow range of acts open to the conservatives: without a mass basis, only a *coup d'état* or an assassination could bring about their aim—an authoritarian and powerful Germany without Hitler—and such means were repugnant to them.

When the war began to appear lost in 1943 and 1944 and the threat of a Bolshevized Europe took shape, the conservative opposition overcame its scruples. An assassination attempt in March 1943 failed. On July 20, 1944, another attempt was made. Colonel Count Klaus Schenk von Stauffenberg set off a bomb during a briefing in Hitler's headquarters at Rastenberg, near the Russian front. Hitler was only shaken and temporarily deafened. The conspirators, who had meant to close down the concentration camps, abolish the SS., and seek a separate peace with the West, were shot or hung up on meat hooks to die. Only military defeat from the outside would finally bring Hitler down, and all Germany with him.

The Military Impact of the Resistance

The military outcome of the war was influenced only marginally by the European resistance. The impact of the resistance was probably greater in Eastern than in Western Europe. Partisan bands behind the German lines in Russia seriously interfered with transportation and security, and required the diversion of some German troops from the front.

Yugoslavia provided the most militarily effective resistance in Europe. When Yugoslavia was overrun by the Germans in April 1941, the Army did not disband; it took to the hills. The rugged Yugoslav terrain was never an area of German security. As the two sides settled down into stalemate, however, General Draža Mikhailovich's "Chetniks" tended to establish *de facto* truces with the German occupying forces. When the Communists entered the war, a more active resistance movement was created by a Croatian Communist, Josip Broz, better known as Tito. The Yugoslav case posed the issue of two possible resistance strategies: immediate action, with all its risks of reprisals and greater short-term suffering; or a more cautious policy of awaiting the arrival of superior Allied forces. British observers who parachuted in to meet Tito sent back reports of his activism that persuaded the Allies to shift their financial and material aid from Mikhailovich to Tito. In the end, Tito's forces held down ten German divisions. He emerged as the unrivaled postwar leader of Yugoslavia, less ethnically riven than between the wars and committed to a new leadership combining communism and nationalism.

The resistance was less militarily significant in Western Europe. Resistance organizations there did provide essential information on German troop locations, and they helped delay German troop movements during the Allied invasion of Normandy on D-Day, June 6, 1944. The real significance of the resistance in the West, however, was the intellectual renewal that it stimulated.

The Intellectual Impact of the Resistance

Resistance meant thought as well as action. Depression, fascism, and war—the second European fratricide in twenty-five years—all demanded an unsparing criticism of the European experience and hard thought about the new Europe that should be built after Hitler:

> After the Resistance, after the economic, social and political Revolution that each one of us bears within him . . . what republic? What democracy?[24]

Although resistance intellectuals came from widely varied backgrounds, from Catholic to Communist, the enormity of Europe's self-destruction and the risks of clandestine writing and speaking imposed some common characteristics on them. The nature of the enemy identified the resistance firmly with the left after the Soviet Union entered the war in June 1941. The resistance intellectuals rejected prewar Europe almost universally; virtually no one worked to resurrect interwar conditions. Because the totality of the crisis demanded profound change, they prepared nothing less than a transformation of European politics, society, and economy. Most resistance thinkers supported a return to parliamentary democracy, but a system purified of the fumbling and corruption attributed to interwar parliaments. They called for a more open and egalitarian access to schools, jobs, and honors. They rejected the notion of a self-regulating market, blamed now for the depression; but unlike the prewar left, resistance economists accepted some degree of planning and state intervention as essential. (These wartime hopes will be examined more fully in the next chapter.)

A major resistance innovation was the ferment produced in the European churches. Although no Christian denomination entered the resistance en bloc, many younger priests and pastors went beyond the mere struggle for religious autonomy to an active social and political commitment. The churches' previous positions on obedience to secular authority and on socioeconomic issues were challenged as never before. A major Catholic innovation was the worker-priests who exchanged their cassocks for overalls and shared directly in the labor experience. The worker-priest experiment began with ministry to drafted French factory workers in German munitions plants, and thus drew in part on

[24]The French resistance leaflet "Après," No. 2 (July 1943), quoted in Henri Michel and Boris Mirkine-Guetzevitch, *Les idées politiques et sociales de la résistance* (Paris, 1954), p. 87.

Vichy roots as well as on the resistance; in both cases, the worker-priests insisted on breaking decisively with the middle-class existence of the priesthood.

The question of whether to commit unlawful acts against an unjust authority posed serious moral problems for priests and pastors. Every standard precept called for submission to the state. Pastor Dietrich Bonhoeffer, a young German Protestant seminary professor, has made perhaps the profoundest impression on Christian ethical thinking since the war. Bonhoeffer was a follower of the Swiss theologian Karl Barth, who had criticized modern liberal theology as too man-centered and optimistic. The actions of the Nazi regime reinforced Barth's attack on the more facile forms of liberal "social Gospel" theology, calling renewed attention to the depths of human evil and awakening doubts about the reality of social progress on earth. Instead of drawing quietistic conclusions from this, however, Bonhoeffer insisted that Christians should not live separate lives of mere piety but should share fully in the secular world as imitators of Christ. Bonhoeffer was convinced that only the defeat of his country could produce the necessary collective penance, and start the church out afresh in Germany stripped of its surface piety and its property. Bonhoeffer was in touch with the conspirators of July 20, 1944, and was one of four clergymen executed after that assassination attempt on Hitler.

The most important secular ethic to come out of the resistance was existentialism. Its main figure, the French philosopher Jean-Paul Sartre, had avoided political commitment in the 1930s. He had worked on philosophical problems of being and knowing, under the influence of the German phenomenologists Edmund Husserl and Martin Heidegger. The descent into war forced Sartre to realize that no one could be free, not even a philosopher, unless he accepted an active responsibility for the state of the world. Otherwise, decisions of life and death would be made for him by others. How should a person act, however, if, like Sartre, he could believe neither in God, nor in immutable moral laws, nor in a predetermined human nature? Sartre found a philosophy of action in his earlier philosophy of existence. An individual's existence, Sartre thought, was the only certainty. What each person made of his existence was a matter of free choice. "Choices are possible in one direction or another; what is not possible is not to choose." The individual of good faith accepted this burden of choice and "engaged" himself in the situation around him, acting according to his own "project" of what the world should be, conscious that his "act engages all humanity." The individual of bad faith ignored his responsibility and freedom, blaming others for the state of the world; but such a person had made his choice no less than the first.[25]

A simplified existentialism, ignoring the great complexity and subtlety of Sartre's philosophical work, became a kind of fad among resistance

---

[25]Jean-Paul Sartre, *L'Existentialisme est un humanisme* (Paris, 1945), pp. 27, 73.

intellectuals by the end of the war. In fact, Sartre had put his finger on the agony of choice experienced by active resisters. The consequences of one's acts were exposed with brutal clarity in a situation in which one might be tortured, and where "one word sufficed to provide ten, a hundred arrests. This total responsibility in total solitude, is it not the clearest revelation of our freedom?"[26] In Sartre's terms, the resistance was a "Republic of Silence" in which solitary, free men and women engaged their lives and the lives of others by acts of deliberate choice.

[26]Jean-Paul Sartre, "Le République du silence," printed clandestinely in 1944, reprinted in Sartre, *Situations, III* (Paris, 1949), p. 13.

Suggestions for Further Reading

Gordon Wright, *The Ordeal of Total War, 1939–1945** (1968) is a superior general survey. Basil H. Liddell-Hart applies the strategic thinking of a lifetime to *The History of the Second World War** (1971). Peter Calvocoressi and Guy Wint, *Total War** (1972) deals both with the battlefield and with the conference table. H. A. Jacobsen and J. Rohwer, eds., *Decisive Battles of World War II: The German View* (1965) is a useful corrective.

Don W. Alexander, "Repercussions of the Breda Variant," *French Historical Studies*, Vol. 8, No. 3 (Spring 1974) explains the French defeat of 1940 convincingly in terms of strategic errors by the High Command, after a canvass of many other explanations. There is more detail but less analysis in William L. Shirer, *The Collapse of the Third Republic** (1971); Alistair Horne, *To Lose a Battle* (1969); and Guy Chapman, *Why France Fell* (1968). The atmosphere of that collapse is unforgettably evoked in Marc Bloch, *Strange Defeat** (1949), and André Beaufre, *The Fall of France, 1940* (1968).

Derek Wood and Derek Dempster, *The Narrow Margin* (1961) is the best account of British air defense.

Albert Seaton, *The Russo-German War* (1971) is a balanced account by a British officer who used both German archives and Soviet publications. See also Alan Clark, *Barbarossa: The Russian-German Conflict, 1941–1945* (1965), and Trumbull Higgins, *Hitler and Russia: The Third Reich in a Two-Front War, 1937–1943* (1966). Soviet generals' memoirs are excerpted and commented on usefully in Seweryn Bialer, ed., *Stalin and His Generals* (1969). Raymond L. Garthoff,

How Russia Makes War (1953); John Erickson, *The Soviet High Command* (1962); and Basil H. Liddell-Hart, ed., *The Red Army* (1956) are still valuable.

For Hitler as strategist, see Percy Ernst Schramm, *Hitler: The Man and the Military Leader** (1971), and the less scholarly narrative of John Strawson, *Hitler's Battles for Europe* (1971). Basil H. Liddell-Hart examines conflicts between Hitler and his generals in *The German Generals Talk** (1948). Walter Ansel criticizes Hitler's failure to exploit Mediterranean possibilities in *Hitler and the Middle Sea* (1972).

The impression that the German war economy was a smoothly geared machine has been dispelled by Alan S. Milward, *The German Economy at War* (1965). Albert Speer's account of his own success in raising war production, *Inside the Third Reich** (1970), should be corrected by Geoffrey Barraclough, "What Albert Speer Didn't Say," *The New York Review of Books*, Vol. 15, No. 12 (January 7, 1971).

Alexander Dallin, *German Rule in Russia, 1941–1945* (1957) is one of the most revealing monographs about German occupation policies. Werner Warmbrunn, *The Dutch under German Occupation* (1963); Alan S. Milward, *The Fascist Economy in Norway* (1972) and *The New Order and the French Economy* (1970); Robert O. Paxton, *Vichy France: Old Guard and New Order, 1940–1944* (1972); Vojtech Mastny, *The Czechs Under Nazi Rule: The Failure of National Resistance, 1939–1942* (1971); and Mario D. Fenyo, *Hitler, Horthy, and Hungary* (1972) explore German occupation regimes and various degrees of collaboration. John A. Armstrong,

"Collaborationism in World War II: The Integral Nationalist Variant in Eastern Europe," *Journal of Modern History*, Vol. 40, No. 3 (September 1968) draws useful comparisons.

Two novels that reflect the violence of occupied Europe are Jerzy Kosinsky, *The Painted Bird** (1965), and André Schwarz-Bart, *The Last of the Just** (1960).

The most comprehensive general history of European resistance movements is Henri Michel, *The Shadow War: The European Resistance, 1939–1945* (1972). Some good local resistance studies include Charles F. Delzell, *Mussolini's Enemies* (1961); John A. Armstrong *et al.*, *Soviet Partisans in World War II* (1964); and the papers read at two conferences and published under the title *European Resistance Movements, 1939–1945* (1960, 1963). Blake Ehrlich, *The French Resistance* (1966) may be consulted for France, whose resistance has no fully satisfactory study in English. Hans Rothfels, *The German Opposition to Hitler*, 2nd ed. (1962); Gerhard Ritter, *The German Resistance* (1959); and Terence Prittie, *Germans Against Hitler* (1964) are all sympathetic to the conservative German resistance. George K. Romoser, "The Politics of Uncertainty: The German Resistance Movement," *Social Research*, Vol. 31, No. 1 (Spring 1964) criticizes its elitism and its links with anti-Weimar conservatives.

For the two most enduring leaders of the European anti-Hitler movement, see Phyllis Auty, *Tito: A Biography** (1970), and Charles de Gaulle, *The Complete War Memoirs of Charles de Gaulle,** 3 vols. (1968), a literary monument in its own right. Brian Crozier, *De Gaulle* (1973) is the most comprehensive account of the war years, although unsatisfactory for the later period.

FROM HOT WAR
TO COLD WAR
1942–1949

16

Adolf Hitler lost the military initiative during the winter of 1942/43. After that turning point, even though the Nazi war machine was still capable of savage short thrusts, Hitler found himself obliged to respond to Allied initiatives rather than surprise the world as before with his own audacious moves. The war was far from over yet, of course. The Allies disagreed sharply among themselves over the strategy best suited to force Germany to unconditional surrender. Nearly three years of bitter fighting remained before that surrender on May 8, 1945. Nevertheless, by 1943 it was the Allies who chose the time and place of most battles. With that advantage, they gradually overwhelmed the Third Reich with their superior resources.

The military initiative that the Allies regained passed out of the hands of the former Great Powers that had dominated European affairs since the rise of modern states. Even in the First World War, one group of European nations had managed to defeat another only by turning outside Europe for help. The renewed European conflict that broke out in 1939 was even more quickly transformed into a world war with the involvement of Japan (September 1940), Russia (June 1941), and the United States (December 1941). The Second World War demanded vast resources that the traditional European Great Powers, states of 50 million people or so, could no longer provide. The superpowers, industrialized states approaching 200 million people or more, alone commanded sufficient resources under a single political authority to determine the outcome of wars. Hitler's Europe was the first of these superpowers, and the United States and the Soviet Union rose to the challenge as the only states capable of defeating Hitler. In the process, basic decisionmaking about the future of Europe was shifted away from Berlin, London, and Paris to two new capitals: Washington and Moscow. Europe's last civil war destroyed European autonomy.

American Hegemony in the West

In 1940, the United States lagged far behind European states in military power. Its Army was smaller than the Belgian Army. But behind that modest military façade was an immense economic potential. When the United States entered the war in December 1941, more than two years after the fighting had begun in Europe, American productivity and manpower thrust the country into overwhelming domination over the Western European partners of the alliance.

One factor in American hegemony was economic. Even more quickly than in the First World War, the United States became the arsenal of the alliance against Germany. American productive power quadrupled under the stimulus of war production for the alliance, while European productive power was being wrecked by wear and military action. Massive purchases of armaments in the United States forced the anti-Hitler nations once again to liquidate their reserves of gold, foreign exchange, and overseas investments. Even before the United States entered the war, President Franklin Roosevelt sought ways to assist Hitler's enemies to purchase supplies in the United States without exhausting their credit and dislocating the world economy with war debts as in 1914 to 1918. The Lend-Lease Act of March 1941 empowered him to supply friendly nations with war matériel through loans and leases, and in exchange for access to military bases. Eventually $43 billion in war matériel was supplied to the anti-Hitler coalition in this fashion. But this aid was a mere palliative. Accumulated European riches were dispersed, while the United States supplanted Europe as the productive center of the Western world.

The other factor in American hegemony was strategic. Allied strategists were determined not to accept a negotiated settlement with Germany this time. They were resolved to force Hitler to nothing less than unconditional surrender. As early as August 1941 Roosevelt met with British Prime Minister Churchill aboard the cruiser *Augusta* off Newfoundland to spell out their ultimate aims in the Atlantic Charter: to seek no territory for themselves, but to create a world in which people could choose their own form of government and live in freedom and security. These aims could be achieved only after "the final destruction of Nazi tyranny." The principles of the Atlantic Charter helped rally anti-Hitler Europeans to the effort of the second total war in a quarter century. But they could not be realized without opening a second front somewhere in Hitler's Fortress Europe and fighting through to Berlin, an enterprise that would require concentrations of force beyond the reach of any powers except the United States and the Soviet Union.

Planning the Second Front

The Japanese attack on Pearl Harbor, on December 7, 1941, brought the United States into war. Churchill went to Washington at once to begin military planning with Roosevelt. Their meeting in January 1942, code-named Arcadia, was the first of a long series of personal conferences in which the Allied statesmen tried to reconcile their interests around a common strategy. American military planners joined their British counterparts in the Combined Chiefs of Staff Committee. Initially, Churchill, a seasoned war leader, got his way. Roosevelt agreed to a "Europe first" strategy according to which Allied forces would concentrate on defeating Hitler before dealing with Japan. Twenty-four other nations (including the Soviet Union and China) joined with the British and Americans on New Year's Day, 1942, in a United Nations Declaration subscribing to the principles of the Atlantic Charter and pledging their "full resources" to "complete victory over their enemies." Thus the Allies' commitment to unconditional surrender and an assault on Fortress Europe was reaffirmed.

The time and place of that assault remained to be decided, however. This became the central theme of Anglo-American wartime relations over the next three years, a period during which the preponderance of influence gradually slipped from Churchill's London to Roosevelt's Washington. Although the two partners were agreed on fundamentals—the priority of Europe and the necessity of a second front— British and American strategic conceptions reflected their different national experiences and capacities.

Churchill was inclined to feel for soft spots around the edges of Hitler's Europe. The British and French had spent their time during the "phony war" of the winter of 1939/40 looking for openings in Scandinavia or the Balkans as an alternative to a frontal assault across the Rhine. After France was knocked out of the war, Churchill's long imperial experience made him acutely conscious of British interests in the Mediterranean. Moreover, those who had seen battle on the western front in the First World War and during 1940 were understandably reluctant to embark once more on a rash and perhaps premature frontal assault. "The British," wrote United States Secretary of War Henry Stimson in his diary in 1943, "are haunted by shadows of Passchendaele and Dunkirk."[1] These influences kept Churchill keenly interested in securing the Mediterranean Sea and, once the immediate threat to Egypt and the Suez Canal was reduced by an Allied landing in North Africa in November 1942, in exploring feasible invasion routes up through southern Europe.

Some have claimed that Churchill, steeped in the history and practice of European power politics, tried from the beginning to fit strategy to political aims by moving the Anglo-American second front to a point from which the Western Allies might beat the Russians to control of Eastern Europe. In fact, until 1944 Churchill was more nervous about Russian defeat or a separate Russian peace than about Russian conquest of Europe. But there is no question that Churchill was highly sensitive to the second front's political implications for postwar British power.

The Americans concentrated on a frontal assault on Germany with what some British commentators have regarded as a kind of frontier crudity. The Americans tended to see the issue as a technical one of accumulating the necessary force for an overwhelming knock-out blow. "Realist" critics of American foreign policy, such as George Kennan, have argued also that American policymakers naively refused to admit that every strategy contains political implications; they wanted to believe that Americans were rising above European power politics by making "pure" military decisions. Suspicious of the imperial motives lurking behind Churchill's plans for Mediterranean and southern European landings, the Americans preferred to gather a massive force for the earliest possible frontal assault on the Channel coast. At bottom, there remained a Wilsonian vision of the United States, unsullied by "immoral" political calculations, straightening out wicked Europe again with one massive military blow. After a clean decision, the Americans hoped to leave European peacekeeping to a future United Nations organization.

The history of the second front in Western Europe consisted of a gradual evolution toward American strategic conceptions along with American material preponderance. The Soviet Union hastened this evolution by Stalin's desperate need for relief from the one-front war he waged against Germany from June 1941 until D-Day, June 6, 1944, when an Anglo-American force finally came ashore in Normandy. Reeling under the full German onslaught, Stalin made insistent demands for an immediate Allied second front in Western Europe. Indeed, the alliance depended on first preventing Russian defeat and then, after that threat became less immediate, persuading the dubious

---

[1]Passchendaele, a town in Belgium, was the site of particularly bloody and futile British attacks in November 1917; Dunkirk was the city on the French Channel coast from whose beaches the British Expeditionary Force was rescued by a flotilla of small boats in June 1940.

THE DEFEAT OF THE AXIS, 1942-1945

and resentful Stalin that the landing was being prepared for the earliest time that it could be accomplished successfully.

Diversionary Second Fronts: North Africa and Italy

At the beginning of 1942, the tottering Russians needed some kind of diversionary second front in Western Europe. An American proposal to launch a cross-Channel assault despite all risks, if the Russian situation

A shattered Mussolini with the German commando that rescued him in September 1943 after his exclusion from power by King Victor Emmanuel and Marshal Pietro Badoglio in July. Mussolini then set up the Republic of Saló under German protection in northern Italy until he was captured and killed by partisans in April 1945.

became desperate, was set aside in favor of a more Churchillian strategy, a probe toward a weaker flank. Operation TORCH, the first Anglo-American initiative of the war, landed troops in North Africa and opened up the Mediterranean Sea.

Up to the end of 1942, Germany and Italy had threatened to shut the Allies completely out of the Mediterranean. At the western entrance, two neutrals determined to remain in Hitler's good graces—Franco's Spain and Vichy French North Africa—stood watch over the Straits of Gibraltar. At the eastern entrance, a brilliant German general, Erwin Rommel, whose troops had been reinforcing the Italians in Libya since 1941, twice pushed eastward to within 100 miles of the Suez Canal. During the night of November 8, 1942, however, an American force with some British support landed in three places in French Morocco and Algeria. The best efforts of the poorly equipped Vichy French troops to keep North Africa out of Allied–Axis contention could not prevent Allied capture of those two colonies. Then, assisted by those Frenchmen ready to return to war, the Allies advanced eastward into Tunisia. From there, Rommel's *Afrika Korps* could be taken from behind. Allied access to the Mediterranean was thereby assured, and southern Europe lay open to Allied thrusts from the sea.

TORCH has been sharply criticized as an attack on a potentially friendly neutral, but the move made much sense. It was psychologically important for the United States to take some conspicuous but successful initiative as early as possible. Vichy French North Africa, neutral and thinly defended, was an area into which inexperienced American troops could move quickly, successfully, and usefully. The main disappointment in TORCH was that delays in obtaining French cooperation in Morocco and Algeria gave the Axis time to reinforce Tunisia. The rest of North Africa, therefore, did not fall into Allied hands until May 1943.

After the defeat of Rommel's *Afrika Korps,* the central issue was what to do next with the Allied forces concentrated in North Africa. Stalin refused to admit that TORCH had reduced any pressure on the eastern front, despite Churchill's efforts at persuasion. Over dinner in the Kremlin in August 1942, Churchill had attempted to convince Stalin of the advantages of a peripheral strategy. Drawing a crocodile on the tablecloth, he had pointed to the "soft belly." After TORCH, Churchill proposed that the Allies move north against the next weak link—Italy—and strike at the "underbelly" of the Axis.[2]

Roosevelt accepted Churchill's idea at the Casablanca Conference of January 1943. In public, the Casablanca Conference produced a ringing affirmation that the Allies would accept nothing less than Axis unconditional surrender. In private, Anglo-American military planners were more cautious. German submarine successes against Allied supply ships continued to rise to their highest levels of the war in the spring of 1943. In March 1943 alone, more than 1 million tons of Allied shipping sank in the North Atlantic, about twice as much as shipyards could replace in the same length of time. The business of assembling enough men and matériel in Britain to blast an entry into Europe was proving a more massive task than anyone had foreseen in 1942. The only way to make any move at all in 1943 was to delay the cross-Channel invasion another year, disappoint Stalin once more, and attack Italy.

In July 1943, Allied forces (American, British, and Free French) landed in Sicily. At first, the Italian campaign promised to yield enormous dividends. On July 25, Mussolini was overthrown in a *coup d'état* led by the former chief of staff of the Army, Marshal Pietro Badoglio. He was supported by the king and those members of the Fascist Grand Council who preferred to capitulate to the Allies than see Italy become a battleground. But before arrangements could be made for a rapid Allied advance into the Italian vacuum, the Germans rushed in major reinforcements, rescued Mussolini in a daring light-plane operation, and turned Italy into an occupied country. Allied forces could not cross from Sicily to the Italian mainland until September 2. Thereafter, they inched forward through rough terrain tenaciously defended by the Germans. In the end, the Italian campaign brought the miseries of protracted war to Italy without opening an easy route into central Europe for the Allies.

[2]Winston Churchill, *The Hinge of Fate* (New York, 1950), pp. 430–34, and Robert S. Sherwood, *Roosevelt and Hopkins* (New York, 1948), p. 674.

The long-awaited second front was finally opened in Western Europe with an immense amphibious landing on the Normandy coast on June 6, 1944, D-Day. Even at that late date, landing troops from the rough English Channel onto a steep coast bristling with fortifications involved enormous risks. Aside from the sheer mass of their forces, the Allies were aided by elaborate counterintelligence, including false papers planted on bodies, that persuaded the Germans to expect the landings on the flat plains of northern France. Convinced that the Normandy landing was a feint, Hitler held Rommel's tank divisions in northern France too long to throw the landing forces back in their first vulnerable days. During that time, the Allies managed to construct three artificial harbors out of old ships and floating concrete caissons ("Mulberries"). The Allies then proceeded to make the most of American productive capacity. In the first 100 days after D-Day, 2.2 million men, 450,000 vehicles, and 4 million tons of supplies went ashore through the Mulberries and the port of Cherbourg, captured on June 27. By early July, Allied forces had fought their way out of the Normandy hedgerow country into the open plains of northern France.

In the final assault on the German heartland, American production and strategic and tactical thinking assumed clear predominance on the western front. Whereas Churchill wanted the Allied troops in Italy to invade central Europe through a pass at the east end of the Alps (the Ljubljana Gap, in Yugoslavia), the Americans insisted on taking troops out of Italy for a supplementary landing in southern France on August 15, 1944. This move reflected American uncertainty in Normandy as well as hostility to Churchill's supposed schemes for protecting British

spheres of influence in Eastern Europe, an enterprise that Washington feared would require protracted occupation duties and political complications at the end of the war.

An American general, Dwight D. Eisenhower, now commanded all Allied forces—American, British, and French. Eisenhower's preference for advance on a broad front, cautiously supported by thorough build-up of supplies, prevailed over the more audacious proposals for a concentrated strike deep into Germany suggested by the senior British commander, General Bernard Law Montgomery, and by an American general, George S. Patton. In the British view, Eisenhower followed the "strategy of an elephant leaning on an obstacle to crush it."[3] Eisenhower and the American chief of staff, George C. Marshall, were particularly opposed to Churchill's suggestions that the Anglo-American forces capture Berlin and Prague before the Russians. According to American thinking, such proposals injected political considerations into what should be a purely military enterprise. Eisenhower told Marshall, "I shall not attempt any move I deem militarily unwise merely to gain a political prize unless I receive specific orders from the Combined Chiefs of Staff." No such orders came, for General Marshall wrote, "Personally . . . I would be loath to hazard American lives for purely political purposes."[4]

An Allied advance was delayed still further by the Battle of the Bulge, a massive German counterattack westward into Luxembourg and Belgium that took place in late December 1944. When bad weather

[3]London *Economist,* quoted in Diane Shaver Clemens, *Yalta* (New York, 1970), p. 99.
[4]Dwight D. Eisenhower, telegram of May 1, 1945, and George C. Marshall, telegram of April 28, 1945, quoted in Forrest C. Pogue, *George C. Marshall: Organizer of Victory, 1943–45* (New York, 1973), p. 573.

D-Day. The first wave of the invasion force approaches the Normandy beach in the face of waiting German guns, June 6, 1944.

*A stunned German family is
helped by a home guard
after an Allied bombing raid
on Mannheim.*

prevented the Allies from using their air superiority, it looked for a moment as though the Germans might break through to the Channel again. Even after the German "Bulge" was hammered back, it was not until March 7, 1945, that American soldiers, dashing across a railroad bridge at Remagen as German defenders tried to dynamite it, secured a way across the Rhine.

**Soviet
Hegemony
in the East**

While the United States was emerging as the dominant partner of the Anglo-American alliance, the Soviet Union was becoming the other great superpower of postwar Europe. That prospect seemed much less evident in 1941 than it does in retrospect. Although Russian economic growth had been impressive in the 1930s, foreign public opinion had been much more strongly impressed by the social costs of collectivizing the farms and, above all, by the purges that decimated the country's leaders. These impressions of a Soviet Union tottering at the brink of internal dissolution were reinforced by Stalin's choice of neutrality over the risk of war with Hitler in August 1939, and by the poor showing the Russians made against the Finns in the Winter War of 1939/40. Hitler calculated in June 1941 that the Soviet Union would fall apart under the blows of his invasion, and Western observers feared the same result. The Joint Intelligence Committee in London estimated that Hitler would be in Moscow within six weeks.[5]

Soviet Survival, 1941–43

The battles that followed Hitler's invasion of Russia were the most gigantic of the war. The Soviets assembled 3 million men for the defense of Moscow in late 1941, for example. They sent 6000 tanks against the Germans in the Battle of Kursk-Orel in July 1943. In a sense, the Russians played in the Second World War the role of the French in the First World War. They endured the most massive battles on their own soil, suffered the largest loss of life (perhaps 12 million dead), and claimed the leading postwar role on the Continent. With justification, the Russians have looked on the eastern front as the main theater of the Second World War.

It was at Stalingrad at the end of 1942 that the Russians were able to turn the tide. In November, a German army advanced into the very streets of Stalingrad, the principal city of the lower Volga River and gateway to the oil-rich Caucasus region. If they broke through, the Germans would consolidate their hold on half the Russian supply of oil and wheat. Instead, Soviet troops clung to Stalingrad, street by street and house by house, while the Russian command launched encircling counterattacks under the cover of oncoming winter. When Hitler refused to allow the surrounded German force in Stalingrad even the slightest strategic retreat, the entire sixth army (twenty-two divisions, whose 500,000 men had been reduced to 80,000 by casualties) was taken prisoner along with its commander, Field Marshal Friedrich Paulus, on February 2, 1943. It was the first time in history that a German field marshal had been captured in battle. During the same weeks, at the northern end of the eastern front, on the Baltic Sea, Russian troops managed to open a precarious supply route into Leningrad, which had been tightly ringed by German forces for 506 days, the longest siege ever endured by a modern city.[6]

---

[5]Sherwood, pp. 304, 327.

[6]Leningrad remained under German shellfire for more than another year, although the period of most severe starvation was over. (Harrison Salisbury, *The 900 Days: The Siege of Leningrad* [New York, 1969], pp. 550, 567.)

The Germans pushed forward once again on several fronts in the spring of 1943, but the Soviets were able to gain their first summer victory in the great tank battle of Kursk-Orel in July 1943. The grim endurance phase of the Russo-German war had come to an end. From the summer of 1943 on, the Russians began the relentless advance that brought them to the old Polish frontier by February 1944. From there they entered central Europe just as the Western Allies were embarking on the French coast. With the elimination of Germany and Japan in 1945, for the first time no major powers stood across Russian paths to the sea to the east and west.

What had brought the Soviet Union to this position? How had it survived? Three basic Soviet achievements stand out: industrial reconstruction, mass citizen support, and the emergence of new officer talent. Soviet survival seems to have been more a product of internal resources than of outside assistance, in the form of both Western aid and Nazi errors.

A major difficulty had been presented by the German occupation of the most productive areas of the Soviet Union. Forty percent of the Soviet population and perhaps 75 percent of its productive capacity lay in the occupied western border areas. The Soviets moved whole populations eastward and built 1360 factories in new industrial centers east of the Urals. The Soviet economy emerged strengthened, in the long run, from newly tooled, more evenly spread urban-industrial development.

The enormous population of the Soviet Union was an asset only if the Soviet leaders managed to keep it united and willing to undergo the greatest sacrifices of any Allied nation. Stalin drew on deep nationalist feelings for this purpose. Reviewing the customary parade on the anniversary of the Bolshevik Revolution in November 1941, this time

The battle of Stalingrad, November 1942. Soviet troops hold the city in house-to-house fighting.

with German armies in the suburbs of Moscow, Stalin invoked "our great ancestors," including those of Tsarist Russia. The portraits of the tsarist generals who had fought Napoleon, Alexander Souvarov and Mikhail Kutuzov, hung in Stalin's office.[7] In 1938 film director Sergei Eisenstein and composer Sergei Prokofiev had joined to create a brilliant film evoking the thirteenth-century defense against the Teutonic knights, *Alexander Nevsky.* Rather than a war to defend the homeland of communism, the war against Hitler became the Great Patriotic War, as all Soviet writers refer to it now.

The brutality of the German occupation helped forestall tendencies to collaborate within the Soviet populations. Instead of attempting to garner support from Soviet peasants in the occupied areas, the Germans tried to extort a maximum amount of grain from them and threatened to displace them with German settlers. The result was passive resistance to the Germans by the same peasants who had resisted Soviet collectivization a decade before. In late 1941, the Germans got less grain from direct exploitation of their occupied areas of the Soviet Union than they had been getting under the Nazi-Soviet Pact in early 1941.[8] Some Soviet dissidents were willing to collaborate with the Germans, such as General Andrei Vlasov, who tried to form an anti-Communist army among Russian prisoners of war. But they were never given much independence by the Nazis, who considered them all Slavic *Untermenschen* (subhumans).

The mass of Soviet citizenry rallied to the defense of Russian soil, whatever their attitudes toward Stalin's regime. One measure of the

[7] Seweryn Bialer, *Stalin and His Generals* (New York, 1969), p. 516.
[8] Alexander Dallin, *German Rule in Russia, 1941–45: A Study in Occupation Policies* (New York, 1957), p. 369.

Soviet population's solidarity was Leningrad's endurance of ghastly suffering during its two-and-a-half year siege. Starvation and disease reduced the population from 4 million to 2.5 million. Another sign of the regime's viability under pressure was the emergence of a new generation of talented officers only a few years after over half the officer corps had been purged. Georgi Zhukov, for example, the defender of Moscow in 1941, rose from colonel to marshal in three years.

Outside assistance also helped the Soviet Union survive and then turn the tide. At the time Hitler launched his Operation Barbarossa in 1941, Churchill, still enduring Britain's "darkest hour," threw off his traditional anticommunism and offered alliance to Stalin within hours. After November 1941, the United States included the Soviet Union in its shipment of lend-lease supplies. Even so, such outside assistance seems to have been only a marginal factor in Stalin's success. Western aid was limited by harsh conditions along two available routes: through Iran, and by ship around Arctic Norway to the northern Russian port of Murmansk. The Murmansk run, open at best only during the brief ice-free months of summer, had to be suspended in 1942 and again in 1943 after heavy losses to German air and submarine attacks. Although Western material aid was more substantial than the Soviets have wanted to admit,[9] that aid was effective only because internal Soviet resiliency in maintaining a one-front war against Hitler for three years made it usable.

Hitler's mistakes contributed another form of outside assistance. One might first question whether Hitler's decision to invade the Soviet Union was not a fatal act of overreaching. Once launched, however, the eastern campaign had to succeed quickly or lapse into a long war of attrition in which the immense Soviet Union had long-term advantages. Hitler's judgment that the Soviet Union would collapse under pressure was ideologically distorted. Moreover, the opportunity to strike a knock-out blow in 1941 was diminished by a late start, on June 22, 1941, following spring diversions into Yugoslavia, Greece, and Crete. Surviving German generals have blamed Hitler for advancing into Russia on a broad front rather than striking directly at Moscow, and then for diverting forces from the Moscow front in mid-July 1941 to the rich oil and grain areas of the south, permitting Zhukov to organize the defense of Moscow in November. By then, the Germans were suffering from their lack of winter equipment.

Hitler's errors as a defensive strategist are more widely agreed on than his possible mistakes as an offensive strategist. His refusal to withdraw from Moscow to the Polish frontier in November 1941, as some of his generals advised, was probably correct. But his failure to make a strategic withdrawal from Stalingrad in November 1942 cost him an

---

[9]About $9.5 billion out of a total of $43 billion in lend-lease went to the Soviet Union. The Russians estimate that 5 percent of their vital supplies came from the West; the United States estimates about 15 percent. The single most important item was 425,000 American trucks.

Leningrad during the siege, 1942. A couple is dragging the body of a child down Nevsky Prospect on a sled.

entire army. The same dogged refusal to shorten his defensive lines in 1943 probably helped the Russians break through into their final advance to the west. Even Hitler's most obvious errors are not the major explanation for Soviet success, however. Once the Soviet Union survived its first winter of German assault, the Soviet leaders acquired a far larger margin of possible error. When the war of attrition set in, the smallest errors on the German side were fatal ones.

Soviet Advance to the West

By the time the Allies were finally landing at the western edge of Hitler's Europe, in June 1944, Soviet forces had been advancing relentlessly to the west for nearly a year, since their breakthrough in July 1943. In the winter of 1943/44 they recaptured most of their 1939 territory. In the spring of 1944 they reached their 1914 frontiers in the interwar Baltic States and in Poland. Then, from September to November 1944, halting their advance in Poland, they turned to the south and broke through into the Danube Valley in Yugoslavia and Hungary, farther west than any Russian troops had stood since the Napoleonic Wars. In January 1945 the Russians resumed their advance into Poland. When the Allied leaders met at Yalta in February 1945, the Western Allies were still bogged down on the far side of the Rhine, while the Russians were within 100 miles of Berlin. The postwar settlement was already being shaped by the respective positions of the Allied armies.

The Big Three and the Future of Europe

In the early years of the Second World War, when the central issue of the anti-Hitler coalition was the survival of Britain and the Soviet Union, the exact configuration of postwar Europe seemed a distant and academic issue to Americans. President Roosevelt and his Secretary of State Cordell Hull shrank from premature political commitments that recalled the unhappy precedent of the encumbering secret treaties of the First World War. As long as possible, the American leaders attempted to confine wartime diplomacy to "military" matters, as if these decisions in themselves had no political implications.

Insofar as they made overtly "political" agreements in those early years, the American leaders limited themselves to broad statements of principle—the Atlantic Charter of August 14, 1941, for example—and to committing all the Allies to a projected new international organization—the United Nations—within which postwar political issues could be worked out in a climate of cooperation. The Americans were determined to do Woodrow Wilson's work right this time.

When Soviet Foreign Minister V. M. Molotov tried to get his new American and British allies to recognize the Soviet Union's 1941 frontiers (and thus its 1939 and 1940 gains with Hitler's help), he was forced to settle in May 1942 for a purely military alliance. The first major wartime Allied leaders' conference at Casablanca, Morocco, in January 1943[10] limited itself to immediate military decisions and to establishing the principle of accepting nothing less than Axis unconditional surrender. Meanwhile, the future of Europe continued to be shaped informally on the battlefield.

Gathering Political Implications

The political implications of the unfolding military campaigns could no longer be held in abeyance after the summer of 1943. The Russians had begun their drive to the west. One of the Axis partners, Italy, had withdrawn from the war, not by unconditional surrender, but by secret negotiations between some of Mussolini's dissident associates and the Anglo-American leaders, negotiations in which the Soviet Union had played no part. Another German ally, Romania, was sending peace-feeler signals to the West. Stalin was deeply suspicious about delays in opening the second front in the west, about the suspension of Allied convoys to Murmansk, and about the postwar plans of the bitterly anti-Communist Polish government in exile in London. An Allied political conference could no longer be deferred.

The foreign ministers of the United States, Britain, and the Soviet Union met in Moscow in October 1943—the first political conference of the main Allied powers.[11] The conference's outcome was an uneasy compromise between simple matters of general principle and thorny matters of future boundaries and regimes. Secretary of State Hull

---

[10]Roosevelt, Churchill, and the French leaders de Gaulle and Giraud; Stalin was invited but declined to leave his command post.
[11]China was also represented.

guided the conference resolutely onto the high ground of principle. Most public attention was fixed on the Declaration of General Security reaffirming the determination of the anti-Hitler allies to resolve their postwar problems cooperatively in a United Nations Organization. In more concrete matters, the foreign ministers restated their resolution to force Hitler to unconditional surrender, followed by the military occupation of Germany, a complete purge of all Nazi officials, and the total demobilization of Germany's armed forces. The foreign ministers set up a permanent working group—the European Advisory Commission—to work out more specific terms of the postwar settlement. Thus the Russians had been brought into participation in postwar planning before any of the major policy questions had been settled. As Secretary of State Hull saw it, that success justified skirting the tougher issues— postwar frontiers and spheres of influence in central and Eastern Europe.

The Teheran Conference, November 1943

None of these issues, of course, could be solved without the personal assent of Joseph Stalin. It was highly desirable, from a Western point of view, to draw Stalin more fully into confident participation in the United Nations in advance of the actual postwar settlement. In addition, Stalin clearly needed to be reassured about plans for a second front, while the Anglo-American leaders needed to be reassured that Stalin would remain in the coalition to the end, even against Japan. Roosevelt, who seems to have believed that he was more capable than diplomats of charming Stalin into a more open partnership, energetically promoted a personal meeting of the three heads of state. He suggested a number of midway points for a conference, including a warship in the Bering Strait. Stalin finally agreed to come no further than the Iranian capital of Teheran, where Soviet troops could help maintain tight security.

Stalin, Churchill, and Roosevelt met in the large walled garden of the Soviet Embassy in Teheran for three days at the end of November 1943. Never before had wartime leaders traveled half way around the globe to confer on strategy and the future shape of the world. As for Stalin, it was his only trip outside Russia except for a congress of exiled Russian socialists in London in 1903 and the Potsdam Conference in July 1945.

Over long state banquets in the evening, the three leaders sized one another up and talked expansively about the future of Europe. Churchill and Stalin needled each other with evident relish. In this relaxed mood and with Russian and Anglo-American armies still far from German soil, it was easy to agree generally on harsh punishment for the Nazis. The other leaders raised no objection when Stalin declared that 50,000 to 100,000 Nazis would have to be executed after the war. Even Churchill, who was later to work for a united Germany as a counterweight to Russian expansion in Europe, agreed with the others that Germany should be partitioned. But there were also glimpses of future differences. Roosevelt found that he was closer to Stalin than to

Churchill on some issues, such as the future disposition of European overseas empires. The Polish question already seemed too sensitive to touch, even before the Russian armies had reached Polish soil. Roosevelt refused to discuss it; 6 or 7 million Polish-Americans, he told Stalin, would vote in the American presidential elections of 1944. Churchill, however, saw no objection to recognizing the 1940 Polish–Soviet frontier in the east provided that an independent Poland were compensated at German expense in the west. With three matches on the tablecloth, he illustrated how all the Polish frontiers could be moved westward, like a "closing left" maneuver on a parade ground.

In retrospect, those conversations sounded to one Cold War observer like "a flourish of knives over the body of Europe."[12] But no concrete frontier settlements were reached. The Americans still preferred to leave what Hull called "that Pandora's Box of infinite troubles" to the happier future when the Russians would be fully integrated into a United Nations. Stalin said that he had "no desire to speak at the present time about any Soviet desires, but when the time comes, we will speak."[13]

Stalin seemed primarily interested in military plans. The second front in the west, promised him in 1942, had still not been opened in 1943. Churchill, more anxious than ever about the cost of a frontal assault into France, was profuse with eastern Mediterranean plans: opening up the Black Sea, giving aid to Yugoslavia, or sending a force north through the Ljubljana Gap at the head of the Adriatic Sea into the Danube Basin, to "extend our right hand along the Danube."[14] Roosevelt and Stalin overrode his eloquence. The invasion of Western Europe (code-named operation OVERLORD), so many times deferred, was now firmly set for May 1, 1944.

That decision—the major concrete result of Teheran—meant that Russian and Western European armies would divide Europe along north–south lines, roughly in the middle. Later, from a Cold War perspective, that looked like "Stalin's supreme triumph":[15] a military division of Europe in which Anglo-American influence was kept out of the Balkans and Eastern Europe. Those long-term implications may have been less clear at the end of 1943, when the Russians had still not yet recaptured their 1941 frontiers. Churchill never denied that the English Channel coast must become the main western theater of war, a point the Germans were soon to reinforce by launching a new generation of rocket bombs—V2's—on London from occupied Holland. Moreover, the craggy Balkans were not considered an easy route into Eastern Europe for the Anglo-American troops; General Marshall later growled drily that the "soft underbelly had chrome-steel sideboards."[16] Above all,

---

[12]Herbert Feis, *Churchill, Roosevelt, and Stalin: The War They Waged and the Peace They Sought* (Princeton, N.J., 1957), p. 275.
[13]U.S., Department of State, *The Conferences at Cairo and Teheran* (Washington, D.C., 1961), p. 555.
[14]Feis, p. 229.
[15]Isaac Deutscher, *Stalin: A Political Biography,* 2nd ed. (New York, 1967), p. 508.
[16]Quoted in Pogue, p. 415. Marshall used these words in an interview in 1956.

Roosevelt shrank from projects that might involve the United States in postwar troop duty in Europe. After Teheran, it was clear that all Eastern Europe and the Balkans would be liberated by the Russians.

Soviet Moves in the Balkans

The Russian armies began to do just that in the year following the Teheran Conference. They crossed the old Polish frontiers in January 1944. When the Anglo-American forces landed on the French coast on June 6, 1944, as planned, Stalin kept his promise to conduct a simultaneous offensive toward Warsaw that would prevent Hitler from shifting troops to the west. Then, in August 1944, the Soviet armies stopped short of Warsaw for five months, even though the city rose against its German occupiers in anticipation of liberation. The main Soviet advance shifted south, where the surrender of Romania on August 23, 1944, opened the way to the Balkans. During September and October 1944, Russian armies took the lower Danube basin, up to the gates of Budapest, the capital of Hungary. By November 1944, Soviet Russian armies occupied Balkan territory far beyond the wildest dreams of Imperial Russia.

Churchill was determined to pin Stalin down to a concrete agreement on future spheres of influence in the Balkans, without United States assent if necessary. He flew to Moscow on October 9, 1944. With armies advancing against Hitler from both east and west, the conversation was easy and expansive. After dinner Churchill said, "Let us settle our affairs in the Balkans." He proposed a frank division of influence, with the Soviet Union predominant in Romania and Bulgaria, Britain predominant in Greece, and a "fifty-fifty" division in Yugoslavia and Hungary. Stalin quickly agreed, putting a large blue pencil mark on Churchill's scrap of paper.

The Yalta Conference, February 1945

Nothing, of course, was official without Roosevelt's agreement. The "Big Three" met again in February 1945, in the former Livadia Palace of Tsar Nicholas II at the Russian Black Sea resort of Yalta. At the time, with victory approaching, the Yalta Conference seemed one more celebration of growing Allied cooperation and harmony, the "dawn of the new day we had all been praying for and talking about for so many years."[17] But later, in the highly charged Cold War climate of the 1950s, the view was widespread that Roosevelt, through careless negotiation, ill health (he died two months later), or outright treason within his staff,[18]

[17]Harry Hopkins, quoted in Clemens, pp. 279–80.
[18]Alger Hiss, the State Department officer responsible for drawing up United States proposals at the Yalta Conference for the future United Nations organization, was accused in 1948 by members of the House Un-American Activities Committee of having given secret documents to Communist agents, in what became the most celebrated Cold War trial in the United States. When he denied the charges, Hiss was convicted of perjury.

simply handed over Eastern and central Europe to Stalin at Yalta. Yalta seemed "the high point of Soviet diplomatic success and correspondingly the low point of American appeasement."[19]

A soberer examination shows that the major lines of postwar influence in Europe had already been drawn by the Allied armies. At the time the three leaders met in Yalta, the Anglo-American armies were still west of the Rhine, recovering from the Battle of the Bulge, while the Russian armies were within 100 miles of Berlin. In any event, a war devoted to Germany's destruction could hardly fail to enhance the power of Germany's main eastern neighbor.

Another problem was that while Roosevelt could offer Stalin relatively little in February 1945, he had much to ask. The United States military leaders wanted Russian help against Japan "at the earliest possible date."[20] When two atomic bombs subsequently brought Japanese surrender a mere three months after Germany surrendered, it was difficult to remember how formidable the Japanese had still seemed at the time of Yalta. American military planners expected to lose as many as 1 million men in another D-Day, an amphibious landing in the Japanese home islands. Roosevelt therefore agreed to an expanded Soviet role in the Far East—possession of Sakhalin and the Kurile Islands, a share in postwar influence in Korea, and support in negotiating two warm water ports and railroad rights in Manchuria with the Chinese—in return for a promise of Soviet military assistance against Japan and of American air bases in Siberia.

EASTERN AND WESTERN FRONTS AT TIME OF YALTA CONFERENCE, FEBRUARY 1945

The establishment of the United Nations was a major American preoccupation at Yalta. Roosevelt knew that American public opinion would not permit him to commit troops to Europe for any length of time after Germany's defeat. Along with Secretary of State Hull, he wanted to draw the Big Three into a postwar international organization before particular postwar issues could divide them into opposing camps.

[19]William Chamberlin, quoted in Clemens, p. 280.
[20]U.S., Department of State, *Foreign Relations of the United States. The Conferences at Malta and Yalta* (Washington, D.C., 1955), pp. 388ff. General Douglas MacArthur, commander of United States forces in the Pacific, denied in the later atmosphere of the Cold War that he had asked for Russian help against Japan.

Through the United Nations, he hoped to achieve a self-enforcing peace settlement that would not require American troops, as well as an open world without spheres of influence in which American enterprise could work freely. To American staff members of the Yalta delegation, Imperial Britain seemed a more immediate threat to this prospect than Soviet Russia. They were afraid that a British attempt to set up spheres of influence in Europe would provoke the Russians to do the same. The resulting conflicts might well produce "a war which we could not win."[21] The British and French empires also seemed obstacles to the future open world Roosevelt envisioned, and he talked freely to Stalin of dissolving the old European empires in Asia.

Roosevelt and the American delegation spent much more time pinning down the details of the future United Nations than on resolving immediate problems in Poland and Germany. Their design for the organization was heavily weighted with members friendly or subordinate to the United States, and it provided for the right of veto over any actions taken against the wishes of any one of the Big Three, a procedure necessary for ratification by the United States Congress and willingly accepted of course by Stalin and Churchill. Stalin accepted the rest of the design, without showing much interest, after a compromise had been reached on Poland and after the addition of two Russian states—the Ukraine and Byelorussia—as voting members. Churchill accepted the rest after being promised that the trusteeship provisions for United Nations supervision of former colonies would apply to "not one scrap of British Territory."

The immediate issues of Germany and Eastern Europe were treated much less conclusively. Differences among the Allies were beginning to emerge. The Big Three reaffirmed their agreement that Germany must surrender unconditionally, be disarmed, and be denazified. Occupation zones were allocated. France was brought in to occupy one zone at the insistence of Churchill, who foresaw Britain left alone facing Russia in Europe. But was Germany to be dismembered, or administered as a single unit? With Churchill now doubtful about the effects of an atomized central Europe, the question was left unanswered. No agreement could be reached on reparations either. Stalin, supported by Roosevelt, proposed that a total of $20 billion in reparations from Germany plus forced labor be drawn from all the occupation zones; Russia would get half of this total. Churchill found these plans excessive. These unsettled issues were to cause much grief later on.

The Yalta compromises on Eastern Europe attempted to reconcile two irreconcilable goals: nations governed by authentically democratic regimes and at the same time friendly to the Soviet Union. Agreement was possible only if this fundamental contradiction were glossed over. The Russians had tried to predetermine the Polish settlement by recognizing

[21]Admiral William D. Leahy, quoted in *Ibid.*, p. 108.

The Big Three—Churchill, Roosevelt, and Stalin—on the patio of the Livadia Palace at Yalta, February 1945. Roosevelt died two months later.

a hand-picked government in the areas already occupied by Soviet troops. The Anglo-American leaders got Stalin to accept the "reorganization" of this new government to include some pro-Western Poles, and to promise future elections. Elsewhere in Eastern Europe, three-power Allied Control Commissions were to oversee the establishment of new governments. In the absence of any stronger presence there, however, the Anglo-American members eventually found the authority of these commissions to be ephemeral.

At Yalta, hospitality and the euphoria of approaching victory covered over the latent conflicts. Three months later, when Hitler committed suicide on April 30, 1945, and the remnants of his Army surrendered on May 8, the linchpin of the anti-Hitler alliance was removed. The Big Three met one last time in July 1945 in the very capital of the country they had defeated, in the Berlin suburb of Potsdam where Frederick the Great had built his palace.

The Potsdam Conference, July 1945

Much had changed since Yalta. Roosevelt had died on April 12. The unknown and inexperienced vice president, a former senator from Missouri, Harry S. Truman, was just getting his bearings when the Potsdam Conference began on July 17. Winston Churchill, voted out of office in a general election during the conference, was replaced by the Labour leader, Clement Attlee. None of the old conviviality of Teheran and Yalta brightened this meeting. Immediate decisions on the future of

Europe could no longer be set aside in favor of more congenial discussions of military progress. Germany and its satellites had been defeated; now they had to be administered.

One more major change had occurred. The day before the Potsdam Conference opened, the first of three experimental atomic bombs was successfully exploded in the New Mexico desert at Alamagordo. Truman was informed immediately:

> The test was successful beyond the most optimistic expectations of anyone. . . . For a brief period there was a lightning effect within a radius of twenty miles equal to several suns at midday; a huge ball of fire was formed which lasted for several seconds. This ball mushroomed and rose to a height of over 10,000 feet before it dimmed. The light from the explosion was seen clearly at Albuquerque, Santa Fe, Silver City, El Paso and other points generally to about 180 miles away. The sound was heard to the same distance in a few instances but generally to about 100 miles. Only a few windows were broken although one was some 125 miles away. . . . Dr. Kistiakowsky . . . threw his arms around Dr. Oppenheimer and embraced him with shouts of glee. . . . All seemed to feel that they had been present at the birth of a new age.[22]

The other two bombs could now be dropped on Japan. The British chief of staff saw the implications at once: "It was no longer necessary for the Russians to come into the Japanese war. . . . Furthermore we now had something in our hands which would redress the balance with the Russians."[23]

Whether the Alamagordo explosion itself stiffened Truman in the Potsdam negotiations, as the American New Left historian Gar Alperovitz has claimed in his *Atomic Diplomacy* (1965), is a hotly disputed point. In any case, it is difficult to imagine leaders of such different social systems finding much common ground in discussions of the political, social, and economic structure of postwar Europe. Agreements at Potsdam were largely limited to reaffirming previous general understandings: that Germany should be demilitarized, denazified, and its leaders brought before an International War Crimes Tribunal. Positive new arrangements could be agreed on only by phrasing them in ambiguous terms that the two sides soon interpreted in their own way.

Both sides already felt that the other had violated earlier agreements. For example, Truman no longer supported the reparations arrangements that Roosevelt had accepted at Yalta. Under a new arrangement the Russians could draw reparations only from their own zone, along with 25 percent of the "unnecessary" capital equipment of the Western zones—a formula bound to lead to different interpretations. The Russians had added only two pro-Western ministers to the Polish

---

[22]General L. R. Groves, "Memorandum for the Secretary of War," July 18, 1945, Potsdam Document No. 1305. This letter was read directly to Truman and Churchill at Potsdam; Stalin was given only brief information about a new bomb.
[23]Lord Alanbrooke, diary entry of July 23, 1945, quoted in Arthur Bryant, *Triumph in the West* (London, 1959), p. 363.

government, which they now ceased to call "provisional." Each side had a long list of alleged acts of bad faith.

The two victorious superpowers now eyed each other across the rubble.

Origins of the Cold War

Several burning issues had to be settled at the war's end in the summer of 1945. Those that could not be settled by agreement were settled by *fait accompli.* Time had run out on the use of wartime camaraderie to smooth over these issues. The Allies' attention had turned from the relatively technical business of defeating Hitler's Europe to the overtly political business of installing Hitler's successors. Who would become the presidents, governors, or mayors of the liberated territories? What form of government should be set up? Who owned the properties there? Who would make these decisions? Did each Allied power have the right to impose regimes of its own choosing in the areas liberated by its blood? If the liberated populations had any choice in the matter, how would their opinions be ascertained?

At bottom lay a basic question no one dared ask publicly: Were United States and Russian aims in postwar Europe fundamentally unreconcilable? To each side, its own peace aims seemed reasonable, even self-evident; only an ally of bad faith could object to them. Europe, of course, was only one part of a world stage on which the superpowers now calculated their interests, but it was a central part. Europe's future depended in large measure on how Washington and Moscow got along with each other.

Soviet Peace Aims

Stalin's aims in Europe in 1945 were at the heart of the matter. The Soviet Union had obviously transformed its world power position. How did the Soviet leaders intend to use that power? During the Cold War, many Americans assumed that Stalin's aims were constant and insatiable. From this perspective, whatever limits Stalin accepted in 1945 were those forced on him by countervailing power. Stalin's aims no doubt grew during the Cold War, but a good case can be made for the view that initially they were limited and largely defensive. The security of the Soviet state rather than the spread of Communist regimes far and wide seems to have had first priority in 1945.

No one challenged the Soviet intention to regain some former Russian soil lost to the Japanese in 1905, to the Germans in 1918, and to the successor states in 1919 and 1920. Some of Stalin's western frontier claims were less extensive than those Tsarist Russia had asked its Allies to approve in 1914 to 1917, when it had wanted to annex the Dardanelles and expected to keep its broad Polish lands. In other places the new western frontiers ran along those of 1914 (such as much of the frontier with Romania). In some places (Finland and the Baltic region in the north, and across the Carpathian Mountains in the center) the new Soviet frontiers lay west of any previous Russian soil. In the Far East, Stalin regained approximately the frontiers Russia had prior to its defeat by Japan in 1905. By and large, Stalin avenged the humiliations of Tsushima, Brest-Litovsk, and Versailles and reestablished the frontiers of Tsarist Russia at its height.[24]

Around those frontiers, Stalin seems to have worked for contiguous rings of friendly states. Some of those adjoining states had made war on the Soviet Union alongside the Germans after 1941: Romania, Hungary, and Finland; other adjoining states, such as Poland, had been invasion routes into Russia for centuries. Romania and Finland had to give up territory. Poland was moved bodily westward. Czechoslovakia lost its easternmost extremity, Trans-Carpathian Ruthenia. And Stalin insisted, above all, that "friendly" governments rule these border states.

One problem with these arrangements was that regaining part of the tsarist frontiers required snuffing out the national independence of

[24]See maps below. Finland had been an independent duchy under the tsar's personal rule between 1809 and 1914. The Ruthenians of the newly acquired trans-Carpathian region spoke a language close to Ukrainian. Even here, therefore, Soviet claims were not entirely without basis.

RUSSIA IN THE TWENTIETH CENTURY

some of the successor states carved out of Eastern Europe in 1918 and 1919: most conspicuously, the Baltic nations of Lithuania, Latvia, and Estonia. Another crucial problem was the nature of the "friendly" governments that Stalin demanded on his frontiers. Could they be freely elected, pluralistic regimes open to Western trade and travel and still "friendly" on Stalin's terms? Must they be Communist to be "friendly"?

Outside the immediately contiguous states, Stalin appears to have accepted the spheres of influence that he and Churchill had so easily agreed to after dinner on October 9, 1944.[25] In Greece, he allowed the British to settle the civil war between Communist and pro-Western groups in their own favor. In Western Europe, up to 1947, Stalin ordered local Communist parties to work within democratically elected Popular Fronts. He accepted Chiang Kai-shek without question as the legitimate ruler of China. Suspicious as always to distant Communist parties not under his direct control, Stalin seems to have given no orders for revolution abroad.

American Peace Aims

Most Americans are accustomed to think that the United States wanted nothing in postwar Europe except the peaceful self-government that would come naturally unless the superpowers interfered. In this spirit, American armed forces were reduced from 3.5 million to 500,000 within less than ten months at the end of the war. But there was a design for Europe, and the world, reflected in American statements and actions: a world without barriers to trade and investment; an open, pluralistic world, favorable to American economic predominance as well as in keeping with American emotional preferences. These goals resembled earlier Open Door policies in China, extended now to the whole world. Stalin's conception of closed spheres of influence was anathema to these goals.

American peace aims in Europe come into sharper relief when contrasted with the aims of allied Western democracies, especially Britain and France. One conflict concerned colonies. Roosevelt spoke frankly at Yalta and elsewhere about his hopes of seeing the European colonies in Asia replaced by trusteeships. At that stage, for example, American officials in China enjoyed good relations with the exiled Vietnamese nationalist leader, Ho Chi Minh. The French, not illogically, claimed that the Americans simply wanted to replace French economic presence in Indochina with their own.

The United States and its Western European allies also disagreed on the economic conditions of recovery. Postwar British and French governments assumed that restoration of the prewar economy was impossible without extensive government control. The United States, by

---

[25]See above, p. 485.

contrast, insisted that Britain lift currency controls and return the pound to free international trading in 1947 as a condition for receiving an American loan. It is now almost universally agreed that this step was premature. The pound rapidly declined on its reappearance in a free world currency market. Despite British efforts to cut their consumption

TERRITORIAL ADJUSTMENTS AFTER THE SECOND WORLD WAR 1945

To Russia
FINLAND
Lake Ladoga
Leased to Russia until 1955
Leningrad
NORWAY
SWEDEN
ESTONIA
To Russia
RUSSIA
LATVIA
To Russia
NORTH SEA
DENMARK
BALTIC SEA
LITHUANIA
To Russia
EAST PRUSSIA
To Russia
Occupied by Poland
Occupied by Poland
U.S.
Berlin
BRITISH ZONE
RUSSIAN ZONE
NETH.
GERMANY
To Russia
POLAND
BELG.
FRENCH ZONE
UNITED STATES ZONE
CZECHOSLOVAKIA
NORTHERN BUKOVINA
From Hungary to Czech.
RUSSIAN ZONE
Vienna
U.S. ZONE
SUBCARPATHIAN RUTHENIA
BESSARABIA
To Russia
FRANCE
BRATISLAVA BRIDGEHEAD
FRENCH ZONE
AUSTRIA
SWITZ.
BRITISH ZONE
HUNGARY
ROMANIA
VENEZIA GIULIA
To Yugoslavia
Trieste
YUGOSLAVIA
DOBRUJA
To Bulgaria
To France
BLACK SEA
ITALY
ADRIATIC SEA
BULGARIA
ALBANIA
GREECE
The boundaries shown on this map date from the beginning of World War II.
MILES
0
200
DODECANESE IS.
To Greece from Italy
Axis nations after World War II
Lands which changed hands after World War II

of imported goods (including food) to a bare minimum, the pound had to be devalued from $4.03 to $2.80 in September 1949. Since most funds and materials for reconstruction had to be imported from the United States, scarce dollars acquired very high values in European currencies. It became inexpensive for American tourists to travel in Europe and for American firms to buy up European branches. The reign of the dollar in Europe lasted for a whole generation after 1945, until the late 1960s when long years of American spending in Europe began to produce large trade deficits with prosperous European economies.

These conflicts of interest between the United States and the Western European democracies suggest that American peace aims after 1945 included, at least implicitly, the creation of an open world economy in which the dollar was the strongest currency and in which American firms could operate most freely. American power was sufficient to get its way over the objections of former Great Powers like Britain and France. The Soviet Union, however, was strong enough to set up its own immense sphere of influence from which American investors, traders, and tourists were excluded.

Seeds of Antagonism

Economic conflict coincided with the ideological clash between capitalism and communism. If the Russian sphere of influence had been merely authoritarian, one could still have expected United States–Russian friction like the Open Door conflict among the United States and Britain and Germany over China at the turn of the century. Old ideological suspicions made the United States–Soviet clash of interests assume the emotional dimensions of a crusade. Each side came to believe that an aggressive enemy wanted to extinguish its whole way of life. Soviet leaders increasingly told their people after 1945 that the capitalist powers, led by the United States, were encircling them. The American people increasingly came to believe that the Communist bloc, led by the Soviet Union, was trying to overthrow every free-enterprise regime in the world by subversion. Encirclement and subversion: these twin specters took on reality as the acts of each side seemed to confirm suspicions. For example, the Russians viewed America's return to armaments in 1947, coupled with its creation of a worldwide system of military bases and alliances, as confirmation of an ever tightening capitalist encirclement. These growing, self-fulfilling suspicions slipped easily into old grooves of ideological conflict dating back to 1917. In that sense, the Cold War was one more installment in a long history of revolution versus containment going back to Lenin and Woodrow Wilson.

Who struck the first blow in the Cold War, and where? The possible answers differ as widely as interpretations of the Cold War itself. From the Russian point of view, the capitalist powers first showed their determination to crush the Soviet regime with their military intervention of 1919 and 1920.[26] Stalin's suspicions of the West were never entirely allayed during the war. When the Western allies excluded him from the secret surrender negotiations with Italy in July 1943, Stalin could well assume that each liberating army was arranging matters to its own tastes. Stalin followed the same course with the Romanian and Bulgarian surrenders in September 1944; he subsequently felt aggrieved that the Western allies wanted to interfere in the regimes of states bordering the Soviet Union. In May 1945, President Truman cut off lend-lease aid so abruptly that ships already bound for Soviet ports were called back. At Potsdam, Truman seemed to the Soviets to have hardened the American position on German reparations since Yalta.

From the American point of view, the first sign of Stalin's apparent aim to impose Communist regimes on countries liberated by the Red Army was deeply chilling. Just before the Yalta Conference, for example, Stalin unilaterally recognized his hand-picked Communist Lublin Committee as the legitimate government of Poland. Even more alarming were hints that Communists would foment insurrections after the war even beyond the range of the Red Army. The first of these was the mutiny in the Greek naval units at Alexandria, Egypt, on April 4, 1944, and the uprisings in Athens in December 1944. These events suggested to some Western Europeans and Americans that Communist aims went far beyond mere security for the Soviet Union to revolutionary change throughout Europe and the world. Even before the German surrender at Reims on May 8, 1945, therefore, both sides regarded each other with mutual distrust.

Poland

First Battlegrounds of the Cold War

No question aroused more distrust and bitterness among the Allies at the end of the war than the future of Poland. The Polish issue is an ideal case for observing in detail how conflicting interests between Russia and the Western Allies generated a spiral of mutual suspicion and antagonism.

Poland's frontiers were part of the problem. This issue went back to the re-creation of Poland at the Versailles Conference. The Versailles experts had drafted a proposed Soviet–Polish frontier in 1919, the Curzon Line, which ran approximately along ethnic lines. After the Soviet–Polish war of 1919 to 1921, however, the Versailles powers agreed to an expanded Poland whose frontier, 150 miles east of the proposed Curzon Line, included many Ukrainians and White Russians.[27] Stalin watched for his first opportunity to rectify a Soviet–Polish frontier that many, even outside the Soviet Union, could regard as a violation of national self-determination. His first chance came with the

[26]See Chapter 5, pp. 138–42.
[27]See Chapter 5, p. 141.

Nazi-Soviet Pact of August 1939, with its secret clauses in which Hitler agreed to Soviet aims in Eastern Europe.

When Germany defeated Poland in September 1939, Stalin quickly moved into the eastern part, up to approximately the Curzon Line. Later, when Stalin was fighting against Hitler, he tried to persuade his new British and American allies to recognize his 1939 gain. They refused to make any firm frontier settlements as long as the war continued. The Curzon Line was not unreasonable on either ethnic or historic terms, however, and a Poland moved bodily westward was better from the Western point of view than no Poland at all. At the Teheran Conference in November 1943, therefore, both Churchill and Roosevelt led Stalin to believe that a Poland stretching from the Curzon Line in the east westward to the Oder and Neisse rivers, including former German territory in the west, was a reasonable basis for discussion.[28]

Behind the territorial question lay a political one: What kind of regime would govern Poland? The Western Allies regarded the Polish government in exile in London as the legitimate future government. The London Poles and their leader, General Wladyslaw Sikorski, were remnants of the Polish Army along with former middle-class political leaders who had escaped to the West. They had useful contacts with the internal resistance, and a Polish Army under General Wladyslav Anders was giving assistance to the British in the Middle East and later in Italy. The London Poles (like many Poles at home) were determined not to relinquish an inch of their swollen 1921 frontiers. Indeed, some of the London Poles had dreams of an even greater Poland that would take advantage of a mutually exhausted Germany and Russia. They shared the anti-Soviet feelings of the Polish Army, now made even sharper by the Soviet annexation of the eastern territories with Hitler's help in 1939. Thus General Sikorski and the London Poles were both a help and a potential embarrassment to the wartime coalition.

Stalin considered the London Poles both hostile and expansionist, the heirs of the Polish leaders who had fought the Russians from 1919 to 1921. He found his opportunity to break with them over the Katyn Massacre. In April 1943, the Germans announced the discovery of the bodies of 10,000 Polish officers in a mass grave in the Katyn Forest, near Smolensk, Russia, and claimed that the Russians had executed them in 1940. The London Poles called for an international investigation. Stalin was enraged—he reverted often to the claim that the London Poles were working for the Nazis—and refused to have anything more to do with Sikorski.[29]

Instead, the Soviet government recognized a group of Polish Communists in Moscow as the legitimate future government of Poland—a Poland that remained west of the Curzon Line, to be sure. When Soviet

---

[28]Roosevelt did not know that there was an eastern Neisse River and a western Neisse River; the Soviets claimed they meant the western Neisse. Roosevelt refused any public discussion of this question for fear of offending Polish-American voters in the 1944 election.

[29]It is now generally admitted outside the Soviet Union that the Russians did execute these officers during their occupation of eastern Poland from 1939 to 1941.

American and Russian officers dance with Red Army girls following a dinner celebrating the meeting of the two armies at Torgau, Germany, April 25, 1945. Note spelling of Amerikan *on the Russians' banner.*

armies reached Poland in July 1944, the pro-Soviet Poles set up a provisional government in the liberated town of Lublin.

There remained a substantial independent force in Poland: those resistance groups in sympathy with the London Poles. As the Soviet Army approached Warsaw at the end of August 1944, the Home Army—a resistance unit under former officers supported from London —rose against the Germans in anticipation of Soviet aid. But instead of rushing into Warsaw to join forces with the Home Army, the Soviet Army stopped outside the city on the other side of the Vistula River. For two months the Home Army held out alone against the Germans, while Western efforts to airdrop supplies were hampered by Russian refusals to allow the planes to land behind Russian lines. After sixty-three desperate days, the last of the Polish Home Army was liquidated. Westerners have been convinced that Stalin knowingly allowed the Germans to wipe out his main rivals for future control of Poland. There is some evidence, however, that the Soviet Army had genuine problems crossing the river against fierce German resistance. In any event, the results left the Lublin Poles in sole control of liberated Poland, under the Red Army. Stalin extended official diplomatic recognition to the Lublin Committee just before going to Yalta in January 1945.

At the Yalta Conference the Western allies tried to trade territorial concessions for political concessions. They recognized the Curzon Line in the east, and the right of the Poles to "administer" former German soil up to the Oder-Neisse rivers in the west as compensation, while awaiting a future more definite settlement. In exchange, they insisted that the Lublin Committee be expanded to include some representatives of the

London Poles and that free elections be held in Poland. Stalin no doubt deeply resented his Western allies' insistence on dealing with Poles who represented for him the expansionist Poland of 1919 to 1921. Moreover, at Potsdam President Truman went beyond the Yalta agreements in calling for a "new" Polish government rather than merely a "reorganized" one.

Stalin included only two London Poles in the Polish government, and by the time elections were finally held in January 1947, all businesses employing more than fifty persons had been nationalized, and police action had been taken against the middle-class parties. Stalin had gotten his way, but not before his suspicions were confirmed that the West wanted an anti-Soviet buffer government in Poland; the West, in its turn, felt that Stalin had reneged on the Yalta terms regarding Poland.

Germany

Germany was the other main arena of Cold War conflict in Europe in 1945. It was against Germany that the American–Soviet alliance had formed; it was in Germany, at the village of Torgau along the Elbe River, that American and Russian soldiers had first met and grasped hands on April 25, 1945; it was the future of Germany that would test and then break the alliance.

Allied determination to accept nothing less than unconditional German surrender had decided some matters about the future of Germany in advance. This time, unlike 1918, Germany would be entirely occupied by its victors, and it would be administered by the victors rather than by indigenous German officials. Beyond that, however, two major decisions remained to be made about how the occupation of Germany would work. Should the emphasis of occupation policy fall on retribution or rehabilitation? And should Germany be dismembered or occupied as a single unit? The details of occupation zones, reparations, and the machinery of interallied cooperation in Germany depended on these two major questions.

All of Hitler's enemies in 1945 wanted to prevent the resurgence of an armed, expansive Germany. Russia, Stalin said, could not afford to fight the Germans once in every generation, and his Western allies readily agreed. How to prevent that revival was more controversial. Early in the war, a number of dismemberment schemes had been drawn up in the West. President Roosevelt's Treasury Secretary Henry Morgenthau proposed to split Germany into a half dozen small states with primarily agrarian economies. Churchill suggested separating Prussia from the rest of Germany and creating a new Catholic south Germany centered on Vienna. By the war's end, however, the British began to resist the atomization of central Europe in order to pit a counterweight against Russia. At Yalta, Churchill held out against the dismemberment plans of Roosevelt and Stalin. The Yalta decision was ambiguous: Germany was to be "dismembered" in some unspecified way, but a single unified Allied

German civilians are forced by United States soldiers to view the bodies of Jewish women who starved during a 300-mile march, April 1945. Many Germans believed that such atrocities were invented by the Allies for propaganda purposes.

Control Commission was supposed to coordinate the policies of the four occupation zones (now including France).

In fact, the opposite happened. Germany was never formally dismembered; indeed, no formal peace terms for Germany could ever be agreed on. Instead, the various occupation zones went their own way in a *de facto* dismemberment.

Divergent economic aims soon set the occupation zones on irreconcilable paths. While all the Allies still agreed on dismantling German armed forces and war production, and attempted, more or less clumsily, to denazify German society with new education schemes and purges of personnel, they differed sharply about Germany's economic future. Britain and the United States wanted to restore normal productivity as quickly as possible; the Soviet Union and France wanted to extract a maximum of German wealth and labor to rebuild their ravaged countries.

Calvin B. Hoover, chief economic advisor in the American zone, pointed out as early as December 1945 that without the recovery of German industry, the United States would have to feed and supply Germany and Europe for a long time. Other local American officials observed that economic chaos would help spread communism in Europe. American occupation authorities promoted German industrial exports that would make Germany self-sufficient, help rebuild all of Europe, and make it immune to communism. Wartime punitive schemes like the Morgenthau Plan seemed simply irrelevant to those involved in the immediate tasks of feeding and sheltering a prostrate Europe. Meanwhile, in the Soviet zone, the Russians were dismantling the German industrial system and beginning the breakup of the great East Elbian estates, but Western occupation authorities found that they were systematically excluded from finding out what was going on there.

Reparations produced the most immediate friction. It had been agreed at the Yalta Conference that Germany must pay reparations to those who suffered war damage. President Roosevelt accepted Stalin's figures as a basis for discussion: $20 billion, of which half would go to the Russians. Stalin expected to collect reparations from the whole of Germany in two forms: a share of the whole existing German industrial plant, and a share of current production. At Potsdam, in July 1945, President Truman drew back from the Yalta position. The Soviets were cut back to 25 percent of "unneeded" industrial equipment in the Western zones and to a share of current production from their zone only. That formula was impossible to apply. What was "unneeded" industrial plant in the Western zones depended on one's opinion of the proper standard of industrial production for the Germans. The Soviet leaders felt justified in demanding their full pound of flesh from all the occupation zones of Germany because that had been agreed to at Yalta, because much of Germany's wealth lay in the west, because Russia had borne the brunt of the land war, and because the alternative was to seek economic aid for Russian reconstruction directly from the United States, aid that might well be tied to political conditions. From the American point of view, the Russians were simply stripping Germany of the means to live in a private-enterprise world. In May 1946, General Lucius Clay closed the American zone to any further Soviet extraction of reparations.

Thereafter, all general discussions of the German question broke down over the reparations issue and the irreconcilable aims for the German economic future that it entailed. Meetings of the four Allied foreign ministers in Moscow in March and April 1947 and in London in November and December 1947 ended in openly hostile disagreement over German peace terms. Meanwhile, the two sides went their separate ways in the day-to-day administration of the zones. In early 1947 the Americans and British united their two zones in a new economic unit ("Bizonia") and set 1936 levels as their goals for German production. Local German representatives were given increased responsibility. The Russians countered with an Economic Council in their zone and the beginnings of German political life with the German Peoples' Congress for Unity and a Just Peace. In February 1948 the three Western occupying powers agreed to proceed toward a separate constitution for revived German political authority in the west. In response to this, the Soviets walked out of the Allied Control Commission on March 20, 1948. Even the pretense of a united four-power occupation had come to an end.

A direct confrontation ensued in the summer of 1948. The immediate cause was again economic policy, the key to each side's aims for the German future. When a new currency was issued for the now united western zones in June 1948, it circulated in Berlin at much more favorable rates than the eastern zone's currency. The city of Berlin, under its own four-power arrangement, was buried deep within the eastern zone. The Soviets faced a choice of either allowing Berlin to become an outpost of the reviving West German economy or sealing off Berlin. They blocked all Western traffic to Berlin. The Allies responded to the blockade with an airlift. For the next 324 days, hundreds of planes ferried the necessities of life to

GERMANY AFTER TWO WARS

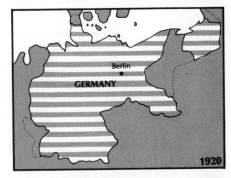

Berlin from the West, averaging 8000 tons per day. General Clay reflected the tone of the now open East–West conflict:

> When Berlin falls, western Germany will be next. . . . If we withdraw, our position in Europe is threatened. If America does not understand this now, does not know that the issue is cast, then it never will and Communism will run rampant.[30]

Although the successful airlift forced the Russians to back down in May 1949, the Berlin crisis had hastened the formation of two Germanies. Each side called for union, but on its own terms. Unable to get its own terms, each side built a bastion on that part of Germany that it controlled. The western Federal Republic of Germany became a sovereign state in September 1949. The eastern German Democratic Republic came into existence the following month.

A World in Two Blocs, 1947–49

As early as March 1946, former British Prime Minister Winston Churchill lent his gift for phrase-making to the opening East–West conflict in Europe:

> From Stettin in the Baltic to Trieste in the Adriatic, an iron curtain has descended across the continent.[31]

Western observers were already deeply disturbed by their exclusion from any role in the states bordering on the Soviet Union (Poland, Romania, Bulgaria) and from those self-liberated states with powerful Communist movements (Yugoslavia, Albania). American policy had carried forward into peacetime the basic assumption that, as Roosevelt warned Stalin in a telegram in October 1944, "there is in this global war literally no question, either military or political, in which the United States is not interested."[32] Stalin, who observed that the Soviet Union had equally little to say in the occupation policies applied to Italy and Japan, worked on quite different premises.

> This war is not as in the past; whoever occupies a territory also imposes his own social system. Everyone imposes his own system as far as his armies can reach. It cannot be otherwise.[33]

While the West could do nothing about Eastern Europe short of marching in a new army, the southern frontiers of the Soviet Union were much more fluid. The three areas of contention there from 1945 to 1947 were Iran and the two states that controlled access to the Black Sea, Turkey and Greece. Emerging conflicts in these areas led the United

---

[30]Lucius D. Clay, *Decision in Europe* (Garden City, N.Y., 1950), p. 361.
[31]Excerpt from a speech given at Westminster College, Fulton, Missouri, March 6, 1946.
[32]Sherwood, p. 834.
[33]Quoted in Milovan Djilas, *Conversations with Stalin,* trans. Michael B. Petrovich (New York, 1962), p. 114.

States to create a new policy of military alliances and worldwide armed intervention to match its postwar ideal of "one world," a global Open Door accessible to American trade and influence.

Soviet and British troops had been stationed in Iran since 1941 to counter German influence. In 1946 the Russians sponsored independence movements among northern border minorities, the Kurds and Azerbaijanis, and demanded a share in Iranian oil rights. With British support and a favorable United Nations resolution behind it, the Iranian government suppressed the border nationalities and then cancelled the draft oil contract, while Stalin decided not to press the issue.

Turkey controlled passage from the Black Sea to the Mediterranean, and the Soviet government brought pressure to bear on the Turkish government to revise the Treaty of Montreux (1936) by which the Turks could close the Straits to warships in time of war, thereby sealing the Russians up in the Black Sea. The Turks refused, again with British support.

The British were also deeply involved in the extremely bitter civil war between the Greek royal government and Communist movements spawned by the wartime resistance. Although Stalin had given the Greek Communists little support at the beginning (apparently honoring his understanding with Churchill of October 1944), important aid began to come from Greece's neighbor, Communist Yugoslavia.

In the spring of 1947, beset by worldwide commitments and dwindling resources, the British passed all these responsibilities to the United States. On March 12 President Truman laid down the new principles of American foreign policy in a message to Congress asking for emergency appropriations to aid Turkey and Greece:

> I believe that it must be the policy of the United States to support free people who are resisting attempted subjugation by armed minorities or by outside pressures.

Although Congress voted funds only for the specific purpose of aiding Greece and Turkey, the Truman Doctrine committed the United States publicly to intervene in any area in the world that threatened to come under Communist control.

The economic counterpart to this new active American involvement was the Marshall Plan, a sweeping program of economic aid to Europe announced by Secretary of State George C. Marshall in a commencement speech at Harvard in June 1947. The United States offered substantial sums of money for restoring European prosperity—both East and West—on condition that the European recipient states join together to plan its most effective use. The American aim, Marshall said, was "the revival of a working economy in the world so as to permit the emergence of political and social conditions in which free institutions can exist."

From a Soviet point of view, Marshall Plan aid seemed likely to draw any nation that received it into the American economic orbit. When Czechoslovakia agreed to participate, and Poland and Hungary appeared interested, the Soviet Union stepped in and blocked them. Over the next four years, the United States contributed $12 billion for the European Recovery Program, all of which went to Western Europe. The Soviet reaction had helped solidify the division of Europe into two closed camps.

Looking at the world in 1947, Stalin could see that Russian aspirations had been checked in the south, and that his experiment with multiparty regimes under Communist supervision in a ring of "friendly" states on the western borders[34] did not afford iron-clad security. The desire of some Eastern European states to affiliate with the Marshall Plan revealed the Western economies' powers of attraction. And the vagaries of multiparty systems left open the possibility of Communist electoral setbacks. In late 1947 and early 1948, therefore, Stalin cracked down hard on Eastern Europe. He replaced the multiparty regimes with full Communist control in all the areas he could influence.

The assumption of outright Communist power in Czechoslovakia in February 1948 may have been Stalin's defensive response to the prospect of serious Communist losses in forthcoming elections. But the "Prague *coup*" did more than any other single act to convince the West that Stalin's expansionist appetite was insatiable. The independence of Czechoslovakia was a tender point for all who remembered the West's betrayal at Munich in 1938. Czechoslovakia's President Eduard Beneš had aroused cautious optimism in the West by his success between 1945 and 1948 in trading off subordination in foreign policy to the Soviet Union against an internal political system that provided some degree of personal freedom and electoral expression. When Stalin brought that compromise to an end, he persuaded most Westerners that no compromise was possible with him.

The establishment of full Communist control in Hungary during the summer of 1948 and the Berlin Blockade of June 1948 confirmed Western alarm. The response was a military alliance against the Soviet Union. The North Atlantic Treaty Organization of twelve Western states (1949) faced 250 Russian divisions in Eastern Europe, later organized into the Warsaw Pact (1955). The real strength of these two alliances, however, lay with the two superpowers who faced each other as mortal enemies. Europe, split in two, seemed likely to become their battleground.

---

[34]The evolution from multiparty National Fronts in Eastern Europe in 1946 to outright Communist control by 1948 is explored more fully in Chapter 17, pp. 528–35.

Suggestions for Further Reading

Allied strategy is ably reviewed, on the basis of official United States archives, by Forrest C. Pogue, *The Supreme Command* (1954). Winston S. Churchill, *The Second World War,** 6 vols. (1948–53) contains a rich collection of wartime papers and correspondence illustrating the British leader's role in setting Allied strategy, as well as the grandest narrative of the war yet written.

For the circumstances of Russian victory, in addition to the works of Seaton, Bialer, and Liddell-Hart cited at the end of Chapter 15, see Georgi Zhukov, *The Memoirs of Marshal G. Zhukov* (1971). The sufferings endured by the Russian people are vividly depicted by Alexander Werth, *Russia at War: 1941–1945** (1964), and Harrison Salisbury, *The 900 Days: The Siege of Leningrad** (1969).

The most comprehensive account of the wartime summit conferences of the Big Three are the works of a former State Department economist, Herbert Feis, written from a viewpoint sympathetic to Roosevelt and Truman: *Churchill, Roosevelt, and Stalin: The War They Waged and the Peace They Sought** (1957) and *Between War and Peace: The Potsdam Conference** (1960). Diane Shaver Clemens, *Yalta** (1970), who has weighed United States documents against Soviet publications, gives more weight than Feis to Soviet concessions and to Truman's retractions of earlier agreements.

These books take us into the heart of the controversy over the origins of the Cold War. Herbert Feis continued to argue that Allied leaders were interested only in the defeat of the Axis until forced by Soviet expansion to alter their perspectives: *The Atomic Bomb and the End of World War II,** rev. ed. (1966) and *From Trust to Terror: The Onset of the Cold War, 1945–50** (1970). See also W. H. McNeill, *America, Britain, and Russia: Their Cooperation and Conflict, 1941–1946* (1953), and Norman A. Graebner, *Cold War Diplomacy, 1945–1960** (1960). These authors were largely concerned with refuting earlier charges that Roosevelt and Truman had conceded too much to Stalin. In the late 1960s, New Left historians changed the focus of debate by charging that American promotion of a worldwide "open door" favorable to United States industrial supremacy forced Stalin to choose between economic dependence and an admittedly harsh but defensive closed sphere of influence in Eastern Europe. William Appleman Williams, *The Tragedy of American Diplomacy,** 2nd ed. (1972); Gabriel Kolko, *The Politics of War** (1968); and Gabriel and Joyce Kolko, *The Limits of Power** (1972) all argue the primacy of American economic aims. Gar Alperovitz, *Atomic Diplomacy: Hiroshima and Potsdam** (1965) contends that the atomic bomb permitted Truman to take a much firmer line against Stalin. David Horowitz, *The Free World Colossus*, rev. ed. (1971) portrays United States policy as counterrevolutionary rather than merely opposed to Russian expansion. Some of these authors have been accused of wrenching archival excerpts out of context by Robert J. Maddox, *The New Left and the Origins of the Cold War* (1973). See also the judicious assessment of Charles S. Maier, "Revisionism and the Interpretation of Cold War Origins," *Perspectives in American History*, Vol. 4 (1970).

Other authors trace Cold War origins to the containment of Bolshevism in 1917. See André Fontaine, *History of the Cold War,** 2 vols. (1968–69). D. F. Fleming, writing before American archives were open, found evidence in American newspapers of consistent overreaction to Soviet acts in *The Cold War and its Origins, 1917–1960*, 2 vols. (1968). Raymond Aron, *The Century of Total War** (1954) puts the Cold War into a long historical perspective more favorable to the West.

John L. Gaddis, *The United States and the Origins of the Cold War, 1941–1947** (1972) is the most carefully researched assessment of the American role; while taking the revisionists' views into account, Gaddis accepts few of their conclusions. For the Soviet side, the work of Ulam cited on page 431 is the latest and fullest account.

Thomas G. Paterson, ed., *The Origins of the Cold War** (1970), and Lloyd C. Gardner, *et al., Origins of the Cold War** (1970) assemble recent articles on both sides.

Shortcomings of the postwar settlement are reviewed in John W. Wheeler-Bennett and Anthony Nicholls, *The Semblance of Peace: The Political Settlement After the Second World War** (1972).

Street scene in Warsaw, April 1946.

17

RUIN AND RECONSTRUCTION 1945–1953

Europe in 1945 was an even more desolate landscape than it had been in 1918. Although proportionally fewer soldiers had died in Europe during the faster moving Second World War, civilians had suffered far more bitterly. Strategic bombing and the sweep of motorized armies made major battlefields of cities. More English civilians than soldiers were killed between June 1940 and September 1941 during the Battle of Britain.[1] More than 135,000 Germans perished in the firebombing of Dresden on February 13, 1945, the largest number of victims of any single military action of the war.[2] The Soviet Union suffered the highest casualty rate of all the belligerents, perhaps 7 million civilians and 11 million soldiers killed. In all, 18 million European noncombatants died from bombing, shelling, disease, malnutrition, overwork, and outright genocide between 1939 and 1945.

In September 1945, the American diplomat George Kennan passed

[1]A. J. P. Taylor, *English History, 1914–45* (Oxford, 1965), p. 502.
[2]Seventy-eight thousand were killed in the atomic bombing of Hiroshima.

through the ruins of the Finnish city of Vyborg, which had been fought over twice since 1939.

> The onetime modern Finnish town of Vyborg . . . was, so far as I could see, devoid of habitation. . . . I left the train in early morning when it stopped at the Vyborg station and roamed about among the ruins of the place. While I was doing this it began to rain heavily. I took refuge from the rain in what had been the doorway of a fine modern department store, now gutted and wrecked. Not having seen a living being on my entire walk, I was surprised, standing there in the doorway, to hear a noise behind me. Looking around, I discovered that I was sharing the shelter of the doorway with a goat. The two of us, it seemed, were for the moment the sole inhabitants of this once thriving modern city.[3]

Similar scenes of urban desolation were spread across Europe from downtown London to Stalingrad.

Food remained scarce through 1947. The war-ravaged soil brought forth a little over half its prewar crop in 1946. Livestock had been killed off, and fertilizer was nonexistent. To make matters worse, the winter of 1947/48 was the coldest in fifty years. Hunger was most severe in Eastern Europe. Soon after the war, doctors in a Vienna hospital were reported to be getting "unsweetened coffee, a very thin soup, and bread. Less than 500 calories in all."[4] The French ration allowed Parisians three more slices of bread per day in 1946 than the Nazis had granted in 1942.[5]

[3]George F. Kennan, *Memoirs: 1925–50* (New York, 1967), p. 280.
[4]George Orwell, *In Front of Your Nose* (New York, 1968), p. 83.
[5]Janet Flanner, *Paris Journal, 1944–65* (New York, 1965), p. 51.

Production and marketing were too disrupted to give useful jobs to those Europeans who wanted to work. In many parts of Europe, the black market was more lucrative than honest labor, and barter brought more than money. The hero of Gunter Grass's novel *The Tin Drum* (1959) sold his mother's ruby necklace for "a real leather briefcase and twelve cartons of Lucky Strikes, a fortune." His employer, the tombstone carver, would provide his clients "a plain but good-sized stone of Grenzheim shell lime" for five sacks of potatoes.

Runaway inflation, as in the years after the First World War, discouraged saving and pauperized those members of the middle class who depended on past savings. The most prestigious French literary prize, the Goncourt Prize, of 5000 francs had been worth $1000 when it was created in 1903. In 1953, the same number of francs was worth $14.29.

**THE EXPULSION OF
GERMANS FROM
CENTRAL EUROPE, 1945–1947**

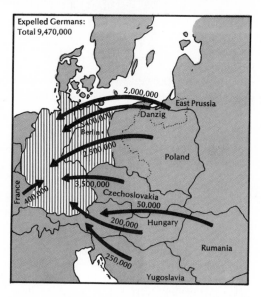

Political and moral dislocations added to the turmoil. Some members of resistance movements, including a few last-minute adherents, wreaked vengeance on former collaborators. Homeless youths who had known nothing but violence in their short lives formed gangs in the ruined cities. The uncertainty of the future, in both the Western and Soviet-dominated areas, discouraged purposeful activity.

The most desperate Europeans of all were the nearly 11 million destitute wanderers, "displaced persons" or "DP's" in the impersonal jargon of the relief agencies. These uprooted people included liberated prisoners of war, Jews who had survived the extermination camps, the forced labor that had been taken from all over Europe to work in German factories, and, most numerous of all, those who had fled before the advance of the Russian armies. It took more than a decade for such relief agencies as UNRRA (United Nations Relief and Rehabilitation

Agency) to repatriate or resettle all the refugees of five years of war. The last DP camps were closed in the early 1960s.

Vast exchanges of populations swelled the numbers of the uprooted. Instead of trying to fit borders to nationality as at Versailles in 1919, the victorious powers fit nationality to borders. Almost 20 million Europeans were moved out of disputed frontier areas in the postwar settlement: 13 million Germans were expelled from ancestral homes in the Sudetenland, Silesia, and the lands east of the Oder-Neisse rivers destined to become Polish; 6.5 million people were moved to fit new borders between Russia and its western neighbors, Poland and Czechoslovakia.[6] The result, wrote Arnold Toynbee, "was to cancel the ethnic effects of a thousand years of German, Polish and Lithuanian conquest and colonization and to restore the ethnic map to something like the *status quo ante* A.D. 1200."[7]

The Work of Reconstruction

A prodigious work of reconstruction was necessary before most Europeans could even be assured of the basic necessities of life. But reconstruction did not mean simply restoring Europe to its condition before 1939 or 1933. The depression of the 1930s, no less than the war, had discredited the self-regulating liberal market, laissez-faire politics, and the international anarchy of competitive sovereign states. Even if it had not, the ruin and scarcities caused by the war made necessary the continuation of war government into the indefinite future. By both conviction and necessity, liberated Europe began to rebuild along new lines of socialist or mixed economies and state intervention in the public welfare.

New Leaders and Parties

Europe's old leadership was leavened by an unusually large infusion of new men and new parties. The purge of Hitler's allies and collaborators opened up more places than had been normal after earlier, less ideological wars. In France, nearly 125,000 collaboration cases were heard before special courts after the liberation; 767 persons were executed and thousands sentenced to prison. Even though Holland, Denmark, and Norway had long since abolished the death penalty, they restored it for a few dozen top collaborators, including the Dutch and Norwegian fascist leaders Anton Adriaan Mussert and Vidkun Quisling. Several Western countries imprisoned an even larger proportion of their populations for collaboration than did the French: 633 per 100,000 in Norway, 596 in Belgium, 419 in Holland, and 94 in France. That part of the prewar Western European leadership that had collaborated with

[6]Joseph R. Schechtman, *Postwar Population Transfers in Europe, 1945–55* (Philadelphia, 1962), p. 363.
[7]Quoted in Hans Gatzke, *The Present in Perspective,* 3rd ed. (New York, 1965), p. 16.

Hitler was in disgrace. Not even those prewar leaders who had led the Allies to victory were guaranteed leadership roles after the liberation. The indomitable Churchill was voted out of office in the election of July 26, 1945, even while he was conferring with Truman and Stalin at Potsdam.

Into the vacancies stepped a new generation of resistance leaders, new parties, and a greatly strengthened socialist and Communist left. The resistance contributed fewer important leaders than might have been expected from the movement's vigor and popularity. Only two active leaders of resistance forces actually ruled their countries after the liberation: France's General Charles de Gaulle and Yugoslavia's Marshal Tito. De Gaulle headed the Provisional Government of liberated France until January 1946 and then returned to power in 1958 during the crisis of the Algerian War and served as president of a Fifth French Republic until 1969. Josip Broz, alias Marshal Tito, a former metal worker who commanded the Communist resistance in Yugoslavia, the Partisans, has ruled that country almost without contest for thirty years. Elsewhere the most successful underground fighters did not always thrive in postwar politics, and other resistance leaders, especially the intellectuals, preferred to return to their chosen occupations. The resistance was more significant for the climate it created in 1945 than for its leaders: it provided a union of Catholic, Communist, socialist, and liberal anti-Nazis determined to create a new Europe, socially just and free from the threat of war.

The most important new parties on the Continent were progressive Catholic parties, usually called Christian Democrats. The war and the fascist experience had profoundly transformed Catholicism in Europe. An older generation willing to accept any allies, even fascist, against Godless communism, was discredited, and a younger generation of progressive Catholic resistance veterans was brought forward. Combining traditional paternalism with the economic and social radicalism of the resistance, some of the new Catholic leaders tried to free the Church from too close an identification with capitalism. Christian Democrat leaders were also in the forefront of the European unity movement after the war, in part out of genuine internationalism, in part as a response to what some saw as a Soviet danger.

As a religion-based party rather than a class-based party, Christian Democrats ran up very large votes in the Catholic areas of liberated Europe after 1945. They appealed to Catholics of both the working class and the middle class. For want of alternatives, many conservatives also voted for them. Women's suffrage in France and Italy (1946) helped swell the totals. In Germany, a special situation was created by the Communist grip on the old Protestant regions. The Catholic Rhineland and Bavaria dominated postwar West German politics just as Protestant Prussia had dominated the old Reich.

Under Konrad Adenauer, who had been mayor of Cologne in the 1920s and who had been interned under Hitler, the Christian Democrats governed in Germany from 1949 to 1969.[8] The Italian Christian Democrats, led by Alcide De Gasperi, dominated every government of Italy for thirty years after the liberation. The French Catholic left (*Mouvement républicain populaire,* MRP) comprised the largest party in France briefly in 1946 and remained powerful until the early 1950s.

The other dominant postwar parties in Continental Europe came from the Marxist left, both socialist and Communist. Their major roles in the resistance prepared the way for a new Popular Front era of broad left cooperation. After the German invasion of the Soviet Union in June 1941, Communists had enjoyed particular success in the resistance; they were well equipped for clandestine activity and prepared to submerge the call of revolution within the broader appeal of national liberation. The Italian Communist party became the largest in the West; it grew from about 10,000 underground members in 1943 to 400,000

[8]Under Adenauer's successors after 1963.

*Josip Broz, better known
as Marshall Tito, the
Yugoslav partisan leader,
1944.*

members in 1944 and to 2 million members in 1947. The Communists were the largest party in France at one point in 1945, and their vote total never fell much below 25 percent until 1958. The reformist left, rather than the Communist left, was strengthened in West Germany and Britain. In the Western-occupied zones of Germany, the Communist party drew only 5.7 percent of the vote in 1949; it was eventually outlawed by Adenauer in 1956. In Britain, the Labour party maintained its traditional grasp on the British left. In Eastern Europe, Communist parties flourished under Russian encouragement. Socialists remained mass parties in most of liberated Europe, but they were constricted by more active competitors to the right and left.

Despite the Marxist resurgence, Western Europe was not at the brink of social revolution in 1945, as it had been from 1918 to 1920. Perhaps the most urgent revolutionary drives had spent themselves in Europe after the First World War: the overthrow of the last traditional autocracies, the national independence movements of Eastern Europe, land seizures by desperate peasants. However, the desire for social change was apparent, and the resistance emerged from underground in some parts of Europe with the material capacity to take power and in a climate approaching social revolution: in northern Italy and some parts of southern French hill country, and in Brussels, which experienced general strikes immediately after the Germans withdrew. But only in Yugoslavia and Albania, out of the reach of both Russian and Allied armies, did the resistance lead on to social revolution.

The major difference from the previous postwar period was the Soviet Union's rejection of the revolutionary course in 1945. Stalin was, by all evidence, working for control rather than social revolution then. As if on order, the Communist resistance units in Western Europe stacked their arms. All Western European Communist parties participated in reformist regimes until 1947. Eastern European Communists also worked with reformist parties in National Fronts under Russian occupation until 1947. The Western Allies stood ready, of course, to throttle social revolution wherever it showed itself within their reach (as Britain did in Greece in 1944), but they were never seriously challenged. There were no new waves of soldiers', sailors', and workers' councils on this second armistice day.

Economic Recovery

Most Europeans turned their hand to the daunting tasks of reconstruction. In 1945 it was easy to suppose that Europeans would not enjoy normal life for many decades, and perhaps never again experience the serene comforts of the privileged before 1914. As late as 1953, an American journalist was able to arouse curiosity with a book suggesting that Europe was beginning to show signs of "fire in the ashes."[9] But by the mid-1950s, it was evident that Western Europe, at least, had entered a period of unprecedented economic growth.

[9]Theodore H. White, *Fire in the Ashes* (New York, 1953).

Even the Second World War had failed to destroy the basic elements of European dynamism. To be sure, many former European markets and resources in Latin America, Africa, and the Pacific had slipped into United States hands, and European businessmen surveying the wreckage of their continent could hardly expect to compete in the future with the new Western colossus. In Eastern Europe, reparations to Russia and the diversion of old trade patterns to the Soviet bloc were additional burdens. The very destruction of war, however, offered opportunities to rebuild with the latest technology. The skills and imagination of these sophisticated peoples were intact. Refugees offered cheap and willing labor. The European birth rate was rising, a sign of revived hope and a stimulus to buying.

Marshall Plan aid from the United States further stimulated the pace of recovery in Western Europe. Over seven years, from 1947 to 1954, the European Recovery Program poured $12 billion into the sixteen participating nations. This aid amounted to $29 for each inhabitant of West Germany, $33 per capita for Italy, $72 for France, $77 for England, and $104 for Austria. At American insistence, the aid was funneled into European development through an international agency, the Organization for European Economic Cooperation (OEEC), which attempted to encourage freer trade and rational planning on a continentwide basis, steps toward the open world market that was an aim of American policymakers. Their more immediate aim was to provide an emergency remedy for hopeless poverty, which Americans believed could only feed revolution and aid communism. The Marshall Plan was clearly intended to serve the interests of the United States, but it just as clearly served the material interests of those Western Europeans who began to prosper again in the early 1950s.

Even critics of the Marshall Plan do not deny its share in Western European economic revival. The direct injection of capital funds for reconstruction in a temporarily dislocated but advanced region had far more effect than similar aid to underdeveloped regions. "The Marshall Plan had worked because the Europeans had the technical know-how and capital resources to turn every dollar of American aid into six dollars of capital formation."[10]

Critics have charged the Marshall Plan, however, with subjecting Western Europe to the American economy. That subordination, of course, was the result of far wider forces. While Europe was economically prostrate, the necessity of importing food, fuel, and manufactured goods (mostly from the United States) produced an enormous dollar gap: Europeans had to spend more dollars to import necessities than they could earn by selling goods to Americans. This gap was the reason for the great scarcity of dollars in European hands and the very high value of dollars in exchange for pounds, francs, marks, or lire. In the long run, no doubt, the Marshall Plan helped prepare the way for greater European economic independence by stimulating production; in

[10]Walter La Feber, *America, Russia and the Cold War, 1945–67* (New York, 1967), p. 180.

the short run, however, its stimulus widened the dollar gap, since revived prosperity only promoted more imports from the United States.

During the depression of the 1930s or under fascist autarky, such disparities in currency values would have been taken care of by trade restriction, barter devices, and currency controls. The Americans, supported by liberal European economists, were determined to replace these closed economic defenses with a free international market in the postwar world. The Bretton Woods Agreement of July 1944 was the cornerstone of this system: the forty-four participating nations committed themselves to the freest possible trade and currency exchange after the war, and to fixed currency exchange rates, with the International Monetary Fund[11] standing by to smooth over temporary maladjustments in international monetary exchange and keep exchange rates steady. These "administered" exchange rates were an attempt to achieve the commercial freedom of the nineteenth-century gold standard without the dangers of that system's cyclical fluctuations in a highly distorted postwar world economy.

Under the Bretton Woods Agreement, the dollar retained a privileged place in Europe for twenty-five years after the war. Individual Americans could live better than kings in Europe. They casually bought up centuries' accumulation of silver and art objects. American firms could purchase European subsidiaries with ease, threatening the independence of European economies. American economic power made it more difficult for European governments to oppose American policies, such as German rearmament, or resist repeated devaluations of the pound, the franc, or the lira to keep the open economy going.

The Soviet Union declined to participate in the Bretton Woods system. And, as noted in the preceding chapter, when some of its Eastern European clients (Poland, Hungary, and Czechoslovakia) showed interest in the Marshall Plan, the Soviet leaders began in 1947 to install one-party regimes and tie the Eastern European economies more tightly to Russia. A measure of prosperity came to Eastern Europe only in the 1960s. Thus the reconstruction of Europe took place under conditions that widened the differences between East and West.

The Labour Government in Britain, 1945–51

After the bitter 1930s, few Europeans believed that a free market could regulate an economy both justly and effectively in peacetime. Most of them believed that some degree of governmental direction and planning was a permanent necessity. Moreover, virtually all European governments now accepted the basic welfare of all citizens—health, housing, education, a living income—as part of their normal responsibilities.

[11]The IMF is an international fund intended to provide temporary support to currencies under heavy selling pressure in international exchanges and thus avoid forced devaluations, such as that of the pound in 1931. It began operating in 1946 with assets of $8.5 billion, 25 percent supplied by the United States, and kept non-Communist currencies convertible at fixed rates, by periodic support or devaluation, until the early 1970s.

This was no less true in Britain than it was on the Continent, even though Britain had had no occupation, resistance, or armed liberation, and the doggedly respectable Labour party had retained firm control of the British left. Even in the best years between the wars, no less than 10 percent of British workers had been unable to find jobs, leaving nearly 2 million families in despair. British citizens voted against a return to prewar arrangements in July 1945 when they gave the Labour party its first outright majority in history. That Clement Attlee, former professor at the London School of Economics and a scholarly reformist, replaced Churchill in the very moment of Churchill's war triumph showed how decisively the British public rejected the domestic *status quo*.

The Beveridge Report: "Full Employment"

Persistent unemployment had been the shame of twentieth-century Britain. "Full Employment in a Free Society," the title of Sir William Beveridge's[12] February 1943 report on postwar social security arrangements, set the priorities for the Labour government of 1945 to 1951. Even for a liberal economist like Beveridge, the "unplanned market economy" stood condemned for "its failure to generate sufficient steady demand for its products." The experience of two wars had shown that unemployment vanished when the state set up "unlimited demand for a compelling common purpose." On these pragmatic grounds, Beveridge (following Keynes) proposed that the state accept its responsibility even in peacetime to generate sufficient purchasing power to keep everyone employed.

Putting full employment first thrust new obligations on the Labour government. In domestic policy, the state undertook to forecast what level private investment was likely to attain and then make sufficient public outlay to close the foreseen employment gap, even if the budget did not balance. In international economic policy, this meant standing the depression policies of both Labour and the Conservatives on its head. Instead of mollifying international bankers and thwarting currency speculators with balanced budgets and reduced social services, the welfare state resolved to attain full employment and then take whatever measures (currency control, devaluation) might be necessary on the international money market.

In Beveridge's terms, full employment could be assured "in a free society," without all the compulsions of a war economy or a totalitarian regime. A majority of Labour party members, the trade union mass more fully than the intellectual wing, accepted Beveridge's view that it was "sufficient to . . . socialize demand" and not necessary to "socialize production. . . . The need for socialism has not yet been demonstrated."[13] State control of part of the economy would provide sufficient leverage over the rest.

[12]Beveridge was the director of the London School of Economics.
[13]William H. Beveridge, *Full Employment in a Free Society* (New York, 1945), pp. 21, 28–30, 37.

Therefore, the Labour government limited its nationalization to the permanently ailing coal industry and some basic commodities like steel and transportation, plus a few service enterprises (some public restaurants, a few breweries). Eighty percent of British industry remained in private hands. Considering the extent to which even the Conservatives had brought such ailing businesses as coal and steel under government coordination between the wars, Labour's limited nationalization was a relatively minor departure.

The Welfare State

The most sweeping Labour innovations provided basic social services to all British subjects on the principle of universal right rather than need. This departed sharply both from humiliating charity and from previous Labour emphasis on welfare for wage earners. After 1948, the National Health Service provided medical services free to everyone in Britain who wished to use it. Although Health Minister Aneurin Bevan made no attempt to replace private medical practice with a single system of salaried state doctors, by 1950, 95 percent of the British public went to doctors enrolled in the National Health Service. Social security arrangements dating back to Lloyd George were rounded out with family assistance. The British welfare state also built on several major wartime reforms. The English Education Act of 1944 made some form of secondary education available to all, although an examination taken after grade school (the "eleven-plus examination") channeled students into technical or classical secondary schools in a way that tended to perpetuate class distinctions. The Town and Country Planning Act of 1943 gave the government power to set aside green space and prevent speculation in land values distorted by the anticipated post-*blitz* housing shortage.

The cost of these new programs was met in part by very steep income and inheritance taxes. Between 1938 and 1949, taxes increased fourfold. In 1938, 7000 persons had admitted to annual incomes after taxes of over £6000 (about $30,000 at the time); in 1947 and 1948 there were only 70 incomes this large.[14] The very wealthy could still thrive by spending capital, and businessmen quickly learned expense-account living, but the spread of wealth in Britain was narrowed for a time. The nobleman who opened his ancestral home to tourists at two shillings a visit became a familiar feature of postwar England.

Economic Maladjustment

Britain's immediate postwar years were a time of almost unending crisis. This was less the result of Labour's social policies than of painful adjustment to Britain's fundamentally changed place in the world. This small island's economic hegemony in the nineteenth century had owed

[14]Arthur Marwick, *Britain in the Century of Total War* (Boston, 1968), p. 359.

much to temporary preeminence in coal, textiles, shipping, and finance. Even before 1914 other countries were catching up with Britain, and even passing it with the benefits of leapfrogging technological stages. The First World War had liquidated much of Britain's nineteenth-century accumulation of overseas investment; the Second World War had reduced it still further. After 1945, the British economy struggled with almost permanent deficits in international accounts. In a country that had to import much of its food, fuel, and raw materials, and that no longer drew much income from overseas investments, the slightest slack in production or the slightest release of consumer buying threw imports ahead of exports.

Under these conditions, British survival depended on getting the British people to work as hard as possible and consume as little as possible. Even basic foods like bread continued to be rationed for years; Englishmen could not buy butter and sugar freely until 1954. While writing his novel *1984* on the Scottish island of Jura in the fall of 1947, George Orwell wrote a friend that he was gathering wood and peat to eke out his small hoard of coal for the "pretty bleak" winter he expected.[15] The official British policy was called "austerity," and for the British who endured those grim years, austerity was indelibly associated with the severe black-coated figure and dour expression of Chancellor of the Exchequer Sir Stafford Cripps, a Labour party intellectual of upper–middle-class origin from the party's left wing.

British recovery was complicated by some unnecessary burdens. The record winter cold of 1947/48 required spending precious foreign exchange to import coal; it was a case literally of "carrying coals to Newcastle." Since a majority of Labour leaders were reluctant to withdraw from those parts of Britain's overseas possessions outside India and the Middle East, heavy military expenditures (especially after the Korean War began in 1950) diverted funds away from productive investment. Finally, when the United States forced Britain to restore the pound to free international trading in 1947, trade deficits and heavy speculation against the pound caused a devaluation in 1949. Although British exporters could sell their goods more cheaply, imports became more expensive, one of the costs of belonging to the American economic sphere.

The British people had freely consented to sacrifices when the enemy was Hitler. Sacrifices were harder to extract against that less discernible enemy, economic maladjustment. Strikes, notably of dock workers in 1949, put the Labour government in the awkward position of opposing union demands. The more radical wing of the Labour party, led by the intransigent and blunt-spoken Welshman Aneurin Bevan, broke with the government in 1950 over the restoration of partial medical fees (for eyeglasses and false teeth) and over defense expenditure that "dragged" Britian, Bevan said, "behind the wheels of American diplomacy."[16]

[15]Orwell, p. 376.
[16]Michael Foot, *Aneurin Bevan*, Vol. 2 (New York, 1974), p. 335.

The opposition Conservatives also attacked Labour unmercifully for alleged mismanagement of the nationalized industries. How was it possible, for example, that coal-exporting England had had to import coal in the winter of 1947/48? The notorious inefficiency of the coal industry before the war, however, makes it unlikely that the Conservatives would have dealt more successfully with the insoluble problems confronting Britain after 1945. In any event, when the Conservatives won the election of October 1951, they returned only steel and road transport (the only profitmaking industries that Labour had nationalized) to private companies. Coal and railroads remained nationalized. Welfare provisions remained intact, although more medical fees were instituted in 1957. The British Conservatives accepted the major elements of the welfare state, adding only a dash of state planning for greater productivity.

The French Fourth Republic

Liberated France had even less desire than Britain to return to the institutions of the discredited 1930s. The French people voted almost 20 to 1 in a referendum in October 1945 against reviving the prewar Third Republic, which had failed both to remedy the depression and to stop Hitler. The new Fourth Republic (1946–58) had to satisfy a number of French aspirations after the liberation: it must be a parliamentary republic, in reaffirmation of French libertarian values against the hated collaborationist Vichy state, but it must be more efficient and more socially progressive than the Third Republic had been. Efficiency, freedom, and social welfare would be difficult goals to reconcile even without the wreckage left by four years of occupation and the bitter divisions left by collaboration and resistance. Creating the Fourth Republic was even more complicated by the search for a new leadership among the varied groups that had cooperated in the liberation of France.

The Search for Leadership

The preeminent French liberation leader was General Charles de Gaulle. That austere, brilliant, aloof officer had pursued since June 1940 the mission of personifying an invisible French grandeur. As the head of the Free French in London, de Gaulle had insisted that eternal France had been only temporarily eclipsed by defeat and that the collaborationist Vichy regime (despite its superficial marks of legality) automatically forfeited its legitimacy for lack of independence. Almost alone at first, he took comfort in the certainty of his convictions. His stand as an advocate of tank warfare in the French Army before the war had been lonely but correct; he believed he was still correct, although alone in London in June 1940. Gradually he imposed his leadership on one after another of the elements of the French resistance. He waged his most difficult battle against his American and British allies, who tried to treat him as a subordinate instead of as the embodiment of France.

The Free French leader, General Charles de Gaulle (left) walks from the Arc de Triomphe to Notre Dame, the day after the surrender of the German general commanding the Paris garrison, August 26, 1944.

By a combination of luck, skill, and inflexibility, de Gaulle outdistanced all potential rivals for powering during the liberation of France. He could ignore the Americans' interest in resurrecting some Third Republic stalwarts, such as Edouard Herriot. He could not ignore the dream of some *maquis* units to assume control over the regions they helped liberate. De Gaulle sent handpicked senior civil servants— Commissioners of the Republic—into each major town as the German and Vichy officials were withdrawing. Thus he forstalled local takeovers by either the *maquis* or the United States Army, although, in the same process, he also assured the continuity of France's centralized professional administrative system.

His moral authority equalled in French history only by that of the first Napoleon, de Gaulle presided over the French Provisional Government in 1945, while an elected constitutional assembly drafted the basic charter of the new republic. In January 1946, however, General de Gaulle abruptly resigned as head of the Provisional Government, disgusted by the revival of party bickering and of civilian meddling in Army affairs. The assembly produced a Fourth Republic all too similar to the Third, in which parliament had its way against a weak executive. De Gaulle issued occasional declarations that indicated he had hoped to replace multiparty parliamentarism with something more authoritarian.

The fighters of the resistance also had a small role in the new republic. Expertise and experience were needed to assure the transition from Vichy to the Fourth Republic. Except for the most conspicuous collaborators, the bureaucracy remained substantially intact. Resistance personnel were largely shunted to the sidelines because of their inexperience or distaste for politics.

The Fourth Republic, therefore, was created by three political parties and run by the traditional bureaucracy. The revived Third Republic Marxist parties—Communists and Socialists—and the French version of the Christian Democratic parties of Catholic Western Europe, the MRP, continued their cooperation born in the resistance. These three parties divided the French vote about equally among them and governed France in a three-way coalition (*tripartisme*) until 1947.

The constitution of the Fourth Republic combined the preferences of these three parties. A parliamentary regime like the Third Republic, the Fourth Republic placed even more weight in the Chamber of Deputies. List voting gave more power than before to political parties. The president had largely ceremonial functions, while the prime minister, reluctant by tradition to use the power of dissolution, had no influence over the Chamber except the promise of cabinet seats in the government coalition of the moment. The multiparty conditions of the Fourth Republic did not allow the forceful political leadership that Frenchmen had wanted after the war. In its twelve years of existence, the Fourth Republic had twenty-six cabinets, all of them coalitions. The cabinets were often chosen after a prolonged "crisis" during which France had no government while a coalition was being laboriously pieced together.

Nationalization and Planning

The three parties took a number of major steps toward creating a mixed economy and a welfare state even before the Fourth Republic's constitution was drawn up. Nationalization went further in France than in England. The French railroads were already public (as in all Continental countries), while the aviation and armaments industries had been partially nationalized by the Popular Front. Added to these after the war were the Bank of France, the largest insurance companies, coal, steel, electricity, and gas. The Renault automobile firm was nationalized while Louis Renault awaited trial for having built tanks for the Germans. Because he died before his trial, the company remained in public hands. As the purge impulse waned, other major firms that had produced matériel for the Germans during the occupation remained private. There were no nationalizations after 1946.

The Fourth Republic extended social services further than had been possible under the Third Republic, with its small-town, small-property majority. The social security system, created in 1931, now included free medical services for everyone enrolled. Concerned by its low birth rate, France granted larger family allocations (begun in 1939) than most Western countries.

The major economic innovation of postwar France was the adoption of planning. As in Britain, the economy was mixed; most productive capacity remained in private hands, but the state could use its important nationalized sector to influence the rest. A new planning agency, the *Commissariat du Plan*, was created by executive decree, a reflection of the increasing role given to nonelected experts and the diminishing ability of parliament to deal with complex economic questions. Under Jean Monnet, the *Commissariat* launched a vigorous program to modernize French productive capacity, debilitated by years of neglect during the depression and by German pillage. Mere replacement did not satisfy the energetic Monnet and his expert staff. They injected an element of planned stimulation for productivity. Beyond controlling the state's share of the economy, the *Commissariat* could apply "indicative" (but not "coercive") planning to the whole economy by setting goals, providing accurate economic forecasts, inhibiting investment in mere gimmickry, and providing incentives for investment in needed sectors, such as automobiles and chemicals. According to Monnet's gospel, "Productivity is not a state of affairs; it is a state of mind."[17] French businessmen, who had long preferred some degree of state-aided coordination over cutthroat competition, participated, as did government experts and representatives of trade unions. By the end of the First Plan (1947–52) French gross national product was 14 percent higher than it had been in 1938.

Tripartisme became a casualty of the Cold War when the Communists were forced out of the government in May 1947. The national elections of 1951 revived moderate and conservative parties. Thereafter the Fourth Republic was governed by centrist coalitions as in the Third Republic. But state welfare and planning had become permanent features of French life. As the private sector prospered, the planning agency simply became more "indicative," and the state continued to encourage growth industries.

Postwar Italy

Italy faced reconstruction under special circumstances. As the battleground of a long, bitterly contested land campaign (1943–45), Italy had suffered more war damage than any other Western nation except Germany. Italy was also a defeated enemy. The Peace Treaty of 1947 gave somewhat less recognition than many Italians had hoped to the fact that Marshal Badoglio and King Victor Emmanuel III had removed Mussolini from power in July 1943 and had shifted to support of the

[17]République française. Commissariat-général du Plan de modernisation et d'équipement, *Rapport général sur le premier plan* (Paris, 1946), p. 6.

Allies. The Peace Treaty stripped Italy of its African and Aegean empires, and transferred the area around Trieste to Yugoslavia.[18]

The Contest for Political Power

It was certain that the new regime in postwar Italy would be anti-Fascist. Two very different anti-Fascist groups had some claim on power, however. In the expanding Allied-controlled areas of the south, the revived parties of pre-Fascist Italy, under the temporary government of the former Fascist Marshal Badoglio, expected to restore parliamentary monarchy. In the north, armed resistance units and local Committees of Liberation, in which the Communist party had a large role, exercised *de facto* control over large areas that they liberated ahead of the Allied armies in the spring of 1945. They expected to transform Italy by social revolution and moral regeneration.

Within a few months of the war's end, it was clear that the resistance movement would have no more say in postwar Italy than anywhere else in Western Europe. The encouragement that the Anglo-American military government gave to the existing parliamentary parties was only one explanation for the absence of revolutionary change. Many resistance leaders had no political experience and wished only to return to

[18]The fate of Trieste itself was not finally settled until 1954, when it was restored to full Italian sovereignty under the new conditions of the Cold War.

Alcide De Gasperi, the postwar Italian Christian Democratic leader.

private life. Most importantly, Palmiro Togliatti, the leader of the Italian Communist party, returned in 1944 from his many years of exile in Moscow with orders to cooperate with the provisional regime in the south, even with Marshal Badoglio. At the end of the war, the Committees of Liberation for the most part gave up their arms as directed by the provisional government.

Italy's first postwar elections in June 1946 produced a constituent assembly in which three parties predominated, not unlike the French political spectrum: Christian Democrats (207), Socialists (115), and Communists (104). Together they drafted a parliamentary constitution similar to that of the 1919 to 1922 period. The major changes were the election of the upper house (formerly appointed), the vote for women, and the dismissal of the royal house. Fifty-four percent of the Italian voters having rejected a continuation of the monarchy in June 1946, Italy became a republic.

The two giants of postwar Italy were the Communist leader, Palmiro Togliatti, and the new leader of the Christian Democrats, Alcide De Gasperi. De Gasperi, a veteran of the Catholic *Popolari* of the 1920s, had passed the war years in more or less open opposition to Mussolini from the shelter of his post as Vatican librarian. In 1945 the Communist party was far more powerful in Italy than it had been in the years 1919 to 1922. Its leadership of anti-Fascist Italians in the Spanish Civil War and its control over the anti-Fascist trade unions at the end of the war made it the largest Communist party outside areas directly controlled by Russian armies, with around 2 million members and nearly a quarter of the popular vote throughout the postwar period. When the Communist party went into opposition at the beginning of the Cold War in 1947,[19] it was De Gasperi who emerged with predominant power over postwar Italy.

In April 1948, in the first parliamentary elections held under the new constitution, De Gasperi's Christian Democrats won an absolute majority, the first (and so far only) single party majority in modern Italian parliamentary history. The extension of the vote to women in that Catholic country, where women were traditionally more religious than men, probably helped him. As the one alternative to communism, De Gasperi also benefited from political and economic support from the United States and from the Italian clergy. De Gasperi remained prime minister until 1953, and his Christian Democrats continued to dominate the governing coalition thereafter.

Reconstruction

The reconstruction of postwar Italy took place under the auspices of a Catholic party whose commitment to a free-enterprise economy was strongly colored by social paternalism and corporatism. After a period of disastrous inflation and black-marketeering, the regime used Mar-

---

[19]See Chapter 18, p. 544.

shall Plan aid to stablize an economy relatively free of wartime controls after 1947. By 1952 worker income had risen well above 1938 levels, almost as much by increased welfare payments as by wages. Italian worker families received only an average of 59 percent of their income from wages; the rest came from various forms of welfare payments, the highest proportion in Western Europe.[20] As usual, it was middle-class recipients of civil service salaries and holders of savings who had suffered most severely as the costs of fascism were liquidated by inflation (the lira was stablized at about one-fiftieth of its prewar value), but in a country where fascism had just been discredited, they had no leaders to turn to except De Gasperi.

As in all Western European welfare states, private enterprise and government managed the economy together in De Gasperi's Italy. The role of the state was larger in Italy, however, in part through the legacy of Fascist economic institutions. Italy was more openly "neocorporatist" than the other welfare states. There was no nationalization. The manufacturers' association (*Confindustria*), its personnel unchanged, retained a powerful role in economic management, under an umbrella of benevolent state assistance. The major public holding company of the 1930s—IRI, the Institute for Industrial Reconstruction—continued to own a large share of Italian metallurgy, chemicals, shipbuilding, and airlines, while leaving administration to businessmen. Two-fifths of all capital invested in Italy by the early 1960s was channeled through IRI and the state oil company. Only the giant FIAT automobile works remained fully private among major Italian corporations. By contrast, the workers' factory councils created at the liberation ceased to function.

The major economic problems of postwar Italy were the backwardness of the south and land hunger. Prodded by another wave of land occupations in the south, De Gasperi distributed 1.75 million acres bought (on generous terms) from large uncultivated estates in the south. About 85,000 families were settled as owner-farmers, far fewer than had expected help. The major social change—the movement of millions of southern Italians to the industrial cities of northern Italy and the rest of Western Europe—had to await the great boom of the 1960s.

The Two Germanies

As the occupation zones of Germany hardened into *de facto* partition, the German people could look forward to little better than an animal existence. Weeds grew around the foundations of what had been city blocks; two-thirds of the homes in most larger cities lay in ruins. The first foreign correspondents to enter Berlin were appalled by the stench

---

[20]The average Western European working-class family received 63 percent of its income in wages; the British working-class family, 84 percent. (Anthony Sampson, *The Anatomy of Europe* [New York, 1968], p. 358.)

of corpses buried in mounds of rubble that almost obliterated the traces of former streets.

> Nothing is left in Berlin. There are no homes, no shops, no transportation, no government buildings. Only a few walls. . . . Berlin can now be regarded only as a geographical location heaped with mountainous mounds of debris.[21]

The survivors, their numbers swollen by millions of refugees, camped in exposed corners of basements and hallways. Barter and the black market were the main sources for the necessities of life. The cigarettes an American GI casually gave his German girlfriend could keep her family alive by barter. Only the grotesque seemed adequate to describe the immediate postwar years, such as the misshapen but clairvoyant dwarf hero of Gunter Grass' novel *The Tin Drum.*

Separate Statehood

As East and West seized on their parts of Germany as Cold War chess pieces, German national life revived along the tensest frontier of the emerging Cold War. Each side encouraged those German political elements favorable to itself in its own area of control. The result was an accelerated drive toward separate and distorted statehood.

German officials had been brought into state and city governments from the beginning. The major issues were whether and how federal German administration would develop and what would be the conditions of economic revival. After the Moscow Conference of spring 1947, the French dropped their objections to central German authorities in the west. A central German Economic Council was set up in the British and American zones in May 1947. The Russians countered with a similar body in the east in June 1947. Central political institutions followed in 1948. The East Germans called a Peoples' Congress on March 18, 1948, the hundredth anniversary of the 1848 revolution, to promote a unified socialist Germany. After the Russians began to blockade Berlin, a West German constitutional convention met in September 1948. Under the new constitution of the Federal Republic of Germany (May 1949), the first West German government (still subject to the intervention of the occupying powers) took office in September 1949. Under a constitution drawn up in March 1949 by another Peoples' Congress, the German Democratic Republic was created in October 1949.

Two competing Germanies had come into existence. Inevitably, their internal politics were polarized by their Cold War origins. The Russian hand in the new German Democratic Republic was blatant. Although the unified Social Democratic-Communist movement (Socialist Unity Party, SED) that the Russians had pushed together did not have a majority in

---

[21]*New York Herald Tribune,* May 3, 1945, quoted in Koppel Pinson, *Modern Germany* (New York, 1954), p. 533.

the one free election held in the Russian zone,[22] it had the lion's share of places in the single-list elections held in the new German Democratic Republic. Furthermore, the smaller Communist party controlled leadership positions and policymaking in the SED even though the Social Democrats were more numerous. The German Democratic Republic was a one-party state whose authority rested on twenty Russian divisions and the Communist party apparatus under Walter Ulbricht, who had spent the war in Moscow. Ulbricht was to rule East Germany as party secretary from 1945 to 1969.

The Federal Republic of Germany was governed by the Christian Democrats under Konrad Adenauer and his successors for twenty years, from 1949 to 1969. Adenauer was hardly forced on West Germany by the Allies, since the Christian Democrats won a plurality in free elections in 1949 and improved their position steadily to an outright majority by 1957.[23] The division of Germany did give the Christian Democrats an artificial advantage, however. It prevented the Social Democrats, the largest party of the Weimar Republic, from playing the same role after 1945. Outnumbered in Catholic West Germany, the Social Democrats were forced into the SED in East Germany and deprived of any national role in their old stronghold, the occupied former capital, Berlin.

The West German "Miracle"

Under the Christian Democrats, West Germany sprang in less than a decade from rubble to the richest economy in Western Europe. The first step in economic recovery was the currency reform of June 20, 1948. On that Sunday, each West German received forty new *Deutsche Marks* in exchange for forty *Reichsmarks*,[24] along with his ration cards for that month. All West Germans acted as if saving, buying and selling, and investing were worthwhile again. Hoarded goods came out of hiding, and the black market dried up. The West Germans had begun their postwar economic "miracle."

The economic revival was carried out under the direction of Ludwig Erhard, Chancellor Adenauer's Economics Minister and eventual successor, according to a free-market policy vastly different from the welfare states of Britain and France. Britain and France, having failed to solve the depression of the 1930s with a liberal economy, adopted sweeping measures of state intervention in a mixed economy after 1945. West Germany, having associated twelve years of economic management under the Nazis with scarcity and defeat, chose to release competitive

[22]The results of the local election of October 1946 in the Soviet zone were: Socialist Unity party, 45 percent; Christian Democratic party, 24.5 percent; Liberal party, 24.6 percent.
[23]The results of the first federal elections in the western zones in August 1949 were: Christian Democratic party, 31 percent; Social Democratic party, 29 percent; Liberal party, 21 percent; fringe parties, 5 percent; Communist party, 5.7 percent.
[24]About $10. Additional currency, bank deposits, or other holdings, such as insurance policies or pension holdings, were redeemed eventually at about one-fifteenth of face value.

energies by removing most controls and encouraging private enterprise. Erhard called it a *Sozialmarktwirtschaft* (social market economy), which one commentator has translated freely as "a free enterprise economy with a social conscience."[25] The heart of the system was incentive. In addition to the inherent incentive of rebuilding the ruins, all sorts of tax rewards were offered for reinvestment by owners and overtime work by labor. The ultimate incentive was the possibility of riches. Twenty years later, 16,000 Germans admitted to incomes higher than 1 million *Deutsche Marks* per year.[26] The "social conscience" part of the *Sozialmarktwirtschaft* appeared in the Bismarckian tradition of state insurance for all paid workers, rather than in the form of wages. Most West Germans accepted low wages and initially high unemployment in exchange for rapid growth in total wealth.

The West German economic "miracle" is attributable to a mixture of causes. Energetic and disciplined people were stimulated by the possibilities of rebuilding their country. The Western Allies abandoned their efforts to limit the German economy and to break up its giant economic units. The 10 million refugees from Eastern Europe, a ready source of cheap labor, were more a help than a burden. No investment went into military development or colonial wars. Most of all, the Korean

[25] Alfred Grosser, *Germany in Our Time* (New York, 1971), p. 177.
[26] Over $260,000. *Ibid.,* p. 186.

European reconstruction. This view of West Berlin in 1965 shows the Europa Center and the blackened stump of the Kaiser Wilhelm Memorial Church retained, with modern annexes, as a reminder of the Second World War.

War encouraged German machinery exports decisively from 1951 to 1953. Few would attribute the German success solely to free-market policies; indeed, the *Sozialmarktwirtschaft* included increasing economic planning and widespread social security measures and public investment. But the West German success began the gradual swing of all Western Europe back toward laissez faire in the 1950s.

The German Democratic Republic, meanwhile, languished in poverty into the 1950s as the Russians drew reparations totaling an estimated 70 billion marks (at 200 times the rate the Western Allies drew reparations from West Germany after 1945) from that agricultural rump of the old Germany, a region about the size of Ohio. There was as yet little sign of the East German industrial growth of the 1960s. Many of East Germany's skilled young escaped to the West.

Both Walter Ulbricht and Konrad Adenauer governed under constitutions that were meant to be temporary. Both governed longer than Hitler, however. Although the division of Germany was accepted by few Germans, any conceivable form of unification seemed to require the victory of one half of Germany over the other.

Eastern Europe: Successor States as Russian Satellites

The dominant fact of life in Europe east of the Elbe River after 1945 was the Russian presence. Two hundred and fifty Russian divisions occupied Eastern Europe, and nothing could be done there against the will of Russian authorities.

The successor states created by the Versailles settlement of 1919 had been meant to fill the void left by the destruction of three great empires—Austria-Hungary, Germany, and Russia—with happy, prosperous, self-governing nationalities. Instead, the successor states had quarreled among themselves, divided Eastern Europe into closed economic backwaters, and fallen under various foreign influences. Resurgent Germany had established economic dominance over Eastern Europe during the depression and consolidated its hold during the Second World War.

That war replaced Germans with Russians in Eastern Europe. More or less by default, a system had evolved by which each power established its influence over the areas that its troops liberated. However earnestly the Western Allies wanted a say in the affairs of Eastern Europe, they had no physical presence in the area, nor were they inclined to reciprocate with a corresponding Russian say in the areas they had liberated, such as Italy or Japan. The Western Allies were neither physically nor morally prepared to challenge the Russian sphere in Eastern Europe. What was not yet clear in 1945 was how closely the Soviet Union would make these "friendly" states on its borders conform to its own economic and political system.

Eventually, with the exception of Austria, tightly closed Communist regimes controlled all the countries that Russian troops had entered in

1945: Poland, Czechoslovakia, Hungary, Romania, Bulgaria, Yugo- slavia,[27] Albania, and East Germany (known after 1949 as the German Democratic Republic). A region of 90 million people, nearly half as populous as the Soviet Union itself, was virtually annexed to the Russian economic, political, and military system. The Russians called these countries Peoples' Democracies. Hostile Westerners called them satellites.

National Front Regimes, 1945–47

At the outset, the Russians did not install one-party Communist regimes. Until late 1947 or early 1948, the Russians permitted non-Communist elements to share power with indigenous Communists. The main mass movements in post-Hitlerian Eastern Europe—Social Democrats and agrarian or peasant parties—exercised a relatively large freedom of action within National Fronts.

No one could expect Eastern Europe to return to interwar conditions. Few would have even wanted such a restoration. The successor states' initial parliamentary systems had almost all turned into autocracies of various sorts, none of them successful. All were discredited, along with much of the ruling classes, by collaboration with the Germans. This still archaic agricultural region with an overcrowded and underemployed rural population continued to be stirred by intense land hunger. What there was of large-scale commerce and industry, much of it foreign owned and damaged by the war, was riper for nationalization than for a free-market economy, which had never really worked well in that region. Eastern Europe was no less ready to jettison its discredited interwar arrangements than was Western Europe.

There was no major grass-roots revolutionary wave in Eastern Europe in 1945 comparable to that of 1918 to 1920. The Russian liberators were not met by spontaneous soviets or workers' and peasants' councils claiming sovereignty for a revolutionary people, except in Yugoslavia and Albania, which were beyond their control. Nor did they try to stimulate anything of the sort. The Russians were interested in control of the former German empire in Eastern Europe, not a rerun of 1917. However, they did not try to smother all local aspirations for change. The Russians channeled indigenous ferments in ways beneficial to their control.

Land redistribution was the most revolutionary act of the National Front regimes in Eastern Europe. The case of Romania may serve as an example. The agrarian leader Petru Groza, of the Plowman's Front, was more or less forced on King Michael as prime minister, with Communist

[27]Yugoslavia remained Communist but outside the Russian sphere after Marshal Tito refused to accept Russian control over his secret police and Army in 1948. Since Yugoslavia had liberated itself without Russian troops, like Albania, its Communist-led resistance movement carried through a revolutionary seizure of power and assumed one-party rule, unlike the National Front regimes in the Russian-controlled areas up through 1947. Thus Yugoslavia stood first to the left of Soviet policy and then to the right.

support, soon after Romania surrendered. Through a law of March 23, 1945, even before Germany had been defeated, the state expropriated all estates larger than fifty hectares (110 acres), as well as those larger than ten hectares that had not been cultivated for seven years, and the land of collaborators. Nearly 800,000 peasant families were given about three acres apiece. Although the agrarian reform in Romania in 1919 and 1920 had involved more land (over 1 million peasant families had received an average of nearly nine acres apiece), this step in 1945 seemed to complete the triumph of the small farmer. Throughout Eastern Europe, from Poland to Bulgaria, 3 million peasant families shared about 6 million acres of land in similar acts of expropriation.

In ways reminiscent of Lenin's tactic of giving land to the peasants in 1917, the National Front regimes took over the policies of agrarians and reaped a harvest of peasant followers. This dramatic completion of the post-First World War land reforms was not without its dangers for the Communist parties, however. It created a host of inefficient small plots in a region of low agricultural productivity. The mass of small landholders would vigorously resist any turn toward collectivization. And it prepared fertile ground for the Communists' main rivals, the agrarian parties, who could promise the small landholders long-term security more convincingly than the Communists.

The other main domestic work of the National Fronts in Eastern Europe was nationalization of key sectors of the economy. The local Communist parties supported the old program of their Social Democratic allies within the National Fronts. The nationalization of steel, coal, and the major banks and insurance companies met with little opposition in Eastern Europe, where the major industries and mines had been French and British before becoming German, and where the indigenous middle class tended to be small.

Even Czechoslovakia, the only industrialized country in Eastern Europe, and one with a substantial indigenous middle class, had no trouble nationalizing its economy. It had a well-developed trade union movement and Marxist political parties. Moreover, many of the country's major industrial owners were foreigners or collaborationist Czechs, some of whom had fled ahead of the Russian armies. The provisional administration of the first days, in which Communist and socialist workers were prominent, installed temporary state administrators of such property. Much *de facto* nationalization had already taken place, therefore, before the pre-Munich rulers of Czechoslovakia returned after their country's liberation. The presidential decree of October 1945 nationalized all sectors of the economy essential to the national interest (mines, metal production, electric power, armaments works, banks, and insurance companies) as well as all firms that employed more than 120 to 500 workers, depending on the kind of enterprise involved. As in Western Europe, the Czech Social Democrats were more eager for total nationalization than the Czech Communists, who were interested in maintaining broad political alliances at this stage. The National Front settled on nationalizing about three-quarters of Czech industries employing about two-thirds of Czech industrial workers;[28] smaller enterprises and most commerce were left in private hands. Compensation was promised, but when the Communists took power in 1948 it had not yet been paid. The Communists then nationalized all firms with more than fifty workers.

The National Fronts' agrarian and industrial policies both built on local nationalism. Land reform had a particularly nationalist character in Eastern Europe, because the largely Slavic rural population had long endured the exactions of Germanic and Magyar landlords and creditors. The last of the Germanic large farmers in Eastern Europe were now swept away in their home nation's defeat, while the Magyar landlords in Romania were reduced to small landholders. Communist parties successfully placed themselves in the forefront of this marriage of land hunger and nationalism. The Polish Communist Wladislaw Gomulka, later long-term party secretary (1956–70), was put in charge of settling Polish families on lands vacated by the Germans east of the Oder and Neisse rivers in 1945. In this way, Communist parties in Poland and elsewhere got credit for the "revenge of the Slavs and Romanians against the 'master races'."[29] Nationalization of industry was easier, too, in circumstances in which foreigners had come to dominate Eastern European enterprises between the wars.

Finally, the National Fronts profited from the immediate postwar surge of antifascist and anti-German feeling. Peoples like the Poles and the Czechs, who expelled millions of Germans from their ancestral homes in 1945, and all who remembered Nazi brutalities better than they could imagine the consequences of Russian dominance, felt they needed the Russians more than the Russians needed them. The postwar purges helped open the way for new political elites, particularly in former dictatorships and monarchies like Hungary, Romania, and Bulgaria, whose leaders and principal businessmen had collaborated with the Nazis. It is doubtful that the National Front regimes of Eastern Europe actually executed more collaborators than did Western European regimes after the liberation,[30] but the vacant leadership positions were more readily occupied by Communists in Russian-occupied Eastern Europe.

In all these ways, the National Front regimes built on indigenous pressures for change and renovation following the dark night of war and collaboration. And after the failure of the successor states to make democracy work between the wars, there was far less interest in a return to the parliamentary experiments of the 1920s than Western Europeans had felt in their own better established liberties.

[28]Josef Korbel, *The Communist Subversion of Czechoslovakia, 1938–48: The Failure of Coexistence* (Princeton, N.J., 1959), p. 165.

[29]François Fejtö, *Histoire des démocraties populaires* (Paris, 1952), p. 150.

[30]More than 2000 in Bulgaria; 362 in Czechoslovakia, of whom 250 were Germans; 430 in Hungary. France executed 767 collaborators.

Russia did not treat all the states of Eastern Europe alike, of course. Russian control was most direct in the principal border states: Poland, Romania, and Bulgaria. Poland, the key to keeping Germany in check, clearly had the highest priority. We have already seen how Stalin broke with the London Poles as early as 1943 and prepared a Communist provisional government in exile in Moscow. At Yalta and Potsdam, the Western Allies had been able to persuade Stalin to include only two London Poles—including the agrarian leader Stanislaw Mikolajczyk—in the new government. When elections were finally held in January 1947, major industries had already been nationalized and opposition parties were harassed by the police and the Communist party. Following Communist successes in these elections, Mikolajczyk went into exile, in October 1947, and the Polish government could be seen as a Russian satellite regime. The commander in chief of the Polish armed forces from 1949 to 1956, Marshal Konstantin Rokossovsky, was a Russian officer.

The Russians also asserted their will forcefully in Romania, which was not only a major border state but one whose armies had invaded the Ukraine in 1941. Although the young King Michael had hastily changed sides in 1944 (and had received the Russian Order of Victory for it), he was obliged to choose his first postwar prime minister from within the National Democratic Front, a coalition of agrarians and Communists. The first elections a year and a half later, in November 1946, were marked by harassment of the opposition (as oppositions had always been harassed in Romanian elections). The Romanians lost eastern and northern territory to the Russians, but having regained Transylvania from Hungary at Russia's behest, they continued to need Russian support.

Bulgaria was the simplest case. This country of small peasant proprietors, so similar to Russia in language, religion, and culture, had felt strong sentimental ties to Russia even in tsarist times. A relatively free election in November 1945 overwhelmingly replaced the monarchy (which had been a passive Axis satellite) with the Fatherland Front, a coalition of Communists and agrarians.

Russian control remained far looser during this "dualism" period in the less strategically vital Czechoslovakia and Hungary. Czechoslovakia was the exception to every Eastern European rule. It was an industrialized country in the peasant sea of Eastern Europe. It was the one Eastern European nation with a substantial middle class and industrial working class and an experience of political democracy between the wars. Czechoslovakia was the only Eastern European country with a large indigenous Communist party even before the Second World War. And it was the only one in which prewar leaders were restored to power. During the "dualism" period, the prewar democratic leaders—President Eduard Beneš and Foreign Minister Jan Masaryk—proposed to govern a social democracy with domestic political liberty while maintaining close voluntary relations with the Soviet Union in foreign affairs.

As early as December 1943, President Beneš—then in exile in London—visited Moscow and concluded a treaty of alliance and postwar cooperation with Stalin. Beneš told Molotov that in important matters the postwar Czechoslovak government "would always speak and act in a fashion agreeable to . . . the Soviet government."[31] Beneš' deliberate and controversial choice of close cooperation with the Soviet Union was based on his fear of postwar German revival, his disillusion with the failure of England and France to protect him in 1938, and a realistic reading of probable postwar power relationships in Eastern Europe.

The Russians later became much more powerful in Eastern Europe than Beneš (or anyone else) had imagined in 1943, but his calculation seemed to work at first. After the Soviets liberated Prague, they permitted the restoration of the prewar Czechoslovak Republic with its full range of parties and Beneš as president. In return for the cession to the Soviet Union of the eastern tip of his country (whose Ruthenian people spoke a Ukrainian dialect), Beneš had a firm guarantee against future German efforts to regain the Sudetenland, from which he expelled almost the entire German population. At the end of 1945, Soviet troops were withdrawn from Czechoslovakia. In free elections in May 1946, the Communists, building on a strong prewar base, received 38 percent of the vote. Their leader, Klement Gottwald, was the logical choice for prime minister in a coalition cabinet with socialists and Beneš' liberal followers. Beneš' regime was a test of whether it was possible for a relatively open, pluralistic regime to cooperate voluntarily with the Soviet Union as a "friendly" but non-Communist neighbor.

Hungary was an overwhelmingly agricultural country whose upper classes had been deeply implicated in Admiral Horthy's policy of cooperation with the Axis. It was not surprising, then, that in free elections in November 1945—the freest in Hungary's troubled history—the peasant Smallholders' party received an absolute majority, and the Smallholders' leader, Zoltan Tildy, became prime minister of the new Hungarian Republic. The Communist vote was about 20 percent. There seemed to be no effort at that time to tie Hungary to a closed Soviet sphere.

Could these dualist regimes, in which local Communist parties shared power with other parties under the eye of Russian Army units, be permanent? Would the Russians be satisfied with pluralist non-Communist regimes at their borders? Given the disruption and chaos of the immediate postwar years, would the mixed regimes be able to surmount problems that previous regimes had failed to deal with except by some form of autocracy?

These questions soon became academic. From the summer of 1947

[31]Quoted in Vojtech Mastny, "The Beneš-Stalin-Molotov Conversations in December 1943," *Jahrbücher für Geschichte Osteuropas,* Vol. 20 (1970): 373.

into early 1948, all the areas within reach of Soviet soldiers were brought under one-party Communist control.

Soviet Crackdown in Eastern Europe

The first sign of the Soviet crackdown was a concerted attack throughout Eastern Europe on the Communists' main rivals for a mass following, the agrarian parties. In July 1947, the Romanian National Peasant and National Liberal parties were dissolved, and the peasant leader Iuliu Maniu was sentenced to life imprisonment. In the same month the Bulgarian agrarian leader Nikolaj Petkov was brought to trial and executed. In August 1947, elections in Hungary, in which intimidation was widespread, reduced the hold of the majority Smallholders' party. In October 1947, the Polish agrarian leader Mikolajczyk fled abroad. These attacks on the agrarian parties were followed by political changes: King Michael of Romania abdicated at the end of December 1947. The Communists seized power in Czechoslovakia in February 1948. During the six months from late summer 1947 to early 1948, all the National Front, or dualist, regimes were replaced by one-party Communist regimes.

The facts are clear enough. Their meaning is more difficult to be sure of. For those who believe that the Russians meant all along to impose Communist regimes on Eastern Europe, the two years from 1945 to 1947 were mere preparation. It seems likely, however, that the Russians cracked down when confronted by two pressures: their desire to draw on the wealth of Eastern Europe for reconstruction, and their fear of losing control of Eastern Europe unless they governed it more directly. From this point of view, the turning point came with the announcement of the Marshall Plan in June 1947. Czech, Polish, and Hungarian interest in taking part was a warning that the mixed regimes might be tempted to participate in the reviving Western European economy.

The Czech takeover of February 1948 clearly suggests that the Russians feared a decline of their postwar position in Eastern Europe. In early 1948, the non-Communist members of the government proposed to resign in a body and call new elections in which the Communists were unlikely to get the 38 percent they had won in 1946. President Beneš received the resignations on February 21, 1948. The Communist party and trade unions responded by occupying the main government buildings in Prague and preventing the election from taking place. In that sense, the Prague *coup* of February 1948 was a preemptive move designed to keep Czechoslovakia from slipping back into the Western economic orbit. Beyond that, however, the Communists forced Beneš to form a government dominated by Communists under Gottwald. When Foreign Minister Jan Masaryk was found dead in the courtyard of the Foreign Ministry on March 10, an apparent suicide,[32] and when Beneš

---

[32]There is some evidence that he was pushed rather than jumped from the window.

died the following September, there were no further barriers to a one-party Communist regime. The Czech *coup* sent shock waves throughout the world, for it showed that Stalin would not tolerate anything short of outright Communist control of the border states, and it aroused fears of other Communist *coups* in Europe.

Peoples' Democracies

The new Communist regimes in Eastern Europe were called Peoples' Democracies, to distinguish them from the more advanced Russian socialist state. The constitutions provided for parliamentary forms and guarantees of the usual liberties. In practice, the Communist party and the security police lay at the heart of the system. The local Communist parties were brought under direct Russian control in a series of purges in the late 1940s and early 1950s. A number of old-line local Communists (of whom the most celebrated was the Hungarian Laszlo Rajk) and Jewish Communists, such as the Hungarian Anna Pauker, the Czech Rudolph Slansky, and ten other Jewish Communist leaders in Czechoslovakia, were replaced by leaders devoted to the Russians. Only Yugoslavia, which had liberated itself and had no common border with the Soviet Union, preserved a form of national communism separate from the Soviet bloc after 1948, despite efforts by the Russians first to control it and then to eliminate it.

The Eastern European satellites were geared to the economic needs of Soviet reconstruction. This entailed the forced collectivization of small farms after 1948, over vigorous peasant protests. Surplus labor was diverted into factory production under a series of Five Year Plans begun in 1948. Former trade patterns with the West were broken. The Russian share of Czech trade, for example, increased from 6 percent in 1947 to 27.5 percent in 1950 and to 34.5 percent in 1956. By 1947 Eastern Europe as a whole provided a market for nearly half of Russia's exports and supplied more than a third of Russia's imports. Because Russian exports were priced above world prices and imports below, a high degree of forced contributions to Russian reconstruction was extracted from these economies: an amount estimated at $20 billion since the end of the war. These exactions postponed Eastern European recovery and made it a grim and unhappy area long after Western Europe had returned to prosperity.

Reconstruction and Orthodoxy in the Soviet Union

The Soviet Union faced the most gigantic reconstruction task of any belligerent in the war. Up to 20 million people had been killed, and whole regions of western Russia—the most highly developed area before the war—had been devastated by fighting and scorched earth tactics. Stalin was determined not merely to restore the Russian economy to its prewar levels but to build an industrial base appropriate to Russia's new world role as the greatest military force on the Continent and the leader of a group of "friendly" new regimes.

There were two possible routes toward industrial growth. One of them, reconstruction through aid from the West, probably seemed too costly to Stalin's freedom of political action. In any case, Stalin had been reminded of its limitations by the sudden end of lend-lease in 1945 and the disputes over reparations from the Western occupation zones in Germany. The other route was a return to the 1930s policy of extracting development capital from the labor of Soviet citizens. Reconstruction was eased slightly by the unwilling aid of Eastern Europe and by the labor of German prisoners, but it rested mostly on the willingness of most Russians to tighten their belts once more. From 1946 to 1950, while housing remained so desperately short that newly married couples lived for years with in-laws in a single room, and while only the barest minimum of consumer goods was being produced, the Russian leaders poured more capital into investment than they had in the thirteen years following the launching of the First Five Year Plan in 1928. This accomplishment rested on extracting every possible kopek of surplus value from the labor of both men and women. In a population whose males had been decimated by wars and civil wars, women made up most of the doctors, 57 percent of agricultural labor, and a third of heavy manual labor.[33] Russia was on its way to creating the industrial basis for a world power position on the backs of a population crammed into small rooms and barely supplied with the basic necessities.

It might have been expected that the end of the war would open new breathing spaces in Russia's tightly closed society. Quite the contrary happened. A certain ideological relaxation had accompanied the Great Patriotic War. Many Soviet citizens had been exposed to Western contacts, to revived religion, to a resurgence of private farm plots during wartime shortages, and even, in the Western occupied areas, to years of life under non-Communist rule. After the war the Soviet regime perceived these wartime relaxations as a threat to orthodoxy, compounded by the return of Russian prisoners of war (some of them against their will) and the need to assimilate new populations in the lands taken from Poland, Czechoslovakia, and Romania.

Stalin accompanied physical reconstruction with tightened orthodoxy. His chief lieutenant immediately after the war (1946–48) was Andrei Zhdanov, the party boss of Leningrad during the wartime siege and a particularly narrow-minded representative of that new generation of party functionaries whose career had consisted more of serving the Soviet state than of opposing tsardom.[34] The Zhdanov decrees of 1946 subordinated all forms of literary and scientific expression to the political needs of the regime.

The arts declined into numbing conformity. The great filmmaker Sergei Eisenstein, whose *Alexander Nevsky* had helped kindle Russian

---

[33]Isaac Deutscher, *Stalin: A Political Biography,* 2nd ed. (New York, 1967), p. 576.
[34]Zhdanov was twenty-one years old in 1917.

patriotism after 1938, ran into trouble with his striking depiction of a despot's moral decay, *Ivan the Terrible.* The composer Sergei Prokofiev, who had been persuaded to return to Russia from California in the late 1930s, found his work impeded by politicians' criticisms. Many novelists were silent. The novelist Boris Pasternak earned a living by translations. The most celebrated instance of political interference in science was the power that Trofim Lysenko wielded over biology. Lysenko was an agronomist whose conviction that acquired characteristics could be inherited fit Stalin's faith in the possibility of changing mankind by changing the environment. Lysenko's domination of biology crippled the science of genetics in the Soviet Union for a generation.

Even before the Cold War had taken clear shape in international relations, the Russian forced labor camps were filled with actual or potential dissidents. There were returning prisoners of war, some of whom were shipped directly from the camps of Hitler to the camps of Stalin. There were ethnic groups that the Russians had dispersed preventively before the Nazi advance, such as the Volga Germans, and others that had collaborated with the invader, such as the Crimean Tartars. And there were young Russians imprisoned for frank wartime speaking. The young Army Captain Aleksandr Solzhenitsyn, who had been trained as a mathematician before the war, had been arrested in Germany at the war's end for criticizing Stalin in letters to a friend. As he was taken down a long escalator in the Moscow subway, on his way to fourteen years of imprisonment, facing the unknowing faces of other Russians on their way up, he resolved to become a writer to tell his fellow citizens about that other Russia, the world of prisoners, that was growing so rapidly even in the moment of Russian triumph.[35] But things were to become even tighter in the Cold War before Solzhenitsyn's name would be known to many Russians.

[35]Aleksandr Solzhenitsyn, *The Gulag Archipelago, 1918–1956,* trans. Thomas P. Whitney (New York, 1974), pp. 17–18.

Suggestions for Further Reading

Walter Laqueur, *Europe Since Hitler** (1972) is packed with interesting detail. Andrew Shonfield's important *Modern Capitalism: The Changing Balance of Public and Private Power,** corrected ed. (1969) examines the enlarged role of state planning and regulation in the restoration of capitalist economies in Western Europe. The lavishly illustrated Maurice Crouzet, *The European Renaissance Since 1945** (1971) deals with Eastern Europe as well and discusses intellectual life. The best-informed comparative look at postwar welfare states and mixed economies in Western Europe is *Economic Planning and Policies in Britain, France, and Germany* (1968), a volume published by the British study group Political and Economic Planning (PEP).

Charles P. Kindleberger, *Europe's Postwar Growth* (1967), and M. M. Postan, *An Economic History of Western Europe, 1945–1964** (1966) are basic; the latter discusses society as well as economy. Harry E. Price, *The Marshall Plan and Its Meaning* (1955) is the fundamental work on its subject.

For postwar Britain, see Arthur Marwick, *Britain in the Century of Total War* (1968), as well as the more general works cited at the end of Chapter 1. Richard M. Titmuss, *Essays on the Welfare State,** 2nd ed. (1966) contains the stimulating essays of an advocate. The closing chapters of Peter Laslett, *The World We Have Lost** (1965) draws an illuminating comparison between the British welfare state and earlier society.

The complex politics of the French Fourth Republic are most knowledgeably handled by Philip Williams, *Crisis and Compromise** (1966). For economic policy, see Mario Einaudi, Maurice Byé, and Ernesto Rossi, *Nationalization in France and Italy* (1955), and Pierre Bauchet, *Economic Planning: The French Experience* (1964).

Postwar Italy receives a penetrating brief treatment in the last chapter of H. Stuart Hughes, *The United States and Italy*, 2nd ed. (1965). Fuller political histories are Norman Kogan, *A Political History of Postwar Italy* (1966), and Giuseppi Mammarella, *Italy After Fascism: A Political History, 1943–1965*, rev. ed. (1966). See also Elizabeth Wiskemann, *Italy Since 1945* (1971).

Alfred Grosser, *Germany in Our Time** (1971) is the best single volume on postwar Germany. Ralf Dahrendorf, *Society and Democracy in Germany* (1967) is a wide-ranging and suggestive discussion of social and political change in Germany since 1945. Henry C. Wallich, *Mainsprings of German Revival* (1955) applauds the modified free-enterprise economy with which West Germany revived.

Hugh Seton-Watson, *The East European Revolution*, 3rd ed. (1956) is still basic. For individual Eastern European states after 1945, see the book by Roos cited on page 189; Ghita Ionescu, *Communism in Romania, 1944–1962* (1964); and Joseph Rothschild, *The Communist Party of Bulgaria* (1959).

In addition to the excellent brief chapter on the Prague *coup* of 1948 in the work of Mamatey and Luza cited at the end of Chapter 9, there are many longer works, all reflecting the intensity of anger and disillusion in the West: Hubert Ripka, *Czechoslovakia Enslaved* (1950); Dana Adams Schmidt, *Anatomy of a Satellite* (1952); and Josef Korbel, *The Communist Subversion of Czechoslovakia, 1938–1948: The Failure of Coexistence** (1959).

Tito's break with Stalin is treated briefly in John C. Campbell, *Tito's Separate Road* (1964), and, more personally, by an insider, Vladimir Dedijer, *The Battle Stalin Lost: Memoirs of Yugoslavia, 1948–1953** (1971).

EUROPE IN THE COLD WAR: BETWEEN THE SUPERPOWERS 1947–1962

18

The United States and the Soviet Union dropped all pretense of trying to continue their wartime alliance in 1947 and 1948. On the American side, the Truman Doctrine adopted by Congress on March 12, 1947[1], made assistance to any anti-Communist regime in the world the central focus of American foreign policy. United States government leaders thought that up to then they had made concessions to a Soviet alliance, but Secretary of State Dean Acheson now vowed not to make any more. These "concessions . . . have to be written off as appeasement that did not pay," he wrote in 1948.[2]

[1]See Chapter 16, p. 503.
[2]Dean Acheson, introduction to *The United States in World Affairs, 1947–1948* (New York, 1948), p. 6.

On the Soviet side, Stalin abandoned the policy of broad National Fronts in Eastern Europe and sought outright Communist control wherever his troops had the upper hand. It was in 1948 that he brought Czechoslovakia and Hungary into line with the other satellites and attempted to get control of Berlin. Outside his direct military sphere, Stalin ordered local Communist parties to break off participation in mixed postwar governments. After 1947 Western European Communist parties withdrew into an opposition as hermetically closed as that of the "class against class" years after 1928. Whatever one's interpretation of Soviet policy between 1945 and 1947—whether it was meant simply to create a defensive sphere of influence or to lay the first stages of a plan for world domination—no one doubts that after 1947 the Soviet leaders were looking for chances to consolidate and advance their power. The reasons might still be defensive, but the game was now rougher. The Americans answered in kind.

This hardened antagonism between the Communist states and the capitalist states produced a new kind of conflict: the Cold War. The availability on both sides of nuclear weapons capable of annihilating the other[3] made war unthinkable; each side's claim to universal ideological legitimacy made peace impossible. Under an umbrella of mutual nuclear terror, the two sides grappled with each other by every means short of the war that might obliterate them both.

The Cold War conflict was as bitter as war without actual armed combat between the principal powers. Its arena was virtually worldwide, even more than the Second World War. Its techniques included economic assistance, intellectual persuasion, and psychological subversion as well as more traditional forms of political and military influence. Each side lent military and economic assistance to its allies and dependents. The Soviets supported movements for ethnic separatism and colonial independence in the Western sphere; the Americans broadcast encouragement to dissidents behind the Iron Curtain and supported anti-Communist regimes around the world. Both sides struggled for the upper hand in the emerging new nations of Africa and Asia. The result was an unending series of *coups,* guerrilla warfare, and civil wars with more or less open support from Moscow and Washington. Over it all brooded the possibility that the two rivals would come to direct combat, which must inevitably mean nuclear war.

Europe Under the Mushroom Cloud

Europeans had to endure the humiliation of looking on powerlessly as the two giant rivals circled each other. After centuries of confident domination of the world, the Europeans found their fate now dependent on the distant rulers of upstart nations. For fifteen years or so after the war, the possibility of being incinerated by the side effects of remote

---

[3]The Soviets tested an atomic bomb in September 1949 and announced their possession of thermonuclear weapons in August 1953. One thermonuclear weapon had a force about equal to all the bombs dropped on Germany between 1939 and 1945.

power politics haunted every European. As one of the characters in Max Frisch's play *The Chinese Wall* (1946) says:

> A slight whim on the part of the man on the throne, a nervous breakdown, a touch of neurosis, a flame struck by his madness, a moment of impatience on account of indigestion—and the jig is up. Everything! A cloud of yellow or brown ashes boiling up towards the heavens in the shape of a mushroom, a dirty cauliflower—and the rest is silence, radio-active silence.[4]

Europeans' prospects for regaining some control over their destinies looked bleak indeed in the 1950s. Eastern Europeans seemed condemned to indefinite Russian control. Western European dependence, although less direct, was almost more terrifying. The 250 Russian divisions in Eastern Europe could swarm west almost at will unless the Americans intervened. American intervention, however, meant the "massive retaliation" with which Secretary of State John Foster Dulles (1952–59) threatened a Russian advance with conventional arms in Europe: nuclear annihilation of the European battleground in the guise of saving it. Europeans felt threatened by what Arnold Toynbee called "annihilation without representation."[5] Many thinking Europeans reacted to the situation with a sense of cosmic absurdity or with profound pessimism.

George Orwell, depressed already by the tuberculosis he had contracted in Britain's harsh postwar conditions, wondered in a letter to a friend in December 1947 whether it was worth worrying about the crises of the moment.

> This stupid war is coming off in about 10–20 years, and this country will be blown off the map whatever happens. The only hope is to have a home with a few animals in some place not worth a bomb.

A year later he was writing that he hoped his young son would become a farmer. "Of course that may be the only job left after the atom bombs."[6] In Paris, novelist Gilbert Cesbron thought Europe had gone the way of rich, decadent Babylon: "Does anyone remember Babylon?" he asked. "Europe is contracting," wrote Janet Flanner from Paris in October 1946. "The USSR and USA areas of influence are expanding. It is as if Europe were slowly entering a new ice age."[7]

After the Berlin Blockade ended in May 1949 with the United States, Britain, and France still grimly holding on to the western occupation sectors of the city, the Cold War frontiers were frozen in Europe for a generation. Further Soviet gains in the West (assuming that the Soviets really wanted more territory beyond Berlin) were now possible only by outright military action that risked American massive retaliation. The Americans were equally reluctant to disturb the European *status quo,* as United States restraint showed during the uprisings in East Berlin (June

---

[4]Max Frisch, *The Chinese Wall,* trans. James L. Rosenberg (New York, 1955), p. 28.
[5]Quoted in Hans W. Gatzke, *The Present in Perspective,* 3rd ed. (New York, 1965), p. 181.
[6]*The Collected Essays, Letters, and Journalism of George Orwell,* Vol. 4 (New York, 1968), pp. 387, 451, 454.
[7]Janet Flanner, *Paris Journal, 1944–65* (New York, 1965), p. 69.

1953), Poland (October 1956), and Hungary (October 1956). The high cost of change on both sides locked the two European blocs into a precarious stability. But Europeans were still nervous, and Cold War language remained harsh on both sides.

After 1949, the hottest battleground of the Cold War was the Korean War (1950–53), in which United States and Communist Chinese armies fought each other to stalemate by conventional arms without either side daring to expand the conflict. Distant though it was, the Korean War affected Europe deeply. Aside from the small European troop contributions to the United Nations force in Korea, the war stimulated European economic growth and led to the rearmament of Germany within a new Western anti-Communist alliance.

Europe was also deeply affected by the Cold War's stimulus to decolonization. Europe's eclipse in the Second World War, combined with the rapid spread of ideas of national self-determination throughout the world, had made the colonial powers' hold on their overseas possessions far more precarious in 1945 than it had been in 1918. In the Wilsonian and Open Door traditions, President Franklin Roosevelt had openly encouraged the independence of European colonies. Britain had been forced to accede to Indian independence in 1946, and amidst dreadful religious strife between Moslems and Hindus, the new states of Pakistan and India had come into existence in August 1947. The Dutch had lost Indonesia after bitter fighting in 1948.

The Cold War, however, had the effect of swinging the United States into support for colonial defense and the Soviet Union (and, after 1948, Communist China) into support for liberation movements. The French waged an almost incessant, exasperating, bloody, and eventually futile war in their colonies, first against the Communist Vietminh in Indochina (1946–54) and then against the nationalist FLN in Algeria (1954–61). Before the final French defeat in Indochina at Dien Bien Phu, the United States had reached the point of supplying 80 percent of their matériel; after the French departure in 1954, the United States assumed the French role of supporter

© WALT KELLY

"--THEIR SMILES AS WAN AS PRIMROSES GATHER'D AT MIDNIGHT BY CHILLY FINGERED SPRING-"
KEATS

WALT KELLY

The two blocs. Truman and Stalin and their unruly "children" as seen by the American cartoonist Walt Kelly in 1949.

of an anti-Communist regime. The French found that they had spent scarce resources in exchange for little but casualties, frustration, and one more reminder of lost prestige.

The Isolation of Communist Parties

The Cold War split the resistance coalitions that had governed liberated Europe since 1945. On the Continent, the tripartite coalitions of Communists, socialists, and antifascist Catholics whose new found unity in the resistance had been the basis of politics since 1945 did not survive the widening divisions between Communists and anti-Communists. In the spring of 1947, Communist parties went into opposition everywhere in Western Europe. Thereafter, Western European states were governed by centrist or conservative regimes.

Belgium led the way. By March 1947 cooperation between Catholics and Communists had become impossible in the ruling coalition. At that point, Paul-Henri Spaak, an anti-Communist socialist, formed Belgium's first postwar cabinet of socialists and Catholics from which Communists were excluded. Spaak was to dominate Belgian politics and the European unity movement for the next generation.

The French Communist party's departure from the government on May 5, 1947, illustrates how domestic strains and international tensions combined to both push and pull the Western Communist parties into a new isolation. Communist participation in postwar reconstruction had become more and more awkward. "Unite, Work, Struggle!" had been the French Communist party's slogan during the postwar reconstruction period. Having chosen to participate legally in a nonrevolutionary government, the Communist party was obliged to share in that government's austerity reconstruction policies. Controlled wages, price inflation, no strikes, and hard work at rebuilding the country were the workingman's lot. In the spring of 1947, a wildcat strike at the state-owned Renault automobile plant in Paris showed the French Communist leaders that they were in danger of being passed on their own left. It was time to return to the purity of opposition.

The French Communist party leaders could well suppose that they had more to lose than gain from further participation in parliamentary coalitions. Their support for the government's economic austerity program was costing them worker support. And although the Communist party had been the largest party in France briefly in 1945, the other two parties of the liberation—socialists and left Catholics (MRP)—were united in their determination to block Communist access to the premiership or to the major ministries controlling the Army or police.

Here one may see the play of foreign pressures as well. In the immediate postwar years, French governments had relied on Soviet support for their punitive German policy: their desire was to keep

Germany divided and unindustrialized. By the spring of 1947, however, France was getting coal from the British and American occupation zones and had accepted control of the Saar in return for excluding the Russians from a share in occupation policies in the western zones. With those questions settled, France no longer needed Russian cooperation in Germany. Moreover, American economic support was an ever growing necessity during the hardships of the reconstruction years, and the United States made no secret of its nervousness about Communist strength in France. In the spring of 1947, Jean Monnet and the prewar French Popular Front leader Léon Blum, recently returned from a German prisoner of war camp, went to Washington to seek help for French reconstruction. They obtained the renunciation of war debts to the United States (thus avoiding the war debts problem of the 1920s), a promise of surplus goods, and a $650 million reconstruction loan. Although Blum and Monnet declared that they had accepted no political conditions, it was obvious to French political leaders that "it is not to a socialist-communist regime that the United States will grant the loan we need."[8]

When, on May 5, 1947, the Communist ministers tried to square the circle by voting for wage raises opposed by the government to which they belonged, Premier Paul Ramadier, a Socialist, demanded their resignation.

The break came at almost the same moment in Italy under similar pressures. Many Italian socialists, however, led by Pietro Nenni, were more determined than French socialists to avoid a rupture with the Communists. The subsequent split among the socialists left the new Christian Democratic party under Alcide De Gasperi to emerge as the dominant political force of a coalition excluding Communists and relying on United States financial assistance. De Gasperi had visited the United States in January 1947, where he was put under great pressure to exclude the Communists from the coalition. In May 1947 he succeeded in piecing together a Christian Democrat, anti-Communist socialist, and center coalition. De Gasperi won an absolute majority in Italy's first postwar legislative elections in April 1948, with the support of the United States, the clergy, and all those who regarded him as the only alternative to communism in Italy.

The split affected the powerful Marxist trade union federations of both Italy and France, which divided into Communist and anti-Communist factions at the end of 1947. Secret funds from the American labor movement assisted the formation of the *Force ouvrière,* a non-Communist trade union that mobilized about 15 percent of the French work force as compared with about 40 percent for the Communist CGT (*Conféderation géneral du travail*), and about 20 percent for the Catholic Unions. In Italy, during the 1950s, the United States refused to award manufacturing contracts to Italian firms in which a majority of the

---

[8]Left Catholic (MRP) leader P. H. Teitgen, quoted in Jacques Fauvet, *La IVe république* (Paris, 1959), p. 94.

workers supported the Communist union, CGIL (*Confederazione Generale Italiano del Lavoro*). For their part, the Communist unions, no longer required to discipline the work force for reconstruction, embarked on a series of insurrectionary strikes in France and Italy in late 1947 and in 1948.

The Cold War division naturally took a different form in Great Britain, where communism had always been marginal and the war had not involved the polarizing experiences of occupation, collaboration, and liberation. The Labour party split over national defense policy in the Cold War. A majority of the Labour government, supported by the Trades Union Congress, wanted Britain to continue to play a world military role. After the Korean War broke out, Britain contributed a small force, and Prime Minister Clement Attlee proposed a three-year armament program costing nearly £5 billion. Social services began to be cut. In April 1951, Labour Minister Aneurin Bevan and some of his followers, including Harold Wilson, resigned from the government, charging that Britain was being dragged into "the anarchy of American competitive capitalism" by means of an arms race that would actually aid communism by reducing the British standard of living.[9] Divided, the Labour party lost the October 1951 elections to the Conservatives.

Division of the European Left

The result of these developments, in Britain as on the Continent, was the division of the European left. The Western European Communist parties reverted to a position of hostile isolation as complete as that of the early 1930s. Aside from a few intellectual fellow travelers and such socialists as the followers of Pietro Nenni in Italy, the non-Communist left in Western Europe went out of its way to mark its distance from the Communists. It was a socialist Minister of the Interior, Jules Moch, who crushed the French strike wave of 1947 and 1948. The old leader of the French Socialist party, Léon Blum, called the French Communists "the foreign nationalist party." His successor, Guy Mollet, declared that the French Communists were not left but east. Arguing in favor of German arms in 1954, Mollet claimed:

> We have to have them, because since the war Russians have kept millions of men under arms, because in the last ten years Russia has destroyed the liberties of so many people, and because all the troubles today come from Russian expansionism.[10]

In France and Italy, the Communists retained a strong emotional hold on many workers convinced of their permanent exile within a capitalist system; the Communist vote never dropped much below 20 percent. Meanwhile, the French and Italian socialist parties became increasingly dominated by lower civil servants and shopkeepers. So divided, the left

[9] Elaine Windrich, *British Labour's Foreign Policy* (Stanford, Calif., 1952), pp. 232–33.
[10] Flanner, p. 260.

had no chance of electoral victory. By contrast, the West German Social Democratic party set out to win an electoral majority by making as broad an appeal as possible to a population in which workers formed a smaller and smaller proportion. In 1959, at the annual party congress at Bad Godesberg, the party that had once been the most powerful Marxist party in the world formally renounced the teachings of Karl Marx. But revived prosperity reduced its appeal. Either way, sectarian or not, the Western European left was generally out of power during the Cold War years.

Cold War divisions posed a painful dilemma for those Western European intellectuals whom the Popular Front, the Spanish Civil War, and the resistance had drawn into action on behalf of a united left. The debate over correct attitudes toward the United States and the Soviet Union in the 1950s was particularly sharp in Paris, where intellectuals held public attention and where they had been deeply influenced by the anti-Hitler resistance and by Marxist thought. The issue was joined in 1950 when a survivor of one of Hitler's concentration camps published an attack on Stalin's concentration camps. Was Stalin the new tyrant against whom European intellectuals should unite? The novelist Albert Camus concluded after much soul-searching that his ultimate loyalty lay with the West because the Soviet Union permitted no personal liberty.

The existentialist philosopher Jean-Paul Sartre was the most important spokesman for the other side. While admitting the existence of evils at that time in the Soviet Union, Sartre was too hostile to the European bourgeoisie and too predisposed by existentialism to make major choices in terms of ultimate goals to side with the United States. Despite its transitory evils, the Soviet Union represented for Sartre the ultimate promise of a better life. Sartre did not join the Communist party, but preserved his individual freedom while supporting Communist causes. Leon Trotsky had called such intellectual outsiders "fellow travelers," and the term became a current epithet for Sartre and like-minded sympathizers.

The Cold War prompted some intellectuals to renounce the political engagement of the 1930s and 1940s altogether. The Irish playwright Samuel Beckett, living in France, achieved an enormous impact with *Waiting for Godot* (1952), in which two tramps face an empty universe with humor and dogged persistence. To pessimist humanists like Beckett, the Cold War world was simply absurd. At best one could find in it an occasional glimpse of redeeming human perseverance.

Centrist and Conservative Governments

Western Europe in the 1950s was governed largely by centrist or conservative parties. This was the Europe of Alcide De Gasperi and his Christian Democrat followers in Italy; of Konrad Adenauer in Germany; of Churchill, Anthony Eden, and Harold MacMillan in Britain. In France, the collapse of the Fourth Republic at the end of the decade brought back to power General Charles de Gaulle with a more authoritarian constitution.

Italy continued to be ruled through the 1950s by the coalition of center parties of which the Christian Democrats were by far the largest. Since the Christian Democrats never again won an absolute majority of the seats as they had in 1948, Italian politics became a disheartening round of brief coalition governments. After De Gasperi's death in 1954, five governments succeeded one another in as many years. Political strategists continued to piece together Christian Democrat–Liberal coalitions of the center right, refusing to attempt the other alternative of an "opening to the left" offered by Pietro Nenni's left-wing socialists, who moved away from the Communists after the Hungarian uprising of 1956. Basically, Italian citizens showed relatively little interest in matters other than Italy's rapid economic growth (the fastest in Western Europe) and border disputes with Yugoslavia and Austria. The Christian Democrats solidified their hold with patronage and the help of the Church in elections. In 1959 Italy became the first European nation to permit the United States to base intermediate range ballistic missiles (IRBM's) on its soil.

Germany's aged Konrad Adenauer went on from strength to strength in the 1950s. His Christian Democrats' plurality grew with each election until they achieved an absolute majority in September 1957. The extraordinary prosperity of West Germany's free-enterprise economy spread a self-satisfied glow over the country. The stresses of the Cold War brought West Germany into an active international role more quickly than would have been thought possible at the end of the war. After the Korean War began, West Germany was allowed to join the North Atlantic Treaty Organization and was permitted to set up armed forces in 1955.

Those pariahs of Europe, Spain and Portugal, also became respectable allies within the Western anti-Communist alliance in the 1950s. At the end of the war, the United States, Britain, and France had publicly called for Franco's overthrow. By 1953, however, in exchange for the right to build military bases on Spanish soil, the United States extended economic aid to Spain. In 1955 Spain was admitted to the United Nations, although not to NATO. The role of the fascist party, the *Falange,* had never been great under Franco, and it now almost disappeared within a regime of pragmatic technicians, monarchists, and Catholic businessmen (members of a lay order called *Opus dei*) who presided over the beginnings of rapid economic growth.

Portugal's Salazar had always enjoyed a better press than Franco because he had not been personally involved in the 1926 military *coup* against the Portuguese Republic, and because Portugal had provided Allied bases in the Azores during the war. Thus, although flags flew at half-mast in Lisbon following the news of Hitler's death in May 1945, Portugal was a founding member of NATO in 1949. Abandoning his policy of economic stability in the 1950s, Salazar accepted loans from the

United States and undertook economic development that heralded the eventual end of Portugal's static, hierarchical society. Even when Salazar suffered a disabling stroke in September 1968 at the age of seventy-nine, his authoritarian regime remained intact until 1974, with single-candidate elections and strict control of information.

After their electoral victory of October 1951, the British Tories enjoyed power until 1964, the longest unbroken Conservative rule in modern British history.[11] To be sure, this was no reactionary party. British Conservatives under Churchill and his successors (Anthony Eden, 1955–57; Harold MacMillan, 1957–63; Sir Alec Douglas-Home, 1963–64) accepted the main elements of the welfare state. Road transport and steel were denationalized, and partial fees were imposed on medical services in 1957, but on the whole, the Conservatives—especially MacMillan—frankly accepted the mixed economic system created by Labour from 1945 to 1951.

The French Fourth Republic shifted back to the center after conservatives made their first substantial postwar showing in the elections of 1951. Antoine Pinay, premier in 1952 and the first conservative to head a French government after the war, reassured French investors by his very presence, rather like Poincaré in 1926. Pinay reduced French inflation and reestablished a more stable franc on which the postwar economic boom began to build. Although the elections of 1956 gave the French Socialists (SFIO) a strategic position, they could not rule without allies. Refusing Communist support, Socialist Guy Mollet maintained the longest government of the Fourth Republic (sixteen months, February 1956 to June 1957) through the expedient of satisfying the center and right by his vigorous prosecution of the Algerian War.

Colonial Wars

Both France and Britain poured enormous energy in the 1950s into the losing struggle to maintain their world possessions and influence. The French were involved in one colonial war or another from 1945 to 1961, which meant that France, alone among Western European nations, knew incessant war for almost a quarter century after 1939. The Indochina War (1945–54) involved only professional soldiers, but their defeat by the Communist Vietminh generated a passionate anticommunism and a bitterness against the Fourth Republic's ineffectiveness that came to full fruition when the officers found the whole process beginning again in Algeria (1954–61).

French draftees were mobilized for the war against the Algerian independence movement. In this way, French civilians for the first time shared the French Army's frustration at the failure of modern weapons to deal with guerrillas hidden in rocky hills and sympathetic villages. As cases of French atrocities began to be revealed, life in France in the late

[11]Even the Liberal party's eclipse following Gladstone's divisive adoption of Home Rule for Ireland gave the Tories briefer periods of rule: from 1886 to 1892, and from 1895 to 1905.

1950s was poisoned by bitter division between critics of a cruel, fruitless war and those who saw France defending Western civilization against Communist–Arab barbarism. The resentments of officers, ideological anti-Communists, and frightened French settlers in Algeria finally boiled over in an uprising against the ineffective Fourth Republic in Algiers in May 1958. Unable to get the Army or police to obey orders to crush the rebellion, the Fourth Republic gave way, unmourned, to the strong presidency of de Gaulle and a more authoritarian Fifth Republic. The one Cold War revolution in Western Europe had been nationalist and authoritarian.

The British also poured their dwindling resources into imperial holding operations. In the 1950s, they struggled against oil nationalization in Iran, tried to mediate an intractible civil war between Greeks and Turks on Cyprus, and tested the first British atomic bomb in 1952. They were successful in crushing a revolt by Chinese in Malaya, but only at the price of granting Malayan independence.

One of the most spectacular European military operations in the 1950s was the Suez Campaign of 1956. Britain and France had stepped into the vacuum left by the collapse of the Ottoman Empire in 1918. Arab resentment at seeing their national aspirations thwarted by British mandates over Palestine and Iraq and French mandates over Syria and the Lebanon simmered between the wars. It was raised to fever pitch by the Jews' success in creating a separate state in part of Palestine in 1948. A new generation of angry young Arab middle-class leaders, such as the Egyptian Colonel Gamal Abdel Nasser, threw out some of the corrupt pro-Western monarchies of the Middle East and turned to the Soviet Union for aid. Egypt and Syria accepted Soviet arms in 1955. Then, when the United States refused to provide funds to Egypt for a new high dam at Aswan on the Nile, Nasser nationalized the Suez Canal. Britain, France, and Israel devised a joint lightning attack that was supposed to seize the canal and Cairo. When the operation took too long, and the Soviets threatened to intervene, the United States brought pressure on Anthony Eden, Guy Mollet, and Israeli Premier David Ben-Gurion to withdraw their forces and accept United Nations mediation.

The Suez Campaign elicited the first public display of parallel United States–Soviet concern to restrain crises. And it showed Europeans that their prestige and independence were limited, regardless of whether the superpowers got along or whether they quarreled. The humiliation of Suez suggested to many Europeans that the old European states could accomplish nothing by isolated action.

The former Great Powers of Europe no longer had the capacity to act freely on a world stage dominated by superpowers. Many Europeans felt this loss keenly enough to subordinate traditional national identities to the ideal of some larger European unity.

Western Europe: The Movement for Union

There were two possible kinds of response. Europeans could throw themselves into the arms of one superpower to save themselves from the other. Or they could unite their fragmented energies into a larger unit—a united Europe—and become a new superpower in their own right. Europeans did some of both after 1945.

A sense of Continental European identity went back as far as Latin Christendom. After the modern European nation-states had taken shape and had waged repeated wars against one another, there were periodic proposals for some substitute to the system of competing sovereign states. Satisfied powers proposed international organization to preserve the *status quo,* from the European federation and arbitration council proposed by the Abbé de Saint-Pierre at the end of the reign of Louis XIV (1713) through Tsar Alexander I's Holy Alliance of 1815 to the 1930 proposal of a United States of Europe by French leaders Herriot and Briand. After the First World War, European businessmen proposed organizing the European economy against American competition. Europeans on the left, from utopians like Saint-Simon to Marxist internationalists, expected revolution to replace warring dynasties and business firms with a united world of productive workers. The schemes that came closest to realization were those backed by conquest: the spread of the French revolutionary constitution across Europe by Napoleon I, and Hitler's European Economic Sphere (*Grosswirtschafts-raum*) organized against Russia and the United States.

The liberation of 1945 made ideas of European union both current and practicable: current, because Europeans vowed then never to allow their national rivalries to provoke another such war, and practicable, because the totality of destruction left borders fluid. Left-leaning European resistance movements spoke hopefully of a "European federation, democratic, open to all European peoples including England and the USSR."[12] The conservative anti-Hitler movement in Germany, which had hoped for a separate peace with the Anglo-Americans in time to turn together on the Russians, advocated rather a "Europe unified on the base of Christianity and German predominance, designed to avert Bolshevism."[13]

Architects of European Union

When steps were actually taken toward European union in the late 1940s, the Cold War had so intensified that the anti-Bolshevik motive mingled with the desire to end European fratricide. Many of the architects of a new Europe came from the Catholic Rhineland, the border terrain across which Frenchmen and Germans had been killing each other for centuries. On the French side was Robert Schuman, foreign minister ten times in the four years after 1948. Schuman came

---

[12]Henri Michel and Boris Mirkine-Guetzévitch, *Les Idées politiques et sociales de la Résistance* (Paris, 1954), p. 399.
[13]Ernst Jünger, *L'Appel,* quoted in Flanner, p. 273.

from one of those borderland families that had lived under both French and German flags and had seen the horrors of war too often. Schuman himself had been a German officer in the First World War, a French deputy for restored Alsace after 1919, and a founder of the French Christian Democratic party (MRP) in 1945. Indeed, between Schuman and his colleague George Bidault, the MRP controlled the French Foreign Ministry for the first eight years and twenty ministries of the Fourth Republic.

Further down the Rhine on the German side was Konrad Adenauer, the Catholic mayor of Cologne in the 1920s. As an opponent of Protestant Social Democratic Prussia, Adenauer had been at least marginally involved in plans for an autonomous Rhineland state in the early 1920s. The Nazi regime removed him from office and subjected him to periods of internment. As the German Christian Democrat leader and first chancellor of West Germany after 1949, Adenauer was ready to listen to Schuman, as was the Italian Christian Democrat leader Alcide De Gasperi.

These Christian Democrat architects of European unity were joined by some anti-Communist socialists, whose traditional internationalism was colored by fear of further Soviet expansion. The Belgian socialist leader Paul-Henri Spaak, prime minister of his country after 1947, spoke of the "creation of a Europe united economically and politically" as the work to which he gave "the most heart, will, and sustained effort."[14] Spaak was to be the first president of the OEEC, the European organization of recipients of Marshall Plan aid, and later was to be secretary-general of NATO. The Labour government's foreign secretary, Ernest Bevin, supported cooperation among the non-Communist European nations without accepting full British integration into a larger unit.

European union also had fervent supporters among Western European businessmen and high civil servants. Long accustomed to regulated markets and convinced that the individual European states offered too narrow scope for business, scientific, or technological advances, businessmen like the Frenchman Jean Monnet worked for a unified European economy on the scale of the United States.

Pressures for Union

Economic rationalization and Cold War pressures provided the immediate impetus for Western European union. "Europeans, let us be modest. It is the fear of Stalin and the daring views of [General] Marshall which led us into the right path," wrote Spaak.[15] The United States government, committed to efficiency as well as to prevention of a return to the closed economic nationalisms of the 1930s, required that Marshall Plan funds be funneled through an integrated multinational agency, the

[14]Paul-Henri Spaak, *Combats inachevés,* Vol. 2 (Paris, 1969), p. 11.
[15]*Ibid.,* p. 12.

Organization of European Economic Cooperation, rather than given outright to individual states.

Stalin's acts in 1948 stimulated military alliances in Western Europe. The Czech *coup* of February 1948 and the Berlin Blockade of the summer of 1948 convinced a number of Western Europeans that Russia would be more powerful than Germany in the postwar world. Suddenly nothing seemed to stand between the most powerful land army on earth and the English Channel. As de Gaulle said in 1947, the Russian Army was "no further from France than two laps of a bicycle race." It is difficult to convey vividly enough the dread felt by Western Europeans in the late 1940s that the Soviet armies would march west.

The first Western European responses were traditional military alliances. Britain and France had already concluded a mutual defense agreement, the Treaty of Dunkirk, on March 4, 1947: it provided the firm Continental obligation that the British had steadfastly refused after the First World War. This treaty was directed explicitly against German revival. Immediately after the Czech *coup,* on March 17, 1948, Britain

COLD WAR EUROPE

NATO Forces: 2.2 million men.
    21 combat divisions (Incl. 5 U.S. divisions)
    6000 aircraft at 175 airbases in Western
    Europe. Arrays of atomic weapons, including long
    and short range missiles (Thors, Matadors, Redstones,
    and Corporals) and battlefield missiles.

◾ Members of NATO
   (Plus U.S.A. and Canada)

◾ Members of Warsaw Pact

Warsaw Pact Forces: 3.4 million men
    Outside Soviet Union: 101 combat divisions
                (72 satellite, 29 Russian)
    Inside Soviet Union: 146 combat divisions
    1000 or more jet bombers and 600 jet fighters
    based in Eastern Europe.
    Several thousand missiles of the 700-mile range
    and 1500-mile range

and France joined with the Benelux countries[16] in the Treaty of Brussels
to form a common defense system, directed this time at the Soviet threat.

By themselves the Western European nations were no match for the
250 Soviet divisions stationed in Eastern Europe. Only the United States
could begin to match Soviet armed power. At that time America was just
beginning to reverse its postwar demobilization. The major political step
in Washington was the Vandenberg resolution of June 1948,[17] sponsored by Arthur Vandenberg, Republican senator from Michigan who
converted from isolationism. The Vandenberg resolution advocated
American association with regional collective defense arrangements
elsewhere in the world, a striking departure from the rapid American
withdrawal of troops in 1918 and 1919 and in 1945 and 1946, and from
the political isolationism of the prewar Republican party.

Union for Defense: The Creation of NATO

Armed with the promise of bipartisan United States support, British
Foreign Secretary Ernest Bevin led the way in creating a five-nation
defense coordinating command under the Treaty of Brussels. Field
Marshal Bernard L. Montgomery, the greatest British commander of
the Second World War, set up an international command at the palace
of Fontainebleau, outside Paris, in the summer of 1948. By then, Bevin
and Spaak were exploring the idea of a much broader collective defense
arrangement against the Soviet Union. The result was NATO—the
North Atlantic Treaty Organization—created on April 4, 1949.

NATO went far beyond the traditional European military alliance.
The United States, for the first time, was committed to a long-term
military union outside the Americas in peacetime. Together with
Canada and ten European nations, the United States agreed to a
twenty-year alliance in which "an attack upon one" of the members in
Europe, North Africa, or North America would be considered an "attack
upon all" (Article 5). In pooling their military units under international
command, the European members integrated their forces more closely
than they had in any previous military alliance. The participants joined
not merely in the defense of territory but to "safeguard the freedom,
common heritage, and civilization of their peoples" and to bring about
the closer integration of the North Atlantic area. At the end of 1950,
the Supreme Allied Commander–Europe (SACEUR), American General Dwight Eisenhower, set up his international command at Paris.

Problems in European Unity

Uniting the Western democracies for defense raised two very thorny
issues. Who was included in the "free world" (as the phrase soon
described it)? Semifascist Portugal was a NATO member from the

---

[16]Belgium, the Netherlands, and Luxemburg had formed a Customs Union, or free-trade
area, in 1944. Although each nation retained its full sovereignty, Benelux regulated the
economies of the three members as a unit.

[17]Only four senators voted against; seventy-nine for.

beginning; Greece and Turkey joined in October 1951; should West Germany be included? And how far should the European nations go in submerging their individual sovereignties in a supranational body?

The issue of Germany's role in the anti-Soviet alliance dominated Western European foreign policy from the formation of the Federal German Republic in May 1949 until West Germany's inclusion in NATO in October 1954. The issue of supranational authority was entwined with it. If Germany were rearmed, would German officers then command French or Dutch or British troops within NATO? Should European soldiers be organized by national units or should a genuine European army be formed in which German, French, British, Italian, Belgian, and Dutch soldiers mingled in the same unit?

The French were the most sensitive on both points. A probable majority of Frenchmen of all political persuasions was opposed to rearming Germans in any form. But partisans of European unity reasoned that since Germany would eventually rearm in some fashion, the best safeguard for the future was to submerge German soldiers in a fully integrated European army. The outbreak of the Korean War in June 1950 made the question urgent, as the United States pressed vigorously for West German rearmament. To block the creation of a separate Germany Army, the French Premier René Pleven proposed a truly supranational army, the European Defense Community (EDC). Although Pleven's proposal received support in other European states in 1951 and 1952, the French parliament itself voted EDC down in June 1954. After that, the French got what they least wanted. Not only was Germany rearmed, but a separate German Army was recreated only ten years after Hitler's death. Although still forbidden possession of nuclear, biological, and chemical weapons by the terms of its entry into NATO, West Germany was well on its way to becoming a major weight in the Western alliance by 1955.

German officials attended their first NATO ministers' meeting in Paris on May 7, 1955, almost ten years to the day after the German armies' surrender at Reims, May 9, 1945. The chief German military representative, who came discreetly dressed in civilian clothes, was General Hans Speidel, a senior officer in the German occupation of France from 1941 to 1944. It seemed, wrote Janet Flanner, "the strangest week since the end of the war, because all that was postwar ended too."[18]

The other thorny issue, still to be resolved, was the supranational nature of the new Europe. Should Europe remain a coalition of sovereign states or should the new European institutions possess authority to make sovereign decisions affecting defense, foreign policy, and finances? NATO units were international only at the senior command level, and the failure of EDC in 1954 determined that Western European nations would not relinquish sovereignty over their individual armed services. Many Europeans remained passionately committed,

[18]Flanner, p. 272.

however, to the creation of supranational political institutions to form the basis of a new Western European state.

Attempt at Political Union: The Council of Europe

The first attempt to found common political institutions for Europe was a kind of European parliament, the Council of Europe, set up at Strasbourg in May 1949. In some prointegration quarters, the Council of Europe was regarded as the future legislative branch of a United States of Europe. The British, however, under both Labour and Conservative governments, prevented this and all other bodies to which they belonged from acquiring any independent supranational functions during the 1950s and 1960s. The Labour govenment of 1945 to 1951, like the Scandinavian socialist governments, remained suspicious of a Continental integration movement dominated by Catholics and technocrats. Moreover, British leaders of both parties felt that any absorption of British sovereignty in a new European state was incompatible with Britain's special role as head of the Commonwealth. Although less imperial-minded than the Tories, British Labour was strongly attached to the preferential trading agreements that brought inexpensive food from Canada and New Zealand. British Labour was also insular. Its delegate to the creation of the Council of Europe, William Whiteley, had never before been out of England.

The Council of Europe, therefore, was not the step toward political integration that its first president, Paul-Henri Spaak, and others had hoped. Since its members were not elected directly by Europeans but were delegations of parliamentarians sent by each member country prorated by size (three each for Iceland and Luxemburg; eighteen for France, Germany, Italy, Britain), the council represented governments rather than a popular electorate to which it was directly answerable. Its members were chosen more for purposes of political patronage than for their commitment to integrated Europe. And even though the council eventually included parliamentarians of sixteen nations, its annual meetings at Strasbourg were better known for good food and abstract language than for any independent political force. As the British political scientist Wilfrid Pickles observed, the Council of Europe resembled a real parliament about as much as an adulterous weekend at Brighton resembled marriage: "it offers some of the pleasures but none of the responsibilities."[19]

With the parliamentary route to European integration blocked by the stillborn Council of Europe and the European army route to integration blocked by the failure of the European Defense Community, the movement for European unity would have to follow other paths, and it would have to proceed without Britain. Grand designs for political union from the top came to seem utopian. Instead, supranational

[19]Quoted in Howard Bliss, *The Political Development of the European Community: A Documentary Collection* (Waltham, Mass., 1970), p. 5.

institutions took root and grew on the economic level, and with limited functions. Partisans of wider European union could take comfort in the hope that as supranational decisionmaking became established in limited economic sectors, the implications of these decisions might spill over into political arenas and bring about an organic growth of common institutions.

Economic Union: The European Coal and Steel Community and the Common Market

The Marshall Plan had prompted the creation of the multinational OEEC in 1947 to disburse the funds. The OEEC was only advisory, however, and could not make policy for its member states. The first step toward a genuine economic supranational institution was the Schuman Plan. French Foreign Minister Robert Schuman proposed in 1950 that "the entire Franco-German production of coal and steel be placed under a common High Authority," as "the first step in the federation of Europe." In this fashion, war between France and Germany would become "not merely inconceivable but physically impossible." Robert Schuman's daring initiative produced the European Coal and Steel Community (ECSC) of 1951.

The Schuman Plan was a radical departure from other moves toward European unity both in the completeness of the integration proposed and in the limited sector to which integration was to be applied. In that way, it neatly sidestepped the deadlocked debate between political federalists and unionists. Since its functions of economic planning were new, it did not amputate precious prerogatives from existing states nor trespass on sensitive areas of military command or political choice. In political terms, it offered a dramatic gain to those Europeans who longed for some way to transcend the old nationalisms. In economic terms, it promised to replace the marginally profitable steel mills and coal mines previously kept going for national purposes with the most efficient exploitation of Western European coal and steel irrespective of national boundaries. For the French, it offered some degree of international control over the inevitable but feared German economic recovery. For the Germans, it offered a chance to escape from some of the economic interference of the Allied occupation authorities (still dedicated to "decartelizing" Germany) via a voice in the international management of European coal and steel.

The most striking novelty of the European Coal and Steel Community was its top administrative agency, the High Authority. This executive committee of nine technical experts[20] regulated the coal and steel interests of the six member states: France, Germany, Italy, and the Benelux countries. Since they were not subject to electoral control and since they could not be dismissed during their term of office, members of

[20]Eight were named by the six participant governments; the ninth was chosen by cooptation by the other eight members.

the High Authority enjoyed an important measure of power independent of the member state governments. They could set and regulate prices, levy fees to cover the costs of their operations (a form of taxing power), and encourage or discourage investment for the most efficient use of resources according to purely technical criteria. In the one limited sector in its charge, the High Authority introduced genuine supranational decisionmaking to European institutions.

The European Coal and Steel Community was a success. Coinciding with the beginning of the postwar boom in 1953 and no doubt helping to encourage it, the community acquired a reputation for stimulating economic growth that it would have had difficulty winning under depression conditions. Early success overcame the suspicions of both businessmen and labor unions. At the moment when the merger of state sovereignties was suffering an apparently mortal setback with the defeat of the European Defense Community in the French parliament in 1954, the thriving European Coal and Steel Community pointed the way toward a different mode of unification: sector-by-sector economic integration, followed by spillover into such political realms as wages and social policy.

The European Coal and Steel Community provided the roots for the European Common Market. The Common Market's members were the same: France, Germany, Italy, Belgium, Holland, and Luxembourg, known as "the Six." Its concept of economic integration by sectors was a lesson learned from the European Coal and Steel Community. The immediate impetus for its creation was the European humiliation of the Suez Campaign of 1956. The Treaties of Rome (March 25, 1957) united the Six in two agencies: the European Atomic Energy Agency (Euratom) and the European Economic Community (EEC), better known as the Common Market. They went into effect on January 1, 1958, the start of a new generation of European integration.

In its simplest terms, the Common Market proposed to make Western Europe's 175 million people a single free-trade area, with free movement of goods, capital, and workers within an area comparable to that of the United States. Tariffs between the six members were to be lowered to zero in stages over the following twelve to fifteen years. Since no one member could pursue radically different wage or social security policies or support farm prices in a manner substantially different from that of the other partners without distorting the way the Common Market worked, the expected spillover effect led the EEC into the business of harmonizing the economic and social policies of the Six. Thus the Common Market was far more than merely a free-trade zone like the European Free Trade Area (EFTA) that the British, Danes, Norwegians, Swedes, Swiss, Austrians, and Portuguese (known as "the Outer Seven") set up by way of response in 1959.

Harmonizing social and economic policy among the Six obviously suggested some kind of supranational authority and the transfer to the EEC of powers usually reserved to sovereign states. Here the EEC went less far than had the European Coal and Steel Community. Its .top directing agency, the EEC Executive, resembled the Coal and Steel High Authority in that it was a body of international civil servants whose loyalties tended to be attached to the community as a whole rather than to their country of origin. Overall policies, however, were set by the EEC Council of Ministers who spoke for the member state governments, and a unanimity rule in all important matters gave each member state a veto.

The Common Market took root and flourished. It contributed to as well as profited from the unprecedented prosperity of Europe in the 1960s. It met all its economic deadlines ahead of time. The last internal tariffs were abolished in 1968, after nine years instead of the anticipated twelve to fifteen. Trade among the Six grew steeply: trade between France and Germany, for example, increased by about 40 percent over the first nine years of the EEC. Millions of workers from the backward regions of the Six, such as southern Italy, moved freely to work in France and Germany. A corps of dedicated international civil servants emerged in Brussels to staff the agencies of a new bureaucracy. National animosities abated within the Six to the point where German NATO troops trained on French soil in the middle 1960s almost without public notice. Just over ten years after the Common Market had begun, observers could speak of Europe as an "emergent nation."[21]

Debate over European Union

In the context of the Cold War within which Western European unity began to take shape, its achievements have given rise to debate. Some critics have contended that the European community perpetuated and hardened the division of Europe into two satellite blocs. The Six were indeed a "little Europe" solution to the problem of regional or Continental cooperation, conforming to the lines drawn by American and Soviet influence after 1945. The entry of a separate West Germany into NATO in 1955 and into the Common Market in 1958, in particular, placed an armed and economically booming West Germany athwart any proposals for a wider, more neutral form of European unification. In 1957 the Polish Foreign Minister Adam Rapacki proposed the Rapacki Plan for a denuclearized neutral zone in central Europe. It found support from the Bevanites in England and from some socialists on the Continent, but it was inconceivable unless NATO were dismantled, which was certainly one of its intentions. On a more general level, it may be that the very success of the Western European response to the Soviet danger kept the lines drawn longer in Europe than they might otherwise have been. In any case, there was certainly little evidence in the 1950s of Soviet willingness to permit a wider European unification on truly independent terms.

[21]Carl J. Friedrich, *Europe: An Emergent Nation?* (New York, 1969). Chapter 20 takes a closer look at European integration after 1960.

Other critics have charged that European economic unification consolidated the power of giant corporations and of authoritarian experts, without parliamentary control, in a new European economy in which working people had even less opportunity than before to control their own lives. The European Economic Community was bound to reflect the outlook of the Christian Democrats, such as Adenauer, Erhard, Schuman, and De Gasperi, and of the businessmen, like Monnet, who created it. The Common Market, charged a Communist deputy in the French parliament in January 1957, would be "the dream of the German trusts . . . a little Europe under the sponsorship of the Pope."[22]

Even after discounting the partisan sharpness of that charge, there was some ground for concern. The Common Market clearly gave an impetus to the growth of giant corporations. As American investors established branch plants in the new tariff-free area, the Six tolerated and even encouraged the amalgamation of their countries' firms in order to compete on a world scale. Rather than Europeanwide firms, giant enterprises began to appear in each member country. French steel producers were reduced to two giants; the firm of Saint-Gobain-Péchiney combined earlier giants in glass, chemicals, and machinery into a vast new conglomerate. The German firm of Krupp recovered its prewar power and more. Moreover, the technical bureau at Brussels created a new level of decisionmaking that was beyond control of parliament or of concerted strike action by workers still organized largely on national lines. To be sure, the Six continued a high level of social benefits, and wages rose with the general prosperity.

At the level of economic performance, no one could doubt the success of the European Economic Community. The residents of drab, cheerless East Berlin, whose streets were still marked by shell holes in the middle 1950s, could see the lights of the main West Berlin commercial street, the *Kurfürstendamm,* with its sidewalk cafés, neon signs, and traffic jams of Mercedes-Benz and Volkswagens. Under Soviet control, Eastern Europe had taken a quite divergent course toward economic integration and forced Cold War unity.

The Soviet Union: From Stalin to Khrushchev

The tensions of the Cold War tightened the Soviet regime, which had already reasserted orthodoxy and bent the Soviet populations, as we have seen, to a massive task of industrial development. The burden of industrial growth was made still heavier by Russia's Cold War armaments expenditures. Scarce resources were diverted into an enormous effort of military research and development that produced an atomic test (1949), nuclear weapons (1953), high-performance MIG fighters

---

[22]Quoted in F. Roy Willis, *France, Germany, and the New Europe, 1945–67.* rev. ed. (Stanford, Calif., 1968), p. 263.

(1950–53), and the world's first space satellite, *Sputnik* (1957). The international challenges of the Cold War only heightened Stalin's penchants for secrecy, iron autocracy, and all-pervasive police control. Russians lived out Stalin's last years in the shadow of anticipated war and harsh repression.

Lavrentii Beria's secret police kept even Stalin's highest associates ill at ease. It seemed as though a new purge was beginning, and a more overtly anti-Semitic one, when a group of nine Jewish doctors were arrested in January 1953 on charges of shortening the lives of Soviet officials. Before the "doctors' plot" could be developed further, however, Stalin died of a stroke on March 9, 1953. The doctors were released. The man who had been more powerful than any tsar was buried beside Lenin in the great mausoleum in the Kremlin wall in a mixture of awe and relief.

The Struggle for Power, 1953–58

Stalin's death set off an internal struggle for power at the top of the Soviet system, the outlines of which can still be only dimly glimpsed. Russia was ruled from 1953 to 1957 by "collective leadership," perhaps less from conviction than from the inability of any one of Stalin's successors to dominate the others. The first to disappear was Beria, the secret police head, who was dismissed from his posts and the party in July 1953 and executed in December. George Malenkov seemed the principal heir to Stalin. A man of bourgeois origins who had learned flexibility in Stalin's personal entourage, Malenkov set a new course by increasing the availablity of consumer goods for the first time since the war. As premier from 1953 to 1955, Malenkov appeared to lean more fully on the postrevolutionary engineers and technicians than on the party.

Nikita Khrushchev had governed the Ukraine for Stalin from 1939 to

Stalin's successors line up at his funeral, March 6, 1953: from left to right, Molotov, Voroshilov, Beria, Malenkov, Bulganin, Khrushchev, Kaganovich, and Mikoyan.

1950 and then directed Soviet agriculture before serving after 1954 as party secretary, the strategic post from which Stalin had earlier risen to power. After Malenkov resigned in 1955 under accusations by party leaders of "anti-Party activity," Khrushchev took on a more and more conspicuous role. In July 1957 he managed to maneuver a number of the old guard (Molotov in particular) out of power. When he assumed the office of premier in 1958, Khrushchev became the first since Stalin's death to unite the political and party offices in his own hands.

Khrushchev never wielded the same power as Stalin, however. A miner's son, he had not learned to read and write until he was in his twenties, but he combined quick intelligence and a keen sense of power with an irrepressible gregariousness. With all the confidence of a successful autodidact, Khrushchev loved to talk, to listen, and to spar verbally with everyone from collective farmers to the General Assembly of the United Nations, to whom he once punctuated his words by pounding on a desk with his shoe. One important reason why Khrushchev lacked the power Stalin had was that the society Stalin had ruled had been transformed. Only 10 percent urban in 1920, Russia was in the late 1950s half city dwellers; once mostly illiterate, Russians now included a large elite of engineers, professionals, and technicians who were loyal to the regime but who demaded more scope for their activity. Stalin's successors had to bring party, military, and elite elements into cooperation; they could no longer simply be bludgeoned into obedience.

The Post-Stalin "Thaw"

The most striking change after Stalin's death was the intellectual "thaw." In the more urban and literate society that Russia had become, a regime had to encourage more voluntary participation if it were not to stagnate; however, Soviet regimes were unaccustomed to criticism and quick to reimpose censorship. The "thaw" was uneven and halting, therefore, but it at least became impossible to return to the intellectual torpor of Stalin's last years. The most celebrated authorized new novel was Vladimir Dudintsev's *Not By Bread Alone* (1957), a rather commonplace morality tale of an idealistic inventor's frustrations at the hands of bureaucracy. The novelty of Dudintsev's book was not in its literary quality, which was mediocre, but in its suggestion that progress came from individualists rather than from the party, and in the fact that its publication was permitted. The far more sophisticated and troubling *Dr. Zhivago* by Boris Pasternak (1957) was published only abroad, and Pasternak was warned that if he went to Stockholm to accept his Nobel Prize in person he would not be allowed to return to the Soviet Union.

The most celebrated moment in the "thaw" was Party Secretary Khrushchev's secret denunciation of Stalin to the Twentieth Party Congress in 1956. This speech, whose contents soon leaked out to the general public, was probably the most influential single utterance in Russia since Lenin's speech at the Finland Station in April 1917. The cruelties of Stalin's purges and police system (in which Khrushchev had participated) were known to all, but for the first time Russians were told by their Communist leaders that Stalin had been not only cruel but incompetent as a war leader in 1941. Tongues were untied. Once some degree of internal criticism was permitted, Stalin's successors found themselves struggling awkwardly during the next generation to set the proper limit between permissible constructive criticism and nonpermissible attacks on the regime.

One way to keep the system on the track was to promise more consumer goods. Khrushchev announced that the Soviet Union would surpass the United States in total production by the 1970s. He replaced the whole centralized economic planning system in 1957 with more flexible regional planning offices to reduce administrative bottlenecks. Admitting that Soviet agriculture had never recovered the precollectivization levels of 1928,[23] Khrushchev launched a characteristically bold cornraising program for animal feed and sent students and soldiers to the southeastern frontier to turn 90 million acres of pastoral land into wheat in his Virgin Lands project. Even though these grandiose schemes fell far short, the lot of the Soviet consumer was clearly improved under Khrushchev.

Another way to keep the system on its track, no doubt, was a vigorous foreign policy. Immediately after Stalin's death, the Soviet leaders had sought a reconciliation with Yugoslavia and had met President Eisenhower in the first Cold War Summit Conference in Geneva in 1955. Once settled in power, however, Khrushchev lashed out aggressively against the West. Between 1958 and 1961 Berlin was the focal point of Soviet pressure. Harrassing Western traffic to Berlin and threatening to

---

[23]Khrushchev admitted in 1953 that the Soviet Union still had 3.5 million fewer cows than in 1941 and 9 million fewer than in 1928. (Edward Crankshaw, *Khrushchev's Russia,* 2nd ed. [London, 1962], p. 83.)

The Berlin Wall, erected by the Russians in 1961, divided many families. Here a wedding party in West Berlin waves to relatives isolated on the other side.

transfer Soviet occupation rights in Berlin unilaterally to the East Germans, Khrushchev tried to force the Western occupying powers out of the city. He established close ties with Syria, Egypt, and the African state of Guinea. In 1960 he used the American blunder of allowing a U-2 spy plane to be caught over the Soviet Union as an excuse to break up another Summit Conference with Eisenhower in Paris. In 1962 he began constructing missile sites in Cuba.

Stalin's successors apparently had to appease several different constituencies by assuring rising output, by reconciling some degree of freedom with internal order, and by winning overseas successes. As the 1960s began, with Khrushchev telling Americans ebulliently that "we will bury you," the Cold War did not seem to be abating.

Eastern Europe: Consolidation and Rebellion 1948–56

Stalin seems to have decided in 1947 and 1948 that Russia must control the Eastern European borderlands tightly or not at all. The initial postwar policy of dual control in which Communists shared power with Social Democrats and peasant parties in National Fronts gave way to one-party Communist regimes, peoples' democracies.

In economic terms, this turning point bore some resemblance to Stalin's decision to collectivize Russian agriculture in 1929. Both industrial growth and agricultural productivity in Eastern Europe had been pressing against constricting ceilings. The postwar land redistribution had left a high proportion of the population in the countryside, occupying small inefficient family farms that produced little surplus wealth to generate industrial growth. The crackdown in Eastern Europe in 1947 and 1948 might be seen in part, then, as an attempt to break this vicious economic circle. Collectivizing and mechanizing agriculture would supposedly enable a small number of farm workers to produce more crops, thereby releasing both surplus population and surplus wealth for faster industrial development.

Forced Consolidation

In one Eastern European country after another after 1947, coercion replaced persuasion in the effort to convert family farms into collectives. The process went furthest in Bulgaria, the closest of the satellites. In one year, 370,000 Bulgarian farms were collectivized. By the end of 1952, 52 percent of the country's arable land was collectivized. The process was slower in Poland, Hungary, and Romania, but the final goal was clear.

The land collectivization, although less violent than it had been in the Soviet Union from 1929 to 1931, did require force and aroused anguished opposition. After initial overt resistance, the peasants adopted the devious strategy of devoting intense care to the one-acre plot authorized for each family's own use, and giving lax attention to the collective lands. With productivity low, agriculture remained the great failure of Eastern European regimes through the 1950s, as in the Soviet Union. More than half the agricultural productivity of the Polish collective farms, for example, is estimated to have come from the peasants' small private plots.

Without surplus wealth from agriculture, industrial growth had to be financed out of low public consumption. The Five-Year Plans adopted by all the peoples' democracies after 1949 placed major emphasis on heavy capital goods, so that consumer goods were extremely scarce. The austerity of life was aggravated by the terms of trade with the Soviet Union. Under commercial treaties between the state trading offices of the Communist bloc countries, the Soviet Union paid low prices for industrial products shipped to Russia, while the peoples' democracies paid higher than world market prices for raw materials imported from the Soviet Union. Under any social system, of course, predominantly agricultural Eastern Europe would have lagged behind Western Europe in economic growth. But economic ties to the Soviet Union, engaged in a gigantic effort not only to recover from the war but to surpass the West, imposed an almost unbearably drab and laborious life on the peoples of Eastern Europe.

In response to Western European unification movements, the Soviet Union led Eastern Europe into supranational organizations. The economic response to the Marshall Plan was the Council for Mutual Economic Assistance (COMECON), established in 1949 to harmonize the socialist economies. Unlike the later Western European Common Market, COMECON included its related superpower, which had a far larger say in COMECON decisions than any one country had in the Common Market. The response to NATO was the military coordination agreement known as the Warsaw Pact (1955), in which the Soviet military weight resembled much more closely that of the United States in NATO.

Peasant grievances, low wages, harsh working conditions, and lack of consumer goods made life in Eastern Europe immensely frustrating. In the absence of any organized opposition these frustrations tended to be expressed in the nationalist terms still so vivid in the successor states. With the unifying German threat largely in abeyance, and with ethnic minorities greatly diminished, discontents were focused on the Soviet

COMMON MARKET AND COMECON

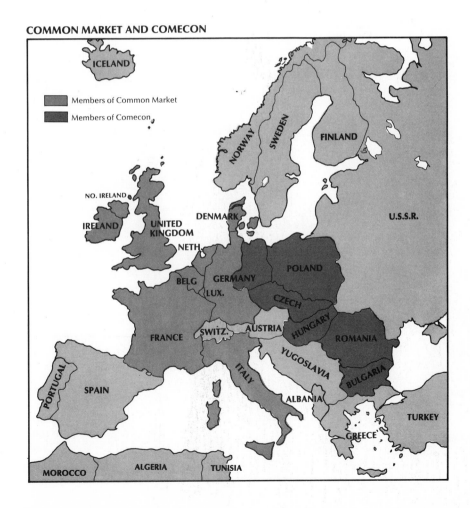

presence. That made the effects of Stalin's death in 1953 particularly volatile in Eastern Europe.

Thaw and Rebellion

The first serious disorders within the peoples' democracies broke out soon after Stalin's death. Continued efforts to squeeze more productivity out of Eastern European workers aroused resentments that were both economic and nationalist. In Czechoslovakia, where worker morale and productivity were extremely low, the regime attempted to force the population to work harder by confiscating savings in May 1953. The result was a massive demonstration in Pilsen, in which workers displayed pictures of Beneš and Masaryk. The most serious troubles occurred in East Berlin. The government's announcement of new norms for construction workers on June 16, 1953, led to a strike that grew on June 17 into a full-fledged revolt. It had to be put down at the cost of twenty-five dead and some six hundred subsequent executions.

Warned by these events, and in consonance with the promise of more consumer goods in the Soviet Union announced by Stalin's successor Malenkov, most of the peoples' democracies announced a new course toward less repressive conditions. Hungarian Premier Imre Nagy (1953–55) went furthest in the quest for a more relaxed, more national

Two East Berlin youths stone a Russian tank during the demonstrations of June 17, 1953.

variant of socialism within the Soviet bloc. Nagy announced a halt in land collectivization and permitted some collectives to disband, so that about 70 percent of the farm land in Hungary remained in private hands at the end of 1953. Nagy also diverted more resources into consumer goods. He relaxed police control to the point where Budapest became one of the most outspoken of Eastern European capitals. Nagy said that Hungary must find its own way to socialism, "to cut our coat according to our cloth." When Nagy's model, Malenkov, fell in the Soviet Union, Nagy's enemies, led by Hungarian Party Secretary Mátyás Rákosi, removed him from office.

Reactions to Khrushchev's de-Stalinization speech in 1956 were even more frightening to the Soviet leadership. In both Poland and Hungary, Communist intellectuals took the lead in exploring ways to make their regimes more open and more national within the socialist system. In Poland, the former Stalinist poet Adam Wazyk formed the Crooked Circle Club, which soon spread a libertarian, national message. His "Poem for Adults" of August 1956 demanded

> Clear truths
> The bread of liberty,
> And resplendent reason.[24]

Workers in Poznan, Poland, demonstrated in July 1956 carrying banners reading "bread and liberty," and the police and Army could not be relied on to use force. The Soviet regime accepted the recall of Wladyslav Gomulka, who had been out of favor since 1947 for advocating a Polish way to socialism. In what many Poles referred to as "spring in October," Gomulka stopped the collectivization of land, set a more moderate course toward the Church (Poland is the most Catholic country of Eastern Europe), and established himself as the indispensable guarantor until 1970 of a regime that would be both loyal to the Russian alliance and socialist in its own way—peasant and Catholic.

Polish de-Stalinization was carried through peacefully; in Hungary, de-Stalinization led to insurrection followed by harsh repression. The Budapest Communist intellectuals formed the Petöfi Circle, named for a poet of the 1848 revolutions, to spread their message. The ironworkers of Csepel Island in the Danube led demonstrations for better conditions. When the authorities forbade a demonstration on October 20, 1956, in sympathy for Gomulka's new program, 200,000 protestors, mostly students, gathered in Budapest chanting Petöfi's verse, "We shall never again be slaves." That night Imre Nagy was recalled to be premier.

Events might have been channeled into something parallel to the Polish compromise, but shots were fired, and the demonstrations became uncontrollable. Soviet flags and Stalin's statue were pulled down in Budapest, revolt spread to the rural collectives, and Revolutionary and Workers' Councils assumed control of some localities. On October

---

[24]Quoted in François Fejtö, *Histoire des démocraties populaires,* Vol. 2 (Paris, 1969), p. 71.

29 it was announced that Soviet troops were being withdrawn. On October 30, 1956, Nagy announced a return to a multiparty system and a coalition government of Communists, Social Democrats, and smallholders "as in 1945." The Russians, however, unwilling to accept the loss of Hungary and covered by the diversion of international attention to the Suez Campaign, withdrew only to organize the military reconquest of Hungary. After November 4, a Soviet armed force including 2500 tanks spread through Hungary, shelling thousands of buildings in Budapest and killing at least 3000 Hungarians.[25] An estimated 200,000 refugees, or nearly 2 percent of the total population, fled to the West. A deeply wounded Hungary was restored to firm Communist rule under János Kádár.

The agony of Hungary in November 1956 showed clearly that while the Soviet Union would permit some leeway within the satellite countries, as in Poland, it would go to almost any lengths to preserve the essence of Russian control of the Socialist bloc. It showed, too, that the United States would not intervene behind the Iron Curtain. Whatever change was to come in the peoples' democracies would have to come by internal evolution.

[25]Hungarian government statistics, in United Nations, General Assembly, *Report of the Special Committee on the Problem of Hungary*, Suppl. 18 (A/3592) (New York, 1957), p. 33. Outside estimates ran as high as 20,000 Hungarians and 7000 Russians killed.

The great bronze statue of Stalin tumbled by the crowd in Budapest, November 1956.

Suggestions for Further Reading

In addition to works cited at the end of Chapter 17, the following are especially useful for the history of Western European nations in the 1950s and 1960s: Philip Williams and Martin Harrison, *Politics and Society in de Gaulle's Republic** (1972), the best study of the French Fifth Republic; Stanley Payne, *Franco's Spain** (1967); and George Hills, *Spain* (1970), both relatively informative on the recent period.

Good brief introductions to the Western European unification movement are Wilfrid F. Knapp, *Unity and Nationalism in Europe Since 1945** (1969), and Roger Morgan, *Western European Politics Since 1945** (1973). Ernst Haas, *Beyond the Nation-State** (1968) proposed the spillover theory of integration, whereby success in integrating one function would help draw other functions into coordination. Much contemporary writing on European integration becomes quickly dated, but among the more recent or enduring works on the earlier phases are: Miriam Camps, *European Unification in the Sixties** (1966); Uwe Kitzinger, *The European Common Market and Community** (1967); Richard Mayne, *The Community of Europe** (1963); and Howard Bliss, ed., *The Political Development of the European Community: A Documentary Collection** (1970).

F. Roy Willis, *France, Germany, and the New Europe, 1945–1967,** rev. ed. (1968) is the best account of relations between the two major partners in Western European integration. The same author's *Italy Chooses Europe** (1971) is a model study of the internal implications of participation in the European Community.

Robert McGeehan, *The German Rearmament Question* (1971) surveys one of the most pressing European conflicts of the 1950s.

On Eastern European integration, see Michael Kaser, *Comecon* (1965).

Wolfgang Leonhard, *The Kremlin Since Stalin* (1962) is the best account of the struggle for power in Russia after 1953. See also Edward Crankshaw, *Khrushchev* (1966).

The most comprehensive work on Eastern Europe after 1953 is François Fejtö, *A History of the Peoples' Democracies: Eastern Europe Since Stalin* (1971). See also J. F. Brown, *The New Eastern Europe* (1967), and Stephen Fischer-Galati, *Eastern Europe in the Sixties* (1967).

On Hungary in 1956, see Paul E. Zinner, *Revolution in Hungary* (1962); Ferenc A. Vali, *Rift and Revolution in Hungary* (1961); United Nations, General Assembly, *Report of the Special Committee on the Problem of Hungary,* Suppl. 18 (A/3592), 1957. Janos Radványi, *Hungary and the Superpowers* (1972) examines the international ramifications.

For Poland, see Nicholas Bethell, *Gomulka: His Poland and His Communism* (1969).

THE "NEW EUROPE": CONSUMER SOCIETIES AND MASS CULTURE IN THE 1960S

19

After the First World War, Europeans had struggled to regain the prosperity of 1914, that *belle epoque* to which men of property, at least, looked back with nostalgia. In the best years of the late 1920s boom, European production had not far exceeded that of 1914. During the depressed 1930s, production figures had fallen lower. In 1938 only Germany and Russia were producing much more than they had produced in 1914.

After the Second World War, the Western European economies not only recovered those long-sought 1914 levels; they surged ahead to reach the highest levels of prosperity they had ever known. Postwar recovery was completed by about 1953 in most of Western Europe, and the harsh late 1940s began to recede into memory. That milestone passed, the Western European economies burst into spectacular growth. By the mid-1960s, production in Italy, Germany, and Holland, for example, was three times the 1914 level. Although the pace of growth slackened at times (as in the minor "recessions" of 1966 and 1967 in England and Germany), modern Europe had never experienced so long a period of growth uninterrupted by depression or financial crisis. Poverty was still very real in southern Italy, the Balkans, and Spain, and the Eastern European economies remained far behind, but there were now whole regions in Europe, such as Scandinavia, where poverty was virtually unknown. The 1914 figures—along with nostalgia for some past *belle epoque*—had become simply irrelevant for Europeans of the 1960s. Riches had never been so great or so widespread.

A quarter century of almost uninterrupted boom by the early 1970s was a phenomenon that the business cycle specialists of the 1930s had not trained economists to interpret. Postwar reconstruction was bound to stimulate the European economies for a time. But economic growth continued long after that immediate impetus had been spent, and beyond what past history of boom and bust had permitted anyone to expect. What sustained this latest boom?

The credit claimed by state planners and Keynesian economists in France, Italy, and England could not be extended to Germany, where the success of "Social Market Economy" required some explanation other than state economic intervention. Even there, however, the state increased public investment when German economic growth slowed down alarmingly in the "recession" of 1966 and 1967. Each government's determination to keep employment high had something to do with maintaining the boom.

The increasing speed of technological advance also deserved credit for continued growth. Technical innovation moved much faster from idea to commercial application in the twentieth century, especially after the technological stimulus of the Second World War. It had taken more than a century for the steam engine to evolve from the first sketches to the first practical devices of the eighteenth century; nuclear power, by contrast, went from theory to producing electricity in less than a generation. Similarly, in the electronic field, radio tubes had not gone into mass production until the 1920s, even though Thomas Edison had made a prototype in 1884. By contrast, transistors (1948) and integrated circuits (1958) went into widespread use almost at once in radios and computers.[1] Wider technical education and commercial expectations hastened the application of inventions, which in turn generated new production.

The most decisive changes seem to have occurred in the realm of attitudes. After a long generation of relative stagnation, from 1914 to about 1953, Europeans recaptured some of the feverish energy of the

[1]These examples come from David S. Landes, *The Unbound Prometheus* (Cambridge, Mass., 1969), pp. 518–19.

Industrial Revolution's beginnings of the late eighteenth and early nineteenth centuries. Governments and businessmen began to value growth more than security. Consumers who snapped up television sets, refrigerators, and automobiles, and then replaced them every few years, formed what looked like a permanent boom market.

The result was what Andrew Shonfield, a defender of the apparent success of "neocapitalism" in Western Europe in the 1960s, has called "supergrowth."[2] Supergrowth was not simply an expanded version of prewar European economies. It did not resemble the normalcy of the late 1920s. It built on two elements with self-sustaining momentum: high mass comsumption, and continued state welfare and planning policies. And it was accompanied by an apparent decline in class conflict.

Consumer Societies

British rationing, the last vestige of wartime controls in Western Europe, ended in 1954.[3] Until then, no British boy or girl under eighteen had ever known free shopping. The end of fifteen years of scarcity would have produced something of a buying spree under any conditions. Among the young, it was accompanied by new ideas about saving and spending. In the British postwar welfare state no one need starve in unemployment or old age, or go without medicine. So, unlike their elders, young workers began to spend what they earned. This British pattern was common to much of Europe.

In the early 1950s, an American social anthropologist, Lawrence Wylie, lived with his family for a year in a remote village in southern France. He found the villagers cautious and parsimonious, distrustful of the state and of their neighbors, and conditioned by ages of war and revolution against flaunting their little savings in conspicuous consumption. The men were so pessimistic about renewed war that they would not make any long-term investment.

> Plant an apricot orchard so the Russians and Americans can use it as a battlefield? Thanks, not so dumb.[4]

Then the Wylies returned for a visit in 1961. They found the old women in black shawls beginning to be outnumbered by noisy children and brightly clad young women. The men were now willing to borrow to buy tractors in the expectation that economic growth and political stability could be counted on. Their wives were trying out washing machines.

In both examples, the demand function of the economy had been transformed. Purchases did not decline when wartime destruction had been replaced, because welfare states diminished the necessity to save against disaster, because planned economies seemed to reduce the risk

[2] Andrew Shonfield, *Modern Capitalism: The Changing Balance of Public and Private Power,* corrected ed. (Oxford, 1969).
[3] Rationing continued in some Eastern European countries into the 1960s.
[4] Lawrence Wylie, *Village in the Vaucluse,* 2nd ed. (Cambridge, Mass., 1964), p. 33.

Naples in the early 1970s. The automobile approaches the saturation point in Europe.

of depression, because young people spent more and more, and rising birth rates produced more young people. Two decades of full employment and rising real wages bred still further confidence.

One prominent sign of that confidence was the spread of installment buying, or purchases on credit. Frugal artisans and close-handed peasants had considered it a calamity in the past when the need for raw materials or seed forced them into debt with its attendant ruinous interest and risks of foreclosure by the moneylender. By contrast, postwar Western European consumers embraced new schemes for paying for television sets or automobiles over time. The British, to take one example, purchased goods worth over £400 million "on the never-never" in 1957; the figure had tripled by 1965.[5]

The most coveted consumer goods were television sets and automo-

[5]Pauline Gregg, *The Welfare State* (Amherst, Mass., 1969), pp. 240, 350.

biles. Television figures are most accurate for Britain, where the state requires a license for each radio or television receiver. While nearly 11 million radio licenses were sold in 1947, only 14,500 television licenses were sold. In 1965, the British public bought 13 million television licenses.[6] Once a rich sportsman's toy, the automobile had already reached a large middle-class market in Western Europe between the wars. But the consumer economy truly arrived in the 1960s when the lower middle class and skilled workers, in their turn, stepped up from bicycles to motorcycles and then, increasingly, to inexpensive automobiles. Such simple mass-produced cars as the Citroën 2CV ("two horsepower"), a kind of latter day Model T Ford whose highly sophisticated front-wheel drive and clutchless transmission were planted in an ungainly rudimentary body, enabled millions of Frenchmen to own cars for the first time. By the early 1970s, seven French adults in ten owned a car. Other Western European nations whose density of automobiles began to approach that of the United States were Sweden, West Germany, and Britain.[7]

Such goods as refrigerators, washing machines, and alcohol and tobacco also claimed high shares of consumer spending. Food, once the preponderant expenditure of the poor, now accounted for less than 50 percent of personal spending in most Western European countries for the first time. The main public amusement of the 1920s, the cinema, declined in favor of television.

Total production and total national wealth had grown dramatically in all the European nations. By 1967 the national income per capita had reached $2480 in Switzerland, $2046 in France, and $2010 in West Germany. But these aggregate figures do not tell us all we need to know about how the long Western European boom of the 1950s and 1960s affected society. We must look more closely at the distribution of wealth and at social mobility.

Distribution of Wealth in Western Europe

At the top, new fortunes were made in Western Europe. There was relatively little room for quick wealth in basic industry, unlike the opportunities opened by the early nineteenth-century Industrial Revolution. Railroads, airlines, and coal mines were state property almost everywhere in Europe, and major steel companies remained in private hands only in West Germany and in post-Labour Britain from 1951 to 1966, at which time the Labour government nationalized steel again. Several of the largest automobile manufacturers (Renault; Volkswagen until 1956) were state firms.

[6] *Ibid,* p. 353.

[7] Motor Vehicles per 1000 population (1970):

United States	532	Britain	244
Sweden	283	Italy	206
West Germany	253	Japan	172

New York Times, April 8, 1973, Section 1a, p. 8, and *Statistisk Årsbok för Sverige* (Stockholm, 1971), p. 176.

Some of the great European industrial dynasties saw their family firms slip into the hands of managers and technicians. The German metal and armaments firm of Krupp, which had survived Allied prosecution and plans for dismemberment after the Second World War, and had recovered great economic power in West Germany, encountered financial difficulties in 1969 and was put under state-appointed management on behalf of the shareholders. Other European family firms, such as Peugeot automobiles, were forced by competition into larger conglomerates. Of course, many of the industrial dynasties navigated these flood waters of the European boom successfully, such as FIAT's Giovanni Agnelli and the business machine magnate Arrigo Olivetti. The top managers and technicians of the new European enterprises also became wealthy men, although perhaps not on the scale of the heads of the former large family firms.

The new millionaires of postwar consumer societies were usually neither captains of industry in basic commodities nor the managers of huge firms. They were ambitious entrepreneurs in real estate, electric household appliances, mass communications, and entertainment. Some of the most spectacular of these new fortunes flourished in the relatively open market economy of West Germany. Axel Springer found himself at the end of the war with the ruins of his father's small printing shop in Hamburg and an idea: to sell printed schedules for radio programs. With the profits from this modest enterprise and a permit to publish from the Allied occupation authorities, Springer proceeded to build an empire of newspapers and slick magazines that by the 1960s was the fifth largest in the world. His *Bildzeitung,* a popular Sunday photo sheet, had the largest circulation of any European newspaper.

Another spectacular example was Max Grundig, a radio salesman before the war. He assembled a wheelbarrow-load of tools in an old courtyard in the Nuremberg suburb of Fürth in 1945, and, with seven helpers, he put together the first Grundig radio. This was a simple assemble-it-yourself kit that the public bought eagerly, since old radios had often been confiscated, and new ones were rationed. Twenty years later, Grundig owned the largest television factory in Germany, the largest radio factory in Europe, and the largest sound-track factory in the world.

Some fortunes were built around the careers of successful popular musicians like the Beatles. An occasional fortune could be built in partnership with the state, such as Marcel Dassault's success in designing and building civil aircraft for Air France and Mirage fighter bombers for General de Gaulle's nuclear attack force, the *force de frappe.*

At the bottom, there was more disposable wealth than ever before. Even though prices rose almost constantly after the war, average real wages rose ahead of them through the 1950s and 1960s in Western Europe. Even in Great Britain, whose economic performance fell behind that of the Continent, average weekly earnings more than doubled between 1950 and 1961, while retail prices advanced by only about 50 percent.[8] Increased social services, such as free medical care, education, and subsidized public transportation, helped to bring some degree of security and even modest comfort to broad ranges of working people. In Continental Western Europe, an average of 36 percent of working families' income came from various fringe benefits paid by state social welfare agencies; in Italy, that figure was 51 percent.[9] Seebohm Rowntree, who observed social conditions in the British city of York, found soon after the war that only 3 percent of the citizens of York were in real need.[10] All of those were aged, the only group neglected by youth-oriented postwar British society. The institution of the welfare state during and after the war had made the decisive difference.

The last pockets of traditional poverty began to be drawn into the economic mainstream. During the summer of 1973, a Paris museum displayed the recent history of Minot, a village in Burgundy devoted to primitive subsistence agriculture that "could be described as late neolithic" until after the Second World War. Then consumer society broke in with a rush.

> The last horse collar was made in Minot in 1949; the last horse trod its streets in 1968. The old water mill closed down in 1952. The washing machine replaced the wash house—and broke up the community of women —in the nineteen sixties. In 1968, the anthropologists moved in, as into some Amazonian jungle tribe, and in 1973 Minot entered the museum.[11]

The main lever of change in the remaining preindustrial corners of Europe was the movement of young men from Spain, Portugal, southern Italy, and Turkey to the factories of northern Europe. Some 6 million southern Italians moved to northern Italian industrial cities in the 1960s. Foreigners made up 37 percent of the manual labor population of Switzerland by 1967. Although these workers were concentrated in the lowest forms of manual labor, and although there was friction with East Indians in Britain, Algerians in France, and Turks in Germany, some of this "subproletariat" returned home with savings and training and began middle-class lives as, for instance, automobile mechanics or television repairmen.

Wealth remained remarkably concentrated in a few hands in prosperous Western Europe, probably more so than during the enforced egalitarianism of war and reconstruction. British inheritance tax figures in 1971 showed that the top 1.2 percent of persons (about 61,000 individuals) owned 21.44 percent of the total personal wealth in Great Britain, and the top quarter owned about three-quarters of the total personal wealth.[12] Disparity was greater in West Germany, where the

[8]Gregg, p. 236.
[9]Anthony Sampson, *Anatomy of Europe* (New York, 1969), p. 238.
[10]As compared to 31 percent in 1936. See Chapter 1, p. 18.
[11]*New York Times,* June 13, 1973, p. 58.
[12]Murray Forsyth, "Property and Property Distribution Policy," *PEP Broadsheet,* No. 528 (July 1971). The top 1.2 percent of Americans owned 33 percent of the total personal wealth and 54 percent of investment assets in 1962, according to a Federal Reserve study.

top 1.7 percent owned 35 percent of the total wealth. Since those described as independent were accumulating wealth faster than those described as dependent (that is, salaried or wage workers), the disparity of wealth was probably widening in the Western Europe of the early 1970s.

Social Mobility in Western Europe

In between the richest and the poorest, the mass of Western Europeans gave evidence of greater homogeneity and easier social mobility. The twentieth-century trend toward fewer outward signs of social distinction was accelerated after the war by informal habits of dress, especially among the young, by inexpensive standardized clothing, and by widening access to such status symbols as the automobile. A lower–middle-class European commented to an interviewer that at his job he was a nobody; at the wheel of his car, he felt he was treated with respect.[13]

The two most powerful forces of egalitarianism were education and leisure. Mass primary education had been the work of the late nineteenth century. Secondary and university systems remained narrowly selective until after the Second World War. By deeply rooted European tradition, secondary schooling had consisted of rigorous training in literary expression based on the classics; it was accessible only to upper-class youths and a few poor youths of exceptional literary talent. After the war there were powerful movements in two complementary directions: toward greater democracy in higher education, and toward more technical competence in the skills of science, engineering, and business. The first sign of change was an enormous increase of enrollment in secondary schools. The French had abolished fees for state secondary schools in 1929; the British abolished them in 1947. The right of all to a free secondary education up to the age of fifteen was recognized for the first time in British history. The French raised their school-leaving age to sixteen in 1967. Education became the fastest growing item in Western European budgets. The proportion of gross national product devoted to education in Britain rose from 2.8 percent in 1938 to 5.4 percent in 1965, and in France, from 2 percent in 1952 to 4.6 percent in 1965.

But what should be taught in the now crowded secondary schools? Since aptitudes and backgrounds in the schools became less uniform, the standard Western European solution was to divide the curriculum into different tracks: classical and "modern" for the more gifted, and vocational for the less intellectually gifted. In France, the traditional, rigorous *lycées* were supplemented by more egalitarian *collèges d'éducation secondaire,* but it was clear to all that very different degrees of prestige were attached to the different schools, that family background had much to do with the school that one attended, and that the choices made there often committed a student to his lifetime social level. High tensions

[13]*New York Times,* April 8, 1973, Section 1a, p. 8.

developed around examinations for entry into one school or the other. The "eleven-plus" examination in England was an awesome hurdle, for the entry at eleven years of age into a vocational "secondary modern" school instead of a more prestigious "grammar" school might well limit one's future status for good. When the Labour party returned to power in Britain in 1964, it began phasing out the "eleven-plus" examination and providing for freer transfer among schools as a student's talents developed. Even with modification of this sort, however, Western European secondary schools had clearly become an arena of fierce status pressure among the young.

The experience of mass schooling showed that the children of literate or cultivated parents performed better, from the first classes on, than children of workers or peasants. As schooling became more and more important for jobs in a technical society, few people of poor backgrounds actually advanced far beyond their parents' social standing. A study of top executives in France in 1968 showed that 40 percent of them had been born in Paris, and that three-quarters were sons (none were women) of high ranking business or professional families; only about 10 percent had come from modest backgrounds. The fact that more than a third had grandparents of modest social position suggested that the narrow path to social advancement was a matter of at least two generations.[14]

Enrollment also increased rapidly in Western European universities. The number of British universities increased from sixteen in 1935 to fifty-two in 1965, and university enrollment from 50,000 to 168,000. University enrollment in France more than tripled in fifteen years after 1950, West German enrollment almost tripled, and Italian enrollment more than doubled. Western European nations sent between 8 percent and 15 percent of the age group twenty to twenty-four to universities in 1965, compared with 3 percent to 5 percent in 1950.[15] The prospects were for continued growth, as university education was nearly free (except for living expenses). Governments subsidized higher education because high skills were an advantage in the race for prosperity. The educational disparity between middle-class and working-class or peasant youths was further accentuated by university admissions, however, and university study was even more clearly geared to access to professions than was secondary-school education.

The spread of leisure was a more genuine egalitarian development than the spread of education. The establishment of leisure as a right of working people in the 1930s[16] was followed during the postwar boom by major development of leisure travel. As paid vacations became standard among the working class, the sheer numbers of those looking for escape to the sea or the mountains climbed prodigiously. Among the West Germans, the most avid foreign travelers in Western Europe, a fifth of

[14]*Le Monde,* October 1, 1968.
[15]In the United States, 43 percent attend some form of higher education at least for a time.
[16]See Chapter 10. pp. 285–90.

La Grande Molle, a new tourist holiday development on the French Mediterranean coast.

the whole population goes abroad each year. In 1966, 5.5 million Germans visited Italy alone. Catering to tourists became a big business in itself, as tourism was the largest foreign-exchange earner in Spain, Italy, and Greece. Thinly settled coastal land around the Mediterranean became the object of frantic speculation for hotels, second homes, and campsites. While most tourists carefully preserved their national and class surroundings in tours or vacation communities, a highly successful French enterprise, the *Club Méditerranée,* built more than forty-five imitation Tahitian villages around the world where those seeking escape from middle-class conformity could live in mock austerity, using beads for money and enjoying a brief fling without forms of social ostentation or hierarchy.

Consumer Society in the Soviet Bloc

The Soviet Union and Eastern Europe also entered the age of mass consumption, but a bit later. As the grim postwar years of forced growth in heavy industry began to show results in the 1960s, popular pressures for a less harsh existence began to receive some official response.

Even though Malenkov's slightly more consumer-oriented new course in 1953 had been brief, all the post-Stalin leaders in the Soviet Union attended to the need for more food of better quality, clothing, housing, and a few amenities. Khrushchev (first secretary of the party and premier, 1958–64) gave special attention to agriculture, which had never recovered the 1928 level of output. The new party program of July 1961 promised to complete the "transition to communism" for the Soviet Union by 1980 by surpassing the United States in steel, agricultural production, and other essential basic commodities. According to Khrushchev, by 1980 all Russians could look forward to having apartments of their own, "even newlyweds."

The Cold War and the expensive Soviet space program postponed any significant shift to consumer goods, however. Although the Soviet Union retained its space lead by orbiting the first man around the earth, Yuri Gagarin, in April 1961,[17] Khrushchev continued to oppose mass production of private automobiles—"those armchairs on wheels"—for Soviet citizens. Khrushchev's impulsive and overextended ploughing of unsuitable steppe (the Virgin Lands scheme) and his introduction of American corn to areas unsuited to it exacerbated a bad harvest in 1963. A slowdown in economic growth, combined with the fiasco of the Cuban missile crisis and the deterioration of relations with China, led his associates to remove him quietly from power in October 1964.

Khrushchev's blander successors turned Soviet priority for the first time to improving the quantity and quality of consumer goods. Alongside the clerkish Premier Aleksei Kosygin and the impassive President Nikolay Podgorny, it was Party Secretary Leonid Brezhnev (general secretary of the Communist party of the Soviet Union, 1964–   ) who clearly dominated this new collective leadership. Brezhnev was a product of the generation that had not really known Tsarist Russia (he was eleven years old in 1917), a pragmatic technician trained in both agronomy and engineering rather than in party doctrine. The Twenty-third Party Congress (March and April 1966) announced that for the first time in Soviet history consumer goods production was planned to rise more rapidly than basic investment in productive equipment.

Brezhnev proposed to reach this goal by turning frankly to the West for technical aid and capital. The Soviet Union's industrial plant was now sufficiently powerful and its regime sufficiently sound to use Western assistance without any feeling of inferiority, as long as the cultural isolation of Soviet citizens was maintained. In 1966 the Soviets

[17]The United States astronaut John Glenn orbited the earth in February 1962.

concluded major foreign contracts, including one with FIAT for a vast automobile plant (its town was renamed Togliatti after the late Italian Communist leader) that would triple Soviet automobile output, and cooperation with the French in developing color television.

Brezhnev's other innovation was a loosening of the strangling central planning system, as proposed by Yevsei Liberman, a professor at Kharkov University. Liberman began developing in 1962 a theory of applying market mechanisms to a socialist economy. Growth and efficiency would be stimulated, Liberman argued, if more decisions were restored to the directors of individual enterprises. Greater liberty to administer required a better device to measure success or failure than the previous norms imposed from above. Liberman proposed that the enterprise's profits be the measure of its success, and that part of the profits be shared among managers and workers as incentives to better work. In case of losses, managers' (but not workers') pay would be reduced. Profits, of course, required a price system. The state set prices on certain basic goods, allowed them to fluctuate within fixed limits on others, and in the case of some luxuries, freed them. Managers of industrial and agricultural enterprises were supposed to obtain their raw materials on the best terms possible and make the best bargain possible for their finished products. Liberman and his supporters argued that no return to capitalism was involved here, since basic productive capacity remained in the hands of the state and could neither be acquired nor inherited by individuals. By 1967, 40 percent of Soviet industrial output was functioning on these terms, and Khrushchev's giant collective farms (only twenty-eight for all Russia) had been reorganized into smaller units committed to "economic self-reliance."

Soviet productivity continued to rise in many areas (the Soviet Union passed the United States in steel production in 1971), but the pace slowed after the 1960s. Agriculture continued to be the Achilles heel of the regime. In 1972 Brezhnev concluded a gigantic wheat purchase (400 million bushels) with the United States, and traveled to America in June 1973 to conclude agreements for more American capital investment. The search for some way to stimulate lagging economic growth was taking precedence over autarky.

The Eastern European countries had turned to Libermanism even before the Soviet Union: East Germany in 1963, and the others in 1965 (except for Romania and Albania). East Germany emerged in the late 1960s as the tenth industrial producer in the world, an astonishing achievement. By 1967, 60 percent of East German households had television sets, and 38 percent had refrigerators and washing machines. The other East European countries became more urban than rural for the first time, joining Czechoslovakia as genuinely industrialized economies. The drabness of Eastern European life seemed less inevitable in the 1960s and, therefore, perhaps less bearable.

The "End of Ideology"

"The affluent society banks the fires of indignation," observed the French political scientist Raymond Aron in 1957.[18] Compared to the reconstructing zeal of the liberation years and to the impassioned divisions of the Cold War, the prosperous late 1950s seemed a time of ideological simmering-down in Europe. In Western Europe, sociologists talked about the "end of ideology";[19] in the Soviet Union after 1964, Party Secretary Brezhnev, his own garage stocked with a Rolls Royce, a Mercedes, a Citroën-Maserati, and a Cadillac, called on Western firms to supply his people with consumer goods.

One could argue that prosperous times and the access of more and more salaried workers to material comfort had merely reduced social frictions for a while. To an extent, that was true. Even at the turn of the century, the German economist Werner Sombart had tried to explain the failure of ideological socialism in the United States in part by sheer abundance: "On the reefs of roast beef and apple pie socialist Utopias of every sort are sent to their doom."[20] Marxists had had no difficulty disposing of this argument by predicting coming depression or a widening disparity between the rich and the rest.

Beyond a mere temporary prosperity, however, it seemed possible in the late 1950s and early 1960s that lasting social, economic, and political changes were in the process of making the "end of ideology" permanent. One important structural change was the faster growth of white-collar than of blue-collar workers as a proportion of the total population. This process, in fact, had begun in the 1890s in the most advanced industrial countries. Factory workers leveled off at about a third of the population, instead of becoming the predicted absolute majority; by contrast, the number of clerical and service workers began growing rapidly. In the 1950s it seemed that white-collar workers might actually outnumber blue-collar workers in advanced industrial countries. The "proletariat" was being replaced by a "salariat."[21] On the theory that white-collar workers were less alienated from middle-class aspirations, some Frénch businesses actually tried to hasten this process in the early 1970s by paying a number of factory workers a monthly salary rather than a weekly wage.

Another element of the "end of ideology" view was a new confidence that planned economies and welfare states had conquered the business cycle. Up to 1945 depression and unemployment had discredited the European system as much as war had. If the postwar planners could

[18]Raymond Aron, *The Opium of the Intellectuals,* trans. Terence Kilmartin (New York, 1962), p. xv.
[19]Daniel Bell, *The End of Ideology: The Exhaustion of Political Ideals in the Fifties* (Glencoe, Ill., 1960). While Bell applied the phrase mostly to the United States, it is equally apt for Western Europe.
[20]Werner Sombart, *Warum gibt es in den Vereinigten Staaten keinen Sozialismus?* (Tübingen, 1906), p. 126.
[21]Bell, p. 217. The United States passed this landmark in 1956.

replace the old boom-and-bust rhythm with steady growth in both productivity and incomes, the gnawing insecurity that had dominated proletarian life even during interludes of prosperity would be vanquished. As the Western European welfare states approached their second decade since 1945 without a serious depression and with virtually full employment, the growing prosperity seemed more than a mere interlude.

A final element in the "end of ideology" position was the discrediting of the vigorous ideologies of earlier times. Laissez faire had been discredited during the Great Depression to the point where European businessmen above the neighborhood shop level rarely talked of the values of individual enterprise. A whole range of Integralist Catholic and racial ideologies (although not nationalism) had been discredited by the defeat of fascism. On the left, the harsh realities of Stalinist practice stripped Marxism of some of its attraction. Even before de-Stalinization began in Moscow, many Western sympathizers were stopped short by Albert Camus' question: "Do you, yes or no, regard the Soviet Union as having fulfilled the revolutionary 'project'?"[22] De-Stalinization hastened this critical reevaluation after 1956, and the Soviet interventions in Hungary (1956) and Czechoslovakia (1968) accelerated it even more. Doubts about collectivism were heightened in Western Europe by the disillusioning experience of partial nationalization. Working for a large state-owned firm resembled all too closely working for a large privately owned firm, in terms of job boredom, low pay, and lack of advancement. But if collectivism did not necessarily bring more personal freedom, it might at least bring higher productivity. Even the promise of more productivity through collectivism was belied when Western European growth rates persistently led Soviet growth rates in the 1960s.

Consensus Politics

The main political mark of the "end of ideology" years was the emergence of a broad consensus around pragmatic, technical management of public affairs for sustained economic growth. Both right and left in Western Europe seemed to agree on the virtues of a mixed economy, welfare state, and pragmatic planning. Even the West and the Soviet Union seemed to differ mainly on the means to attain the same end: an economy of abundance.

In practice, this consensus was expressed in Western Europe by conservatives in power through the late 1950s and 1960s. In this sense, the "end of ideology" years built on the conservative Cold War victories in Western Europe in the early 1950s. Germany continued to be ruled by Konrad Adenauer (1948–63), followed by his economics minister and the deviser of the German economic "miracle," Ludwig Erhard (1963–66). In England, the longest-lived Tory government of modern times

[22]Albert Camus, letter in *Les Temps modernes*, August 1952.

ruled from 1951 to 1964 under Churchill and his successors. Italy was governed by the Christian Democratic successors of Alcide De Gasperi. France, the one nation in Western Europe to change its political system substantially in these years, turned to a strong executive under General Charles de Gaulle (1958–69).

It was less the governments than the oppositions that changed during the "end of ideology" period. The Western European left became more gradualist and pragmatic; in some instances, it shared power with the center. Western European socialists talked less about nationalization after the late 1950s and more about technical problems of planned economic growth, about worker participation in the decisions of a managed economy, about how to reconcile automation with satisfying work, and about the organization of leisure in the welfare state.

The most striking transformation was that of the West German Social Democratic party (SPD). The first Marxist party of Western Europe (1879) and until 1933 the largest, it was the repository of orthodox Marxist social democracy after the death of Marx and Engels. But the SPD decided at its 1959 annual congress at Bad Godesberg to renounce Marxist doctrine as the party's main guide. "The SPD, which was a party of the working class, is now a party of the whole people." The program described democratic socialism as a set of values rooted in "Christian ethics, humanism, and classic philosophy," and a set of pragmatic political aims designed to "establish a way of life," not to carry out a revolution. The new SPD opposed great concentrations of economic power in either private or state hands; hence, there was less talk of nationalization than of shared, decentralized decisionmaking. "As much competition as possible, as much planning as necessary" for economic abundance was the party's motto. Like the British Labour party and the Swedish Socialist party, the new SPD after Bad Godesberg was designed to appeal to a majority of an electorate in which factory workers remained a minority.[23]

In practice, the Bad Godesberg program meant the replacement of the old Social Democratic survivors of Weimar with a new generation of SPD leaders. The indomitable Kurt Schumacher, marked by the First World War and by Hitler's concentration camps with the loss of a leg and an arm, was the last strong representative of Weimar social democracy until his death in 1953. The main new leader was Willy Brandt. As a student, Brandt had left Germany when Hitler came to power and spent hard years in Norway (where he took the name Brandt from an Ibsen play) and in Sweden. In 1957 he was elected mayor of West Berlin where he made his mark more by youth and energy than by doctrine.

In 1966, seven years after the adoption of the Bad Godesberg program and two years after Willy Brandt became leader of the German

[23]SPD Bad Godesberg program, quoted in Alfred Grosser, *Germany in our Time* (New York, 1971), p. 151.

SPD, the flagging Christian Democrats joined with the SPD in a "Great Coalition" government in which Brandt was foreign minister. It was the first time the German Christian Democrats had shared power with another political party since 1948, and Brandt was the first SPD minister in Germany since 1930.

The British Labour party, reformist since its beginning, also entered a more pragmatic period with the death in 1960 of the miners' leader Aneurin Bevan, Labour's gadfly, and with the replacement of Clement Attlee as party leader by the scholarly Hugh Gaitskell, a proponent of a mixed economy run by experts. Indeed, the distinctions between the welfare state Toryism of R. A. Butler, the Conservative Chancellor of the Exchequer (1951–55), and Gaitskell's ideas of a planned mixed economy were so slight that bemused Englishmen simply called both parties' programs "Butskellism." When Gaitskell died prematurely, an Oxford economics professor, Harold Wilson, brought Labour back to power in 1964, after thirteen years of Tory government. Wilson renationalized steel and democratized secondary education, but the main platform of the second postwar Labour government (1964–70) was scientific and technological contributions to further economic growth.

In Italy, the independent socialist leader Pietro Nenni, whose determination to cooperate with the Italian Communist party in 1948 and 1949 had split the Italian socialists, also evolved toward a more centrist position in the 1960s. When the ruling Christian Democrats proposed an "opening to the left" to broaden their coalition, the Nenni socialists even participated in the government for a time (1963–68).

Western European Communist parties found themselves with aging leaders and members, isolated from the rest of the left, and approaching their lowest point since the Second World War. When de Gaulle came to power in June 1958, the French Communist party retained only 19 percent of the popular vote, its lowest percentage since 1936. Many sympathetic Western intellectuals had cooled to the party since the Soviet invasion of Hungary and the revelations of de-Stalinization in 1956. The years of Cold War passion and intellectual *engagement* that Simone de Beauvoir had described in her prize-winning novel of 1957, *Les Mandarins,* seemed in the 1960s very remote in time. The new leaders of Europe were no longer *engagé* intellectuals, like de Beauvoir and Sartre, but pragmatic experts, the bright young men who designed Europe's high-speed trains and nuclear power plants. The future seemed to hold out a long vista of sustained growth and stability.

The "postideological" stability promised in the late 1950s and early 1960s began to look less certain at the end of the decade. The events of 1968 proved that point in both Western and Eastern Europe. Student demonstrations in Paris, joined by the most massive general strike in

**Discontents in
Consumer
Societies
Since 1968**

France since 1936, very nearly brought the Gaullist regime to its knees in May 1968 and showed how easily an advanced consumer society can be paralyzed by discontented workers, lower managers, and students. In Czechoslovakia, a movement toward a more open and tolerant socialist society mushroomed beyond the capacity of the government to control it or of the Russians to tolerate it. In August 1968, 500,000 Russian troops and several thousand tanks entered Czechoslovakia to restore authoritarian rule. These were only the most massive outbursts of a turbulence that affected almost every advanced industrial nation in the late 1960s and early 1970s.

What had happened to the satisfactions promised by prosperous consumer societies in both the Communist and capitalist worlds?

Worker and Consumer Discontents

In Western Europe, several very different forms of discontent coincided to produce periodic stirrings of restlessness. Boring work was one basic cause of dissatisfaction. The emotional fatigue of endlessly repeating trivial parts of a fragmented process was no new problem. Assembly-line boredom had been a standard charge leveled against the factory system since the nineteenth century, and it had been brilliantly satirized in the 1930s by Charlie Chaplin's film *Modern Times* (1936) and René Clair's *A Nous la Liberté* (1931). But as the number of people engaged in whole tasks grew even fewer and those performing fragmented tasks for huge organizations (whether public or private) became the standard,[24] boring work produced a latent anger that could intensify other discontents. There seemed no practical solution to the problem. Both the German SPD and the French Gaullist regime showed interest in more worker participation in profits and even in some decisionmaking, but did nothing to change the essentially passive and monotonous quality of most work. The experiment of the SAAB motor works in Sweden in the early 1970s to replace assembly lines with teams responsible for larger segments of each car was admittedly expensive. The only escape for most workers was the frenetic quest for leisure recreation.

The old problem of boring work was complicated by the postwar need for better educated workers. As the technical skills required to operate automated equipment increased, and as white-collar jobs proliferated more rapidly than blue-collar, young, highly qualified workers confronted jobs that were not necessarily fulfilling. It was the workers in the most advanced sectors of French industry—automobiles and aviation—who led the strike movement of May 1968, along with the technicians and staffs of state radio and television who felt confined by governmental direction. Before 1968, the neo-Marxist Herbert Marcuse

[24]As one partial illustration, self-employed persons declined in England from 14 percent of the work force in 1911 to 7 percent in 1955. (E. H. Phelps-Brown, *Pay and Profits* [Manchester, 1968], p. 4.)

had argued that marginal groups in society—students, ethnic minorities—were more likely than wage workers to form the kernel of future revolutionary movements.[25] After May 1968, Marxist Roger Garaudy predicted a "new historic bloc" of dissatisfied skilled technicians and the students in training for such work, while sociologist Serge Mallet believed that the highly skilled workers would lead the "new working class" rather than become the satisfied "worker aristocracy" that Lenin had feared. Any predictions of stability in consumer societies would have to rest on the extent to which they could satisfy the growing stratum of skilled but wage-earning experts.

Inflation provided an additional spur to discontent in Western Europe. The long European boom had been accompanied by regular inflation produced by rising purchasing power under full employment conditions. As long as it remained small, inflation encouraged a sensation of growing prosperity. At the end of the 1960s, however, inflation spun out of control in much of Western Europe.

Among the immediate causes were international monetary instability and the increasing cost of imported oil for rapidly growing energy needs. But there was also a sense that the economic planners had lost control. Efforts to regulate wages and prices only sharpened conflict between unions and government to the point where parliamentary systems could hardly function. A conspicuous example was the effort of British Conservative Prime Minister Edward Heath to freeze wages and prices in November 1972. After a coal miners' strike had paralyzed the British economy, Heath's Conservatives lost their majority in the election of February 1974. The realization that price increases of 10 percent to 15 percent per year would far outstrip wage increases had much to do with the round of strikes in Italy that repeatedly brought the country to a standstill after 1969. Since no state dealt successfully with inflation, the comfortable notion of the early 1960s that Keynesian economic managers had found the key to economic security was called into question.

Student Discontent

A dissident youth culture contributed to the turbulence of the late 1960s. Since alienated young people were a worldwide phenomenon, it would be a mistake to look for purely European explanations. The American anthropologist Margaret Mead found an intelligible general explanation[26] in the rapid pace of technological change. She argued that in stable societies the young had believed that their own lives would resemble the lives of their parents; hence, the parents' experiences provided lessons worth transmitting. Not so in an age in which the conditions of life changed beyond recognition within a few years. Whereas it had taken a generation to assimilate the automobile into

[25]Herbert Marcuse, *One Dimensional Man* (Boston, 1964).
[26]Margaret Mead, *Culture and Commitment: A Study of the Generation Gap* (Garden City, N.Y., 1970).

public life, the airplane had moved from plaything to basic transportation in less time, atomic energy had been put to practical use in two decades, and space travel ceased to arouse wonder in a few years. Mead believes that in the 1960s young people had simply ceased to believe that their elders had anything to teach them.[27]

There were, of course, particular reasons for European student dissent. Students occupied an ambiguous social position: although not yet integrated into society, they were subject to its pressures in a brutally competitive, career-oriented educational system; scornful of materialism, they nevertheless saw their future material possibilities being set by examination performance.

These elements took acute form in European consumer societies. The university students of the late 1960s had known nothing but prosperity. Suffering in earlier depressions and wars were so many proofs of their parents' failure, while the last stages of the Cold War seemed further evidence of incompetence and bad faith among their elders. Questions about moral responsibility for Nazism and the crass materialism of the German revival further widened the generation gap in Germany. European universities were among the most selective and competitive in the world; having grown very rapidly in enrollment, they left students without faculty contact or adequate facilities, while sharpening their critical capacities.

[27]See Chapter 4, p. 122 for an earlier form of conflict between generations.

Students and police in Paris, May 11, 1968.

All these discontents came into focus in France in May 1968. Troubles began when a minority of students opposed the French universities' role as selector and producer of docile technocrats, as "an initiation into bourgeois affairs," and as an old-fashioned vehicle for "only the acquisition of a cultural heritage" inadequate to keep up with the "New Industrial Revolution."[28] Priding itself more on spontaneity than doctrine, the group took the name "March 22 Movement" from the date of the first sit-in at the new, raw campus of Nanterre in suburban Paris, led by a German exchange student, Daniel Cohn-Bendit. The movement won its first mass base when police overreacted during a demonstration at the Paris Sorbonne campus on the night of May 11, 1968; 367 persons were wounded and 460 arrested. Encouraged by widespread public sympathy, the students sought allies in the factories, and some industries began strikes on May 14 over quite different issues of boring work and inflation. By late May, 10 million people were on strike in France, the largest social outburst since May 1936 and a spontaneous one, without the leadership of the Communist or socialist unions.

As France became paralyzed by shortages of gas and food, General de Gaulle's regime was thought to be finished when the general disappeared on May 29. It turned out that he had gone secretly to West Germany to assure the loyalty of French Army units stationed there. At that point, however, de Gaulle saw his chance for survival in the incompatibility of the wage demands of consumer-oriented workers and the more fundamental social criticism of the students. The students were isolated when a majority of the workers finally accepted a large wage raise in early June. Elections held on June 23 gave de Gaulle the benefit of a backlash of frightened and angry Frenchmen who had been plunged suddenly from an imperfect but relative abundance into a nightmare of stalled automobiles, food hoarding, and uncongenial youthful life styles. For the first time in French history, a single party—the Gaullists—received an absolute majority of parliamentary seats.

The immediate effect of the Paris May, then, was to solidify the *status quo*. For the moment, most workers seemed to want mere wage raises and most other Frenchmen to want mere stability. But the fragility of highly technological consumer societies had been clearly demonstrated. De Gaulle's image had been severely battered, and a year later, at the age of seventy-nine, he left office after a relatively minor constitutional proposal was rejected at the polls.

Other Social Tensions in Western Europe

The Paris May of 1968 was only the most spectacular display of Western European social tensions of the late 1960s and early 1970s. German universitites, where traditionally powerful academic hierarchies en-

---

[28]*Bulletin du mouvement du 22 mars,* April 1968. Statement of the *Syndicat national de l'Enseignement supérieur* (Instructors' Union), May 1968.

gaged in a tug of war with student radical groups, were brought to virtual deadlock from 1967 to 1971. In 1972, Italy, subject to both inflation and growing unemployment, ran through its thirty-second, thirty-third, and thirty-fourth governments since the Second World War under the pressure of repeated strikes and the desire of reformist socialists to explore ways to cooperate with the large Italian Communist party. A return to Tory government in England in 1970 was followed by efforts to limit union power. In January 1972, British miners struck nationwide for the first time since the great General Strike of 1926, and in February and March 1973 the British underwent their first civil servants' strike. Unemployment reached 3.4 percent, the highest since the depression. Finally, a prolonged miners' strike and the fuel crisis of the winter of 1973/74 brought the Conservative government down. Even Spain, silent as a tomb since the end of the Civil War in 1939, experienced a powerful increase in linguistic nationalism, strikes, and intellectual opposition to the regime in the late 1960s and early 1970s.

At the time of these more urban-centered discontents, Western European agriculture was undergoing the stresses of rapid modernization. The economic planners had encouraged the abandonment of traditional peasant dwarf holdings and the mechanization of large family farms and corporate farms. For the first time, the farm population dropped to below a third of the working population in France, and approached that figure in Italy. Improved methods produced surpluses, however, and the remaining farmers were pinched between low farm prices and inflated prices for the items they needed to buy. While the Communist party had some success in organizing the declining small farmers in France and Italy (a short-term success but a long-term risk in tying communism to technical backwardness), the larger farmers resorted to direct action in France. They blocked highways and occupied local government offices on several occasions in the late 1960s. The problems of farm supply and pricing also seemed to be beyond the capacities of the planners in prosperous Western Europe.

Discontent in Eastern Europe

The discontents of Eastern Europe in the late 1960s were not identical to those in the West, of course. There was a high degree of frustrated nationalism at work in the discontents of Czechoslovakia, Poland, and Romania. Intellectuals and students in Eastern Europe and the Soviet Union were struggling for basic rights of expression that were widely enjoyed in the West. Western public opinion was generally shocked when the state forbade expression of dissent, as in the cases of censorship in the French national radio and television systems, or when dissenters were directly attacked by their foes, as in the shooting of the German radical student leader Ohnesorg by an angry war veteran in 1970. In Eastern Europe, by contrast, efforts for freer expression turned on such basic matters as writing or speaking in any way critical of the regime, or even of deviating from orthodox realism in the arts. Eastern and Western European social discontents in the late 1960s and early 1970s cannot simply be considered as two variants of the same consumer society malaise.

The discontents clearly overlapped in many respects, however. Having begun to taste abundance in the 1960s, Eastern Europeans wanted more. The routine of labor in state factories was not very much different in its fragmentation, boredom, dependence, long hours, and low wages from work for a capitalist owner. A dissident youth culture became prominent, marked in part by serious criticism of regimentation and hierarchy within socialism, and in part by flaunting Western-style blue jeans and rock music. To this extent, the frustrations of Czechoslovak workers in the Skodka factories were similar to those of French workers at Renault, and those of Czech students to Parisian students. The questions of alienated labor, social hierarchy, and control over the planners' use of resources bridged the Iron Curtain.

The troubles in Poland in December 1970—the most severe since 1956—stemmed directly from living conditions. Premier Gomulka, whose regime had begun as a liberalizing compromise in 1956, had governed more and more repressively in the next fourteen years, resorting even to anti-Semitism in the late 1960s as a means to divert popular lassitude and disgruntlement (half the remaining Jews were forced into exile from 1968 to 1970). When steep food price increases were announced just before Christmas 1970, the workers in the Lenin shipyard at Gdansk (formerly Danzig) began demonstrations that spread to Szczecin (formerly Stettin) and other Baltic port cities. After 300 people had been killed in futile efforts to put down the revolts, Edward Gierek replaced Gomulka as party secretary. Gierek reduced food prices and abandoned an unpopular wage incentive system, but industrial unrest continued into 1971.

The Romanian–Soviet dispute of the 1960s was almost purely nationalist. The Romanian regime boldly rejected economic integration into COMECON in the name of national communism, while maintaining firm internal political control. Since the conflict concerned state relations within the Soviet bloc more than internal dissent (except indirectly, insofar as Party Secretary Ceauscescu managed to divert internal unrest into nationalist channels), this case will be considered more fully in Chapter 20.

The Czechoslovak Springtime of 1968

The most direct challenge to the Communist regimes of Eastern Europe since 1956 took place in Czechoslovakia in 1968 as a result of a combination of stresses: nationalism, desire for freer expression, and demand for better working conditions.

The Czechoslovak regime of Klement Gottwald (1948–53) and his successor as first secretary of the Czechoslovak Communist party, Antonín Novotný (1953–68), had been the most reliably Stalinist of the peoples' democracies, with the possible exception of Walter Ulbricht's East Germany. Novotný survived the troubles of 1956 and subsequent de-Stalinization with only minor adjustments, such as rehabilitating in 1963 some of the surviving victims of the 1951 and 1952 party purges. In late 1967, however, Novotný simply lost his capacity to have orders obeyed in the face of two obstinate grass-roots movements: a desire of the Slovaks for more autonomy, and a clamor for greater self-expression among younger intellectuals and administrators.

It was striking that effective opposition to Novotný's Stalinism came from the top, from within the younger generation of skilled technicians, state administrators, and intellectuals that the regime itself had produced. In that way, the Czechoslovak crisis reflected a problem common to all the peoples' democracies and the Soviet Union itself. The party officials who had created the new regime, mostly men of little education, toughened by wartime resistance and postwar revolution, had raised up a younger generation of administrators who had known less struggle and whose training was better suited to the technical progress and managed economic growth of the 1960s than to the Cold War struggles of the 1940s. The young scientists, agronomists, journalists, and economists who came of age in the 1960s wanted freer rein to apply their skills in a pragmatic fashion.[29] They were supported from below by workers who resented quotas, norms, steeply graduated piecework wage scales, and distant authority. Such groups wanted, for the most part, to reform rather than abolish the socialist system in Czechoslovakia. It was a majority of the Czech Communist party's Central Committee that eased Novotný out of office in January 1968 and replaced him as party secretary with a young spokesman for Slovak autonomy, Alexander Dubček.[30]

Alexander Dubček was no Western liberal. He wanted to make the party more national, more popular, and more responsive without its ceasing to be the only party. Nor did he have any intention of dismantling the economic structures of socialism. He wanted only to prove that the Czech Communist party was "capable of exercising political direction by means other than bureaucratic and police methods." The new program of the Czech Communist party (April 6, 1968) announced a "Czechoslovak way to socialism," reflecting a burgeoning sense of national distinctiveness.

> We engage ourselves in the construction of a new model of socialist society, profoundly democratic, and adapted to Czechoslovak conditions.

Without permitting a legal opposition, the new program authorized the "expression of different points of view" by the parties that had cooperated with the Communists in the National Front of 1945 to 1948:

[29]For an analysis of a similar development in the German Democratic Republic, see Peter C. Ludz, *The Changing Party Elite in East Germany* (Cambridge, Mass., 1972).
[30]Novotný remained president until March 1968.

Anti-Russian demonstrators at Saint Wenceslaus Square, Prague, August 1968. The sign says: "Dubček Hurray! USSR go home."

the Social Democrats and the late President Beneš' party, the Socialist National party. In that sense, part of the "Czechoslovak spring" harkened back to the immediate postwar pluralist regime voluntarily aligned with the Soviet Union. In other ways, the Dubček experiments tried to break new ground in the organization of work and in the devolution of decisionmaking. Trade unions, youth groups, and other popular organizations were encouraged to take an active role in a more decentralized administration.

Dubček's problem was to steer Czechoslovakia between two rising tides. A wave of free debate and discussion swelled up in this traditionally vivacious people that had repressed its intellectual curiosity for twenty years. After censorship was abolished on June 25, 1968, there was no restraining Czech imaginations. The incautious burst into print with suggestions for a multiparty system, national neutrality (withdrawal from the Warsaw Pact), and artistic experiment, all of which went further than Dubček, a convinced if pragmatic Communist, was willing to go. The other tide was the growing alarm of Czechoslovakia's neighbors, especially East Germany and Poland, who watched nervously for the contagion to spread to their populations.

Soviet Party Secretary Leonid Brezhnev attempted to put pressure on Dubček, evidently hoping for a compromise along the Gomulka lines of 1956 rather than a repeat of the Hungarian explosion of 1956. Although Soviet troops had been withdrawn from Czechoslovakia in 1945, some units entered the country briefly in June 1968 for Warsaw Pact "maneuvers." Finally, Dubček's determination to proceed with an open Party Congress in September seemed too grave a danger. On August 21, 1968, the Russians (supported by troops from East Germany, Poland, Hungary, and Bulgaria) moved 500,000 men and several thousand tanks into Czechoslovakia in a smoothly organized airborne operation. The Russians justified the military solution of the Czech challenge with the Brezhnev doctrine of limited national independence among socialist countries: a threat to a socialist regime in any one of them was a threat to all.

Although the Czechs offered no armed opposition (thus avoiding a disaster on the scale of Hungary in 1956), they received the invading soldiers with almost unanimous passive resistance. Briefed to expect West German anti-Communists at work in Czechoslovakia, the Russian soldiers had no idea how to deal with the "legions of young blue-jeaned Czechs sitting in their serried ranks in the roadways, jeering and whistling at the boot-faced troops."[31] Or with the workers who went ahead and held the promised Party Congress secretly in a factory. Dubček was arrested at first, but after President Ludvík Svoboda, a tough-minded old general, refused to cooperate, and no Czech collaborators stepped forward as János Kádár did in Hungary in 1956, Brezhnev elected to let Dubček govern under close control. A delicate process of gradually tightening repression followed. Dubček was removed from office in September 1969 and expelled from the party in 1970, along with nearly 500 other members. Trials went on through 1972. The Russians clearly preferred an unpopular but obedient communism in Eastern Europe to a popular, nationalist one.

Discontent in the Soviet Union

Only seven of the world's ninety Communist parties, outside the five participants, supported the Russian military destruction of Dubček's regime. Most of the Western European Communist parties denounced it publicly. The protests of foreign Communists and the criticism of fellow-traveling intellectuals could be shrugged off as they had been in

[31]*Economist,* August 31, 1968.

1956. This time, however, the Russian action in Czechoslovakia called attention to dissent at home. Pavel Litvinov, the grandson of Stalin's foreign minister in the 1930s, and several others were arrested for demonstrating in Moscow's Red Square. The difficulties that the Soviet regime had faced with dissident writers and scientists were sharply increased.

Conflict between the Soviet regime and intellectuals was, in part, the product of uncertainty over de-Stalinization. Once some of the restraints had been removed, Soviet officials did not know just where to draw the line between legitimate discussion of problems (as in the devastating cartoons in *Krokodil* against some lesser abuses) and impermissible deviation (as in the novels of Aleksandr Solzhenitsyn). Beyond the question of artistic freedom, however, was the more intractable problem of how a new generation of technical experts could run the machinery of a pragmatic Russia without the kind of free discussion that practical solutions to problems seemed to demand. How could the sciences function without free inquiry? Yet, the regime depended heavily on technical innovation to provide the material abundance that it had to deliver to its citizens.

The most penetrating criticism of post-Stalinist orthodoxy came from two physicists, Andrei Sakharov and V. F. Turchin, and a historian, Roy Medvedev. In a letter of March 1970 circulated widely among educated Russians by *samizdat*,[32] the physicists warned that the Soviet Union was falling behind scientifically and economically because of official "distrust of those who think critically, creatively, and actively." Whereas other intellectuals warned that political control of the arts might "close down the heart of the nation,"[33] the scientists argued that technical progress would be delayed without free exchange of information, free travel abroad, and a society that encouraged inquiry. The letter of Sakharov and his colleagues proposed fourteen steps toward democratization that the scientists justified as necessary for Russian technical advancement and material abundance.

The Soviet leaders reacted toughly to these criticisms, especially those that took public form or were smuggled out to be published in the West. It was perhaps progress that prominent dissidents, such as General Pyotr Grigorenko, who demonstrated publicly on behalf of the Tartars who wanted to return to their former region, and Roy Medvedev's brother Zhores, a biologist, should be confined to mental institutions rather than simply disappear into the living death of a Siberian labor camp as in Stalin's day. But the Soviet Union under Brezhnev had still not solved the problem of how to provide abundance to its people and how to educate many of them to the highest technical competence without also letting them speak their minds.

[32]The hand-to-hand circulation of officially forbidden documents and literature, a play on the name of the state publishing agency.
[33]Aleksandr Solzhenitsyn's undelivered Nobel Prize acceptance speech of 1970.

**Mass Culture
and High
Culture in the
"New Europe"**

Popular Culture

The young and wage earners with spare cash to spend provided a mass market for an emerging worldwide popular culture in the 1960s. Its modes of transmission were television, cheap transistor radios, recordings, films, and inexpensive international travel. Its content was casual, spontaneous enjoyment of leisure and the senses. Its forms of expression were drawn, for the most part, from American models: jazz and rock music, informal clothing, western movies. This popular culture received wide acceptance in all of Europe, including Eastern Europe where it was officially discouraged. It was the basis of enormous new fortunes. It finished off the remains of traditional regional folk cultures (except for a few artificial nostalgic "folk" songs), further increased the homogeneity of European young people, and widened the gap between the tastes of the young and their elders.

The most celebrated figures in 1960s mass culture were a quartet of

The Americanization of Western Europe. Three French "cowboys" on the Champs Elysées.

young singers from the British port city of Liverpool, the Beatles. Their infectious, relaxed enthusiasm, combined with highly expert recordings and publicity, made the Beatles among the best-known personages in the world of the late 1960s. Their original tunes and movies carried a vaguely antiauthoritarian, antimilitarist, antihierarchical message. They leveled gentle ridicule at a status-conscious middle class, sanctioned the use of consciousness-affecting drugs, and publicized a life of apparently carefree, good-humored hedonism.

It was significant that the Beatles came from working-class backgrounds, from a provincial city outside any of the traditional cultural capitals, and that their art bore almost no relation to traditional high culture. The British historian Eric Hobsbawm observed that with the Beatles, British culture had become working-class.[34] In truth, the Beatles stood less for anything properly British than for an international culture of youth and leisure. It is doubtful that any entertainers had ever before transcended national boundaries so fully. The Beatles enjoyed their first success in a Hamburg nightclub, made films that were dubbed into dozens of languages, and toured the world in person and on records. The British government's recognition of their export value with the award of the Order of the British Empire simply called attention to the anachronism of national cultures and middle-class deference and manners.

The Beatles, of course, were only the most celebrated example of an international phenomenon. The young Muscovites who tried to buy blue jeans from Western tourists showed that the international culture of youth and leisure was more powerful than bureaucracies and national cultural establishments.

The Fine Arts

It is difficult to discern any fundamentally new departure in the fine arts after the Second World War. Artists continued for the most part to work the mine of private expression, as they had done since the century had opened. Art historian E. H. Gombrich holds that "no revolution in art has been more successful than that which started before World War I."[35] That revolution had consisted in setting artists free of learned conventions, allowing them to explore every possible medium of self-expression. The variety of subject matter, technique, and medium made it impossible to call any one of them characteristic of the postwar period. What was important was the virtual disappearance of the angry shock that had greeted experiment as late as 1914, and the universal acceptance of the belief that artistic success was measured in terms of expressing oneself in an original idiom. Even Gombrich, fundamentally sympathetic to the modern arts, could wonder whether the obligation to be "new" had not become the new conformity of the later twentieth century.

[34]Eric Hobsbawm, *Industry and Empire* (New York, 1968), p. 276.
[35]E. H. Gombrich, *The Story of Art,* 12th ed. (Garden City, N.Y., 1972), p. 483.

Not all postwar art was nonfigurative, of course. The horrors of that war cried out for expression. The Italian sculptor Marino Marini made concentrated expressions of desolation from a series of human figures on horseback, inspired by Italian peasants fleeing from air raids. The British sculptor Henry Moore adapted his monumental figures to portray the endurance of Londoners waiting out air raids in the subway. Some painters in the 1960s tried to bridge the gap between art and commercial mass culture with pop art, which incorporated bits of comic strips or commercial advertising. Its spirit mocked the sanctimonious pretensions of fine arts with some of the vigor of 1920s dada. For the most part, however, painters concentrated on the abstract techniques of the earlier twentieth century.

The same fragmentation of vision occurred in the novel. The "new novel" of French writers like Alain Robbe-Grillet and Natalie Sarraute focused on concrete details without plot, character development, or a clear sense of the observer's identity. The traditional novel also enjoyed continued vigor in Britain, Italy, and Germany. The German postwar realists still wrote satirical social novels; Heinrich Böll won the Nobel Prize for his *Group Portrait with Lady* (1973), which follows fifty years of the ups and downs of Cologne in the twentieth century through the life of a young woman.

Despite the serious inroads television made on the cinema as popular entertainment, films continued to be a vigorous form of artistic expression in the 1960s, and one that preserved a vision accessible to a wider audience than painting. Paris and Rome were centers of experimental filmmaking in the 1960s. The most provocative works were the savage exposés of empty urban life by Jean-Luc Godard and Michelangelo Antonioni, Luchino Visconti's brooding explorations of decadence, the dark psychological dramas of the Swedish director Ingmar Bergman, and the Catholic-Freudian allegories of the Spaniard Luis Buñuel.

Composers continued their search for new sounds to complete their liberation from tone and harmony. The most important postwar developments did not differ in kind from their interwar predecessors, but the composers did discover new ranges of sound. Electronic music, begun between the wars by Edgard Varèse, was given immense new range by the application of computers and electronic instruments like the Moog synthesizer. Another new trend was the use of silence and of chance in "aleatory" music that the performers improvised according to the composer's general instructions. "Concrete" music shared the fragmented vision of the 1960s with its concentration on individual sounds. The Frenchman Pierre Boulez was the most distinguished exponent of atonal composition, but, as in the other arts, there was abundant room for variety. The German Carl Orff reduced his choral settings to highly ritualized, almost hypnotic repetitions of a few harmonic patterns. The German Karl-Heinz Stockhausen and the Italian Luigi Nono used electronic and atonal music to express their left political position in the late 1960s.

The most accessible of the fine arts was architecture, which postwar reconstruction and expansion gave great scope. For the most part, the architects of the postwar period continued to develop the main ideas of the period just before and after the First World War. Italian architect Pier Luigi Nervi continued to produce magnificent free forms in concrete; Ludwig Mies van der Rohe and other Bauhaus disciples carried on functionalism; Le Corbusier put some of his thoughts about the social functions of buildings into practice in housing projects in the south of France.

Religious Revival

The churches emerged from the war strengthened by the moral revulsion against Nazism. Even though much of the high culture had been materialistic and at least agnostic for two centuries, there were signs of religious revival.

The death of Pope Pius XII, (1938–58), a cautious, aristocratic administrator, allowed wartime and postwar currents to be expressed at the top of the Church hierarchy. The new pope, John XXIII (1958–63), was his predecessor's opposite: a jovial, robust man of peasant origins, whose overflowing human warmth radiated in all directions. Pope John's brief papacy incorporated much of the postwar ferment in a wave of up-dating (*aggiornamento*). Pope John called the first world Catholic council since 1870 at the Vatican, soon known as "Vatican II" (1961–63), which authorized the use of local languages rather than Latin in the celebration of the Mass, approved ecumenical approaches to other Christians, and vested more power in Church councils. Pope John's two major encyclicals, *Mater et Magistra* (1961) and *Pacem in Terris* (1963), emphasized the need for social justice and more worker participation in the decisions that affected them, and called for an end to international conflict.

Pope John's successor, Pope Paul VI (1964–   ), exhibited a papal style strongly marked by an administrative career. He was more cautious about modern doctrinal trends, as he showed, for example, in his continued rejection of birth control. This conservative style created difficulties in some of the more progressive sections of the Church, such as in Holland. But Pope Paul traveled all over the world in carrying out a more active ecumenism than any of his predecessors. Withdrawing the excommunication pronounced on all Marxists by Pope Pius in 1949, Pope Paul established better relations with the prelates of Iron Curtain countries and moved the Church away from the position that Christianity could exist only under one social system.

Among Protestant theologians, the Second World War had deepened a concern with the pervasiveness of human evil, original sin. The comfortable liberal Protestantism of the late nineteenth century, too submerged in its own time to resist Nazism, was discredited, along with an easy belief in human moral progress.

There were two possible directions to go from there. For the Swiss theologian Karl Barth, the liberal belief that man's reason could save him was a treacherous slope on which one soon slid to the notion that man made whatever religion he needed. Barth resisted this train of thought with a vigorous fundamentalism, which reasserted the primacy of revelation and the powerlessness of man to save himself without God's grace. Barth gave intellectual and moral leadership to the Protestant opposition to Hitler. Dietrich Bonhoeffer, who was executed by the Nazis in 1945, was the most influential of his German pupils.

The other path led, like nineteenth-century liberalism, through human reasoning, but, unlike the liberal Protestantism of that century, it was not content with individual piety, the "historical Jesus," and reasoned moral progress. Theologians like Rudolf Bultmann argued that the biblical message was presented in the cultural terms of a time that could no longer be understood. Modern Christians must extract the inner meaning from these myths and apply them to each situation of modern life. For some, such as the British theologian John Robinson, this meant that "God was dead" in the sense that pious Sunday school myths would have to be rephrased in a language suitable for our own day.

Both churches approached each other, the Catholics in an ecumenical broadening, and the Protestants in a rediscovery of the importance of liturgy and rite. In both, there was a revival of public worship.

Scientific Achievements

European science recovered only slowly from the effects of depression, war, and "brain drain" to the United States. Western European supranational scientific efforts began to show some results in the 1960s. CERN (The European Center for Nuclear Research) built one of the world's most powerful nuclear accelerators in Switzerland, and ELDO (European Launch Development Organization) began to develop a heavy rocket launching device so that Western Europe could catch up in space science. Western European universities were not always well equipped for modern research, however, and a far smaller proportion of the national income was devoted to pure science than in the United States and the Soviet Union. In spite of the disasters of Stalin's meddling in linguistics and genetics, Soviet applied technology scored striking successes in nuclear energy and rocketry, and Russian physics and chemistry were highly creditable.

Whereas physics continued, often brilliantly, to develop the implications of the great leaps made at the beginning of the century, the most profound changes occurred in biology and biochemistry. Study of the basic structure of the proteins that make living cells and of the biochemical structure of genetic elements opened up the possibility of synthesizing living tissue and, beyond that, raised the moral question of how to control experiments modifying the human body or personality. The Nobel Prize in Medicine and Physiology in 1962 was given to Sir Francis Crick of Cambridge University along with the American James

Watson, for working out the structure of DNA, the basic protein element of genetic material.

The social sciences and philosophy, less dependent than the physical sciences on massive research expenditure, were areas of European brilliance after the Second World War. With the decline of immediate postwar ideologies, there were fewer Europeans who clung to vast overarching philosophical or sociological systems. The logical positivists, followers of Ludwig Wittgenstein and Bertrand Russell, such as the Oxford philosopher A. J. Ayer, shied away from large ethical or metaphysical questions to study with mathematical precision the structure of the logic of individual statements. The same fragmentation, although less deliberate, governed research in the social sciences, which became heavily influenced by American pragmatic, detailed observation. No major figures emerged to take the place of the great masters of social thought who had dominated the earlier generation: Marx, Weber, Freud.

The closest thing to a powerful new influence in the social sciences was structuralism, to which the French anthropologist Claude Lévi-Strauss gave the most sophisticated expression. While teaching in Brazil in the 1930s and in exile in New York from Vichy France in the 1940s, Lévi-Strauss became profoundly moved by the Brazilian Indian tribes that he saw gradually vanishing before the advance of "civilization." Already doubtful of the superiority of that civilization, Lévi-Strauss set out to discover the basic elements of all thought processes among primitive peoples. By analyzing the detailed content of myths about food, cooking, and smoking, Lévi-Strauss thought he could discover and catalogue a finite number of concrete logical processes that were the basic structure of all human thought: pairing, opposites, and the like. His interest was in the structure of thought, not in its history, in attempting to "decipher a code rather than tracing a pedigree."[36] In *The Savage Mind* (1962) he argued that the logical processes of thought of unchanging ("primitive") societies were as complex, and as valid, as those of changing or developed societies. In his most accessible work, *Tristes Tropiques* (1955), Lévi-Strauss mused about the clash of cultures, suggested his doubts about the relative validity of Western civilizations, and maintained that the nature of human thought could best be approached by finding the code of inner logical structure than by tracing a history.

Lévi-Strauss's taste for detailed, concrete research and for rather mechanistic explanations became widely influential. Anthropology and linguistics developed into more active centers of interest than traditional philosophy and history, although history itself was stimulated by contact with the social sciences. Even literary criticism, as in the work of French critic Roland Barthes, turned away from impressionistic commentary to the search for concrete, "positive" logical structures in plot and character.

The words *fragmented* and *concrete* have appeared often in this brief

[36]George Lichtheim, *Europe in the Twentieth Century* (New York, 1972), p. 180.

discussion. While popular culture dominated mass attention, high culture after the Second World War found itself divided among scientists pursuing ever more specialized and inaccessible studies in minute detail.

In Britain in the 1960s, vigorous debate centered on a celebrated exchange between a scientist, C. W. Snow, and a literary critic, F. W. Leavis. Snow had argued that there were "two cultures," the scientific and the literary, and in its more elementary form, the debate turned around which was superior. In fact, there were many cultures, mostly inaccessible to even the educated. Europeans had lost not only their assurance of cultural superiority, but their vision of a whole culture.

Suggestions for Further Reading

The works by Shonfield and Crouzet cited at the end of Chapter 17 are essential for study of the prosperous Europe of the 1960s. Shonfield argued that the mixed, planned economies of Europe were capable of sustained growth and full employment in the long run; Crouzet was more skeptical. No informative book on the problems of inflation in Europe has yet been published. Stephen Graubard, ed., *A New Europe?** (1964) contains many important articles written from the more optimistic perspective of the early 1960s.

Anthony Sampson, *Anatomy of Europe** (1969) is an impressionistic survey of Western European life amidst plenty. Studies of the effects of prosperity on individual countries include the same author's *Anatomy of Britain Today** (1965) and *The New Anatomy of Britain** (1972); Vernon Bogdanor and Robert Skidelsky, eds., *The Age of Affluence, 1951–1964** (1970); and John Ardagh, *The New French Revolution: A Social and Economic Study of France, 1945–1968** (1969).

There are several interesting studies of the modernization of Western European villages: Lawrence Wylie, *Village in the Vaucluse,** 2nd ed. (1964) and, edited by the same author, *Chanzeaux: A Village in Anjou* (1966); Edgar Morin, *Red and White: Report from a French Village** (1970); Benjamin R. Barber, *The Death of Communal Liberty: A History of Freedom in a Swiss Mountain Canton*

(1974); and Julian A. Pitt-Rivers, *People of the Sierra,** rev. 2nd ed. (1971).

Economic change in Eastern Europe is examined in Michael Gamarnikow, *Economic Reform in Eastern Europe* (1968).

J. Peter Nettl, *The Soviet Achievement** (1967) is a good brief introduction to Russian material gains, with interesting illustrations. Alec Nove, *The Soviet Economy,** 2nd ed. (1969) and *Economic History of the USSR** (1972) are basic. See also Margaret Miller, *The Rise of the Soviet Consumer* (1965).

Among attempts to fathom the social effects of European prosperity are John Goldthorpe *et al., The Affluent Worker: Political Attitudes and Behavior* (1968); Richard M. Titmuss, *Income Distribution and Social Change* (1962); and Richard F. Hamilton, *Affluence and the French Worker in the Fourth Republic* (1967), which shows that French workers did not vote according to income but according to the political affiliation of the union to which they belonged.

Changes in social mobility and social stratification are examined statistically in Albert E. Halsey, ed., *Trends in British Society Since 1900* (1971). See also T. B. Bottomore, "Class Structure in Western Europe," in Margaret Scotford Archer and Salvador Giner, eds., *Contemporary Europe: Class, Status, and Power* (1971).

The basic statements of the "end of ideology" thesis are Daniel Bell, *The End of*

Ideology* (1960), and Raymond Aron, *The Opium of the Intellectuals** (1957). Recent doubts about the thesis are examined in Frank E. Myers, "Social Class and Political Change in Western Industrial Systems," *Comparative Politics*, Vol. 2, No. 3 (April 1970).

Two penetrating studies of the European left under conditions of affluence are George Lichtheim, *Marxism in Modern France** (1966), and Annie Kriegel, *The French Communists: Profile of a People* (1972). Sidney Tarrow, *Peasant Communism in Southern Italy* (1967) is illuminating.

On the French uprisings of 1968, see Raymond Aron, *The Elusive Revolution* (1969), and the more sympathetic Alain Schnapp and Pierre Vidal-Nacquet, *French Student Uprising, November 1967–June 1968* (1971), a collection of documents with commentary.

The basic work on the generation gap is John R. Gillis, *Youth and History: Tradition and Change in European Age Relations, 1770 to the Present* (1974).

Among many works on the Czech "springtime" of 1968, see Ivan Svitak, *The Czechoslovak Experiment, 1968–1969* (1971).

The latest scholarly survey of dissidence in the Soviet Union is Abraham Rothberg, *The Heirs of Stalin: Dissidence and the Soviet Regime, 1953–1970* (1972).

Two European intellectuals disappointed with the uses to which working people put mass culture and leisure are Ignazio Silone, *Emergency Exit* (1968), and Richard Hoggart, *The Uses of Literacy* (1957).

20 EUROPE IN THE WORLD TODAY

This book began with a period in which Europe was the richest, most intellectually innovative, and most militarily powerful region of the earth. After a half century of wars, revolution, and depression, that preeminence had all but vanished. As the French political commentator Raymond Aron observed in the 1950's, Europe had "finished conquering" and was "succumbing to its victory."[1] It was an ambiguous victory, in that European techniques and civilization had so spread throughout the world that offshoots and former colonies had become more powerful than the old Continent. One partly-European superpower, the Soviet Union, held Eastern Europe under its sway. The rest of Europe was dependent for military defense on the other superpower, the United States; it was also permeated by popular culture of mostly American provenance, and enormously influenced by American economic power.

[1]Raymond Aron, *The Opium of the Intellectuals,* trans. Terence Kilmartin (New York, 1962), p. 314.

Yet Europeans were too energetic, skillful, and imaginative to remain passive in the world. By the 1960s, after twenty years of parochial concern with reconstruction and recovery, Europeans found that their new industrial and commercial power restored their independent voice in the world. And that world had become less rigidly bipolar, leaving more room for Europeans to maneuver between the superpowers. Although almost the last of the European colonies had been lost, there were increased opportunities for European cultural and economic influence in the Third World.

The Cold War Thaw

In the 1960s the Western and Communist blocs lost some of the cement that had hardened the two sides. First, the cement of fear began to soften. After nearly twenty years of Cold War, the United States and the Soviet Union repeatedly demonstrated their determination to limit their conflicts to local skirmishes. Late in the 1960s, few Europeans would remember how much they had feared a Soviet march westward or a massive American retaliation, as late as the erection of the Berlin Wall in 1961. Both Eastern and Western Europeans began to feel less passive before the military decisions of the superpowers. At the same time, the cement of economic dependence softened. Eastern and Western Europeans discovered that their own economic power gave them increased leverage in dealing with their "protectors."

There is something artificial in designating any moment as the turning point, but the Cuban missile crisis, the hottest moment of the Cold War, did appear to end an old era and begin a new one. In October 1962, United States reconnaissance planes discovered that the Soviet Union was placing ballistic missiles in Cuba, as close to Florida as United States missiles in Turkey were to the Soviet frontier. Unlike the Korean War, indeed unlike any Cold War confrontation since the Berlin Airlift of 1948, Cuba set the armed forces of the two nuclear powers against each other, without intermediaries. Overreaction could lead to a nuclear strike if either side had reason to believe that the other was about to strike first.

Despite obstacles of unclear communication, time pressure, and fatigue, both Soviet Premier Khrushchev and United States President Kennedy managed to convey their desire for settlement short of war and to control their own partisans of overreaction. Kennedy postponed the air strike on the missile sites urged by both his military advisors and former Secretary of State Dean Acheson; instead, he adopted the more limited riposte of a naval blockade of Cuba. Khrushchev turned sixteen Cuba-bound Russian ships around in midocean on the strength of a positive American reply to his offer to remove the missiles in exchange for an American agreement not to invade Cuba. The Russians gave up active military presence in Cuba, without insisting on the removal of United States missiles in Turkey in exchange; the Americans accepted the continued existence of Communist Cuba as an exception to the Monroe Doctrine. Each side could claim to have won its essential point without going to war.

The Cuban crisis reminded the superpowers that they had more interest in jointly preserving the *status quo* and their advantageous postwar positions than in precipitating a fatal duel. That awareness had been evident when the United States and the Soviet Union, separately and for their own reasons, worked to avert war over the Suez Canal in October 1956. The next year Communist leaders began talking publicly of "peaceful coexistence." Representatives of twelve Communist parties, assembled in Moscow for the fortieth anniversary of the Bolshevik Revolution in November 1957, had declared:

> At the present time the forces of peace have grown to such an extent that there is a real possibility of averting wars. . . . The Communist and Workers' Parties taking part in this meeting declare that the Leninist principal of peaceful coexistence of the two systems, "socialist and capitalist," . . . is the sound basis of the foreign policy of socialist countries and the dependable pillar of peace and friendship among the peoples.[2]

That common interest had been lost from view during successive crises over Berlin, Lebanon, and Southeast Asia from 1958 to 1961. But the last-minute step back from the brink of war in the Cuban confrontation opened the way for more substantial relaxation of tensions than during the 1955 to 1957 thaw. The climate of relief was conducive to wider agreements.

In the summer of 1963, the United States and the Soviet Union signed a partial Nuclear Test Ban Treaty ending all but underground explosions. A "hot line" telephone was installed between the Kremlin and the White House to prevent poor communication from needlessly complicating future confrontations. Most importantly for Europeans, the Soviet Union ceased to set deadlines for ending the four-power presence in Berlin and turning Berlin into a free city. To be sure, there was shock and outrage in August 1968 when the Soviet Union crushed the Dubček regime in Czechoslovakia by armed force. Although that action proved Russian determination to maintain its sphere of influence intact, there were no apparent Soviet territorial aims west of the Iron Curtain after the Berlin issue was dropped in the early 1960s.

Polycentrism in the Communist World

The Sino-Soviet Split

Along with relaxation came independent stirrings by members of both blocs. The most striking evidence of dissension on the Communist side was the Sino-Soviet split. The Chinese Communists had won their victory of 1948 without Soviet support, and their leaders had bitter memories of Stalin's withdrawal of support in 1927.[3] Economic difficul-

---

[2]Moscow Declaration of November 16, 1957, quoted in O. Edmund Clubb, Jr., *China and Russia: The Great Game* (New York, 1970), p. 442.
[3]See Chapter 13, p. 376.

ties and Cold War unity kept these frictions hidden until the late 1950s. Mao Tse-tung even signed the Moscow Declaration of Peaceful Existence of November 1957 in person. But as the Chinese began their "great leap forward" into agricultural communes in 1958, and as they engaged in more active military confrontations with the nationalist Chinese on Taiwan against Soviet advice, they began to enunciate a separate Maoist Communist doctrine.

Mao objected to the ideology of peaceful coexistence and to the Soviets' belief that their model applied to Chinese experience. He proposed a policy of active attacks on imperialism, in which reformist socialists or Third World bourgeois-nationalist states were as dangerous enemies as the great bourgeois states themselves—in other words, a return to the 1928 to 1934 policy of "class against class," as opposed to Khrushchev's new variant of Popular Front alliances. Mao also argued that the peasant communism that had produced the Chinese victory of 1948 was as valid as the Russian model, and indeed more applicable to future revolutionary situations—hence, Russia was no longer an example for other Communists. In fact, Mao charged the Soviet Union with "economism"—putting its own economy of abundance ahead of promoting world revolution.

Behind these doctrinal differences lay Chinese–Russian antagonisms that were practical, territorial, and even nationalist. Mao wanted the Soviets to cease all aid to Third World bourgeois-nationalist states (such as India, with whom China waged a border war in 1962) so that all Soviet economic surplus could be devoted to Chinese needs. Anxious to reassert ancient Chinese influence over central Asia, Mao accused the Russians of having overrun Chinese lands in its nineteenth-century expansion eastward. Mao, finally, expressed national pride in the autonomy of China's own revolutionary pattern and set out to supplant the Soviet Union as the leader of Communist movements in the Third World.

The disagreement was mutual. In July 1960, the Soviet Union withdrew all of its 1390 technicians from China and suspended its economic aid. Khrushchev's hard line of 1960 and 1961, including the resumption of nuclear testing, was intended as much to threaten as to outflank the Chinese. Up until October and November 1962 they attacked each other only indirectly. The Chinese denounced the Yugoslavs; the Soviet replies were directed at Albania, China's only European ally. In October and November 1962, however, came both the Russian failure in Cuba and the China–India border war, in which the Soviets continued to supply arms to the Indians. Thereafter, the Soviet Union and China attacked each other openly. Disagreement over the Nuclear Test Ban Treaty of July 1963 broke off all contact between the two. The Chinese accused the Russians of "capitulation to United States imperialism"; Khrushchev charged the Chinese with the "madness" of wanting to unleash a nuclear war that only the Chinese masses would survive. By 1969 Chinese and Soviet troops were skirmishing in two places on their long border: along the Amur River to the north of Manchuria, and along the Ussuri River in central Asia. One encounter cost over 800 casualties. There were rumors that the Soviets had plans to bomb the Chinese nuclear research center, where the Chinese tested their first nuclear bomb in 1964.

The break with China sent a rift all the way through the Communist parties of the world. The number of European Maoists was always small, although these splinter groups diverted some of the young and the active from Communist parties in Italy and France. Only one European state—Albania—entered wholly into the Maoist camp. More important for Europe was the indirect support given by the Sino-Soviet split to the Eastern European movement toward national communism.

National Communism in Eastern Europe

Just after Khrushchev's denunciation of Stalin in June 1956, the Italian Communist leader Palmiro Togliatti had proposed that world communism become "polycentric":

> The Soviet model cannot and must not any longer be obligatory. . . . The whole system becomes polycentric, and even in the Communist movement itself we can not speak of a single guide.[4]

Khrushchev was obliged to accept publicly the validity of a "multiplicity of forms of socialist development" in an effort at reconciliation with Tito in June 1956. Soviet intervention in Hungary in November 1956, however, revealed the limits of permissible divergence within the Soviet bloc. The Moscow Declaration of November 1957 continued to refer to the Soviet Union as leader of the "socialist camp."

Aided by Chinese attacks on the Soviet right of leadership in the 1960s, tendencies toward nationally independent forms of communism reappeared in Eastern Europe. The two examples of dissidence in the 1950s, one limited and peaceful (Poland) and the other uncontrolled and crushed (Hungary), had two equivalent examples in the 1960s. The Czechoslovakian attempt to move rapidly toward political and intellectual freedom within a socialist economy provoked the brutal Soviet invasion of August 21, 1968. But the Romanians followed the opposite course of political autocracy combined with economic independence, with far more success.

Romania, in fact, achieved an extraordinary degree of economic leeway. In 1962 the Eastern European economic organization, COMECON, adopted a division of labor by which some Communist nations would produce finished products and the other would supply raw materials. As a primarily agricultural state with large oil reserves, Romania foresaw itself condemned to perpetual economic backwardness by this plan. At a meeting of COMECON in February 1963, Romania refused to accept the sacrifices demanded of it in the name of a "socialist divison of labor"; that is, to renounce its own economic development in

[4]Palmiro Togliatti, "Nine Questions of Stalinism." Polycentrism was launched in a Togliatti interview in an Italian party publication, *Nuovi Argomenti,* on June 16, 1956. Although Togliatti himself later recanted, polycentrism was irreversible.

commodities that would compete with the more industrial Czechoslovakia and East Germany.

In 1964 the Romanian leaders publicly declared the independence of all Communist nations and the obligation of noninterference in others' affairs, a warning to the Soviet Union to allow Romanian economic development to follow its own course. In the same year, the Romanians sought economic and technical aid from France and the United States. By the early 1970s Romania was following an independent position in foreign policy, voting against the Soviet Union in the United Nations on disarmament projects.

There was nothing politically liberal about Romanian national communism. Party Secretary Gheorghe Gheorghiu-Dej (1944–65) was one of the strictest of the Eastern European Stalinists; he supported the Soviet Union fully in its struggles with China. His successor, Nicolai Ceausescu (1965–   ), followed a similar course, supporting the Soviet Union against Czechoslovakia while exchanging visits with United States President Nixon.

By 1970 it had long been impossible to talk of a single Communist bloc. Since 1963 there had been at least two blocs: Soviet and Chinese. By the late 1960s, the term *satellites* became inappropriate to describe the wide variety of Eastern European Communist regimes, whose support the Soviet Union could not automatically count on. In Poland and Yugoslavia, about 85 percent of the arable land was in private family farms. Every successive Polish leader had had to come to terms with the bedrock Catholicism of the Poles. Poland, Yugoslavia, and Romania were receiving American economic aid. Albania was in the Chinese camp. Hungary, having learned how far dissent could be stretched in 1956, enjoyed far more access to Western literature and goods than the Soviet Union. The invasion of Czechoslovakia in August 1968 proved that the Soviet Union would fight to prevent the introduction of unlimited political and cultural liberalism, far sooner than it would to enforce economic uniformity. But there was a limit to the number of times the Soviet Union could afford to offend its foreign followers so deeply for any purpose.

By the early 1970s, the challenge for the Eastern European Communist regimes was to find some way of assuring abundance, even through exchanges with the West, without catching what they considered to be the cultural malaise, divisions, and critical spirit of the West.

The integration movement in Western Europe had been intended at first to end the civil war among nation-states in Europe; after 1948 it had been stimulated by the fear of Soviet invasion. Always present was a latent apprehension of "America the Menace."[5] That fear of the

The Emerging Western "Third Force"

[5]Georges Duhamel, *America: The Menace. Scenes from the Life of the Future,* trans. Charles Miner Thompson (Boston, 1931).

enormous American power was masked only when America's arms seemed to be defending Europe and when its aid appeared vital for economic recovery.

The climate changed somewhat around 1962. The fear of Soviet invasion was much reduced after Russia quietly abandoned its Berlin demands and revealed in the Cuban crisis its fundamental determination to avoid war. The Cuban missile crisis also conveyed a more specific message to Europeans: the United States and Russia could stake the lives of Europeans without their even knowing. The United States had sent emissaries to European capitals to "inform" European leaders, not to "consult" with them, about a crisis in which Europe might well become one of the battlegrounds. Even the NATO council was critical. Finally, in the summer of 1962 France at last emerged from the drain and distraction of eight years of very painful colonial war: it was the last important step in European decolonization, and it freed France and its president, General Charles de Gaulle, to turn to other matters.

Indeed, it was France that led the way toward a more independent Western European role and General de Gaulle who personified the European "Third Force" policy after 1962.

Gaullism: An Independent Europe

The first area in which European policy began to take an independent line was military and foreign policy, which is curious considering the small proportion of their national income that Western European states spent on the military. That, of course, was part of the problem. Western Europe's defense depended on the "tripwire" of a relatively small number of United States troops in Europe to bring American force into play. But that force would be used in ways that would destroy Europe. According to the United States' graduated deterrent strategy of the 1960s, American force would be deployed in gradually ascending steps against a Soviet advance. While this strategy left open a far greater opportunity for limiting a conflict in Europe to conventional weapons than the 1950s strategy of massive retaliation on the Russian heartland, it had the grave disadvantage in European eyes of making their continent the main battleground. Western Europeans could recover some control over their own security by raising a massive conventional force themselves, and depend on the Americans only in case of nuclear war. Or they could build a nuclear force themselves.

Only two Western European states had attempted to build a modern nuclear armed force after the war: Britain and France. The British tested their first atomic bomb in October 1951 and their first nuclear bomb in March 1957. The burden was immense, however, for a country whose economic growth rate fell below that of the Continent. In 1957 the British government renounced all pretense of independent military resources and accepted missiles from the United States. The British defense effort had served mainly to maintain influence with the United

States, but it was an effort that required British coordination with American policy, which meant that Britain could not use this force against American wishes.

The French went a separate way, not entirely by choice: the United States refused to provide technical defense information to the French government, deemed less secure than the British. The French Fourth Republic went ahead with independent nuclear research, and de Gaulle hastened the program when he returned to power in 1958. The first French atomic bomb was exploded in the Sahara in 1960, and the first nuclear weapon in the French Pacific islands in 1968.

De Gaulle saw no point in a European country having a major military force unless it had unlimited power to give it orders. The British armed force was tied to American policy; all the NATO forces were under the command of integrated staffs and ultimately under an American general, the Supreme Allied Commander–Europe. De Gaulle's rejection of this state of affairs seemed to many observers a kind of archaic nationalism. At the same time, his separate path struck a responsive chord in many Europeans outside France as well.

Two grand old men of the New Europe. Former West German Chancellor Konrad Adenauer and French President Charles de Gaulle in Paris, 1966.

De Gaulle had begun to remove French armed forces from NATO command as early as 1959, when he pulled out the fighter aircraft squadrons and the Mediterranean fleet. He removed the Atlantic and Channel fleets from NATO command in June 1963, and in 1966 he withdrew all French participation from NATO (while proclaiming that France would remain a member of the Atlantic Alliance, of which NATO was the military arm). NATO headquarters moved from near Paris to Brussels in 1966.

By the time of the sudden Soviet move into Czechoslovakia in August 1968, NATO had ceased to be a very active center of military initiative among its members. After Czechoslovakia, the French military cooperated informally with some NATO operations, such as air defense communication. But Europe had neither a truly integrated military force nor sufficient national forces to counterbalance a possible Russian move. The American plan to promote a multinational nuclear force using United States-controlled warheads was rejected by France and other European governments in the late 1960s. Inflation-burdened Holland reduced its NATO participation by half in 1974.

Another area of some expression of European independence from America was cultural. Was European culture being submerged in American advertising, packaging, and incessant novelty? There was a good deal of discussion about this; the French actually tried to reduce "Franglais," the assimilation of English words into their language. But little that governments could do was likely to change the tastes of the newly affluent majority of young Europeans, who had not received the classical education of the elite.

The most important area of independence from the United States was economic. Europe had ceased to be directly dependent on American aid in the early 1950s; most aid after 1950 was military, and that ended by 1956. By the 1960s, Western Europe had emerged as a major economic power in its own right, an industrialized region of 175 million highly skilled people, comparable in rough general magnitude to the superpowers' economic weight.

The Common Market

Western Europe's growing economic power focused attention on its economic union, the Common Market. European integration entered a new phase in which economic independence from the United States became the most powerful motive for progress.

The European desire for economic independence coincided, to some degree, with General de Gaulle's struggle in the 1960s to reduce the influence of the superpowers on France and Europe. A less complex European statesman than de Gaulle might have found in the thriving Common Market the ideal vehicle for raising a Great Europe, stretching "from the Atlantic to the Urals," to the status of a third superpower. De

Gaulle, however, threw his will and intelligence into two different and in some ways contradictory aims: an independent France within an independent Europe. He was determined to avoid French submersion in a nameless, faceless new state whose inhabitants, he said in a scornful speech, would speak "Esperanto or Volapuk," instead of French, German, or Italian. De Gaulle tried in the early 1960s to assure that integrated Europe would remain a "Europe of States."

The question of the direction of the European integration movement was joined again. On the one hand lay the possibility that, having succeeded brilliantly in its initial economic assignment,[6] the European Common Market would make its supranational elements (common social policy, common agricultural policy) the germ cell of a genuine political union. That was the hope of the aged survivors of the European integration movement's heroic days, such as Jean Monnet, and of the growing body of supranational officials, such as Walter Hallstein, president of the Common Market's Commission for the first ten years (1958–67). Hallstein liked to speak of the Treaty of Rome (1958) as a "constitutional document," the "first chapter of a European constitution."[7] From this point of view, the Common Market should take on not only new functions but new members. For example, it should assume powers of taxation, and it should expand to include Britain and other members of the European Free Trade Association who had changed their minds about European integration.

On the other hand lay the idea of a more limited cooperation among states, for which de Gaulle was the most conspicuous but by no means the only spokesman. Despite his clear aversion to supranationality, de Gaulle did not want to dissolve the Common Market or other European groups. He wanted to use the Common Market for his own goals: to make powerful again a Europe led by France. Using France's veto power to block any decisions until he got his way, de Gaulle prodded the Common Market in directions favorable to French interests. The Common Market members were forced into the uncomfortable choice of doing things his way or not at all.

As the main agricultural producer of the Six, France insisted that the Common Market absorb French agricultural surpluses. France wanted Common Market overseas development funds directed largely to French Africa. De Gaulle vetoed British entry into the Common Market in January 1963 and again in 1967, because British imports of Commonwealth agricultural products were a threat to French agriculture and because he felt that Britain was too closely tied to United States policy. When Hallstein attempted to increase the Common Market's budgetary independence by collecting some customs duties and disbursing agricultural subsidies directly, de Gaulle brought the whole

[6]See Chapter 18, pp. 556–58.
[7]European Economic Community, *Bulletin,* No. 7-1967 (July 1967), p. 8.

Conservative Prime Minister Edward Heath, flanked by former Labour Prime Minister Harold Wilson, pass before the statue of the indomitable Churchill as they lead members of the House of Commons into the House of Lords to hear Queen Elizabeth II address the opening of Parliament, July 2, 1970.

machinery to a halt for seven months, from July 1965 to January 1966. De Gaulle effectively blocked the step forward to majority voting in the Council of Ministers scheduled for 1966. This was a grave setback, for it appeared to leave the Common Market stalled at the stage of unanimous voting. At issue was whether a policy could be forced on one recalcitrant member, or whether all members were to keep their veto power.

It is possible that even without de Gaulle the Common Market would not have developed beyond a free-trade area to genuine economic and political union in the 1960s. The earlier pan-European enthusiasms had somewhat diminished as the Common Market settled into technical routine and Europe into a less passionate era. It was not proven that the theory of spillover, according to which the Common Market and other European institutions would generate new functions in daily practice, would actually extend beyond the easier areas of common tariff policy. In times of economic difficulty, for example, there was still a tendency for member states to fall back on individual solutions. The clearest case occurred at the time of the recession in the overproducing coal fields in

1958. When the High Authority of the European Coal and Steel Community proposed stern measures, requiring all six member states to reduce coal imports and set production quotas to aid distressed mining operations in Belgium and Germany, the High Authority was overruled by the member governments acting through the Coal and Steel Community's Council of Ministers. Later, the Coal and Steel Community's High Authority was merged with the Common Market and Euratom commissions (1967), which had less broad supranational powers. Even where de Gaulle was not involved, the European communities did not automatically grow beyond the level of a forum for the cooperation of sovereign member states.

Nevertheless, the European communities not only survived but prospered. In 1967 the European Coal and Steel Community and Euratom were merged with the Common Market into an enlarged European Economic Community under a single executive Commission. Daily practice continued to expand the community's legitimacy, and no one seriously proposed to go back to the old European free-for-all. The community's Court of Justice built up a body of case law and obliged several member states, including France, to bring some actions (such as certain kinds of export subsidy) into line with community policy. After 1969, although General de Gaulle's successor as president of France, Georges Pompidou (1969–74), continued to oppose majority voting, there was renewed talk about monetary union, about increasing taxation powers, and about the eventual direct election of the community legislature at Strasbourg. Most important of all, Britain, Ireland, and Denmark joined the Common Market on January 1, 1973.

The United States and Europe: Economic Rivals

The United States had dominated the world economy virtually without challenge for twenty years after the Second World War. In 1945 the United States accounted for half the world's productive capacity. Then the prosperity that the United States had encouraged in Western Europe (and Japan) began to narrow that lead. In the 1960s, for the first time since the war, the United States was troubled not by European poverty but by European economic rivalry.

The changed relationship showed itself in several important ways. One was the balance of payments. Throughout the 1950s, the European economies struggled against a chronic "dollar gap." Europeans needed desperately to buy food, coal, and machinery from dollar areas at a time when they obtained dollars only from foreign aid, American travel abroad, and the small American imports from Europe. To prevent disastrous declines in their own currencies' relative value, Western European governments had to limit imports and control their citizens' access to dollars. Around 1960, the United States began running a deficit in its balance of payments with Western Europe. Americans spent more abroad on items like Volkswagens, which eventually accounted for

10 percent of the American automobile market; even more importantly, the United States government spent vast sums abroad in military operations. By the end of 1970, the United States deficit with Europe had risen to over $10 billion per year.

Related to the shift in the balance of payments was the shift in productive capacity. The European automobile industry cut deeply into the American market in the late 1960s. During that decade, Western European steel production ran ahead of American production:

	1959	1971[8]
United States	93 million tons	141 million tons
Europe (the Six plus Britain)	88 million tons	147 million tons

Europe's growth in productive capacity was not merely quantitative. Postwar reconstruction had equipped Western Europe with more technically advanced plants for such processes as continuously cast steel.

As late as 1955, some observers could still believe that the economic gap was widening between the United States and Europe.[9] A decade later, the gap was rapidly closing, and by 1970 the dollar had been forced into its first devaluation since 1934. Mental habits changed slowly, of course, but the United States–Western European relationship was clearly transformed in the 1960s. Strategically, the United States seemed less immediately necessary as a protector; economically, Western Europe was no longer the threadbare poor relation needing charity, but was now an industrial Great Power. As the economic relationship took increasing precedence over the strategic one, the United States and Western Europe began to look on each other in the dual roles of market and rival.

The United States' emerging conflict with the Common Market took three forms. In order of increasing complexity, they were a dispute over the Common Market's external tariffs, the power of United States business branches within the Common Market countries, and monetary stability.

The tariff question surfaced almost as soon as the balance of trade had shifted in the early 1960s. The first harbinger of the new relationship was the "Chicken War" of 1961. When the Common Market external tariffs damaged American farmers' exports of chicken to Europe, the larger issue was posed of whether the Common Market would erect protectionist barriers against the outside world, while providing free trade within. President Kennedy engaged in tough negotiations with the Common Market to reduce tariffs substantially on both sides over a wide range of products. The "Kennedy Round" of tariff negotiations, which continued long after the president's death, until 1967, marked the first time that the United States and the Common Market had dealt with each other as economic equals.

[8]Michael Mandelbaum and Daniel Yergin, "Balancing the Power," *Yale Review,* Vol. 62, No. 3 (March 1973): 324.
[9]Aron, p. 222.

The problem of American investments in the Common Market countries was more difficult. As the European market flourished, United States companies established branches within the Six in order to avoid the external tariff. By 1965, the EEC Commission in Brussels estimated that American branches or subsidiaries accounted for 80 percent of computer production in Europe, 24 percent of automobiles, 15 percent of synthetic rubber, and 10 percent of petrochemicals.[10] The prospect that overseas American firms would become the main beneficiaries of the Common Market boom, controlling vital sectors of the Western European economy, raised an alarm that can be measured by the way in which French journalist Jean-Jacques Servan-Schreiber's *The American Challenge* (1967)[11] became the best-seller in French publishing history.

The Six were torn between their desire for American investment and their fear of losing control of their main industries. The response was mostly an individual national one of limiting American branches (as in France) or of encouraging the merger of European firms into giants capable of competing with the Americans.

American branches in Europe were linked to the monetary issue. The international monetary system set up after the Second World War at the Bretton Woods Conference[12] made the dollar virtually equivalent to gold as a reserve currency to be held by national banking systems. This gold exchange standard, unlike the pre-1914 pure gold standard, meant that national banks in Europe did not have to cash their dollars in for gold, for the dollar was "as good as gold." When the balance of trade changed around 1960, European banking systems and firms began accumulating large dollar reserves. If all these dollar reserves had been presented at Fort Knox for gold at once, the United States would have experienced a large gold loss during the 1960s that would have made it more difficult to keep up the high rate of military spending, tourist spending, and business investment that was continuing to pour American dollars overseas. In that sense, the dollar was beginning to be overvalued; and in that sense, the gold exchange standard permitted American firms to invest more freely in Europe than they could have if all European-held dollars had been redeemed for gold at once.

General de Gaulle first called attention to the fact that the dollar was overvalued, that "the emperor was wearing no clothes." At the beginning of 1965, he advocated a return to a pure gold standard, and to prove his point, the French government began redeeming several hundred million dollars for gold. Such was the emotional power of the dollar, however, after many years of "dollar gap" in Europe, that the issue was still understood only on a technical level. The International

[10]Ernest Mandel, quoted in George Lichtheim, *Europe in the Twentieth Century* (New York, 1972), p. 314.
[11]The book did not, of course, examine only American investments in Europe. It also warned against the power of American technological and management skill on a world level, and urged Europeans to emulate it.
[12]See Chapter 17, p. 514.

Monetary Fund, the chief regulating office for monetary matters set up at Bretton Woods, tried to smooth the matter over by creating a new reserve fund in 1969, a paper reserve called Special Drawing Rights, and by allowing individuals to buy gold at a floating rate, while the official rate for government dealings remained at $32 per ounce of gold.

As far as ordinary citizens were concerned, the postwar mystique of the dollar came to an end in a massive wave of speculation against the dollar in May 1971. The wild selling of dollars by Swiss bankers, the "gnomes of Zurich," American speculators, and oil-rich Arabs was the first revelation to the public that the dollar would have to be looked at in terms of hard facts and not reputation. The hard facts were that the annual American trade deficit had reached $10.68 billion in 1970 and was going even higher in 1971. Moreover, inflation in the United States, combined with low interest rates there, encouraged American speculators to shift funds to Germany where interest rates were high. In 1970, $6 billion was transferred in this fashion from the United States to Germany. Instability was further increased by the enormous growth of Eurodollars, which had reached $50 billion by 1971, mostly since 1969. Eurodollars were dollars held by Europeans or by American firms doing business in Europe. They were lent to other Europeans or to American branches in a great expansion of credit in Europe. The holders of Eurodollars were tempted to exchange them for German marks when the dollar began to look weak in May 1971, which added enormously to the mass of speculation. The final hard fact was the dwindling United States gold and foreign currency reserves. The gold reserve had fallen to about $11 billion in Fort Knox in May 1971; at that time, there was $20 billion afloat in West Germany alone. If every holder of dollars in West Germany had demanded gold at once, the United States would have been technically bankrupt.

On May 5, 1971, most European central banks, overwhelmed in the rush, simply stopped foreign exchange trading. The Bretton Woods system had broken down. Since the West German mark was allowed to "float" upward to find its proper exchange value, the exchange rates were in chaos. President Nixon tried to persuade Europe to solve the problem by assuming more NATO defense costs, by lowering EEC tariffs, and by buying more United States goods. In the end, however, the United States was obliged to devalue the dollar by 8.57 percent at the Smithsonian Conference in December 1971. A second devaluation of 10 percent followed in February 1973. These steps made European goods more expensive in the United States and American goods cheaper abroad. But above all, they meant that the dollar would not be held as a reserve currency abroad with the same faith as before, and that the monetary system that had allowed the United States to spend beyond its earnings abroad for a decade had come to an end.

Western Europe was now capable of dealing with the United States as an economic equal. The relationship was an ambiguous one. The two sides of the Atlantic dealt with each other carefully, knowing that the prosperity of each depended on the prosperity of all. But they pushed and shoved at each other in ways that would not have been dreamed of a decade earlier. The Common Market convicted the United States Continental Can Company of monopoly practices in Europe in 1972; the United States brought suit before the Geneva Agreement on Trade and Tariffs (GATT) against some forms of European agricultural surcharges that damaged American farm exports. Western Europe had now acquired the economic weight to go its own way in the world, a less clearly demarcated world than the bipolar system of 1945 to 1962.

West Meets East: Willy Brandt and Ostpolitik

The most profound transformation in the dependent, two-bloc Europe of the Cold War came not from General Charles de Gaulle but from the most dynamic European statesman to follow him, West German Chancellor Willy Brandt. Brandt had become foreign minister in a "Great Coalition" with the Christian Democrats in 1966. In October 1969, new elections gave a narrow majority for the first time to a coalition of Brandt's Social Democrats and a splinter party, the Free Democrats. Although the Free Democrats supported laissez-faire economic policies at home, they were willing to work with the SPD for broad relaxation with the Communist countries in international relations. With Brandt as chancellor, the German Social Democrats held power in Germany for the first time since Chancellor Hermann Müller (1928–30).

Brandt's *Ostpolitik* (eastern policy) was intended to change dramatically West Germany's relations with Eastern Europe and the Soviet Union, and to thaw the main Cold War frontier across the center of Europe. Brandt, aged fifty-eight in 1969, was in an exceptionally strong position to sweep with a new broom. He had spent the years from 1933 to 1945 in Norway and Sweden, where he participated in underground resistance to Hitler. While there, he became impressed with the pragmatic welfare state social democracy of Scandinavia. As mayor of West Berlin after 1957, he enjoyed an advantageous stage from which to show himself young, imaginative, and energetic. In 1964 he became leader of the German Social Democratic party and changed it into a pragmatic mass party.[13] As chancellor of a heavily one-sided coalition after October 1969, Brandt enjoyed much more leeway than had Müller. To be sure, his Free Democrat partners prevented any major social change, but Brandt's priority was the dismantling of the wall across central Europe. In this task, he fended off both the student and radical left, who attacked him for working within capitalism, and the Christian Democrats, who were shocked at any deviation from Adenauer's rigid position against dealing with anyone who recognized East Germany.

Brandt's first major breakthrough took place in Moscow, for the Soviet Union held the key to any change in the Eastern European

[13]See Chapter 19, p. 584.

relationship. In any case, the Soviet Union was eager for détente. The Moscow Treaty of August 1970 provided for mutual recognition of existing frontiers. This was tantamount to German renunciation of the lost lands east of the Oder-Neisse River, now in Poland, and of such former Germanic territories as the Czech Sudetenland, which Hitler acquired at Munich and which some German nationalists still claimed. This giant step made subsequent treaties with Poland and Czechoslovakia almost anticlimactic. A new era had dawned, however, when a German chancellor could place a wreath on the monument to the Polish victims of Nazi barbarism in Warsaw, as Brandt did in 1970. In early 1973, he agreed with the Czech government to renounce the Munich settlement of 1938 and thereby any German claim to the Sudetenland, from which so many German-speaking people had been evicted in 1945.

With East Germany, negotiations went somewhat more awkwardly. When Brandt first met East German Chancellor Willy Stoph at Erfurt in March 1970, the East German crowd surged forward shouting Brandt's name. This demonstration of enthusiasm was highly embarrassing to those who claimed legitimacy for East Germany. The East German leaders, who had built the Berlin Wall only nine years earlier out of fear of the corrosive effect of Western contacts on their people, had second thoughts about détente. But the way seemed more open again after Walter Ulbricht, the tough first secretary of the East German Socialist Unity party (SED), retired in 1971 at the age of seventy-seven. Now both Adenauer and Ulbricht, the twin personifications of Cold War rigidity in the two Germanies, were gone.

Even though Ulbricht's successor, Erich Honnecker, was an old-line party functionary who also feared Western contacts, progress was made in ways that would have seemed unthinkable before 1969. At Christmas 1972, the first major movement of persons across the border took place after eleven years of isolation. Many divided families were reunited as an estimated 500,000 West Germans took advantage of the permission to visit East Germany for up to thirty days. East Germans, however, could still not travel. In June 1973, the two Germanies were admitted simultaneously to the United Nations after their mutual diplomatic recognition. It was the most decisive negotiated change in European state relations since the Locarno Agreements of 1925.

The major question, of course, was whether a few visits across the Berlin Wall plus diplomatic recognition would lead to the reunification of Germany. Although that possibility seemed nearer than at any time since 1948, formidable obstacles remained to a step that would completely transform the balance of power within Europe. A reunited Germany would combine the greatest industrial powers of both Eastern and Western Europe into a major new state larger than any of its neighbors except the Soviet Union. Neither Russia nor France could be expected to take pleasure in that prospect. Each would prefer to absorb

A dramatic moment in West German Chancellor Willy Brandt's Ostpolitik. *Brandt kneels before the memorial to Jewish victims of the Nazis in Warsaw, December 1970, shortly before West Germany and Poland established diplomatic relations.*

the new Germany into some supranational unit, but a reunited Germany could hardly belong either to the Common Market and NATO or to COMECON and the Warsaw Pact. Nor could the two social systems be merged without the dismantling of one. Thus Europeans contemplated a transformation of their state system from afar, and while the possibilities of radical change seemed greater than at any time since the war, their import was uncertain.

Decolonization and "Informal Empire"

The major European colonial empires were dismantled after the Second World War. By 1962, only the Portuguese still fought to maintain direct rule of overseas possessions. In retrospect, the Italian seizure of Ethiopia in 1935 and 1936 had been the last overt European conquest of overseas territory, and that had been short lived.

At the close of the First World War there had already been powerful independence movements in areas like British India, where the lawyer Mohandas K. Gandhi perfected techniques of nonviolent civil disobedience during 1919 and 1920 that forced the British authorities either to make concessions or to appear more harshly repressive than British public opinion would accept. The ideal of national self-determination propagated by the Versailles Peace Conference contributed to the growth of national independence movements in the colonies, even though the Versailles settlement actually perpetuated colonial regimes under the mandate system.[14]

Although the German colonies had been distributed among the Allies as mandates, the other colonial powers had relatively little difficulty maintaining their empires throughout the interwar period by means of a mixture of minor concessions to local self-government and armed force. Iraq, under British mandate, was the only non-Western state to attain independence between the wars (1932). Indeed, the rise of fascism stimulated renewed interest in colonies. Hitler claimed the return of German colonies, and Mussolini avenged the old Italian defeat at Adowa by the conquest of Ethiopia. Colonies came to seem more important than ever to the British and Free French during the Second World War for recruiting forces and establishing strategic bases. The British and French clearly expected to retain their empires after the war, perhaps with greater local authority as dominions, but tied nonetheless to the imperial system.

Instead, the European empires were almost all swept away in the years between 1945 and 1960. The eclipse of the power of European states during the war destroyed whatever legitimacy their colonial regimes had possessed, and the exhaustion of Britain and France after the war precluded any successful efforts to reestablish that authority. The United States was favorably inclined at the end of the war to colonial self-determination, for reasons of both sentiment and self-interest. The

[14]See Chapter 6, pp. 175–76.

Soviet Union and, after 1948, Communist China offered support and encouragement to colonial revolutions. There emerged in the Third World a generation of skilled guerrilla tacticians and nationalist political leaders who successfully exploited the heightened expectations, the swollen populations, and the land hunger that European contact itself had generated. No European state had lost a colony to insurrection between 1815 and 1940; no European state won a colonial war after 1945.

Asian Decolonization

The first breaks occurred in the Asian areas that had been occupied by the Japanese. In 1945 the departing Japanese left local nationalist leaders in control of both Dutch Indonesia and French Indochina. The Dutch and the French each tried unsuccessfully to reestablish their presence. After a bitter two-year war in Indonesia, the Dutch had to accept the creation of a Republic of Indonesia, which became independent in December 1949 under the nationalist leader Sukarno.

The French effort to return to Indochina led to a far longer war, because the United States aided the French after the Communists took power in China in 1948. The Indochinese nationalist leader Ho Chi Min, who had become a Communist as a young worker in Paris during the First World War, was already active in the 1930s. During the Japanese occupation, Ho waited in southern China. When the Japanese withdrew in 1945, he proclaimed the Republic of Vietnam with a declaration of independence closely modeled on the United States document of 1776. Meanwhile, French forces moved in, and while the Vietnamese leaders negotiated their future status in Paris, French and Vietnamese units on the scene began to fight. The war lasted until 1954, with the United States providing up to 80 percent of the supplies. After the French left in 1954, the United States supplanted them as the main influence in the southern areas outside Ho Chi Min's control. Thus the Cold War drew decolonization into a confrontation between traditional elites supported by the United States and independence movements supported by the Russians and later the Chinese.

India had been the most troubled part of the British Empire between the wars. It was clear before 1940 that mere dominion status would not satisfy Gandhi and the more radical wing of the Congress party led by Jawaharlal Nehru. During the Second World War, Indian troops contributed to the British war effort, for few Indian leaders saw any advantages in an Axis victory. After the war, the British Labour government was ready to grant independence, but the process was enormously complicated by clashes between Hindu and Moslem populations in India. Unable to reach agreement on a single new state acceptable to both Hindus and Moslems, the British simply announced in early 1947 their intention of transferring sovereignty within a year. A partition plan was hastily agreed on, and in August 1947, amidst great loss of life as Hindu and Moslem populations struggled through hostile regions to reach their new state areas, the two independent nations of India and Pakistan were created. Ceylon achieved independence from Britain at the same time.

Arab Decolonization

The Arab peoples underwent a cultural renaissance in the twentieth century that heightened their sense of identity. By the 1930s they focused their antagonisms against the colonial powers, on the broken promises of independence of 1914 and 1918, and on the settlement of Jewish refugees in Palestine. In 1945 the French grudgingly gave up the mandated territories of Syria and the Lebanon, but the Palestine

DECOLONIZATION

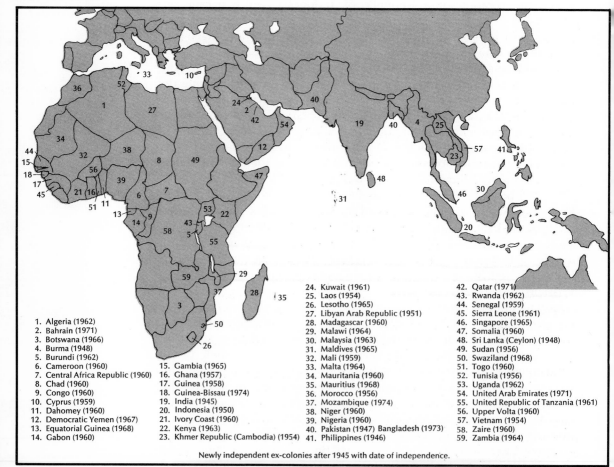

1. Algeria (1962)
2. Bahrain (1971)
3. Botswana (1966)
4. Burma (1948)
5. Burundi (1962)
6. Cameroon (1960)
7. Central Africa Republic (1960)
8. Chad (1960)
9. Congo (1960)
10. Cyprus (1959)
11. Dahomey (1960)
12. Democratic Yemen (1967)
13. Equatorial Guinea (1968)
14. Gabon (1960)
15. Gambia (1965)
16. Ghana (1957)
17. Guinea (1958)
18. Guinea-Bissau (1974)
19. India (1945)
20. Indonesia (1950)
21. Ivory Coast (1960)
22. Kenya (1963)
23. Khmer Republic (Cambodia) (1954)
24. Kuwait (1961)
25. Laos (1954)
26. Lesotho (1965)
27. Libyan Arab Republic (1951)
28. Madagascar (1960)
29. Malawi (1964)
30. Malaysia (1963)
31. Maldives (1965)
32. Mali (1959)
33. Malta (1964)
34. Mauritania (1960)
35. Mauritius (1968)
36. Morocco (1956)
37. Mozambique (1974)
38. Niger (1960)
39. Nigeria (1960)
40. Pakistan (1947) Bangladesh (1973)
41. Philippines (1946)
42. Qatar (1971)
43. Rwanda (1962)
44. Senegal (1959)
45. Sierra Leone (1961)
46. Singapore (1965)
47. Somalia (1960)
48. Sri Lanka (Ceylon) (1948)
49. Sudan (1956)
50. Swaziland (1968)
51. Togo (1960)
52. Tunisia (1956)
53. Uganda (1962)
54. United Arab Emirates (1971)
55. United Republic of Tanzania (1961)
56. Upper Volta (1960)
57. Vietnam (1954)
58. Zaire (1960)
59. Zambia (1964)

Newly independent ex-colonies after 1945 with date of independence.

question erupted into civil war in 1948. The British kept hands off while the Jewish settlers carved out the independent state of Israel.

After that defeat, the Arabs looked for unity and new leadership. The young colonels, led by Gamal Abdel Nasser, who took over Egypt and nationalized the Suez Canal in 1956, were idolized by many young Arabs elsewhere, but local political elites kept their separate state identity. The Algerian insurrection that began in 1954 and wore the French down to acceptance of independence by 1962 helped neighboring Tunisia and Morocco win independence from France in 1956.

African Decolonization

In the late 1950s and 1960s, the African colonies gained independence. The signs of modern nationalism appeared as early as 1939, when the Martinique deputy in the French parliament, Aimé Césaire, announced his pride in "negritude" in the poem "Return to my native country." Even by the 1950s, however, African nationalist movements had not yet overcome tribal localisms and economic backwardness sufficiently to defeat European armies by any major insurrectionary movement. When Britain negotiated independence with the Gold Coast (Ghana) in 1957, Belgium with the Congo in 1960, and France with all its remaining African states in 1960, they were attempting to run ahead of popular opinion to grant political independence while preserving cultural and economic influence. Portugal, the only colonial state that attempted to maintain political control by armed force after 1961, began to negotiate a settlement in 1974.

"Informal Empire"

The former colonial powers in Europe preserved a large degree of influence in their former colonies after the 1960s, surprisingly large in view of the bitterness with which colonial wars had been fought. Certain aspects of the national liberation movements had been drawn from European models: nationalism, the state, political parties, even the tactics of guerrilla warfare. More importantly, every newly independent people aspired to economic development on European urban and industrial models. The modernization of the ex-colonies was not only a cause of their political independence but a cause of their subsequent economic and cultural dependence.

European influence persisted, therefore, and even grew in much of the Third World. Freed from the burden of colonial wars, the former colonial powers could afford to share their prosperity. In the 1960s, many European states contributed a higher proportion of their national product to foreign aid than did the United States. Education missions, economic and technical assistance, and private investment came from Europe. In the former French-ruled areas of West Africa, more French

The energy crisis in Italy, 1973. Note the brand names of American and international corporations active in Italy.

people lived and worked in the newly independent states of Senegal and the Ivory Coast than there had been in colonial days. Europe enjoyed the advantages of what might be called "informal empire" in an expanding role in the Third World.

Europe in the 1970s

Europe's Role in the World

By the 1970s, Europeans constituted only about 9 percent of the world's population. Nevertheless they produced about 30 percent of the world's goods. Once again they were influential far beyond mere numbers.

That influence still remained less than wealth or tradition might suggest. There were several harsh reminders in the early 1970s of Europeans' imperfect control over their own destinies. Following the Yom Kippur war of October 1973 between Israel and the Arab states, an Arab embargo on oil and the subsequent quadrupling of oil prices revealed that much of the 1960s boom had been built on a shift from domestic coal to foreign oil. The fact that Syria and Egypt had fielded more tanks and aircraft in that war than NATO possessed underscored the disparity between Western Europe's wealth and its capacity to control its own destiny. More immediately, the oil price rise greatly exacerbated inflation in Western Europe, the most serious internal problem affecting welfare states. As European gold and hard currency flowed out to the Arab states and Iran in the largest international monetary transfer in history, Europeans wondered how the oil producers' new wealth would affect European trade and finance.

At the same time, further relaxation of tensions between the United States and the Soviet Union unexpectedly diminished rather than increased Europeans' control over their world position. The desire of the American and Soviet leaders for détente after the Cuba confrontation had survived both the American war in Vietnam and the Soviet repression of Czechoslovakia. Soviet leaders wanted technical expertise and investment capital from the West, and as the Soviet missile capability built up close to parity with the American capability, they began to want to limit the vast expenditure involved in building offensive and defensive missile systems. American policymakers, under the Johnson, Nixon, and Ford administrations, were also reluctant to incur the expense and political liabilities of installing gigantic antiballistic missile defense systems. After long negotiations, Strategic Arms Limitation Talks (SALT) got under way in Helsinki in May 1969. In May 1972, President Nixon and Secretary Brezhnev signed in Moscow the first SALT treaty, an agreement to freeze offensive missiles at approximate parity and to forego defensive missile systems altogether.

Europeans, especially the NATO allies, had ambiguous reactions. On the one hand, they could hardly fail to applaud a reduction in international tensions. On the other hand, "SALT is the only major East–West transaction that has lacked European participation."[15] SALT had grown out of a triangular negotiation not involving the European states. When President Nixon's foreign affairs advisor Henry Kissinger succeeded in reestablishing relations with China in the fall of 1971, the Russians became more eager than ever to reach agreement with the United States. Western Europeans felt suspicion and resentment at not being consulted on major decisions concerning them.

These public displays of powerlessness left the Western European states still groping toward some appropriate form of political expression. Gaullist Europe, the Europe of States, was supposed to speak with one voice through consultation at the top. But the energy crisis set off by the Arabs' oil embargo showed that it could not do even that. When the Arab oil exporters attempted to cut off oil shipments altogether to Holland, a member of the European Economic Community, the other members dealt separately with the Arabs rather than defend their

[15]John Newhouse, "SALT," *The New Yorker,* June 2, 1973, p. 101.

interests as a bloc. It was possible, however, that the shock of that display of disunity within the European Economic Community would galvanize the members once again around common institutions, as much motivated by a desire for independence from the United States as by the need for a common policy to supply energy needs and fight inflation.

Changing Political Scenes

As the Western European states grappled unsuccessfully with inflation in the mid-1970s, their ability to continue rapid economic growth within the existing political and social system was called into question.

Italy, whose inflation rate of nearly 20 percent per year was the highest in the Common Market, seemed almost ungovernable by 1974. The centrist coalition government formed by Christian Democrat Mariano Rumor in March 1974 was the thirty-sixth ministry in the thirty-one years since the fall of Mussolini. It proved no more able than its predecessors to persuade Italians to reduce imports and restrain their life styles in order to end an enormous deficit in international payments. It lasted only three months. In the summer of 1974, the city of Rome announced that it was unable to pay its bills. No political force seemed capable of controlling both the Italian middle classes and the highly politicized trade unions.

While social and economic pressures were somewhat less urgent in France, it still was not clear what direction the strong presidency created by de Gaulle's Fifth Republic would take after de Gaulle's departure. After the death of de Gaulle's immediate successor, Georges Pompidou, Valéry Giscard d'Estaing, an urbane aristocrat trained in the senior civil service, won the presidency for French conservatives in April 1974. The failure of the united left's candidate, François Mitterand, to win a majority raised doubts about whether an orderly alternation of government and opposition was possible in French politics. President Giscard d'Estaing began to give more apparent flexibility to the French administration by such acts as dividing the state radio and television monopoly into competitive branches and by appointing Françoise Giroud as Europe's first Minister for the Status of Women. But the Fifth Republic had not yet provided a way out of the recurrent French pattern of strong presidencies interrupted by periodic popular outbursts.

After the British Conservatives lost their majority in February 1974, the Labour party under Harold Wilson, without an absolute majority of its own, attempted to cope with a 14 percent inflation rate and a decline in national production.

Although West Germany had the lowest inflation rate in the Common Market (7 percent), Chancellor Willy Brandt was unexpectedly forced out of public life in May 1974 by the discovery of an East Germany spy on his office staff. Brandt's successor, the former SPD Finance Minister Helmut Schmidt, continued the Social Democrat-Free Democrat coalition but without the same personal ascendancy Brandt had displayed.

The Iberian Peninsula began to emerge from thirty years of enforced silence. In ill health at the age of eighty-one, General Franco handed over power in Spain in July 1974 to his carefully chosen successor, Prince Juan Carlos de Borbón, grandson of the king who had left the throne in 1931, but he resumed it again in October. It was not clear that he could master the pent-up forces of reawakening Spanish political life. The Portuguese dictatorship under Salazar's successor Marcello Caetano was overthrown in April 1974 by army officers who had become convinced that only an end to the protracted colonial war in Africa could permit Portugal to progress at home. The new Portuguese government was quickly split between left and right in the unaccustomed freedom of political action, and the attempt to achieve a negotiated settlement in Africa after so many years of bitter warfare was a difficult task.

The future course of Europe remained uncertain in the mid-1970s. What was certain was that Europeans would continue to be dynamic and creative and worthy of close attention by Americans.

Suggestions for Further Reading

O. Edmund Clubb, Jr., *China and Russia: The Great Game* (1970) is the most recent study. For "polycentrism," see D. L. M. Blackmer, *Unity in Diversity: Italian Communism and the Communist World* (1968). For diversity within the Communist bloc, see Zbigniew K. Brzezinski, *The Soviet Bloc: Unity and Conflict** (1967), and the closing chapters of the work by François Fejtö cited at the end of Chapter 18.

Michel Tatu, *Power in the Kremlin: From Khrushchev to Kosygin* (1969) is the work of a well-informed French journalist. See also Robert Conquest, *Russia After Khrushchev* (1965).

Stanley Hoffmann, *Decline or Renewal? France Since the 1930s* (1974) contains the most penetrating analysis of de Gaulle as a national leader and a world political strategist.

The most recent developments in Western European integration are surveyed in Stuart de la Mahotière, *Towards One Europe** (1970). The fervently prointegration *Europe in the Making* (1973) by Walter Hallstein, former chairman of the European Economic Community Commission, can be balanced by the estimate in Leon N. Lindberg and Stuart Scheingold, *Europe's Would-be Polity* (1970) that the momentum has slackened. Carl J. Friedrich, *Europe: An Emergent Nation?* (1969) examines the unofficial integration of attitudes, pressure groups, and economies within Western Europe.

For Willy Brandt, see Lawrence L. Whetten, *Germany's Ostpolitik* (1971).

The best general survey of European decolonization up to 1960 is Rupert Emerson, *From Empire to Nation** (1961). See also Rudolf von Albertini, *Decolonization: The Administration and Future of the Colonies, 1919–1960* (1971).

Reflections on Europe's place in the world range from the pessimistic Hajo Holborn, *Political Collapse of Europe** (1950), to John L. Lukacs, *The Decline and Rise of Europe** (1965).

PICTURE CREDITS

2 Henri L'Artigue, Rapho Guillumette Pictures
11 Radio Times Hulton Picture
Library
16–17 Radio Times Hulton Picture
Library
26 Radio Times Hulton Picture
Library
29 Süddeutscher Verlag, Munich
31 Roger Viollet
42 Collection Kees Van Dongen
52 Gernsheim Collection
55 P. A. Reuter
66 The Press Association Ltd.
74 Süddeutscher Verlag, Munich
79 Radio Times Hulton Picture
Library
81 L'Illustration
82 Süddeutscher Verlag, Munich
83 L'Illustration
84 L'Illustration
85 Musée de la Guerre, Paris
87 Bayerisches Hauptstaatarchiv,
Munich
88 Radio Times Hulton Picture
Library
89 Imperial War Museum, London
91 Imperial War Museum, London
105 Imperial War Museum, London
106–07 Popperfoto
112 United States National Archives
116 Radio Times Hulton Picture
Library
120 Imperial War Museum, London

126 The Bettman Archive
131 L'Illustration
134 United Press International
135 Culver Pictures
136 Radio Times Hulton Picture
Library
139 Charles Phelps Cushing
149 (top and bottom) Archiv für Kunst
und Geschichte/Katherine
Young
154 L'Illustration
167 L'Illustration
172 Radio Times Hulton Picture
Library
179 Imperial War Museum, London
180 Historical Pictures Service
185 L'Illustration
190–91 Brown Brothers
194 Archiv für Kunst und Geschich-
te/Katherine Young
199 United Press International
204 Zeitgeschichtliches Bildarchiv
Heinrich Hoffman
205 Zeitgeschichtliches Bildarchiv
Heinrich Hoffman
207 United Press International
224 Institute of Social History, Amsterdam
227 (top) Herman Axelbank
227 (bottom) Archiv für Kunst und
Geschichte/Katherine Young
231 Erich Salomon, Magnum
236 Bild-Archiv, Österreichische
Nationalbibliothek, Vienna

248   Gernsheim Collection
256   Radio Times Hulton Picture Library
268   Gernsheim Collection
272   Radio Times Hulton Picture Library
278   Gallatin Collection, Philadelphia Museum of Art
282   Bundesarchiv, Koblenz
287   Süddeutscher Verlag, Munich
294   Lucien Hervé
297   Museum of Modern Art Film Stills Archive
298   Copyright French Reproduction Rights
299   The Tel-Aviv Museum
301   Collection, Museum of Modern Art, New York (purchase)
312   Radio Times Hulton Picture Library
320   Central Press Photo
322   Radio Times Hulton Picture Library
328   Süddeutscher Verlag, Munich
329   Süddeutscher Verlag, Munich
337   Illustrated Newspapers Ltd.
342–43   Katherine Young
349   Katherine Young
350   Katherine Young
352   Katherine Young
357   Süddeutscher Verlag, Munich
367   Wide World Photos
375   United Press International
385   Alan Band Associates
388–89   Alan Band Associates
392   Alan Band Associates
393   Cartoon by David Low by arrangement with the Trustees and the London Evening Standard
394   Keystone Press Agency
404   Wide World Photos
407   Zeitgeschichtliches Bildarchiv Heinrich Hoffmann
409   Brown Brothers

420   Radio Times Hulton Picture Library
422   Wide World Photos
429   United Press International
432   Ullstein Bilderdienst
437   United Press International
440–41   Fox Photos
443   Imperial War Museum, London
444   Imperial War Museum, London
446   Sovfoto
456   Wide World Photos
472   Wide World Photos
474–75   United States Coast Guard Official Photo
476   Ullstein Bilderdienst
478–79   Sovfoto
481   Novosti Press Agency
488   United States Army Photo
497   United States Army Photo
499   United States Army Photo
506–07   United Press International
511   Brown Brothers
519   Henri Cartier-Bresson, Magnum
522   David Seymour, Magnum
527   Landesbildstelle, Berlin
542   Copyright Walt Kelly
560–61   Sovfoto
563   I. N. Bild—Bad Godesberg
566   Wide World Photos
568   Wide World Photos
573   Jan Lukas, Rapho Guillumette Pictures
579   George Gerster, Rapho Guillumette Pictures
588   J. A. Pavlovsky, Rapho Guillumette Pictures
593   Bullaty-Lomeo, Rapho Guillumette Pictures
596   Wide World Photos
611   Wide World Photos
614   United Press International
621   United Press International
626   J. P. Paireault, Magnum

INDEX

Acerbo Election Law, 200
Acheson, Dean, 539, 605
Action française, 38, 208, 212, 356, 364
Adams, Henry, 36
Adenauer, Konrad, 178, 510, 512, 526, 528, 546, 547, 551, 559, 583, 619, 620
Adler, Friedrich, 380
Adler, Fritz, 109
Adowa, Battle of, 10, 409, 622
Advertising, 285
Aehrenthal, Alois van, 54–55
Afrika Korps, 472–73
Agnelli, Giovanni, 575
Agrarian party (Romania), 362
Agrarian revolutionaries (SR's), 32, 133, 134, 137
Agriculture, 14–15, 590, 609
    collectivization, 335–37, 564, 567, 583
    Eastern European, 261–64
    Great Depression, 313–14
    Iberian Peninsula, 266
    Soviet Union, 335–37, 562, 580, 581
Airplanes, 36, 289
    First World War, 91
    Second World War, 435, 436
Albania, 33, 55, 56, 502, 529, 607–09
Alcock, John, 289
Alexander I (king of Yugoslavia), 264–65
Alexander of Battenberg, 28
Alexandra Feodorovna (empress of Russia), 107–08

Alfonso XIII (king of Spain), 215, 267, 390
Algeria, 472–73
Algerian War, 510, 542, 548–49, 625
All Quiet on the Western Front (Remarque), 86–87, 114, 122
Allen, William Sheridan, 346
Allied Control Commission, 488, 501
Alperovitz, Gar, 489
Alsace-Lorraine, 167, 168, 177, 178, 230, 403, 406, 448
American Challenge, The (Servan-Schreiber), 617
Amundsen, Roald, 10
Anders, Wladyslaw, 496
Anschluss, 403–05, 414–15
Anticapitalism, 37, 38, 204, 209–10
Anti-Semitism, 37, 38, 204, 207, 208, 213–14, 291, 345, 353, 360, 361, 362, 367, 436, 591
Antonescu, Ion, 363, 448, 453
Antonioni, Michelangelo, 598
Aosta, Duke of, 198
Appeasement policy, 416–19, 424
Arabs, 169–70
Aragon, Louis, 124, 377, 459
Arcadia meeting, 469
Architecture, 45, 279, 293, 295, 303, 599
Aristocracy, 18–20, 111
Armenia, 142

Army
    British, 101
    French, 102–03, 119, 143
    German, 104
    Russian, 127, 438
    See also First World War; Second World War
Aron, Raymond, 582, 604
Artists
    mass audience and, 302–04
    social status of, 301–02
Asquith, Herbert, 70, 99–100, 101, 245
Astor, Lady, 111
Atlantic Alliance, 612
Atlantic Charter, 469, 482
Atomic bombs, *see* Nuclear weapons
Atomic Diplomacy (Alperovitz), 489
Attlee, Clement, 488, 515, 545
Australia, 27, 176
Austria
    Anschluss with Germany, 403–05, 414–15
    Christian Social dictatorship, 357–59
    economy, 215, 315, 358
    fascist movement, 343
    Great Depression, 315, 358
    Nazi activities in, 358, 359
    parliamentary democracy, 260
    post-Second World War, 528
    Prussian wars, 50
    suffrage, 29, 243
    Triple Alliance, 71

Versailles peace settlement, 180, 182, 184, 186, 226, 329
Austria-Hungary
  Austro-Serbian war, 51–63
  dissolution of, 150–53
  First World War, 82–85, 99, 108–10, 119, 125, 143, 168
  monarchy, 28
  nationalism, 33, 34
  Russia and, 52, 54–55
Austro-Serbian war, 51–63
Autarky, 331, 333, 412–13
Automobiles, 573–74, 580, 581, 615–16
Ayer, A. J., 601
Azaña, Manuel, 380, 390–91, 393
Azerbaijan, 142

Badoglio, Pietro, 473, 521, 522
Bainville, Jacques, 173
Balbo, Italo, 197, 214
Baldwin, Stanley, 246–48, 282–83, 321, 367–68, 417, 418
Balfour Declaration, 170
Balkan Wars, 34, 50, 55–56, 59, 68, 77
Ball, Albert, 91
Bank of England, 321
Bank of France, 329
Barnes, George, 112
Barrès, Maurice, 13
Barth, Karl, 464, 600
Barthes, Roland, 601
Baudelaire, Charles, 14, 39, 46
Bauer, Otto, 153, 343, 358
Baumont, Maurice, 266
Bavaria, 145, 148, 150, 160, 205, 255, 258, 259
Beatles, the, 575, 597
Beauvoir, Simone de, 585
Beck, Josef, 425
Beck, Ludwig, 424, 461–62
Beckett, Samuel, 546
Beer hall *Putsch* (1923), 205–06, 257–59
Belgian Neutrality Treaty (1839), 66
Belgium, 28
  Cold War politics, 543
  decolonization, 625
  fascist movement in, 368–69
  First World War, 66–67, 76, 79

imperialism, 6
movement for European union, 551, 553, 556–58
Second World War, 439–41, 455
suffrage, 29
Versailles peace settlement, 176–79
war debts, 314
Benedict XV (pope), 143
Beneš, Edouard, 187, 416, 420, 421, 504, 532–34
Ben-Gurion, David, 549
Bennet, Arnold, 20
Berchtold, Leopold, 56
Berg, Alban, 293, 295, 296, 300
Bergman, Ingmar, 598
Bergson, Henri, 43
Beria, Lavrentii, 560
Berlin, 562–63
  Blockade (1948), 501–02, 504, 541, 552, 605
  cultural life, 300–01, 303
Berlin-to-Baghdad Railway, 65, 68, 69
Bernhardi, Friedrich von, 68–69
Bernstein, Edouard, 78
Berthelot, Marcellin, 36
Bessarabia, 53, 173, 185, 187, 361–63, 427, 438
Bethlen, Count Istvan, 208
Bethmann-Hollweg, Theobald von, 56, 66, 106, 144
Bevan, Aneurin, 366, 516, 517, 545, 585
Beveridge, Sir William, 515
Bevin, Ernest, 156, 551, 553
Bianchi, Michele, 197
Bidault, George, 551
Bienvenu-Martin, Jean-Baptiste, 62
Birdsall, Paul, 186
Birth control, 24–25
Birth rate, 23, 24
Bismarck, Otto von, 30, 71, 211, 253, 353
Black Hand, 51, 54
Blériot, Louis, 36, 289
Blitzkrieg, 434–36, 439, 445, 450
Blomberg, Werner von, 353
Blum, Léon, 325–26, 376, 377, 382–89, 418, 419, 424, 544, 545
Boccioni, Umberto, 43, 123
Boer War, 9, 64, 235

Bohemia, 153, 182, 186, 187
Bohemia-Moravia, 423, 459–60
Bohr, Niels, 40, 305
Böll, Heinrich, 598
Bolo, Paul, 119
Bolsheviks, 128–42, 152, 172–73, 269–71
Bonhoeffer, Dietrich, 464, 600
Bonnet, Georges, 419
Borbón, Juan Carlos de, 629
Boris III (king of Bulgaria), 265, 361
Bosnia, 51, 52, 54, 59, 68, 71, 77
Boulez, Pierre, 598
Bradbury, Sir John, 224
Brandt, Willy, 584–85, 628
  Ostpolitik, 619–20
Braque, Georges, 42
Brasillach, Robert, 453
Brecht, Bertolt, 293, 302, 311
Brest-Litovsk, Treaty of (1918), 135, 139, 142, 161, 180
Breton, André, 123, 124, 296
Bretton Woods Agreement (1944), 514, 617, 618
Brezhnev, Leonid, 580–81, 582, 594, 627
Briand, Aristide, 229–32, 235–36, 253, 550
Bright, John, 117
Britain, Battle of, 442–45, 506
British Union of Fascists (BUF), 366–68
Brooke, Rupert, 121, 122
Brown, Arthur, 289
Broz, Josip (Marshal Tito), 462–63, 519
Brüning, Heinrich, 328–30, 346–48, 403, 412
Brusilov, Alexei, 85–86, 107, 131
Brussels, Treaty of (1948), 553
Buchan, John, 97–98, 370
Buddenbrooks (Mann), 20
Bukharin, Nikolai, 135, 270, 272, 274, 335, 338
Bukovina, 438
Bulgaria, 28, 53, 362, 363
  agrarian population, 261
  authoritarian rule, 361
  Balkan Wars, 55
  collectivization, 564
  communist uprising (1925), 274

First World War, 85, 153
   independence, 52, 54
   National Front regime, 531
   nationalism, 33, 34
   parliamentary democracy, 260
   Second World War, 495
   Soviet Union and, 502, 529,
      532, 534
   Stamboliski regime, 262–64
   Versailles peace settlement,
      182, 184, 186, 187
Bulge, Battle of the, 475–76, 486
Bülow, Bernhard von, 235
Bultmann, Rudolf, 600
Buñuel, Luis, 598
Burgenland, 218
Butler, R. A., 585
Butler, Samuel, 20
Byelorussia, 487

Caetano, Marcello, 629
Caillaux, Joseph, 119
Camelots du roi, 38
Cameroons, 176
Campbell, Roy, 398
Camus, Albert, 546, 583
Capitalism, 9, 68, 70, 376
Capitulations, 6, 9
Caporetto, Battle of, 143, 152
Carol I (king of Romania), 28
Carol II (king of Romania), 265,
   362, 363
Cartel des gauches, 250–52, 324,
   326
Cartels, 242, 331, 332, 333–34
Casablanca Conference (1943),
   473, 482
Castellane, Boni de, 19
Casualty rates
   First World War, 113
   Second World War, 506
Catholic Church, 39, 354–56,
   599–600
   in Austria, 359
   in France, 211, 355, 463–64
   in Germany, 353, 461
   in Italy, 110, 211, 269, 355
   in Poland, 567
   in Portugal, 266
   in Spain, 266, 391
Cavell, Edith, 76
Ceausescu, Nicolai, 591, 609
Center party (Germany), 255,
   257, 258, 330, 352, 354

Césaire, Aimé, 625
Cesbron, Gilbert, 541
Cézanne, Paul, 41
Chagall, Marc, 300
Chamberlain, Austen, 229–31
Chamberlain, Neville, 417–22,
   424–27, 438, 447, 462
Champagne offensive, 87, 88,
   90, 143
Champs Magnétiques, Les (Breton),
   123
Chaplin, Charlie, 311
Charterhouse of Parma, The
   (Stendhal), 33
Chiang Kai-shek, 376, 492
Chicherin, George, 221, 237
Chicken War (1961), 616
China, 6, 160
   China–India border war, 607
   Korean War, 542
   Sino-Soviet split, 606–08
   United States relations with,
      627
Christian Democratic party
   French (MRP), 511, 520, 543,
      551
   Italian, 511, 523, 544, 546,
      547, 585
   West German, 510–11, 526,
      547, 585, 619
Christian Social party (Austria),
   358
Christian X (king of Denmark),
   455
Churchill, Lord Randolph, 19
Churchill, Sir Winston, 249, 336,
   417, 485, 546, 548, 584
   Arcadia meeting, 469
   Casablanca Conference, 473
   as Chancellor of Exchequer,
      247
   election of 1945, 488, 510,
      515
   First World War, 72, 84, 94
   postwar German issue, 487,
      488
   quoted, 22, 50, 94, 249, 442,
      502
   Second World War, 442–43,
      445, 469–70, 473–75, 480,
      483–84, 496
   Teheran Conference, 483–84,
      496
   Yalta Conference, 485–88,
      498

Ciano, Galeazzo, 411
Cities, 12–14
Civil war (Russian), 136, 138–42,
   269
Civilization and Its Discontents
   (Freud), 297
Clair, René, 311
Class, 15–23, 111, 115, 212
Clay, Lucius, 501, 502
Clemenceau, Georges, 103, 119,
   121, 143, 152, 165, 170–71,
   176, 178, 185
Clercq, Staf de, 368
Clerical authoritarianism, 354–
   69
Clothing, 111, 290, 577
Coal industry, 248–49, 314, 516,
   518
Codreanu, Corneliu, 208, 211,
   361–63
Cohn-Bendit, Daniel, 589
Cold War, 172, 374, 539–68
   antagonism, seeds of, 494–95
   centrist and conservative gov-
      ernments, 546–48
   colonial wars, 548–49
   Communist parties, isolation
      of, 543–45
   decolonization and, 542
   division of left, 545–46
   Eastern European consolida-
      tion and rebellion (1948–
      56), 563–68
   German issue, 498–502
   Marshall Plan, 503–04
   movement for European
      union, 549–59
   NATO, 504
   origins of, 490–95
   Polish issue, 491, 495–98
   Soviet peace aims, 490–92
   Summit Conferences, 562,
      563
   thaw, 605–06, 619
   Truman Doctrine, 503, 539
   United States peace aims,
      492–95
   Warsaw Pact, 504
Cole, G. D. H., 323
Collaboration, 453–57, 509
Collective bargaining, 384, 385
Collectivization, 335–37, 564,
   567, 583
Comintern, 161–63, 237, 250,
   264, 370, 376–79, 458

Common Market, 557–58, 559, 612–15
  United States and, 616–17, 619
Communications, 280–85
Communist party
  Belgian, 543
  British, 237, 376, 381
  Bulgarian, 263
  Chinese, 376
  Czech, 381, 530–34, 592
  French, 125, 163, 325, 364, 375–78, 381–82, 399, 512, 520, 543, 545, 585
  German, 148, 201, 223, 257, 258, 259, 327, 330, 344, 346, 347, 350–53, 377, 460, 461
  Hungarian, 533
  Italian, 162, 511–12, 522, 523, 544, 545, 585, 590
  Polish, 531, 532
  Romanian, 362
  Russian, 237, 273–74
  Spanish, 393, 396
  West German, 512
  See also Comintern
Concerning the Spiritual in Art (Kandinsky), 41
Congo, 176, 625
Congress of Berlin (1878), 51, 52
Conscription, 101, 102, 111
Conservatism, 37–38, 215
Conservative party (Britain), 225, 244–47, 518, 545, 548, 585, 628
Consumer societies, 572–95
  discontent in, 585–95
  egalitarianism, 577–95
  politics in (1953–68), 582–85
  in Soviet bloc, 580–81
  wealth, distribution of, 574–77
Cooperatives, 319
Corfu, 200
Cornford, John, 398
Corporatism, 318, 324, 333–35, 355, 409
Coty, François, 365
Council for Mutual Economic Assistance (COMECON), 565, 591, 608
Council of Europe, 555–56

Creative Evolution (Bergson), 43
Credit-Anstalt, 315, 329, 358
Crete, 445, 480
Crick, Sir Francis, 600–01
Cripps, Sir Stafford, 517
Croatia, 448, 454
Croats, 54, 151, 184, 186, 187, 264
Croix de feu, 364, 382, 384
Crowe, Sir Eyre, 65
Cuba, 160, 563
  missile crisis, 605–06, 610
Cubism, 42, 295
Culture, 39–46, 280–85, 290–308, 536–37, 561–62, 596–97, 602
Cuno, Wilhelm, 257
Curzon Line, 495, 496, 497
Curzon, Lord, 247
Cyprus, 549
Czechoslovakia, 138, 280, 620
  agrarian population, 261
  crisis (1938), 416–17, 419–24
  Great Depression, 416
  industry, 581
  Karlsbad program, 419
  land reform, 262
  Little Entente, 220
  National Front regime, 530–31
  nationalism, 33, 61
  nationality problem, 414–16
  nation-building, 153–55
  parliamentary regime, 260, 265–66
  Prague *coup* (1948), 504, 534–35, 552
  "springtime" (1968), 591–94
  Soviet Union and, 491, 504, 514, 529, 532–35, 540, 583, 586, 591–94, 606, 608, 609, 627
  suffrage, 243
  Versailles peace settlement, 169, 170, 173, 180, 182–88, 206, 226
Czechs, 139–40, 150–53, 218

Dada, 122–23
Daladier, Edouard, 365, 376, 380, 382, 419, 421, 422, 438
Dalí, Salvador, 297
Dangerfield, George, 100

D'Annunzio, Gabriele, 110, 158, 192
Danzig, 184, 186, 226, 424–26
Darwin, Charles, 305
Dassault, Marcel, 575
Dawes, Charles G., 228
Dawes Plan, 228, 232, 259, 314
Dawson, Geoffrey, 418
D-Day, 474
De Ambris, Alceste, 194
Déat, Marcel, 318, 324, 364–65
De Bono, Emilio, 197
Decline of the West, The (Spengler), 292
Decolonization, 542, 622–26
Defence of the Realm Act (DORA), 119
Deflation, 316, 317, 346
De Gasperi, Alcide, 511, 523, 524, 544, 546, 547, 551, 559, 584
de Gaulle, Charles, 617
  Common Market and, 612–15
  Fifth Republic, 547, 549, 589, 610–15
  Free French, leader of, 455, 456, 460, 518
  NATO and, 611–12
  Provisional Government, head of, 510, 519
  tank warfare, 441, 518
Degrelle, Léon, 368–69
Democratic party (Germany), 255, 258
Democritus, 39
Denikin, Anton, 141, 142
Denmark
  Common Market, 615
  fascist movement, 343
  Great Depression, 319
  Prussian Wars, 50
  reconstruction, 509
  Second World War, 439, 451, 455, 459
  Versailles peace settlement, 178
Depression, *see* Great Depression
d'Esperey, Franchet, 155
De-Stalinization, 562, 567–68, 583, 595
Devaluation, 322, 324, 386
De Vecchi, Cesare, 198
Diaghilev, Sergei, 300
Dickens, Charles, 12

Disarmament Conference, 403
Djilas, Milovan, 15
Dr. Zhivago (Pasternak), 562
Dollar gap, 615, 617
Dollfuss, Engelbert, 358–59, 361, 404, 414
Doriot, Jacques, 364, 365
Dorten, Hans Adam, 177
Douglas-Home, Sir Alec, 548
Doumergue, Gaston, 365
Dreyfus Affair, 103, 251, 366, 379, 383
Dreyfus, Alfred, 251
Dubček, Alexander, 592–94
DuBois, W. E. B., 170
Duchamp, Marcel, 123
Duclos, Jacques, 377
Dudintsev, Vladimir, 562
Dulles, John Foster, 541
Duma, 28, 108, 127
Dunkirk, 441–42
Dunkirk, Treaty of (1947), 552

East Germany (German Democratic Republic), 529, 581
    economy, 528
    reconstruction, 524–28
    revolt (1953), 566
    West Germany and, 620
    See also Germany
East Prussia, 180, 424
Easter Rebellion, 117, 119
Ebert, Friedrich, 146–48, 150, 201, 243, 255, 256, 259, 347
Economic Consequences of the Peace, The (Keynes), 171, 223, 407
Economy, 4–5, 236–37, 241–42
    Austrian, 215, 315, 358
    British, 247–48, 493–94, 514–18, 526, 587
    classical-liberal, 35
    Common Market, 557–58, 559, 612–17, 619
    consumer societies, 572–83, 587
    deflation, 316, 317, 346
    devaluation, 322, 324, 386
    dollar gap, 615, 617
    East German, 528
    First World War and, 114–16
    French, 214–15, 252–53, 385–86, 387, 520–21, 526, 548

German, 215, 222–23, 225–26, 255, 257, 259, 311, 314, 315, 327–33, 344, 353, 354, 412, 434, 450
    gold exchange standard, 617
    gold standard, 5, 242, 247, 253, 275, 321, 617
    inflation, 114–16, 157, 215, 222–23, 226, 236, 242, 252, 259, 508, 587, 618, 627, 628
    Italian, 333–35, 523–24, 571, 628
    liberal, 316–17
    Marshall Plan, 503–04, 513–14, 523–24, 534, 551, 556
    neoliberal, 241–42
    reconstruction, 512–14
    Romanian, 608–09
    Russian, 270, 271, 273, 275
    Second World War and, 450, 454–55, 468, 478
    Soviet Union, 335–37, 478, 535–36, 562
    Spanish, 547
    United States, 242, 468, 494, 503–04, 513–14, 615–19
    United States–European rivalry, 615–19
    Versailles peace settlement and, 187–88
    West German, 526–28, 571, 628
    See also Great Depression
Eddington, Sir Arthur, 306
Eden, Anthony, 416, 546, 548, 549
Edison, Thomas, 571
Education, 24, 35, 304–05, 577–78
Egalitarianism, 577–79
Egypt, 9, 10, 93, 549, 563, 625
Eichmann, Adolf, 453
Einstein, Albert, 40–41, 45, 305–06
Eisenhower, Dwight D., 475, 553, 562
Eisenstein, Sergei, 303, 308, 479, 536–37
Eisner, Kurt, 146, 148
Eliot, T. S., 124, 398
Eminent Victorians (Strachey), 122
Energy crisis, 626–28
Engels, Friedrich, 21, 191

Epp, Franz X. von, 201, 203
Erhard, Ludwig, 526, 527, 559, 583
Erzberger, Mathias, 255, 258
Estonia, 173, 180, 427, 437, 438, 492
Ethiopia, 10, 236, 386, 408–10, 610
Eurodollars, 618
European Advisory Commission, 483
European Atomic Energy Agency (Euratom), 557, 615
European Center for Nuclear Research (CERN), 600
European Coal and Steel Community (ECSC), 556–57, 615
European Defense Community (EDC), 554, 555
European Economic Community (EEC), *see* Common Market
European Free Trade Area (EFTA), 557
European Launch Development Organization (ELDO), 600
European Recovery Program, 504, 513
European union, movement for architects of, 550–51
    Common Market, 557–58, 559, 619–17, 619
    Council of Europe, 555–56
    debate over, 558–59
    European Coal and Steel Community (ECSC), 556–57, 615
    NATO, creation of, 553
    pressures for, 551–53
    problems in, 553–55
Existentialism, 464–65, 546
Expressionism, 41–42

Facta, Luigi, 197, 198
Faisal, Prince, 170
Faisceau, 208
Falange, 360, 392, 547
Falkenhayn, Erich von, 85, 86, 88, 89, 90, 104
Fallada, Hans, 311–12, 345
Family, 23–27
Farinacci, Roberto, 269
Fascism, 190–216, 339, 583, 622
    appeal of, 370–71

Austrian, 343
Belgian, 368–69
British, 343, 366–68
Danish, 343
Dutch, 369–70
early, 193–95
in Eastern Europe, 360–63
French, 363–66, 382
Hungarian counterrevolution, 206–08
Italian, 192–201, 210, 215, 268–69, 343
meaning of, 209–11
Norwegian, 343, 370
Popular Front and, 374, 380, 386–87, 399
Portuguese, 343, 357
Romanian, 208–09, 361–63
roots of, 211–15, 307
spread of, 342–71
Swedish, 343
See also Nazi party
Fatherland Front, 359, 532
Fatherland party (Germany), 121
Fauves, 41–42, 296
February Revolution, 127–28, 152
Feder, Gottfried, 354
Federal Republic of Germany, *see* West Germany
Ferdinand of Saxe-Coburg, 28
Ferenczi, Sandor, 307
Finland, 180, 427, 491
Second World War, 437–39, 448, 477
suffrage, 27, 243
First World War, 49–125, 127, 135, 139–40, 143–45
casualty rates, 113
as catalyst of fascism, 214
causes of, 67–72
Champagne offensive, 87, 88, 90, 143
Eastern Front, 82–86
economy, 114–16
escalation, 60–67
First Battle of the Marne, 79–82
intellectual impact of, 121–24
internal order, impact on, 116–21
July crisis of 1914, 51–60
mobilization, 60–62

Schlieffen Plan, 63–64, 72, 79, 81, 104, 439
at sea, 94–95
secret treaties, 166–67, 168–70
social impact of, 110–14
Somme campaign, 87, 88, 90
trench warfare, 81, 82, 86, 88
Verdun offensive, 88–89, 104
war fever, 75–79
war governments, 99–110
wartime aims, 166–67, 235
weapons, 90–91
Western Front, search for breakthrough, 86–91
widening of, 92–94
Fischer, Fritz, 68
Fiume, 158, 192, 200, 218
Five Year Plans, 336, 337
Flanner, Janet, 541, 554
Flemish National Union, 368
Foch, Ferdinand, 86, 144, 177, 178
Fokker, A. H. G., 91
Forster, E. M., 23, 339
Four Year Plan (Germany), 413
Fourteen Points, 145, 152, 167–68, 169, 171–72, 177, 179, 182, 232, 235
France
Algerian War, 542, 548–49, 625
alliance politics, 220, 411
anti-Marxism, 208
appeasement policy, 416–19
aristocracy, 19
Bank of, 329
Battle of, 439–42
cartel des gauches, 250–52, 324, 326
Catholic Church in, 211, 355, 463–64
Cold War politics, 543–45, 546–47, 548
Common Market, 613–15
consumer society, 572, 576
Czech crisis (1938), 416–19, 421, 423–24
decolonization, 622–23, 625
disarmament issue, 232–34
economy, 214–15, 252–53, 315, 323–26, 364, 385–86, 387, 520–21, 526, 548
education, 304, 305, 577–78
electoral shifts, 225

Ethiopian crisis, 410
fascist minority in, 363–66, 382
Fifth Republic, 547, 549, 584, 585–86, 589, 610–15, 628
First World War, 61–64, 76, 78–82, 84–95, 98, 99, 102–03, 115, 119–21, 125, 139, 140, 143, 144, 159, 167, 168
Fourth Republic, 518–21, 546, 548
Franco-German War (1871), 221
Franco-Prussian War (1870), 178
Franco-Russian Alliance (1892), 57, 61, 62, 71, 219
Franco-Soviet Pact (1935), 379, 386
Gaullism, 610–15
Great Depression, 315, 323–26, 364, 385
imperialism, 6, 9
Indochina War, 542–43, 548, 623
labor unions, 31–32, 113, 384, 385
Locarno Agreements, 229–32
mandatory powers, 175, 176, 549
middle class, 22
Moroccan crises, 50, 68, 69, 235
movement for European union, 550–58
nationalism, 32–33
NATO and, 611–12
New Deal, 383–88
nuclear weapons, 610–11
peace aims (1945), 492–94
Polish crisis, 425–27
Popular Front, 325–26, 364, 375–76, 381–89, 398–99, 455
Prussian Wars, 50
radicalism, 379, 380
reconstruction, 509, 518–21, 544
resistance, 459–60
revolution (1789), 37
Rhineland crisis (1936), 406–07
Ruhr, occupation of, 222,

223–25, 254, 255, 257
Second World War, 434–36,
438–42, 445, 448, 451, 453,
455–59
social-welfare systems, 18
Spanish Civil War, 387, 389
Stresa Front, 405
strikes, 116–17, 156, 326, 384,
388, 543, 545, 585–86, 589
student discontent, 585–86,
589
Suez Campaign, 549
suffrage, 27, 29, 243
Versailles peace settlement,
165, 170–71, 173, 177–79,
184, 219–21
Vichy regime, 455–57
war debts, 222, 314
France, Battle of, 439–42
Franco, Francisco, 359–60, 391–
93, 410–11, 443, 445, 547
Franco-German War (1871), 221
Franco-Prussian War (1870), 178
Franco-Russian Alliance (1892),
57, 61, 62, 71, 219
Franco-Soviet Pact (1935), 379,
386
Franz Ferdinand (archduke of
Austria-Hungary), 51, 56,
85, 151
Franz Josef (emperor of Austria-
Hungary), 28, 33, 56, 109,
152
Free Democratic party (West
Germany), 619
Free French, 455, 456, 460, 518
Freikorps, 148, 150, 173, 201–03,
254, 255
French, John, 86
French Revolution (1789), 37
Freud, Sigmund, 44, 45, 123,
297–99, 601
Friedrich, Karl, 403
Fritsch, Werner von, 353
Functionalism, 293, 296
Fundamentalism, 600
Futurist movement, 42–43, 123

Gagarin, Yuri, 580
Galicia, 82, 83, 84, 107, 166
Gallagher, John, 10
Gallipoli, 84, 85, 93
Gamelin, Maurice, 440
Gandhi, Mohandas K., 622, 623

Garaudy, Roger, 587
Gauguin, Paul, 41
Gaullism, 610–15
Gay, Peter, 293
*General Theory of Employment, In-
terest, and Money* (Keynes),
323
Geneva Agreement on Trade
and Tariffs (GATT), 619
Geneva Protocol, 228–29
Gentleman's Agreement, 411
George V (king of England), 65
Georgia, 142
German Democratic Republic,
see East Germany
German-National movement, 38,
213, 416
Germany
aristocracy, 19
beer hall *Putsch*, 205–06, 257–
59
disarmament issue, 232–34
economy, 215, 222–23, 225–
26, 255, 257, 259, 311, 314,
315, 327–33, 344, 353, 412,
434, 450
education, 304–05
First World War, 56–57, 63–
67, 76–84, 87–91, 93–5,
103–07, 113–15, 121, 125,
135, 139, 140, 143–45, 166
Freikorps, 148, 150, 173, 201–
03, 254, 255
Gleichschaltung, 352–54, 403
Great Coalition, 257–60, 327
Great Depression, 311, 314,
315, 327–33, 344
imperialism, 6, 9
industry, 254, 259, 331–32
Jews in, 204, 353, 450, 452–53
Kapp *Putsch*, 202, 254, 257,
351
labor unions, 31–32, 113
League of Nations and, 228,
230, 231
Locarno Agreements, 229–32
mass media, 280, 281, 283,
284
middle class, 22
monarchy, 28
Moroccan crisis, 50, 68, 69
nationalism, 33
Nazism, revival of (1929–32),
344–47

Nazi-Soviet Pact (1939), 426–
27, 438, 447, 479, 496
occupation zones, 498–502
policy of "fulfillment," 225–
26, 228
presidential government
(1930–33), 347–51
Rapallo, Treaty of, 221, 237,
378
rearmament, 331, 403, 405
reparations, 179–80, 221–23,
228, 232, 252, 314, 487,
489, 500–01
revolution in (1918–19), 145–
50, 160
Ruhr, occupation of, 222,
223–25, 254, 255, 257
Second World War, 428–29,
433, 434–36, 438–63, 467–
81, 483, 488
social-welfare systems, 18
Spanish Civil War, 394–95
strikes, 116–17
suffrage, 27, 243
Triple Alliance, 71
Versailles peace settlement,
171, 173, 177–80, 184–87,
218, 221–23
Weimar Coalition, 255–57
Weimar Constitution (1919),
243
See also East Germany; Hitler,
Adolf; West Germany
Gheorghiu-Dej, Gherghe, 609
Gibraltar, 448
Gierek, Edward, 591
Gil Robles, José María, 391
Giolitti, Giovanni, 110, 157, 195,
196, 198, 199, 379
Giroud, Françoise, 628
Giscard d'Estaing, Valéry, 628
Gleichschaltung, 352–54, 403
Godard, Jean-Luc, 598
Goebbels, Josef, 283, 354, 454
Goering, Hermann, 203, 331,
412–13, 414, 419, 444
Gold Coast (Ghana), 625
Gold exchange standard, 617
Gold standard, 5, 242, 247, 253,
275, 321, 617
Goldie, Sir George, 9
Goltz, Rüdiger von der, 173
Gömbös, Gyula, 207–08, 211,
359, 361

Gombrich, E. H., 597
Gomulka, Wladislaw, 531, 567, 591
Goremykin, Ivan, 108
Gort, Lord, 441
Gottwald, Klement, 533, 591
Gould, Jay, 20
Gramsci, Antonio, 157
Graves, Robert, 75, 398
Great Britain
　anti-Hitler alliances, 411
　appeasement policy, 416–19
　Boer War, 9, 64, 235
　Cold War, 496, 500, 501, 503, 545, 548
　Common Market, 613, 615
　consensus politics, 585
　consumer society, 572–77
　Czech crisis (1938), 416–21, 424
　decolonization, 622, 623–24, 625
　disarmament issue, 234
　economy, 247–48, 311, 315–16, 319–23, 366, 493–94, 514–18, 526, 587
　education, 304, 577–78
　electoral shifts, 225
　Ethiopian crisis, 410
　fascist movement, 343, 366–68
　First World War, 64–67, 72, 76, 78, 80, 81, 84, 85, 87, 88, 90–95, 98–101, 112–13, 115, 119, 121, 139, 140, 144, 159, 166, 168–70
　Great Depression, 311, 315–16, 319–23, 366
　imperialism, 6, 9, 10
　India and, 542, 622, 623–24
　industry, 248–49, 314, 516, 518
　internal dissent, 70
　Ireland and, 117, 119
　Jews in, 367
　Korean War, 545
　labor unions, 31, 112–13
　Labour government, 245–46, 514–18
　Locarno Agreements, 229–31
　mandatory powers, 175, 176
　mass culture, 280, 283, 284, 597
　middle class, 21, 22
　monarchy, 28
　movement for European union, 551–55
　Munich settlement, 421–22
　nuclear weapons, 610–11
　peace aims (1945), 492–94
　Polish crisis, 425–27
　reconstruction, 514–18
　Rhineland crisis (1936), 406–07
　Second World War, 434–36, 438–45, 469, 470, 472–74, 480, 483–89
　social-welfare systems, 18
　Stresa Front, 405
　strikes, 116–17, 156, 249, 517, 587, 590
　Suez Campaign, 549
　suffrage, 27, 28, 243
　three-way party system, 244–45
　unrest of 1919–20, 156
　Versailles peace settlement, 165, 171
　war debts, 222, 314
Great Coalition, 327
Great Depression, 264, 275, 310–12, 429
　origins and course of, 313–16
　politics in authoritarian states, 330–39
　politics in liberal states, 319–30
　remedies, 316–19
Greece, 28, 554
　Balkan Wars, 55
　Communists in, 495, 503
　nationalism, 33, 34
　Second World War, 445, 480
Grey, Sir Edward, 65, 427
Grigorenko, Pyotr, 595
Groener, Wilhelm, 105, 113, 146, 148
Gropius, Walter, 279, 293, 300, 302, 303
Grosz, George, 301–02
Group Portrait with Lady (Böll), 598
Groza, Petru, 529
Grundig, Max, 575
Guderian, Heinz, 439, 440
Guérin, Daniel, 373
Guernica (Picasso), 397
Guerrilla warfare, 623, 625
Guesde, Jules, 112
Guinea, 563
Guynemer, Georges, 91

Haakon VII (king of Norway), 455
Hague Conferences (1899 and 1904), 27, 117
Hahn, Otto, 436
Haigh, Sir Douglas, 86, 90
Haile Selassie (emperor of Ethiopia), 410
Haldane, J. B. S., 398
Halévy, Elie, 120, 121
Halifax, Lord, 418, 419, 420, 424
Hamburg uprising (1923), 271
Harding, Warren G., 219, 241
Hardy, Thomas, 290
Harmsworth, Alfred, 281, 285
Hart, B. H., 90
Heath, Edward, 587
Heidegger, Martin, 306, 464
Heisenberg, Werner, 40
Hemingway, Ernest, 300
Henderson, Arthur, 100, 112
Henderson, Sir Neville, 421
Henlein, Konrad, 416, 419, 421
Herriot, Edouard, 225, 228, 233, 251–52, 325, 380, 519, 550
Hervé, Gustave, 78
Herzegovina, 51, 52, 54
Himmler, Heinrich, 452
Hindenburg, Paul von, 83, 84, 90, 95, 104–06, 144, 146, 186, 259, 327, 328, 330, 347–50, 353
Hipper, Franz von, 94
History of Bohemia (Palacký), 33
Hitler, Adolf, 38, 135, 187, 192, 201, 208, 211, 226, 228, 260, 622
　accession to office of chancellor, 348–51
　Anschluss with Austria, 403–05, 414–15
　appeasement policy, 416–19
　art styles and, 307, 308
　assassination attempt, 462, 464
　beer hall *Putsch*, 205–06, 257–59
　Czechoslovakia and, 416, 420–24

economic considerations, 412–13
emergence of, 202–03
ideological motives, 412
mass electoral following, 344–46
meeting with Stalin (1939), 362
Mussolini and, 411, 414–15, 427, 433
Nazi-Soviet Pact, 426–27
New Order, 448–53
Poland and, 403, 425–27
radio speeches, 283
revolution after power (1933–39), 351–54
Rhineland, remilitarization of, 405–08
Second World War, 428–29, 433, 434, 436, 438, 439, 442–63, 467–69, 474, 480–81
suicide, 488
Hlinka, Andrej, 186, 454
Ho Chi Minh, 492, 623
Hoare, Sir Samuel, 410
Hobsbawm, Eric, 597
Hobson, John A., 9
Hodge, John, 112
Hoffmann, Stanley, 251
Hoggart, Richard, 291
Holland
economy, 571
energy crisis, 627
fascist movement in, 369–70
First World War, 64
imperialism, 6
Indonesia and, 623
NATO and, 612
reconstruction, 509
Second World War, 439–41, 451, 455
"Hollow Men, The" (Eliot), 124
Holy Alliance (1815), 550
Honegger, Arthur, 295
Honnecker, Erich, 620
Hoover, Calvin B., 500
Hoover, Herbert, 315
Horthy, Miklós, 156, 187, 207, 208, 361, 448, 453, 454, 533
Hötzendorf, Conrad von, 56, 83, 85
Howard's End (Forster), 23

Hugensburg, Alfred, 346
Hugo, Victor, 36
Hull, Cordell, 482, 483, 484, 486
Hundred Years' War, 50
Hungary, 160, 363
agrarian population, 261
collectivization, 564, 567
counterrevolution, 206–08
de-Stalinization, 567–68
Gömbös regime, 361
as independent republic, 154–55
Jews in, 206, 208, 261, 361
Kun regime, 155–56, 161, 173, 206, 262
National Front regimes, 531
nationalism, 33
October Republic (1918), 206, 207
Second World War, 448, 453, 454, 481
Soviet Union and, 491, 504, 514, 529, 533, 534, 540, 566–68, 583, 585, 608, 609
suffrage, 30, 260
Versailles peace settlement, 173, 180, 182, 184–87, 362
Husserl, Edmund, 306, 464
Huxley, Thomas Henry, 39

Imperialism, 6–10, 68–69
Imperialism: The Highest Stage of Capitalism (Lenin), 9, 68
Import Duties Act (1932), 322
Inchcape, Lord, 241
Independent Labour Party (ILP) (Britain), 118, 246
Independent Social Democratic party (USPD) (Germany), 118, 146, 162
Indeterminacy theory, 40, 305
India, 10, 93
China–India border war (1962), 607
independence, 542, 622, 623
Second World War, 623
Indochina, 6, 9, 492
Indochina War, 542–43, 623
Indonesia, 542, 623
Industrial Revolution, 12
Industry
British, 248–49, 314, 516, 518

in consumer societies, 574–75
Czech, 581
German, 254, 259, 331–32
Italian, 334–35
Russian, 138, 269–75
Soviet, 335–37
Inflation, 114–16, 157, 215, 222–23, 226, 236, 242, 252, 259, 508, 587, 618, 627, 628
Installment buying, 573
International Court of Arbitration, 117
International Monetary Fund, 514, 618
International War Crimes Tribunal, 489
Interpretation of Dreams, The (Freud), 44
Invergordon Mutiny, 321
Iran, 502, 503, 549
Iraq, 170, 175, 176, 446, 549, 622, 627
Ireland, 70, 117, 119, 615
Iron Guard, 361–63, 453
Isherwood, Christopher, 330
Ismail (khedive), 9
Israel, 170, 549, 625, 626
Italy
aristocracy, 19
Catholic Church in, 110, 211, 269, 355
Cold War politics, 544, 546, 547
consensus politics, 585
corporatism, 318, 333–35
disarmament issue, 234
economy, 333–35, 523–24, 571, 628
Ethiopian War, 236, 386, 408–10, 622
Fascism, 192–201, 210, 215, 268–69, 343
First World War, 67, 78, 83, 85, 93–94, 110, 143, 151–53, 167, 168
Great Depression, 333–35
imperialism, 9, 10
industry, 334–35
internal dissent, 69–70
leisure activities, 286–87
mass media, 283, 284
middle class, 22
monarchy, 28

movement for European union, 551, 555–58
nationalism, 33
Paris Peace Conference (1919), 165
radicalism, 379, 380
reconstruction, 521–24
Second World War, 445, 448, 472, 473, 482, 495
Spanish Civil War, 394, 395, 410–11
Stresa Front, 405, 411
strikes, 117, 157, 545, 587, 590
suffrage, 27, 29, 243
tourism, 579
Triple Alliance, 71
unrest of 1919–20, 156–59
Ivory Coast, 626
Izvolsky, Alexander, 54–55, 60, 62

Jacobins, 382
James, William, 11
Japan, 140, 237
decolonization, 623
disarmament issue, 234
industrialization, 9
Kellogg-Briand Pact, 231
Manchuria and, 238, 378
mandatory powers, 176
mass media, 280, 284
Paris Peace Conference (1919), 165
Second World War, 468, 469, 486, 489
Jaurès, Jean, 160, 383
Jellicoe, John, 94–95
Jerome, Jennie, 19
Jessner, Leopold, 303
Jeunesses patriotes, 208
Jews
in Britain, 367
in Germany, 204, 353, 450, 452–53
in Hungary, 206, 208, 261, 361
in Poland, 261, 591
in Romania, 209, 261, 361–63
in Russia, 214
Jodl, Alfred, 407
Joffre, Joseph, 62, 80, 81, 85, 86, 90, 103
John XXIII (pope), 599

Jordan, 170
Joyce, James, 297
Juarez, Benito, 192
Judenich, Nicolai, 141
July crisis (1914), 51–60
Jutland, Battle of, 94–95

Kádár, János, 568, 594
Kahr, Gustav von, 202, 205
Kamenev, Lev, 132, 271, 274, 338
Kandinsky, Wassily, 41, 279, 300
Kapp *Putsch,* 202, 254, 257, 351
Kapp, Wolfgang, 202
Karl (emperor of Austria-Hungary), 109, 152, 154, 207
Karlsbad program, 419
Karolyi, Prince Michael, 154, 155, 161, 206
Kazakstan, 142
Kellogg-Briand Pact (1928), 231–32
Kennan, George, 338, 470, 506
Kennedy, John F., 605, 616
Kennedy Round, 616
Kerensky, Alexander, 28, 130–33
Kessler, Harry, 301–02
Keynes, John Maynard, 5, 171, 223, 318, 407, 515
Khrushchev, Nikita, 337–38, 446, 560–63, 580, 605, 607
Kierkegaard, Sören, 39
Kipling, Rudyard, 10
Kirchner, Ludwig, 300
Kirov, Sergei, 337
Kissinger, Henry, 627
Kitchener, Horatio, 121
Klee, Paul, 293, 294, 300, 301, 304
Kluck, Alexander von, 81
Koestler, Arthur, 397, 400
Kolchak, Alexander, 141, 157
Komsomol, 287
Korea, 486
Korean War, 517, 527–28, 542, 554
Kornilov, Lavr, 132
Kosygin, Aleksei, 580
Kreisau Circle, 461
Kronstadt uprising, 270
Kulaks, 272, 335

Kun, Béla, 155–56, 161, 173, 187, 206, 262
Kuomintang party, 376
Kurile Islands, 486
Kursk-Orel, Battle of, 477, 478
Kutuzov, Mikhail, 479

Labor unions, 31–32, 112–13, 242, 249, 384, 385, 544
Labour party (Britain), 32, 162, 225, 237, 244–46, 317, 320–21, 366, 381, 512, 545, 555, 584, 585, 628
Labour party (Norway), 163
Lampedusa, Giuseppe de, 210
Land reform, 262, 391, 529–31, 564
Land Without Justice (Djilas), 15
Largo Caballero, Francisco, 393
La Rochelle, Pierre Drieu, 289, 453
Laslett, Peter, 22
Lateran Pact (1929), 269
Latvia, 173, 180, 427, 437, 438, 492
Laval, Pierre, 325, 379, 382, 386, 410
Law, The (Vailland), 21–22
Lawrence, D. H., 46, 299, 302
Lawrence, T. E., 170
League of Nations, 217, 218, 219, 228, 230, 231, 238, 378, 403, 406, 410, 423
Covenant, 172, 175–77, 232, 235
Lebanon, 170, 175, 624
Le Corbusier, 279, 293, 295, 599
Leeb, Wilhelm von, 447
Léger, Fernand, 293, 295
Legion of the Archangel Michael, 361
Lehideux, François, 455
Leighton, Lord, 45
Leisure time, 285–92, 384–85, 577, 578–79, 596
effects of, 290–92
organized, 286–87
sports, 288
travel, 289–90
Lend-Lease Act (1941), 468
Lenin, Nikolai, 141, 142, 143, 155, 156, 158, 166, 235, 273–74, 303, 308
April theses, 130

Bolshevik regime, 133–38
Bolshevik Revolution (1917),
129–33
Brest-Litovsk, Treaty of, 135
death, 270
on imperialism, 9–10
land redistribution, 134–35,
161
one-party rule, 137, 147, 273
in Switzerland, 118
Third International, 161–63
War Communism, 137
Leningrad, siege of, 477, 480
Leo XIII (pope), 211, 333, 355
Leopard, The (Lampedusa), 210
Leopold III (king of Belgium),
455
Leopold of Saxe-Coburg, 28
Leroy-Beaulieu, Paul, 77
Levi, Carlo, 15
Lévi-Strauss, Claude, 601
Liberal•economics, 316–17
Liberal party (Britain), 99, 244–
45
Liberal party (Romania), 362
Liberalism, 34–37, 117–18, 213,
370, 379–80, 600
Liberman, Yevsei, 581
Libya, 9, 168, 193, 446, 472
Liddell-Hart, Basil H., 233
Liebknecht, Karl, 117, 148, 253
Life expectancy, 18, 25
Literacy, 35, 36
Literature, 297, 311–12, 562,
598
Lithuania, 141, 173, 180, 185,
186, 218, 220, 427, 437,
438, 492
Little Entente, 220, 221, 230
Little Man, What Now? (Fallada),
311–12, 345
Litvinov, Maxim, 378, 423, 426,
427
Litvinov, Pavel, 595
Lloyd George, David, 102, 237,
242, 245, 283
collapse of majority, 244
First World War, 100–01, 111
"khaki election" (1918), 180,
219, 244
Liberal party, leadership of,
18, 30, 291
Versailles peace settlement,
165, 171, 178, 185–86

Locarno Agreements (1925),
229–32, 406, 408, 620
London, Treaty of (1915), 93,
168
London Naval Conference
(1930), 234
Longuet, Jean, 377
Lorraine, 61
Lubbe, Marinus van der, 351
Ludendorff, Erich, 83, 84, 90,
95, 97, 104–06, 144, 145,
205, 206, 259
Luftwaffe, 444
Lukacs, Georg, 155
Lunacharsky, Anatole, 275, 308
Lusitania, 94
Lutheran churches, 39, 353
Lüttwitz, Walther von, 202
Luxemburg, 553, 556–58
Luxemburg, Rosa, 136, 146,
147, 148, 160, 162, 253
Lvov, Prince George, 127, 130
Lysenko, Trofim, 537

MacDonald, Ramsay, 78, 225,
228, 245–46, 251, 320, 321
Macedonia, 53, 55
McKenna, Reginald, 100
Macmillan, Harold, 21, 546, 548
Madariaga, Salvador de, 234
Maginot Line, 233, 421, 435,
439
Magritte, René, 297
Magyars, 54, 151, 152, 154, 206,
416
Malaya, 549
Malenkov, George, 560, 566,
567, 580
Malinowski, Bronislaw, 306
Mallet, Serge, 587
Malraux, André, 398
Malvy, Eugène, 119
Man, Henri de, 318
Manchuria, 238, 378, 486
Mandarins, Les (Beauvoir), 585
Mandates, 175–76
Maniu, 534
Mann, Thomas, 20
Mannerheim, Karl Gustav, 448
Man's Hope (Malraux), 398
Manstein, Fritz Erich von, 439,
440
Manuilski, Dimitri, 378

Mao Tse-tung, 607
Maquis, 459, 519
March 22 Movement, 589
Marconi, Guglielmo, 280
Marcuse, Herbert, 587
Marinetti, Filippo, 43, 194, 196,
213
Marini, Marino, 598
Marne, First Battle of the, 79–
82, 86, 97
Marne, Second Battle of the, 144
Marshall, George C., 475, 484,
503
Marshall Plan, 503–04, 513–14,
523–24, 534, 551, 556
Martinique, 625
Marx, Karl, 21, 32, 153, 160,
191, 212, 306, 546, 601
Marx, Wilhelm, 259
Marxism, 370, 399, 400, 583
Masaryk, Jan, 532, 534
Masaryk, Thomas G., 151, 265–
66
Mass audience
creation of, 280–82
search for, 302–04
Mass culture, 280–85
effects of, 290–92
in "New Europe," 596–97
Mass media
control of, 284–85
political uses of, 282–83
technological basis for, 280–81
Masurian Lakes, Battle of the,
83, 104
Mater et Magistra (John XXIII),
599
Matignon Agreements, 384
Matisse, Henri, 42, 293, 299
Matteotti, Giacomo, 200, 268
Maurras, Charles, 38, 212, 268,
356, 363–64, 369
Max of Baden, 145, 147, 177
Maximalism, 158–59, 162
Mayakovsky, Vladimir, 304, 308
Mayer, Arno, 172
Mead, Margaret, 587–88
Medvedev, Roy, 338, 595
Medvedev, Zhores, 595
Mein Kampf (Hitler), 202, 260,
412
Meinecke, Friedrich, 253
Meitner, Lise, 436
Mensheviks, 128, 132

Meunier, Paul, 119
Mexico, 394
Meyerhold, Vsevelod, 304, 308
Michael (king of Romania), 529, 532, 534
Michaelis, Georg, 106
Michel, Henri, 439
Middle class, 20–22, 111, 115, 212
Mies van der Rohe, Ludwig, 293, 599
Mikhailovich, Draža, 462
Mikolajczyk, Stanislaw, 532, 534
Milhaud, Darius, 293
Miliukov, Pavel, 28, 127, 130
Mill, John Stuart, 35, 397
Mitchell, Wesley Clair, 311
Mitterand, François, 628
Moch, Jules, 545
Modernism, 279, 294–96
Moldavia, 51, 52
Mollet, Guy, 545, 548, 549
Molotov, V. M., 482, 533, 561
Moltke, Helmut von, 57, 63, 64, 69, 79, 81, 86, 461
Monarchies, 27–28, 243
Mondrian, Piet, 295
Monnet, Jean, 521, 544, 559, 613
Monopoly, 9, 68
Monroe Doctrine, 172, 606
Montenegro, 53, 55
Montesquiou, Robert de, 19
Montgomery, Bernard Law, 475, 553
Montreux, Treaty of (1936), 503
Moore, Henry, 598
Morgan, J. P., and Company, 321
Morgenthau, Henry, 498
Morgenthau Plan, 500
Morocco, 50, 68, 69, 77, 235, 472, 473, 625
Moscow Declaration of Peaceful Existence (1957), 607, 608
Moscow Treaty (1970), 620
Mosley, Sir Oswald, 322–23, 324, 366–68
Motion pictures, 280–85, 296, 303, 598
Mouvement républicain populaire (MRP), 511, 520, 543, 551
Müller, Hermann, 77, 260, 327, 347, 619

Munich settlement, 421–23, 462, 620
Music, 279, 293, 295, 300, 301, 302, 598
Mussert, Anton Adriaan, 369–70, 453, 509
Mussolini, Benito, 78, 124, 208, 318, 334, 361, 369, 438, 622
    Austria and, 358–59, 404
    Fascism and, 192–201, 268–69
    Hitler and, 411, 414–15, 427, 433
    radio speeches, 283
    removal from power, 521
    Second World War, 445, 473
Mustapha Kemal (Ataturk), 218

Nagy, Imre, 566–67, 568
Napoleon I, 550
Napoleon III, 211
Napoleonic Code, 25, 27
Napoleonic Wars, 50
Nasser, Gamal Abdel, 549, 625
National-Christian Socialism, 208–09
National Front regimes (1945–47), 529–31
National Government (1931–35) (Britain), 321–22
National Insurance Act (1911), 99
National People's party (DNVP) (Germany), 256, 260, 352, 353
National Socialist German Workers' party, *see* Nazi party
National-Socialist League (NSB) (Holland), 369
Nationalism, 32–34, 37, 38, 53, 70, 153, 161, 194, 195, 203, 213, 625
Nationalization, 516, 518, 520, 530, 531, 574, 583
Nature of the Physical Universe (Eddington), 306
Naumann, Friedrich, 30
Navy
    British, 64, 69, 94–95, 321, 435
    French, 435
    German, 64, 69, 94–95, 405, 434, 443

Nazi party, 232, 255
    Austria, activities in, 358, 359, 404, 405, 414
    economic system, 330–33
    revival of (1929–32), 344–47
    revolution after power (1933–39), 351–54
    Twenty-Five Points, 203–04, 210
    See also Hitler, Adolf
Nazi Seizure of Power, The: The Experience of a Single German Town (Allen), 346
Nazi-Soviet Pact (1939), 426–27, 438, 447, 479, 496
Nehru, Jawaharlal, 623
Nenni, Pietro, 544, 547, 585
Nervi, Pier Luigi, 599
Neuilly, Treaty of (1919), 174
    See also Versailles peace settlement (1919)
Neurath, Konstantin von, 353, 403
New Economic Policy (NEP), 270, 271, 273
New Order, 448–53
New party (Britain), 366
New Zealand, 176
Newspapers, 281, 284–85
Newton, Sir Isaac, 34
Nicholas II (tsar of Russia), 28, 61, 107–08, 126, 127
Nicolson, Arthur, 60
Nicolson, Harold, 166
Niemöller, Martin, 353, 461
Nietzsche, Friedrich, 39
Nigeria, 9
Nivelle, Robert, 88, 90, 103
Nixon, Richard M., 618, 627
Nizan, Paul, 397
Nono, Luigi, 598
North Africa, 472–73
North Atlantic Treaty Organization (NATO), 504, 547, 553, 554, 558, 565, 610–12
Norway
    fascist movement, 343, 370
    Great Depression, 319
    reconstruction, 509
    Second World War, 439, 451, 455
    suffrage, 27, 29
Noske, Gustav, 148, 201

Not By Bread Alone (Dudintsev), 562
Novotný, Antonin, 591–92
Nuclear Test Ban Treaty (1963), 606, 607
Nuclear weapons, 485, 489, 540, 541, 559, 606–08, 610–11
Nuremberg Decrees, 353

October Revolution, 132, 152
Oil prices, 626–27
Olivetti, Arrigo, 575
On Liberty (Mill), 35
Operaio Nazionale Dopolavoro, 286–87
Operation Barbarossa, 445–48, 480
Operation OVERLORD, 445–48, 480
Operation TORCH, 472–73
Orff, Carl, 598
Organization for European Economic Cooperation (OEEC), 513, 551, 552, 556
Orlando, Vittorio Emanuele, 165
Ortega y Gasset, José, 292
Orthodox Church of Russia, 39
Orwell, George, 312, 517, 541
Ostpolitik, 619–20
Otto of Bavaria, 28
Ottoman Empire, 33, 34, 51, 52, 55, 93, 99, 169
Owen, Wilfred, 122, 123

Pacem in Terris (John XXIII), 599
Pacifism, 78
Pact of Steel (1939), 411
Painting, 41–43, 45, 279, 294–96, 300–02, 397, 598
Pakistan, 542, 624
Palacký, František, 33
Paléologue, Maurice, 62
Palestine, 170, 175, 549, 624–25
Pankhurst, Emmeline, 27
Panzer divisions, 436, 439, 440
Papen, Franz von, 330, 347–51, 403
Paris Commune (1871), 31
Paris Peace Conference (1919), *see* Versailles peace settlement (1919)

Parliamentary democracies, broadening of, 242–44
Parliaments, role of, 28–30
Parti populaire français, 364
Pashich, Nicholas, 54
Pasternak, Boris, 537, 562
Patton, George S., 475
Pauker, Anna, 535
Paul VI (pope), 599
Paulus, Friedrich, 477
Pavelić, Ante, 454
Pearl Harbor, 469
Peary, Robert, 10
Peasant party (Croatia), 263
Peasant party (Poland), 263
Peasantry, 14–15, 261–64, 270–72, 275, 335–37, 391, 393, 479, 564
Péguy, Charles, 122
People's party (Germany), 256, 258
Pétain, Philippe, 89, 365, 442, 443, 445, 453, 455–57, 460
Petkov, Nikolaj, 534
Philosophes, 34
Philosophy, 43, 306, 601
Phony war, 438, 469
Physics, 39–41, 305–06, 600
Picasso, Pablo, 42, 279, 293, 299, 397
Pickles, Wilfrid, 555
"Pig War," 54, 56
Pilsudski, Josef, 169, 184, 265
Pinay, Antoine, 548
Pirelli, Alberto, 334
Piscator, Erwin, 303
Pius IX (pope), 211
Pius X (pope), 211
Pius XI (pope), 355–56
Pius XII (pope), 599
Pivert, Marceau, 384
Planck, Max, 40, 305
Pleven, René, 554
Podgorny, Nikolay, 580
Poetry, 121–22
Poincaré, Raymond, 58, 60, 62, 63, 219, 223, 225, 228, 252–53, 548
Poland, 130, 138, 154, 220, 403, 620
  agriculture, 261, 564, 609
  collectivization, 564
  crisis (1939), 424–26
  de-Stalinization, 567

discontent (1970), 591
Jews in, 261, 591
nationalism, 34, 161
parliamentary regime, 260, 265
Pilsudski's *coup,* 265
rights of passage, 423, 426
Russo-Polish War, 141, 162, 173, 218
Second World War, 436–37, 451, 460, 481, 482, 484, 487
Soviet Union and, 491, 495–98, 502, 504, 514, 529, 532, 608, 609
Versailles peace settlement, 169, 170, 172, 180, 182–83, 184–87, 218, 495
Police power, 119–20
Polish Corridor, 226, 324–25
Polycentrism, 606–09
Pompidou, Georges, 615, 628
Pop art, 598
Popular Front, 373–401, 455
  in France, 325–26, 364, 375–76, 381–89, 398–99, 455
  intellectuals and, 397–98
  liberal reaction, 379–80
  resistance movements, 399
  socialist reaction, 380–81
  in Spain, 387, 389, 390, 392–96
  Stalin and, 379
Popular sovereignty, 32
Population, 3–4, 12
Population control, 23–25
Portugal, 215, 553
  Army *coup* (1974), 629
  colonies, 622, 625
  fascist movement, 343, 357
  First World War, 266
  Republic of 1910, 266, 267–68
  Salazar regime, 268, 356–57, 547–48
  Second World War, 448
  strikes, 267
Positivism, 38
Potsdam Conference (1945), 488–90, 498, 500
Poulenc, Francis, 302
POUM *(Partido Obrero de Unificación Marxista),* 395, 396
Pound, Ezra, 398
Poverty, 16–18, 571

Prague *coup* (1948), 504, 534–35, 552
Preuss, Hugo, 243, 255
Primo de Rivera, José Antonio, 360, 392
Primo de Rivera, Miguel, 215, 267, 389, 390
Princip, Gavrilo, 51, 56
Prokofiev, Sergei, 479, 537
Protestantism, 39, 353, 599–600
Proust, Marcel, 19, 44, 297
Prussia, 29–30, 69, 106, 145, 166, 243
Prussian Wars, 50
Psychoanalysis, 44, 297–98, 306
Psychological warfare, 435
Purges, 337–38, 400, 447
Pygmalion (Shaw), 14

Quadragesimo Anno (Pius XI), 355–56, 359
Quantum theory, 40
Quisling, Vidkun, 370, 454, 509

Radič, Stepan, 186, 263, 264
Radical party (France), 250–52, 324, 325, 375–76, 380, 382–83, 387, 398–99
Radicalism, 194, 195, 379–80
Radio, 280–85, 571
Raeder, Erich, 443
Rajk, Laszlo, 535
Rákosi, Mátyás, 567
Ramadier, Paul, 544
Rapacki, Adam, 558
Rapacki Plan, 558
Rapallo, Treaty of (1922), 221, 237, 378
Rasputin, 108
Rathenau, Walther, 104, 114, 221, 222, 255, 258
Rauschning, Hermann, 209
Rearmament, 331, 403, 405, 554
Reconstruction, 571
   British Labour government (1945–51), 514–18
   Eastern Europe, 528–35
   economic recovery, 512–14
   French Fourth Republic, 509, 518–21, 544
   Germany, 524–28
   Italy, 521–24
   new leaders and parties, 509–12

Soviet Union, 535–37
Red and the Black, The (Stendhal), 13
Red Guards, 132
"Red Orchestra" group, 461
Reich, Wilhelm, 298
Reichsrat, 109, 152, 243
Reichstag, 28, 29, 32, 69, 78, 119, 243
Reinhardt, Max, 303
Relativity theories, 40–41, 305–06
Religion
   organized, 38–39
   revival, 599–600
   See also names of churches
Remarque, Erich Maria, 86–87, 114, 122
Remembrance of Things Past (Proust), 19, 44, 297
Renault, Louis, 520
Reparations, 179–80, 221–23, 228, 232, 252, 314, 487, 489, 500–01, 528
Republicanism, 27, 28
Rerum Novarum (Leo XIII), 333, 355
Resistance, 457–65, 510
   intellectual impact of, 463–65
   military impact of, 462–63
   outside Germany, 458–60
   within Germany, 460–62
Revolt of the Masses, The (Ortega y Gasset), 292
Rexism, 369
Reynaud, Paul, 442
Rhineland, 171, 177–78, 219, 230
   remilitarization of (1936), 405–08
Ribbentrop, Joachim von, 353, 426, 437
Richthoven, Manfred von, 91, 203
Riefenstahl, Leni, 283
Riga, Peace of (1920), 141
Robbe-Grillet, Alain, 598
Robinson, John, 600
Robinson, Ronald, 10
Rocque, François de la, 364, 382
Roentgen, Wilhelm, 40
Röhm, Ernst, 203, 205, 354
Rokossovsky, Konstantin, 532

Rolland, Romain, 76, 77
Romains, Jules, 76, 89, 114
Romania, 28, 33, 52, 53, 138, 161, 206
   agrarian population, 261
   Balkan Wars, 55
   collectivization, 564
   economy, 608–09
   fascist movement in, 208–09, 361–63
   First World War, 151, 168–69
   independent position, 608–09
   Jews in, 209, 261, 361–63
   land reform, 262, 529–30, 531
   Little Entente, 220
   National Front regime, 529–30, 531
   parliamentary democracy, 260
   peasant uprising (1907), 261–62
   revolution (1917–20), 154–56
   Second World War, 363, 448, 454, 482, 495
   Soviet Union and, 491, 502, 532, 534, 591, 608–09
   Versailles peace settlement, 173, 182, 184–87
Rome, Treaties of (1957), 557
Rome, Treaty of (1958), 613
Rommel, Erwin, 446, 472
Roosevelt, Franklin D., 384, 542
   Arcadia meeting, 469
   Casablanca Conference, 473, 482
   cash and carry policy, 434
   lend-lease, 468
   Teheran Conference, 483–84, 496
   Yalta Conference, 485–88, 498, 500
Rosenberg, Alfred, 203, 307
Rossi, Cesare, 200
Rossoni, Edmondo, 334
Rousseau, Henri, 43
Rowntree, Seebohm, 17–18, 576
Ruhr, occupation of, 222, 223–25, 254, 255, 257
Rumor, Mariano, 628
Runciman, Lord, 99, 417
Rundstedt, Gerd von, 446
Russell, Bertrand, 37, 601
Russia, 28
   Austria-Hungary and, 52, 54–55

Bolshevik regime, 133–42, 269–71
Bosnian crisis, 54, 59, 68, 71
civil war, 136, 138–42, 269
economy, 270, 271, 273, 275
First World War, 60–61, 63, 76, 78, 79, 82–86, 92, 93, 99, 107–08, 125, 127, 135, 166–68
Franco-Russian Alliance (1892), 57, 61, 62, 71, 219
imperialism, 6
industry, 138, 269–75
Jews in, 214
Kronstadt uprising, 270
nationalism, 34
New Economic Policy, 270, 271, 273
political dictatorship, consolidation of, 273
provisional government, 128–32
Revolution (1905), 126
Revolutions (1917), 119, 126–33, 152, 159–61, 166
Russo-Japanese War (1905), 54, 57, 69, 70
Russo-Polish War (1920–21), 141, 162, 173, 218
soviets, 128–30, 132
strikes, 117
suffrage, 30
Versailles peace settlement, 182, 186, 187
War Communism, 137, 269–70
See also Union of Soviet Socialist Republics
Russian Revolution (1905), 126
Russian Revolutions (1917), 119, 126–33, 152, 166
Russo-Japanese War (1905), 54, 57, 69, 70
Russo-Polish War (1920–21), 141, 162, 173, 218
Ruthenians, 173, 416, 533
Rutherford, Ernest, 40, 305

SA. *(Sturmabteilungen)*, 346, 353
Saar, 178, 403
Saint Germain, Treaty of (1919), 174, 357–58
See also Versailles peace settlement (1919)

Saint-Simon, Comte de, 550
Sakhalin, 486
Sakharov, Andrei, 595
Salandra, Antonio, 110, 157, 198, 199
Salazar, Antonio de Oliveira, 268, 356–57
Salisbury, Lord, 247
Salvemini, Gaetano, 286
Samuel, Herbert, 249
Sarrault, Albert, 406
Sarraute, Natalie, 598
Sartre, Jean-Paul, 36–37, 292, 464–65, 546, 585
Sassoon, Siegfried, 123
Satie, Erik, 301
Savage Mind, The (Lévi-Strauss), 601
Saxony, 257, 258
Sazanov, Sergei, 60, 61, 62, 63, 70
Schacht, Hjalmar, 257, 259, 331, 412
Scheer, Reinhard, 94–95
Schlageter, Leo, 257
Schleicher, Kurt von, 347, 349, 354
Schleswig-Holstein, 217, 255, 344
Schlieffen, Alfred von, 64, 77, 80
Schlieffen Plan, 63–64, 72, 79, 81, 104, 439
Schmidt, Helmut, 628
Schoenberg, Arnold, 279, 295
Schönerer, Georg von, 38, 213, 416
Schorske, Carl, 46
Schumacher, Kurt, 584
Schuman Plan, 556
Schuman, Robert, 556, 559
Schuschnigg, Kurt, 359, 405, 414
Science, 11, 34, 36, 435–36, 600–01
revolution in, 39–41, 45
Sculpture, 45, 598
Second International, 77, 118, 161
Second World War, 433–90
aftermath, 506–09
American hegemony in West, 468–76
Atlantic Charter, 469, 482

Blitzkrieg, 434–36, 439, 445, 450
Britain, Battle of, 442–45, 506
Casablanca Conference, 473, 482
casualty rates, 506
collaboration, 453–57, 509
D-Day, 474
Dunkirk, 441–42
in the East (1939–42), 436–38, 445–48
economy, 450, 454–55, 468, 478
France, fall of, 439–42
morale, 435
New Order, 448–53
occupation policy, 450–51
Operation Barbarossa, 445–48, 480
Operation OVERLORD, 484
Operation TORCH, 472–73
origins of, 428–29
Pearl Harbor, 469
phony war, 438, 469
Potsdam Conference, 488–90, 498, 500
racial extermination, 452–53
resistance, 457–65, 510
Russo-Finnish "winter war," 437–39, 477
Soviet hegemony in East, 476–81
Teheran Conference, 483–85, 496
weapons, 435–36
in the West (1940), 438–45
Yalta Conference, 481, 485–88, 496, 498, 500
Sedan, Battle of, 86
Seeckt, Hans von, 202, 221, 257–59
Seipel, Father Ignaz, 358
Sembat, Marcel, 112
Senegal, 626
Serbia
Austro-Serbian war, 51–63
Balkan Wars, 55
First World War, 72, 82, 83, 85, 93
Versailles peace settlement, 182, 184, 186
Serbs, Croats, and Slovenes, Kingdom of, *see* Yugoslavia

Servan-Schreiber, Jean-Jacques, 617
Sèvres, Treaty of (1920), 174
See also Versailles peace settlement (1919)
Sexuality, 44, 297–99
Seyss-Inquart, Artur von, 414
Shaw, George Bernard, 16
Shonfield, Andrew, 572
Siberia, 139–41, 237
Sikorski, Wladyslaw, 496
Silesia, 180, 183, 185–86, 187, 255, 425
Sima, Horia, 363
Sinn Fein, 117, 158
Slansky, Rudolph, 535
Slovakia, 448, 454
Slovaks, 33, 54, 155, 184, 186, 187, 206, 416, 423
Slovenes, 33, 184, 186, 264
Smallholders' party (Hungary), 262–63, 533, 534
Smith, Adam, 35
Smithsonian Conference (1917), 618
Snowden, Philip, 78, 118, 320–21, 323
Social class, 15–23, 111, 115, 212
Social Democratic party
  Austrian, 32, 162, 358, 359
  Czech, 530
  German (SPD), 32, 69, 77–78, 118, 121, 146, 147, 162, 255–58, 327, 330, 344, 346, 347, 350–53, 380, 460, 461, 546, 584, 619
  Norwegian, 381
  Polish, 153
  Russian, 32, 137
  Swedish, 162, 381
Socialist National party (Czechoslovakia), 593
Socialist parties, 31–32
  fascism and, 194, 195, 209–10
  First World War and, 77–78, 118
  French (SFIO), 32, 250–52, 324, 325, 364, 375–77, 381–83, 399, 520, 543, 548
  Great Depression and, 317
  Italian, 110, 193, 194, 523, 544
  Norwegian, 370
  Popular Front, reaction to, 380–81

Swedish, 584
Socialist Unity party (SED) (East Germany), 525–26
Social-welfare systems, 18
Solidarité française, 365
Solzhenitsyn, Aleksandr, 338, 537, 595
Sombart, Werner, 76, 582
Somme campaign, 87, 88, 90
Sonnino, Sidney, 93, 110
Sorel, George, 192
South Slavs, 33, 51, 150, 152, 155, 169, 185, 206, 264
Souvarov, Alexander, 479
Sovereignty, 27, 68
Soviets, 128–30, 132, 137
Spaak, Paul-Henri, 543, 551, 553, 555
Space programs, 580
Spain, 27
  Civil War, 386–87, 389, 394–96, 398, 410–11
  economy, 547
  fascist movements, 343
  First World War, 266
  Franco regime, 359–60, 547, 629
  parliamentary monarchy, 266
  Popular Front, 387, 389, 390, 392–96
  Primo de Rivera dictatorship, 215, 267
  radicalism, 379, 380
  Second Spanish Republic, 389–94
  strikes, 266–67, 590
  suffrage, 29, 243
  tourism, 579
Spartacists, 146–48, 173, 253, 255
Special Drawing Rights, 618
Speer, Albert, 450, 454
Speidel, Hans, 554
Spender, Stephen, 115, 397
Spengler, Oswald, 13, 292
Sports, 288
Springer, Axel, 575
Squadristi, 195–200, 269
SS. *(Schutzstaffel),* 354, 452
Stakhanov, Aleksey, 337
Stalin, Josef, 135, 308
  Cold War, 495–98, 500, 502–04
  death, 560
  economy and, 335–36

on foreign Communists, 376–78
German issue, 498, 500
meeting with Hitler (1939), 362
Nazi-Soviet Pact, 426–27
peace aims, (1945), 490–92
Polish issue, 495–98
Popular Front and, 379, 400
purges, 337–38, 400
reconstruction, 535–36
rise of, 274–75
Second World War, 437, 446–47, 470–71, 473, 477–79, 482–88
on social democracy, 377
Stalingrad, Battle of, 477, 480–81
Stamboliski, Alexander, 262–64
Stanislavsky, Konstantin, 304, 308
Starhemberg, Prince Ernst Rüdiger von, 414
Stauffenberg, Klaus Schenk von, 462
Stavisky Affair, 365
Stavisky, Alexander, 365
Stendhal, 13, 33
Stimson, Henry, 470
Stinnes, Hugo, 116
Stockhausen, Karl-Heinz, 598
Stoph, Willy, 620
Strachey, John, 366
Strachey, Lytton, 122
Strasser, Gregor, 349, 350, 354
Strategic Arms Limitation Talks (SALT), 627
Strauss, Richard, 45
Stravinsky, Igor, 279, 293, 300
Stresa Front, 405, 411
Stresemann, Gustav, 226, 228–32, 251, 256, 257–59, 403, 412
Strikes
  British, 116–17, 156, 249, 517, 587, 590
  French, 116–17, 156, 326, 384, 388, 543, 545, 585–86, 589
  German, 116–17
  Italian, 117, 157, 545, 587, 590
  Portuguese, 267
  Spanish, 266–67, 590
  United States, 156

Student discontent, 585–91
Sturgkh, Karl, 109
Sturzo, Luigi, 196
Submarines, 94, 95, 473
Sudetenland, 187, 416, 419–24, 533, 620
Suez Campaign, 549, 568
Suffrage, 27, 29–30, 35, 137, 211, 212, 242, 243, 362
Summit Conferences, 562, 563
Surrealism, 123, 296–97, 397
Svoboda, Ludvik, 594
Sweden
  fascist movement, 343
  Great Depression, 319
  middle class, 22
  Second World War, 439, 448
  suffrage, 29
Switzerland, 243, 448, 574
Sykes-Picot Agreement (1916), 169–70, 175
Syndicalism, 192–93, 333, 334
Syria, 170, 175, 446, 549, 563, 624, 627
Szálasy, Ferenc, 453
Szamuelly, Tibor, 155, 156

Taittinger, Pierre, 208
Tanganyika, 176
Tanks, 90–91, 436, 440–41
Tannenberg, Battle of, 83, 104
Tanzania, 176
Tariffs, 314
Tatlin, Vladimir, 303
Taxation, 21, 101, 102, 516
Taylor, A. J. P., 81, 206, 275
Technology, 36, 571, 587
Teheran Conference (1943), 483–85, 496
Telegraph, 280
Telephone, 280
Television, 281, 573, 574, 598
Terauchi, Count Seiki, 165
Teschen, 182–83, 185, 218, 220, 425
Tess of the D'Ubervilles (Hardy), 290
Thälmann, Ernst, 259
Theater, 296, 303, 304, 311
Third International, *see* Comintern
Thirty Years' War, 49, 50
Thompson, J. J., 40
Thorez, Maurice, 376, 382, 384
Thuringia, 257, 258

Thyssen, Fritz, 346
Tildy, Zoltan, 533
Time Machine, The (Wells), 36
Tiso, Joseph, 454
Tito, Marshal, 462–63, 510
Todt, Fritz, 450
Togliatti, Palmiro, 523, 608
Togo, 176
Toller, Ernst, 148
Toynbee, Arnold, 509, 541
Trade, 4–5, 35–36
Trans-Carpathian Ruthenia, 491
Transcaucasia, 142
Trans-Siberian Railroad, 6, 140
Transylvania, 54, 155, 161, 169, 173, 185, 363, 454, 532
Travel, 289–90
Trench warfare, 81, 82, 86, 88
Trianon, Treaty of the (1920), 174, 206
  See also Versailles peace settlement (1919)
Trieste, 522
Triple Alliance, 71
Triple Entente, 93
Tristes Tropiques (Lévi-Strauss), 601
Trotsky, Leon, 118, 133, 135, 141, 160, 161, 166, 271, 274–75, 303, 384, 397, 546
Truman Doctrine, 503, 539
Truman, Harry S., 488–89, 495, 498, 500
Tukhachevsky, Michael, 141
Tunisia, 9, 472, 473, 625
Turchin, V. F., 595
Turkestan, 142
Turkey, 554
  Balkan Wars, 55
  conflict (1947–49), 502–03
  First World War, 84, 85, 92–93, 168, 169
  nationalism, 34, 218
  Young Turk movement, 54
  See also Ottoman Empire
Twittering Machine (Klee), 301
Two Cheers for Democracy (Forster), 339
Tzara, Tristan, 122

Ukraine, 141, 142, 172, 185, 447, 487
Ulbricht, Walter, 526, 528, 620
Ulysses (Joyce), 297

Unemployment, 275, 311, 321, 322, 323, 329, 330, 515
Union of Democratic Control (Britain), 118, 168
Union of Soviet Socialist Republics
  agriculture, 335–37, 562, 580, 581
  arms limitations, 606, 607, 627
  Cold War, 494–96, 498–504, 537, 539–42, 546, 549, 559–60, 562–63, 605
  Comintern, 161–63, 237, 250, 264, 370, 376–79, 458
  Cuban missile crisis, 605–06, 610
  culture, 303–04, 308, 536–37, 561–62
  Czech crisis (1938), 423–24
  and Czech "springtime," 594
  de-Stalinization, 562, 567–68, 583, 595
  disarmament issue, 234
  discontent, 594–95
  economy, 335–37, 478, 535–36, 562
  Franco-Soviet Pact (1935), 379, 386
  industry, 335–37
  League of Nations and, 228, 378
  leisure activities, 287
  mass media, 284
  Nazi-Soviet Pact (1939), 426–27, 438, 447, 479, 496
  organization of, 142
  orthodoxy, 536–37
  peace aims (1945), 490–92
  peaceful coexistence, ideology of, 607
  post-Stalin "thaw," 561–63
  purges, 337–38, 400, 447
  Rapallo, Treaty of, 221, 237, 378
  reconstruction, 535–37
  satellites, 491, 495–98, 502, 504, 514, 525, 528–35, 540, 562–68, 583, 585, 586, 591–94, 606, 608–09, 627
  Second World War, 437–39, 445–48, 454, 459, 468–71, 475–81, 486–90
  Sino-Soviet split, 606–08
  Spanish Civil War, 394, 396

Stalin, rise of, 274–75
struggle for power (1953–58), 560–61
West Germany, relations with, 619–20
See also Russia
United African Company, 9
United Nations, 482, 483, 486–87, 547, 620
United Nations Relief and Rehabilitation Agency (UNRRA), 508–09
United States of America
arms limitations, 606, 607, 627
cash and carry policy, 434
China, relations with, 627
Cold War, 494–96, 498, 500–04, 539–42, 546, 549, 563, 605
Common Market and, 616–17, 619
Cuban missile crisis, 605–06, 610
disarmament issue, 234
economy, 242, 311, 313, 314, 327, 468, 494, 503–04, 513–14, 615–19
European economic rivalry, 615–19
European independence from, 610–12
exports, 4
First World War, 95–96, 144
foreign investments, 6
Great Depression, 311, 313, 314, 327
in Indochina, 542, 623
Kellogg-Briand Pact, 231
Korean War, 542
Marshall Plan, 503–04, 513–14, 523–24, 534, 551, 556
mass media, 280, 284
NATO, 553
New Deal, 384
peace aims (1945), 492–95
Second World War, 450, 468–76, 480, 482–90
Soviet wheat purchase, 581
strikes, 156
suffrage, 27
Treaty of Versailles, refusal to ratify, 218, 220
Truman Doctrine, 503, 539

Versailles peace settlement, 165, 171–72
war debts, 222, 314
Upper Silesia, 217, 218, 220, 226
Uprooted, The (Barrès), 13
U-2 incident, 563
Uzbekistan, 142

Vailland, Roger, 21–22
Valéry, Paul, 4
Valois, Georges, 208
Vandenberg, Arthur, 553
Vandenberg resolution (1948), 553
Van Gogh, Vincent, 41, 300
Van Severen, Joris, 368
Van Zeeland, Paul, 369
Varèse, Edgard, 598
Verdun (Romains), 76, 89, 114
Verdun offensive, 88–89, 104
Versailles, Treaty of (1919), 174
See also Versailles peace settlement (1919)
Versailles peace settlement (1919), 165–89
anti-Bolshevism, 172–73
assessment of, 186–88
demilitarization of Germany, 178–79
discrimination among nationalities, 184–86
dismantled (1933–39), 402–31
Eastern European settlement, 180–88
Fourteen Points, 145, 162, 167–68, 169, 171–72, 177, 179, 182, 232, 235
frontier problems, 182–84
League of Nations Covenant, 172, 175–77
national interests, 170–72
Neuilly, Treaty of (1919), 174
in practice, 217–38
reparations, 179–80, 221–23, 228
Saint-Germain, Treaty of (1919), 174, 357–58
Sèvres, Treaty of (1920), 174
territorial changes, 178, 180–88
Trianon, Treaty of the (1920), 174, 206

Versailles, Treaty of (1919), 174
wartime treaties and promises, 168–70
Western European settlement, 177–80
Vichy regime, 455–57, 518
Victor Emmanuel II (king of Italy), 410
Victor Emmanuel III (king of Italy), 110, 198, 199, 521
Vienna Conference (1815), 180
Vietnam, Republic of, 623
Vietnam War, 627
Vilna, 218, 220, 437
Visconti, Luchino, 598
Vittorio Veneto, Battle of, 153
Viviani, René, 58, 62, 63
Vlasov, Andrei, 479
Voltaire, 34

Wages, 17, 115, 326, 332, 575
Waiting for Godot (Beckett), 546
Wallachia, 51, 52
War Communism, 137, 269–70
War debts, 222, 314, 544
War of the Worlds, The (Wells), 36
Warsaw Pact (1955), 504, 565
Washington Naval Conference (1921 and 1922), 234
Waterloo, Battle of, 86
Watson, James, 600–01
Waugh, Evelyn, 398
Way of All Flesh, The (Butler), 20
Wazyk, Adam, 567
Wealth, 18–20, 574–77
Weapons
First World War, 90–91
nuclear, 485, 489, 540, 541, 559, 605–08, 610–11
Second World War, 435–36
Webb, Beatrice, 338
Webb, Sidney, 338
Weber, Eugen, 363
Weber, Max, 25, 243, 306, 601
Webern, Anton, 295
Weill, Kurt, 293, 302, 311
Weimar Coalition, 255–57
Weimar Constitution (1919), 243
Weizmann, Chaim, 170
Welfare state, 516, 518, 520–31, 572, 576, 582–83
Wells, H. G., 36, 166

West Germany (Federal Republic of Germany), 512, 554
Cold War, 547
consensus politics, 583, 584
consumer society, 574–77, 583
East Germany and, 620
economy, 526–28, 571, 628
movement for European union, 554–58
Ostpolitik, 619–20
rearmament, 554
reconstruction, 524–28
student discontent, 588, 589–90
Weygand, Maxime, 440, 442
Wheatley Act (1924), 322
Wheatley, John, 246
White Russians, 138, 141, 142
Whiteley, William, 555
Wilberforce, Samuel, 39
Wilhelm II (kaiser of Germany), 28, 45, 56, 57, 61, 63, 65, 66, 79, 106, 144–46
Wilhelmina (queen of the Netherlands), 455
Wilson, Harold, 545, 585, 628
Wilson, Sir Horace, 418

Wilson, Woodrow, 96, 109, 140, 143, 150, 154, 165
Fourteen Points, 145, 152, 167–69, 171–72, 177, 179, 182, 232, 235
opposition to, 218–19
Witos, Wincenty, 263, 265
Wittgenstein, Ludwig, 306, 601
Women, 25–27, 101, 111, 243
Woolf, Leonard, 37, 49
Worker discontent, 586–87, 589
Workers' International, *see* Second International
World Disarmament Conference, 232, 234
Wozzeck (Berg), 293, 296, 300
Wrangel, Peter, 141, 269
Wylie, Lawrence, 572

Yalta Conference (1945), 481, 485–88, 497, 498, 500
Yom Kippur war (1973), 626
Young Plan, 232, 344, 346
Young Turk movement, 54
Ypres, Battle of, 87

Yugoslavia, 154, 155, 206, 243, 260, 522
agriculture, 261, 609
aid to Greece, 503
Fiume and, 158, 200, 218
Little Entente, 220
national minorities, problem of, 264–65
nationalism, 161
resistance in, 462–63
Second World War, 445, 454, 462–63, 480, 481, 484
Soviet Union and, 502, 529, 535, 562, 609
Versailles peace settlement, 169, 170, 182, 185–87

Zhdanov, Andrei, 436
Zhukov, Georgi, 447, 480
Zimmermann, Arthur, 95
Zimmermann Note, 95
Zimmerwald Conference (1915), 118
Zinoviev, Gregory, 132, 246, 271, 274, 338
Zinoviev Letter, 246
Zola, Emile, 299

EUROPE IN 1975

ICELAND
Reykjavik

NORWAY
Oslo

SWEDEN
Stockholm

GULF OF BOTHN

BALTIC SEA

ATLANTIC OCEAN

NORTH SEA

NO. IRELAND
Glasgow
Belfast
IRELAND
Dublin
UNITED
KINGDOM
Liverpool
Birmingham
London

DENMARK
Copenhagen

EAST
Berlin
GERMANY
Cologne
Leipzig
Elbe
WEST
Frankfurt
Rhine

Hamburg

Gdánsk
Poznan
Vistula
Warsaw
POLAND
Oder
Prague
Cra
CZECHOSLOVAKIA

ENGLISH CHANNEL
Le Havre

NETH.
Amsterdam
Brussels
BELG.
LUX.

Seine
Paris
Loire

BAY OF BISCAY

FRANCE
Bordeaux

Lyons
Rhône

SWITZ.
A L P S
Munich
Vienna
AUSTRIA
Budapest
HUNGA

Milan
Trieste
Venice
Genoa
Drava
YUGOSLA

PORTUGAL
Lisbon
Tagus
Madrid
SPAIN

Vigo
Ebro
PYRENEES
ANDORRA

Marseilles
Barcelona
Balearic Is.

Corsica
(Fr.)

Florence
ITALY
Rome
Naples

ADRIATIC SEA

Tirana
ALBAN

Strait of Gibraltar
Gibraltar
(Brit.)

Casablanca
MOROCCO

Algiers
ALGERIA

Sardinia

MEDITERRANEAN SEA

Sicily

Tunis
TUNISIA
Malta